FACTS ON FILE
BIBLIOGRAPHY
OF
AMERICAN FICTION
1866-1918

Edited by
James Nagel
and
Gwen L. Nagel

With the Assistance of
Judith S. Baughman

A MANLY, INC., BOOK

Facts On File
New York • Oxford

For Alfred Bendixen, Alan Gribben, Harrison T. Meserole, and David Nordloh

Facts On File Bibliography of American Fiction: 1588–1865
edited by Kent P. Ljungquist.

Facts On File Bibliography of American Fiction: 1919–1988
edited by Matthew J. Bruccoli and Judith S. Baughman.

FACTS ON FILE BIBLIOGRAPHY OF AMERICAN FICTION 1866–1918

Copyright © 1993 by Manly, Inc., and Facts On File, Inc.

Facts On File, Inc.   Facts On File Limited
460 Park Avenue South   c/o Roundhouse Publishing Ltd.
New York NY 10016   P. O. Box 140
USA   Oxford OX2 7SF
                           United Kingdom

Library of Congress Cataloging-in-Publication Data

Bibliography of American fiction, 1866–1918 / edited by James Nagel
   and Gwen L. Nagel ; with the assistance of Judith S. Baughman.
      p.   cm.
      Includes index.
      ISBN 0-8160-2116-3
      1. American fiction—19th century—Bibliography. 2. American
   fiction–20th century—Bibliography. I. Nagel, James. II. Nagel,
   Gwen L. III. Facts on File, inc.
   Z1231.F4B46   1992
   [PS377]
   016.813'4—dc20   92–32466

A British CIP catalogue record for this book is available from the British Library.

Facts On File books are available at special discounts when purchased in bulk
quantities for businesses, associations, institutions or sales promotions. Please call
our Special Sales Department in New York at 212/683-2244 (dial 800/322-8755
except in NY, AK or HI) or in Oxford at 865/728399.

Manufactured by the Maple-Vail Book Manufacturing Group
Printed in the United States of America

10 9 8 7 6 5 4 3 2 1

This book is printed on acid-free paper.

Contents

Facts On File
Bibliography of American Fiction

Author Entries

Andy Adams (1859-1935)

Samuel Hopkins Adams (1871-1958)

George Ade (1866-1944)

Louisa May Alcott (1832-1888)

Thomas Bailey Aldrich (1836-1907)

Horatio Alger, Jr. (1832-1899)

James Lane Allen (1849-1925)

Sherwood Anderson (1876-1941)

Gertrude Atherton (1857-1948)

Jane Goodwin Austin (1831-1894)

Mary Austin (1868-1934)

Irving Bacheller (1859-1950)

John Kendrick Bangs (1862-1922)

L. Frank Baum (1856-1919)

Rex Beach (1877-1949)

Edward Bellamy (1850-1898)

Ambrose Bierce (1842-1914?)

Earl Derr Biggers (1884-1933)

Sherwood Bonner (1849-1883)

Hjalmar Hjorth Boyesen (1848-1895)

Alice Brown (1856-1948)

Charles Farrar Browne (Artemus Ward)
    (1834-1867)

H. C. Bunner (1855-1896)

Thornton W. Burgess (1874-1965)

Frances Hodgson Burnett (1849-1924)

Edgar Rice Burroughs (1875-1950)

James Branch Cabell (1879-1958)

George Washington Cable (1844-1925)

Abraham Cahan (1860-1951)

Guy Wetmore Carryl (1873-1904)

Willa Cather (1873-1947)

Mary Hartwell Catherwood (1847-1902)

Robert W. Chambers (1865-1933)

Charles Waddell Chesnutt (1858-1932)

George Randolph Chester (1869-1924)

Kate Chopin (1851-1904)

Winston Churchill (1871-1947)

Samuel Langhorne Clemens (Mark Twain)
    (1835-1910)

Irvin S. Cobb (1876-1944)

Rose Terry Cooke (1827-1892)

Stephen Crane (1871-1900)

F. Marion Crawford (1854-1909)

James Oliver Curwood (1878-1927)

Olive Tilford Dargan (1869-1968)

Rebecca Harding Davis (1831-1910)

Richard Harding Davis (1864-1916)

John William De Forest (1826-1906)

Margaret Deland (1857-1945)

Thomas Dixon, Jr. (1864-1946)

Mary Mapes Dodge (1831?-1905)

Ignatius Donnelly (1831-1901)

Theodore Dreiser (1871-1945)

Alice Moore Dunbar-Nelson (1875-1935)

Finley Peter Dunne (1867-1936)

Edward Eggleston (1837-1902)

Edgar Fawcett (1847-1904)

Dorothy Canfield Fisher (1879-1958)

Mary Hallock Foote (1847-1938)

Paul Leicester Ford (1865-1902)

John Fox, Jr. (1862 or 1863-1919)

Harold Frederic (1856-1898)

Mary E. Wilkins Freeman (1852-1930)

Alice French (Octave Thanet) (1850-1934)

Henry Blake Fuller (1857-1929)

Zona Gale (1874-1938)

Hamlin Garland (1860-1940)

Katharine Fullerton Gerould (1879-1944)

Charlotte Perkins Gilman (1860-1935)

Ellen Glasgow (1873-1945)

Susan Glaspell (1876?-1948)

Anna Katharine Green (1846-1935)

Zane Grey (1872-1939)

Sutton Elbert Griggs (1872-1930)

Edward Everett Hale (1822-1909)

Lucretia Peabody Hale (1820-1900)

Henry Harland (Sidney Luska) (1861-1905)

Joel Chandler Harris (1848?-1908)

Constance Cary Harrison (1843-1920)

Bret Harte (1836-1902)

Lafcadio Hearn (1850-1904)

Joseph Hergesheimer (1880-1954)

Robert Herrick (1868-1938)

Marietta Holley (Josiah Allen's Wife) (1836-1926)

Pauline Elizabeth Hopkins (1859-1930)

Emerson Hough (1857-1923)

E. W. Howe (1853-1937)

William Dean Howells (1837-1920)

Helen Hunt Jackson (H. H., Saxe Holm)
    (1830-1885)

Henry James (1843-1916)

Sarah Orne Jewett (1849-1909)

James Weldon Johnson (1871-1938)

Owen Johnson (1878-1952)

Mary Johnston (1870-1936)

Richard Malcolm Johnston (1822-1898)

Clarence Budington Kelland (1881-1964)

Grace King (1852-1932)

Joseph Kirkland (1830-1893)

Peter B. Kyne (1880-1957)

Alfred Henry Lewis (1857-1914)

Joseph C. Lincoln (1870-1944)

David Ross Locke (Petroleum V. Nasby)
    (1833-1888)

Jack London (1876-1916)

Harriet M. Lothrop (Margaret Sidney) (1844-1924)

Charles Major (1856-1913)

Don Marquis (1878-1937)

Brander Matthews (1852-1929)

George Barr McCutcheon (1866-1928)

William McFee (1881-1966)

Oscar Micheaux (1884-1951)

S. Weir Mitchell (1829-1914)

Clarence E. Mulford (1883-1956)

Mary Noailles Murfree (Charles Egbert Craddock)
    (1850-1922)

Meredith Nicholson (1866-1947)

Frank Norris (1870-1902)

Edgar Wilson (Bill) Nye (1850-1896)

Thomas Nelson Page (1853-1922)

David Graham Phillips (1867-1911)

Ernest Poole (1880-1950)

Eleanor H. Porter (1868-1920)

Gene Stratton Porter (1863-1924)

William Sidney Porter (O. Henry) (1862-1910)

Howard Pyle (1853-1911)

Eugene Manlove Rhodes (1869-1934)

Alice Hegan Rice (1870-1942)

Mary Roberts Rinehart (1876-1958)

Elizabeth Madox Roberts (1881-1941)

Edward Payson Roe (1838-1888)

Edgar Saltus (1856-1921)

Henry Wheeler Shaw (Josh Billings) (1818-1885)

Upton Sinclair (1878-1968)

Charles Henry Smith (Bill Arp) (1826-1903)

F. Hopkinson Smith (1838-1915)

Harriet Prescott Spofford (1835-1921)

Frank R. Stockton (1834-1902)

Booth Tarkington (1869-1946)

Maurice Thompson (1844-1901)

Albion Winegar Tourgée (1838-1905)

Lew Wallace (1827-1905)

Elizabeth Stuart Phelps Ward (1844-1911)

Edward Noyes Wescott (1846-1898)

Edith Wharton (1862-1937)

Stewart Edward White (1873-1946)

Brand Whitlock (1869-1934)

Kate Douglas Wiggin (1856-1923)

Harry Leon Wilson (1867-1939)

Owen Wister (1860-1938)

Constance Fenimore Woolson (1840-1894)

Harold Bell Wright (1872-1944)

Elizabeth (Lillie) Buffum Chace Wyman
    (1847-1929)

SERIES INTRODUCTION

The *Bibliography of American Fiction* lists published writings in English by and about writers in what is now the United States of America, from the first immigrants to 1988. The compilation of these volumes was motivated by the ambition to publish a reference work that provides the first resource for the study of American fiction writers.

Easy access to seemingly limitless bits of information necessitates the winnowing of data for literary research. Thus, there is an increasing need for a bibliographical reference work that provides an organized guide to the most useful material.

In his preface to volume 4 of the *New Cambridge Bibliography of English Literature* (1972), I. R. Willison points out that *CBEL* is a bibliography of literature, not of publications; i.e., the content of the material listed has been selected to serve the purposes of literary history and research. *BAF* observes the same distinction, which has added significance some twenty years later. The availability of bibliographic resources in various electronic forms has revolutionized the process of generating lists of publications by and about an author. It is possible now, for example, in a five-minute period with the aid of a computer and without leaving one's desk, to generate lists of at least 1,370 articles on Henry James and 833 articles on Mark Twain published between 1981 and 1991. Such electronic checklists are an enormous convenience, replacing weeks or even months of hand compilation. For certain types of research these uninterpreted inventories are mandatory; but such lists provide little or no evaluation of the items they include. *BAF* entries are compiled by scholar-specialists who have read the works they select and include them because of their significance.

BAF is designed to provide an accurate record of essential primary and secondary bibliographical information for students seeking an introduction to an author's work and the research or criticism it has generated; scholars seeking general information outside their field of specialization; and scholars seeking a reliable ready reference within their field.

Fiction has been broadly interpreted to include children's writers and humorists when their work is primarily fictional in nature or involves the creation of fictional personas (e.g., Henry Wheeler Shaw's Josh Billings). The authors included in *BAF* were selected by the volume editors from lists circulated to the Advisory Board and to other scholars.

BAF does not attempt to establish the canon of American fiction. It does provide a record for the figures included.

I. PLAN OF THE WORK

BAF is organized by author entries into three periods:

through 1865—one volume
1866-1918—one volume
1919-1988—two volumes

The cut-off date for all *BAF* volumes is 31 December 1988. Nothing published after that date is listed in the primary or secondary lists.

The volumes are independent of each other. A researcher working on eighteenth-century fiction will normally be required to consult only one volume of *BAF*. Chronological placement of an author is determined by the publication date of his or her earliest significant volume of fiction. Willa Cather produced work into the 1940s; but since three of her best-known books were published before 1919, she is placed in the 1866-1918 volume. All English-language books by a fiction writer in all genres are listed in the entry; but books written in other languages and never translated into English are omitted.

The author entries are supplemented by two general bibliographical sections: 1) a vade mecum of one hundred basic reference tools for the literature of the United States—not restricted to the study of fiction; 2) a general bibliography of reference, historical, and background works for the period covered by each volume. These two lists-in-progress were circulated to the volume editors and Advisory Board.

The contributor responsible for an entry is identified. Each entry has been checked and—when necessary—revised by the in-house editors. Bibliographies compiled from bibliographies perpetuate errors; a considerable effort has been made to examine every item in every entry. The resources of the following libraries have been routinely utilized: the Thomas Cooper Library, University of South Carolina; the South Carolina State Library; the Richland County Public Library, Columbia, South Carolina; the University of Georgia Library; the Widener Library, Harvard University; the Northeastern University Library; Boston University Library; the Boston Public Library; Wellesley College Library; Brandeis University Library; Bates College Library; Massachusetts Institute of Technology Library; Tufts University Library; Bowdoin College Library; Bridgton, Maine, Public Library; Fryeburg, Maine, Public Library; the Lilly Library, Indiana University; the Library of Congress; the British Library; and the Bodleian Library, Oxford University. The services of the Interlibrary-Loan Department of the Cooper Library have been crucial to this project.

II. ENTRY FORMAT

All authors receive the same treatment. No attempt has been made to indicate the stature of an author by the form of the entry. The length and scope of each *BAF* entry is determined by the author's career.

The brief headnotes for entries are intended to place authors in terms of their reputations in their own times and now.

Author entries have two main categories: *Primary Works* (books and other significant publications by the author) and *Secondary Items* (books and shorter writings about the author).

The first rubric in an entry is BIBLIOGRAPHIES & CATALOGUES, listing primary and secondary bibliographies or checklists and exhibition or dealer catalogues *that have reference value*. Superseded bibliographies are omitted. Checklists in subject reference works (e.g., *Fiction, Folklore, Fantasy & Poetry for Children, 1876-1985*) have been excluded. Except for the *Bibliography of American Literature* and *First Printings of American Authors*, multi-author tools listed in the "General Bibliography" are excluded from the author entries.

PRIMARY WORKS

PRIMARY WORKS are listed chronologically and organized under the following headings:

BOOKS: a complete listing of the first American editions of the author's books in all genres. The genre of a primary book is stipulated, except when the genre is specified in the book's title or the work defies simple categorization. The primary lists record the first printing of each first edition; but no attempt has been made to differentiate printings, issues, or states. Keepsakes, privately printed items, and limited editions are included when—in the judgment of the contributor—the material is significant in terms of the author's career. Substantially revised primary books are listed with the first printings of those books. Subtitles are included when they clarify the nature of the volumes.

The first British or Commonwealth edition is listed: 1) if the book was never published in the United States; 2) if it precedes the American edition by at least one year; 3) if there is a title change—or a byline change—between the American and British editions; 4) if the volume contains material that is not in the American edition.

The BOOKS rubric includes posthumously published volumes of previously unpublished or uncollected writings. Book-length facsimiles of manuscripts are also listed here.

The date of publication is that printed on the title page. When the book was actually published earlier or later than the date specified on the title page, the title-page date is retained in the *BAF* citation. If no printed publication date appears on the title page, the copyright date or the Library of Congress deposit date has been used. When it has proved impossible to verify publication date, the putative year of publication has been listed with a question mark. When three or more cities are printed on the title page of a primary book, they are cited thus: NY & c. Only the main city of publication is provided for secondary volumes.

LETTERS, DIARIES, NOTEBOOKS: normally restricted to book-length publications.

OTHER: books in which the figure had substantial participation, such as translations by or books edited by the author. Uncollected shorter works of particular interest or significant works published only in anthologies may also be included in the rubric. OTHER is not an all-inclusive category: the items qualify on the basis of their importance in the author's canon.

EDITIONS & COLLECTIONS: the standard edition(s) of the author's works and influential collections of material that had previously appeared in books by the author (e.g., *The Best Stories of Sarah Orne Jewett, The Edith Wharton Reader*).

MANUSCRIPTS & ARCHIVES: the locations of the major institutional repositories of the author's papers.

SECONDARY WORKS

SECONDARY WORKS are listed alphabetically by author, editor, or compiler of the items and are organized under the following rubrics:

CONCORDANCES;

BIOGRAPHIES, divided into two subheadings: **Books** and **Book Sections & Articles**;

INTERVIEWS, a rubric employed when a substantial body of material exists; otherwise, such items are listed under CRITICAL STUDIES **Book Sections & Articles**;

CRITICAL STUDIES, four subheadings— a) **Books**, b) **Collections of Essays**, c) **Special Journals**, d) **Book Sections & Articles**. The secondary items are selective. *BAF* contributors were instructed to restrict these items to the most useful publications: book-length studies are not automatically included. Unpublished dissertations (Ph.D.) and theses (M.A.) are listed only if they have reference value. Reviews of primary books are included when the review or the reviewer was influential.

Full citations are provided for secondary books and articles. Subtitles for books are included when they clarify the scope of the books. To facilitate Interlibrary-Loan procurement of periodical articles, these citations include the volume number, the full date of the issue, and complete pagination for the article. The issue number is provided for a journal when there is no volume number or there is no month or season for the issue. In most cases MLA acronyms are used for journal titles. If there is no MLA acronym for a frequently cited journal or for a journal with an unwieldy title, *BAF* has supplied one. A key to all acronyms appears in each volume.

The appearances of secondary essays under **Collections of Essays** are identified by the names of the volume editors. Thus "Rpt Tanner, Stone" indicates that the essay is reprinted in two volumes listed in the entry. When the editor has compiled more than one collection, the volume is normally identified by stipulating its date: "Rpt Powers (1973)." In certain cases, however, clarity requires that a collection be identified by editor and short title.

The **Book Sections & Articles** rubric includes articles that appeared originally in books (Morris, Wright. "Use of the Past: Henry James." *The Territory Ahead* [NY: Harcourt, Brace, 1958], 93-112) and articles that were originally published in journals or newspapers (Garland, Hamlin. "Sanity in Fiction." *NAR*, 176 [Mar 1903], 336-348). If an article that first appeared in a hard-to-find periodical was reprinted in a readily available general collection, this volume may be noted: Rpt *Literary Opinion in America,* ed Morton Dauwen Zabel (NY: Harper, 1961).

TABLE OF ABBREVIATIONS

C = College
comp = compiler or compiled by
ed = edition, editor, or edited by
intro = introduction
nd = no date
no = number
Npl = no place
npub = no publisher
ns = new series
P = Press
Repub = Republished
Retrans = Retranslated
Rev = Revised
Rev ed = Revised edition
Rpt = Reprinted
Sect = Section
trans = translator or translated by
U = University
UK = United Kingdom
U P = University Press
Vol = volume

Editors' Note

This volume of the *Bibliography of American Fiction* consists of entries on writers who published their important works between 1866 and 1918. Traversing the inception of realism following the Civil War, through the emergence of naturalism at the end of the century, to the beginnings of modernism at the end of World War I, this period is bountiful for American fiction. These years also contributed the local-color movement, the first important urban novels, the full development of the short story as a vital genre, the establishment of women writers as a principal cultural force, and the vital early contributions to African-American fiction.

Since there were thousands of writers who published books during these years, far more than could be practically covered in any bibliography, we have sought the counsel of colleagues, especially those listed on the Advisory Board, in establishing principles for choosing the writers to be included. We are cognizant of the fact that this book will appear at a time when the canon is in the process of revision and when neglected figures are receiving attention in scholarly books and articles with impressive and heartening frequency. As a result, we have attempted to include writers within this time frame who have produced at least one major work that has been given consistent attention and about whom there is a growing body of scholarship. Although we have added scores of writers who have not appeared in standard bibliographies in the past, we recognize that we have not covered everyone who will receive attention by the end of this decade. Such omissions should be taken as the vagaries of prognostication, not the attempt to diminish or neglect any particular writer or group; we do not suggest that the writers included in this volume are the only ones worthy of consideration.

A collateral issue is the attempt to record what Americans were reading in these years between the wars, what stories and novels achieved sufficient exposure to warrant contemporary comment and response. Some of the authors who achieved this standing wrote what is now regarded as "popular" or "genre" fiction, some of it focused on a particular region, some on specific historical events or utopian projections; but all of these writers have received at least some serious critical recognition.

Each entry in the *Bibliography of American Fiction: 1866-1918* begins with a brief headnote placing the writer in the context of American literary history and suggesting the current assessment of that writer. These statements reflect the judgments of the contributing scholars and will, no doubt, require adjustment in ensuing decades. Anyone who has observed the course of critical commentary knows that the canon has changed in every decade and will continue to do so and that any bibliography can be presented only as a record of what seemed worthy of attention by a given generation of scholars. For whatever contributions the inclusion of neglected writers might make to literary study in the future, we share our satisfaction with many colleagues and friends who played a role in the development of this volume. Fundamental to the presentation of this bibliography, however, is the belief that American fiction from the Civil War through World War I is a vital legacy, equal to that of any nation of the time, and impressive even in list form.

J.N.
G.L.N.

A VADE MECUM
FOR STUDENTS OF AMERICAN LITERATURE

One hundred works and ten periodicals essential to the study of American literature.

These reference sources are intended to aid research on general aspects of American literature and its connections with other fields. Tools specific to genres, periods, and authors are listed under those rubrics in the appropriate *BAF* volumes, along with many useful books excluded here because of space considerations. Library of Congress call numbers and availability through computer technology are noted, with annotations as needed. Certain works listed here also appear in the General Bibliographies.

HISTORICAL BACKGROUND

1. *American Studies: An Annotated Bibliography*, ed Jack Salzman. Cambridge & c: Cambridge U P, 1986. 3 vols. Supplement, 1990. [Z 1361 .C6 A4]
Summaries of books on U.S. society & culture; well-organized, useful index.

2. *Dictionary of American Biography*, ed Allen Johnson, Dumas Malone et al. NY: Scribners, 1928-   . 20 vols, 8 supplements & index. [E 176 .D563]
Generally excellent, scholarly essays with brief bibliographies.

3. *Dictionary of American History*, ed Louise B Katz. NY: Scribners, 1976-1978. 7 vols & index. [E 174 .D52]
Careful identification of events, places & movements. For biographies, use *DAB* (# 2).

4. *Encyclopedia of American Facts and Dates* by Gorton Carruth. 8th ed, NY & c: Harper & Row, 1987. [E 174.5 .C3]
Best chronology of American history.

5. *Guide to the Study of the United States of America: Representative Books Reflecting the Development of American Life and Thought*, ed Roy P Basler et al. Washington: Library of Congress, 1960. Supplement, 1976. [Z 1215 .U53]
Annotated list of titles.

6. *Harvard Guide to American History*, ed Frank Freidel. Cambridge: Harvard U P, rev 1974. 2 vols. [Z 1236 .F743]
Selective topical bibliographies.

7. *Oxford Companion to American History*, ed Thomas H Johnson. NY: Oxford U P, 1966. [E 174 .J6]

8. *Oxford History of the American People* by Samuel Eliot Morison. NY: Oxford U P, 1965. [E 178 .M855]

THE AMERICAN LANGUAGE

9. *The American Language: An Inquiry into the Development of English in the United States* by H L Mencken. 4th ed, NY: Knopf, 1936. Supplements, 1945 & 1948. [PE 2808 .M4]
Personalized narrative on history & quirks of written & spoken American English.

10. *Dictionary of American English on Historical Principles*, ed William A Craigie & James R Hulbert. Chicago: U Chicago P, 1938-1944. 4 vols. [PE 2835 .C72]
American complement to *OED* (# 13).

11. *Dictionary of American Regional English*, ed Frederic G Cassidy. Cambridge & London: Harvard U P, 1985-   . 2 vols to date. [PE 2843 .D52]

12. *New Dictionary of American Slang*, ed Robert L Chapman. NY & c: Harper & Row, 1986. [PE 2846 .C46]

13. *Oxford English Dictionary*. 2nd ed, ed J A Simpson & E S C Weiner, Oxford: Oxford U P, 1989. 20 vols. [PE 1625 .O87]
An historical dictionary, chronicling meanings & usage of 500,000 words over a millenium. Heavily British, so balanced by Craigie & Hulbert (# 10).

LITERATURE

Quotations

14. *Familiar Quotations: A Collection of Passages, Phrases, and Proverbs Traced to their Sources*

in Ancient and Modern Literature by John Bartlett. 15th ed, ed Emily Morison Beck, Boston & Toronto: Little, Brown, 1980. [PN 6081 .B27]
Standard, updated compilation, arranged by author & date; well-indexed.

15. *A New Dictionary of Quotations on Historical Principles from Ancient and Modern Sources* by H L Mencken. NY: Knopf, 1942. [PN 6081 .M49]
Among the many books of quotations, this may rank highest for literary interest.

Literary Histories

16. *Annals of American Literature 1602-1983*, ed Richard M Ludwig & Clifford A Nault, Jr. NY & Oxford: Oxford U P, 1986. [PS 94 .L83]
Chronology of significant literary events & publications.

17. *Cambridge History of American Literature*, ed William Peterfield Trent el al. Cambridge: Cambridge U P / NY: Putnam, 1917-1921. 4 vols. [PS 88 .C3]
Exhaustive treatment for 17th through 19th centuries.

18. *Columbia Literary History of the United States*, ed Emory Elliott. NY: Columbia U P, 1988. [PS 92 .C64]
Essays on selected writers, movements & periods.

19. *Literary History of the United States: History*. 4th ed, ed Robert E Spiller et al, NY: Macmillan / London: Collier Macmillan, 1974. [PS 88 .L522]
Particularly strong for pre-WWI literature & background. See # 69.

Literary Dictionaries

20. *Benét's Reader's Encyclopedia* by William Rose Benét. 3rd ed, NY: Harper & Row, 1987. [PN 41. B4]
Companion to varieties of world literature.

21. *Brewer's Dictionary of Phrase and Fable*, centenary ed, rev by Ivor H Evans. NY: Harper & Row, 1981. [PN 43 .B65]
Unique guide to allusions & expressions; earlier editions still useful.

22. *A Handbook to Literature* by C Hugh Holman. 5th ed, NY: Macmillan, 1986. [PN 41 .H6]
Essential dictionary of literary terminology. Comprehensive, with useful appendixes.

23. *Oxford Companion to American Literature*. 5th ed, ed James D Hart, NY & Oxford: Oxford U P, 1983. [PS 21 .H3]
Oxford Companions are standards of pithy identifications of authors, works, characters in literature & may also contain useful appendixes.

24. *Oxford Companion to Classical Literature*. 2nd ed, ed M C Howatson, Oxford & NY: Oxford U P, 1989. [PA 31 .H69]
Among many uses, explains modern allusions to classical writings.

25. *Oxford Companion to English Literature*. 5th ed, ed Margaret Drabble, Oxford & c: Oxford U P, 1985. [PR 19 .D73]
Also includes entries on major American writers.

26. *Oxford Companion to the Theatre*. 4th ed, ed Phyllis Hartnoll, Oxford & c: Oxford U P, 1983. [PN 2037 .O95]
Emphasis on staged drama, especially British & American. International, historical in scope.

27. *Princeton Encyclopedia of Poetry and Poetics*, enlarged ed, ed Alex Preminger. Princeton: Princeton U P, 1974. [PN 1021 .E5]

Literary Biographies

28. *American Authors, 1600-1900*, ed Stanley J Kunitz & Howard Haycraft. NY: Wilson, 1938. [PS 21. K8]

29. *American Women Writers: A Critical Reference Guide from Colonial Times to the Present*, ed Lina Mainiero. NY: Ungar, 1979-1982. 4 vols. [PS 147 .A4]
Critical biography & selected bibliography for 1,000 writers, many not covered elsewhere.

30. *American Writers*. NY: Scribners, 1974. 4 vols. 2-vol supplements, 1979, 1981, 1991. [PS 55 .A44]
Scholarly essays with selective bibliographies. Based on the *U Minnesota Pamphlets on American Writers*.

31. *Black American Writers, Past and Present: A Biographical and Bibliographical Dictionary*, ed Theressa Gunnels Rush et al. Metuchen, NJ: Scarecrow, 1975. [Z 1229 .N39 R87]
Uneven guide to 2,000 writers.

32. *Contemporary Authors: A Bio-Bibliographical Guide to Current Writers in Fiction, General*

NonFiction, Poetry, Journalism, Drama, Motion Pictures, Television, and Other Fields. Detroit: Gale, 1962- . 160 vols to date. [Z 1224. C615]
Biographical, occasionally critical information, regularly revised, very current. *Bibliographic Series*, 2 volumes to date, provides extensive bibliographies on authors.

33. *Dictionary of Literary Biography.* Detroit: Bruccoli Clark Layman/Gale, 1978- . 160 vols to date.
Scholarly, illustrated, critical biographical essays with bibliographies. Individual volumes cover international literatures by nationality, genre & period. Includes *Yearbooks* and *Documentary Series* volumes. Also *Concise DALB, 1987-1989,* 6 vols. [PS 129 .C66] Cumulatively indexed.

34. *Twentieth Century Authors,* ed Stanley J Kunitz & Howard Haycraft. NY: Wilson, 1942. Supplement, ed Kunitz & Vineta Colby, 1955. [PN 451 .K8]

35. *World Authors, 1950-1970,* ed John Wakeman. NY: Wilson, 1975. Supplements, *1970-1975* (1980); *1975-1980,* ed Vineta Colby (1985); *1980-1985,* ed Colby (1991). [PN 451 .W3]

Primary Bibliographies

36. *American Bibliography: A Chronological Dictionary of All Books, Pamphlets and Periodical Publications Printed in the United States of America from the Genesis of Printing in 1639 down to and including the year 1820, with Bibliographical and Biographical Notes* by Charles Evans. Chicago: Blakeley, 1903-1934 (vols 1-12); Worcester, Mass: American Antiquarian Society, 1955-1959 (vols 13-14). [Z 1215. E923]
Chronological listing with good indexes. Many libraries have the cited material in microform. Supplemented by the following:
American Bibliography: A Preliminary Checklist for 1801-1819 by Ralph R Shaw & Richard H. Shoemaker. Metuchen, NJ: Scarecrow, 1958-1983. 20 vols & 3 indexes.
A Checklist of American Imprints for 1820-1829 by Richard H Shoemaker. Metuchen, NJ: Scarecrow, 1964-1973. 10 vols & 2 indexes.
A Checklist of American Imprints for 1830 by Gayle Cooper. Metuchen, NJ: Scarecrow, 1972.
A Checklist of American Imprints for 1831-33 by Scott Bruntjen & Carol Rinderknecht Bruntjen. Metuchen, NJ: Scarecrow, 1975-1979. 3 vols.

A Checklist of American Imprints for 1834 by Carol Rinderknecht. Methuen, NJ: Scarecrow, 1982.
A Checklist of American Imprints for 1835-1839 by Rinderknecht. Metuchen, NJ: Scarecrow, 1985. 5 vols.
A Checklist of American Imprints for 1830-1839: Author Title Indexes by Rinderknecht. Metuchen, NJ: Scarecrow, 1989. 4 vols.
Supplement to Charles Evans' American Bibliography by Roger P Bristol. Charlottesville: U P Virginia, 1971.

37. *American Fiction, 1774-1900: A Contribution,* 3 vols, ed Lyle H Wright. San Marino, Calif: Huntington Library, 1965-1969. [Z 1231 .F4 W9]
11,000 novels, listed by author, briefly described. Indexed by title. Microfilm of titles available at many libraries.

38. *American Literary Manuscripts: A Checklist of Holdings in Academic, Historical, and Public Libraries, Museums, and Authors' Homes in the United States.* 2nd ed, ed J Albert Robbins, Athens: U Georgia P, 1977. [Z 6620. U5 M6]
Papers of 2,800 authors in 600 locations.

39. *Bibliography of American Literature,* ed Jacob Blanck. New Haven, Conn: Yale U P, 1955-1991. 9 vols. [Z 1225 .B55]
Primary bibliographies of books by nearly 300 authors who died before 1931.

40. *Bibliotheca Americana: A Dictionary of Books Relating to America from Its Discovery to the Present Time* by Joseph Sabin. NY: Sabin, 1868-1936. 29 vols. [Z 1201. S22]
Annotated listing of material about America. Usefulness enhanced by:
Author-Title Index to Joseph Sabin's Dictionary of Books Relating to America by John Edgar Molnar. Metuchen, NJ: Scarecrow, 1974. 3 vols.

41. *Books in Print.* NY: Bowker, 1948- . Annually with updates. [Z 1215 .P972]*
Listing by author, title & subject of books available from or projected by major American publishers.

*Asterisks indicate works that are at least partly available by computer. See note on "Computer Availability" at the end of the "Vade Mecum."

42. *Cumulative Book Index.* NY: Wilson, 1933-   .
Quarterly, cumulated annually. [Z 1219.
M78]*
English language books published internationally. See   49.

43. *First Printings of American Authors: Contributions toward Descriptive Checklists.* Detroit: Bruccoli Clark/Gale, 1977-1987. 5 vols.
[Z 1231 .F5 F57]
Listings for many authors not found elsewhere.

44. *Literary Writings in America: A Bibliography,*
ed Edward H O'Neill. Millwood, NY: KTO,
1977. 8 vols. [Z 1225 .L58]
Index to materials by & about 600 authors,
in thousands of books & periodicals, 1850-
1940.

45. *National Union Catalog, Pre-1956 Imprints.*
London: Mansell, 1968-1980. 685 vols. Supplementary vols 686-754. [Z 881 .A1 U518]
Listing by author of all books published before 1956 & owned by American research libraries, including the Library of Congress.
Basic bibliographical information with locations.

46. *National Union Catalog, 1956-1967,* 125 vols,
Totowa, NJ: Rowman & Littlefield, 1972;
1968-1972, 104 vols, Ann Arbor, Mich:
Edwards, 1973; *1973-1977,* 135 vols,
Totowa, NJ: Rowman & Littlefield, 1978.
Annual, 1974-   . [Z 881. A1 U517]
Continuation of #45 in book form; since
1983 issued on microfiche. Large portion of
NUC available in MARC database.

47. *New Serial Titles, 1950-70: A Union List of
Serials Commencing Publication after December 31, 1949.* Washington: Library of Congress, 1973. 4 vols. Updates: *1971-75* (1976),
2 vols; *1976-80* (1981), 2 vols; *1981-85*
(1986), 6 vols; *1986-89* (1990), 6 vols. [Z
6945 .U5 .S42]

48. *Union List of Serials in Libraries of the United
States and Canada.* 3rd ed, NY: Wilson,
1965. 5 vols. [Z 6945 .U45]
Limited by age, but best listing of major libraries' holdings of journals that began before
1950.

49. *United States Catalog: Books in Print.* NY:
Wilson, 1899-1928. 4 vols, 7 supplements.
[Z 1219 .M78]

Periodic cumulation from publishers' catalogues, arranged by author, title & subject.
Continued by *CBI* (#42).

50. *United States Newspaper Program National
Union List.* 3rd ed, Dublin, Ohio: OCLC,
1989. [Z 6945. U5]
Ongoing cooperative listing of all library
holdings, with locations & exact holdings,
both paper & microfilm.

Indexes to Primary Sources

51. *Columbia Granger's Index to Poetry,* ed Edith
P Hazen & Deborah J Fryer. 9th ed, NY: Columbia U P, 1990. [PN 1022. G7]*
Listing by title & first line, indexing anthologies of poetry. Previous editions must be used
for older anthologies.

52. *Nineteenth-Century Reader's Guide to Periodical Literature, 1890-1899, With Supplementary Indexing, 1900-1922,* ed Helen Grant
Cushing & Adah V Morris. NY: Wilson,
1944. 4 vols. [AI 3 .R47]
Indexes American & British general magazines, many not in Poole's (#55), by author
& standardized subject listings.

53. *Ottemiller's Index to Plays in Collections: An
Author and Title Index to Plays Appearing in
Collections Published Between 1900 and
1985.* 7th ed, ed Billie M Connor & Helene
G. Mochedlover, Metuchen, NJ: Scarecrow,
1988. [Z 5781 .O8]
Reliable one-volume guide, best source for
pre-1949 anthologies.

54. *Play Index.* NY: Wilson, 1953-   . 7 vols to
date. [Z 5781 .P53]
Far more extensive than Ottemiller (#53) for
recently published works, each volume covering publications of specific years. Useful indexes.

55. *Poole's Index to Periodical Literature, 1802-
1906* by William Frederick Poole et al. NY:
Smith, 1882-1908. 6 vols in 7. [AI 3 .P7]
Index to 500 American & British periodicals
is by subject only. Following is needed to locate articles by the author:
Cumulated Author Index for Poole's Index to Periodical Literature 1802-1906, ed C Edward
Wall. Ann Arbor, Mich: Pierian, 1971.

56. *Reader's Guide to Periodical Literature: An Author and Subject Index.* NY: Wilson, 1900-   .
Monthly, with quarterly & annual
cumulations. [AI 3 .R4]*
Guide to popular, non-technical magazines.

57. *Short Story Index: An Index to Stories in Collections and Periodicals.* NY: Wilson, 1953- . [Z 5917 .S5 C62]
Annual, periodic cumulations.

Bibliographies of Criticism

58. *American and British Poetry: A Guide to the Criticism, 1925-1978,* comp Harriet Semmes Alexander. Athens, Ohio: Swallow, 1984. [Z 1231 .P7 A44]
Good index to studies of entire poems under 1000 lines. Useful supplement to *Guide to American Poetry Explication* (#68).

59. *American Drama Criticism: Interpretations, 1890-1977* by Floyd Eugene Eddleman. 2nd ed, Hamden, Conn: Shoe String, 1979. Supplements, 1984, 1989. [Z 1231 .D7 P3]
Good index to popular magazines, books & some scholarly journals.

60. *The American Novel 1789-1959: A Checklist of Twentieth-Century Criticism* by Donna L Gerstenberger & George Hendrick. Denver: Swallow, 1961. *Volume II: Criticism Written 1960-1968.* Chicago: Swallow, 1970. [Z 1231 .F4 G4]
Listing by novelist & by novel. Good starting point.

61. *American Short-Fiction Criticism and Scholarship, 1959-1977: A Checklist* by Joe Weixlmann. Chicago: Swallow, 1982. [Z 1231 .F4 W43]
Comprehensive, accurate & usable.

62. *Articles on Twentieth-Century Literature: An Annotated Bibliography, 1954-70,* ed David E Pownall. Millwood, NY: Kraus, 1973-1980. 7 vols. [Z 6519 .P66]
International in scope of subject & journals indexed.

63. *The Contemporary Novel: A Checklist of Critical Literature on the British and American Novel Since 1945* by Irving Adelman & Rita Dworkin. Metuchen, NJ: Scarecrow, 1972. [Z 1231 .F4 A34]
Criticism of 200 authors, listed by novelist & novel.

64. *Dissertations in American Literature, 1891-1966,* ed James L Woodress. Durham, NC: Duke U P, 1968. [Z 1225 .W8]
Organized by author, genre & subject.

65. *Drama Criticism: Volume I: A Checklist of Interpretation since 1940 of English and Ameri-* can *Plays* by Arthur Coleman & Gary R Tyler. Denver: Swallow, 1966. [Z 5781 .C65]
Broad, excellent coverage.

66. *Eight American Authors: A Review of Research and Criticism,* ed James L Woodress. NY: Norton, rev 1971. [PS 201 .E4]
Bibliographies for Poe, Emerson, Hawthorne, Thoreau, Melville, Whitman, Twain & James.

67. *Fifteen American Authors Before 1900: Bibliographical Essays on Research and Criticism,* ed Earl N Harbert & Robert A Rees. Madison: U Wisconsin P, rev 1984. [PS 201 .R38]
H Adams, Bryant, Cooper, S Crane, Dickinson, Edwards, Franklin, Holmes, Howells, Irving, Longfellow, Lowell, Norris, Taylor & Whittier.

68. *Guide to American Poetry Explication.* Volume 1: *Colonial and Nineteenth-Century,* ed James Ruppert; Volume 2: *Modern and Contemporary,* ed John R Leo. Boston: Hall, 1989. [Z 1231. P7]
Alexander (#58) often can add items.

69. *Literary History of the United States: Bibliography.* 4th ed, ed Robert E Spiller et al, NY: Macmillan / London: Collier Macmillan, 1974. [PS 88 .L522 Vol 2]
Awkward but important combination of three previously published bibliographies covering pre-1948, 1948-1958, 1958-1970. See   19.

70. *Major Writers of Early American Literature,* ed Everett H Emerson. Madison: U Wisconsin P, 1972. [PS 185 .E4]
Bradford, Bradstreet, Taylor, Mather, Byrd, Edwards, Franklin, Freneau & C B Brown.

71. *Short Fiction Criticism: A Checklist of Interpretation Since 1925 of Stories and Novelettes (American, British, Continental), 1800-1958,* ed Jarvis Thurston et al. Denver: Swallow, 1960. [Z 5917 .S5 T4]
Useful for early criticism; updated by Weixlmann (#61).

72. *Sixteen Modern American Authors: A Survey of Research and Criticism,* ed Jackson R Bryer. Durham, NC: Duke U P, rev 1974. Vol 2 (1989) covers 1972-1988. [PS 221 .F45]
Anderson, Cather, S Crane, Dreiser, Eliot, Faulkner, Fitzgerald, Frost, Hemingway, O'Neill, Pound, Robinson, Steinbeck, Stevens, W C Williams & Wolfe.

73. *Twentieth-Century Short Story Explication, 1900-1975* by Warren S Walker. 3rd ed,

Hamden, Conn: Shoe String, 1977. Supplements, *1976-1978* (1980), *1977-1981* (1984), *1981-1984* (1987), *1984-1986* (1989), *1987-1988* (1991). [Z 5917 .S5 W33]
Extensive, but difficult to use. Journal abbreviations defined in supplements.

Periodical Guides to Criticism

74. *Abstracts of English Studies.* Calgary: U Calgary P, 1958- . Quarterly. [PE 25 .A16]
International guide to articles & essays, many not indexed elsewhere, on English & American literature.

75. *American Literary Scholarship.* Durham, NC: Duke U P, 1965- . Annual. [PS 3 .A47]
Bibliographic essays on genres, authors, periods.

76. *Annual Bibliography of English Language and Literature.* Cambridge, UK: Modern Humanities Research Association, 1920- . Annual. [Z 2011 .M69]
International, arranged by topic. This & *YWES* (#86) supplement *MLAIB* (83).

77. *Book Review Digest.* NY: Wilson, 1905- . 10 times per year, cumulated annually. [Z 1219 .C96]*
Excerpts from reviews of popular books in magazines & newspapers.

78. *Book Review Index.* Detroit: Gale, 1965- . Bi-monthly, cumulated. [Z 1035 .A1 B6]*
Far more comprehensive than #77; especially good for scholarly books & novels receiving limited attention.

79. *Combined Retrospective Index to Book Reviews in Humanities Journals, 1802-1974.* Woodbridge, Conn: Research Publications, 1982-1984. 10 vols. [Z 6265 .C65]
500,000 reviews from 150 journals listed; especially strong in literature.

80. *Contemporary Literary Criticism: Excerpts from the Criticism of Today's Novelists, Poets, Playwrights and Other Creative Writers.* Detroit: Gale, 1973- . [PN 771 .C59]
International coverage, long excerpts from criticism. Format similar to NCLC (84) & TCLC (#85).

81. *Essay and General Literature Index.* NY: Wilson, 1900- . Semi-annual, cumulated. [AI 3 .E752]*
Index by author & subject to essays published in collections. Many fields, genres covered.

82. *Humanities Index.* NY: Wilson, 1974- . Quarterly, cumulated annually. [Z 6941 .H84]*
Not as comprehensive as *MLAIB* (#75), but interdisciplinary, covering history, philosophy, theology, as well as language & literature. Valuable for timeliness. Supersedes *International Index* (1907-1965) & *Social Sciences and Humanities Index* (1965-1974).

83. *MLA International Bibliography of Books and Articles on the Modern Languages and Literature.* NY: MLA, 1921- . Annual. [Z 7006. M64]*
Extensive, international coverage of American literature & since 1981 enhanced by subject index. Arrangement by nationality & period. Must be supplemented by other indexes.

84. *Nineteenth-Century Literary Criticism: Excerpts from Criticism of the Works of Novelists, Poets, Playwrights, Short Story Writers, and Other Creative Writers who lived between 1800 and 1900, from the First Published Critical Appraisals to Current Evaluations.* Detroit: Gale, 1981- . [PN 761 .N56]

85. *Twentieth-Century Literary Criticism: Excerpts from Criticism of the Works of Novelists, Poets, Playwrights, Short Story Writers, and Other Creative Writers, 1900-1960, from the First Published Critical Appraisals to Current Evaluations.* Detroit: Gale, 1978- . [PN 771 .G27]

86. *The Year's Work in English Studies.* London: English Association, 1921- . Annual. [PE 58 .E6]
Two chapters provide bibliographic essays on American literary scholarship.

Bibliographies of Bibliographies

87. *Bibliographic Index: A Cumulative Bibliography of Bibliographies.* NY: Wilson, 1937- . 3 times per year, annually cumulated. [Z 1002 .B595]*
Usuable tool for staying current.

88. *Bibliography of Bibliographies in American Literature* by Charles H Nilon. NY: Bowker, 1970. [Z 1225 .A1 N5]
Aging but vital, updated by #87.

Guides to Research

89. *Bibliographical Guide to the Study of the Literature of the U.S.A.* by Clarence L Gohdes &

Sanford E Marovitz. 5th ed, Durham, NC: Duke U P, 1984. [Z1225 .G6]
Annotated listing, especially good for topical approach.

90. *Literary Research Guide: A Guide to Reference Sources for the Study of Literatures in English and Related Topics* by James L Harner. NY: MLA, 1989. [Z 2011 .H34 1989]
Useful manual for using the library. Hundreds of annotations on selected reference books; appendixes.

Books & Publishing

91. *American Journalism: A History, 1690-1960* by Frank Luther Mott. 3rd ed, NY: Macmillan, 1962. [PN 4855 .M63]

92. *The Book in America: A History of the Making and Selling of Books in the United States* by Hellmut Lehmann-Haupt et al. 2nd ed, NY: Bowker, 1952. [Z 473 .L522]

93. *Copyright Handbook* by Donald F Johnston. 2nd ed, NY: Bowker, 1982. [KF 2994 .J63]

94. *Glaister's Glossary of the Book* by Geoffrey Ashall Glaister. 2nd ed, London & c: Allen & Unwin, 1979. [Z 118 .G55]
Treats all aspects of the book & publishing. Illustrations & appendixes.

95. *Guide to the Study of United States Imprints* by G Thomas Tanselle. Cambridge: Harvard U P, 1971. 2 vols. [Z 1215 .A2 T3]
Comprehensive checklists of materials on all aspects of printing & publishing history. See also *DLB* (#33), vol 46.

96. *A History of American Magazines* by Frank Luther Mott. Cambridge: Harvard U P, 1938-1968. 5 vols. [PN 4877 .M63]
Covers 1741-1930, by period, genre & specific titles.

97. *History of Book Publishing in the United States* by John W Tebbel. NY: Bowker, 1973-1981. 4 vols. [Z 473 .T42]

Directories

98. *Literary Market Place: The Directory of American Book Publishing.* NY: Bowker, 1940- . Annual. [Z 282 .L584]
Addresses & information for publishers, agents, reviewers, book clubs, etc.

99. *MLA Directory of Periodicals: A Guide to Journals and Series in Languages and Litera-*

tures. NY: MLA, 1979- . Annual. [Z 7006 .M632]
Listing of all serials indexed by MLAIB (#83).

100. *Ulrich's International Periodicals Directory.* NY: Bowker, 1932- . Annual. [Z 6941 .U5]*
Best listing of currently published titles by subject; valuable for listing of indexes that cover each journal.

IMPORTANT JOURNALS

J-1. *American Literature: A Journal of Literary History, Criticism, and Bibliography.* Durham, NC: Duke U P, 1929- . Quarterly. [PS 1 .A6]
Critical articles, book reviews, research in progress; formerly thorough, now selective bibliography.

J-2. *American Literary Realism, 1870-1910.* Jefferson, NC: McFarland, 1967- . Semiannual. [PS 228 .R3]

J-3. *American Quarterly.* Philadelphia: U Pennsylvania P, 1949- . Quarterly. [AP 2 .A39]
Explores the cultural background of literature. Bibliographical essays.

J-4. *ESQ: A Journal of the American Renaissance.* Pullman: Washington State U P, 1955- . Quarterly. [PS 1629 .E6]

J-5. *Early American Literature.* Chapel Hill: U North Carolina P, 1966- . 3 times per year. [PS 1 .E1]

J-6. *Journal of American Studies.* Cambridge: Cambridge U P, 1967- . Quarterly. [E 151 .J6]
General topics.

J-7. *Modern Fiction Studies.* West Lafayette, Ind: Purdue U, Department of English, 1955- . Quarterly. [PS 379 .M55]

J-8. *Resources for American Literary Study.* College Park: U Maryland, Department of English, 1971- . Semiannual. [Z 1225 .R46]

J-9. *Studies in American Fiction.* Boston: Northeastern U, Department of English, 1973- . Semiannual. [PS 370 .S87]

J-10. *Studies in the American Renaissance.* Charlottesville: U P Virginia, 1977- . Annual. [PS 201 .S86]

COMPUTER AVAILABILITY

Reference works useful to students of American literature are increasingly available through computer technology. Some are "on-line" tools, used via telephone linkage to computer centers or data bases; others can be used either on-line or on compact disc or tape. The advantages of such computer resources include speed and the ability to use and combine specific subject headings. Factors that determine the utility of these tools include scope, reliability of both data and method, and ease of use.

Titles in the Vade Mecum that are at least partially available by computer are marked with the * symbol. Reference librarians will be able to provide guidance. Other major computer tools include:

OCLC (OnLine Computer Library Center): A network including nearly all American libraries and many foreign ones. Lists millions of books, serials, maps, recordings, and archival materials. Especially useful for identifying libraries with specific titles.

RLIN (Research Libraries Network): Listing of items held by the leading American research libraries, the Research Libraries Group. Good for all library materials, especially archival materials.

Both the OCLC and RLIN databases include the recent Library of Congress cataloguing, called MARC (Machine-Readable Cataloguing). The strength of OCLC is its broad coverage of libraries, but RLIN is more carefully catalogued. Also, RLIN offers searching by subject, whereas OCLC has just begun to accommodate this procedure. Research libraries have access to both data-bases, which complement each other.

Daniel Boice

GENERAL BIBLIOGRAPHY:
REFERENCE & RESEARCH WORKS

This selective checklist covers three areas: 1) histories and bibliographies of American literature, to provide context for the study of American fiction; 2) histories and bibliographies of American fiction; 3) works specific to American fiction between the Civil War and World War I. The enormous number of possible items necessitated general policies on limitation. Literary criticism has been restricted to the most influential titles. Books not in English have been generally excluded, as have titles judged to be too narrow in scope (those treating a single theme or a small group of authors) and books deemed too broad (those covering several genres or those treating American and foreign fiction). Anthologies of fiction and articles in periodicals have also been excluded.

An early version of this bibliography was prepared by Robert C. Leitz III (Louisiana State University) and Kenneth Price (Texas A&M University) and augmented by Gwen L. Nagel and James Nagel. This material was conflated with the bibliography prepared by Daniel Boice (Thomas Cooper Library, University of South Carolina) for *BAF: 1919-1988*; the setting copy was prepared by Daniel Boice.

OUTLINE

I. BASIC TOPICS
   A. Bibliographies
      1. Primary
      2. Secondary
   B. Handbooks & Guides
   C. Intellectual & Social Background
   D. Relations with Other Art Forms
   E. Relations with Other Countries: Cross Influences & Critical Reception

II. LITERARY & HISTORICAL STUDIES
   A. General Studies: 19th-Century American Literature
   B. The Novel
   C. The Short Story

III. MOVEMENTS IN FICTION
   A. Realism
   B. Naturalism

IV. INFLUENCES
   A. Politics
   B. Psychology
   C. Religion

V. FICTION ON SPECIAL TOPICS

VI. AUTHORS
   A. Collective Biography & Biographical Dictionaries
   B. Women Writers
   C. African-American Writers
   D. Other

VII. REGIONS & REGIONALISM
   A. General Studies
   B. The South
   C. New England
   D. The Midwest
   E. The West & Southwest

VIII. GENRES
   A. Mystery & Espionage
   B. Science Fiction
   C. Fantasy & Horror
   D. Historical Fiction
   E. Westerns
   F. Children's Literature
   G. Humor
   H. Romantic Fiction

IX. PUBLISHING & AUTHORSHIP
   A. Publishing
   B. Magazines
   C. Popular Fiction
   D. Censorship

I.   BASIC TOPICS

A. Bibliographies

1. PRIMARY
Blanck, Jacob, comp. *Bibliography of American Literature*. New Haven: Yale U P, 1955-1991. 9 vols.

Books in Print. NY: Bowker, 1948- . Annual with updates.

Fiction 1876-1983: A Bibliography of United States Editions. NY: Bowker, 1983. 2 vols.

First Printings of American Authors: Contributions Toward Descriptive Checklists. Detroit: Bruccoli Clark/Gale, 1977-1987. 5 vols.

O'Neill, Edward H, ed. *Literary Writings in America: A Bibliography.* Millwood, NY: KTO, 1977.

Robbins, J Albert, ed. *American Literary Manuscripts: A Checklist of Holdings in Academic, Historical, and Public Libraries, Museums, and Authors' Homes in the United States,* 2nd ed. Athens: U Georgia P, 1977.

Wright, Lyle, ed. *American Fiction, 1774-1900: A Contribution Toward a Bibliography.* San Marino, Calif: Huntington Library, 1965-1969. 3 vols.

Wright, R Glenn. *Author Bibliography of English Language Fiction in the Library of Congress Through 1950.* Boston: Hall, 1973. 8 vols.

Wright. *Chronological Bibliography of English Language Fiction in the Library of Congress Through 1950.* Boston: Hall, 1974. 8 vols.

Wright. *Title Bibliography of English Language Fiction in the Library of Congress Through 1950.* Boston: Hall, 1976. 9 vols.

Yaakov, Juliette, ed. *Fiction Catalog,* 11th ed. NY: Wilson, 1986. Annual supplements, 1986 & 1987.

2. SECONDARY

Gabel, Gernot U & Gisela R Gabel. *Dissertations in English and American Literature: Theses Accepted by Austrian, French and Swiss Universities, 1875-1970.* Hamburg: npub, 1977. *Supplement, 1971-1975, and Additions.* Köln, Gemini, 1982.

Gohdes, Clarence L & Sanford E Marovitz. *Bibliographical Guide to the Study of the Literature of the USA,* 5th ed. Durham, NC: Duke U P, 1984.

Havlice, Patricia Pate. *Index to American Author Bibliographies.* Metuchen, NJ: Scarecrow, 1972.

Koster, Donald N. *American Literature and Language: A Guide to Information Sources.* Detroit: Gale, 1982.

Leary, Lewis, ed. *Articles on American Literature, 1900-1950.* Durham, NC: Duke U P, 1954. Supplements, *1950-1967* (1970), *1968-1975* (1979).

McNamee, Lawrence F. *Dissertations in English and American Literature: Theses Accepted by American, British and German Universities, 1865-1964.* NY: Bowker, 1968. Supplements, *1964-1968* (1969), *1969-1973* (1974).

Nilon, Charles H. *Bibliography of Bibliographies in American Literature.* NY: Bowker, 1970.

Patterson, Margaret C. *Author Newsletters and Journals: An International Annotated Bibliography of Serial Publications Concerned With the Life and Works of Individual Authors.* Detroit: Gale, 1979. Supplements in *Serials Review,* 8, no 4 (1982), 61-72; 10, no 1 (1984), 51-59; 11, no 3 (1985), 31-44.

Pownall, David E. *Articles on Twentieth-Century Literature: An Annotated Bibliography, 1954-1970.* Millwood, NY: Kraus, 1973-1980. 7 vols.

Salzman, Jack, ed. *American Studies: An Annotated Bibliography.* Cambridge: Cambridge U P, 1986. 3 vols.

Wortman, William A. *A Guide to Serial Bibliographies for Modern Literature.* NY: MLA, 1982.

B. Handbooks & Guides

Bradbury, Malcolm, Eric Mottram & Jean Franco, eds. *The Penguin Companion to American Literature.* NY: McGraw-Hill, 1971.

Hart, James D, ed. *Oxford Companion to American Literature,* 5th ed. NY: Oxford U P, 1983.

Inge, M Thomas, ed. *Handbook of American Popular Culture.* Westport, Conn: Greenwood, 1978-1981. 3 vols.

Jones, Howard Mumford & Richard M Ludwig. *Guide to American Literature and Its Backgrounds Since 1890,* 3rd ed. Cambridge: Harvard U P, 1964.

Kirkpatrick, D L. *Reference Guide to American Literature,* 2nd ed. Chicago: St James, 1987.

Leary, Lewis & John Auchard. *American Literature: A Study and Research Guide.* NY: St Martin, 1976.

Ludwig, Richard M & Clifford A Nault, Jr, eds. *Annals of American Literature, 1602-1983.* NY: Oxford U P, 1986.

Rogal, Samuel J. *A Chronological Outline of American Literature.* NY: Greenwood, 1987.

Rood, Karen L, ed. *American Literary Almanac, From 1608 to the Present: An Original Compendium of Facts and Anecdotes About Literary Life in the United States of America.* NY: Bruccoli Clark Layman/Facts on File, 1988.

C. Intellectual & Social Background

Banta, Martha. *Failure & Success in America: A Literary Debate.* Princeton: Princeton U P, 1978.

Bradbury, Malcolm & Howard Templeton, eds. *Introduction to American Studies.* London: Longman, 1981.

Cargill, Oscar. *Intellectual America: Ideas on the March.* NY: Macmillan, 1941.

Commager, Henry Steele. *The American Mind: An Interpretation of American Thought and Character Since the 1880's.* New Haven: Yale U P, 1950.

Curti, Merle. *The Growth of American Thought.* NY: Harper, 1943.

Horton, Rod W & Herbert W Edwards. *Backgrounds of American Literary Thought*, 3rd ed. Englewood Cliffs, NJ: Prentice-Hall, 1974.

Lasch, Christopher. *The New Radicalism in America, 1899-1963: The Intellectual as a Social Type.* NY: Knopf, 1965.

Maxwell, D E S. *American Fiction: The Intellectual Background.* NY: Columbia U P, 1963.

Weiss, Richard. *The American Myth of Success: From Horatio Alger to Norman Vincent Peale.* NY: Basic Books, 1969.

D. Relations With Other Arts

Nye, Russel B. *The Unembarrassed Muse: The Popular Arts in America.* NY: Dial, 1970.

Peary, Gerald & Roger Shatzkin, eds. *The Classic American Novel and the Movies.* NY: Ungar, 1977.

Tichi, Cecelia. *Shifting Gears: Technology, Literature, Culture in Modernist America.* Chapel Hill: U North Carolina P, 1987.

E. Relations With Other Countries: Cross Influences & Critical Reception

Anderson, Carl L. *The Swedish Acceptance of American Literature.* Philadelphia: U Pennsylvania P, 1957.

Lalli, Biancamaria Tedeschini, Robert Perrault & Alessandra Pinto Surdi, eds. *Repertorio Bibliografico della Letteratura Americana in Italia.* Rome: Edizioni di Storia e Letteratura, 1966-1982. 4 vols in 3.

Libman, Valentina A, comp. *Russian Studies of American Literature: A Bibliography*, ed Clarence Gohdes; trans Robert V Allen. Chapel Hill: U North Carolina P, 1969.

Pochmann, Henry A. *German Culture in America: Philosophical and Literary Influences, 1600-1900.* Madison: U Wisconsin P, 1957.

II. LITERARY & HISTORICAL STUDIES

A. General Studies

Berkovitch, Sacvan & Myra Jehlen, eds. *Ideology and Classic American Literature.* Cambridge: Cambridge U P, 1986.

Blair, Walter et al. *American Literature: A Brief History,* rev ed. Chicago: Scott, Foresman, 1964.

Blankenship, Russell. *American Literature as an Expression of the National Mind,* rev ed. NY: Holt, 1958.

Boynton, Percy H. *A History of American Literature.* Boston: Ginn, 1919.

Brooks, Van Wyck. *America's Coming-of-Age.* NY: Huebsch, 1915.

Brooks. *New England: Indian Summer: 1865-1915.* NY: Dutton, 1940.

Brooks. *The Confident Years: 1885-1915.* NY: Dutton, 1952.

Brooks. *The Dream of Arcadia: American Writers and Artists in Italy, 1760-1915.* NY: Dutton, 1958.

Clark, Harry Hayden, ed. *Transitions in American Literary History.* Durham, NC: Duke U P, 1953.

Clough, Wilson O. *The Necessary Earth: Nature and Solitude in American Literature.* Austin: U Texas P, 1964.

Conn, Peter. *The Divided Mind: Ideology and Imagination in America, 1898-1917.* Cambridge: Cambridge U P, 1983.

Dickinson, Thomas H. *The Making of American Literature.* NY: Century, 1932.

Elliott, Emory, ed. *Columbia Literary History of the United States.* NY: Columbia U P, 1988.

Falk, Robert. *The Victorian Mode in American Fiction, 1865-1885.* East Lansing: Michigan State U P, 1965.

Haney, John L. *The Story of Our Literature: An Interpretation of the American Spirit.* NY: Scribners, 1923.

Hartwick, Harry. *The Foreground of American Fiction.* NY: American Book, 1934.

Hicks, Granville. *The Great Tradition: An Interpretation of American Literature Since the Civil War,* rev ed. NY: Macmillan, 1935.

Hook, Andrew. *American Literature in Context, III: 1856-1900.* London: Methuen, 1983.

Howard, Leon. *Literature and the American Tradition.* Garden City, NY: Doubleday, 1960.

Hughson, Lois. *From Biography to History: The Historical Imagination and American Fiction, 1880-1940.* Charlottesville: U P Virginia, 1988.

Jones, Howard Mumford. *The Theory of American Literature,* rev ed. Ithaca, NY: Cornell U P, 1965.

Jones. *The Age of Energy: Varieties of American Experience, 1865-1915.* NY: Viking, 1971.

Knight, Grant C. *The Critical Period in American Literature.* Chapel Hill: U North Carolina P, 1951.

Knight. *The Strenuous Age in American Literature.* Chapel Hill: U North Carolina P, 1954.

Lee, Brian. *American Fiction: 1865-1940.* London: Longman, 1987.

Lewisohn, Ludwig. *Expression in America*. NY: Harper, 1932.

Martin, Jay. *Harvests of Change: American Literature, 1865-1914*. Englewood Cliffs, NJ: Prentice-Hall, 1967.

Martin, Ronald E. *American Literature and the Universe of Force*. Durham, NC: Duke U P, 1981.

Massa, Ann. *American Literature in Context, IV: 1900-1930*. London: Methuen, 1982.

Mumford, Lewis. *The Golden Day: A Study in American Experience and Culture*. NY: Boni & Liveright, 1926.

Nagel, James, ed. *American Fiction: Historical and Critical Essays*. Boston: Northeastern U P, 1977.

Pattee, Fred Lewis. *A History of American Literature Since 1870*. NY: Century, 1915.

Pattee. *The New American Literature, 1890-1930*. NY: Century, 1930.

Quinn, Arthur Hobson. *American Fiction: An Historical and Critical Survey*. NY: Appleton-Century, 1936.

Rankin, Thomas E & Wilford M Aikin. *American Literature*. NY: Harcourt, Brace, 1922.

Rathbun, John W & Monica M Grecu, eds. *American Literary Critics and Scholars, 1880-1900: Dictionary of Literary Biography, Volume 71*. Detroit: Bruccoli Clark Layman/Gale, 1988.

Rourke, Constance. *American Humor: A Study of the National Character*. NY: Harcourt, Brace, 1931.

See, Fred G. *Desire and the Sign: Nineteenth-Century American Fiction*. Baton Rouge: Louisiana State U P, 1987.

Snell, George. *The Shapers of American Fiction, 1798-1947*. NY: Dutton, 1947.

Spencer, Benjamin T. *The Quest for Nationality: An American Literary Campaign*. Syracuse, NY: Syracuse U P, 1957.

Spiller, Robert. *The Cycle of American Literature: An Essay in Historical Criticism*. NY: Macmillan, 1956.

Spiller et al, eds. *Literary History of the United States*, 4th rev ed, NY: Macmillan / London: Collier-Macmillan, 1974. 2 vols.

Taylor, Walter Fuller. *A History of American Letters*, rev ed. Boston: American Book, 1956.

Tyler, Moses Coit. *A History of American Literature*. NY: Putnam, 1878.

Wager, Willis. *American Literature: A World View*. NY: NYU P / London: U London P, 1968.

Ward, Alfred C. *American Literature, 1880-1930*. NY: Dial / London: Methuen, 1932.

Wendell, Barrett. *A Literary History of America*. NY: Scribners, 1900.

Ziff, Larzer. *The American 1890s: Life and Times of a Lost Generation*. NY: Viking, 1966.

B. The Novel

Cowie, Alexander. *The Rise of the American Novel*. NY: American Book, 1948.

Fiedler, Leslie A. *Love and Death in the American Novel*. NY: Criterion, 1960.

Geismar, Maxwell. *Rebels and Ancestors: The American Novel, 1890-1915*. Boston: Houghton Mifflin, 1953.

Hatcher, Harlan. *Creating the Modern American Novel*. NY: Farrar & Rinehart, 1935.

Hoffman, Frederick J. *The Modern Novel in America, 1900-1950*, rev ed. Chicago: Regnery, 1963.

Holman, C Hugh. *The American Novel Through Henry James*, 2nd ed. Arlington Heights, Ill: AHM, 1979.

Rubin, Louis D, Jr & John Rees Moore, eds. *The Idea of an American Novel*. NY: Crowell-Collier, 1961.

Stegner, Wallace, ed. *The American Novel From James Fenimore Cooper to William Faulkner*. NY: Basic Books, 1965.

Van Doren, Carl. *Contemporary American Novelists, 1900-1920*. NY: Macmillan, 1923.

Van Doren. *The American Novel, 1789-1939*, rev ed. NY: Macmillan, 1940.

SPECIAL JOURNALS

American Literature (1929-   ). Quarterly.
Journal of American Studies (1967-   ). Quarterly.
Resources for American Literary Study (1971-   ). Semiannual.
Studies in American Fiction (1973-   ). Semiannual.

C. The Short Story

Pattee, Fred L. *The Development of the American Short Story: An Historical Survey*. NY: Harper, 1923.

Stevick, Philip, ed. *The American Short Story, 1900-1945: A Critical History*. Boston: Twayne, 1984.

Voss, Arthur. *The American Short Story: A Critical Survey*. Norman: U Oklahoma P, 1973.

SPECIAL JOURNAL

Studies in Short Fiction (1963-   ). Quarterly.

III. MOVEMENTS IN FICTION

A. Realism

Benardette, Jane, ed. *American Realism: A Shape for Fiction*. NY: Putnam, 1972.

Berthoff, Warner. *The Ferment of Realism: American Literature, 1884-1919*. NY: Free P / London: Collier-Macmillan, 1965.

Cady, Edwin H. *The Light of Common Day: Realism in American Fiction*. Bloomington: Indiana U P, 1971.

Habegger, Alfred. *Gender, Fantasy and Realism in American Literature.* NY: Columbia U P, 1982.

Kaplan, Amy. *The Social Construction of American Realism.* Chicago: U Chicago P, 1988.

Kolb, Harold H, Jr. *The Illusion of Life: American Realism as a Literary Form.* Charlottesville: U P Virginia, 1969.

McKay, Janet Holmgren. *Narration and Discourse in American Realistic Fiction.* Philadelphia: U Pennsylvania P, 1982.

Parrington, Vernon Louis. *The Beginnings of Critical Realism in America, 1860-1920.* Vol. 3 of *Main Currents in American Thought.* NY: Harcourt, Brace, 1930.

Pizer, Donald. *Realism and Naturalism in Nineteenth-Century American Literature,* rev ed. Carbondale: Southern Illinois U P, 1984.

Pizer & Earl Harbert, eds. *American Realists and Naturalists: Dictionary of Literary Biography, Volume 12.* Detroit: Bruccoli Clark/Gale, 1982.

Stein, Allen. *After the Vows Were Spoken: Marriage in American Literary Realism.* Columbus: Ohio U P, 1984.

Sundquist, Eric J, ed. *American Realism: New Essays.* Baltimore, Md: Johns Hopkins U P, 1982.

SPECIAL JOURNALS
American Literary Realism (1967-   ). Frequency varies.

B. Naturalism
Ahnebrink, Lars. *The Beginnings of Naturalism in American Fiction: A Study of the Works of Hamlin Garland, Stephen Crane, and Frank Norris With Special Reference to Some European Influences, 1891-1903.* Uppsala, Sweden: U Uppsala / Cambridge: Harvard U P, 1950.

Boller, Paul F, Jr. *American Thought in Transition: The Impact of Evolutionary Naturalism, 1865-1900.* Chicago: Rand McNally, 1969.

Conder, John J. *Naturalism in American Fiction: The Classic Phase.* Lexington: U P Kentucky, 1984.

Hakutani, Yoshinobu & Lewis Fried, eds. *American Literary Naturalism: A Reassessment.* Heidelberg: Carl Winter, 1975.

Howard, June. *Form and History in American Literary Naturalism.* Chapel Hill: U North Carolina P, 1985.

Krause, Sydney J, ed. *Essays on Determinism in American Literature.* Kent, Ohio: Kent State U P, 1964.

Lamprecht, Sterling P. *The Metaphysics of Naturalism.* NY: Appleton-Century-Crofts, 1967.

Michaels, Walter B. *The Gold Standard and the Logic of Naturalism: American Literature at the Turn of the Century.* Berkeley: U California P, 1987.

Schneider, Robert W. *Five Novelists of the Progressive Era.* NY: Columbia U P, 1965.

Stone, Edward, ed. *What Was Naturalism? Materials for an Answer.* NY: Appleton-Century-Crofts, 1959.

Walcutt, Charles Child. *American Literary Naturalism: A Divided Stream.* Minneapolis: U Minnesota P, 1956.

Westbrook, Perry D. *Free Will and Determinism in American Literature.* Rutherford, NJ: Fairleigh Dickinson U P / London: Associated U Presses, 1979.

IV. INFLUENCES

A. Politics
Blake, Fay M. *The Strike in the American Novel.* Metuchen, NJ: Scarecrow, 1972.

Gilbert, James B. *Writers and Partisans: A History of Literary Radicalism in America.* NY: Wiley, 1968.

Rideout, Walter B. *The Radical Novel in the United States, 1900-1954: Some Interrelations of Literature and Society.* Cambridge: Harvard U P, 1956.

Taylor, Walter Fuller. *The Economic Novel in America.* Chapel Hill: U North Carolina P, 1942.

B. Psychology
Kiell, Norman, ed. *Psychoanalysis, Psychology, and Literature: A Bibliography.* 2nd ed. Metuchen, NJ: Scarecrow, 1982. 2 vols.

Taylor, Gordon O. *The Passages of Thought: Psychological Representation in the American Novel, 1870-1900.* NY: Oxford U P, 1969.

SPECIAL JOURNAL
Literature and Psychology (1951-   ). Quarterly.

C. Religion
Frederick, John T. *The Darkened Sky: Nineteenth-Century American Novelists and Religion.* Notre Dame, Ind: U Notre Dame P, 1969.

Gunn, Giles. *The Interpretation of Otherness: Literature, Religion, and the American Imagination.* NY: Oxford U P, 1979.

Hintz, Howard W. *The Quaker Influence in American Literature.* NY: Revell, 1940.

O'Connor, Leo F. *Religion in the American Novel: The Search for Belief, 1860-1920.* Lanham, Md: U P America, 1984.

Stewart. Randall. *American Literature and Christian Doctrine.* Baton Rouge: Louisiana State U P, 1958.

SPECIAL JOURNAL

Christianity and Literature (1973-   ). Quarterly.
Literature and Belief (1981-   ). Annual.

V. FICTION ON SPECIAL TOPICS

Aaron, Daniel. *The Unwritten War: American Writers and the Civil War.* NY: Knopf, 1973.

Aichinger, Peter. *The American Soldier in Fiction, 1880-1963: A History of Attitudes Toward Warfare and the Military Establishment.* Ames: Iowa State U P, 1975.

Barnett, James Harwood. *Divorce and the American Divorce Novel, 1858-1937: A Study in Literary Reflections of Social Influences.* Philadelphia: U Pennsylvania P, 1939.

Bender, Bert. *Sea-Brothers: The Tradition of American Sea Fiction From Moby-Dick to the Present.* Philadelphia: U Pennsylvania P, 1988.

Boas, Ralph Philip & Katherine Burton. *Social Backgrounds of American Literature.* Boston: Little, Brown, 1933.

Burns, Grant. *The Sports Pages: A Critical Bibliography of Twentieth-Century American Novels and Stories Featuring Baseball, Basketball, Football, and Other Athletic Pursuits.* Metuchen, NJ: Scarecrow, 1987.

Cady, Edwin Harrison. *The Gentleman in America: A Literary Study in American Culture.* Syracuse, NY: Syracuse U P, 1949.

Chamberlain, John. *Farewell to Reform: The Rise, Life and Decay of the Progressive Mind in America,* 2d ed. Gloucester, Mass: Smith, 1958.

Coan, Otis W & Richard G Lillard. *America in Fiction: An Annotated List of Novels That Interpret Aspects of Life in the United States, Canada, Mexico,* 5th ed. Palo Alto, Calif: Pacific, 1967.

Flory, Claude Reherd. *Economic Criticism in American Fiction, 1792 to 1900.* Philadelphia: U Pennsylvania P, 1937.

Frohock, W M. *The Novel of Violence in America,* 2nd ed. Dallas: Southern Methodist U P, 1957.

Good, Howard. *Acquainted With the Night: The Image of Journalists in American Fiction, 1890-1930.* Metuchen, NJ: Scarecrow, 1986.

Grobani, Anton, ed. *Guide to Baseball Literature.* Detroit: Gale, 1975.

Grobani, ed. *Guide to Football Literature.* Detroit: Gale, 1975.

Herron, Ima Honaker. *The Small Town in American Literature.* Durham, NC: Duke U P, 1939.

Higgs, Robert J. *Laurel & Thorn: The Athlete in American Literature.* Lexington: U P Kentucky, 1981.

Holman, C Hugh. *Windows on the World: Essays on American Social Fiction.* Knoxville: U Tennessee P, 1979.

Kaul, A N. *The American Vision: Actual and Ideal Society in Nineteenth-Century Fiction.* New Haven: Yale U P, 1963.

Kramer, John E, Jr. *The American College Novel: An Annotated Bibliography.* NY: Garland, 1981.

Lindberg, Gary. *The Confidence Man in American Literature.* NY: Oxford U P, 1982.

Lively, Robert A. *Fiction Fights the Civil War: An Unfinished Chapter in the Literary History of the American People.* Chapel Hill: U North Carolina P, 1957.

Long, Elizabeth. *The American Dream and the Popular Novel.* Boston: Routledge & Kegan Paul, 1985.

Messenger, Christian K. *Sport and the Spirit of Play in American Fiction: Hawthorne to Faulkner.* NY: Columbia U P, 1981.

Millgate, Michael. *American Social Fiction: James to Cozzens.* NY: Barnes & Noble, 1964.

Milne, Gordon. *The Sense of Society: A History of the American Novel of Manners.* Rutherford, NJ: Fairleigh Dickinson U P / London: Associated U Presses, 1977.

Mukherjee, Arun. *The Gospel of Wealth in the American Novel: The Rhetoric of Dreiser and Some of His Contemporaries.* Totowa, NJ: Barnes & Noble, 1987.

Oriard, Michael. *Dreaming of Heroes: American Sports Fiction, 1868-1980.* Chicago: Nelson-Hall, 1982.

Parrington, Vernon Louis, Jr. *American Dreams: A Study of American Utopias.* Providence, R I: Brown U P, 1947.

Pfaelzer, Jean. *The Utopian Novel in America, 1886-1896: The Politics of Form.* Pittsburgh, Pa: U Pittsburgh P, 1984.

Ransom, Ellene. *Utopus Discovers America; or, Critical Realism in American Utopian Fiction, 1798-1900.* Nashville, Tenn: Joint U Libraries, 1947.

Regier, C C. *The Era of the Muckrakers.* Chapel Hill: U North Carolina P, 1932.

Roemer, Kenneth M. *The Obsolete Necessity: America in Utopian Writings, 1888-1900.* Kent, Ohio: Kent State U P, 1976.

Rose, Lisle A. *A Survey of American Economic Fiction, 1902-1909.* Chicago: U Chicago Libraries, 1958.

Shulman, Robert. *Social Criticism & Nineteenth-Century American Fictions.* Columbia: U Missouri P, 1987.

Smith, Henry Nash ed. *Popular Culture and Industrialism, 1865-1890.* NY: NYU P, 1967.

Smith, Myron J, Jr. *War Story Guide: An Annotated Bibliography of Military Fiction.* Metuchen, NJ: Scarecrow, 1980.

Spindler, Michael. *American Literature and Social Change: William Dean Howells to Arthur Miller.* Bloomington: Indiana U P / London: Macmillan, 1983.

Stineback, David C. *Shifting World: Social Change and Nostalgia in the American Novel.* Lewisburg, Pa: Bucknell U P / London: Associated U Presses, 1976.

Tuttleton, James W. *The Novel of Manners in America.* Chapel Hill: U North Carolina P, 1972.

Westbrook, Wayne W. *Wall Street in the American Novel.* NY: NYU P, 1980.

Wilson, Edmund. *Patriotic Gore: Studies in the Literature of the American Civil War.* NY: Oxford U P, 1962.

VI. AUTHORS

A. Collective Biography & Biographical Dictionaries

Baldwin, Charles C. *The Men Who Make Our Novels,* rev ed. NY: Dodd, Mead, 1924.

Kunitz, Stanley J & Howard Haycraft, eds. *American Authors, 1600-1900.* NY: Wilson, 1938.

Kunitz & Haycraft, eds. *Twentieth Century Authors.* NY: Wilson, 1942. Supplement, 1955.

Martine, James J, ed. *American Novelists, 1910-1945: Dictionary of Literary Biography, Volume 9.* Detroit: Bruccoli Clark/Gale, 1981. 3 parts.

Millett, Fred B. *Contemporary American Authors: A Critical Survey and 219 Bibliographies.* NY: Harcourt, Brace, 1940.

Vinson, James. *American Writers Since 1900.* Chicago: St James, 1983.

B. Women Writers

Auchincloss, Louis. *Pioneers & Caretakers: A Study of 9 American Women Novelists.* Minneapolis: U Minnesota P, 1965.

Baym, Nina. *Woman's Fiction: A Guide to Novels By and About Women in America, 1820-1870.* Ithaca, NY: Cornell U P, 1978.

Deegan, Dorothy Yost. *The Stereotype of the Single Woman in American Novels: A Social Study with Implications for the Education of Women.* NY: Columbia U P, 1951.

Duke, Maurice, Jackson R Bryer, & M Thomas Inge, eds. *American Women Writers: Bibliographic Essays.* Westport, Conn: Greenwood, 1983.

Earnest, Ernest. *The American Eve in Fact and Fiction, 1775-1914.* Urbana: U Illinois P, 1974.

Huf, Linda. *A Portrait of the Artist as a Young Woman: The Writer as Heroine in American Literature.* NY: Ungar, 1983.

Jones, Anne Goodwyn. *Tomorrow Is Another Day: The Woman Writer in the South, 1859-1936.* Baton Rouge: Louisiana State U P, 1981.

Kieniewicz, Teresa. *Men, Women, and the Novelist: Fact and Fiction in the American Novel of the 1870s and 1880s.* Washington: U P America, 1982.

Kinney, James. *Amalgamation!: Race, Sex, and Rhetoric in the Nineteenth-Century American Novel.* Westport, Conn: Greenwood, 1985.

Lee, L L & Merrill Lewis, eds. *Women, Women Writers, and the West.* Troy, NY: Whitston, 1980.

Mainiero, Lina, ed. *American Women Writers: A Critical Reference Guide From Colonial Times to the Present.* NY: Ungar, 1979. 4 vols.

McNall, Sally A. *Who Is in the House? A Psychological Study of Two Centuries of Women's Fiction in America, 1795 to the Present.* NY: Elsevier, 1981.

Shapiro, Ann R. *Unlikely Heroines: Nineteenth-Century American Women Writers and the Woman Question.* Westport, Conn: Greenwood, 1987.

SPECIAL JOURNALS

Frontiers: A Journal of Women Studies (1975-). Triquarterly.

Legacy: A Journal of Nineteenth-Century Women Writers (1984-). Semiannual.

Tulsa Studies in Women's Literature (1982-). Semiannual.

Women & Literature (1974-). Semiannual.

Women's Studies: An Interdisciplinary Journal. (1972-). Triquarterly.

C. African-American Writers

Adams, Wm. *Afro-American Authors.* Boston: Houghton Mifflin, 1972.

Bell, Bernard W. *The Afro-American Novel and Its Tradition.* Amherst: U Massachusetts P, 1987.

Bone, Robert. *Down Home: A History of Afro-American Short Fiction From Its Beginnings to the End of the Harlem Renaissance.* NY: Putnam, 1975.

Brawley, Benjamin Griffith. *The Negro in Literature and Art in the United States,* 3rd ed. NY: Duffield, 1929.

Brown, Lloyd W, ed. *The Black Writer in Africa and the Americas.* Los Angeles: Hennessy & Ingalls, 1973.

Brown, Sterling A. *The Negro in American Fiction.* Washington: Associates in Negro Folk Education, 1937.

Callahan, John F. *In the African-American Grain: The Pursuit of Voice in Twentieth-Century Black Fiction.* Urbana: U Illinois P, 1988.

Campbell, Jane. *Mythic Black Fiction: The Transformation of History.* Knoxville: U Tennessee P, 1986.

Canady, Joan. *Black Images in American Literature.* Rochelle Park, NJ: Hayden, 1977.

Carby, Hazel V. *Reconstructing Womanhood: The Emergence of the Afro-American Woman Novelist.* NY: Oxford U P, 1987.

Cooke, Michael G. *Afro-American Literature in the Twentieth Century: The Achievement of Intimacy.* New Haven: Yale U P, 1984.

Davis, Arthur P. *From The Dark Tower: Afro-American Writers, 1900-1960.* Washington: Howard U P, 1974.

Elder, Arlene A. *The "Hindered Hand": Cultural Implications of Early African-American Fiction.* Westport, Conn: Greenwood, 1978.

Gates, Henry Louis, Jr, ed. *Black Literature and Literary Theory.* NY: Methuen, 1984.

Gates. *The Signifying Monkey: A Theory of Afro-American Literary Criticism.* NY: Oxford U P, 1988.

Gayle, Addison, Jr. *The Black Aesthetic.* Garden City, NY: Doubleday, 1971.

Gayle. *The Way of the New World: The Black Novel in America.* Garden City, NY: Doubleday, 1975.

Gibson, Donald B. *The Politics of Literary Expression: A Study of Major Black Writers.* Westport, Conn: Greenwood, 1981.

Gloster, Hugh M. *Negro Voices in American Fiction.* Chapel Hill: U North Carolina P, 1948.

Hemenway, Robert, ed. *The Black Novelist.* Columbus, Ohio: Merrill, 1970.

Harris, Trudier, ed. *Afro-American Writers Before the Harlem Renaissance: Dictionary of Literary Biography, Volume 50.* Detroit: Bruccoli Clark/Gale, 1986.

Hill, Herbert, ed. *Anger and Beyond: The Negro Writer in the United States.* NY: Harper & Row, 1966.

Locke, Alain, ed. *The New Negro: An Interpretation.* NY: Boni, 1925.

Loggins, Vernon. *The Negro Author: His Development in America to 1900.* NY: Columbia U P, 1931.

Margolies, Edward & David Bakish. *Afro-American Fiction, 1853-1976: A Guide to Information Sources.* Detroit: Gale, 1979.

Payne, Ladell. *Black Novelists and the Southern Literary Tradition.* Athens: U Georgia P, 1981.

Pryse, Marjorie & Hortense J Spillers, eds. *Conjuring: Black Women, Fiction, and Literary Tradition.* Bloomington: Indiana U P, 1985.

Rush, Theressa Gunnels, Carol Fairbanks Myers & Esther Spring Arata. *Black American Writers Past and Present: A Biographical and Bibliographical Dictionary.* Metuchen, NJ: Scarecrow, 1975.

Shockley, Ann Allen. *Afro-American Women Writers, 1746-1933: An Anthology and Critical Guide.* Boston: Hall, 1988.

Southgate, Robert L. *Black Plots & Black Characters: A Handbook for Afro-American Literature.* Syracuse, NY: Gaylord, 1979.

Starke, Catherine Juanita. *Black Portraiture in American Fiction: Stock Characters, Archetypes, and Individuals.* NY: Basic Books, 1971.

Stepto, Robert B. *From Behind the Veil: A Study of Afro-American Narrative.* Urbana: U Illinois P, 1979.

Trimmer, Joseph F. *Black American Literature: Notes on the Problem of Definition.* Muncie, Ind: Ball State U P, 1971.

Turner, Darwin T. *Afro-American Writers.* NY: Appleton-Century-Crofts, 1970.

Whiteman, Maxwell. *A Century of Fiction by American Negroes, 1835-1952: A Descriptive Bibliography.* Philadelphia: npub, 1955.

Williams, Kenny J. *They Also Spoke: An Essay on Negro Literature in America, 1787-1930.* Nashville, Tenn: Townsend, 1970.

Willis, Susan. *Specifying: Black Women Writing the American Experience.* Madison: U Wisconsin P, 1987.

SPECIAL JOURNALS

Black American Literature Forum (1977-   ). Previous title: *Negro American Literature Forum* (1967-1976). Quarterly.

CLA Journal (1957-   ). Quarterly.

Studies in Black Literature (1970-1976). Semiannual.

D. Other

Martínez, Julio A & Francisco A Lomelí, eds. *Chicano Literature: A Reference Guide.* Westport, Conn: Greenwood, 1985.

Nadel, Ira Bruce. *Jewish Writers of North America: A Guide to Information Sources.* Detroit: Gale, 1981.

VII. REGIONS & REGIONALISM

A. General Studies

Burke, John Gordon, ed. *Regional Perspectives: An Examination of America's Literary Heritage.* Chicago: American Library Association, 1973.

Davidson, Donald. *The Attack on Leviathan: Regionalism and Nationalism in the United States.* Chapel Hill: U North Carolina P, 1938.

Gohdes, Clarence. *Literature and Theater of the States and Regions of the USA: An Historical Bibliography*. Durham, NC: Duke U P, 1967.

B. The South

Bain, Robert, Joseph M Flora & Louis D Rubin, Jr, eds. *Southern Writers: A Biographical Dictionary*. Baton Rouge: Louisiana State U P, 1979.

Bain & Flora, eds. *Fifty Southern Writers Before 1900: A Bio-Bibliographical Sourcebook*. NY: Greenwood, 1987.

Flora & Bain, eds. *Fifty Southern Writers After 1900: A Bio-Bibliographical Sourcebook*. NY: Greenwood, 1987.

Gray, Richard. *Writing the South: Ideas of an American Region*. NY: Cambridge U P, 1986.

Hobson, Fred. *Tell About the South: The Southern Rage to Explain*. Baton Rouge: Louisiana State U P, 1983.

Holman, C Hugh. *The Roots of Southern Writing: Essays on the Literature of the American South*. Athens: U Georgia P, 1972.

Holman. *The Immoderate Past: The Southern Writer and History*. Athens: U Georgia P, 1977.

Hubbell, Jay B. *The South in American Literature, 1607-1900*. Durham, NC: Duke U P, 1954.

Hubbell. *Southern Life in Fiction*. Athens: U Georgia P, 1960.

I'll Take My Stand: The South and the Agrarian Tradition by Twelve Southerners. NY: Harper, 1930.

MacKethan, Lucinda Hardwick. *The Dream of Arcady: Place and Time in Southern Literature*. Baton Rouge: Louisiana State U P, 1980.

McIlwaine, Shields. *The Southern Poor-White From Lubberland to Tobacco Road*. Norman: U Oklahoma P, 1939.

Rose, Alan Henry. *Demonic Vision: Racial Fantasy and Southern Fiction*. Hamden, Conn: Archon, 1976.

Rubin, Louis D, Jr, ed. *A Bibliographical Guide to the Study of Southern Literature*. Baton Rouge: Louisiana State U P, 1969.

Rubin, ed. *The History of Southern Literature*. Baton Rouge: Louisiana State U P, 1985.

Rubin & C Hugh Holman, eds. *Southern Literary Study: Problems and Possibilities*. Chapel Hill: U North Carolina P, 1975.

Skaggs, Merrill Maguire. *The Folk of Southern Fiction*. Athens: U Georgia P, 1972.

Stein, A F & T N Walters, eds. *The Southern Experience in Short Fiction*. Glenview, Ill: Scott, Foresman, 1971.

SPECIAL JOURNALS
Notes on Mississippi Writers (1968-   ). Semiannual.

Southern Literary Journal (1968-   ). Semiannual.
Southern Quarterly (1962-   ).
Southern Review (1965-   ). Quarterly.
Southern Studies. (1961-   ). Quarterly.

C. New England

Donovan, Josephine. *New England Local Color Literature: A Women's Tradition*. NY: Ungar, 1983.

Eakin, Paul John. *The New England Girl: Cultural Ideals in Hawthorne, Stowe, Howells and James*. Athens: U Georgia P, 1976.

Nagel, James & Richard Astro. *American Literature: The New England Heritage*. NY: Garland, 1981.

Westbrook, Perry D. *Acres of Flint: Sarah Orne Jewett and Her Contemporaries*, rev ed. Metuchen, NY: Scarecrow, 1981.

Westbrook. *The New England Town in Fact and Fiction*. Rutherford, NJ: Fairleigh Dickinson U P / London: Associated U Presses, 1982.

SPECIAL JOURNAL
ATQ (1969-   ). Quarterly. Formerly *American Transcendental Quarterly*.
New England Quarterly (1928-   ).

D. The Midwest

Bray, Robert C. *Rediscoveries: Literature and Place in Illinois*. Urbana: U Illinois P, 1982.

Duffey, Bernard. *The Chicago Renaissance in American Letters: A Critical History*. East Lansing: Michigan State U P, 1954.

Faulkner, Virginia & Frederick C Luebke, eds. *Vision and Refuge: Essays on the Literature of the Great Plains*. Lincoln: U Nebraska P, 1982.

Fuson, Ben W. *Centennial Bibliography of Kansas Literature, 1854-1961*. Salina: Kansas Wesleyan U, 1961.

Karolides, Nicholas J. *The Pioneer in the American Novel, 1900-1950*. Norman: U Oklahoma P, 1967.

Kramer, Dale. *Chicago Renaissance: The Literary Life in the Midwest, 1900-1930*. NY: Appleton-Century, 1966.

Meyer, Roy W. *The Middle Western Farm Novel in the Twentieth Century*. Lincoln: U Nebraska P, 1965.

Nemanic, Gerald, ed. *A Bibliographical Guide to Midwestern Literature*. Iowa City: U Iowa P, 1981.

Paluka, Frank. *Iowa Authors: A Bio-Bibliography of Sixty Native Writers*. Iowa City: Friends of the U of Iowa Libraries, 1967.

Rusk, Ralph Leslie. *The Literature of the Middle Western Frontier*. NY: Columbia U P, 1925. 2 vols.

Smith, Carl S. *Chicago and the American Literary Imagination, 1880-1920*. Chicago: U Chicago P, 1984.

SPECIAL JOURNAL
Midamerica: The Yearbook of the Society for the Study of Midwestern Literature (1973-   ). Annual.
Midwestern Miscellany (1974-   ). Annual.

E. The West & Southwest

Anderson, John Q, Edwin W Gaston, Jr & James W Lee, eds. *Southwestern American Literature: A Bibliography*. Chicago: Swallow, 1980.

Baird, Newton D & Robert Greenwood. *An Annotated Bibliography of California Fiction, 1644-1970*. Georgetown, Calif: Talisman, 1971.

Branch, Douglas. *The Cowboy and His Interpreters*. NY: Appleton, 1926. Rpt NY: Cooper Square, 1961.

Coleman, Rufus A, ed. *Northwest Books*, 2nd ed. Lincoln: U Nebraska P, 1949.

Durham, Philip & Everett L Jones, eds. *The Frontier in American Literature*. NY: Odyssey, 1969.

Durham & Jones. *The Western Story: Fact, Fiction and Myth*. NY: Harcourt Brace Jovanovich, 1975.

Erisman, Fred & Richard W Etulain, eds. *Fifty Western Writers: A Bio-Bibliographical Sourcebook*. Westport, Conn: Greenwood, 1982.

Etulain, Richard W. *Western American Literature: A Bibliography of Interpretive Books and Articles*. Vermillion, SD: Dakota, 1972.

Etulain. *A Bibliographical Guide to the Study of Western American Literature*. Lincoln: U Nebraska P, 1982.

Everson, William. *Archetype West: The Pacific Coast as Literary Region*. Berkeley, Calif: Oyez, 1976.

Ferlinghetti, Lawrence & Nancy J Peters. *Literary San Francisco: A Pictorial History From Its Beginnings to the Present*. San Francisco: City Lights/Harper & Row, 1980.

Fussell, Edwin. *Frontier: American Literature and the American West*. Princeton: Princeton U P, 1965.

Gurian, Jay. *Western American Writing: Tradition and Promise*. De Land, Fla: Everett/Edwards, 1975.

Hazard, Lucy Lockwood. *The Frontier in American Literature*. NY: Crowell, 1927.

Hinkel, Edgar J, ed. *Bibliography of California Fiction, Poetry, Drama. Criticism of California Literature: A Digest and Bibliography, Biographies of California Authors and Indexes of California Literature*, 3 vols. Oakland, Calif: Alameda County Library, 1938. Vol 1 covers fiction.

Kurtz, Kenneth. *Literature of the American Southwest: A Selective Bibliography*. Los Angeles: Occidental C, 1956.

Lamar, Howard R, ed. *The Reader's Encyclopedia of the American West*. NY: Crowell, 1977.

Lee, Robert Edson. *From West to East: Studies in the Literature of the American West*. Urbana: U Illinois P, 1966.

Lewis, Merrill & L L Lee, eds. *The Westering Experience in American Literature: Bicentennial Essays*. Bellingham: Western Washington U P, 1977.

A Literary History of the American West. Fort Worth: Texas Christian U P, 1987.

Love, Glen A. *New Americans: The Westerner and the Modern Experience in the American Novel*. Lewisburg, Pa: Bucknell U P, 1982.

Major, Mabel & T M Pearce. *Southwest Heritage: A Literary History With Bibliography*, 3rd ed. Albuquerque: U New Mexico P, 1972.

Milton, John R. *The Novel of the American West*. Lincoln: U Nebraska P, 1980.

Pilkington, William T. *My Blood's Country: Studies in Southwestern Literature*. Fort Worth: Texas Christian U P, 1973.

Pilkington, ed. *Critical Essays on the Western American Novel*. Boston: Hall, 1980.

Powell, Lawrence C. *Heart of the Southwest: A Selective Bibliography of Novels, Stories, and Tales Laid in Arizona and New Mexico and Adjacent Lands*. Los Angeles: Dawson's Book Shop/Plantin, 1955.

Smith, Henry Nash. *Virgin Land: The American West as Symbol and Myth*. Cambridge: Harvard U P, 1950.

Vinson, James & D L Kirkpatrick, eds. *Twentieth-Century Western Writers*. Detroit: Gale, 1982.

Walker, Franklin. *San Francisco's Literary Frontier*. NY: Knopf, 1939.

Walker. *A Literary History of Southern California*. Berkeley: U California P, 1950.

Walker. *The Seacoast of Bohemia: An Account of Early Carmel*. San Francisco: Book Club of California, 1966. Rev ed, Santa Barbara, Calif: Smith, 1973.

West, Ray B, Jr. *Writing in the Rocky Mountains*. Lincoln: U Nebraska P, 1947.

SPECIAL JOURNAL
Western American Literature (1966-   ). Quarterly.

VIII. GENRES

A. Mystery & Espionage

Albert, Walter. *Detective and Mystery Fiction: An*

International Bibliography of Secondary Sources. Madison, Ind: Brownstone, 1985.

Barzun, Jacques & Wendell Hertig Taylor. *A Catalogue of Crime.* NY: Harper & Row, 1971.

Cawelti, John G. *Adventure, Mystery and Romance: Formula Stories as Art and Popular Culture.* Chicago: U Chicago P, 1976.

Hagen, Ordean A. *Who Done It? A Guide to Detective, Mystery and Suspense Fiction.* NY: Bowker, 1969.

Hubin, Allen J. *Crime Fiction, 1749-1980: A Comprehensive Bibliography.* NY: Garland, 1984. *1981-1985 Supplement to Crime Fiction, 1749-1980,* 1988.

Johnson, Timothy W & Julia Johnson, eds. *Crime Fiction Criticism: An Annotated Bibliography,* NY: Garland, 1981.

Olderr, Steven. *Mystery Index: Subjects, Settings, and Sleuths for 10,000 Titles.* Chicago: American Library Association, 1987.

Queen, Ellery. *The Detective Short Story: A Bibliography.* NY: Biblo & Tannen, 1969.

Steinbrunner, Chris & Otto Penzler. *Encyclopedia of Mystery and Detection.* NY: McGraw-Hill, 1976.

Steinbrunner, Charles Shibuk & Penzler. *Detectionary: A Bibliographical Dictionary of the Leading Characters in Detective and Mystery Fiction,* rev ed. Woodstock, NY: Overlook, 1977.

SPECIAL JOURNALS

The Armchair Detective (1967-   ). Quarterly.

Clues: A Journal of Detection (1980-   ). Semiannual.

B. Science Fiction

Allen, Dick & Lori Allen, eds. *Looking Ahead: The Vision of Science Fiction.* NY: Harcourt Brace Jovanovich, 1975.

Ash, Brian. *Who's Who in Science Fiction.* NY: Taplinger, 1976.

Barron, Neil. *Anatomy of Wonder: A Critical Guide to Science Fiction,* 3rd ed. NY: Bowker, 1987.

Bleiler, E F, ed. *Science Fiction Writers: Critical Studies of the Major Authors From the Early Nineteenth Century to the Present Day.* NY: Scribners, 1982.

Clareson, Thomas D. *Science Fiction Criticism: An Annotated Checklist.* Kent, Ohio: Kent State U P, 1972.

Clareson. *Some Kind of Paradise: The Emergence of American Science Fiction.* Westport, Conn: Greenwood, 1985.

Contento, William. *Index to Science Fiction: Anthologies and Collections.* Boston: Hall, 1978.

Currey, L W. *Science Fiction and Fantasy Authors: A Bibliography of First Printings of Their Fiction and Selected Nonfiction.* Boston: Hall, 1979.

Currey & R Reginald. *Science Fiction & Fantasy Reference Guide: An Annotated List of Critical, Bibliographical, and Biographical Works.* San Bernardino, Calif: Borgo, 1980.

Dictionary Catalog of the J Lloyd Eaton Collection of Science Fiction and Fantasy Literature. Boston: Hall, 1982. 3 vols.

Gunn, James, ed. *The New Encyclopedia of Science Fiction.* NY: Viking, 1988.

Hall, H W, ed. *Science Fiction and Fantasy Reference Index, 1878-1985.* Detroit: Gale, 1987.

Justice, Keith L. *Science Fiction Master Index of Names.* Jefferson, NC: McFarland, 1986.

Moskowitz, Sam. *Seekers of Tomorrow: Masters of Modern Science Fiction.* Cleveland: World, 1966.

Nicholls, Peter, ed. *The Science Fiction Encyclopedia.* Garden City, NY: Doubleday, 1979; *The Encyclopedia of Science Fiction: An Illustrated A to Z.* London: Granada, 1979.

Parrinder, Patrick, ed. *Science Fiction: A Critical Guide.* London & NY: Longman, 1979.

Parrinder. *Science Fiction: Its Criticism and Teaching.* NY: Methuen, 1980.

Pierce, Hazel Beasley. *A Literary Symbiosis: Science Fiction/Fantasy Mystery.* Westport, Conn: Greenwood, 1983.

Reginald, R. *Science Fiction and Fantasy Literature: A Checklist, 1700-1974: With Contemporary Science Fiction Authors II.* Detroit: Gale, 1979. 2 vols.

Tymn, Marshall B & Mike Ashley, eds. *Science Fiction, Fantasy, and Weird Fiction Magazines.* Westport, Conn: Greenwood, 1985.

Tymn & Roger C Schlobin. *The Year's Scholarship in Science Fiction and Fantasy: 1972-1979.* Kent, Ohio: Kent State U P, 1979. *The Year's Scholarship in Science Fiction, Fantasy and Horror Literature, 1980-   * (Annual, 1983-   ).

Tymn, Schlobin & L W Currey, eds. *A Research Guide to Science Fiction Studies: An Annotated Checklist of Primary and Secondary Sources for Fantasy and Science Fiction.* NY: Garland, 1977.

Wolfe, Gary K. *Critical Terms for Science Fiction and Fantasy: A Glossary and Guide to Scholarship.* NY: Greenwood, 1986.

SPECIAL JOURNALS

Extrapolation: The Newsletter of the MLA Seminar on Science Fiction (1959-   ). Quarterly.

Foundation: The Review of Science Fiction. (1972-   ). Frequency varies.

Science Fiction Studies (1973-   ). Frequency varies.

SF Horizons (1968-   ). Frequency varies.

C. Fantasy & Horror

Attebery, Brian. *The Fantasy Tradition in American Literature: From Irving to LeGuin*. Bloomington: Indiana U P, 1980.

Bleiler, E F. *The Guide to Supernatural Fiction*. Kent, Ohio: Kent State U P, 1983.

Kerr, Howard, John W Crowley & Charles L Crow, eds. *The Haunted Dusk: American Supernatural Fiction, 1820-1920*. Athens: U Georgia P, 1983.

Tymn, Marshall B. *Horror Literature: A Core Collection and Reference Guide*. NY: Bowker, 1981.

Tymn, Kenneth J Zahorski & Robert H Boyer. *Fantasy Literature: A Core Collection and Reference Guide*. NY: Bowker, 1979.

D. Historical Fiction

Dekker, George. *The American Historical Romance*. NY: Cambridge U P, 1987.

Gerhardstein, Virginia Brokaw. *Dickinson's American Historical Fiction*, 5th ed. Metuchen, NJ: Scarecrow, 1986.

Leisy, Ernest E. *The American Historical Novel*. Norman: U Oklahoma P, 1958.

VanDerhoof, Jack. *A Bibliography of Novels Related to American Frontier and Colonial History*. Troy, NY: Whitston, 1971.

E. Westerns

Bold, Christine. *Selling the Wild West: Popular Western Fiction, 1860 to 1960*. Bloomington: Indiana U P, 1987.

Cawelti, John G. *The Six-Gun Mystique*. Bowling Green, Ohio: Bowling Green U Popular P, 1970.

Dinan, John A. *The Pulp Western: A Popular History of the Western Fiction Magazine in America*. San Bernardino, Calif: Borgo, 1983.

Drew, Bernard A, Martin H Greenberg & Charles G Waugh. *Western Series and Sequels: A Reference Guide*. NY: Garland, 1986.

Etulain, Richard W & Michael T Marsden, eds. *The Popular Western: Essays Toward a Definition*. Bowling Green, Ohio: Bowling Green U Popular P, 1974.

Folsom, James K. *The American Western Novel*. New Haven, Conn: College & U P, 1966.

Folsom, ed. *The Western: A Collection of Critical Essays*. Englewood Cliffs, NJ: Prentice-Hall, 1979.

Jones, Daryl. *The Dime Novel Western*. Bowling Green, Ohio: Bowling Green State U Popular P, 1978.

F. Children's Literature

Carpenter, Humphrey & Mari Prichard. *The Oxford Companion to Children's Literature*. NY: Oxford U P, 1984.

Cech, John, ed. *American Writers for Children, 1900-1960: Dictionary of Literary Biography, Volume 22*. Detroit: Bruccoli Clark/Gale, 1983.

Doyle, Brian, ed. *The Who's Who of Children's Literature*. NY: Schocken, 1968.

Estes, Glenn E, ed. *American Writers for Children Before 1900: Dictionary of Literary Biography, Volume 42*. Detroit: Bruccoli Clark/Gale, 1985.

Haviland, Virginia. *Children's Literature: A Guide to Reference Sources*. Washington: Library of Congress, 1966.

Helbig, Alethea K & Agnes Regan Perkins. *Dictionary of American Children's Fiction, 1859-1959: Books of Recognized Merit*. Westport, Conn: Greenwood, 1985.

Hendrickson, Linnea. *Children's Literature, A Guide to the Criticism*. Boston: Hall, 1987.

Lystad, Mary. *From Dr. Mather to Dr. Seuss: 200 Years of American Books for Children*. Boston: Hall, 1980.

Rahn, Suzanne. *Children's Literature: An Annotated Bibliography of the History of Criticism*. NY: Garland, 1981.

Welch, D'Alte. *A Bibliography of American Children's Books*. Worcester, Mass: American Antiquarian Society & Barre, 1972.

SPECIAL JOURNALS

Children's Literature (1975-). Previous titles: *Children's Literature: The Great Excluded* (1972); *Great Excluded: Children's Literature* (1973-1974). Annual.

Children's Literature Abstracts (1973-). Quarterly.

Children's Literature Association Quarterly (1976-).

Horn Book (1925-). Quarterly.

G. Humor

Bier, Jesse. *The Rise and Fall of American Humor*. NY: Holt, Rinehart & Winston, 1968.

Blair, Walter. *Horse Sense in American Humor: From Benjamin Franklin to Ogden Nash*. Chicago: U Chicago P, 1942.

Blair. *Native American Humor*, rev ed. San Francisco: Chandler, 1960.

Blair & Hamlin Hill. *America's Humor: From Poor Richard to Doonesbury*. NY: Oxford U P, 1978.

Brown, Carolyn S. *The Tall Tale in American Folklore and Literature*. Knoxville: U Tennessee P, 1987.

Dudden, Arthur Power. *American Humor*. NY: Oxford U P, 1987.

Sloane, David E E, ed. *American Humor Magazines and Comic Periodicals*. Westport, Conn: Greenwood, 1987.

Trachtenberg, Stanley, ed. *American Humorists, 1800-1950: Dictionary of Literary Biography, Volume 11.* Detroit: Bruccoli Clark/Gale, 1982. 2 parts.

SPECIAL JOURNAL
Studies in American Humor (1974-   ). Quarterly.

H. Romantic Fiction
Mussell, Kay. *Women's Gothic and Romantic Fiction: A Reference Guide.* Westport, Conn: Greenwood, 1981.
Radway, Janice A. *Reading the Romance: Women, Patriarchy, and Popular Literature.* Chapel Hill: U North Carolina P, 1984.

IX. PUBLISHING & AUTHORSHIP
A. Publishing
Denning, Michael. *Mechanic Accents: Dime Novels and Working-Class Culture in America.* London: Verso, 1987.
Dzwonkoski, Peter, ed. *American Literary Publishing Houses, 1900-1980: Trade and Paperback: Dictionary of Literary Biography, Volume 46.* Detroit: Bruccoli Clark Layman/Gale, 1986.
Lehmann-Haupt, Hellmut et al. *The Book in America: A History of the Making and Selling of Books in the United States,* 2nd ed. NY: Bowker, 1952.
Tebbel, John W. *History of Book Publishing in the United States.* NY: Bowker, 1973-1981. 4 vols.

B. Magazines
Chielens, Edward E, ed. *American Literary Magazines: The Eighteenth and Nineteenth Centuries.* Westport, Conn: Greenwood, 1986.
Hoffman, Frederick J, Charles Allen & Carolyn F Ulrich, eds. *The Little Magazine: A History and a Bibliography,* 2nd ed. Princeton: Princeton U P, 1947.
Mott, Frank Luther. *A History of American Magazines.* Cambridge: Harvard U P, 1957-1968. 5 vols.

SPECIAL JOURNAL
Publishers Weekly (1872-   ).

C. Popular Fiction
Girgus, Sam B. *The American Self: Myth, Ideology, and Popular Culture.* Albuquerque: U New Mexico P, 1981.
Hackett, Alice Payne & James Henry Burke. *80 Years of Best Sellers, 1895-1975.* NY: Bowker, 1977.
Hart, James D. *The Popular Book: A History of America's Literary Taste.* NY: Oxford U P, 1950
Inge, M Thomas, ed. *Handbook of American Popular Literature.* Westport, Conn: Greenwood, 1988.
Löfroth, Erik. *A World Made Safe: Values in American Best Sellers, 1895-1920.* Uppsala, Sweden: U Uppsala P, 1983.
Mott, Frank Luther. *Golden Multitudes: The Story of Best Sellers in the United States.* NY: Macmillan, 1947.
Pearson, Edmund L. *Dime Novels; or, Following an Old Trail in Popular Literature.* Boston: Little, Brown, 1929.
Smith, Herbert F. *The Popular American Novel, 1865-1920.* Boston: Twayne, 1980.

D. Censorship
Boyer, Paul S. *Purity in Print: The Vice Society Movement and Book Censorship in America.* NY: Scribners, 1968.

AUTHOR ENTRIES

ANDY ADAMS

Thorncreek Township, Ind, 3 May 1859-Colorado Springs, Colo, 26 Sep 1935

As a young man Andy Adams migrated to Texas where he spent several years as a cowboy; he then moved to Colorado during the mining boom. His first novel, *The Log of a Cowboy*, was his most popular and best work, but all his trail-drive and ranching stories are remarkable for their authenticity. Although Adams was dismayed by readers who confused his fiction with history, historians J. Frank Dobie and Walter Prescott are credited with bringing his works to the attention of a national audience.

BIBLIOGRAPHIES

"AA: A Bibliography." Hudson (1964), 259-265. Primary.

First Printings of American Authors, Vol 4 (Detroit: Bruccoli Clark/Gale, 1979), 3-5. Primary.

BOOKS

The Log of a Cowboy: A Narrative of the Old Trail Days. Boston & NY: Houghton Mifflin, 1903. Abridged ed, 1927. New abridged ed, *A True Narrative of Cowboy Life From AA's Log of a Cowboy Trail Drive,* ed Glen Rounds. NY: Holiday House, 1965. Novel.

A Texas Matchmaker. Boston & NY: Houghton, Mifflin, 1904. Novel.

The Outlet. Boston & NY: Houghton, Mifflin, 1905. Novel.

Cattle Brands: A Collection of Western Camp-Fire Stories. Boston & NY: Houghton, Mifflin, 1906.

Reed Anthony, Cowman: An Autobiography. Boston & NY: Houghton, Mifflin, 1907. Novel.

Wells Brothers: The Young Cattle Kings. Boston & NY: Houghton Mifflin, 1911. Children's novel.

The Ranch on the Beaver: A Sequel to Wells Brothers. Boston & NY: Houghton Mifflin, 1927. Children's novel.

Why the Chisholm Trail Forks and Other Tales of the Cattle Country, ed with intro by Wilson M Hudson. Austin: U Texas P, 1956. Repub as *AA's Campfire Tales,* ed with new preface by Hudson. Lincoln & London: U Nebraska P, 1976.

The Corporal Segundo, ed with intro by Hudson. Austin, Tex: Encino, 1968. Play.

MANUSCRIPTS & ARCHIVES

State Historical Society of Colorado, Denver.

BIOGRAPHIES

Book

Hudson, Wilson M. *AA: His Life and Writings.* Dallas, Tex: Southern Methodist U P, 1964.

Articles

Dobie, J Frank. "Frank Dobie Recounts What He Knew of AA, Texas Cowboy Writer." *AustinAmS* (6 Oct 1935), 21.

Molen, Dayle. "AA . . . Log of a Cowboy." *Persimmon Hill,* 9 (Spring 1979), 48-57.

CRITICAL STUDIES

Book

Hudson, Wilson M. *AA: Storyteller and Novelist of the Great Plains.* Austin, Tex: Steck-Vaughn, 1967.

Book Sections & Articles

Barton, Sandra L. "*Log of a Cowboy* and *In Cold Blood* as Nonfiction Novels." *AFFWord,* 1 (Jul 1971), 1-6.

Borland, Hal. "The Magnetic West." *NYTBR* (15 Aug 1943), 6, 18.

Brunvand, Jan H. "Sailors' and Cowboys' Folklore in Two Popular Classics." *SFQ,* 29 (Dec 1965), 266-283.

Brunvand. "The Hat-in-Mud Tale." *The Sunny Slopes of Long Ago,* ed Wilson M Hudson & Alan Maxwell (Dallas, Tex: Southern Methodist U P, 1966), 100-109.

Capps, Benjamin. "A Critical Look at a Classic Western Novel." *Roundup,* 12 (Jun 1964), 2, 4.

Davidson, Levette J. "The Unpublished Manuscripts of AA." *ColMag,* 28 (Apr 1951), 97-107.

Dobie, J Frank. "AA: Cowboy Chronicler." *SWR,* 11 (Jan 1926), 92-101.

Frantz, Joe B & Julian Ernest Choate, Jr. "The Literature After 1900." *The American Cowboy* (Norman: U Oklahoma P, 1955), 158-177.

Graham, Don. "Old and New Cowboy Classics." *SWR*, 65 (Summer 1980), 293-303.

Hudson, Wilson M. "A, Dobie, and Webb on the Use of Regional Material." *American Bypaths,* ed Robert G Collmer & Jack W Herring (Waco, Tex: Baylor U P, 1980), 57-78.

Molen, Dayle H. "AA: Classic Novelist of the Trail." *Montana,* 19 (Jan 1969), 24-35.

Quissell, Barbara. "AA and the Real West." *WAL,* 7 (Fall 1972), 211-219.

Taylor, Archer. "Americanisms in *The Log of a Cowboy.*" *WF,* 18 (Jan 1959), 39-41.

Webb, Walter Prescott. *The Great Plains* (NY: Ginn, 1931), 266-269.

Christine M. Bernsen

SAMUEL HOPKINS ADAMS

Dunkirk, NY, 26 Jan 1871-Beaufort, SC, 16 Nov 1958

Samuel Hopkins Adams first made his reputation as a muckraking journalist with a series of articles in *Collier's* exposing the patent medicine industry. During a writing career that spanned more than six decades, Adams published novels, short stories, histories, and biographies. Under the pseudonym Warner Fabian, he wrote a series of novels—commencing with *Flaming Youth*—that were considered daring for the 1920s. Adams's *Revelry*, a fictional account of the presidency of Warren G. Harding, was banned in Philadelphia and Washington but was a best-seller. Although most of his published work is forgotten today, Adams continues to be remembered as a muckraker and as a chronicler of the "flaming youth" of the 1920s.

BOOKS

Blinky: A Story of the East Side. NY: Department of Hygiene, New York Association for Improving the Condition of the Poor, 1897. Nonfiction.

The Great American Fraud. Chicago: AMA, 1906. Nonfiction.

The Mystery, with Stewart Edward White. NY: McClure, Phillips, 1907. Novel.

The Flying Death. NY: McClure, 1908. Novel.

Average Jones. Indianapolis: Bobbs-Merrill, 1911. Novel.

The Secret of Lonesome Cove. Indianapolis: Bobbs-Merrill, 1912. Novel.

The Health Master. Boston & NY: Houghton Mifflin, 1913. Nonfiction.

The Clarion. Boston & NY: Houghton Mifflin, 1914. Novel.

Little Miss Grouch. Boston & NY: Houghton Mifflin, 1915. Novel.

The Adams Articles. NY: Tribune Association, 1916. Nonfiction.

The Unspeakable Perk. Boston & NY: Houghton Mifflin, 1916. Novel.

Our Square and the People in It. Boston & NY: Houghton Mifflin, 1917. Stories.

The Beggar's Purse: A Fairy Tale of Familiar Finance. Boston: Smith & Porter, 1918.

Invaded America. NY: National Americanization Committee, 1918. Essay.

Common Cause: A Novel of the War in America. Boston & NY: Houghton Mifflin, 1919.

Wanted: A Husband. Boston & NY: Houghton Mifflin, 1920. Novel.

Success. Boston & NY: Houghton Mifflin, 1921. Novel.

From a Bench in Our Square. Boston & NY: Houghton Mifflin, 1922. Stories.

Flaming Youth (as by Warner Fabian). NY: Boni & Liveright, 1923. Novel.

Siege. NY: Boni & Liveright, 1924. Novel.

Sailors' Wives (as by Fabian). NY: Boni & Liveright, 1924. Novel.

The Piper's Fee. NY: Boni & Liveright, 1926. Novel.

Summer Bachelors (as by Fabian). NY: Boni &
Liveright, 1926. Novel.

Revelry. NY: Boni & Liveright, 1926. Novel.

Unforbidden Fruit (as by Fabian). NY: Boni &
Liveright, 1928. Novel.

The Flagrant Years: A Novel of the Beauty Market.
NY: Liveright, 1929.

The Men in Her Life (as by Fabian). NY: Sears,
1930. Novel.

The Godlike Daniel. NY: Sears, 1930. Biography.

Week-end Girl (as by Fabian). NY: Macaulay,
1932. Novel.

The Gorgeous Hussy. Boston & NY: Houghton
Mifflin, 1934. Novel.

Widow's Oats (as by Fabian). NY: Macaulay,
1935. Novel.

Perfect Specimen. NY: Liveright, 1936. Novel.

Maiden Effort. NY: Liveright, 1937. Novel.

The World Goes Smash. Boston: Houghton Mifflin,
1938. Novel.

Both Over Twenty-one. NY: Liveright, 1939.
Novel.

*Incredible Era: The Life and Times of Warren Ga-
maliel Harding.* Boston: Houghton Mifflin,
1939.

Whispers. NY: Liveright, 1940. Novel.

The Harvey Girls. NY: Random House, 1942.
Novel.

Tambay Gold. NY: Messner, 1942. Novel.

Canal Town. NY: Random House, 1944. Novel.

A. Woollcott: His Life and His World. NY: Reynal
& Hitchcock, 1945; *Alexander Woollcott: His
Life and His World.* London: Hamilton, 1946.

Banner by the Wayside. NY: Random House, 1947.
Novel.

Plunder. NY: Random House, 1948. Novel.

*Safe Money: The Record of One Hundred Years of
Mutual Savings at the Auburn Savings Bank.*
Auburn, NY: Auburn Savings Bank, 1949.

Sunrise to Sunset. NY: Random House, 1950.
Novel.

The Pony Express. NY: Random House, 1950.
Children's history.

The Santa Fe Trail. NY: Random House, 1951.
Children's history.

The Erie Canal. NY: Random House, 1953.
Children's history.

*Wagons to the Wilderness: A Story of Westward Ex-
pansion.* Philadelphia: Winston, 1954. Children's novel.

Grandfather Stories. NY: Random House, 1955.

General Brock and Niagara Falls. NY: Random
House, 1957. Children's history.

Chingo Smith of the Erie Canal. NY: Random
House, 1958. Children's history.

Tenderloin. NY: Random House, 1959. Novel.

OTHER

Who and What: A Book of Clues for the Clever, ed
SHA. NY: Boni & Liveright, 1927.

MANUSCRIPTS & ARCHIVES

The major collections are at Syracuse U Library &
Hamilton C Library.

CRITICAL STUDIES

Articles

Cassedy, James H. "Muckraking and Medicine:
SHA." *AQ,* 16 (Spring 1964), 85-99.

Coren, Robert W. "SHA, His Novel *Revelry,* and
the Reputation of Warren G. Harding." *Courier,* 11 (Spring 1974), 3-10.

Hillman, Serrell. "SHA: 1871-1958." *SatR,* 41 (20
Dec 1958), 15, 37.

Perrick, Josephus. "A *Grandfather Stories* Glossary." *Verbatim,* 10 (Spring 1984), 10-12.

Philip B. Eppard

GEORGE ADE

Kentland, Ind, 9 Feb 1866-Brook, Ind, 16 May 1944

George Ade was one of the most popular and influential American humorists in the period between Mark Twain and James Thurber. His greatest success came from his *Fables,* which adapted Aesop's form to American comedy by employing slang, incongruity, and an ironic moral. He also wrote stories and plays that once attracted a wide audience. During the first decade of the twentieth century, the freshness of his technique garnered respect from many critics, but his popularity soon declined. Nevertheless, Ade's reputation as an important humorist endures.

BIBLIOGRAPHIES

First Printings of American Authors, Vol 2 (Detroit: Bruccoli Clark/Gale, 1978), 1-12. Primary.

Russo, Dorothy. *A Definitive Bibliography of GA.* Indianapolis: Indiana Historical Society, 1947. Primary.

BOOKS

The Chicago Record's "Stories of the Streets and of the Town" (Anon). Chicago: Chicago Daily News, 1894.

Second Series of the Chicago Record's "Stories of the Streets and of the Town" (Anon). Chicago: Chicago Daily News, 1894.

Third Series of the Chicago Record's "Stories of the Streets and of the Town" (Anon). Chicago: Chicago Daily News, 1895.

Fourth Series of the Chicago Record's "Stories of the Streets and of the Town" (Anon). Chicago: Chicago Daily News, 1895.

The Chicago Record's Staff Correspondent in Europe: What a Man Sees Who Goes Away From Home (Anon). Chicago: Chicago Daily News, 1896.

Artie: A Story of the Streets and Town. Chicago: Stone, 1896. Novel.

Circus Day. Chicago & NY: Werner, 1896. Stories.

Stories From History (as by John Hazelden). Chicago & NY: Werner, 1896.

Pink Marsh: A Story of the Streets and Town. Chicago & NY: Stone, 1897. Novel.

Fifth Series of the Chicago Record's "Stories of the Streets and of the Town" (Anon). Chicago: Chicago Daily News, 1897.

Sixth Series of the Chicago Record's "Stories of the Streets and of the Town" (Anon). Chicago: Chicago Daily News, 1898.

Seventh Series of the Chicago Record's "Stories of the Streets and of the Town" (Anon). Chicago: Chicago Daily News, 1899.

Doc' Horne: A Story of the Streets and Town. Chicago & NY: Stone, 1899. Novel.

Fables in Slang. Chicago & NY: Stone, 1900.

Eighth Series. The Chicago Record's Stories of the Streets and of the Town (Anon). Chicago: Chicago Daily News, 1900.

More Fables. Chicago & NY: Stone, 1900.

Forty Modern Fables. NY: Russell, 1901.

Grouch at the Game, or Why He Changed His Colors. Chicago?: Miller & Mabbett, 1901. Story.

The Girl Proposition: A Bunch of He and She Fables. NY: Russell, 1902.

The Sultan of Sulu: A Musical Comedy, lyrics by GA; music by Alfred G Wathall. NY & c: Witmark, 1902. Repub without music as *The Sultan of Sulu: An Original Satire in Two Acts.* NY: Russell, 1903.

Clarence Allen, the Hypnotic Boy Journalist. . . . NY: Bandar Log, 1903. Story.

Handsome Cyril; or The Messenger Boy With the Warm Feet. NY: Bandar Log, 1903. Story.

In Babel: Stories of Chicago. NY: McClure, Phillips, 1903.

Peggy From Paris: A Musical Comedy in Two Acts, book & lyrics by GA; music by William Loraine. NY & c: Witmark, 1903.

People You Know. NY: Russell, 1903. Stories.

Rollo Johnson, the Boy Inventor. . . . NY: Bandar Log, 1904. Story.

Breaking into Society. NY & London: Harper, 1904. Stories.

True Bills. NY & London: Harper, 1904. Stories.

The Sho Gun: An Original Comic Opera, book & lyrics by GA; music by Gustav Luders. NY: Witmark, 1904.

In Pastures New. NY: McClure, Phillips, 1906. Sketches.

The Slim Princess. Indianapolis: Bobbs-Merrill, 1907. Story.

The Fair Co-Ed, book & lyrics by GA; music by Luders. NY: Witmark, 1908. Play.

I Knew Him When—A Hoosier Fable. . . . Chicago: Indiana Society of Chicago, 1910. Sketches.

Hoosier Handbook and True Guide for the Returning Exile. Chicago: Indiana Society of Chicago, 1911.

Verses and Jingles. Indianapolis: Bobbs-Merrill, 1911.

Knocking the Neighbors. Garden City, NY: Doubleday, Page, 1912. Stories.

Ade's Fables. Garden City, NY: Doubleday, Page, 1914.

Marse Covington. Washington: Commission on Training Camp Activities, Department of Dramatic Activities Among the Soldiers, 1918. Repub, NY & London: French, 1923. Play.

Hand-Made Fables. Garden City, NY: Doubleday, Page, 1920. Stories.

Single Blessedness and Other Observations. Garden City, NY: Doubleday, Page, 1922. Stories.

The Mayor and the Manicure: Play in One Act. NY & London: French, 1923.

Speaking to Father. NY & London: French, 1923. Play.

Nettie: A Play in One Act. NY & London: French, 1923.

The College Widow: A Pictorial Comedy in Four Acts. NY & London: French, 1924. Play.

Just Out of College: A Light Comedy in Three Acts. NY & London: French, 1924. Play.

Father and the Boys: A Comedy-Drama. NY & London: French, 1924. Play.

The County Chairman: A Comedy-Drama. NY & London: French, 1924. Play.

Bang! Bang! NY: Sears, 1928. Stories.

The Old-Time Saloon: Not Wet-Not Dry, Just History. NY: Long & Smith, 1931. Nonfiction.

Notes & Reminiscences, with John T McCutcheon. Chicago: Holiday, 1940. Memoir.

Mrs. Peckham's Carouse. Nappanee, Ind: Indiana Kid, 1961. Play.

LETTERS

Letters of GA, ed Terence Tobin. West Lafayette, Ind: Purdue U P, 1973.

OTHER

A Souvenir, Fifteenth Anniversary, Purdue University, Lafayette, Ind., May 1890, ed & largely written by GA. Lafayette, Ind: Delta Delta Chapter of Sigma Chi, 1890.

Monon Madrigals, ed with intro by GA. Npl: npub, 1911. Verse.

An Invitation to You and Your Folks From Jim and Some More of the Home Folks, comp with intro by GA. Indianapolis: Bobbs-Merrill, 1916. Miscellany.

COLLECTIONS

Thirty Fables in Slang. NY: Arrow, 1933.

Stories of the Streets and of the Town. Chicago: Caxton Club, 1941.

The Permanent A: The Living Writings of GA, ed Fred C Kelly. Indianapolis: Bobbs-Merrill, 1947.

The America of GA (1866-1944): Fables, Short Stories, Essays, ed with intro by Jean Shepherd. NY: Putnam, 1960.

Fables in Slang and More Fables in Slang, intro by E F Bleiler. NY: Dover, 1960.

Artie, and Pink Marsh: Two Novels, intro by James T Farrell. Chicago & London: U Chicago P, 1963.

Chicago Stories, ed with intro by Franklin J Meine. Chicago: Regnery, 1963.

The Best of GA, ed A L Lazarus. Bloomington: Indiana U P, 1985.

MANUSCRIPTS & ARCHIVES

Purdue U Library.

BIOGRAPHIES

Book
Kelly, Fred C. *GA, Warmhearted Satirist.* Indianapolis: Bobbs-Merrill, 1947.

Article
Matson, Lowell. "Ade—Who Needed None." *LitR,* 5 (Autumn 1961), 99-114.

CRITICAL STUDIES

Books
Coyle, Lee. *GA.* NY: Twayne, 1964.

DeMuth, James. *Small Town Chicago: The Comic Perspective of Finley Peter Dunne, GA, and Ring Lardner.* Port Washington, NY: Kennikat, 1980.

Nordhus, Philip B. "GA: A Critical Study." Dissertation: State U Iowa, 1957.

Book Sections & Articles
Ashforth, Albert. "Hoosier Humorist, Three Letters." *ASch,* 56 (Autumn 1987), 565-573.

Bauerle, R F. "A Look at the Language of GA." *AS,* 33 (Feb 1958), 77-79.

Brenner, Jack. "Howells and A." *AL,* 38 (May 1966), 198-207.

Clark, John Abbot. "A's Fables in Slang: An Appreciation." *SAQ,* 46 (Oct 1947), 537-544.

Daniels, R Balfour. "GA as Social Critic." *MissQ,* 12 (Fall 1959), 194-204.

Evans, Bergen. "GA: Rustic Humorist." *AMercury,* 70 (Mar 1950), 321-329.

Franklin, Phyllis. "GA." *ALR,* 8 (Summer 1975), 188-189.

Howells, W D. "Certain of the Chicago School of Fiction." *NAR*, 176 (May 1903), 734-746.

Kelly, Fred C. "GA, Master of Warmhearted Satire." *MichAQR*, 61 (Winter 1955), 156-160.

Kolb, Harold H, Jr. "GA (1866-1944)." *ALR*, 4 (Spring 1971), 157-169.

McKee, James H. "The A Family and Newton County." *IHB*, 39 (Feb 1962), 27-32.

Mencken, H L. "GA." *Prejudices: First Series* (NY: Knopf, 1919), 114-122.

Salzman, Jack. "Dreiser and Ade: A Note on the Text of *Sister Carrie*." *AL*, 40 (Jan 1969), 544-548.

Tarkington, Booth. "A Guess at GA." *The American Spectator Year Book*, ed George Jean Nathan et al (NY: Stokes, 1934), 64-67.

Van Doren, Carl. "Old Wisdom in a New Tongue." *Century*, 105 (Jan 1923), 471-480.

Yates, Norris W. "GA, Student of 'Success.' " *The American Humorist: Conscience of the Twentieth Century* (Ames: Iowa State U P, 1964), 61-80.

Patricia R. New

LOUISA MAY ALCOTT

Germantown, Pa, 29 Nov 1832-Boston, Mass, 6 Mar 1888

Louisa May Alcott, daughter of the Transcendentalist philosopher and educator Amos Bronson Alcott, is best known for her novel *Little Women* and her other works for children. The recent discoveries of "blood-and-thunder" tales she published anonymously or pseudonymously for a popular audience, though, have shown her to be a much more versatile author than previously supposed. Recent scholarship has explored the feminist stance of her writings and how her works embody the cultural values of her times.

BIBLIOGRAPHIES

Bibliography of American Literature, comp Jacob Blanck. New Haven: Yale U P, 1955-1991. Primary.

"Bibliography." Stern (1950), 343-360. Rev in *Louisa's Wonder Book: An Unknown Alcott Juvenile*, ed Stern (Mount Pleasant: Central Michigan U, 1975), 25-52. Primary.

Gulliver, Lucille. *LMA: A Bibliography*. Boston: Little, Brown, 1932. Primary & secondary.

Payne, Alma J. *LMA: A Reference Guide*. Boston: Hall, 1980. Secondary.

Ullom, Judith C. *LMA: An Annotated, Selected Bibliography*. Washington: Library of Congress, 1969. Primary.

BOOKS

Flower Fables. Boston: Briggs, 1855. Stories.

Hospital Sketches. Boston: Redpath, 1863. Journalism.

The Rose Family. A Fairy Tale. Boston: Redpath, 1864. Novel.

On Picket Duty, and Other Tales. Boston: Redpath, 1864.

Moods. Boston: Loring, 1865. Rev ed, Boston: Roberts, 1882. Novel.

The Mysterious Key, and What It Opened. Boston: Fuller, 1868. Novella.

Morning-Glories, and Other Stories. Boston: Fuller, 1868.

Three Proverb Stories. Boston: Loring, 1868.

Little Women or Meg, Jo, Beth and Amy. Boston: Roberts, 1868. Novel.

Little Women or Meg, Jo, Beth and Amy. Part Second. Boston: Roberts, 1869. Novel.

Hospital Sketches and Camp and Fireside Stories. Boston: Roberts, 1869.

An Old-Fashioned Girl. Boston: Roberts, 1870. Novel.

Will's Wonder Book (Anon). Boston: Fuller, 1870. Facsimiled in *Louisa's Wonder Book: An Unknown Alcott Juvenile*, ed Madeleine B Stern (Mount Pleasant: Central Michigan U, 1975). Novella.

V. V.: or, Plots and Counterplots. By A. M. Barnard. Boston: Thomes & Talbot, 1870? Rpt in *Plots and Counterplots: More Unknown Thrillers by LMA*. Novella.

Little Men: Life at Plumfield With Jo's Boys. Boston: Roberts, 1871. Novel.

Aunt Jo's Scrap-Bag: My Boys. Boston: Roberts, 1872. Stories.

Aunt Jo's Scrap-Bag: Shawl-Straps. Boston: Roberts, 1872. Stories.

Work: A Story of Experience. Boston: Roberts, 1873. Novel.

Aunt Jo's Scrap-Bag: Cupid and Chow-Chow. Boston: Roberts, 1874. Stories.

Eight Cousins; or, The Aunt-Hill. Boston: Roberts, 1875. Novel.

Silver Pitchers: And Independence, a Centennial Love Story. Boston: Roberts, 1876. Novel.

Rose in Bloom. A Sequel to "Eight Cousins." Boston: Roberts, 1876. Novel.

A Modern Mephistopheles (Anon). Boston: Roberts, 1877. Augmented as *A Modern Mephistopheles and A Whisper in the Dark*, 1889. Novel.

Under the Lilacs, 11 parts. London: Low, 1877-1878; 1 vol, Boston: Roberts, 1878. Novel.

Aunt Jo's Scrap-Bag: My Girls. Boston: Roberts, 1878. Stories.

Aunt Jo's Scrap-Bag: Jimmy's Cruise in the Pinafore. Boston: Roberts, 1879. Stories.

Jack and Jill: A Village Story. Boston: Roberts, 1880. Novel.

Aunt Jo's Scrap-Bag: An Old-Fashioned Thanksgiving. Boston: Roberts, 1882. Stories.

Spinning-Wheel Stories. Boston: Roberts, 1884.

Lulu's Library: Vol. I. A Christmas Dream. Boston: Roberts, 1886. Stories.

Jo's Boys, and How They Turned Out. A Sequel to "Little Men." Boston: Roberts, 1886. Novel.

Lulu's Library: Vol. II. The Frost King. Boston: Roberts, 1887. Stories.

A Garland for Girls. Boston: Roberts, 1888. Stories.

Lulu's Library: Vol. III. Recollections. Boston: Roberts, 1889. Stories.

Comic Tragedies Written by "Jo" and "Meg" and Acted by the "Little Women." Boston: Roberts, 1893. Plays.

Behind a Mask: The Unknown Thrillers of LMA, ed Madeleine B Stern. NY: Morrow, 1975. Novellas.

Plots and Counterplots: More Unknown Thrillers by LMA, ed Stern. NY: Morrow, 1976. Novellas.

Diana and Persis, ed Sarah Elbert. NY: Arno, 1978. Novel.

A Double Life: Newly Discovered Thrillers by LMA, ed Stern; assoc eds Joel Myerson & Daniel Shealy. Boston: Little, Brown, 1988. Novellas.

LETTERS

The Selected Letters of LMA, ed Joel Myerson & Daniel Shealy; assoc ed Madeleine B Stern. Boston: Little, Brown, 1987.

"A Calendar of the Letters of LMA," ed Myerson, Shealy & Stern. *Studies in the American Renaissance 1988*, ed Myerson (Charlottesville: U P Virginia, 1988), 361-399.

COLLECTION

Glimpses of Louisa: A Centennial Sampling of the Best Short Stories by LMA, ed Cornelia Meigs. Boston: Little, Brown, 1968.

MANUSCRIPTS & ARCHIVES

The major collections are at the Houghton Library, Harvard U & U of Virginia Library.

BIOGRAPHIES

Books
Anthony, Katharine. *LMA.* NY: Knopf, 1938.

Bedell, Madelon. *The Alcotts: Biography of a Family.* NY: Potter, 1980.

Bonstelle, Jessie & Marian De Forest, eds. *Little Women: Letters From the House of Alcott.* Boston: Little, Brown, 1914.

Cheney, Ednah Dow. *LMA: Her Life, Letters, and Journals.* Boston: Roberts, 1889. Includes selections from letters & journals.

Gowing, Clara. *The Alcotts as I Knew Them.* Boston: Clark, 1909.

MacDonald, Ruth K. *LMA.* Boston: Twayne, 1983.

Meigs, Cornelia. *Invincible Louisa: The Story of the Author of Little Women.* Boston: Little, Brown, 1933.

Moses, Belle. *LMA: Dreamer and Worker.* NY: Appleton, 1909.

Papashvily, Helen Waite. *LMA.* Boston: Houghton Mifflin, 1965.

Saxton, Martha. *Louisa May: A Modern Biography of LMA.* Boston: Houghton Mifflin, 1977.

Stern, Madeleine B. *LMA.* Norman: U Oklahoma P, 1950. Rev 1971.

Willis, Frederick L H. *Alcott Memoirs*, ed Edith Willis Linn & Henry Bazin. Boston: Badger, 1915.

Worthington, Marjorie. *Miss Alcott of Concord: A Biography*. Garden City, NY: Doubleday, 1958.

Articles

Hawthorne, Julian. "The Woman Who Wrote *Little Women*." *LadiesHJ*, 39 (Oct 1922), 25, 120-124.

Myerson, Joel & Daniel Shealy. "LMA on Vacation: Four Uncollected Letters." *RALS*, 14 (Spring-Autumn 1984), 113-141.

Myerson & Shealy. "Three Contemporary Accounts of LMA, With Glimpses of Other Concord Notables." *NEQ*, 59 (Mar 1986), 109-122.

Porter, Maria S. "Recollections of LMA." *NEMag*, 6 (Mar 1892), 2-19.

Pratt, A A. "About Little Women." *St. Nicholas*, 30 (May 1903), 631.

Sanborn, F B. "Reminiscences of LMA." *Independent*, 72 (7 Mar 1912), 496-502.

Schlesinger, Elizabeth Bancroft. "The Alcotts Through Thirty Years: Letters to Alfred Whitman." *HLB*, 11 (Autumn 1957), 363-385.

Stern, Madeleine B. "LA, Civil War Nurse." *Americana*, 37 (Apr 1943), 296-325.

Stern. "LA, Trouper." *NEQ*, 16 (Jun 1943), 175-197.

Strickland, Charles. "A Transcendentalist Father: The Child-Rearing Practices of Bronson Alcott." *PAH*, 3 (1969), 5-73.

Talbot, Marion. "Glimpses of the Real LMA." *NEQ*, 11 (Dec 1938), 731-738.

Whitman, Alfred. "Miss A's Letters to Her 'Laurie.' " *LadiesHJ*, 18 (Sep 1901), 5-6; 18 (Oct 1901), 6.

CRITICAL STUDIES

Books

Elbert, Sarah. *A Hunger for Home: LMA and Little Women*. Philadelphia: Temple U P, 1984. Rev as *A Hunger for Home: LMA's Place in American Culture*. New Brunswick, NJ: Rutgers U P, 1987.

Marsalla, Joy A. *The Promise of Destiny: Children and Women in the Short Stories of LMA*. Westport, Conn: Greenwood, 1983.

Meigs, Cornelia. *LMA and the American Family Story*. London: Bodley Head, 1970.

Shealy, Daniel. "The Author-Publisher Relationships of LMA." Dissertation: U South Carolina, 1985.

Strickland, Charles. *Victorian Domesticity: Families in the Life and Art of LMA*. University: U Alabama P, 1985.

Collection of Essays

Stern, Madeleine B, ed. *Critical Essays on LMA*. Boston: Hall, 1984.

Book Sections & Articles

Alberghene, Janice M. "A's Psyche and Kate: Self-Portraits Sunny Side Up." *Proceedings of the Seventh Annual Conference of the Children's Literature Association*, ed Priscilla A Ord (New Rochelle, NY: Iona C, 1982), 37-43.

Baum, Freda. "The Scarlet Strand: Reform Motifs in the Writings of LMA." Stern (1984), 250-255.

Bedell, Jeanne F. "The Necessary Mask: The Sensation Fiction of LMA." *PMPA*, 5 (1980), 8-14.

Blackburn, William. " 'Moral Pap for the Young'?: A New Look at LMA's *Little Men*." *Proceedings of the Seventh Annual Conference of the Children's Literature Association*, ed Priscilla A Ord (New Rochelle, NY: Iona C, 1982), 98-106.

Boaden, Ann. "The Joyful Woman: Comedy as a Mark of Liberation in *Little Women*." *The Masks of Comedy* (Rock Island, Ill: Augustana C Library, 1980), 47-52, 56-57.

Cadogan, Mary. " 'Sweet, if somewhat tomboyish': The British Response to LMA." Stern (1984), 275-279.

Carpenter, Lynette. " 'Did They Never See Anyone Angry Before?': The Sexual Politics of Self-Control in A's 'A Whisper in the Dark.' " *Legacy*, 3 (Fall 1986), 31-41.

Crowley, John W. "*Little Women* and the Boy-Book." *NEQ*, 58 (Sep 1985), 384-389.

Dalke, Anne. " 'The House Band': The Education of Men in *Little Women*." *CE*, 47 (Oct 1985), 571-578.

Douglas, Ann. "Mysteries of LMA." *NYRB*, 25 (28 Sep 1978), 60-63.

Fetterley, Judith. "*Little Women*: A's Civil War." *FSt*, 5 (Summer 1979), 369-383.

Gay, Carol. "The Philosopher and His Daughter: Amos Bronson Alcott and Louisa." *ELWIU*, 2 (Fall 1975), 181-191.

Goldman, Suzy. "LMA: The Separation Between Art and Family." *L&U*, 1, no 2 (1977), 91-97.

Habegger, Alfred. "Precocious Incest: First Novels by LMA and Henry James." *MR*, 26 (Summer-Autumn 1985), 233-262.

Halttunen, Karen. "The Domestic Drama of LMA." *FSt*, 10 (Summer 1984), 233-254.

Hamblen, Abigail Ann. "LMA and the Racial Question." *UniversityR*, 37 (Summer 1971), 307-313.

Heilbrun, Carolyn G. "LMA: The Influence of *Little Women*." *Women, the Arts, and the 1920s in Paris and New York*, ed Virginia Lee

Lussier & Kenneth W Wheeler (New Brunswick, NJ: Transaction, 1982), 20-26.

Hollander, Anne. "Reflections on *Little Women*." *ChildL*, 9 (1981), 28-39.

Kaledin, Eugenia. "LMA: Success and the Sorrow of Self-Denial." *WS*, 5, no 3 (1978), 251-263.

Keyser, Elizabeth Lennox. "A's Portraits of the Artist as Little Woman." *IJWS*, 5 (Nov-Dec 1982), 445-459.

Keyser. "Women and Girls in LMA's *Jo's Boys*." *IJWS*, 6 (Nov-Dec 1983), 457-471.

Keyser. " 'Playing Puckerage': A's Plot in *Cupid and Chow-Chow*." *ChildL*, 14 (1986), 105-122.

Langland, Elizabeth. "Female Stories of Experience: A's *Little Women* in Light of *Work*." *The Voyage In: Fictions of Female Development*, ed Elizabeth Abel et al (Hanover, NH: U P New England, 1983), 112-127.

MacDonald, Ruth K. "The Progress of the Pilgrims in *Little Women*." *Proceedings of the Seventh Annual Conference of the Children's Literature Association*, ed Priscilla A Ord (New Rochelle, NY: Iona C, 1982), 114-119.

MacDonald. "*Moods*, Gothic and Domestic." Stern (1984), 74-78.

Moers, Ellen. "Money, the Job, and Little Women." *Commentary*, 55 (Jan 1973), 57-65.

Myerson, Joel. " 'Our Children Are Our Best Works': Bronson and LMA." Stern (1984), 261-264.

Myerson & Daniel Shealy. "LMA's 'A Wail': An Unrecorded Satire of the Concord Authors."

PBSA, 80 (First Quarter 1986), 93-99.

Rostenberg, Leona. "Some Anonymous and Pseudonymous Thrillers of LMA." *PBSA*, 37 (Apr-Jun 1943), 131-140.

Saxton, Martha. "The Secret Imaginings of LMA." Stern (1984), 256-260.

Stern, Madeleine B. "The Witch's Cauldron to the Family Hearth: LMA's Literary Development, 1848-1868." *MB*, 18 (Oct 1943), 363-380.

Stern. "LMA: An Appraisal." *NEQ*, 22 (Dec 1949), 475-498.

Stern. "LMA in Periodicals." *Studies in the American Renaissance 1977*, ed Joel Myerson (Boston: Twayne, 1977), 369-386.

Stern. "LA's Feminist Letters." *Studies in the American Renaissance 1978*, ed Joel Myerson (Boston: Twayne, 1978), 429-452.

Stern. "LA's Self-Criticism." *Studies in the American Renaissance 1985*, ed Joel Myerson (Charlottesville: U P Virginia, 1985), 333-382.

Turner, Lorenzo Dow. "LMA's 'M. L.' " *JNH*, 14 (Oct 1929), 495-533.

Van Buren, Jane. "LMA: A Study in Persona and Idealization." *Psychohistory*, 9 (Summer 1981), 282-299.

Yellin, Jean Fagan. "From *Success* to *Experience*: LMA's *Work*." *MR*, 21 (Fall 1980), 527-539.

Joel Myerson

THOMAS BAILEY ALDRICH

Portsmouth, NH, 11 Nov 1836-Boston, Mass, 19 Mar 1907

During the last half of the nineteenth century, Thomas Bailey Aldrich was a popular and esteemed poet, fiction writer, and editor. As a poet he was associated with the genteel school of Bayard Taylor and E. C. Stedman and noted for his polished light verse. Aldrich gained international fame as a humorist with his fiction. His most popular novel, *The Story of a Bad Boy,* passed through forty-seven editions and was translated into five languages; it was regarded as the first realistic treatment of an American boy. As editor of the *Atlantic Monthly,* Aldrich preferred traditional form, quiet tone, and craftsmanship to the harsher, more unconventional subjects and forms of the developing realists and naturalists. He quickly lost popularity in the early twentieth century.

BIBLIOGRAPHIES & CATALOGUE

Bartlett, Francis. *A Catalogue of the Works of TBA.* Boston: Merrymount, 1898.

Bibliography of American Literature, comp Jacob Blanck. New Haven: Yale U P, 1955-1991. Primary.

Sherman, Frederic Fairfield. *A Check List of First Editions of the Works of TBA.* NY: Privately printed, 1921.

Ward, Annette P. *Annotated List of the Works of TBA.* NY: Church of the Ascension, 1900.

BOOKS

The Bells: A Collection of Chimes. NY: J C Derby / Boston: Phillips, Sampson / Cincinnati: H W Derby, 1855. Poetry.

Daisy's Necklace: And What Came of It (A Literary Episode). NY: Derby & Jackson / Cincinnati: H W Derby, 1857. Novel.

The Course of True Love Never Did Run Smooth. NY: Rudd & Carleton, 1858. Poetry.

The Ballad of Babie Bell and Other Poems. NY: Rudd & Carleton, 1859.

Pampinea and Other Poems. NY: Rudd & Carleton, 1861.

Out of His Head, a Romance. NY: Carleton, 1862. Excerpted in *Père Antoine's Date Palm.* Cambridge, Mass: Welch, Bigelow, 1866. Novel.

Poems. NY: Carleton / London: Low, 1863.

Pansy's Wish: A Christmas Fantasy, With a Moral. Boston: Marion, 1870. Story.

The Story of a Bad Boy. Boston: Fields, Osgood, 1870. Novel.

Marjorie Daw and Other People. Boston: Osgood, 1873. Augmented as *Marjorie Daw and Other Tales.* Leipzig: Tauchnitz, 1879. Rpt as *Marjorie Daw and Other Stories.* Boston & NY: Houghton, Mifflin, 1885. Individual stories excerpted as *Miss Mehetabel's Son* & *A Rivermouth Romance.* Boston: Osgood, 1877.

Prudence Palfrey: A Novel. Boston: Osgood, 1874.

Flower and Thorn: Later Poems. Boston: Osgood, 1877.

A Midnight Fantasy, and The Little Violinist. Boston: Osgood, 1877. Sketches.

The Queen of Sheba. Boston: Osgood, 1877. Stories.

The Stillwater Tragedy. Boston: Houghton, Mifflin, 1880. Novel.

From Ponkapog to Pesth. Boston & NY: Houghton, Mifflin, 1883. Travel.

Mercedes, and Later Lyrics. Boston & NY: Houghton, Mifflin, 1884. *Mercedes: A Drama in Two Acts,* rev & separately published. Boston & NY: Houghton, Mifflin, 1894. *Later Lyrics* separately published, Boston & NY: Houghton, Mifflin, 1896. Play & poetry.

The Second Son, with M O W Oliphant. Boston & NY: Houghton, Mifflin, 1888. Novel.

Wyndham Towers. Boston & NY: Houghton, Mifflin, 1890. Poetry.

The Sisters' Tragedy With Other Poems, Lyrical and Dramatic. Boston & NY: Houghton, Mifflin, 1891.

An Old Town by the Sea. Boston & NY: Houghton, Mifflin, 1893. Nonfiction.

Two Bites at a Cherry With Other Tales. Boston & NY: Houghton, Mifflin, 1894.

Unguarded Gates and Other Poems. Boston & NY: Houghton, Mifflin, 1895.

Judith and Holofernes: A Poem. Boston & NY: Houghton, Mifflin, 1896.

On Influence of Books. Boston: Hall & Locke, 1901. Essay.

A Sea Turn and Other Matters. Boston & NY: Houghton, Mifflin, 1902. Stories.

Ponkapog Papers. Boston & NY: Houghton, Mifflin, 1903. Essays.

Judith of Bethulîa: A Tragedy. Boston & NY: Houghton, Mifflin, 1904. Rev ed, 1905. Play.
Pauline Pavlovna: A Drama in One Act. Boston & NY: Houghton, Mifflin, 1907?
For Bravery in the Field of Battle. London: Covent Garden, 1970.

OTHER

Every Saturday (1865-1874), ed TBA. Magazine.
Cameos Selected From the Works of Walter Savage Landor, ed TBA & E C Stedman. Boston: Osgood, 1874.
The Story of a Cat by Émile de la Bédollierre; trans TBA. Boston: Houghton, Mifflin, 1879.
Atlantic Monthly (1881-1890), ed TBA. Magazine.
"Introduction." *Poems of Robert Herrick* (NY: Century, 1900), xv-l.
The Young Folks' Library, 20 vols, ed TBA. Boston: Hall & Locke, 1901-1902.

EDITIONS & COLLECTIONS

The Poems of TBA. Boston: Ticknor & Fields, 1865. Rev as *Cloth of Gold and Other Poems.* Boston: Osgood, 1874. Rev again as *The Poems of TBA.* Boston & NY: Houghton, Mifflin, 1882. Rev & augmented ed, Boston & NY: Houghton, Mifflin, 1885. Rev as Vols 1 & 2 of *The Writings of TBA.*
XXXVI Lyrics and XII Sonnets: Selected From Cloth of Gold and Flower and Thorn. Boston: Houghton, Mifflin, 1881.
Friar Jerome's Beautiful Book: Selected From Cloth of Gold and Flower and Thorn. Boston: Houghton, Mifflin, 1881.
The Writings of TBA, 9 vols. Vols 1-8, Boston & NY: Houghton, Mifflin, 1897; Vol 9, Boston & NY: Hall & Locke, 1901-1902. Rev ed, Ponkapog Edition, 9 vols, Boston & NY: Houghton, Mifflin, 1907.
A Book of Songs and Sonnets, Selected From The Poems of TBA. Boston & NY: Houghton, Mifflin, 1906.
The Shadow of the Flowers From The Poems of TBA. Boston & NY: Houghton Mifflin, 1912.

MANUSCRIPTS & ARCHIVES

The major collections are at the Aldrich Memorial Museum, Portsmouth, NH; the Houghton Library, Harvard U; & Cornell U Library.

BIOGRAPHIES
Books
Greenslet, Ferris. *The Life of TBA.* Boston: Houghton Mifflin, 1908.
Mangam, Charles. "A Critical Biography of TBA." Dissertation: Cornell U, 1950.

Book Section & Article
Aldrich, Mrs Thomas Bailey. *Crowding Memories* (Boston: Houghton Mifflin, 1920), passim.
Rideing, William H. "Glimpses of TBA." *Putnam'sM,* 7 (Jan 1910), 398-406.

CRITICAL STUDIES
Books
Gick, Paulo Worth. "An Annotated, Critical Edition of the Unpublished Letters by TBA." Dissertation: Pennsylvania State U, 1982.
Samuels, Charles E. *TBA.* NY: Twayne, 1965.
Tuttle, Donald R. "TBA's Editorship of the *Atlantic Monthly.*" Dissertation: Western Reserve U, 1939.

Book Sections & Articles
Bellman, Samuel I. "Riding on Wishes: Ritual Make-Believe Patterns in Three 19th-Century American Authors: A, Hale, Bunner." *Ritual in the United States,* ed Don Harkness (Tampa, Fla: American Studies, 1985), 15-20.
Brooks, Van Wyck. "A and His Circle." *New England: Indian Summer, 1865-1915* (NY: Dutton, 1940), 296-315.
Cowie, Alexander. "Indian Summer Novelist." *NEQ,* 15 (Dec 1942), 608-621.
Cowie. "TBA (1836-1907)." *The Rise of the American Novel* (NY: American Book, 1948), 579-591.
Fawcett, Edgar. "Mr. A's Poetry." *Atlantic,* 34 (Dec 1874), 671-675.
Geller, Evelyn. "Tom Sawyer, Tom Bailey, and the Bad-Boy Genre." *WilsonLB,* 51 (Nov 1976), 245-250.
Grattan, C Hartley. "TBA." *AMercury,* 5 (May 1925), 41-45.
Gribben, Alan. " 'I Did Wish Tom Sawyer Was There': Boy-Book Elements in *Tom Sawyer* and *Huckleberry Finn.*" *One Hundred Years of Huckleberry Finn,* ed Robert Sattelmeyer & J Donald Crowley (Columbia: U Missouri P, 1985), 149-170.
Howells, William Dean. "Mr. A's Fiction." *Atlantic,* 46 (Nov 1880), 695-698.
More, Paul Elmer. "TBA." *Shelburne Essays, Seventh Series* (NY: Putnam, 1910), 138-152.
Pattee, Fred Lewis. *The Development of the American Short Story* (NY: Harper, 1923), 211-216.
Perry, Bliss. "TBA." *Park-Street Papers* (Boston: Houghton Mifflin, 1908), 141-170.
Tanasoca, Donald. "*The Stillwater Tragedy:* A Socio-Detective Novel." *AN&Q,* 1 (Jun 1963), 148-150.

Catherine Schultz

HORATIO ALGER, JR.

Chelsea, Mass, 13 Jan 1832-Natick, Mass, 18 Jul 1899

Horatio Alger, Jr., was regarded by his contemporaries as a prolific and didactic writer of moral tracts for boys. After his death he was gradually reinvented as a capitalist ideologue and American mythmaker whose name became an eponym for the American success story. His best-known rags-to-riches boy hero was Ragged Dick. Although Alger has often been thought of as a best-selling author, he earned in his lifetime only a modest income from his work. By 1910 more copies of Alger's books were sold annually than were sold in total during his career.

BIBLIOGRAPHIES

Bennett, Bob. *HA, Jr: A Comprehensive Bibliography.* Mount Pleasant, Mich: Flying Eagle, 1980. Primary.

First Printings of American Authors, Vol 5, ed Philip B Eppard (Detroit: Bruccoli Clark Layman/Gale, 1987), 3-25. Primary.

Gardner, Ralph D. *Road to Success: The Bibliography of the Works of HA.* Mendota, Ill: Wayside, rev 1971.

Scharnhorst, Gary & Jack Bales. *HA, Jr: An Annotated Bibliography of Comment and Criticism.* Metuchen, NJ: Scarecrow, 1981.

BOOKS

Bertha's Christmas Vision: An Autumn Sheaf. Boston: Brown, Bazin, 1856. Poetry & stories.

Nothing to Do: A Tilt at Our Best Society (Anon). Boston: French, 1857. Satirical poem.

Frank's Campaign; or, What Boys Can Do on the Farm for the Camp. Boston: Loring, 1864; *Frank's Campaign: A Story of the Farm and the Camp.* London: Aldine, 1887. Novel.

Paul Prescott's Charge: A Story for Boys. Boston: Loring, 1865; *Paul Prescott the Runaway.* London: Aldine, 1887. Novel.

Timothy Crump's Ward; or, The New Years Loan, and What Came of It (Anon). Boston: Loring, 1866. Repub as *Timothy Crump's Ward: A Story of American Life* (Anon), 1866. Novel.

Helen Ford. Boston: Loring, 1866. Novel.

Charlie Codman's Cruise: A Story for Boys. Boston: Loring, 1867; *Bill Sturdy—or—The Cruise of Kidnapped Charlie.* London: Aldine, 1887. Novel.

Ragged Dick; or, Street Life in New York With the Boot-Blacks. Boston: Loring, 1868; *Ragged Dick! or The Early Life of Richard Hunter, Esq.* London: Aldine, 1887. Novel.

Fame and Fortune; or, The Progress of Richard Hunter. Boston: Loring, 1868. Novel.

Mark, the Match Boy; or, Richard Hunter's Ward. Boston: Loring, 1869. Novel.

Ralph Raymond's Heir; or, The Merchant's Crime (as by Arthur Hamilton). Boston: Gleason, 1869. Repub as *The Merchant's Crime.* NY: Lupton, 1888. Novel.

Luck and Pluck; or, John Oakley's Inheritance. Boston: Loring, 1869. Novel.

Rough and Ready; or, Life Among the New York Newsboys. Boston: Loring, 1869. Repub in *Rough and Ready: His Fortunes and Adventures.* London: Aldine, 1887. Novel.

Ben, the Luggage Boy; or, Among the Wharves. Boston: Loring, 1870. Novel.

Rufus and Rose; or, The Fortunes of Rough and Ready. Boston: Loring, 1870. Repub in *Rough and Ready: His Fortunes and Adventures.* London: Aldine, 1887. Novel.

Sink or Swim; or, Harry Raymond's Resolve. Boston: Loring, 1870; *Paddle Your Own Canoe; or, "Harry Raymond's Resolve."* London: Aldine, 1887. Novel.

Tattered Tom; or, The Story of a Street Arab. Boston: Loring, 1871. Novel.

Strong and Steady; or, Paddle Your Own Canoe. Boston: Loring, 1871; *Strong and Steady: A Tale of Self-Help.* London: Aldine, 1887. Novel.

Paul, the Peddler; or, The Adventures of a Young Street Merchant. Boston: Loring, 1871; *Plucky Paul.* London: Aldine, 1888. Novel.

Phil, the Fiddler; or, The Story of a Young Street Musician. Boston: Loring, 1872. Novel.

Strive and Succeed; or, The Progress of Walter Conrad. Boston: Loring, 1872. Novel.

Slow and Sure; or, From the Street to the Shop. Boston: Loring, 1872. Novel.

Try and Trust; or, The Story of a Bound Boy. Boston: Loring, 1873; *Trials and Adventures of Herbert Mason; or, Try and Trust.* London: Aldine, 1887. Novel.

Bound to Rise; or, Harry Walton's Motto. Boston: Loring, 1873. Repub in *Bound to Rise; or, Live and Learn.* London: Aldine, 1888. Novel.

Julius; or, The Street Boy Out West. Boston: Loring, 1874. Novel.

Risen From the Ranks; or, Harry Walton's Success. Boston: Loring, 1874. Repub in *Bound to Rise; or, Live and Learn.* London: Aldine, 1888. Novel.

Brave and Bold; or, The Fortunes of a Factory Boy. Boston: Loring, 1874; *Brave and Bold or the Fortunes of Robert Rushton.* London: Aldine, 1887. Novel.

The Young Outlaw; or, Adrift in the Streets. Boston: Loring, 1875. Novel.

Herbert Carter's Legacy; or, The Inventor's Son. Boston: Loring, 1875; *George Carter's Legacy or the Inventor's Son.* London: Aldine, 1887. Novel.

Grand'ther Baldwin's Thanksgiving With Other Ballads and Poems. Boston: Loring, 1875.

Jack Ward; or, The Boy Guardian. Boston: Loring, 1875. Novel.

Sam's Chance; and How He Improved It. Boston: Loring, 1876; *Sam's Chance and What He Made of It.* London: Aldine, 1887. Novel.

Shifting for Himself; or, Gilbert Greyson's Fortunes. Boston: Loring, 1876; *"How His Ship Came Home."* London: Aldine, 1887. Novel.

Life of Edwin Forrest, the American Tragedian (Anon), with William Rounseville Alger. Philadelphia: Lippincott, 1877. Biography.

The New Schoolma'am; or, A Summer in North Sparta (Anon). Boston: Loring, 1877. Novel.

Wait and Hope; or, Ben Bradford's Motto. Boston: Loring, 1877. Novel.

The Young Adventurer; or, Tom's Trip Across the Plains. Boston: Loring, 1878. Repub in *The Young Adventurer; or, Tom Nelson in California.* London: Aldine, 1887. Novel.

The Western Boy; or, The Road to Success. NY: Carleton/Street & Smith/American News, 1878. Novel.

The Telegraph Boy. Boston: Loring, 1879. Novel.

The Young Miner; or, Tom Nelson in California. Boston: Loring, 1879. Repub in *The Young Adventurer; or, Tom Nelson in California.* London: Aldine, 1887. Novel.

The Young Explorer; or, Among the Sierras. Boston: Loring, 1880. Repub in *Ben Stanton, the Explorer.* London: Aldine, 1887. Novel.

Tony, the Hero. NY: Ogilvie, 1880. Novel.

From Canal Boy to President; or, The Boyhood and Manhood of James A. Garfield. NY: Anderson, 1881. Biography.

From Farm Boy to Senator; Being the History of the Boyhood and Manhood of Daniel Webster. NY: Ogilvie, 1882. Biography.

Ben's Nugget; or, A Boy's Search for Fortune. A Story of the Pacific Coast. Philadelphia: Porter & Coates, 1882. Repub in *Ben Stanton, the Explorer.* London: Aldine, 1887. Novel.

Abraham Lincoln, the Backwoods Boy; or, How a Young Rail-Splitter Became President. NY: Anderson & Allen, 1883. Biography.

The Train Boy. NY: Carleton/Street & Smith/New York Weekly, 1883. Novel.

The Young Circus Rider; or, The Mystery of Robert Rudd. Philadelphia: Porter & Coates, 1883. Novel.

Dan, the Detective. NY: Carleton/Street & Smith/New York Weekly, 1884; *Dutiful Dan, the Brave Boy Detective.* London: Aldine, 1895. Novel.

Do and Dare; or, A Brave Boy's Fight for Fortune. Philadelphia: Porter & Coates, 1884. Novel.

Hector's Inheritance; or, The Boys of Smith Institute. Philadelphia: Porter & Coates, 1885; *Never Despair! ("Nil Desperandum!"); or, Courage Against the World.* London: Aldine, 1887. Novel.

Helping Himself; or, Grant Thornton's Ambition. Philadelphia: Porter & Coates, 1886. Novel.

Joe's Luck; or, A Boy's Adventures in California. NY: Burt, 1887. Novel.

The Store Boy; or, The Fortunes of Ben Barclay. Philadelphia: Porter & Coates, 1887; *The Fortunes of Ben Barclay, the Store Boy.* London: Aldine, 1896. Novel.

Number 91; or, The Adventures of a New York Telegraph Boy (as by Arthur Lee Putnam). NY: Munsey, 1887. Novel.

Frank Fowler, the Cash Boy. NY: Burt, 1887. Novel.

The Young Acrobat of the Great North American Circus. NY: Munsey, 1888; *He Would Be a Mountebank.* London: Aldine, 1888. Novel.

Tom Temple's Career. NY: Burt, 1888. Novel.

Tom Tracy; or, The Trials of a New York Newsboy (as by Putnam). NY: Munsey, 1888. Novel.

Tom Thatcher's Fortune. NY: Burt, 1888. Novel.

The Errand Boy; or, How Phil Brent Won Success. NY: Burt, 1888. Novel.

Bob Burton; or, The Young Ranchman of the Missouri. Philadelphia: Porter & Coates, 1888; *The Young Ranchman of the Missouri.* London: Aldine, 1888. Novel.

Luke Walton; or, The Chicago Newsboy. Philadelphia: Porter & Coates, 1889. Novel.

Ned Newton; or, The Fortunes of a New York Bootblack (as by Putnam). NY: United States Book, 1890. Novel.

Mark Stanton (as by Putnam). NY: United States Book, 1890. Novel.

The Erie Train Boy. NY: United States Book, 1890; *Straight Ahead; or, Life on the Open Road.* London: Aldine, 1891. Novel.

A New York Boy (as by Putnam). NY: United States Book, 1890. Novel.

Dean Dunham; or, The Waterford Mystery. NY: United States Book, 1890; *Wait Til the Clouds Roll By.* London: Aldine, 1890. Novel.

The Odds Against Him; or, Carl Crawford's Experience. Philadelphia: Penn, 1890. Novel.

Struggling Upward; or, Luke Larkin's Luck. Philadelphia: Porter & Coates, 1890; *Struggling Upward; or, A Brave Boy's Purpose.* London: Aldine, 1891. Novel.

$500; or, Jacob Marlowe's Secret. NY: United States Book, 1890. *Uncle Jacob's Secret; or, The Boy Who Cleared His Father's Name.* London: Aldine, 1890. Novel.

Val Vane's Victory! or Well Won! London: Aldine, 1890. Repub in *Facing the World; or, The Haps and Mishaps of Harry Vane & In a New World; or, Among the Gold-Fields of Australia.* Philadelphia: Porter & Coates, 1893. Novel.

The Young Boatman of Pine Point. Philadelphia: Penn, 1892. Novel.

Digging for Gold: A Story of California. Philadelphia: Porter & Coates, 1892. Novel.

Tom Ruff: Who He Was and What He Did. London: Aldine, 1892; *Tom Brace: Who He Was and How He Fared.* NY: Street & Smith, 1901. Novel.

Only an Irish Boy; or, Andy Burke's Fortunes and Misfortunes. Philadelphia: Porter & Coates, 1894. Novel.

Victor Vane, the Young Secretary. Philadelphia: Porter & Coates, 1894. Novel.

The Disagreeable Woman: A Social Mystery (as by Julian Starr). NY: Dillingham, 1895. Novel.

Adrift in the City; or, Oliver Conrad's Plucky Fight. Philadelphia: Porter & Coates, 1895. Novel.

Frank Hunter's Peril. Philadelphia: Coates, 1896. Novel.

The Young Salesman. Philadelphia: Coates, 1896. Novel.

Frank and Fearless; or, The Fortunes of Jasper Kent. Philadelphia: Coates, 1897. Novel.

Walter Sherwood's Probation. Philadelphia: Coates, 1897. Novel.

A Boy's Fortune; or, The Strange Adventures of Ben Baker. Philadelphia: Coates, 1898. Novel.

The Young Bank Messenger. Philadelphia: Coates, 1898. Novel.

Rupert's Ambition. Philadelphia: Coates, 1899. Novel.

Silas Snobden's Office Boy. NY: Ogilvie, 1899. Novel.

Mark Mason's Victory: The Trials and Triumphs of a Telegraph Boy. NY: Burt, 1899. Novel.

Jed, the Poorhouse Boy. Philadelphia: Coates, 1899. Novel.

A Debt of Honor: The Story of Gerald Lane's Success in the Far West. NY: Burt, 1900. Novel.

Out for Business; or, Robert Frost's Strange Career. NY: Mershon, 1900. Completed by Edward Stratemeyer (as by Arthur M Winfield). Novel.

Falling in With Fortune; or, The Experiences of a Young Secretary. NY: Mershon, 1900. Completed by Stratemeyer (as by Winfield). Novel.

Making His Mark. Philadelphia: Penn, 1901. Novel.

Ben Bruce: Scenes in the Life of a Bowery Newsboy. NY: Burt, 1901. Novel.

Lester's Luck. Philadelphia: Coates, 1901. Novel.

Striving for Fortune; or, Walter Griffith's Trials and Successes. NY: Street & Smith, 1901. Repub as *Walter Griffith; or, The Adventures of a Young Street Salesman.* NY: Street & Smith, 1901. Novel.

Andy Grant's Pluck. Philadelphia: Coates, 1902. Novel.

Tom Turner's Legacy: The Story of How He Secured It. NY: Burt, 1902. Novel.

The World Before Him. Philadelphia: Penn, 1902. Novel.

A Rolling Stone; or, The Adventures of a Wanderer. Chicago: Thompson & Thomas, 1902. Novel.

Bernard Brook's Adventures: The Story of a Brave Boy's Trials. NY: Burt, 1903. Novel.

Chester Rank; or, A New Path to Fortune. Philadelphia: Coates, 1903. Novel.

Forging Ahead. Philadelphia: Penn, 1903. Novel.

Adrift in New York; or, Tom and Florence Braving the World. NY: Street & Smith, 1904. Novel.

Finding a Fortune. Philadelphia: Penn, 1904. Novel.

Jerry, the Backwoods Boy; or, The Parkhurst Treasure. Rahway, NJ: Mershon, 1904. Rev by Stratemeyer (as by Winfield). Novel.

Mark Manning's Mission: The Story of a Shoe Factory Boy. NY: Burt, 1905. Novel.

The Young Musician. Philadelphia: Penn, 1906. Novel.

In Search of Treasure: The Story of Guy's Eventful Voyage. NY: Burt, 1907. Novel.

Wait and Win: The Story of Jack Drummond's Pluck. NY: Burt, 1908. Novel.

Ben Logan's Triumph; or, The Boys of Boxwood Academy. NY: Cupples & Leon, 1908. Novel.

Robert Coverdale's Struggle; or, On the Wave of Success. NY: Street & Smith, 1910. Novel.

Alger Street: The Poetry of HA, Jr, ed Gilbert K Westgard, II. Boston: Canner, 1964.

Cast Upon the Breakers, foreword by Ralph D Gardner. Garden City, NY: Doubleday, 1974. Novel.

Mabel Parker; or, The Hidden Treasure, a Tale of the Frontier Settlements, ed with preface by

Gary Scharnhorst. Hamden, Conn: Archon, 1986. Novel.

BIOGRAPHIES

Books
Mayes, Herbert R. *Alger: A Biography Without a Hero*. NY: Macy-Masius, 1928. Repub, with new intro by Mayes & afterword by Jack Bales, Des Plaines, Ill: Westgard, 1978.

Scharnhorst, Gary & Jack Bales. *The Lost Life of HA, Jr*. Bloomington: Indiana U P, 1985.

Book Section & Articles
Bales, Jack. "Herbert R. Mayes and HA, Jr: Or the Story of a Unique Literary Hoax." *JPC*, 8, no 2 (1974), 317-319.

Henderson, William. "A Few Words About HA, Jr." *PW*, 203 (23 Apr 1973), 32-33.

Huber, Richard M. ". . . Religion Demands Success." *The American Idea of Success* (NY: McGraw-Hill, 1971), 42-61.

Munsey, Frank A. "Two Veteran Authors." *Munsey's*, 8 (Oct 1892), 58-61.

Scharnhorst, Gary. "The Alger Problem: The Hoax About Horatio Revealed." *BSUF*, 15 (Spring 1974), 61-65.

Scharnhorst. "Biographical Blindspots: The Case of the Cousins Alger." *Biography*, 6 (Spring 1983), 136-147.

CRITICAL STUDIES

Book
Scharnhorst, Gary. *IIA, Jr*. Boston: Twayne, 1980.

Special Journal
Newsboy (monthly, 1974-1986).

Book Sections & Articles
Behrman, S N. "Introduction." *Strive and Succeed: Two Novels by HA* (NY: Holt, Rinehart & Winston, 1967), v-xii.

Billman, Carol. "McGuffey's Reader and Alger's Fiction: The Gospel of Virtue According to Popular Children's Literature." *JPC*, 11, no 3 (1977), 614-619.

Bode, Carl. "Introduction." *Ragged Dick & Struggling Upward* (NY: Penguin, 1985), ix-xxi.

Bowerman, Richard. "HA, Jr; or, Adrift in the Myth of Rags to Riches." *JAmC*, 2 (Spring 1979), 83-112.

Brucker, Carl W. "Virtue Rewarded: The Contemporary Student and HA." *JGE*, 35, no 4 (1984), 270-275.

Cawelti, John G. "Portrait of the Newsboy as a Young Man: Some Remarks on the Alger Stories." *WMH*, 45 (Winter 1961-1962), 79-83.

Cawelti. "From Rags to Respectability: HA." *Apostles of the Self-Made Man* (Chicago: U Chicago P, 1965), 101-123.

Cowley, Malcolm. "HA: Failure." *Horizon*, 12 (Summer 1970), 62-65. Rpt as "The Real HA Story." *A Many-Windowed House*, ed Henry Dan Piper (Carbondale: Southern Illinois U P, 1970).

Coyle, William. "Introduction." *Adrift in New York & The World Before Him* (NY: Odyssey, 1966), v-xvii.

Crouse, Russel. "Introduction." *Struggling Upward and Other Works* (NY: Crown, 1945), vii-xiv.

Falk, Robert. "Notes on the 'Higher Criticism' of HA, Jr." *ArQ*, 19 (Summer 1963), 151-167.

Fink, Rychard. "HA as a Social Philosopher." *Ragged Dick & Mark, the Match Boy* (NY: Collier, 1962), 5-31.

Fiore, Jordan D. "HA, Jr as a Lincoln Biographer." *JISHS*, 46 (Autumn 1953), 247-253.

Garrison, Dee. "Cultural Custodians of the Gilded Age: The Public Librarian and HA." *JLH*, 6 (Oct 1971), 327-336.

Graham, John. "Struggling Upward: *The Minister's Charge* and *A Cool Million*." *CRevAS*, 4 (Fall 1973), 184-196.

Holland, Norman N. "Hobbling With Horatio, or the Uses of Literature." *HudR*, 12 (Winter 1959-1960), 549-557.

Kramer, Victor A. "Alger's Call for Resignation." *MarkhamR*, 6 (Spring 1977), 49-54.

Kruse, Horst. "Der Aufstiegsmythos in der amerikanischen Trivialliteratur des 19. Jahrhunderts im literarhistorischen Kontext." *Amst*, 23, no 2 (1978), 213-229.

Lemeunier, Yves. "Vision of Poverty and the Poor in the Novels of HA." *All Men Are Created Equal*, ed Jean-Pierre Martin (Aix-en-Provence: Pubs U de Provence, 1983), 121-135.

Lhamon, W T, Jr. "HA and American Modernism: The One-Dimensional Social Formula." *AmerS*, 17 (Fall 1976), 11-27.

Lindberg-Seyersted, Brita. "Three Variations of the American Success Story: The Careers of Luke Larkin, Lemuel Barker, and Lemuel Pitkin." *ES*, 53 (Apr 1972), 125-141.

Lohof, Bruce A. "*Helen Ford*: HA, Jr's Book for Girls." *JPC*, 17 (Spring 1984), 97-105.

Monkkonen, Eric. "Socializing the New Urbanites: HA, Jr's Guidebooks." *JPC*, 11, no 1 (1977), 77-87.

Moon, Michael. "'The Gentle Boy From the Dangerous Classes': Pederasty, Domesticity, and Capitalism in HA." *Representations*, no 19 (Summer 1987), 87-110.

Pauly, Thomas N. "*Ragged Dick* and *Little Women*: Idealized Homes and Unwanted Marriages." *JPC*, 9 (Winter 1975), 583-592.

Pickering, Sam. "A Boy's Own War." *NEQ,* 48 (Sep 1975), 362-377.

Robertson, James O. "HA, Andrew Carnegie, Abraham Lincoln, and the Cowboy." *MQ,* 20 (Spring 1979), 241-257.

Scharnhorst, Gary. "The Boudoir Tales of HA, Jr." *JPC,* 10, no 1 (1976), 215-226.

Scharnhorst. "A Note on the Authorship of Alger's *Life of Edwin Forrest.*" *TheatreS,* 23 (1976-1977), 53-65.

Scharnhorst. "Scribbling Upward: Fitzgerald's Debt of Honor to HA, Jr." *FHA* (1978), 161-169.

Scharnhorst. "From Rags to Patches, or *A Cool Million* as Alter-Alger." *BSUF,* 21 (Autumn 1980), 58-65.

Scharnhorst. "Demythologizing Alger." *MarkhamR,* 10 (Fall-Winter 1980-1981), 20-27.

Scharnhorst. "Howells's *The Minister's Charge:* A Satire of Alger's 'Country-Boy Myth.' " *MTJ,* 20 (Winter 1980-1981), 16-17.

Scharnhorst. "Had Their Mothers Only Known: HA, Jr, Rewrites Cooper, Melville and Twain." *JPC,* 15, no 3 (1981), 175-182. Rpt *JAmC,* 5 (Summer 1982), 91-95.

Scharnhorst. "Dickens and HA, Jr." *DQu,* 2 (Jun 1985), 50-53.

Schroeder, Fred. "America's First Literary Realist: HA, Junior." *WHR,* 17 (Spring 1963), 129-137.

Seelye, John. "Who Was Horatio? The Alger Myth and American Scholarship." *AQ,* 17 (Winter 1965), 749-756.

Seelye. "Introduction." *Digging for Gold* (NY: Collier, 1968), vii-xx.

Shepard, Douglas H. "Nathanael West Rewrites HA, Jr." *SatireN,* 3 (Fall 1965), 13-28.

Shuffelton, Frank. "Bound to Rise—But Not Too Far." *IllQ,* 39 (Fall 1976), 51-64.

Walden, Daniel. "The Two Faces of Technological Utopianism: Edward Bellamy and HA, Jr." *JGE,* 33 (Spring 1981), 24-30.

Walters, Thomas N. "Twain's Finn and Alger's Gilman: Picaresque Counter-Directions." *MarkhamR,* 3 (May 1972), 53-58.

Weiher, Carol. "HA's Fiction: American Fairy Tales for All Ages." *CEA,* 40 (Jan 1978), 23-27.

Weiss, Richard. "HA, Jr, and the Response to Industrialism." *The Age of Industrialism in America,* ed Frederic Cople Jaher (NY: Free P, 1968), 304-316.

Wohl, R Richard. "The 'Rags to Riches Story': An Episode of Secular Idealism." *Class, Status and Power,* ed Reinhard Bendix & Seymour Martin Lipset (Glencoe, Ill: Free P, 1953), 388-395.

Wohl. "The 'Country Boy' Myth and Its Place in American Urban Culture: The Nineteenth-Century Contribution," ed Moses Rischin. *PAH,* 3 (1969), 75-156.

Zuckerman, Michael. "The Nursery Tales of HA." *AQ,* 24 (May 1972), 191-209.

Gary Scharnhorst

JAMES LANE ALLEN

Lexington, Ky, 21 Dec 1849-New York City, NY, 18 Feb 1925

Although he was one of America's most popular writers during the late nineteenth and early twentieth centuries, James Lane Allen is largely unread today. His first collection of short stories, *Flute and Violin and Other Kentucky Tales and Romances*, suggests the subjects that Allen concentrated on in his fiction: romanticism, the love of nature, and the local color of Kentucky. Allen's belief that the techniques of realism could be adapted to the romance shaped his fiction and his essays on literary theory. He is best known for his romances set in Kentucky, especially *A Kentucky Cardinal*. His later novels, more realistic in technique, show a growing interest in Darwinism, determinism, anthropology, and mythology.

BIBLIOGRAPHIES

"Bibliography." Knight, 288-304. Primary & secondary.
Bibliography of American Literature, comp Jacob Blanck. New Haven: Yale U P, 1955-1991. Primary.

BOOKS

Flute and Violin and Other Kentucky Tales and Romances. NY: Harper, 1891. Stories.
The Blue-Grass Region of Kentucky and Other Kentucky Articles. NY: Harper, 1892.
John Gray: A Kentucky Tale of the Olden Time. Philadelphia: Lippincott, 1893. Novel.
A Kentucky Cardinal: A Story. NY: Harper, 1895. Novel.
Aftermath: Part Second of "A Kentucky Cardinal." NY: Harper, 1896. Novel.
Summer in Arcady: A Tale of Nature. NY & London: Macmillan, 1896. Novel.
The Choir Invisible. NY & London: Macmillan, 1897. Rev ed, 1898. Novel.
The Reign of Law: A Tale of the Kentucky Hemp Fields. NY & London: Macmillan, 1900; *The Increasing Purpose*. London & NY: Macmillan, 1900. Novel.
The Mettle of the Pasture. NY & London: Macmillan, 1903. Novel.
The Bride of the Mistletoe. NY: Macmillan, 1909. Novel.

The Doctor's Christmas Eve. NY: Macmillan, 1910. Novel.
The Heroine in Bronze; or, A Portrait of a Girl, a Pastoral of the City. NY: Macmillan, 1912. Novel.
The Last Christmas Tree: An Idyl of Immortality. Portland, Maine: Mosher, 1914. Story.
The Sword of Youth. NY: Century, 1915. Novel.
A Cathedral Singer. NY: Century, 1916. Novel.
The Kentucky Warbler. Garden City, NY: Doubleday, Page, 1918. Novel.
The Emblems of Fidelity: A Comedy of Letters. Garden City, NY: Doubleday, Page, 1919.
The Alabaster Box. NY & London: Harper, 1923. Novel.
The Landmark. NY: Macmillan, 1925. Stories.

COLLECTIONS

A Kentucky Cardinal, and Aftermath. London: Osgood, McIlvaine, 1896. Rev ed, with new preface by Hugh Thomson, NY & London: Macmillan, 1900.
A Kentucky Cardinal, Aftermath, and Other Selected Works by JLA, ed with intro by William K Bottorff. New Haven, Conn: College & University P, 1967.

MANUSCRIPTS & ARCHIVES

The major collections are at the U of Kentucky Library; Kentucky Historical Society, Frankfort; Duke U Library; U of Virginia Library; the Houghton Library, Harvard U; & the Lilly Library, Indiana U.

BIOGRAPHY

Books
Knight, Grant C. *JLA and the Genteel Tradition*. Chapel Hill: U North Carolina P, 1935.
Townsend, John Wilson. *JLA: A Personal Note*. Louisville, Ky: Courier-Journal, 1928.

CRITICAL STUDIES

Book
Bottorff, William K. *JLA*. NY: Twayne, 1964.

Book Sections & Articles
Bottorff, William K. "JLA (1849-1925)." *ALR*, 2 (Summer 1969), 121-124.

Clemens, Cyril. "An Unpublished Letter From JLA." *AL,* 9 (Nov 1937), 355-356.

Finley, John H. "JLA." *AmRofR,* 71 (Apr 1925), 419-420.

Hancock, Albert E. "The Art of JLA." *Outlook,* 74 (15 Aug 1903), 953-955.

Harding, Lee. "From Romance to Realism: JLA's Revisions of *A Kentucky Cardinal.*" *MissQ,* 39 (Winter 1985-1986), 41-52.

Henneman, Joel Bell. "JLA: A Study." *Shakespearean and Other Papers* (Sewanee, Tenn: U P Sewanee, 1911), 112-166.

Maurice, Arthur Bartlett. "JLA's Country." *Bookman,* 12 (Oct 1900), 154-162.

Payne, L W, Jr. "The Stories of JLA." *SR,* 8 (Jan 1900), 45-55.

Quinn, Arthur Hobson. "JLA and the Novel of the Spirit." *American Fiction* (NY: Appleton-Century, 1936), 472-483.

Eric Damon Larison

SHERWOOD ANDERSON

Camden, Ohio, 13 Sep 1876-Colón, Panama Canal Zone, 8 Mar 1941

Before World War I Sherwood Anderson positioned himself among the Chicago Renaissance writers who rebelled against constraints over their private lives and their subject matter and writing styles. After publishing unsuccessful conventional novels about unhappy men who rebel in searches for life's meaning, Anderson unexpectedly presented in *Winesburg, Ohio* the first modern American short stories—cyclic stories organic in form and revolutionary in subject matter that treated in tenderly simple prose the buried and shunned aspects of the lives of Americans in an imaginary small town of the 1890s. Although he continued to publish distinguished short fiction, Anderson yielded to the recurring critical demand that to be important in America he must produce significant novels; he wrote several disappointing novels, only one of which—*Dark Laughter*—achieved financial success. With the revival of interest in Anderson that began in the 1960s, new attention has been paid to his importance in the development of the American short story and his considerable talent as a memoirist and social commentator.

BIBLIOGRAPHIES

First Printings of American Authors, Vol 2 (Detroit: Bruccoli Clark/Gale, 1978), 13-20. Primary.

Modlin, Charles, Hilbert Campbell & Kenichi Takada. "SA: Additions to the Bibliography." *SB,* 39 (1986), 266-268. Primary.

Rogers, Douglas G. *SA: A Selective, Annotated Bibliography.* Metuchen, NJ: Scarecrow, 1976. Primary & secondary.

Sheehy, Eugene P & Kenneth A Lohf. *SA: A Bibliography.* Los Gatos, Calif: Talisman, 1960. Primary & secondary.

White, Ray Lewis. *The Merrill Checklist of SA.* Columbus, Ohio: Merrill, 1969. Primary & secondary.

White. "A Checklist of SA Studies, 1959-1969." *NewberryLB,* 6 (Jul 1971), 288-302. Primary & secondary.

White. "*Winesburg* in Translation." *OhioanaQ,* 19 (Summer 1976), 58-60. Primary.

White. *SA: A Reference Guide.* Boston: Hall, 1977. Secondary.

White. "SA: Fugitive Pamphlets and Broadsides, 1918-1940." *SB,* 31 (1978), 257-263. Primary.

BOOKS

Windy McPherson's Son. NY: Lane / London: Lane, Bodley Head, 1916. Rev ed, NY: Huebsch, 1922. Novel.

Marching Men. NY: Lane / London: Lane, Bodley Head, 1917. Novel.

Mid-American Chants. NY: Lane / London: Lane, Bodley Head, 1918. Poems.

Winesburg, Ohio. NY: Huebsch, 1919. Story cycle.

Poor White. NY: Huebsch, 1920. Novel.

The Triumph of the Egg. NY: Huebsch, 1921. Stories.

Horses and Men. NY: Huebsch, 1923. Stories.

Many Marriages. NY: Huebsch, 1923. Novel.

A Story Teller's Story. NY: Huebsch, 1924. Autobiography.

Dark Laughter. NY: Boni & Liveright, 1925. Novel.

The Modern Writer. San Francisco: Gelber, Lilienthal, 1925. Essay.

SA's Notebook. NY: Boni & Liveright, 1926. Essays.

Tar: A Midwest Childhood. NY: Boni & Liveright, 1926. Novel.

A New Testament. NY: Boni & Liveright, 1927. Poems.

Alice and The Lost Novel. London: Mathews & Marrot, 1929. Stories.

Hello Towns! NY: Liveright, 1929. Columns.

Nearer the Grass Roots and *Elizabethton.* San Francisco: Westgate, 1929. Essays.

The American County Fair. NY: Random House, 1930. Essay.

Perhaps Women. NY: Liveright, 1931. Essays.

Beyond Desire. NY: Liveright, 1932. Novel.

Death in the Woods and Other Stories. NY: Liveright, 1933.

No Swank. Philadelphia: Centaur, 1934. Essays.

Puzzled America. NY & London: Scribners, 1935. Essays.

Kit Brandon: A Portrait. NY & London: Scribners, 1936. Novel.

Plays: Winesburg and Others. NY & London: Scribners, 1937.

A Writer's Conception of Realism. Olivet, Mich: Olivet C, 1939. Essay.

Home Town. NY: Alliance, 1940. Essay.

SA's Memoirs. NY: Harcourt, Brace, 1942.

LETTERS & DIARIES

Letters of SA, ed with intro by Howard Mumford Jones in association with Walter B Rideout. Boston: Little, Brown, 1953.

SA/Gertrude Stein: Correspondence and Personal Essays, ed with intro by Ray Lewis White. Chapel Hill: U North Carolina P, 1972.

SA: Selected Letters, ed with intro by Charles E Modlin. Knoxville: U Tennessee P, 1984.

Letters to Bab: SA to Marietta D. Finley, 1916-33, ed William A Sutton; foreword by Rideout. Urbana: U Illinois P, 1985.

The SA Diaries, 1936-1941, ed with intro by Hilbert H Campbell. Athens & London: U Georgia P, 1987.

OTHER

Marion Democrat (Marion, Va, 1927-1929), ed SA. Newspaper.

Smyth County News (Marion, Va, 1927-1929), ed SA. Newspaper.

EDITIONS & COLLECTIONS

The SA Reader, ed with intro by Paul Rosenfeld. Boston: Houghton Mifflin, 1947.

The Portable SA, ed with intro by Horace Gregory. NY: Viking, 1949.

SA: Short Stories, ed with intro by Maxwell Geismar. NY: Hill & Wang, 1962.

Mid-American Chants: 6 Midwestern Chants by SA/11 Midwest Photographs by Art Sinsabaugh, note by Edward Dahlberg. Highlands, NC: Nantahala Foundation, 1964.

Winesburg, Ohio: Text and Criticism, ed with intro by John H Ferres. NY: Viking, 1966.

Return to Winesburg, ed with intro by Ray Lewis White. Chapel Hill: U North Carolina P, 1967.

A Story Teller's Story: A Critical Text, ed with intro by White. Cleveland, Ohio: P Case Western Reserve U, 1968.

SA's Memoirs: A Critical Edition, ed with intro by White. Chapel Hill: U North Carolina P, 1969.

Tar: A Midwest Childhood—A Critical Text, ed with intro by White. Cleveland, Ohio & London: P Case Western Reserve U, 1969.

The Buck Fever Papers, ed with intro by Welford Dunaway Taylor. Charlottesville: U P Virginia, 1971.

Marching Men: A Critical Text, ed White. Cleveland, Ohio & London: P Case Western Reserve U, 1972.

The "Writer's Book" by SA: A Critical Edition, ed with intro by Martha Mulroy Curry. Metuchen, NJ: Scarecrow, 1975.

France and SA: Paris Notebook, 1921, ed with intro by Michael Fanning. Baton Rouge: Louisiana State U P, 1976.

SA: The Writer at His Craft, ed with intro by Jack Salzman, David D Anderson & Kichinosuke Ohashi. Mamaroneck, NY: Appel, 1979.

The Complete Works of SA, 21 vols, ed Ohashi. Kyoto: Rinsen, 1982.

The Teller's Tales, ed with intro by Frank Gado. Schenectady, NY: Union C P, 1983.

MANUSCRIPTS & ARCHIVES
Newberry Library, Chicago.

BIOGRAPHIES
Books

Carlson, G Bert, Jr. "SA's Political Mind: The Activist Years." Dissertation: U Maryland, College Park, 1966.

Schevill, James. *SA: His Life and Work*. Denver: U Denver P, 1951.

Sutton, William A. "SA's Formative Years (1876-1913)." Dissertation: Ohio State U, 1943.

Sutton. *The Road to Winesburg: A Mosaic of the Imaginative Life of SA*. Metuchen, NJ: Scarecrow, 1972.

Townsend, Kim. *SA*. Boston: Houghton Mifflin, 1987.

Williams, Kenny J. *A Storyteller and a City: SA's Chicago*. DeKalb: Northern Illinois U P, 1988.

Book Sections & Articles

Anderson, Elizabeth & Gerald R Kelley. *Miss Elizabeth* (Boston: Little, Brown, 1969), passim.

Anderson, Margaret. *My Thirty Years' War* (NY: Covici-Friede, 1930), passim.

Buchanan, Annabel Morris. "SA: Country Editor." *World Today*, 53 (Feb 1929), 249-253.

Dell, Floyd. "On Being SA's Literary Father." *NewberryLB*, 5 (Dec 1961), 315-321.

Farrell, James T. "A Memoir on SA." *Perspective*, 7 (Summer 1954), 83-88.

Hecht, Ben. "About SA." *Letters From Bohemia* (Garden City, NY: Doubleday, 1964), 85-103.

Hemingway, Ernest. "Une Generation Perdue." *A Moveable Feast* (NY: Scribners, 1964), 23-31.

Holtz, William. "SA and Rose Wilder Lane: Source and Method in *Dark Laughter*." *JML*, 12 (Mar 1985), 131-152.

Kramer, Dale. *Chicago Renaissance* (NY: Appleton-Century, 1966), passim.

Rideout, Walter B. "SA's Political Pilgrimage." *LAmer*, 5 (Autumn 1984), 181-199.

Rideout. " 'The Most Cultural Town in America': SA and New Orleans." *SoR*, ns 24 (Winter 1988), 79-99.

Rideout. "The Break Between SA and William Faulkner." *WE*, 13 (Summer 1988), 2-5.

Sullivan, John H. "Winesburg Revisited." *AR*, 20 (Summer 1960), 213-221.

White, Ray Lewis. "Hemingway's Private Explanation of *The Torrents of Spring*." *MFS*, 13 (Summer 1967), 261-263.

White. "SA (1876-1941)." *The Politics of Twentieth-Century Novelists*, ed George A Panichas (NY: Hawthorn, 1971), 251-262.

White. "A's Private Reaction to *The Torrents of Spring*." *MFS*, 26 (Winter 1980-1981), 635-637.

White. " 'Implications of Obscenity': The English Trial of *Many Marriages*." *JML*, 10 (Mar 1983), 153-158.

White. " 'As His Home Town Knew Him': SA's Last Trip Home." *Midamerica*, 14 (1987), 74-88.

White. "SA and the Real Winesburg, Ohio." *WE*, 12 (Apr 1987), 1-4.

CRITICAL STUDIES
Books

Anderson, David D. *SA: An Introduction and Interpretation*. NY: Holt, Rinehart & Winston, 1967.

Bruyère, Claire. *SA: L'Impuissance Créatrice*. Paris: Klincksieck, 1985.

Burbank, Rex. *SA*. NY: Twayne, 1964.

Chase, Cleveland. *SA*. NY: McBride, 1927.

Fagin, N Bryllion. *The Phenomenon of SA: A Study in American Life & Letters*. Baltimore, Md: Rossi-Bryn, 1927.

Howe, Irving. *SA*. NY: Sloane, 1951.

Miller, William Vaughn. "The Technique of SA's Short Stories." Dissertation: U Illinois, 1969.

Taylor, Welford Dunaway. *SA*. NY: Ungar, 1977.

Weber, Brom. *SA*. Minneapolis: U Minnesota P, 1964.

Collections of Essays

Anderson, David D, ed. *SA: Dimensions of His Literary Art*. East Lansing: Michigan State U P, 1976.

Anderson, ed. *Critical Essays on SA*. Boston: Hall, 1981.

Appel, Paul P, ed. *Homage to SA: 1876-1941*. Mamaroneck, NY: Appel, 1970.

Campbell, Hilbert H & Charles E Modlin, eds. *SA: Centennial Studies*. Troy, NY: Whitston, 1976.

Ohashi, Kichinosuke, ed. *SA*. Tokyo: Kenkyusha, 1968.

Rideout, Walter B, ed. *SA: A Collection of Critical Essays*. Englewood Cliffs, NJ: Prentice-Hall, 1974.

White, Ray Lewis, ed. *The Achievement of SA: Essays in Criticism*. Chapel Hill: U North Carolina P, 1966.

White, ed. *The Merrill Studies in Winesburg, Ohio*. Columbus, Ohio: Merrill, 1971.

Special Journals

AN&Q, 15 (Sep 1976). SA issue.
MMisc, 12 (1984). SA issue.
NewberryLB, Series 2, no 2 (Dec 1948). SA issue.
NewberryLB, 6 (Jul 1971). SA issue.

Shenandoah, 13 (Spring 1962). SA issue.
Story, 19 (Sep-Oct 1941). SA issue.
TCL, 23 (Feb 1977). SA issue.
Winesburg Eagle: The Official Publication of the Sherwood Anderson Society, 1 (Nov 1975-).

Book Sections & Articles
Anderson, David D. "SA's Ohio." *ON,* 5 (Summer 1979), 181-189.
Anderson. "SA, Chicago, and the Midwestern Myth." *Midamerica,* 11 (1984), 56-68.
Anderson. "SA's Grotesques and Modern American Fiction." *MMisc,* 12 (1984), 53-65.
Anderson, Maxwell. "A Country Town." *NewR,* 19 (25 Jun 1919), 257, 260. Rpt White (1966), Anderson (1981).
Ardat, Ahmad K. "The Prose Style of Selected Works by Ernest Hemingway, SA, and Gertrude Stein." *Style,* 14 (Winter 1980), 1-21.
Baker, Carlos. "SA's *Winesburg:* A Reprise." *VQR,* 48 (Autumn 1972), 568-579.
Bort, Barry D. "*Winesburg, Ohio:* The Escape From Isolation." *MQ,* 11 (Summer 1970), 443-456.
Bredahl, A Carl. " 'The Young Thing Within': Divided Narrative and SA's *Winesburg, Ohio.*" *MQ,* 27 (Summer 1986), 422-437.
Bresnahan, Roger J. "The 'Old Hands' of Winesburg." *MMisc,* 11 (1983), 19-27.
Brooks, Van Wyck. *The Confident Years, 1885-1915* (NY: Dutton, 1952), passim.
Calverton, V F. "SA: A Study in Sociological Criticism." *ModernQ,* 2 (Fall 1924), 82-118.
Cargill, Oscar. *Intellectual America* (NY: Macmillan, 1941), passim.
Cowley, Malcolm. Introduction. *Winesburg, Ohio* (NY: Viking, 1960), 1-15. Rpt Rideout.
Curry, Sister Martha. "SA and James Joyce." *AL,* 52 (May 1980), 236-249.
Dondore, Dorothy Anne. *The Prairie and the Making of Middle America* (Cedar Rapids, Iowa: Torch, 1926), passim.
Enniss, Stephen C. "The Implied Community of *Winesburg, Ohio.*" *ON,* 11 (Spring-Summer 1985), 51-60.
Fanning, Michael. "New Orleans and SA." *SoSt,* 17 (Summer 1978), 199-207.
Faulkner, William. "SA: An Appreciation." *Atlantic,* 191 (Jun 1953), 27-29. Rpt *Essays, Speeches and Public Letters* by Faulkner; ed James B Meriwether (NY: Random House, 1966). Rpt White (1966), Rideout.
Frank, Waldo. "Emerging Greatness." *The Seven Arts,* 1 (Nov 1916), 73-78. Rpt White (1966), Rideout, Anderson (1981).
Fussell, Edwin. "*Winesburg, Ohio:* Art and Isolation." *MFS,* 6 (Summer 1960), 106-114. Rpt White (1966), Rideout.

Geismar, Maxwell. "SA: Last of the Townsmen." *The Last of the Provincials* (Boston: Houghton Mifflin, 1947), passim.
Hansen, Harry. "SA, Corn-Fed Mystic, Historian of the Middle Age of Man." *Midwest Portraits* (NY: Harcourt, Brace, 1923), 109-179.
Hatcher, Harlan. "SA." *Creating the Modern American Novel* (NY: Farrar & Rinehart, 1935), 155-171.
Herron, Ima Honaker. *The Small Town in American Literature* (Durham, NC: Duke U P, 1939), passim.
Hicks, Granville. *The Great Tradition* (NY: Macmillan, 1933), passim.
Hilfer, Anthony Channell. "Masters and A." *The Revolt From the Village, 1915-1930* (Chapel Hill: U North Carolina P, 1969), 137-157.
Hilton, Earl. "SA and 'Heroic Vitalism.' " *NOQ,* 29 (Spring 1957), 97-107.
Ingram, Forrest L. "SA: *Winesburg, Ohio.*" *Representative Short Story Cycles of the Twentieth Century* (The Hague: Mouton, 1971), 143-199.
Joselyn, Sister M. "SA and the Lyric Story." *The Twenties,* ed Richard E Langford & William E Taylor (De Land, Fla: Everett/Edwards, 1966), 70-73.
Karsner, David. "SA, Mid-West Mystic." *WE,* 6 (Apr 1981), 1-6; 7 (Nov 1981), 6-8.
Kazin, Alfred. "The New Realism: SA and Sinclair Lewis." *On Native Grounds* (NY: Reynal & Hitchcock, 1942), 205-226, passim.
Ladenson, Joyce R. "Gender Reconsiderations in Three of SA's Novels." *MSE,* 6, nos 1-2 (1978), 90-102.
Lewis, Wyndham. *Paleface* (London: Chatto & Windus, 1929), passim.
Love, Glen A. "*Winesburg, Ohio* and the Rhetoric of Silence." *AL,* 40 (Mar 1968), 38-57.
MacDonald, Dwight. "SA." *YLM,* 93 (Jul 1928), 209-243.
Mahoney, John J. "An Analysis of *Winesburg, Ohio.*" *JAAC,* 15 (Dec 1956), 245-252.
Mainsard, Joseph. "SA." *Etudes,* 190 (5 Feb 1927), 303-325.
Maresca, Carol J. "Gestures as Meaning in SA's *Winesburg, Ohio.*" *CLAJ,* 9 (Mar 1966), 279-283.
Marriner, Gerald L. "SA: The Myth of the Artist." *TQ,* 14 (Spring 1971), 105-116.
Mellard, James M. "Narrative Forms in *Winesburg, Ohio.*" *PMLA,* 83 (Oct 1968), 1304-1312.
Morgan, H Wayne. "SA: The Search for Unity." *Writers in Transition* (NY: Hill & Wang, 1963), 82-104.
Murphy, George D. "The Theme of Sublimation in A's *Winesburg, Ohio.*" *MFS,* 13 (Summer 1967), 237-246.

Papinchak, Robert Allen. "Something in the Elders: The Recurrent Imagery in *Winesburg, Ohio*." *WE*, 9 (Nov 1983), 1-7.

Pfeiffer, William S. "*Mary Cochran:* SA's Ten-Year Novel." *SB*, 31 (1978), 248-257.

Phillips, William L. "How SA Wrote *Winesburg, Ohio*." *AL*, 23 (Mar 1951), 7-30. Rpt White (1966), Rideout.

Quinn, Arthur Hobson. *American Fiction* (NY: Appleton-Century, 1936), passim.

Raymund, Bernard. "The Grammar of Not-Reason: SA." *ArQ*, 12 (Spring 1956), 48-60; 12 (Summer 1956), 136-148.

Richardson, H Edward. "A and Faulkner." *AL*, 36 (Nov 1964), 298-314.

Rideout, Walter B. " 'I Want to Know Why' as Biography and Fiction." *MMisc*, 12 (1984), 7-14.

Rigsbee, Sally Adair. "The Feminine in *Winesburg, Ohio*." *SAF*, 9 (Autumn 1981), 233-244.

Savin, Mark. "Coming Full Circle: SA's 'The Egg.' " *SSF*, 18 (Fall 1981), 454-457.

Sherman, Stuart. "SA's Tales of the New Life." *Critical Woodcuts* (NY: Scribners, 1926), 3-17.

Shilstone, Frederick W. "Egotism, Sympathy, and George Willard's Development as Poet in *Winesburg, Ohio*." *WVUPP*, 28 (1982), 105-113.

Stouck, David. "*Many Marriages* as a Postmodern Novel." *MMisc*, 12 (1984), 15-22.

Stouck. "SA and the Postmodern Novel." *ConL*, 26 (Fall 1985), 302-316.

Thurston, Jarvis. "A and 'Winesburg': Mysticism and Craft." *Accent*, 16 (Spring 1956), 107-128.

Trilling, Lionel. "SA." *KR*, 3 (Summer 1941), 293-302. Rpt White (1966), Rideout.

Van Antwerp, Margaret A, ed. "SA." *Dictionary of Literary Biography Documentary Series*, Vol 1 (Detroit: Bruccoli Clark/Gale, 1982), 3-56.

Van Doren, Carl. "Sinclair Lewis and SA: A Study of Two Moralists." *Century*, 110 (Jul 1925), 362-369.

Voss, Arthur. *The American Short Story* (Norman: U Oklahoma P, 1973), passim.

Ward, A C. *American Literature, 1889-1930* (NY: Dial, 1932), passim.

Weiss, Daniel. *The Critic Agonistes*, ed Eric Solomon & Stephen Arkin (Seattle: U Washington P, 1985), 108-132.

White, Ray Lewis. "Of Time and *Winesburg, Ohio*: An Experiment in Chronology." *MFS*, 25 (Winter 1979-1980), 658-666.

White. "*Winesburg, Ohio*: The Unique Alternate Draft of 'Nobody Knows.' " *WE*, 8 (Nov 1982), 3-5.

White. "The Revisions of *Windy McPherson's Son*, SA's First Novel." *MMisc*, 12 (1984), 23-52.

White. "*Winesburg, Ohio*: The Table of Contents." *NMAL*, 8 (Autumn 1984), item 8.

White. "*Winesburg, Ohio*: The Story Titles." *WE*, 10 (Nov 1984), 6-7.

White. "The Manuscripts of *Winesburg, Ohio*." *WE*, 11 (Nov 1985), 4-10.

White. "Socrates in *Winesburg*." *NMAL*, 10 (Spring-Summer 1986), item 2.

Winther, S K. "The Aura of Loneliness in SA." *MFS*, 5 (Summer 1959), 145-152.

Ray Lewis White

GERTRUDE ATHERTON

San Francisco, Calif, 30 Oct 1857-San Francisco, Calif, 14 Jun 1948

Gertrude Atherton's literary reputation was established by her fictional rendering of American social history from the 1890s to the 1940s. During more than fifty years of writing novels, short fiction, and journalistic pieces, she provided romantic-realistic characterizations of independent women, thereby revealing social and economic changes in American life. Atherton divided her writing efforts between historical and popular themes and experimented with such forms as the biographical novel and the mystery and horror story. Despite her thirty-four novels and collections of short stories, Atherton's work was largely forgotten until feminist scholarship revived interest in her fictional analyses of concerns and experiences of women.

BIBLIOGRAPHY

McClure, Charlotte S. "A Checklist of the Writings of and About GA." *ALR,* 9 (Spring 1976), 103-162.

BOOKS

What Dreams May Come: A Romance (as by Frank Lin). Chicago & c: Belford, Clarke, 1888. Novel.

Hermia Suydam. NY: Current Literature, 1889; *Hermia: An American Woman.* London: Routledge, 1889. Novel.

Los Cerritos: A Romance of the Modern Time. NY: Lovell, 1890. Novel.

A Question of Time. NY: Lovell, 1891. Novel.

The Doomswoman. NY: Tait, 1893. Novel.

Before the Gringo Came. NY: Tait, 1894. Augmented as *The Splendid Idle Forties: Stories of Old California.* NY & London: Macmillan, 1902. Abridged as *The Splendid Idle Forties: Six Stories of Spanish California,* preface by Oscar Lewis. Kentfield, Calif: Allen, 1960.

A Whirl Asunder. NY & London: Stokes, 1895. Novel.

Patience Sparhawk and Her Times: A Novel. London & NY: Lane, Bodley Head, 1897.

His Fortunate Grace. NY: Appleton, 1897. Novel.

The Californians. NY: Grosset & Dunlap, 1898. Novel.

American Wives and English Husbands: A Novel. NY: Dodd, Mead, 1898. Rev as *Transplanted,* 1919.

The Valiant Runaways. NY: Dodd, Mead, 1898. Novella.

A Daughter of the Vine. London & NY: Lane, Bodley Head, 1899. Novel.

Senator North. NY & London: Lane, Bodley Head, 1900. Novel.

The Aristocrats, Being the Impression of Lady Helen Pole During Her Sojourn in the Great North Woods as Spontaneously Recorded in Her Letters to Her Friend in North Britain, the Countess of Edge and Ross. London & NY: Lane, 1901. Novel.

The Conqueror, Being the True and Romantic Story of Alexander Hamilton. NY & London: Macmillan, 1902. Rev as *The Conqueror: A Dramatized Biography of Alexander Hamilton.* NY: Stokes, 1916. Novel.

Mrs. Pendleton's Four-in-Hand. NY & London: Macmillan, 1903. Story.

Rulers of Kings: A Novel. NY & London: Harper, 1904.

The Bell in the Fog and Other Stories. NY & London: Harper, 1905.

The Travelling Thirds. NY & London: Harper, 1905. Novel.

Rezánov. NY & London: Authors & Newspapers Association, 1906. Novel.

Ancestors: A Novel. NY & London: Harper, 1907.

The Gorgeous Isle, A Romance; Scene: Nevis, B.W.I., 1842. NY: Doubleday, Page, 1908.

Tower of Ivory: A Novel. NY: Macmillan, 1910.

Julia France and Her Times: A Novel. NY: Macmillan, 1912.

California: An Intimate History. NY & London: Harper, 1914. Augmented ed, NY: Boni & Liveright, 1927.

Perch of the Devil. NY: Stokes, 1914. Novel.

Life in the War Zone. NY: npub, 1916. Nonfiction.

Mrs. Balfame: A Novel. NY: Stokes, 1916.

The Living Present. NY: Stokes, 1917. Essays.

The White Morning: A Novel of the Power of the German Women in Wartime. NY: Stokes, 1918.

The Avalanche: A Mystery Story. NY: Stokes, 1919. Novel.

The Sisters-in-Law: A Novel of Our Time. NY: Stokes, 1921.

Sleeping Fires: A Novel. NY: Stokes, 1922; *Dormant Fires.* London: Murray, 1922.

Black Oxen. NY: Boni & Liveright, 1923. Novel.

The Crystal Cup. NY: Boni & Liveright, 1925. Novel.

The Immortal Marriage. NY: Boni & Liveright, 1927. Novel.

The Jealous Gods: A Processional Novel of the Fifth Century B.C. (Concerning One Alcibiades). NY: Liveright, 1928; *Vengeful Gods.* London: Murray, 1928.

Dido, Queen of Hearts. NY: Liveright, 1929. Novel.

The Sophisticates. NY: Liveright, 1931. Novel.

Adventures of a Novelist. NY: Liveright, 1932. Autobiography.

The Foghorn: Stories. Boston & NY: Houghton Mifflin, 1934.

Golden Peacock. Boston & NY: Houghton Mifflin, 1936. Novel.

Can Women Be Gentlemen? Boston: Houghton Mifflin, 1938. Essays.

The House of Lee. NY & London: Appleton-Century, 1940. Novel.

The Horn of Life. NY & London: Appleton-Century, 1942. Novel.

Golden Gate Country. NY: Duell, Sloan & Pearce, 1945. History.

My San Francisco: A Wayward Biography. Indianapolis: Bobbs-Merrill, 1946.

OTHER

A Few of Hamilton's Letters, Including His Description of the Great West Indian Hurricane of 1772 by Alexander Hamilton; ed GA. NY & London: Macmillan, 1903.

"Why Is American Literature Bourgeois?" *NAR*, 178 (May 1904), 771-781. Essay.

"Concha Arguëllo, Sister Dominica." *The Spinsters' Book of Fiction* (San Francisco & NY: Elder, 1906), 1-23. Story.

"Wanted: Imagination." *What Is a Book? Thoughts About Writing*, ed Dale Warren (Boston & NY: Houghton Mifflin, 1935), 43-60. Essay.

COLLECTIONS

Before the Gringo Came. NY: Stokes, 1915 (*Rezánov & The Doomswoman*).

Rezánov and Doña Concha. NY: Stokes, 1937 (*Rezánov & "Concha Arguëllo, Sister Dominica"*).

MANUSCRIPTS & ARCHIVES

U of California, Berkeley, Library.

BIOGRAPHIES

Book
Jackson, Joseph Henry. *GA.* NY: Appleton-Century, 1940.

Book Section & Articles
Forrey, Carolyn. "GA and the New Woman." *CaHSQ*, 55 (Fall 1976), 194-209.

Richey, Elinor. "The Flappers Were Her Daughters: The Liberated World of GA." *AWest*, 11 (Jul 1974), 4-10, 60-63.

Starr, Kevin. "GA, Daughter of the Elite." *Americans and the California Dream, 1850-1915* (NY: Oxford U P, 1973), 345-364.

CRITICAL STUDIES

Books
Forrey, Carolyn D. "GA and the New Woman." Dissertation: Yale U, 1971.

McClure, Charlotte S. *GA.* Boise, Idaho: Boise State U, 1976.

McClure. *GA.* Boston: Twayne, 1979.

Book Sections & Articles
Bradley, Jennifer. "Woman at the Golden Gate: The Last Words of GA." *WS*, 12 (Feb 1986), 17-30.

Budd, Louis J. "GA on Mark Twain." *MTJ*, 21 (Spring 1983), 18.

Canby, Henry Seidel. "Mrs. A's *Black Oxen*." *Definitions*, Series 2 (NY: Harcourt, Brace, 1924), 237-241.

Cooper, Frederic Taber. "Some Representative American Story Tellers IX—GA." *Bookman*, 30 (Dec 1909), 357-363.

Courtney, W L. "GA." *The Feminine Note in Fiction* (London: Chapman & Hall, 1904), 115-134.

Forman, Henry James. "A Brilliant California Novelist, GA." *CaHSQ*, 40 (March 1961), 1-10.

Hapke, Laura. "The Problem of Sensual Womanhood: Three Late Nineteenth-Century Fictional Solutions." *NR*, 4, no 2 (1981), 86-95.

Leider, Emily. "A Tale of Two Gertrudes." *SanFSE&C* (30 Nov 1980), *California Living Mag* sect, 70-73.

Leider. " 'Your picture hangs in my salon': The Letters of GA to Ambrose Bierce." *CaH*, 60 (Winter 1981-1982), 332-349.

McClure, Charlotte S. "GA (1857-1948)." *ALR*, 9 (Spring 1976), 94-101.

McClure. "GA's California Woman: From Love Story to Psychological Drama." *Itinerary: Criticism*, ed Charles L Crow (Bowling Green, Ohio: Bowling Green State U P, 1978), 1-9. Rpt *Women, Women Writers and the West*, ed L L Lee & Merrill Lewis (Troy, NY: Whitston, 1979).

McElderry, B R, Jr. "GA and Henry James." *CLQ,* Series 3 (Nov 1954), 269-272.

Mowbray, J P "That 'Affair' of Mrs. A's." *CriticNY,* 40 (Jun 1902), 501-505.

Overton, Grant. "GA." *The Women Who Make Our Novels* (NY: Moffat, Yard, 1918), 41-53.

Pendennis. " 'My Types'—GA." *Forum,* 58 (Nov 1917), 585-594.

Starr, Kevin. "The Last of the High Provincials." *SanFSE&C* (19 Sep 1976), *California Living Mag* sect, 37-43.

Stevenson, Lionel. "A Versus Grundy: The Forty Years' War." *Bookman,* 69 (Jul 1929), 464-472.

Underwood, John Curtis. "Mrs. A and Ancestry." *Literature and Insurgency* (NY: Kennerley, 1914), 391-446.

Van Vechten, Carl. "Some 'Literary Ladies' I Have Known." *YULG,* 26 (Jan 1952), 97-116.

Walsh, William S. "Mrs. A's Novels: A Dialogue." *Lippincott's,* 50 (Sep 1892), 412-415.

Weir, Sybil. "GA: The Limits of Feminism in the 1890's." *SJS,* 1 (Feb 1975), 24-31.

York, Neil L. "California Girls and the American Eden." *JAmC,* 7 (Winter 1984), 33-43.

Charlotte S. McClure

JANE GOODWIN AUSTIN

Worcester, Mass, 25 Jan 1831-Roxbury, Mass, 30 Mar 1894

Jane Goodwin Austin is noteworthy as the novelist who popularized and formalized many of the Pilgrim legends. Austin, who traced several branches of her family to the *Mayflower,* drew her material from her own family records as well as from William Bradford's *Of Plymouth Plantation.* Her accounts of these early colonials in novels such as *Standish of Standish* and *Betty Alden* have entered the American consciousness by becoming folklore. In addition to her Pilgrim novels, Austin also wrote children's books and adult sensational novels.

BIBLIOGRAPHY

Bibliography of American Literature, comp Jacob Blanck. New Haven: Yale U P, 1955-1991. Primary.

BOOKS

Fairy Dreams; or, Wanderings in Elf-Land. Boston: Tilton, 1859. Stories.

Kinah's Curse! or, The Downfall of Carnaby Cedars. Boston: Elliott, Thomes & Talbot, 1864. Novella.

Dora Darling: The Daughter of the Regiment. Boston: Tilton, 1865. Novel.

The Novice; or, Mother Church Thwarted. Boston: Elliott, Thomes & Talbot, 1865. Novel.

The Outcast; or, The Master of Falcon's Eyrie. Boston: Elliott, Thomes & Talbot, 1865. Novel.

The Tailor Boy: Wreck of the Nautilus. Boston: Tilton, 1865. Novel.

Outpost. Boston: Tilton, 1867. Novel.

Cipher: A Romance. NY: Sheldon, 1869. Novel.

The Shadow of Moloch Mountain. NY: Sheldon, 1870. Novel.

Moonfolk. NY: Putnam, 1874. Novel.

Mrs. Beauchamp Brown. Boston: Roberts, 1880. Novel.

A Nameless Nobleman. Boston: Osgood, 1881. Novel.

The Desmond Hundred. Boston: Osgood, 1882. Novel.

Nantucket Scraps. . . . Boston: Osgood, 1883. Stories.

The Story of a Storm. NY: Lupton, 1886. Story.

Standish of Standish: A Story of the Pilgrims. Boston & NY: Houghton, Mifflin, 1889. Novel.
Dolóres. . . . NY: Lupton, 1890. Story.
Dr. LeBaron and His Daughters. Boston & NY: Houghton, Mifflin, 1890. Novel.
Betty Alden: The First-Born Daughter of the Pilgrims. Boston & NY: Houghton, Mifflin, 1891. Novel.
David Alden's Daughter and Other Stories of Colonial Times. Boston & NY: Houghton, Mifflin, 1892.
It Never Did Run Smooth. NY: Lupton, 1892. Novel.
Queen Tempest. NY: Ivers, 1892. Novel.
The Twelve Great Diamonds. NY: Lupton, 1892. Novel.

The Cedar Swamp Mystery. NY: Lupton, Lovell, 1901. Story.

MANUSCRIPTS & ARCHIVES

The major collections are at the U of Virginia Library; U of Arizona Library; & Stanford U Library.

BIOGRAPHY

Book Section
Swayne, Josephine Latham. *The Story of Concord* (Boston: Ellis, 1923), passim.

Jane Atteridge Rose

MARY AUSTIN

Carlinville, Ill, 9 Sep 1868-Santa Fe, N Mex, 13 Aug 1934

A prolific writer of fiction, poetry, and essays, Mary Austin has always tended to draw extreme reader responses, probably because of the mysticism that runs through much of her fiction as well as her religious writings and landscape studies. Some found her and her work to be pretentious, but a small number of admirers accepted her own view that she was one of the most original geniuses of her day. Austin has attracted attention from naturalists and historians, particularly those advocating Native American culture, a subject that is frequently found in her short fiction. Feminists cherish her emphasis on strong women. In her own time her fictional re-creations of the life of Jesus were also extremely popular, but her religious writing is now largely ignored.

BIBLIOGRAPHIES

Gaer, Joseph, ed. *MA: Bibliography and Biographical Data.* Npl: npub, 1934. Primary.

MHA: *Author, Poet, Lecturer, Naturalist.* Independence, Calif: Mary Austin Home, 1968. Primary.

BOOKS

The Land of Little Rain. Boston & NY: Houghton, Mifflin, 1903. Essays.
The Basket Woman: A Book of Fanciful Tales for Children. Boston & NY: Houghton, Mifflin, 1904.
Isidro. Boston & NY: Houghton, Mifflin, 1905. Novel.
The Flock. Boston & NY: Houghton, Mifflin, 1906. Essays.
Santa Lucia: A Common Story. NY & London: Harper, 1908. Novel.
Lost Borders. NY & London: Harper, 1909. Stories.
Outland (as by Gordon Stairs). London: Murray, 1910; (as by MA). NY: Boni & Liveright. 1919. Novel.
The Arrow Maker: A Drama in Three Acts. NY: Duffield, 1911. Rev as *The Arrow-Maker: A Drama in Three Acts.* Boston & NY: Hough-

ton Mifflin, 1915.

Christ in Italy: Being the Adventures of a Maverick Among Masterpieces. NY: Duffield, 1912. Nonfiction.

A Woman of Genius. Garden City, NY: Doubleday, Page, 1912. Rev ed, Boston & NY: Houghton Mifflin, 1917. Novel.

The Green Bough: A Tale of the Resurrection. Garden City, NY: Doubleday, Page, 1913. Story.

The Lovely Lady. Garden City, NY: Doubleday, Page, 1913. Novel.

California: The Land of the Sun. NY: MacMillan, 1914. Rev as *The Lands of the Sun.* Boston & NY: Houghton Mifflin, 1927. Nonfiction.

Love and the Soul Maker. NY & London: Appleton, 1914. Novel.

The Man Jesus: Being a Brief Account of the Life and Teaching of the Prophet of Nazareth. NY & London: Harper, 1915. Augmented as *A Small Town Man,* 1925.

The Ford. Boston & NY: Houghton Mifflin, 1917. Novel.

The Trail Book. Boston & NY: Houghton Mifflin, 1918. Children's book.

The Young Woman Citizen. NY: Womans, 1918. Essay.

No. 26 Jayne Street. Boston & NY: Houghton Mifflin, 1920. Novel.

The American Rhythm. NY: Harcourt, Brace, 1923. Augmented as *The American Rhythm: Studies and Reëxpressions of Amerindian Songs.* Boston & NY: Houghton Mifflin, 1930. Nonfiction.

The Land of Journey's Ending. NY & London: Century, 1924. Nonfiction.

Everyman's Genius. Indianapolis: Bobbs-Merrill, 1925. Essay.

The Children Sing in the Far West. Boston & NY: Houghton Mifflin, 1928. Poems.

Taos Pueblo, photographs by Ansel Adams. San Francisco: Grabhorn, 1930.

Experiences Facing Death. Indianapolis: Bobbs-Merrill, 1931. Nonfiction.

Starry Adventure. Boston & NY: Houghton Mifflin, 1931. Novel.

Earth Horizon: Autobiography. Boston & NY: Houghton Mifflin, 1932.

Can Prayer Be Answered? NY: Farrar & Rinehart, 1934. Nonfiction.

Indian Pottery of the Rio Grande. Pasadena, Calif: Esto, 1934. Nonfiction.

One-Smoke Stories. Boston & NY: Houghton Mifflin, 1934.

When I Am Dead. Santa Fe, NMex: Rydal, 1935. Poem.

Mother of Felipe and Other Early Stories, ed Franklin Walker. Npl: Book Club of California, 1950. Stories.

Paso Por Aqui. Zelzah, Calif: npub, 1954.

One Hundred Miles on Horseback, intro by Donald P Ringler. Los Angeles: Dawson's Book Shop, 1963. Nonfiction.

The Man Who Didn't Believe in Christmas. Hong Kong: Ford, 1969. Play.

Western Trails, ed Melody Graulich. Reno: U Nevada P, 1987. Stories.

Cactus Thorn, foreword & afterword by Graulich. Reno & Las Vegas: U Nevada P, 1988. Novella.

LETTERS

MA on the Art of Writing, intro by James E Phillips. Los Angeles: Friends of the UCLA Library, 1961.

Literary America, 1903-1934: The MA Letters, ed T M Pearce. Westport, Conn & London: Greenwood, 1979.

OTHER

The Sturdy Oak, ed Elizabeth Jordan. NY: Holt, 1917. Composite novel by 14 American authors, including MA.

"Introduction." *The Path on The Rainbow: An Anthology of Songs and Chants From the Indians of North America,* ed George W Cronyn (NY: Liveright, 1934), xv-xxxii.

COLLECTION

Stories From the Country of Lost Borders, ed with intro by Marjorie Pryse. New Brunswick & London: Rutgers U P, 1987.

MANUSCRIPTS & ARCHIVES

The major collections are at the Huntington Library, San Marino, Calif, & the UCLA library.

BIOGRAPHIES

Books

Doyle, Helen MacKnight. *MA: Woman of Genius.* NY: Gotham House, 1939.

Fink, Augusta. *I-Mary: A Biography of MA.* Tucson: U Arizona P, 1983.

Hougland, Willard, ed. *MA: A Memorial.* Santa Fe, NMex: Laboratory of Anthropology, 1944.

Pearce, T M. *The Beloved House.* Caldwell, Idaho: Caxton, 1940.

Powell, Lawrence Clark. *A Dedication to the Memory of MHA.* Tucson: U Arizona P, 1968.

Ringler, Donald P. *MA: Kern County Days, 1888-1892.* Bakersfield, Calif: Bear Mountain Books, 1963.

Articles

Langlois, Karen S. "MA and Lincoln Steffens." *HLQ,* 49 (Autumn 1986), 357-383.

Major, Mabel. "MA in Fort Worth." *NMQ*, 4 (Nov 1934), 307-310.

CRITICAL STUDIES

Books
Lyday, Jo W. *MA: The Southwest Works.* Austin, Tex: Steck-Vaughn, 1968.
Pearce, T M. *MHA.* NY: Twayne, 1965.

Books Sections & Articles
Anderson, Barbara. "Thoreau and MA." *TSB*, 126 (Winter 1974), 7.
Barker, R L. "MA: Novelist and Ethnologist." *Sunset*, 43 (Sep 1919), 49-50.
Berry, J Wilkes. "MHA (1868-1934)." *ALR*, 2 (Summer 1969), 125-131.
Berry. "Characterization in MA's Southwest Works." *SwAL*, 2 (Winter 1972), 119-124.
Berry. "MA: Sibylic Gourmet of the Southwest." *WestR*, 9 (Winter 1972), 3-8.
Dubois, Arthur E. "MA, 1868-1934." *SWR*, 20 (Apr 1935), 231-264.
Farrar, John. "MA." *The Literary Spotlight,* ed Farrar (NY: Doran, 1924), 165-174.
Ford, Thomas W. "*The American Rhythm*: MA's Poetic Principle." *WAL*, 5 (Spring 1970), 3-14.
Forman, Henry James. "On a Letter From MA." *NMQ*, 31 (Winter 1961-1962), 339-344.
Gelfant, Blanche H. " 'Lives' of Women Writers: Cather, A, Porter / and Willa, Mary, Katherine Anne." *Novel*, 18 (Fall 1984), 64-80.
Hall, Jacqueline D. "MHA." *A Literary History of the American West* (Fort Worth: Texas Christian U P, 1987), 359-369.
Johnson, Lee Ann. "Western Literary Realism: The California Tales of Norris & A." *ALR*, 7 (Summer 1974), 278-280.
Langlois, Karen S. "MA and Houghton Mifflin Company: A Case Study in the Marketing of a Western Writer." *WAL*, 23 (Spring 1988), 31-42.
Langlois. "MA and the New Theatre: The 1911 Production of *The Arrow Maker*." *THStud*, 8 (1988), 71-87.
Pearce, T M. "MA and the Pattern of New Mexico." *SWR*, 22 (Jan 1937), 140-148.

Powell, Lawrence Clark. "Southwest Classics Reread: A Prophetic Passage." *Westways*, 65 (Feb 1973), 60-65.
Robinson, Frank K. " 'From MA to Edgar Lee Masters': A Book Inscription." *LCUT*, no 6 (Dec 1973), 82-85.
Rudnick, Lois. "Re-naming the Land: Anglo-Expatriate Women in the Southwest." *The Desert Is No Lady: Southwestern Landscapes in Women's Writing and Art*, ed Vera Norwood & Janice Monk (New Haven: Yale U P, 1987), 10-26.
Ruppert, James. "Discovering America: MA and Imagism." *Studies in American Indian Literature,* ed Paula Gunn Allen (NY: MLA, 1983), 243-258.
Ruppert. "MA's Landscape Line in Native American Literature." *SWR*, 68 (Autumn 1983), 376-390.
Smith, Henry. "The Feel of the Purposeful Earth: MA's Prophecy." *NMQ*, 1 (Feb 1931), 17-33.
Steffens, Lincoln. "MA and the Desert." *AmerMag*, 72 (Jun 1911), 178-181.
Van Doren, Carl. "The American Rhythm: MA." *Many Minds* (NY: Knopf, 1924), 3-17.
Walker, Franklin. *A Literary History of Southern California* (Berkeley: U California P, 1950), 189-199, 219-222.
White, William Allen. "A Woman of Genius." *SatRL*, 9 (12 Nov 1932), 235-236.
Work, James. "The Moral in A's *The Land of Little Rain*." *Women and Western American Literature*, ed Helen Winter Stauffer & Susan J Rosowski (Troy, NY: Whitston, 1982), 297-310.
Wynn, Dudley. "MA, Woman Alone." *VQR*, 13 (Spring 1937), 243-256.
Young, Vernon. "MA and the Earth Performance." *SWR*, 35 (Summer 1950), 153-163.
Zolla, Elémire. *The Writer and the Shaman: A Morphology of the American Indian*, trans Raymond Rosenthal (NY: Harcourt Brace Jovanovich, 1973), passim.

Emily Schiller

IRVING BACHELLER

Pierrepont, NY, 26 Sep 1859-White Plains, NY, 24 Feb 1950

Irving Bacheller was best known as a prolific author of popular novels, although he was also influential as a journalist. In 1884 he co-directed the New York Press Syndicate, the first such business in metropolitan journalism. After serving as the Sunday editor for the *New York World* from 1898 to 1900, Bacheller published his most successful novel, *Eben Holden,* which sold over a million copies. William Dean Howells commended this tale of an orphaned boy and a rustic hired man who travel from Vermont to New York's St. Lawrence Valley. Bacheller's subsequent fiction and poetry continued to reveal his nostalgia for the rural Northeast while it satirized the excesses of modern urban life. Bacheller also wrote several historical novels about men he considered "the greatest democrat[s]": Christ, Benjamin Franklin, George Washington, and Abraham Lincoln.

BIBLIOGRAPHY

Hanna, A J. *A Bibliography of the Writings of IB.* Winter Park, Fla: Rollins C, 1939. Primary.

BOOKS

The Master of Silence. NY: Webster, 1892. Novel.
The Still House of O'Darrow. London: Cassell, 1894. Novel.
The Story of a Passion. East Aurora, NY: Roycroft, 1899. Story.
Eben Holden. Boston: Lothrop, 1900. Novel.
D'ri and I. Boston: Lothrop, 1901. Novel.
Darrel of the Blessed Isles. Boston: Lothrop, 1903. Novel.
Vergilius. NY & London: Harper, 1904. Novel.
Silas Strong. NY & London: Harper, 1906. Novel.
Eben Holden's Last Day A-Fishing. NY & London: Harper, 1907. Story.
The Hand-Made Gentleman. NY & London: Harper, 1909; *Cricket Heron.* London: Unwin, 1909. Novel.
The Master. NY: Doubleday, Page, 1909. Novel.
In Various Moods. NY & London: Harper, 1910. Poetry.
Keeping Up With Lizzie. NY & London: Harper, 1911. Novel.

"Charge It!" or Keeping Up With Harry. NY & London: Harper, 1912. Novel.
The Turning of Griggsby. NY & London: Harper, 1913. Novel.
The Marryers. NY & London: Harper, 1914. Novel.
The Light in the Clearing. Indianapolis: Bobbs-Merrill, 1917. Novel.
Keeping Up With William. Indianapolis: Bobbs-Merrill, 1918. Novel.
A Man for the Ages. Indianapolis: Bobbs-Merrill, 1919. Novel.
The Prodigal Village. Indianapolis: Bobbs-Merrill, 1920. Novel.
In the Days of Poor Richard. Indianapolis: Bobbs-Merrill, 1922. Novel.
The Scudders. NY: Macmillan, 1923. Novel.
Father Abraham. Indianapolis: Bobbs-Merrill, 1925. Novel.
Opinions of a Cheerful Yankee. Indianapolis: Bobbs-Merrill, 1926. Essays.
Dawn. NY: Macmillan, 1927. Novel.
Coming Up the Road. Indianapolis: Bobbs-Merrill, 1928. Autobiography.
The House of the Three Ganders. Indianapolis: Bobbs-Merrill, 1928. Novel.
A Candle in the Wilderness. Indianapolis: Bobbs-Merrill, 1930. Novel.
The Master of Chaos. Indianapolis: Bobbs-Merrill, 1932. Novel.
Great Moments in the Life of Washington, with Herbert S Kates. NY: Grosset & Dunlap, 1932. Nonfiction.
Uncle Peel. NY: Stokes, 1933. Novel.
The Harvesting. NY: Stokes, 1934. Novel.
The Oxen of the Sun. NY: Stokes, 1935. Novel.
A Boy for the Ages. NY & Toronto: Farrar & Rinehart, 1937. Novel.
From Stores of Memory. NY & Toronto: Farrar & Rinehart, 1938. Stories.
The Winds of God. NY & Toronto: Farrar & Rinehart, 1941. Novel.

OTHER

Best Things From American Literature, ed IB. NY: Christian Herald, 1899. Miscellany.

EDITION

Works, Pine Tree Edition, 7 vols. NY: Harper, 1901-1914.

MANUSCRIPTS & ARCHIVES

The major collections are at Rollins C Library & U of Virginia Library.

CRITICAL STUDIES

Articles

Katz, Joseph. "Stephen Crane and IB's Gold." *SCNews,* 5 (Fall 1970), 4-5.

Samuels, Charles E. "Folklore in *Eben Holden.*" *NYFQ,* 13 (Summer 1957), 100-103.

Watkins, Edna W. "The IB Collection." *NYHSQB,* 26 (Jul 1942), 64.

Rhonda Skillern

JOHN KENDRICK BANGS

Yonkers, NY, 27 May 1862-Atlantic City, NJ, 21 Jan 1922

John Kendrick Bangs enjoyed popular success throughout his long career as poet, novelist, children's author, fantasist, playwright, editor, humorist, and lecturer. Bangs's work cannot be easily assessed because much of his writing in *Puck, Life, Harper's Monthly,* and other periodicals has never been collected. His use of more than a dozen known pseudonyms and his blending of traditional genres complicate the search for and categorization of his work. Bangs is best remembered as the humorist who wrote *Coffee and Repartee* and *A House-Boat on the Styx.* His favorite comic targets were the snobbish, irresponsible wealthy and the ignorant, illiterate masses. Bangs's political activity helped to hone the character of his favorite alter ego, The Idiot. Urbanity and genial social satire were Bangs's literary trademarks.

BIBLIOGRAPHY

Bangs, Frances Hyde. "A List of the First Editions, and Some Others, of JKB, 1862-1922." *YULG,* 7 (Jan 1933), 66-71.

Bibliography of American Literature, comp Jacob Blanck. New Haven: Yale U P, 1955-1991. Primary.

BOOKS

The Lorgnette 1886 (Anon). NY: Coombes, 1886. Sketches.

Roger Camerden: A Strange Story (Anon). NY: Coombes, 1887. Novel.

New Waggings of Old Tales by Two Wags, with Frank Dempster Sherman. Boston: Ticknor, 1888. Stories & verse.

Katherine. Brooklyn, NY: npub, 1888. Augmented as *Katherine: A Travesty.* NY: Gilliss & Turnure/Art Age, 1888. Play.

Mephistopheles: A Profanation. NY: Gilliss & Turnure/Art Age, 1889. Play.

Tiddledywink Tales. NY: Russell, 1891. Children's stories.

The Tiddledywink's Poetry Book. NY: Russell, 1892. Children's verse.

In Camp With a Tin Soldier. NY: Russell, 1892. Children's book.

Coffee and Repartee. NY: Harper, 1893. Stories.

Toppleton's Client; or, A Spirit in Exile. NY: Webster, 1893. Novel.

Half-Hours With Jimmieboy. NY: Russell, 1893. Children's stories.

Three Weeks in Politics. NY: Harper, 1894. Satire.

The Water Ghost and Others. NY: Harper, 1894. Stories.

The Idiot. NY: Harper, 1895. Stories.

Mr. Bonaparte of Corsica. NY: Harper, 1895. Burlesque biography.

The Bicyclers and Three Other Farces. NY: Harper, 1896. Plays.

A House-Boat on the Styx, Being Some Account of the Divers Doings of the Associated Shades. NY: Harper, 1896. Novel.

A Rebellious Heroine: A Story. NY: Harper, 1896. Novel.

The Mantel-Piece Minstrels and Other Stories. NY: Russell, 1896. Children's stories.

A Prophecy and a Plea, Being First a Stygian Prophecy and Second a Plea for Naturalism: Two Poems Read on Divers Occasions. NY: Privately printed, 1897.

The Pursuit of the House-Boat, Being Some Further Account of the Divers Doings of the Associated Shades, Under the Leadership of Sherlock Holmes, Esq. NY: Harper, 1897. Novel.

Paste Jewels, Being Seven Tales of Domestic Woe. NY & London: Harper, 1897. Stories.

Ghosts I Have Met and Some Others. NY & London: Harper, 1898. Stories.

Peeps at People, Being Certain Papers From the Writings of Anne Warrington Witherup. NY & London: Harper, 1899. Satirical interviews.

The Dreamers: A Club, Being a More or Less Faithful Account of the Literary Exercises of the First Regular Meeting of That Organization. NY & London: Harper, 1899. Parodies.

Cobwebs From a Library Corner. NY & London: Harper, 1899. Verse.

The Enchanted Type-Writer. NY & London: Harper, 1899. Novel.

The Booming of Acre Hill and Other Reminiscences of Urban and Suburban Life. NY & London: Harper, 1900. Stories.

The Idiot at Home. NY & London: Harper, 1900. Novel.

Over the Plum-Pudding. NY & London: Harper, 1901. Stories.

Mr. Munchausen, Being a True Account of Some of the Recent Adventures Beyond the Styx of the Late Hieronymus Carl Friedrich, Sometime Baron Munchausen. . . . Boston: Noyes, Platt, 1901. Stories.

Uncle Sam, Trustee. NY: Riggs, 1902. Political tract.

Olympian Nights. NY & London: Harper, 1902. Novel.

Bikey the Skicycle & Other Tales of Jimmieboy. NY: Riggs, 1902. Children's stories.

Mollie and the Unwiseman. Philadelphia: Coates, 1902. Children's book.

Emblemland, with Charles Raymond Macauley. NY: Russell, 1902. Novel.

The Inventions of The Idiot. NY & London: Harper, 1904. Stories.

Monsieur d'En Brochette, Being an Historical Account of Some of the Adventures of Huevos Pasada Par Aqua, Marquis of Pollio Grille, Count of Pate de Foie Gras, and Much Else

Besides, with Bert Leston Taylor & Arthur Hamilton Folwell. NY: Keppler & Schwarzmann, 1905. Novel.

The Worsted Man: A Musical Play for Amateurs. NY & London: Harper, 1905.

Mrs. Raffles, Being the Adventures of an Amateur Cracks-Woman Narrated by Bunny. NY & London: Harper, 1905. Stories.

R. Holmes & Co., Being the Remarkable Adventures of Raffles Holmes, Esq., Detective and Amateur Cracksman by Birth. NY & London: Harper, 1906. Stories.

Andiron Tales. Philadelphia: Winston, 1906. Stories.

Alice in Blunderland: An Iridescent Dream. NY: Doubleday, Page, 1907. Novel.

Potted Fiction, Being a Series of Extracts From the World's Best Sellers Put Up in Thin Slices for Hurried Consumers. NY: Doubleday, Page, 1908. Parodies.

The Genial Idiot: His Views and Reviews. NY & London: Harper, 1908. Stories.

The Real Thing and Three Other Farces. NY & London: Harper, 1909. Plays.

Labor, Cheer, and Love: An Address Delivered by JKB, at the York High School Commencement, Thursday, June Tenth, 1909. York, Maine: York Transcript, 1909.

The Autobiography of Methuselah. NY: Dodge, 1909. Burlesque autobiography.

Songs of Cheer. Boston: Sherman French, 1910. Verse.

Mollie and the Unwiseman Abroad. Philadelphia & London: Lippincott, 1910. Children's book.

Jack and the Check Book. NY & London: Harper, 1911. Stories.

Echoes of Cheer. Boston: Sherman French, 1912. Verse.

A Little Book of Christmas. Boston: Little, Brown, 1912. Stories & verse.

A Line o' Cheer for Each Day o' the Year. Boston: Little, Brown, 1913. Verse.

A Chafing-Dish Party. NY & London: Harper, 1913. Play.

The Foothills of Parnassus. NY: Macmillan, 1914. Verse.

A Quest for Song. Boston: Little, Brown, 1915. Verse.

From Pillar to Post: Leaves From a Lecturer's Notebook. NY: Century, 1916. Memoir.

Half Hours With The Idiot. Boston: Little, Brown, 1917. Stories.

The Cheery Way: A Bit of Verse for Every Day. NY & London: Harper, 1919.

Harper's Lost Reviews: The Literary Notes, with Laurence Hutton et al; comp Clayton L Eichelberger. Millwood, NY: KTO, 1976. Excerpts from *Harper's Weekly.*

OTHER

Literature, an International Gazette of Criticism (1899), ed JKB.
Harper's Weekly (1899-1901), ed JKB.
The New Metropolitan Magazine (1903), ed JKB.
The Gadfly (17 Feb 1907-23 Jun 1907), ed JKB (as by Wilberforce Jenkins). Parody newspaper.
"The Son-in-Law." *The Whole Family: A Novel by Twelve Authors* (NY & London: Harper, 1908), 124-143.

MANUSCRIPTS & ARCHIVES

The major collections are at the U of Virginia Library & the New York Public Library.

BIOGRAPHY

Book
Bangs, Francis Hyde. *JKB, Humorist of the Nineties.* NY: Knopf, 1941.

CRITICAL STUDIES

Book Sections & Articles
Bangs, Francis Hyde. "JKB, Humorist of the Nineties." *YULG*, 7 (Jan 1933), 53-66.
Bangs. "JKB and the Acta Columbiana." *ColUQ*, 28 (Mar 1936), 1-17.
Blair, Walter & Hamlin Hill. "The Turn of the Century, 1895-1905." *America's Humor: From Poor Richard to Doonesbury* (NY: Oxford U P, 1978), 367-387.
Masson, Thomas Lansing. "JKB." *Our American Humorists* (NY: Moffat, Yard, 1922), 26-46.
Stronks, James B. "JKB Criticizes Norris's Borrowings in *Blix.*" *AL*, 42 (Nov 1970), 380-386.
Yates, Norris. "JKB, University Wit." *The American Humorist: Conscience of the Twentieth Century* (Ames: Iowa State U P, 1964), 49-57.

Arthur J. Leo

L. FRANK BAUM

Chittenango, NY, 15 May 1856-Hollywood, Calif, 6 May 1919

With the publication of *The Wonderful Wizard of Oz* in 1900, L. Frank Baum presented American children with what has been called their first home-grown fairy tale. He wished to avoid the darkness and moralizing of his European predecessors and aimed primarily to entertain. Oz is an American landscape peopled with self-reliant, forthright characters who find happiness in their own backyards. Baum wrote thirteen more books in the Oz series to satisfy his clamoring audience, and, after his death, six other writers continued the Oz tradition. Baum, a prolific writer for both adults and children, published books, stories, plays, and poems apart from the Oz books, many of them pseudonymously. They range in subject from stamp collecting and poultry raising to science fiction, adventure, and a series of books for teen-aged girls.

BIBLIOGRAPHIES & CATALOGUES

The Distinguished Collection of LFB and Related Oziana, Including W. W. Denslow, Formed by Justin G. Schiller. NY: Swann Galleries, 1978. Auction catalogue.
Hanff, Peter E & Douglas G Greene. *Bibliographia Oziana: A Concise Bibliographical Checklist of the Oz Books by LFB and His Successors,* founded on and continuing the *Baum Bugle* checklist by Dick Martin, James E Hanff & David L Greene. Kinderhook, Ill: International Wizard of Oz Club, 1976. Primary.
Hearn, Michael Patrick. "Bibliography." *The Annotated Wizard of Oz*, 363-381. Primary & secondary.
Martin, Dick. "LFB: A Chronological Checklist of the Published Writings." *ABC*, Special Number (Dec 1962), 28-31. Primary.

The Wonderful World of Oz: The Works of LFB, His Successors and Illustrators. NY: Books of Wonder, 1983. Catalogue.

BOOKS

(This list omits books written by LFB's successors but published posthumously under his name or under one of his pseudonyms.)

Baum's Complete Stamp Dealers Directory. Syracuse: Baum, Norris, 1873.

The Book of the Hamburgs: A Brief Treatise Upon the Mating, Rearing, and Management of the Different Varieties of Hamburgs. Hartford, Conn: Stoddard, 1886. Nonfiction.

Mother Goose in Prose. Chicago: Way & Williams, 1897. Children's book.

By the Candelabra's Glare. Chicago: Privately printed by Baum, 1898. Facsimile rpt, intro by Peter E Hanff, Delmar, NY: Scholars' Facsimiles and Reprints, 1981. Verse.

Father Goose: His Book. Chicago: Hill, 1899. Verse.

A New Wonderland. NY: Russell, 1900. Repub as *The Surprising Adventures of the Magical Monarch of Mo and His People.* Indianapolis: Bobbs-Merrill, 1903. Children's novel.

The Army Alphabet. Chicago & NY: Hill, 1900. Verse.

The Navy Alphabet. Chicago & NY: Hill, 1900. Verse.

The Songs of Father Goose, music by Alberta N Hall. Chicago & NY: Hill, 1900. Verse.

The Art of Decorating Dry Goods Windows and Interiors. Chicago: Show Window Publishing, 1900.

The Wonderful Wizard of Oz. Chicago & NY: Hill, 1900. Repub as *The New Wizard of Oz.* Indianapolis: Bobbs-Merrill, 1903. Children's novel.

American Fairy Tales. Chicago & NY: Hill, 1901. Augmented as *B's American Fairy Tales.* Indianapolis: Bobbs-Merrill, 1908.

Dot and Tot of Merryland. Chicago & NY: Hill, 1901. Children's novel.

The Master Key: An Electrical Fairy Tale. Indianapolis: Bowen-Merrill, 1901. Children's novel.

The Life and Adventures of Santa Claus. Indianapolis: Bowen-Merrill, 1902. Children's novel.

The Enchanted Island of Yew. Indianapolis: Bobbs-Merrill, 1903. Children's novel.

The Marvelous Land of Oz. Chicago: Reilly & Britton, 1904. Repub as *The Land of Oz,* 1914? Children's novel.

The Fate of a Crown (as by Schuyler Staunton). Chicago: Reilly & Britton, 1905. Novel.

Queen Zixi of Ix. NY: Century, 1905. Children's novel.

The Woggle-Bug Book. Chicago: Reilly & Britton, 1905. Children's novel.

Daughters of Destiny (as by Schuyler Staunton). Chicago: Reilly & Britton, 1906. Novel.

John Dough and the Cherub. Chicago: Reilly & Britton, 1906. Children's novel.

Annabel (as by Suzanne Metcalf). Chicago: Reilly & Britton, 1906. Children's novel.

Aunt Jane's Nieces (as by Edith Van Dyne). Chicago: Reilly & Britton, 1906. Children's novel.

Sam Steele's Adventures on Land and Sea (as by Capt. Hugh Fitzgerald). Chicago: Reilly & Britton, 1906. Repub as *The Boy Fortune Hunters in Alaska* (as by Floyd Akers), 1908. Children's novel.

Bandit Jim Crow (as by Laura Bancroft). Chicago: Reilly & Britton, 1906 ("Twinkle Tales"). Children's story.

Mr. Woodchuck (as by Laura Bancroft). Chicago: Reilly & Britton, 1906 ("Twinkle Tales"). Children's story.

Prairie-Dog Town (as by Laura Bancroft). Chicago: Reilly & Britton, 1906 ("Twinkle Tales"). Children's story.

Prince Mud-Turtle (as by Laura Bancroft). Chicago: Reilly & Britton, 1906 ("Twinkle Tales"). Children's story.

Sugar-Loaf Mountain (as by Laura Bancroft). Chicago: Reilly & Britton, 1906 ("Twinkle Tales"). Children's story.

Twinkle's Enchantment (as by Laura Bancroft). Chicago: Reilly & Britton, 1906 ("Twinkle Tales"). Children's story.

Aunt Jane's Nieces Abroad (as by Edith Van Dyne). Chicago: Reilly & Britton, 1906. Children's novel.

Father Goose's Year Book: Quaint Quacks and Feathery Shafts for Mature Children. Chicago: Reilly & Britton, 1907. Verse.

Ozma of Oz. Chicago: Reilly & Britton, 1907; *Princess Ozma of Oz.* London: Hutchinson, 1942. Children's novel.

Sam Steele's Adventures in Panama (as by Capt. Hugh Fitzgerald). Chicago: Reilly & Britton, 1907. Repub as *The Boy Fortune Hunters in Panama* (as by Floyd Akers), 1908. Children's novel.

Policeman Bluejay (as by Laura Bancroft). Chicago: Reilly & Britton, 1907. Repub as *Babes in Birdland,* 1911. Repub as *Babes in Birdland* (as by LFB), 1917. Children's novel.

Tamawaca Folks (as by John Estes Cooke). Macatawa, Mich: Macatawa, 1907. Novel.

Aunt Jane's Nieces at Millville (as by Edith Van Dyne). Chicago: Reilly & Britton, 1908. Children's novel.

Dorothy and the Wizard in Oz. Chicago: Reilly & Britton, 1908. Children's novel.

The Boy Fortune Hunters in Egypt (as by Floyd Akers). Chicago: Reilly & Britton, 1908. Children's novel.

The Last Egyptian (Anon). Philadelphia: Stern, 1908. Novel.

Aunt Jane's Nieces at Work (as by Edith Van Dyne). Chicago: Reilly & Britton, 1909. Children's novel.

The Boy Fortune Hunters in China (as by Floyd Akers). Chicago: Reilly & Britton, 1909. Children's novel.

The Road to Oz. Chicago: Reilly & Britton, 1909. Children's novel.

Aunt Jane's Nieces in Society (as by Edith Van Dyne). Chicago: Reilly & Britton, 1910. Children's novel.

The Boy Fortune Hunters in Yucatan (as by Floyd Akers). Chicago: Reilly & Britton, 1910. Children's novel.

The Emerald City of Oz. Chicago: Reilly & Britton, 1910. Children's novel.

Aunt Jane's Nieces and Uncle John (as by Edith Van Dyne). Chicago: Reilly & Britton, 1911. Children's novel.

The Boy Fortune Hunters in the South Seas (as by Floyd Akers). Chicago: Reilly & Britton, 1911. Children's novel.

The Flying Girl (as by Edith Van Dyne). Chicago: Reilly & Britton, 1911. Children's novel.

The Sea Fairies. Chicago: Reilly & Britton, 1911. Children's novel.

The Daring Twins. Chicago: Reilly & Britton, 1911. Children's novel.

The Flying Girl and Her Chum (as by Edith Van Dyne). Chicago: Reilly & Britton, 1912. Children's novel.

Aunt Jane's Nieces on Vacation (as by Edith Van Dyne). Chicago: Reilly & Britton, 1912. Children's novel.

Sky Island. Chicago: Reilly & Britton, 1912. Children's novel.

Phoebe Daring. Chicago: Reilly & Britton, 1912. Children's novel.

Aunt Jane's Nieces on the Ranch (as by Edith Van Dyne). Chicago: Reilly & Britton, 1913. Children's novel.

The Patchwork Girl of Oz. Chicago: Reilly & Britton, 1913. Children's novel.

The Cowardly Lion and the Hungry Tiger. Chicago: Reilly & Britton, 1913 ("Little Wizard Series"). Children's story.

Jack Pumpkinhead and the Sawhorse. Chicago: Reilly & Britton, 1913 ("Little Wizard Series"). Children's story.

Little Dorothy and Toto. Chicago: Reilly & Britton, 1913 ("Little Wizard Series"). Children's story.

Ozma and the Little Wizard. Chicago: Reilly & Britton, 1913 ("Little Wizard Series"). Children's story.

The Scarecrow and the Tin Woodman. Chicago: Reilly & Britton, 1913 ("Little Wizard Series"). Children's story.

Tik-Tok and the Nome King. Chicago: Reilly & Britton, 1913 ("Little Wizard Series"). Children's story.

Aunt Jane's Nieces Out West (as by Edith Van Dyne). Chicago: Reilly & Britton, 1914. Children's novel.

Tik-Tok of Oz. Chicago: Reilly & Britton, 1914. Children's novel.

Aunt Jane's Nieces in the Red Cross (as by Edith Van Dyne). Chicago: Reilly & Britton, 1915. Augmented ed, 1918. Children's novel.

The Scarecrow of Oz. Chicago: Reilly & Britton, 1915. Children's novel.

Mary Louise (as by Edith Van Dyne). Chicago: Reilly & Britton, 1916. Children's novel.

Mary Louise in the Country (as by Edith Van Dyne). Chicago: Reilly & Britton, 1916. Children's novel.

Rinkitink in Oz. Chicago: Reilly & Britton, 1916. Children's novel.

Little Bun Rabbit and Other Stories. Chicago: Reilly & Britton, 1916 ("Snuggle Tales"). Children's stories.

The Magic Cloak and Other Stories. Chicago: Reilly & Britton, 1916 ("Snuggle Tales"). Children's stories.

Once Upon a Time and Other Stories. Chicago: Reilly & Britton, 1916 ("Snuggle Tales"). Children's stories.

The Yellow Hen and Other Stories. Chicago: Reilly & Britton, 1916 ("Snuggle Tales"). Children's stories.

The Ginger-Bread Man. Chicago: Reilly & Britton, 1917 ("Snuggle Tales"). Children's story.

Jack Pumpkinhead. Chicago: Reilly & Britton, 1917 ("Snuggle Tales"). Children's story.

The Lost Princess of Oz. Chicago: Reilly & Britton, 1917. Children's novel.

Mary Louise Solves a Mystery (as by Edith Van Dyne). Chicago: Reilly & Britton, 1917. Children's novel.

Mary Louise and the Liberty Girls (as by Edith Van Dyne). Chicago: Reilly & Britton, 1918. Children's novel.

The Tin Woodman of Oz. Chicago: Reilly & Britton, 1918. Children's novel.

The Magic of Oz. Chicago: Reilly & Lee, 1919. Children's novel.

Mary Louise Adopts a Soldier (as by Edith Van Dyne). Chicago: Reilly & Lee, 1919. Children's novel.

Glinda of Oz. Chicago: Reilly & Lee, 1920. Children's novel.

LFB's "Our Landlady." Mitchell: South Dakota
  Writers' Project, 1941. Newspaper columns.
Jaglon and the Tiger Fairies, rev & ed by Jack
  Snow. Chicago: Reilly & Lee, 1953.
  Children's story.
The Musical Fantasies of LFB, ed Alla T Ford &
  Dick Martin. Chicago: Wizard, 1958.
*The High-Jinks of LFB: Being a Selection of
  Songs . . . as Sung by the Uplifters of Los An-
  geles.* Chicago: Wizard, 1959.
A Kidnapped Santa Claus. Indianapolis: Bobbs-
  Merrill, 1961. Children's novel.
The Uplift of Lucifer: or, Raising Hell, ed Manuel
  Weltman; music by Louise Gottschalk. Los
  Angeles: Privately printed, 1963. Play.
Animal Fairy Tales. Chicago: International Wizard
  of Oz Club, 1969.

COLLECTIONS

*LFB's Juvenile Speaker: Readings and Recitations
  in Prose and Verse, Humorous and Other-
  wise.* Chicago: Reilly & Britton, 1910. Repub
  as *B's Own Book for Children,* 1912.
*Twinkle and Chubbins: Their Astonishing Adven-
  tures in Nature-Fairyland* (as by Laura Ban-
  croft). Chicago: Reilly & Britton, 1911
  ("Twinkle Tales").
Little Wizard Stories of Oz. Chicago: Reilly &
  Britton, 1914 ("Little Wizard Series").
Oz-Man Tales. Chicago: Reilly & Lee, 1920
  ("Snuggle Tales").
The Annotated Wizard of Oz, with intro, notes &
  bibliography by Michael Patrick Hearn. NY:
  Potter, 1973.
The Purple Dragon and Other Fantasies, ed David
  L Greene. Lakemont, Ga: Fictioneer, 1976.

MANUSCRIPTS & ARCHIVES

Columbia U Library.

BIOGRAPHIES

Books
Baum, Frank Joslyn & Russell P MacFall. *To Please
  a Child: A Biography of LFB, Royal Historian
  of Oz.* Chicago: Reilly & Lee, 1961.
Baum, Maud Gage. *In Other Lands Than Ours.*
  Chicago: Privately printed, 1907.

CRITICAL STUDIES

Books
Green, David L & Dick Martin. *The Oz Scrap-
  book.* NY: Random House, 1977.
Moore, Raylyn. *Wonderful Wizard, Marvelous
  Land.* Bowling Green, Ohio: Bowling Green U
  Popular P, 1974.

Riley, Michael O'Neal. "Introductory Interiors:
  The Development of LFB's Imaginary World."
  Dissertation: Emory U, 1988.
Snow, Jack. *Who's Who in Oz.* Chicago: Reilly &
  Lee, 1954.
Wagenknecht, Edward. *Utopia Americana.* Seattle:
  U Washington Book Store, 1929.

Collections of Essays
Hearn, Michael Patrick, ed. *The Wizard of Oz.*
  NY: Schocken, 1983.
Nye, Russel & Martin Gardner, eds. *The Wizard of
  Oz and Who He Was.* East Lansing: Michigan
  State U P, 1957.

Special Journal
Baum Bugle (Summer 1957-   ).

Book Sections & Articles
Algeo, John. "Oz and Kansas: A Theosophical
  Quest." *Proceedings of the Thirteenth Annual
  Conference of the Children's Literature Asso-
  ciation,* ed Susan R Gannon & Ruth Anne
  Thompson (West Lafayette, Ind: Purdue U,
  1988), 135-
  139.
Attebery, Brian. "Oz," "The B Tradition." *The
  Fantasy Tradition in American Literature:
  From Irving to Le Guin* (Bloomington: Indi-
  ana U P, 1980), 83-108, 134-153.
Baughman, Roland. "LFB and the 'Oz Books.' "
  CLC, 4 (May 1955), 14-35.
Bauska, Barry. "The Land of Oz and the American
  Dream." *MarkhamR,* 5 (Winter 1976), 21-24.
Beckwith, Osmond. "The Oddness of Oz." *ChildL,*
  5 (1976), 74-91.
Bewley, Marius. "The Land of Oz: America's Great
  Good Place." *Masks and Mirrors* (NY: Athe-
  neum, 1970), 255-267.
Billman, Carol. " 'I've Seen the Movie': Oz Revis-
  ited." *Children's Novels and the Movies,* ed
  Douglas Street (NY: Ungar, 1983), 92-100.
Billman. "LFB: The Wizard Behind Oz." *AmerHI,*
  20 (Sep 1985), 42-48.
Brotman, Jordan. "A Late Wanderer in Oz." *Only
  Connect,* ed Sheila Egoff, G T Stubbs & L F
  Ashley (NY: Oxford U P, 1969), 156-169.
DeLuca, Geraldine & Roni Natov. "Researching
  Oz: An Interview With Michael Patrick
  Hearn." *L&U,* 11 (Oct 1987), 51-62.
Erisman, Fred. "LFB and the Progressive Di-
  lemma." *AQ,* 20 (Fall 1968), 616-623.
Gardner, Martin. "A Child's Garden of Bewilder-
  ment." *Only Connect,* ed Sheila Egoff, G T
  Stubbs & L F Ashley (NY: Oxford U P,
  1969), 150-155.
Griswold, Jerry. "There's No Place But Home: *The
  Wizard of Oz.*" *AR,* 45 (Fall 1987), 462-475.

Hansen, Linda. "Experiencing the World as Home: Reflections on Dorothy's Quest in *The Wizard of Oz.*" *Soundings,* 67 (Spring 1984), 91-102.

Hearn, Michael Patrick. "Discovering Oz (the Great and Terrible) at the Library of Congress." *QJLC,* 39 (Spring 1982), 70-79.

Hearn. "When LFB Was 'Laura Bancroft.' " *ABC,* 8 (May 1987), 11-16.

Jones, Vernon H. "The Oz Parade." *NOR,* 3, no 4 (1973), 375-378.

Littlefield, Henry M. "*The Wizard of Oz:* Parable on Populism." *The American Culture: Approaches to the Study of the United States,* ed Hennig Cohen (Boston: Houghton Mifflin, 1968), 370-382.

McReynolds, Douglas J & Barbara J Lips. "A Girl in the Game: *The Wizard of Oz* as Analog for the Female Experience in America." *NDQ,* 54 (Winter 1986), 87-93.

Plath, David W. "The Wizard of Pilgrimage; or, What Color Is Our Brick Road?" *What Does It Mean to Grow Old?: Reflections From the Humanities,* ed Thomas R Cole & Sally A Gadow (Durham, NC: Duke U P, 1986), 163-178.

Rzepka, Charles. " 'If I Can Make It There': Oz's Emerald City and the New Woman." *SPC,* 10, no 2 (1987), 54-66.

Sackett, S J. "The Utopia of Oz." *GaR,* 14 (Fall 1960), 275-291.

Sale, Roger. "LFB, and Oz." *HudR,* 25 (Winter 1972-1973), 571-592.

Sale. "Baum's Magic Powder of Life." *ChildL,* 8 (1980), 157-163.

Schuman, Samuel. "Out of the Fryeing Pan and into the Pyre: Comedy, Myth, and *The Wizard of Oz.*" *JPC,* 7 (Fall 1973), 302-304.

Starr, Nathan Comfort. "*The Wonderful Wizard of Oz:* A Study in Archetypal Mythic Symbiosis." *Unicorn,* 2 (Summer 1973), 13-17.

St John, Tom. "LFB: Looking Back to the Promised Land." *WHR,* 36 (Winter 1982), 349-360.

Thurber, James. "The Wizard of Chittenango: Oz Books." *NewR,* 81 (12 Dec 1934), 141-142.

Vidal, Gore. "The Oz Books." *The Second American Revolution and Other Essays* (NY: Random House, 1982), 55-82.

Sarah Zavelle Marwil Lamstein

REX BEACH

Atwood, Mich, 1 Sep 1877-Sebring, Fla, 7 Dec 1949

Rex Beach, who joined the gold rush to the Klondike, began his career as an author by writing about his experiences in Alaska. *The Spoilers,* his first novel, became a best-seller. Beach wrote other works about the mining camps, the salmon-fishing industry, and the frontier communities in the Alaskan frontier; but not wanting to be pigeonholed as an Alaskan author, he turned to other settings: Florida, Mexico, New York City, the Canal Zone, New Orleans, San Francisco. Notable for their romanticized, "manly" quality, their authentic settings and dialects, and their portraits of man's struggle to survive the rigors of the wilderness, Beach's works were extremely popular during the first two decades of the twentieth century but have received little attention from critics.

BIBLIOGRAPHY

Tourville, Elsie A. *Alaska: A Bibliography, 1570-1970* (Boston: Hall, 1974), 52-53. Primary.

BOOKS

Pardners. NY: McClure, Phillips, 1905. Stories.

The Spoilers. NY & London: Harper, 1905. Novel.

The Spoilers: A Play in Four Acts, with James MacArthur. NY: Nash, 1906.

The Barrier. NY & London: Harper, 1908. Novel.

The Silver Horde. NY & London: Harper, 1909. Novel.

Going Some: A Romance of Strenuous Affection. NY & London: Harper, 1910. Novel.

The Ne'er-Do-Well. NY & London: Harper, 1911. Novel.

The Net. NY & London: Harper, 1912. Novel.

The Iron Trail: An Alaskan Romance. NY & London: Harper, 1913. Novel.

The Auction Block: A Novel of New York Life. NY & London: Harper, 1914. Novel.

Heart of the Sunset. NY & London: Harper, 1915. Novel.

The Crimson Gardenia and Other Tales of Adventure. NY & London: Harper, 1916. Stories.

Rainbow's End: A Novel. NY & London: Harper, 1916.

Laughing Bill Hyde and Other Stories. NY & London: Harper, 1917.

The Winds of Chance. NY & London: Harper, 1918. Novel.

Too Fat to Fight. NY & London: Harper, 1919. Novel.

Oh, Shoot! Confessions of an Agitated Sportsman. NY & London: Harper, 1921. Repub as *Confessions of a Sportsman. . . .* Garden City, NY: Garden City Publishing, 1927. Essays.

Flowing Gold. NY & London: Harper, 1922. Novel.

Big Brother and Other Stories. NY & London: Harper, 1923.

Going Some: A Play in Four Acts, with Paul Armstrong. NY & c: French, 1923.

North of Fifty-Three. Garden City, NY: Garden City Publishing, 1925. Stories.

The Goose Woman and Other Stories. NY & London: Harper, 1925.

Padlocked. NY & London: Harper, 1926. Novel.

The Miracle of Coral Gables. Nashville, Tenn: Baird-Ward, 1926. Travel.

The Mating Call. NY & London: Harper, 1927. Novel.

Don Careless, and Birds of Prey. NY & London: Harper, 1928. Stories.

Son of the Gods. NY & London: Harper, 1929. Novel.

Money Mad. NY: Cosmopolitan, 1931. Novel.

Beyond Control. NY: Farrar & Rinehart, 1932. Novel.

Men of the Outer Islands. NY: Farrar & Rinehart, 1932. Stories.

Masked Women. NY: Farrar & Rinehart, 1934. Stories.

The Hands of Dr. Locke. NY: Farrar & Rinehart, 1934. Biography.

Jungle Gold. NY: Farrar & Rinehart, 1935. Novel.

Wild Pastures. NY: Farrar & Rinehart, 1935. Novel.

Valley of Thunder. NY & Toronto: Farrar & Rinehart, 1939. Novel.

The Tower of Flame: An Oil Fields Story; Jaraqu of the Lost Islands: A High Seas Story. Los Angeles: Bantam, 1940. Stories.

Personal Exposures. NY & London: Harper, 1941. Autobiography.

The World in His Arms. NY: Putnam, 1946. Novel.

Woman in Ambush. NY: Putnam, 1951. Novel.

COLLECTION

Alaskan Adventures: Three Thrilling Novels of the Far North. NY: Burt, 1909.

MANUSCRIPTS & ARCHIVES

Rollins C Library.

CRITICAL STUDIES

Book

Buske, Frank E. "The Wilderness, the Frontier and the Literature of Alaska to 1914: John Muir, Jack London and RB." Dissertation: U California, Davis, 1976.

Book Sections & Article

Baldwin, Charles C. "RB." *The Men Who Make Our Novels* (NY: Dodd, Mead, rev 1924), 38-41.

Hamilton, Cosmo. "RB: Open at the Neck." *People Worth Talking About* (NY: McBride, 1933), 217-224.

Nye, Russel B. *The Unembarrassed Muse: The Popular Arts in America* (NY: Dial, 1970), 38-39, 129, 365.

Van Gelder, Robert. "An Interview With RB." *NYTBR* (17 Aug 1941), 2, 13. Rpt *Writers and Writing* by Van Gelder (NY: Scribners, 1946).

Gwen L. Nagel

EDWARD BELLAMY

Chicopee Falls, Mass, 26 Mar 1850-Chicopee Falls, Mass, 22 May 1898

Edward Bellamy's reputation rests primarily on his novel *Looking Backward.* Among the most widely read books of its time, it was the second American novel to sell a million copies. The chief difference between contemporary responses and those of today lies in the earlier acceptance of Bellamy's concept of "Nationalism" as a viable political alternative. Nationalist Clubs sprung up by the hundreds and helped to form the Populist Party. Critics now tend to focus on Bellamy's place in the history of the utopian novel, with emphasis on the sociological rather than economic implications of the genre. Much of Bellamy's other fiction can be characterized as fantasy, displaying his interest in parapsychology.

BIBLIOGRAPHY

Bibliography of American Literature, comp Jacob Blanck. New Haven: Yale U P, 1955-1991. Primary.

Griffith, Nancy Snell. *EB: A Bibliography.* Metuchen, NJ: Scarecrow, 1986. Primary & secondary.

Widdicombe, Richard Toby. *EB: An Annotated Bibliography of Secondary Criticism.* NY: Garland, 1988.

BOOKS

Six to One: A Nantucket Idyl. NY: Putnam, 1878. Novel.

Dr. Heidenhoff's Process. NY: Appleton, 1880. Novel.

Miss Ludington's Sister: A Romance of Immortality. Boston: Osgood, 1884. Novel.

Looking Backward, 2000-1887. Boston: Ticknor, 1888. New ed with postscript & corrections by EB, Boston & NY: Houghton, Mifflin, 1889; *Looking Backward (2000-1887), or, Life in the Year 2000 AD.* London: Reeves, 1889. New ed, *Looking Backward, 2000-1887,* ed John L Thomas. Cambridge: Harvard U P, 1967 (Prints 1889 Houghton, Mifflin text, with 1888 Ticknor text in bracketed footnotes). Novel.

Equality. NY: Appleton, 1897. Novel.

The Blindman's World and Other Stories, preface by W D Howells. Boston & NY: Houghton, Mifflin, 1898.

The Duke of Stockbridge: A Romance of Shays' Rebellion, ed with intro by Francis Bellamy. NY & c: Silver, Burdett, 1900. Restoration of the version published serially in the *Berkshire Courier,* 45 (1879), ed Joseph Schiffman. Cambridge: Harvard U P, 1962. Novel.

EB Speaks Again! Articles, Public Addresses, Letters. Kansas City, Mo: Peerage, 1937.

Talks on Nationalism. Chicago: Peerage, 1938. Newspaper columns.

The Religion of Solidarity . . . With a Discussion of EB's Philosophy by Arthur E. Morgan. Yellow Springs, Ohio: Antioch Bookplate, 1940. Essay.

OTHER

New Nation, 1-4 (1891-1894), ed EB. Rpt, 3 vols, NY: Greenwood, 1968.

COLLECTION

Selected Writings on Religion and Society, ed with intro by Joseph Schiffman. NY: Liberal Arts, 1955.

MANUSCRIPTS & ARCHIVES

Houghton Library, Harvard U.

BIOGRAPHIES

Books

Bowman, Sylvia E. *The Year 2000: A Critical Biography of EB.* NY: Bookman, 1958.

Morgan, Arthur E. *EB.* NY: Columbia U P, 1944.

Book Sections & Article

Quint, Howard. "B Makes Socialism Respectable." *The Forging of American Socialism* (Columbia: U South Carolina P, 1953), 72-102.

Seager, Allan. "EB." *They Worked for a Better World* (NY: Macmillan, 1939), 97-116.

Willard, Cyrus Field. "The Nationalist Club of Boston (A Chapter of History)." *Nationalist,* 1 (May 1889), 16-20.

CRITICAL STUDIES

Books

Bowman, Sylvia E. *EB*. Boston: Twayne, 1986.

Lipow, Arthur. *Authoritarian Socialism in America: EB and the Nationalist Movement*. Berkeley: U California P, 1982.

MacNair, Everett W. *EB and the Nationalist Movement, 1889-1894*. Milwaukee: Fitzgerald, 1957.

Morgan, Arthur E. *Plagiarism in Utopia: A Study of the Continuity of the Utopian Tradition, With Special Reference to EB's Looking Backward*. Yellow Springs, Ohio: The Author, 1944.

Morgan. *The Philosophy of EB*. NY: King's Crown, 1945.

Shipley, Marie A Brown. *The True Author of Looking Backward*. NY: Alden, 1890.

Collections of Essays

Bowman, Sylvia E, ed. *EB Abroad: An American Prophet's Influence*. NY: Twayne, 1962.

Patai, Daphne, ed. *Looking Backward, 1988-1888: Essays on EB*. Amherst: U Massachusetts P, 1988.

Book Sections & Articles

Beauchamp, Gorman. "*The Iron Heel* and *Looking Backward*." *ALR*, 9 (Autumn 1976), 307-314.

Bleich, David. "Eros and B." *AQ*, 16 (Fall 1964), 445-459.

Bowman, Sylvia E. "B's Missing Chapter." *NEQ*, 31 (Mar 1958), 47-65.

Gardiner, Jane. "Form and Reform in *Looking Backward*." *ATQ*, ns 2 (Mar 1988), 69-82.

Hansot, Elisabeth. "EB's *Looking Backward* and *Equality*." *Perfection and Progress: Two Modes of Utopian Thought* (Cambridge: MIT P, 1974), 113-144.

Hogan, Robert E. "*Dr. Heidenhoff's Process* and *Miss Ludington's Sister*." *SAF*, 8 (Spring 1980), 51-68.

James, Max H. "The Polarity of Individualism and Conformity, a Dynamic of the Dream of Freedom, Examined in *Looking Backward*." *C&L*, 35 (Fall 1985), 17-59.

Jehmlich, Reimer. "Cog-work: The Organization of Labor in EB's *Looking Backward* and Later Utopian Fiction." *Clockwork Worlds*, ed

Richard D Erlich & Thomas P Dunn (Westport, Conn: Greenwood, 1983), 27-46.

Khouri, Nadia. "The Clockwork and Eros: Models of Utopia in EB and William Morris." *CLAJ*, 24 (Mar 1981), 376-399.

Kumar, Krishnan. "Utopia as Socialism: EB and *Looking Backward*." *Utopia and Anti-Utopia in Modern Times* (Oxford, UK: Blackwell, 1987), 132-167.

Lang, Hans-Joachim. "Paradoxes of Utopian Consciousness: From *Looking Backward* to *Young West*." *Amst*, 25, no 3 (1980), 231-242.

Lang. "Looking Backward at the Second Revolution in Massachusetts: EB's *The Duke of Stockbridge* as Historical Romance." *Amst*, 28, no 3 (1983), 309-322.

McHugh, Christine. "Abundance and Asceticism: Looking Backward to the Future." *AltF*, 1 (Fall 1978), 47-58.

Meier, Paul. "EB." *William Morris: The Marxist Dreamer*, Vol 1 (Sussex, UK: Harvester / Atlantic Highlands, NJ: Humanities, 1978), 73-93.

Morris, William. "*Looking Backward*." *Commonweal*, 5 (22 Jun 1889), 194-195. Rpt *SFS*, 3 (Nov 1976), 287-289.

Parrington, Vernon Louis. "The Precursors of B," "B and His Critics." *American Dreams: A Study of American Utopias* (Providence, RI: Brown U P, 1947), 57-97.

Parssinen, T M. "B, Morris, and the Image of the Industrial City in Victorian Social Criticism." *MQ*, 14 (Apr 1973), 257-266.

Pfaelzer, Jean. "A State of One's Own: Feminism as Ideology in American Utopias 1880-1915." *Extrapolation*, 24 (Winter 1983), 311-328.

Roemer, Kenneth M, ed. *America as Utopia* (NY: Franklin, 1981), passim.

Shurter, Robert L. *The Utopian Novel in America, 1865-1900* (NY: AMS, 1973), passim.

Towers, Tom H. "The Insomnia of Julian West." *AL*, 47 (Mar 1975), 52-63.

Walden, Daniel. "The Two Faces of Technological Utopianism: EB and Horatio Alger, Jr." *JGE*, 33 (Spring 1981), 24-30.

Winters, Donald E. "The Utopianism of Survival: B's *Looking Backward* and Twain's *A Connecticut Yankee*." *AmerS*, 21, no 1 (1980), 23-38.

Barbara L. Berman

AMBROSE BIERCE

Meigs County, Ohio, 24 Jun 1842-Ojinaga, Mexico, 11 Jan 1914?

Ambrose Bierce's short stories reveal him as a pioneer in exploring the epistemology of perception. During his lifetime, however, he was primarily known as an influential journalist. Following his mysterious disappearance in Mexico in 1913, attention focused on his personality. Over the last two decades, inquiry has shifted from the man to his writing. Critics now see him not as a realist but as a satirist, a wit, and—especially—an early impressionist who recognized that the categories of space, time, and causality are relative to the observer, whose perceptions control the reader's awareness.

BIBLIOGRAPHIES

Andrews, William L. "Some New AB Fables." *ALR,* 8 (Autumn 1975), 349-352. Primary.

Bibliography of American Literature, comp Jacob Blanck. New Haven: Yale U P, 1955-1991. Primary.

Fatout, Paul. "AB (1842-1914)." *ALR,* 1 (Fall 1967), 13-19. Secondary.

Fortenberry, George E, ed. "AB (1842-1914?): A Critical Bibliography of Secondary Comment." *ALR,* 4 (Winter 1971), 11-56.

Gaer, Joseph, ed. *AGB, Bibliography and Biographical Data.* Npl: npub, 1935. Repub, NY: Franklin, 1968. Primary.

Monteiro, George. "Addenda to Gaer: B in *The Anti-Philistine.*" *PBSA,* 66 (Jan-Mar 1972), 71-72. Primary.

Monteiro. "Addenda to Gaer: Reprintings of B's Stories." *PBSA,* 68 (Jul-Sep 1974), 330-331. Primary.

Rubens, Philip M & Robert Jones. "AB: A Bibliographic Essay and Bibliography." *ALR,* 16 (Spring 1983), 73-91. Secondary.

Starrett, Vincent. *AB: A Bibliography.* Philadelphia: Centaur Book Shop, 1929. Primary.

Stubbs, John C. "AB's Contributions to *Cosmopolitan:* An Annotated Bibliography." *ALR,* 4 (Winter 1971), 57-59. Primary.

BOOKS

The Fiend's Delight (as by Dod Grile). NY: Luyster, 1873. Sketches.

Nuggets and Dust Panned Out in California (as by Grile). London: Chatto & Windus, 1873. Sketches.

Cobwebs From an Empty Skull (as by Grile). London & NY: Routledge, 1874. Sketches.

The Dance of Death, with Thomas A Harcourt (together as by William Herman). San Francisco: Privately printed, 1877. Rev & augmented ed, San Francisco: Keller, 1877. Satire.

Tales of Soldiers and Civilians. San Francisco: Steele, 1891; *In the Midst of Life.* London: Chatto & Windus, 1892. Rev & augmented ed, NY & c: Putnam, 1898. Rev & augmented again in *The Collected Works of AB,* Vol 2. Excerpted in *A Son of the Gods and A Horseman in the Sky.* San Francisco: Elder, 1907. Stories.

Black Beetles in Amber. San Francisco & NY: Western Authors Publishing, 1892. Rev & augmented in *The Collected Works of AB,* Vol 5. Verse.

Can Such Things Be? NY: Cassell, 1893. Rev & augmented in *The Collected Works of AB,* Vol 3. Stories.

Fantastic Fables. NY & London: Putnam, 1899. Rev & augmented in *The Collected Works of AB,* Vol 6. Fables.

Shapes of Clay. San Francisco: Wood, 1903. Rev & augmented in *The Collected Works of AB,* Vol 4. Verse.

The Cynic's Word Book. NY: Doubleday, Page, 1906. Augmented as *The Devil's Dictionary* in *The Collected Works of AB,* Vol 7. Repub as *Enlarged Devil's Dictionary,* ed Ernest Jerome Hopkins. Garden City, NY: Doubleday, 1967.

The Shadow on the Dial and Other Essays, ed S O Howes. San Francisco: Robertson, 1909. Rev as *Antepenultimata* in *The Collected Works of AB,* Vol 11.

Write It Right: A Little Blacklist of Literary Faults. NY & Washington: Neale, 1909. Stylebook.

Battlefields and Ghosts. Palo Alto, Calif: Harvest, 1931. Reminiscences.

Selections From Prattle, comp Carroll D Hall; foreword by Joseph Henry Jackson. San Francisco: Book Club of California, 1936. Sketches.

The AB Satanic Reader, ed Hopkins. Garden City, NY: Doubleday, 1968. Sketches.

AB—Skepticism and Dissent: Selected Journalism From 1898-1901, ed Lawrence I Berkove. Ann Arbor, Mich: Delmas, 1980. Sketches.

LETTERS

The Letters of AB, ed with intro by Bertha Clark Pope; memoir by George Sterling. San Francisco: Book Club of California, 1922. Repub, NY: Gordian, 1967.

Twenty-one Letters of AB, ed with intro by Samuel Loveman. Cleveland: Kirk, 1922.

"A Collection of B Letters." *UCC,* 34 (Jan 1932), 30-48.

"Seven AB Letters" by M E Grenander. *YULG,* 32 (Jul 1957), 12-18.

"AB and Charles Warren Stoddard: Some Unpublished Correspondence" by Grenander. *HLQ,* 23 (May 1960), 261-292.

" 'Putting You in the Papers': AB's Letters to Edwin Markham" by Joseph W Slade. *Prospects,* 1 (1975), 334-368.

OTHER

The Monk and the Hangman's Daughter [by Richard Voss]; trans Gustav Adolf Danziger; adapted by AB. Chicago: Schulte, 1892. Repub with preface by AB, NY & Washington: Neale, 1907. Repub in *The Collected Works of AB,* Vol 11.

EDITION & COLLECTIONS

The Collected Works of AB, 12 vols. NY & Washington: Neale, 1909-1912.

The Collected Writings of AB, ed with intro by Clifton Fadiman. NY: Citadel, 1946.

AB's Civil War, ed with intro by William McCann. Los Angeles & c: Regnery Gateway, 1956.

In the Midst of Life and Other Tales by AB, afterword by Marcus Cunliffe. NY: NAL/Signet, 1961.

The Sardonic Humor of AB, ed with preface by George Barkin. NY: Dover, 1963.

Ghost and Horror Stories of AB, ed with intro by E F Bleiler. NY: Dover, 1964.

The Complete Short Stories of AB, 2 vols, ed with intro by Ernest Jerome Hopkins. NY: Ballantine, 1970. Repub in 1 vol with intro by Cathy N Davidson, Lincoln & c: U Nebraska P/Bison, 1984.

The Stories & Fables of AB, ed with intro by Edward Wagenknecht. Owings Mills, Md: Stemmer House, 1977.

MANUSCRIPTS & ARCHIVES

The major collections are at the U of California, Berkeley, Library; U of Virginia Library; U of Cincinnati Library; the Huntington Library, San Marino, Calif; New York Public Library; Stanford U Library; Syracuse U Library; & the Beinecke Library, Yale U.

BIOGRAPHIES

Books

Fatout, Paul. *AB, the Devil's Lexicographer.* Norman: U Oklahoma P, 1951.

Fatout. *AB and the Black Hills.* Norman: U Oklahoma P, 1956.

Grattan, C Hartley. *Bitter B: A Mystery of American Letters.* Garden City, NY: Doubleday, 1929.

Hall, Carroll C. *B and the Poe Hoax.* San Francisco: Book Club of California, 1934.

McWilliams, Carey. *AB: A Biography.* NY: Boni, 1929.

O'Connor, Richard. *AB: A Biography.* Boston: Little, Brown, 1967.

Rather, Lois. *Bittersweet: AB & Women.* Oakland, Calif: Rather, 1975.

Starrett, Vincent. *AB.* Chicago: Hill, 1920. Rpt Port Washington, NY: Kennikat, 1969.

Book Sections & Articles

Anderson, David D. "Can Ohio and the Midwest Claim AB?" *OhioanaQ,* 16 (Summer 1973), 84-88.

Bierce, Helen. "AB at Home." *AMercury,* 30 (Dec 1933), 453-458.

Brazil, John R. "AB, Jack London and George Sterling: Victorians Between Two Worlds." *SJS,* 4 (Feb 1978), 19-33.

Brooks, Van Wyck. "The Letters of AB." *Emerson and Others* (NY: Dutton, 1927), 147-157. Rpt Davidson (1982).

Fatout, Paul. "AB, Civil War Topographer." *AL,* 26 (Nov 1954), 391-400.

Follett, Wilson. "Ambrose, Son of Marcus Aurelius." *Atlantic,* 160 (Jul 1937), 32-42. Rpt Davidson (1982).

Goldstein, Jesse Sidney. "Edwin Markham, AB, and 'The Man With the Hoe.' " *MLN,* 58 (Mar 1943), 165-175.

Grenander, M E. "H. L. Mencken to AB." *BClubCalQNL,* 22 (Winter 1956), 5-10.

Grenander. "A London Letter of Joaquin Miller to AB." *YULG,* 46 (Oct 1971), 109-116.

Grenander. "California's Albion: Mark Twain, AB, Tom Hood, John Camden Hotten, and Andrew Chatto." *PBSA,* 72 (Oct-Dec 1978), 455-475.

Harris, Leon. "Satan's Lexicographer." *AH,* 28 (Apr 1977), 57-63.

Hillman, Col Rolfe L, Jr. "AB: He Went to War and to the Devil." *Army,* 24 (Jul 1974), 35-39.

McWilliams, Carey. "The Mystery of AB." *AMercury,* 22 (Mar 1931), 330-337.

McWilliams. "AB and His First Love." *Bookman,* 75 (Jun-Jul 1932), 254-259.

CRITICAL STUDIES

Books
Davidson, Cathy N. *The Experimental Fictions of AB: Structuring the Ineffable.* Lincoln: U Nebraska P, 1984.

Grenander, M E. *AB.* NY: Twayne, 1971.

Wiggins, Robert A. *AB.* Minneapolis: U Minnesota P, 1964.

Collection of Essays
Davidson, Cathy N, ed. *Critical Essays on AB.* Boston: Hall, 1982.

Book Sections & Articles
Aaron, Daniel. "AB and the American Civil War." *Uses of Literature,* ed Monroe Engel (Cambridge: Harvard U P, 1973), 115-131. Rpt *The Unwritten War: American Writers and the Civil War* by Aaron (NY: Knopf, 1973). Rpt Davidson (1982).

Ames, Clifford R. "Do I Wake or Sleep? Technique as Content in AB's Short Story 'An Occurrence at Owl Creek Bridge.' " *ALR,* 19 (Spring 1987), 52-67.

Bahr, Howard W. "AB and Realism." *SoQ,* 1 (Jul 1963), 309-331. Rpt Davidson (1982).

Berkove, Lawrence I. "Arms and the Man: AB's Response to War." *MichA,* 1 (Winter 1969), 21-30.

Berkove. "The Man With the Burning Pen: AB as Journalist." *JPC,* 15, no 2 (1981), 34-40.

Berkove. " 'A Strange Adventure': The Story Behind a Bierce Tale." *ALR,* 14 (Spring 1981), 70-76.

Berkove. "Two Impossible Dreams: AB on Utopia and America." *HLQ,* 44 (Autumn 1981), 283-292.

Berkove. "The Heart Has Its Reasons: AB's Successful Failure at Philosophy." Davidson (1982), 136-149.

Brady, Haldeen. "AB and Guy de Maupassant." *AN&Q,* 1 (Aug 1941), 67-68.

Brazil, John R. "Behind the Bitterness: AB in Text and Context." *ALR,* 13 (Autumn 1980), 225-237.

Bleiler, E F. "Who Was Moxon's Master?" *Extrapolation,* 26 (Fall 1985), 181-189.

Brophy, Brigid. "A Literary History." *The Adventures of God in His Search for the Black Girl* (Boston: Atlantic/Little, Brown, 1974), 20-25.

Crane, John Kenny. "Crossing the Bar Twice: Post-Mortem Consciousness in B, Hemingway, and Golding." *SSF,* 6 (Summer 1969), 361-376.

Davidson, Cathy N. "Re-Structuring the Ineffable and AB's 'The Secret of Macarger's Gulch.' " *MarkhamR,* 12 (Fall 1982), 14-19.

Fatout, Paul. "AB Writes About War." *BClubCalQNL,* 16 (Fall 1951), 75-79.

Follett, Wilson. "America's Neglected Satirist." *Dial,* 65 (18 Jul 1918), 49-52.

Follett. "AB: An Analysis of the Perverse Wit That Shaped His Work." *Bookman,* 68 (Nov 1928), 284-289.

Follett. "B in His Brilliant Obscurity." *NYTBR* (11 Oct 1936), 232.

Grattan, C H. "AB." *Reviewer,* 5 (Oct 1925), 103-104.

Grenander, M E. "*Au Coeur de la vie:* A French Translation of AB." *BUSE,* 1 (Winter 1955-1956), 237-241.

Grenander. "B's Turn of the Screw: Tales of Ironical Terror." *WHR,* 11 (Summer 1957), 257-263. Rpt Davidson (1982).

Grenander. "AB, John Camden Hotten, *The Fiend's Delight,* and *Nuggets and Dust.*" *HLQ,* 28 (Aug 1965), 353-371.

Grenander. "AB and *In the Midst of Life.*" *BC,* 20 (Autumn 1971), 321-331.

Grenander. "AB and *Cobwebs From an Empty Skull:* A Note on BAL 1100 and 1107." *PBSA,* 69 (Jul-Sep 1975), 403-406.

Grenander. " 'Five Blushes, Ten Shudders and a Vomit': Mark Twain on AB's *Nuggets and Dust.*" *ALR,* 17 (Autumn 1984), 169-179.

Hartwell, Ronald. "What Hemingway Learned From AB." *ResearchS,* 38 (Dec 1970), 309-311.

Hartwell. "Fallen Timbers—A Death Trap: A Comparison of B and Munro." *ResearchS,* 49 (Mar 1981), 61-66.

Highsmith, James Milton. "The Forms of Burlesque in *The Devil's Dictionary.*" *SatireN,* 7 (Spring 1970), 115-127. Rpt Davidson (1982).

Kazin, Alfred. "On AB and 'Parker Adderson, Philosopher.' " *The American Short Story,* ed Calvin Skaggs (NY: Dell, 1977), 31-35.

Kunz, Don. "Arthur Barron & Bitter B." *LFQ,* 15, no 1 (1987), 64-68.

Logan, F J. "The Wry Seriousness of 'Owl Creek Bridge.' " *ALR,* 10 (Spring 1977), 101-113. Rpt Davidson (1982).

Marcus, Fred H. "Film and Fiction: 'An Occurrence at Owl Creek Bridge.' " *CalEJ,* 7 (1971), 14-23.

Martin, Jay. "AB." *The Comic Imagination in American Literature,* ed Louis D Rubin, Jr (New Brunswick, NJ: Rutgers U P, 1973), 194-205. Rpt Davidson (1982).

McLean, Robert C. "The Deaths in AB's 'Halpin Frayser.' " *PLL,* 10 (Fall 1974), 394-402.

McWilliams, Carey. "AB." *AMercury,* 16 (Feb 1929), 215-222. Rpt Davidson (1982).

McWilliams. Introduction. *The Devil's Dictionary* (NY: Sagamore, 1957), v-xii.

Mencken, H L. *A Book of Prefaces* (NY: Knopf, 1917), passim.

Mencken. "AB." *Prejudices, Sixth Series* (NY: Knopf, 1927), 259-265. Rpt Davidson (1982).

Miller, A C. "The Influence of Edgar Allan Poe on AB." *AL,* 4 (May 1932), 130-150.

Monaghan, Frank. "AB and the Authorship of *The Monk and the Hangman's Daughter.*" *AL,* 2 (Jan 1931), 337-349.

Nations, L J. "AB: The Grey Wolf of American Letters." *SAQ,* 25 (Jul 1926), 253-268.

Nickell, Joe. "AB and Those 'Mysterious Disappearances' Legends." *InFl,* 13, nos 1-2 (1980), 112-122.

O'Brien, Matthew C. "AB and the Civil War: 1865." *AL,* 48 (Nov 1976), 377-381.

Palmer, James W. "From Owl Creek to *La Rivière du Hibou:* The Film Adaptation of B's 'An Occurrence at Owl Creek Bridge.' " *SHR,* 11 (Fall 1977), 363-371.

Reed, Eugene E. "AB's 'Chickamauga': An Identity Restored." *RLV,* 28 (1962), 49-53.

Roth, Russell. "AB's 'Detestable Creature.' " *WAL,* 9 (Fall 1974), 169-176.

Snell, George. "Poe Redivivus." *ArQ,* 1 (Summer 1945), 49-57.

Solomon, Eric. "The Bitterness of Battle: AB's War Fiction." *MQ,* 5 (Winter 1964), 147-165. Rpt Davidson (1982).

Stein, William Bysshe. "B's 'The Death of Halpin Frayser': The Poetics of Gothic Consciousness." *ESQ,* 18, no 67 (1972), 115-122. Rpt Davidson (1982).

Sterling, George. "The Shadow Maker." *AMercury,* 6 (Sep 1925), 10-19.

Thomas, Jeffrey F. "AB." *ALR,* 8 (Summer 1975), 198-201.

Weimer, David R. "AB and the Art of War." *Essays in Literary History,* ed Rudolf Kirk & C F Main (NY: Russell & Russell, 1965), 229-238.

Williams, S T. "AB and Bret Harte." *AL,* 17 (May 1945), 179-180.

Wilt, Napier. "AB and the Civil War." *AL,* 1 (Nov 1929), 260-285.

Ziff, Larzer. "The Poles of Violence: AB and Richard Harding Davis." *The American 1890s: Life and Times of a Lost Generation* (NY: Viking, 1966), 166-184.

M. E. Grenander

EARL DERR BIGGERS

Warren, Ohio, 26 Aug 1884-Pasadena, Calif, 5 Apr 1933

Earl Derr Biggers, a writer of detective and mystery fiction, created several distinctive characters in this genre but is best known for inventing the Honolulu detective, Charlie Chan. Biggers's Chinese sleuth represented a shift from the way Orientals had been treated in adventure and mystery stories. Chan's intelligence, his position on the side of the law, his role as a family man, even his self-effacing humor put him in clear, positive contrast to Sax Rohmer's Fu Manchu and spawned a whole series of ethnic detectives.

BOOKS

Seven Keys to Baldpate. Indianapolis: Bobbs-Merrill, 1913. Novel.

Love Insurance. Indianapolis: Bobbs-Merrill, 1914. Novel.

Inside the Lines, with Robert Welles Ritchie. Indianapolis: Bobbs-Merrill, 1915. Novel.

The Agony Column. Indianapolis: Bobbs-Merrill, 1916. Repub as *Second Floor Mystery.* NY: Grosset & Dunlap, 1930. Novel.

Inside the Lines. NY & London: French, 1924. Play.

The House Without a Key. Indianapolis: Bobbs-Merrill, 1925. Novel.

The Chinese Parrot. Indianapolis: Bobbs-Merrill, 1926. Novel.

Fifty Candles. Indianapolis: Bobbs-Merrill, 1926. Novel.

Behind That Curtain. Indianapolis: Bobbs-Merrill, 1928. Novel.

The Black Camel. Indianapolis: Bobbs-Merrill, 1929. Novel.

Celebrated Cases of Charlie Chan. Indianapolis: Bobbs-Merrill, 1930.

Charlie Chan Carries On. Indianapolis: Bobbs-Merrill, 1930. Novel.

Keeper of the Keys. Indianapolis: Bobbs-Merrill, 1932. Novel.

EDB Tells Ten Stories. Indianapolis: Bobbs-Merrill, 1933.

OTHER

Quotations From Charlie Chan, comp & ed by Harvey Chertok & Martha Torge. NY: Golden, 1968. Aphorisms from Charlie Chan movies.

CRITICAL STUDIES

Book Sections & Articles

Armato, Douglas M. "Charlie Chan in Books and in Motion Pictures." *ArmD,* 7, no 2 (1974), 97-99.

Benvenuti, Stefano & Gianni Rizzoni. "The Most Exotic: Charlie Chan," trans Anthony Eyre. *The Whodunit* (NY: Macmillan / London: Collier Macmillan, 1980), 77-79.

Breen, Jon L. "Charlie Chan in Qui Nhon." *ArmD,* 2, no 1 (1969), 114.

Breen. "Who Killed Charlie Chan?" *ArmD,* 7, no 2 (1974), 100, 127.

Breen. "Charlie Chan: The Man Behind the Curtain, Part I." *V&R,* 6 (Fall 1974), 29-36.

Breen. "Murder Number One: EDB." *NewR,* 177 (30 Jul 1977), 38-39.

Chin, Frank. "Confessions of a Number One Son." *Ramparts,* 11 (Mar 1973), 41-48.

Chin. "Interview: Roland Winters." *Amerasia,* 2 (Fall 1973), 1-19.

Choy, Christine. "Images of Asian-Americans in Films and Television." *Ethnic Images in American Film and Television,* ed Randall M Miller (Philadelphia: Balch, 1978), 145-155.

Chung, Sue Fawn. "From Fu Manchu, Evil Genius, to James Lee Wong, Popular Hero." *JPC,* 10, no 3 (1976), 534-547.

Connor, Edward. "The 6 Charlie Chans." *Films in Review,* 6 (Jan 1955), 23-27.

Ellman, Neil. "Charlie Chan." *IUB,* 8 (Mar 1967), 91-99.

Ellman. "Charlie Chan Carries On." *ArmD,* 10, no 2 (1977), 183-184.

Everson, William K. "The Oriental Detective." *The Detective in Film* (Secaucus, NJ: Citadel, 1972), 72-85.

Galperin, William. " 'Bad for the Glass': Representation and Filmic Deconstruction in *Chinatown* and *Chan Is Missing.*" *MLN,* 102 (Dec 1987), 1151-1170.

King, Margaret J. "Binocular Eyes: Cross Cultural Detectives." *ArmD,* 13, no 3 (1980), 253-260.

Oehling, Richard A. "The Yellow Menace: Asian Images in American Film." *The Kaleidoscopic Lens,* ed Randall M Miller (Englewood, NJ: Ozer, 1980), 182-206.

Pate, Janet. "Charlie Chan." *The Book of Sleuths* (Chicago: Contemporary, 1977), 55-57.

Penzler, Otto. "Collecting Mystery Fiction." *ArmD,* 15, no 2 (1982), 119-125.

Pitts, Michael R. "Charlie Chan." *Famous Movie Detectives* (Metuchen, NJ: Scarecrow, 1979), 39-84.

Tuska, Jon. "Chinatown, My Chinatown." *The Detective in Hollywood* (Garden City, NY: Doubleday, 1978), 104-157.

Winks, Robin W. "Sinister Orientals." *Murder Ink,* ed Dilys Winn (NY: Workman, 1977), 491-493.

Wu, William F. "Fu Manchu and Charlie Chan." *The Yellow Peril* (Hamden, Conn: Archon, 1982), 164-182, 224-226.

Zinman, David. "Charlie Chan." *Saturday Afternoon at the Bijou* (New Rochelle, NY: Arlington House, 1973), 257-272.

Carl L. Boren

SHERWOOD BONNER

Marshall Co, Miss, 24 Feb 1849-Holly Springs, Miss, 22 Jul 1883

During her brief life, Katharine Sherwood Bonner McDowell, writing as Sherwood Bonner, established a reputation for marketable prose—journalistic essays, travel pieces, children's tales, "black mammy" and other Negro dialect stories, thrillers, romances, and regional fiction set not only in the southern lowlands and the southern mountains but also in the Midwest. For decades after her death, however, she was regarded simply as a writer of quaint southern sketches. Within the last quarter of this century, scholars have acknowledged the complexity of her career, seeing her as more than a pioneer local colorist. Bonner is viewed as a representative figure of her era, and her controversial life has received as much attention as her fiction.

BIBLIOGRAPHY

Biglane, Jean Nosser. "SB: A Bibliography of Primary and Secondary Materials." *ALR*, 5 (Winter 1972), 38-60.

BOOKS

The Radical Club: A Poem Respectfully Dedicated to "The Infinite" by "An Atom." Boston: Times Publishing, 1876.
Like Unto Like. NY: Harper, 1878; *Blythe Herndon*, bound with *Janetta* by Julia Chandler. London: Ward, Lock, 1882. Novel.
Dialect Tales. NY: Harper, 1883. Stories.
Suwanee River Tales. Boston: Roberts, 1884. Stories.
Gran'mammy. Little Classics of the South: Mississippi. NY: Purdy, 1927. Stories.

DIARY

"SB's Diary for the Year 1869," ed William Luke Frank. *NMW*, 3 (Winter 1971), 111-130; 4 (Spring 1971), 22-40; 4 (Fall 1971), 64-83.

MANUSCRIPTS & ARCHIVES

The major collections are at the Mississippi Department of Archives & History, Jackson; Mississippi State U Library; U of Mississippi Library; & the Houghton Library, Harvard U.

BIOGRAPHIES

Book
McAlexander, Hubert H. *The Prodigal Daughter: A Biography of SB*. Baton Rouge: Louisiana State U P, 1981.

Book Section & Articles
Moore, Rayburn S. " 'Merlin and Vivien'?: Some Notes on SB and Longfellow." *MissQ*, 28 (Spring 1975), 181-184.
Polhemus, George W. "The Correct Spelling of SB's Name." *N&Q*, 7 (Jul 1960), 265.
Sutherland, Daniel E. "Some Thoughts Concerning the Love Life of SB." *SoSt*, 26 (Summer 1987), 115-127.
Wagenknecht, Edward. *Longfellow: A Full-Length Portrait* (NY: Longmans, Green, 1955), 280-283.

CRITICAL STUDIES

Book
Frank, William L. *SB*. Boston: Twayne, 1976.

Book Sections & Articles
Bondurant, Alexander L. "SB—Her Life and Place in the Literature of the South." *PMissHS*, 2 (1899), 43-68.
Buck, Paul H. *The Road to Reunion: 1865-1900* (Boston: Little, Brown, 1937), 202-203, 224-225, 228.
Hall, Wade. *The Smiling Phoenix: Southern Humor From 1865 to 1914* (Gainesville: U Florida P, 1965), passim.
McAlexander, Hubert H. "SB (Katharine SB McDowell)." *ALR*, 8 (Summer 1975), 203-204.
McAlexander. "A Reappraisal of SB's *Like Unto Like*." *SLJ*, 10 (Spring 1978), 93-106.
Moore, Rayburn S. "SB's Contributions to *Lippincott's Magazine* and *Harper's New Monthly*." *MissQ*, 17 (Fall 1963-1964), 226-230.
Paine, Gregory Lansing, ed. "SB." *Southern Prose Writers* (NY: American Book, 1947), 273-275.

Simpson, Claude M, ed. *The Local Colorists: American Short Stories, 1857-1900* (NY: Harper, 1960), 289.

Skaggs, Merrill Maguire. *The Folk of Southern Fiction* (Athens: U Georgia P, 1972), passim.

Skaggs. "Southern Compost." *SLJ*, 10 (Spring 1978), 155-160.

Sutherland, Daniel E. *The Confederate Carpetbaggers* (Baton Rouge: Louisiana State U P, 1988), 279-282, 298-299, 321, 331.

Hubert H. McAlexander

HJALMAR HJORTH BOYESEN

Fredriksvaern, Norway, 23 Sep 1848-New York City, NY, 4 Oct 1895

W. D. Howells published Hjalmar Hjorth Boyesen's first novel, *Gunnar,* in the *Atlantic Monthly* four years after the young Norwegian immigrated in 1869. Boyesen became a widely published author of short stories, novels, and poetry and of articles on Norway, on contemporary European writers, and later on American culture. He was embittered by the frequently hostile reaction to his realistic novels and attacked the "empty story-tellers" and critics who praised such writing. Boyesen's chief contribution to American literature was as a liaison between continental European literature and American writing.

BIBLIOGRAPHY

Bibliography of American Literature, comp Jacob Blanck. New Haven: Yale U P, 1955-1991. Primary.

BOOKS

Gunnar: A Tale of Norse Life. Boston: Osgood, 1874. Novel.

A Norseman's Pilgrimage. NY: Sheldon, 1875. Novel.

Tales From Two Hemispheres. Boston: Osgood, 1877.

Falconberg. NY: Scribners, 1879. Novel.

Goethe and Schiller: Their Lives and Works, In-cluding a Commentary on Goethe's Faust. NY: Scribners, 1879.

Ilka on the Hill-top and Other Stories. NY: Scribners, 1881.

Queen Titania. NY: Scribners, 1881. Novella & stories.

Idyls of Norway and Other Poems. NY: Scribners, 1882.

A Daughter of the Philistines. Boston: Roberts, 1883. Novel.

Alpine Roses: A Comedy in Four Acts. . . . NY: Privately printed, 1884.

The Story of Norway. NY & London: Putnam, 1886. Repub as *A History of Norway From the Earliest Times,* augmented by C F Keary, 1900.

The Modern Vikings: Stories of Life and Sport in the Norseland. NY: Scribners, 1887.

The Light of Her Countenance. NY: Appleton, 1889. Novel.

Vagabond Tales. NY: Lothrop, 1889.

Against Heavy Odds: A Tale of Norse Heroism. NY: Scribners, 1890. Augmented as *Against Heavy Odds . . . and A Fearless Trio,* 1894. Novella.

The Mammon of Unrighteousness. NY: Lovell, 1891. Novel.

The Golden Calf. Meadville, Pa: Flood & Vincent, 1892. Novel.

Boyhood in Norway: Stories of Boy-Life in the Land of the Midnight Sun. NY: Scribners, 1892; *The Battle of the Rafts and Other Sto-*

ries of Boyhood in Norway. London: Nelson, 1894.

Essays on German Literature. NY: Scribners, 1892.

Social Strugglers: A Novel. NY: Scribners, 1893.

A Commentary on the Writings of Henrik Ibsen. NY & London: Macmillan, 1894.

Literary and Social Silhouettes. NY: Harper, 1894. Essays.

Norseland Tales. NY: Scribners, 1894.

Essays on Scandinavian Literature. NY: Scribners, 1895.

OTHER

"The Elixir of Pain." *Cosmopolitan,* 11 (May 1891), 62-87; 11 (Jun 1891), 192-218; 11 (Jul 1891), 347-367. Novella.

"A Harvest of Tares." *GLB,* 126 (May 1893), 527-616. Novella.

MANUSCRIPTS & ARCHIVES

The major collections are at Columbia U Library & U of Virginia Library.

BIOGRAPHY

Book

Glasrud, Clarence A. *HHB.* Northfield, Minn: Norwegian-American Historical Association, 1963.

Book Sections & Articles

Howells, William Dean. "HHB." *HB,* 29 (25 Jan 1896), 70-71. Rpt *Literary Friends and Acquaintance* by Howells (NY: Harper, 1900).

Howells. "Some Literary Memories of Cambridge." *Har,* 101 (Nov 1900), 823-839.

Larson, Laurence M. "HHB." *The Changing West and Other Essays* (Northfield, Minn: Norwegian-American Historical Association, 1937), 82-115.

Rideing, William H. "HHB." *The Boyhood of Living Authors* (NY: Crowell, 1887), 163-177.

CRITICAL STUDIES

Books

Fredrickson, Robert S. *HHB.* Boston: Twayne, 1980.

Ratner, Marc. "HHB: Critic of Literature and Society." Dissertation: NYU, 1959.

Collection of Essays

Seyersted, Per. *From Norwegian Romantic to American Realist: Studies in the Life and Writings of HHB.* Oslo: Solum Forlag / Atlantic Highlands, NJ: Humanities, 1984. Includes 8 essays by HHB.

Book Sections & Articles

Glasrud, Clarence A. "B and the Norwegian Immigration." *NAS&R,* 19 (1956), 15-45.

Ratner, Marc. "Georg Brandes and HHB." *SS,* 33 (Nov 1961), 218-230.

Ratner. "Howells and B: Two Views of Realism." *NEQ,* 35 (Sep 1962), 376-390.

Ratner. "The Iron Madonna: HHB's American Girl." *JA,* 9 (1964), 166-172.

Seyersted, Per. "Turgenev's Interest in America, as Seen in His Contacts With HHB, W. D. Howells and Other American Authors." *Scando-Slav,* 11 (1965), 25-39.

Seyersted. "HHB: Outer Success, Inner Failure." *Americana Norvegica,* Vol 1, ed Sigmund Skard & Henry H Wasser (Philadelphia: U Pennsylvania P, 1966), 206-238.

Seyersted. "The Drooping Lily: HHB as an Early American Misogynist." *Americana Norvegica,* Vol 3, ed Harald S Naess & Sigmund Skard (Oslo: Universitetsforlaget, 1971), 74-87.

Turner, Arlin. "A Novelist Discovers a Novelist: The Correspondence of HHB and George W. Cable." *WHR,* 5 (Autumn 1951), 343-372.

White, George Leroy, Jr. "HHB—Immigrant," "Conclusion." *Scandinavian Themes in American Fiction* (Philadelphia: U Pennsylvania, 1937), 174-192.

White. "HHB: A Note on Immigration." *AL,* 13 (Jan 1942), 363-371.

Clarence A. Glasrud

ALICE BROWN

Hampton Falls, NH, 5 Dec 1856-Boston, Mass, 21 Jun 1948

Alice Brown was a prolific novelist, short-story writer, poet, and playwright. In the 1890s she earned a reputation for her stories of rural New England. The early regional stories collected in *Meadow-Grass* and *Tiverton Tales* remain her most enduring work; they possess distinctive style and tone that set her apart from her contemporaries. Yet she cannot be classified exclusively as a recorder of rural New England, for the lives of writers and artists in Boston were the subjects of many of her stories and novels. Her work is suffused with a spiritual dimension that helps distinguish it from the realistic and naturalistic works of her day.

BIBLIOGRAPHIES

Baker, Margaret Ann. "AB: A Bibliography of Books and Uncollected Prose." *ALR*, 17 (Spring 1984), 99-115. Primary.

First Printings of American Authors, Vol 3 (Detroit: Bruccoli Clark/Gale, 1978), 35-41. Primary.

BOOKS

Stratford-by-the-Sea. NY: Holt, 1884. Novel.

Fools of Nature. Boston: Ticknor, 1887. Novel.

Robert Louis Stevenson: A Study, prelude & postlude by Louise Imogen Guiney. Boston: Copeland & Day, 1895. Criticism.

Meadow-Grass: Tales of New England Life. Boston: Copeland & Day, 1895. Stories.

The Road to Castaly. Boston: Copeland & Day, 1896. Augmented as *The Road to Castaly and Later Poems.* NY: Macmillan, 1917.

By Oak and Thorn: A Record of English Days. Boston & NY: Houghton, Mifflin, 1896. Essays.

Mercy Warren. NY: Scribners, 1896. Biography.

The Day of His Youth. Boston & NY: Houghton, Mifflin, 1897. Novel.

Tiverton Tales. Boston & NY: Houghton, Mifflin, 1899. Stories.

King's End. Boston & NY: Houghton, Mifflin, 1901. Novel.

Margaret Warrener. Boston & NY: Houghton, Mifflin, 1901. Novel.

The Mannerings. Boston & NY: Houghton, Mifflin, 1903. Novel.

Judgment. NY & London: Harper, 1903. Novel.

The Merrylinks. NY: McClure, Phillips, 1903. Poetry.

High Noon. Boston & NY: Houghton, Mifflin, 1904. Stories.

Paradise. Boston & NY: Houghton, Mifflin, 1905. Novel.

The Court of Love. Boston & NY: Houghton, Mifflin, 1906. Novel.

The County Road. Boston & NY: Houghton, Mifflin, 1906. Stories.

Rose MacLeod. Boston & NY: Houghton, Mifflin, 1908. Novel.

The Story of Thyrza. Boston & NY: Houghton Mifflin, 1909. Novel.

Country Neighbors. Boston & NY: Houghton Mifflin, 1910. Stories.

John Winterbourne's Family. Boston & NY: Houghton Mifflin, 1910. Novel.

The One-Footed Fairy and Other Stories. Boston & NY: Houghton Mifflin, 1911.

My Love and I (as by Martin Redfield). NY: Macmillan, 1912. Novel.

The Secret of the Clan. NY: Macmillan, 1912. Novel.

Vanishing Points. NY: Macmillan, 1913. Stories.

Robin Hood's Barn. NY: Macmillan, 1913. Novel.

Joint Owners in Spain: A Comedy in One Act. Chicago: Chicago Little Theatre, 1914.

Children of Earth: A Play of New England. NY: Macmillan, 1915.

The Prisoner. NY: Macmillan, 1916. Novel.

Bromley Neighborhood. NY: Macmillan, 1917. Novel.

The Flying Teuton and Other Stories. NY: Macmillan, 1918.

The Loving Cup: A Play in One Act. Boston: Baker, 1918.

The Black Drop. NY: Macmillan, 1919. Novel.

The Buckets in the Sea. Boston: Massachusetts Charitable Eye & Ear Infirmary, 1920. Story.

The Wind Between the Worlds. NY: Macmillan, 1920. Novel.

Homespun and Gold. NY: Macmillan, 1920. Stories.

Louise Imogen Guiney. NY: Macmillan, 1921. Biography.

One Act Plays. NY: Macmillan, 1921.

Old Crow. NY: Macmillan, 1922. Novel.

Louise Imogen Guiney: Appreciations by AB and Robert Haven Schauffler. . . . London: Macmillan, 1923.

Ellen Prior. NY: Macmillan, 1923. Poetry.

Charles Lamb: A Play. NY: Macmillan, 1924.

The Mysteries of Ann. NY: Macmillan, 1925. Novel.

Dear Old Templeton. NY: Macmillan, 1927. Novel.

The Golden Ball. NY: Macmillan, 1929. Play.

The Marriage Feast: A Fantasy. NY: Macmillan, 1931. Play.

The Kingdom in the Sky. NY: Macmillan, 1932. Novel.

The Diary of a Dryad. Boston: npub, 1932. Novel.

Jeremy Hamlin. NY & London: Appleton-Century, 1934. Novel.

The Willoughbys. NY & London: Appleton-Century, 1935. Novel.

Fable and Song. Boston: npub, 1939. Poetry.

Pilgrim's Progress: A Play. Boston: Privately printed, 1944.

OTHER

"Agnes Surriage." *Three Heroines of New England Romance* (Boston: Little, Brown, 1894), 63-105. Biography.

"Peggy." *The Whole Family: A Novel by Twelve Authors* (NY & London: Harper, 1908), 264-292.

"Harriet Eliza Paine." *Old People* by Paine (Boston & NY: Houghton Mifflin, 1910), ix-xxxii. Introduction.

MANUSCRIPTS & ARCHIVES

The major collections are at the Beinecke Library, Yale U; the Houghton Library, Harvard U; & C of the Holy Cross Library.

CRITICAL STUDIES

Books

Langill, Ellen Detering. "AB: A Critical Study." Dissertation: U Wisconsin, Madison, 1975.

Walker, Dorothea. *AB.* NY: Twayne, 1974.

Book Section & Articles

Fisken, Beth Wynne. "Within the Limits of AB's 'Dooryards': Introspective Powers in *Tiverton Tales.*" *Legacy,* 5 (Spring 1988), 15-25.

Thompson, Charles Miner. "The Short Stories of AB." *Atlantic,* 98 (Jul 1906), 55-65.

Toth, Susan Allen. "AB (1857-1948)." *ALR,* 5 (Spring 1972), 134-143.

Toth. "A Forgotten View From Beacon Hill: AB's New England Short Stories." *CLQ,* 10 (Mar 1973), 1-17.

Westbrook, Perry D. "An Armory of Powers: The Countryside of Sarah Orne Jewett and AB." *Acres of Flint: Sarah Orne Jewett and Her Contemporaries* (Metuchen, NJ: Scarecrow, rev 1981), 71-77.

Philip B. Eppard

CHARLES FARRAR BROWNE
(Artemus Ward)
Waterford, Maine, 26 Apr 1834-Southampton, England, 6 Mar 1867

Charles Farrar Browne towered among American comic writers throughout the Civil War years and just afterward, his travels and publications abroad earning international prestige for American "cracker-barrel" humor. Mark Twain eventually surpassed him in the use of a homespun dialect voice, in the cultivation of deadpan comic delivery, in satirical bite, and in the burlesque of pretentious literary forms; but Browne pioneered in developing techniques and mannerisms that Mark Twain refined. Although Browne is not widely read today, his place in American cultural history seems secure. His use of comically perverse orthography, his social criticism, his oblique projection of attitudes and themes through a folksy, semiliterate alter ego—Artemus Ward—and his influence on Mark Twain have been explored with special interest by modern critics.

BIBLIOGRAPHIES

Austin, James C. "CFB (1834-1867, Pseud. Artemus Ward)." *ALR, 5* (Spring 1972), 151-165. Secondary.
Bibliography of American Literature, comp Jacob Blanck. New Haven: Yale U P, 1955-1991. Primary.
Davidson, Janice G. "An Updated List of CFB's ('Artemus Ward's') *Plain Dealer* Journalism, 1857-1860." *BB,* 33 (Jan 1976), 24-31. Primary.
"Selected Bibliography." Pullen, 187-197. Primary & secondary.

BOOKS

Artemus Ward: His Book. . . . NY: Carleton, 1862. Sketches.
Artemus Ward: His Travels. . . . NY: Carleton / London: Low, 1865. Augmented as *Artemus Ward (His Travels) Among the Mormons.* . . . London: Hotten, 1865. Sketches.
Artemus Ward Among the Fenians. . . . London: Hotten, 1866. Essays & sketches.
Artemus Ward in London, and Other Papers. NY: Carleton / London: Low, 1867. Sketches.

Artemus Ward's Lecture. . . , ed T W Robertson & E P Hingston. London: Hotten / NY: Carleton, 1869; *Artemus Ward's Panorama.* . . . NY: Carleton / London: Hotten, 1869.

LETTERS

Letters of Artemus Ward to Charles E. Wilson, 1858-1861. Cleveland: Rowfant Club, 1900.

EDITION

The Complete Works of CFB, Better Known as "Artemus Ward." London: Hotten, 1871. Rev as *The Complete Works of Artemus Ward (CFB).* NY: Dillingham, 1898.

BIOGRAPHIES
Books
Hingston, Edward P. *The Genial Showman.* NY: Harper, 1870.
Pullen, John J. *Comic Relief: The Life and Laughter of Artemus Ward, 1834-1867.* Hamden, Conn: Archon, 1983.
Seitz, Don C. *Artemus Ward (CFB): A Biography and Bibliography.* NY: Harper, 1919.

Book Sections & Articles
Fatout, Paul. "Artemus Ward Among the Mormons." *WHR,* 14 (Spring 1960), 193-199.
Fatout. *Mark Twain on the Lecture Circuit* (Bloomington: Indiana U P, 1960), passim.
Fatout. *Mark Twain in Virginia City* (Bloomington: Indiana U P, 1964), passim.
Jaynes, Bryson L. "Artemus Ward Among the Mormons." *ResearchS,* 25 (Mar 1957), 75-84.
Landon, Melville D. "Artemus Ward: Biography and Reminiscences." *Wise, Witty, Eloquent Kings of the Platform and Pulpit* (Chicago: Werner, 1895), 19-33.
McKee, Irving. "Artemus Ward in California and Nevada, 1863-1864." *PacHR,* 20 (Feb 1951), 11-23.
Richmond, Robert W. "Humorist on Tour: Artemus Ward in Mid-America, 1864." *KHQ,* 33 (Winter 1967), 470-480.
Ryder, James F. "Artemus Ward." *Voigtländer and I* (Cleveland: Cleveland Printing & Publish-

ing/Imperial, 1902), 174-207.

Sandburg, Carl. *Abraham Lincoln: The War Years* (NY: Harcourt, Brace, 1939), passim.

Shaw, Archer H. "Artemus Ward." *The Plain Dealer: One Hundred Years in Cleveland* (NY: Knopf, 1942), 62-72.

Watterson, Henry. "Looking Backward." *SatEP,* 191 (22 Mar 1919), 18-19, 45.

Winter, William. "Old Familiar Faces." *Old Friends* (NY: Moffat, 1909), 284-291.

CRITICAL STUDIES

Books

Austin, James C. *Artemus Ward.* NY: Twayne, 1964.

Reed, John Q. "Artemus Ward: A Critical Study." Dissertation: State U Iowa, 1955.

Book Sections & Articles

Blair, Walter. "Burlesques in Nineteenth-Century Humor." *AL,* 2 (Nov 1930), 236-247.

Blair. *Native American Humor, 1800-1900* (NY: American Book, 1937), passim.

Branch, Edgar M. " 'The Babes in the Wood': Artemus Ward's 'Double Health' to Mark Twain." *PMLA,* 93 (Oct 1978), 955-972.

Clemens, Cyril. "A Convert Humorist." *America,* 67 (26 Sep 1942), 689-690.

Cracroft, Richard H. " 'Ten Wives Is All You Need': Artemus Twain and the Mormons—Again." *WHR,* 38 (Autumn 1984), 197-211.

Dahl, Curtis. "Artemus Ward: Comic Panoramist." *NEQ,* 32 (Dec 1959), 476-485.

De Voto, Bernard. *Mark Twain's America* (Boston: Little, Brown, 1932), passim.

Dutcher, Salem. "Bill Arp and Artemus Ward." *Scott's,* 1-2 (Jun 1866), 472-478.

Eastman, Max. *Enjoyment of Laughter* (NY: Simon & Schuster, 1936), passim.

Estrich, Robert M & Hans Sperber. "Humor in Language." *Three Keys to Language* (NY: Rinehart, 1952), 276-309.

Howe, M A DeWolfe. *American Bookmen* (NY: Dodd, Mead, 1902), 163-171.

Kesterson, David B. "The Literary Comedians and the Language of Humor." *StAH,* ns 1 (Jun 1982), 44-51.

Lorch, Fred W. "Mark Twain's 'Artemus Ward' Lecture on the Tour of 1871-1872." *NEQ,* 25 (Sep 1952), 327-343.

McManus, Kirk. "Artemus Ward: The Legend." *Performance of Literature in Historical Perspectives,* ed David W Thompson (Lanham, Md: U P America, 1983), 683-686.

Nock, Albert J. "Artemus Ward's America." *Atlantic,* 154 (Sep 1934), 273-281.

Rodgers, Paul C, Jr. "Artemus Ward and Mark Twain's 'Jumping Frog.' " *NCF,* 28 (Dec 1973), 273-286.

Rowlette, Robert. " 'Mark Ward on Artemus Twain': Twain's Literary Debt to Ward." *ALR,* 6 (Winter 1973), 13-25.

Tandy, Jennette. "The Funny Men: Artemus Ward and Josh Billings." *Crackerbox Philosophers in American Humor and Satire* (NY: Columbia U P, 1925), 132-157.

Williams, Stanley T. "Artemus the Delicious." *VQR,* 28 (Spring 1952), 214-227.

Robert E. Abrams

H. C. BUNNER

Oswego, NY, 3 Aug 1855-Nutley, NJ, 11 May 1896

One of the minor humorists of the late nineteenth century, Henry Cuyler Bunner, editor of the New York newspaper *Puck: The Comic Weekly,* is all but forgotten today. Modeling his fiction on the tightly structured "contes" of Guy de Maupassant, Bunner wrote frequently of the obstacles hampering young lovers before and after marriage. A strong sentimental strain, a persistent element of optimistic romanticism in the face of adversity, pervades his work. Satire and parody are also found throughout his writings. In addition, Bunner—deeply conscious of his Dutch ancestry in his native region—wrote expressively of the topography of New York City and its environs.

BIBLIOGRAPHY

Bibliography of American Literature, comp Jacob Blanck. New Haven: Yale U P, 1955-1991. Primary.

BOOKS

A Woman of Honor. Boston: Osgood, 1883. Novel.
Airs From Arcady and Elsewhere. NY: Scribners, 1884. Poetry.
In Partnership: Studies in Story-Telling, with Brander Matthews. NY: Scribners, 1884. Criticism & stories.
The Midge. NY: Scribners, 1886. Novella.
The Story of a New York House. NY: Scribners, 1887. Essays.
"Short Sixes": Stories to Be Read While the Candle Burns. NY: Keppler & Schwarzmann, 1891.
Zadoc Pine and Other Stories. NY: Scribners, 1891.
The Runaway Browns: A Story of Small Stories. NY: Keppler & Schwarzmann, 1892.
Rowen: "Second Crop" Songs. NY: Scribners, 1892.
"Made in France": French Tales Retold With a United States Twist. NY: Keppler & Schwarzmann, 1893.
More "Short Sixes." NY: Keppler & Schwarzmann, 1894. Stories.
Jersey Street and Jersey Lane: Urban and Suburban Sketches. NY: Scribners, 1896.

The Suburban Sage: Stray Notes and Comments on His Simple Life. NY: Keppler & Schwarzmann, 1896. Sketches.
Love in Old Cloathes and Other Stories. NY: Scribners, 1896.
The Poems of HCB. NY: Scribners, 1896. Augmented ed, 1897. Augmented again, 1917.
Three Operettas, librettos by HCB, music by Oscar Weil. NY: Harper, 1897.
Our Girls: Poems in Praise of the American Girl. NY: Moffatt, Yard, 1907.

OTHER

Puck: The Comic Weekly (1878-1896), ed HCB.

COLLECTIONS

The Stories of HCB, First Series. NY: Scribners, 1916.
The Stories of HCB, Second Series. NY: Scribners, 1916.
The Stories of HCB: "Short Sixes." NY: Scribners, 1917.
The Stories of HCB: More "Short Sixes," The Runaway Browns. NY: Scribners, 1917.

MANUSCRIPTS & ARCHIVES

The major collections are at the Huntington Library, San Marino, Calif; Columbia U Library; & U of Virginia Library.

BIOGRAPHY

Book
Jensen, Gerard E. *The Life and Letters of HCB.* Durham, NC: Duke U P, 1939.

CRITICAL STUDIES

Book Sections & Articles
Bellman, Samuel I. "Riding on Wishes: Ritual Make-Believe Patterns in Three 19th-Century American Authors: Aldrich, Hale, B." *Ritual in the United States,* ed Don Harkness (Tampa, Fla: American Studies, 1985), 15-20.
Hutton, Laurence. "HCB." *Bookman,* 3 (Jul 1896), 398-402.
Matthews, Brander. "The Uncollected Poems of HCB." *Bookman,* 3 (Aug 1896), 512-516. Rpt *Recreations of an Anthologist* by

Matthews (NY: Dodd, Mead, 1904). Rpt *Bookman,* 43 (Jul 1916), 474-480.

Matthews. "HCB." *Scribner's,* 20 (Sep 1896), 287-294. Rpt *The Historical Novel and Other Essays* by Matthews (NY: Scribners, 1901).

Paine, H G. "HCB as Editor and Story-Writer." *Critic,* ns 25 (23 May 1896), 363.

Parry, Albert. *Garrets and Pretenders: A History of Bohemianism in America* (NY: Dover, rev 1960), passim.

Stronks, James B. "Frank Norris's *McTeague:* A Possible Source in HCB." *NCF,* 25 (Mar 1971), 474-478.

Wells, Benjamin W. "HCB." *SR,* 5 (Jan 1897), 17-32.

Samuel I. Bellman

THORNTON W. BURGESS

Sandwich, Mass, 14 Jan 1874-Hampden, Mass, 5 Jun 1965

A prolific writer of nature stories for children, Thornton W. Burgess published nearly one hundred books during his long career and for forty-four years wrote a daily bedtime-story column for the Associated Newspapers and the New York Herald Tribune syndicates. By his own account Burgess wrote to entertain, to teach nature lore, and to offer moral guidance to his young audience. He viewed his animal characters through an anthropomorphic filter: they operate in a realm at once natural and infused with a human moral code. The formulaic recipe for his tales won him many devoted child readers but little critical attention. A serious conservationist, he used his published works, radio broadcasts, and public lectures to describe the denizens of the Green Meadow, the Laughing Brook, and the Smiling Pool. During the fifty years that he collaborated with his illustrator, Harrison Cady, their books sold more than eight million copies.

BIBLIOGRAPHY

Rahn, Suzanne. "TWB." *Children's Literature: An Annotated Bibliography of the History and Criticism* (NY: Garland, 1981), 182-184. Secondary.

BOOKS

The Bride's Primer, with others. NY: Phelps, 1905. Essays.

Old Mother West Wind. Boston: Little, Brown, 1910. Children's stories.

Mother West Wind's Children. Boston: Little, Brown, 1911. Children's stories.

The Boy Scouts of Woodcraft Camp. Philadelphia: Penn, 1912. Children's novel.

Mother West Wind's Animal Friends. Boston: Little, Brown, 1912. Children's stories.

The Adventures of Johnny Chuck. Boston: Little, Brown, 1913. Children's novel.

The Adventures of Reddy Fox. Boston: Little, Brown, 1913. Children's novel.

The Boy Scouts on Swift River. Philadelphia: Penn, 1913. Children's novel.

Mother West Wind's Neighbors. Boston: Little, Brown, 1913. Children's stories.

The Adventures of Jerry Muskrat. Boston: Little, Brown, 1914. Children's novel.

The Adventures of Mr. Mocker. Boston: Little, Brown, 1914. Children's novel.

The Adventures of Peter Cottontail. Boston: Little, Brown, 1914. Children's novel.

The Adventures of Unc' Billy Possum. Boston: Little, Brown, 1914. Children's novel.

The Boy Scouts on Lost Trail. Philadelphia: Penn, 1914. Children's novel.

The Adventures of Chatterer the Red Squirrel. Boston: Little, Brown, 1915. Children's novel.

The Adventures of Danny Meadow Mouse. Boston: Little, Brown, 1915. Children's novel.

The Adventures of Grandfather Frog. Boston: Little, Brown, 1915. Children's novel.

The Adventures of Sammy Jay. Boston: Little, Brown, 1915. Children's novel.

The Boy Scouts in a Trapper's Camp. Philadelphia: Penn, 1915. Children's novel.

Mother West Wind "Why" Stories. Boston: Little, Brown, 1915.

Tommy and the Wishing Stone. NY: Century, 1915. Children's stories.

The Adventures of Buster Bear. Boston: Little, Brown, 1916. Children's novel.

The Adventures of Old Man Coyote. Boston: Little, Brown, 1916. Children's novel.

The Adventures of Old Mr. Toad. Boston: Little, Brown, 1916. Children's novel.

The Adventures of Prickly Porky. Boston: Little, Brown, 1916. Children's novel.

Mother West Wind "How" Stories. Boston: Little, Brown, 1916.

The Adventures of Paddy the Beaver. Boston: Little, Brown, 1917. Children's novel.

The Adventures of Poor Mrs. Quack. Boston: Little, Brown, 1917. Children's novel.

Mother West Wind "When" Stories. Boston: Little, Brown, 1917.

The Adventures of Bobby Coon. Boston: Little, Brown, 1918. Children's novel.

The Adventures of Jimmy Skunk. Boston: Little, Brown, 1918. Children's novel.

Happy Jack. Boston: Little, Brown, 1918. Children's story.

Mother West Wind "Where" Stories. Boston: Little, Brown, 1918.

The Adventures of Bob White. Boston: Little, Brown, 1919. Children's novel.

The Adventures of Ol' Mistah Buzzard. Boston: Little, Brown, 1919. Children's novel.

The Burgess Bird Book for Children. Boston: Little, Brown, 1919. Abridged as *The Little Burgess Bird Book for Children.* Chicago: Rand McNally, 1941. Stories.

Mrs. Peter Rabbit. Boston: Little, Brown, 1919. Children's novel.

Bowser the Hound. Boston: Little, Brown, 1920. Children's novel.

The Burgess Animal Book for Children. Boston: Little, Brown, 1920. Abridged as *The Little Burgess Animal Book for Children.* Chicago: Rand McNally, 1941. Stories.

Old Granny Fox. Boston: Little, Brown, 1920. Children's novel.

Lightfoot the Deer. Boston: Little, Brown, 1921. Children's novel.

Tommy's Change of Heart. Boston: Little, Brown, 1921. Children's stories.

Tommy's Wishes Come True. Boston: Little, Brown, 1921. Children's stories.

Blacky the Crow. Boston: Little, Brown, 1922. Children's novel.

Whitefoot the Wood Mouse. Boston: Little, Brown, 1922. Children's novel.

The Burgess Flower Book for Children. Boston: Little, Brown, 1923.

Buster Bear's Twins. Boston: Little, Brown, 1923. Children's novel.

Billy Mink. Boston: Little, Brown, 1924. Children's novel.

Little Joe Otter. Boston: Little, Brown, 1925. Children's novel.

The Christmas Reindeer. NY: Macmillan, 1926. Children's story.

Jerry Muskrat at Home. Boston: Little, Brown, 1926. Children's story.

Cubby Bear Has a Mind of His Own. Racine, Wis: Whitman, 1927. Children's story.

Longlegs the Heron. Boston: Little, Brown, 1927. Children's novel.

Baby Possum's Queer Voyage. NY: Stoll & Edwards, 1928. Children's story.

Digger the Badger Decides to Stay. NY: Stoll & Edwards, 1928. Children's story.

Grandfather Frog Fools Farmer Brown's Boy. NY: Eggers, 1928. Children's story.

Grandfather Frog Gets a Ride. NY: Stoll & Edwards, 1928. Children's story.

A Great Joke on Jimmy Skunk. NY: Stoll & Edwards, 1928. Children's story.

Happy Jack Squirrel Helps Unc' Billy. NY: Stoll & Edwards, 1928. Children's story.

The Neatness of Bobby Coon. NY: Stoll & Edwards, 1928. Children's story.

Peter Rabbit Learns to Use His New Coat. NY: Eggers, 1928. Children's story.

The Burgess Seashore Book for Children. Boston: Little, Brown, 1929.

Wild Flowers We Know. Racine, Wis: Whitman, 1929.

The Burgess Big Book of Green Meadow Stories. Boston: Little, Brown, 1932.

Birds You Should Know. Boston: Little, Brown, 1933.

The Wishing-Stone Stories. Boston: Little, Brown, 1935.

The Book of Animal Life, with Thora Stowell. Boston: Little, Brown, 1937.

Tales From the Storyteller's House. Boston: Little, Brown, 1937.

While the Story-Log Burns. Boston: Little, Brown, 1938.

Bobby Coon's Mistake. NY: Platt & Munk, 1940. Children's story.

Paddy's Surprise Visitor. NY: Platt & Munk, 1940. Children's story.

Peter Rabbit Proves a Friend. NY: Platt & Munk, 1940. Children's story.

Reddy Fox's Sudden Engagement. NY: Platt & Munk, 1940. Children's story.

A Robber Meets His Match. NY: Platt & Munk, 1940. Children's story.

The Three Little Bears. NY: Platt & Munk, 1940. Children's story.

Young Flash the Deer. NY: Platt & Munk, 1940. Children's story.

Little Pete's Adventure. Springfield, Mass: McLoughlin, 1941. Children's story.

Animal Stories. NY: Platt & Munk, 1942. Repub as *The Animal World of TB,* 1961.

Little Chuck's Adventure. Springfield, Mass: McLoughlin, 1942. Children's story.

Little Red's Adventure. Springfield, Mass: McLoughlin, 1942. Children's story.

On the Green Meadows: A Book of Nature Stories. Boston: Little, Brown, 1944.

At the Smiling Pool: A Book of Nature Stories. Boston: Little, Brown, 1945.

The Crooked Little Path: A Book of Nature Stories. Boston: Little, Brown, 1946.

The Dear Old Briar-Patch: A Book of Nature Stories. Boston: Little, Brown, 1947.

Along Laughing Brook: A Book of Nature Stories. Boston: Little, Brown, 1949.

Baby Animal Stories. NY: Grosset & Dunlap, 1949.

Nature Almanac. NY: Grosset & Dunlap, 1949.

At Paddy the Beaver's Pond: A Book of Nature Stories. Boston: Little, Brown, 1950.

A TB Picture Story Book. Garden City, NY: Garden City Publishing, 1950.

The Littlest Christmas Tree. NY: Wonder Books, 1954. Children's story.

Peter Rabbit and Reddy Fox. NY: Wonder Books, 1954. Children's story.

Aunt Sally's Friends in Fur; or, The Woodhouse Night Club. Boston & Toronto: Little, Brown, 1955. Pictorial essay.

Now I Remember: Autobiography of an Amateur Naturalist. Boston & Toronto: Little, Brown, 1960.

The Million Little Sunbeams. Toledo, Ohio: Six Oaks, 1963. Story.

COLLECTIONS

Stories Around the Year. NY: Grosset & Dunlap, 1955.

50 Favorite Burgess Stories: On the Green Meadows and the Crooked Little Path. NY: Grosset & Dunlap, 1956.

Bedtime Stories. NY: Grosset & Dunlap, 1959.

The Burgess Book of Nature Lore: Adventures of Tommy, Sue, and Sammy With Their Friends of Meadow, Pool, and Forest. Boston & Toronto: Little, Brown, 1965.

BIOGRAPHIES

Book

Lovell, Russell A, Jr. *The Cape Cod Story of TWB.* Taunton, Mass: Town of Sandwich, TWB Centennial Committee 1874-1974/Sullwold, nd.

Book Section & Articles

Bryan, J. "Mother Nature's Brother." *The Saturday Review Gallery,* ed Jerome Beatty, Jr & the editors of *The Saturday Review* (NY: Simon & Schuster, 1959), 338-344.

Fox, Dorothea Magdalene. "A 90-Year Romance With Nature." *AudM,* 66 (Sep-Oct 1964), 312-313.

Levine, Louis. "Unforgettable TWB." *RDi,* 91 (Oct 1967), 100-105.

O'Neil, Paul. "Fifty Years in the Green Meadow." *Life,* 49 (14 Nov 1960), 112-114, 117-118, 120-121, 124.

Saltford, Herb. "A Man, His Dream, and a Happy Ending." *Yankee,* 37 (Jun 1973), 94.

Lucien L. Agosta

FRANCES HODGSON BURNETT

Manchester, England, 24 Nov 1849-Long Island, NY, 29 Oct 1924

Frances Hodgson Burnett began her career as a novelist for adults, but the publication of *Little Lord Fauntleroy* in 1886 secured her reputation as a writer for children. The book, about a young boy of modest beginnings who inherits an earldom, was one of the biggest sellers of all time. In 1887 Burnett published *Sara Crewe,* a novel for children, which was soon after produced as a play. Because of the play's success, Burnett's editors urged her to extend the original novel, incorporating the new dramatic material. In 1905 the expanded version was published as *A Little Princess,* which proved extremely popular. Burnett's most enduring work, *The Secret Garden,* appeared in 1911 and has never gone out of print.

BIBLIOGRAPHY

Bibliography of American Literature, comp Jacob Blanck. New Haven: Yale U P, 1955-1991. Primary.

BOOKS

That Lass o' Lowrie's. NY: Scribner, Armstrong, 1877. Novel.

"Theo": A Love Story. Philadelphia: Peterson, 1877. Rev ed, NY: Scribners, 1879. Novel.

Surly Tim and Other Stories. NY: Scribner, Armstrong, 1877.

Dolly: A Love Story. Philadelphia: Porter & Coates, 1877. Rev as *Vagabondia: A Love Story.* Boston: Osgood, 1884. Novel.

Pretty Polly Pemberton: A Love Story. . . . Philadelphia: Peterson, 1877. Stories.

Kathleen: A Love Story. . . . Philadelphia: Peterson, 1878. Rev as *Kathleen Mavourneen.* NY: Scribners, 1878. Stories.

Our Neighbour Opposite. London: Routledge, 1878. Stories.

Miss Crespigny: A Love Story. . . . Philadelphia: Peterson, 1878. Rev ed, NY: Scribners, 1879. Stories.

A Quiet Life; and The Tide on the Moaning Bar. . . . Philadelphia: Peterson, 1878. Stories.

Lindsay's Luck. NY: Scribners, 1878. Stories.

Jarl's Daughter; and Other Stories. . . . Philadelphia: Peterson, 1879.

Natalie and Other Stories. London: Warne, 1879.

Haworth's. NY: Scribners, 1879. Novel.

Louisiana. NY: Scribners, 1880. Repub with *That Lass o' Lowrie's.* London: Macmillan, 1880. Novel.

A Fair Barbarian. Boston: Osgood, 1881. Novel.

Esmeralda. . . , with William H Gillette. NY: npub, 1881. Play.

Through One Administration. Boston: Osgood, 1883. Novel.

Little Lord Fauntleroy. NY: Scribners, 1886. Children's novel.

A Woman's Will or Miss Defarge. London: Warne, 1886. Repub with *Brueton's Bayou* by John Habberton. Philadelphia: Lippincott, 1888. Novel.

Sara Crewe or What Happened at Miss Minchin's. NY: Scribners, 1888. Augmented as *Sara Crewe; or, What Happened at Miss Minchin's: and Editha's Burglar.* London & NY: Warne, 1888. *Editha's Burglar* separately published, Boston: Jordan, Marsh, 1888. Children's novel.

The Fortunes of Philippa Fairfax. London: Warne, 1888. Novel.

The Pretty Sister of José. NY: Scribners, 1889. Novel.

Little Lord Fauntleroy, a Drama in Three Acts Founded on the Story of the Same Name by FHB. NY: French, 1889.

Little Saint Elizabeth and Other Stories. NY: Scribners, 1890. Children's stories.

Children I Have Known and Giovanni and the Other. London: Osgood, McIlvaine, 1892; *Giovanni and the Other: Children Who Have Made Stories.* NY: Scribners, 1892. Children's stories.

The Drury Lane Boys' Club. Washington: "The Moon," 1892.

The One I Knew the Best of All: A Memory of the Mind of a Child. NY: Scribners, 1893. Autobiography.

Piccino and Other Child Stories. NY: Scribners, 1894; *The Captain's Youngest Piccino and Other Child Stories.* London: Warne, 1894.

Two Little Pilgrims' Progress: A Story of the City Beautiful. NY: Scribners, 1895. Children's novel.

A Lady of Quality. . . . NY: Scribners, 1896. Novel.

His Grace of Osmonde. . . . NY: Scribners, 1897. Novel.

In Connection With the De Willoughby Claim. NY: Scribners, 1899. Novel.

The Making of a Marchioness. NY: Stokes, 1901. Repub with *The Methods of Lady Walderhurst* in *Emily Fox-Seton. . . .* NY: Stokes, 1909. Novel.

The Methods of Lady Walderhurst. NY: Stokes, 1901. Repub with *The Making of a Marchioness* in *Emily Fox-Seton. . . .* NY: Stokes, 1909. Novel.

In the Closed Room. NY: McClure, Phillips, 1904. Novel.

A Little Princess, Being the Whole Story of Sara Crewe Now Told for the First Time. NY: Scribners, 1905. Substantially revised version of *Sara Crewe.* Children's novel.

The Dawn of a To-morrow. NY: Scribners, 1906. Novel.

Queen Silver-Bell. NY: Century, 1906; *The Troubles of Queen Silver-Bell.* London: Warne, 1907. Children's novel.

Racketty-Packetty House. NY: Century, 1906. Children's novel.

The Cozy Lion, as Told by Queen Crosspatch. NY: Century, 1907. Children's novel.

The Shuttle. NY: Stokes, 1907. Novel.

The Good Wolf. NY: Moffat, Yard, 1908. Children's novel.

The Spring Cleaning, as Told by Queen Crosspatch. NY: Century, 1908. Children's novel.

The Land of the Blue Flower. NY: Moffat, Yard, 1909. Children's novel.

Barty Crusoe and His Man Saturday. NY: Moffat, Yard, 1909. Children's novel.

The Little Princess, a Play for Children and Grown-up Children in Three Acts. NY & London: French, 1911.

The Secret Garden. NY: Stokes, 1911. Children's novel.

My Robin. NY: Stokes, 1912. Novel.

T. Tembarom. NY: Century, 1913. Novel.

The Lost Prince. NY: Century, 1915. Children's novel.

The Little Hunchback Zia. NY: Stokes, 1916. Children's novel.

The Way to the House of Santa Claus: A Christmas Story. . . . NY & London: Harper, 1916. Children's story.

The White People. NY & London: Harper, 1917. Novel.

The Head of the House of Coombe. NY: Stokes, 1922. Novel.

Robin. NY: Stokes, 1922. Novel.

In the Garden. Boston & NY: Medici Society of America, 1925.

Racketty-Packetty House: A Play in Prologue and Three Acts. Boston: npub, 1926.

OTHER

The Children's Book, ed FHB. NY: Moffat, Yard, 1909. Augmented as *Once Upon a Time: Stories-Jingles-Rhymes.* NY: Cupples & Leon, 1915.

COLLECTIONS

Earlier Stories, First Series. NY: Scribners, 1891.
Earlier Stories, Second Series. NY: Scribners, 1891.

MANUSCRIPTS & ARCHIVES

U of Virginia Library.

BIOGRAPHIES

Books

Burnett, Constance Buel. *Happily Ever After: A Portrait of FHB.* NY: Vanguard, 1965.

Burnett, Vivian. *The Romantick Lady (FHB): The Life Story of an Imagination.* NY: Scribners, 1927.

Laski, Marghanita. *Mrs. Ewing, Mrs. Molesworth, and Mrs. HB.* London: Barker, 1950.

Thwaite, Ann. *Waiting for the Party: The Life of FHB, 1849-1924.* NY: Scribners, 1974.

CRITICAL STUDIES

Book Sections & Articles

Adams, Gillian. "Secrets and Healing Magic in *The Secret Garden.*" *Triumphs of the Spirit in Children's Literature,* ed Francelia Butler & Richard Rotert (Hamden, Conn: Library Professional Publications, 1986), 42-54.

Bedard, Roger L. "Sara, Jack, Ellie: Three Generations of Characters." *CLAQ,* 9 (Fall 1984), 103-104.

Bixler, Phyllis. "Idealization of the Child and Childhood in FHB's *Little Lord Fauntleroy* and Mark Twain's *Tom Sawyer.*" *Research About Nineteenth-Century Children and Books,* ed Selma K Richardson (Urbana-Champaign: U Illinois Graduate School of Library Science, 1980), 85-96.

Bixler. "The Oral-Formulaic Training of a Popular Fiction Writer: FHB." *JPC,* 15 (Spring 1982), 42-52.

Bixler. "Continuity and Change in Popular Entertainment." *Children's Novels and Movies,* ed Douglas Street (NY: Ungar, 1983), 69-80.

Downs, Robert Bingham. "Mother's Darling: FHB's *Little Lord Fauntleroy.*" *Famous American Books* (NY: McGraw-Hill, 1971), 172-177.

Keyser, Elizabeth Lennox. "Quite Contrary: FHB's *The Secret Garden.*" *ChildL,* 11 (1983), 1-13.

Keyser. " 'The Whole of the Story': FHB's *A Little Princess.*" *Triumphs of the Spirit in Children's Literature,* ed Francelia Butler & Richard

Rotert (Hamden, Conn: Library Professional Publications, 1986), 230-245.

Knoepflmacher, U C. "Little Girls Without Their Curls: Female Aggression in Victorian Children's Literature." *ChildL,* 11 (1983), 14-31.

Marquis, Claudia. "The Power of Speech: Life in *The Secret Garden.*" *AUMLA,* 68 (Nov 1987), 163-187.

Maurice, Arthur Bartlett. "FHB's *Little Lord Fauntleroy.*" *Bookman,* 34 (Sep 1911), 35-45.

McCarthy, Tom. "The Real Little Lord Fauntleroy." *AH,* 21 (Feb 1970), 50-55, 82-85.

McGillis, Roderick. " 'Secrets' and 'Sequence' in Children's Stories." *SLitI,* 18 (Fall 1985), 35-46.

Molson, Francis J. "FHB (1848-1924)." *ALR,* 8 (Winter 1975), 35-41.

Molson. "Two Little Pilgrims' Progress: The 1893 Chicago Columbian Exposition as Celestial City." *MarkhamR,* 7 (Spring 1978), 55-59.

Nelson, James Malcolm. "The Stage Adaptation of *That Lass o' Lowrie's* and Mid-Victorian Plays of Factory and Mine." *DR,* 61 (Winter 1981-1982), 698-717.

Roxburgh, Stephen D. " 'Our First World': Form and Meaning in *The Secret Garden.*" *Proceedings of the Sixth Annual Conference of the Children's Literature Association, University of Toronto, March, 1979,* ed Priscilla A Ord (Villanova, Pa: Villanova U, 1980), 165-177.

Smedman, M Sarah. "Springs of Hope: Recovery of Primordial Time in 'Mythic' Novels for Young Readers." *ChildL,* 16 (1988), 91-107.

Takita, Yoshiko. "Wakamatsu Shizuko and *Little Lord Fauntleroy.*" *CLS,* 22 (Spring 1985), 1-8.

Wolf, Virginia L. "Psychology and Magic: Evocative Blend or a Melodramatic Patchwork." *Children's Novels and the Movies,* ed Douglas Street (NY: Ungar, 1983), 121-130.

Yaeger, Patricia. "Toward a Theory of Play." *Honey-Mad Women: Emancipatory Strategies in Women's Writing* (NY: Columbia U P, 1988), 207-238.

Sarah Zavelle Marwil Lamstein

EDGAR RICE BURROUGHS

Chicago, Ill, 1 Sep 1875-Encino, Calif, 19 Mar 1950

Edgar Rice Burroughs was one of the most popular writers of his time, and his works continue to sell well in paperback reprints today. A self-taught writer, Burroughs occupies an important place in the history of American science fiction; his tales of other times and worlds, especially those featuring John Carter of Mars, both characterized and shaped the genre during the early twentieth century. Burroughs's greatest achievement was the creation of the character Tarzan of the Apes, whose adventures thrilled readers and several generations of moviegoers. Critics have found little to admire in Burroughs's improbable, repetitious plots, but because of his popularity and influence as a genre writer, he remains a central figure in twentieth-century popular culture.

BIBLIOGRAPHIES

Day, Bradford M, ed. "ERB—A Bibliography." *Bibliography of Adventure* (NY: Arno, rev 1978), 91-125. Primary.

Heins, Henry Hardy, ed. *A Golden Anniversary Bibliography of ERB*. West Kingston, RI: Grant, rev 1964. Primary.

BOOKS

(This list omits republications of books under new titles.)

Tarzan of the Apes. Chicago: McClurg, 1914. Novel.

The Return of Tarzan. Chicago: McClurg, 1915. Novel.

The Beasts of Tarzan. Chicago: McClurg, 1916. Novel.

A Princess of Mars. Chicago: McClurg, 1917. Novel.

The Son of Tarzan. Chicago: McClurg, 1917. Novel.

The Gods of Mars. Chicago: McClurg, 1918. Novel.

Tarzan and the Jewels of Opar. Chicago: McClurg, 1918. Novel.

Jungle Tales of Tarzan. Chicago: McClurg, 1919. Stories.

The Warlord of Mars. Chicago: McClurg, 1919. Novel.

Tarzan the Untamed. Chicago: McClurg, 1920. Novel.

Thuvia, Maid of Mars. Chicago: McClurg, 1920. Novel.

Tarzan the Terrible. Chicago: McClurg, 1921. Novel.

The Mucker. Chicago: McClurg, 1921. Novel.

At the Earth's Core. Chicago: McClurg, 1922. Novel.

The Chessmen of Mars. Chicago: McClurg, 1922. Novel.

The Girl From Hollywood. NY: Macauley, 1923. Novel.

Pellucidar. Chicago: McClurg, 1923. Novel.

Tarzan and the Golden Lion. Chicago: McClurg, 1923. Novel.

The Land That Time Forgot. Chicago: McClurg, 1924. Novel.

Tarzan and the Ant Men. Chicago: McClurg, 1924. Novel.

The Bandit of Hell's Bend. Chicago: McClurg, 1925. Novel.

The Cave Girl. Chicago: McClurg, 1925. Novels.

The Eternal Lover. Chicago: McClurg, 1925. Novel.

The Mad King. Chicago: McClurg, 1926. Novel.

The Moon Maid. Chicago: McClurg, 1926. Novellas.

The Outlaw of Torn. Chicago: McClurg, 1927. Novel.

The Tarzan Twins. Joliet, Ill: Volland, 1927. Novel.

The War Chief. Chicago: McClurg, 1927. Novel.

The Master Mind of Mars. Chicago: McClurg, 1928. Novel.

Tarzan, Lord of the Jungle. Chicago: McClurg, 1928. Novel.

The Monster Men. Chicago: McClurg, 1929. Novel.

Tarzan and the Lost Empire. NY: Metropolitan, 1929. Novel.

Tanar of Pellucidar. NY: Metropolitan, 1930. Novel.

Tarzan at the Earth's Core. NY: Metropolitan, 1930. Novel.

Tarzan the Invincible. Tarzana, Calif: Burroughs, 1931. Novel.

A Fighting Man of Mars. NY: Metropolitan, 1931. Novel.

Jungle Girl. Tarzana, Calif: Burroughs, 1932. Novel.

Tarzan Triumphant. Tarzana, Calif: Burroughs, 1932. Novel.

Apache Devil. Tarzana, Calif: Burroughs, 1933. Novel.

Tarzan and the City of Gold. Tarzana, Calif: Burroughs, 1933. Novel.

Pirates of Venus. Tarzana, Calif: Burroughs, 1934. Novel.

Tarzan and the Lion Man. Tarzana, Calif: Burroughs, 1934. Novel.

Lost on Venus. Tarzana, Calif: Burroughs, 1935. Novel.

Tarzan and the Leopard Men. Tarzana, Calif: Burroughs, 1935. Novel.

Swords of Mars. Tarzana, Calif: Burroughs, 1936. Novel.

Tarzan and the Tarzan Twins, With Jad-bal-ja the Golden Lion. Racine, Wis: Whitman, 1936. Novel.

Tarzan's Quest. Tarzana, Calif: Burroughs, 1936. Novel.

Back to the Stone Age. Tarzana, Calif: Burroughs, 1937. Novel.

The Oakdale Affair & The Rider. Tarzana, Calif: Burroughs, 1937. Novels.

The Lad and the Lion. Tarzana, Calif: Burroughs, 1938. Novel.

Tarzan and the Forbidden City. Tarzana, Calif: Burroughs, 1938. Novel.

Carson of Venus. Tarzana, Calif: Burroughs, 1939. Novel.

Tarzan the Magnificent. Tarzana, Calif: Burroughs, 1939. Novels.

The Deputy Sheriff of Comanche County. Tarzana, Calif: Burroughs, 1940. Novel.

Synthetic Men of Mars. Tarzana, Calif: Burroughs, 1940. Novel.

Land of Terror. Tarzana, Calif: Burroughs, 1944. Novel.

Escape on Venus. Tarzana, Calif: Burroughs, 1946. Novel.

Tarzan and "The Foreign Legion." Tarzana, Calif: Burroughs, 1947. Novel.

Llana of Gathol. Tarzana, Calif: Burroughs, 1948. Stories.

Beyond Thirty & The Man-Eater. S. Ozone Park, NY: Science-Fiction & Fantasy, 1957. Novels.

Savage Pellucidar. NY: Canaveral, 1963. Stories.

Beyond the Farthest Star. NY: Ace, 1964. Novel.

John Carter of Mars. NY: Canaveral, 1964. Novels.

Tales of Three Planets. NY: Canaveral, 1964. Stories.

Tarzan and the Madman. NY: Canaveral, 1964. Novel.

Tarzan and the Castaways. NY: Canaveral, 1965. Stories.

The Girl From Farris's. Kansas City, Mo: House of Greystoke, 1965. Novel.

The Efficiency Expert. Kansas City, Mo: House of Greystoke, 1966. Novel.

I Am a Barbarian. Tarzana, Calif: Burroughs, 1967. Novel.

Pirate Blood. NY: Ace, 1970. Novel.

COLLECTIONS

Three Martian Novels. NY: Dover, 1962 (*Thuvia, Maid of Mars; The Chessmen of Mars; The Mastermind of Mars*).

At the Earth's Core, Pellucidar, Tanar of Pellucidar: Three Science Fiction Novels. NY: Dover, 1963.

MANUSCRIPTS & ARCHIVES

U of Louisville Library.

BIOGRAPHIES

Books

Fenton, Robert W. *The Big Swingers*. Englewood Cliffs, NJ: Prentice-Hall, 1967.

Porges, Irwin. *ERB: The Man Who Created Tarzan*, intro by Ray Bradbury. Provo, Utah: Brigham Young U P, 1975.

CRITICAL STUDIES

Books

Holtsmark, Erling B. *Tarzan and Tradition: Classical Myth in Popular Literature*. Westport, Conn: Greenwood, 1981.

Holtsmark. *ERB*. Boston: Twayne, 1986.

Lupoff, Richard A. *ERB: Master of Adventure*. NY: Canaveral, 1965.

Lupoff. *Barsoom: ERB and the Martian Vision*. Baltimore, Md: Mirage, 1976.

Roy, John Flint, comp. *A Guide to Barsoom*. NY: Ballantine, 1976.

Articles

Cowart, David. "The Tarzan Myth and Jung's Genesis of the Self." *JAmC*, 2 (Summer 1979), 220-230.

Fiedler, Leslie. "Lord of the Absolute Elsewhere." *NYTBR* (9 Jun 1974), 8-17.

Flautz, John T. "An American Demagogue in Barsoom." *JPC*, 1 (Winter 1967), 263-275.

Henighan, Tom. "Tarzan and Rima, the Myth and the Message." *RQ*, 3 (Mar 1969), 256-265.

Hollow, John. "Rereading *Tarzan of the Apes;* or, 'What is it,' Lady Alice whispered, 'a man?'" *DR*, 56 (Spring 1976), 83-92.

Kyle, Richard. "*Out of Time's Abyss:* The Martian Stories of ERB, a Speculation." *RQ*, 4 (Jan 1970), 110-122.

Mandel, Paul. "Tarzan of the Paperbacks." *Life,* 55 (29 Nov 1963), 11-12.

McGreal, Dorothy. "The Burroughs No One Knows." *WCA,* 1 (Fall 1966), 12-15.

Morsberger, Robert E. "ERB's Apache Epic." *JPC,* 7 (Fall 1973), 280-287.

Mullen, Richard D, the Elder. "ERB and the Fate Worse Than Death." *RQ,* 4 (Jun 1970), 186-191.

Romer, Margaret. "ERB, Creator of Tarzan." *Overland,* 92 (Mar 1934), 67, 70.

Slate, Tom. "ERB and the Heroic Epic." *RQ,* 3 (Mar 1968), 118-123.

Topping, Gary. "The Pastoral Ideal in Popular American Literature: Zane Grey and ERB." *Rendezvous,* 12 (Fall 1977), 11-25.

Vidal, Gore. "Tarzan Revisited." *Esquire,* 60 (Dec 1963), 192-193, 262, 264.

Watson, E H Lacon. " 'Tarzan' and Literature." *FR,* 114 (23 Jun 1923), 1035-1045.

William Marderness

JAMES BRANCH CABELL

Richmond, Va, 14 Apr 1879-Richmond, Va, 5 May 1958

James Branch Cabell's chief legacy is the eighteen volumes of what he called the Biography of the Life of Manuel into which was assimilated practically all of his pre-1930 writing. A fantasist who mined myth and folklore for the substance of his generally allegorical fictions, Cabell found himself at odds with practically every prevailing critical school during his long career. Briefly in the 1920s, as a result of the suppression of *Jurgen* at the instigation of the New York Society for the Suppression of Vice, Cabell enjoyed a period of national celebrity. His popularity passed with the passing of the 1920s, although he became something of a literary cult figure. At present, the judgment of Cabell's achievement remains divided between those who consider him a fabricator of pretentious little allegories and those who see him as a creator of a fabulous kingdom that can bear comparison with those of William Faulkner and Gabriel García Márquez.

BIBLIOGRAPHIES

Brewer, Frances Joan. *JBC: A Bibliography of His Writings, Biography and Criticism,* foreword by JBC. Charlottesville: U Virginia P, 1957. Primary & secondary.

Bruccoli, Matthew J. *JBC: A Bibliography, Pt. II: Notes on the C Collection at the University of Virginia.* Charlottesville: U Virginia P, 1957. Primary.

Duke, Maurice. *JBC: A Reference Guide.* Boston: Hall, 1979. Secondary.

First Printings of American Authors, Vol 2 (Detroit: Bruccoli Clark/Gale, 1978), 61-81. Primary.

Hall, James N. "The Biography of Manuel: A Brief Bibliography." *Kalki,* 2, no 1 (1968), 3-5. Primary.

Hall. *JBC: A Complete Bibliography.* NY: Revisionist, 1974. Primary & secondary.

Watson, Ritchie D, Jr. "JBC: A Bibliographical Essay." Inge & MacDonald, 142-179. Essay on secondary sources.

BOOKS

(Between 1932 and 1946 JBC's books were published under the name Branch Cabell.)

The Eagle's Shadow. NY: Doubleday, Page, 1904. Rev ed, NY: McBride, 1923. Novel.

The Line of Love. NY & London: Harper, 1905. Rev ed, NY: McBride, 1921. Stories.

Branchiana. Richmond, Va: Whittet & Shepperson, 1907. Genealogy.

Gallantry. NY & London: Harper, 1907. Rev ed, NY: McBride, 1922. Stories.

The Cords of Vanity. NY: Doubleday, Page, 1909. Rev ed, NY: McBride, 1920. Novel.

Chivalry. NY & London: Harper, 1909. Rev ed, NY: McBride, 1921. Stories.

Branch of Abingdon. Richmond, Va: Jones, 1911. Genealogy.

The Soul of Melicent. NY: Stokes, 1913. Rev as *Domnei: A Comedy of Woman-Worship.* NY: McBride, 1920. Novel.

The Rivet in Grandfather's Neck. NY: McBride, 1915. Novel.

The Majors and Their Marriages. Richmond, Va: Hill, 1915. Genealogy.

The Certain Hour. NY: McBride, 1916. Stories.

From the Hidden Way. NY: McBride, 1916. Rev ed, 1924. Poetry.

The Cream of the Jest. NY: McBride, 1917. Novel.

Beyond Life. NY: McBride, 1919. Essays.

Jurgen. NY: McBride, 1919. Novel.

The Judging of Jurgen. Chicago: Bookfellows, 1920. Nonfiction.

Figures of Earth. NY: McBride, 1921. Novel.

Taboo. NY: McBride, 1921. Nonfiction.

Joseph Hergesheimer: An Essay in Interpretation. Chicago: Bookfellows, 1921.

The Jewel Merchants. NY: McBride, 1921. Play.

The Lineage of Lichfield: An Essay in Eugenics. NY: McBride, 1922.

The High Place. NY: McBride, 1923. Novel.

Straws and Prayer-Books. NY: McBride, 1924. Essays.

The Silver Stallion. NY: McBride, 1926. Novel.

The Music From Behind the Moon. NY: Day, 1926. Novella.

Something About Eve. NY: McBride, 1927. Novel.

Ballades From the Hidden Way. NY: Gaige, 1928. Poetry.

The White Robe. NY: McBride, 1928. Novella.

Sonnets From Antan. NY: Fountain, 1929. Poetry.

The Way of Ecben. NY: McBride, 1929. Novella.

Townsend of Lichfield. NY: McBride, 1930. Stories & nonfiction.

Some of Us. NY: McBride, 1930. Essays.

These Restless Heads. NY: McBride, 1932. Stories & nonfiction.

Special Delivery. NY: McBride, 1933. Essays.

Smirt. NY: McBride, 1934. Novel.

Ladies and Gentlemen. NY: McBride, 1934. Essays.

Smith. NY: McBride, 1935. Novel.

Preface to the Past. NY: McBride, 1936. Nonfiction.

Smire. Garden City, NY: Doubleday, Doran, 1937. Novel.

The Nightmare Has Triplets, an Author's Note on Smire. Garden City, NY: Doubleday, Doran, 1937.

Of Ellen Glasgow: An Inscribed Portrait, with Glasgow. NY: Maverick, 1938.

The King Was in His Counting House. NY & Toronto: Farrar & Rinehart, 1938. Novel.

Hamlet Had an Uncle. NY & Toronto: Farrar & Rinehart, 1940. Novel.

The First Gentleman of America. NY & Toronto: Farrar & Rinehart, 1942; *The First American Gentleman.* London: Lane, Bodley Head, 1942. Novel.

The St. Johns, with A J Hanna. NY & Toronto: Farrar & Rinehart, 1943. History.

There Were Two Pirates. NY: Farrar, Straus, 1946. Novel.

Let Me Lie: Being in the Main an Ethnological Account of the Remarkable Commonwealth of Virginia and the Making of Its History. NY: Farrar, Straus, 1947.

The Devil's Own Dear Son. NY: Farrar, Straus, 1949. Novel.

Quiet, Please. Gainesville: U Florida P, 1952. Nonfiction.

As I Remember It. NY: McBride, 1955. Nonfiction.

LETTERS

Between Friends: Letters of JBC and Others, ed Padraic Collum & Margaret Freeman Cabell; intro by Carl Van Vechten. NY: Harcourt, Brace & World, 1962.

"The Jewel Merchant: A Case History" by Lewis Cheslock. *Cabellian,* 4 (Spring 1972), 68-78. Includes 40-letter exchange among JBC, Cheslock & H L Mencken.

The Letters of JBC, ed with intro by Edward Wagenknecht. Norman: U Oklahoma P, 1975.

"The C-Bailey Correspondence: 1945-49" by Allen R Swope. *Kalki,* 8, no 4 (1986), 293-300.

OTHER

Jurgen and the Censor: Report of the Emergency Committee Organized to Protest Against the Suppression of JBC's Jurgen, preface & "The Judging of *Jurgen*" by JBC. NY: Privately printed, 1920.

"Introduction." *The Queen Pedauque* by Anatole France (NY: Boni & Liveright, 1923), vii-xii.

"About These Books." *A Bibliography of the Writings of JBC* by Guy Holt (Philadelphia: Centaur Book Shop, 1924), 5-9.

The Romaunt of Manuel Pig-Tender From the Quarto of 1559, ed Thomas Horan with alternative readings supplied by JBC. Dalton, Ga: Postprandial, 1931.

EDITIONS & COLLECTIONS

The Works of JBC, Storisende Edition, 18 vols. NY: McBride, 1927-1930.

Between Dawn and Sunrise, ed John Macy. NY: McBride, 1930.

The Witch Woman. NY: Farrar, Straus, 1948.
The Nightmare Has Triplets. Westport, Conn: Greenwood, 1972.

MANUSCRIPTS & ARCHIVES

The major collections are at U of Virginia Library and Virginia Commonwealth U Library.

BIOGRAPHIES

Book Sections & Articles
Godshalk, William L. "JBC at William and Mary: The Education of a Novelist." *W&MR,* 5 (Spring 1967), 1-10.
Godshalk. "Wherein Is Set Forth a Brief Account of C's Early Career, With a Few Even Briefer Comments on Faulkner." *Kalki,* 8, no 3 (1984), 239-243.
MacDonald, Edgar E. "The Glasgow-C Entente." *AL,* 41 (Mar 1969), 76-91.
MacDonald. "C's Richmond Trial." *SLJ,* 3 (Fall 1970), 47-71.
MacDonald. "C as Prospero, Wylie as Miranda in Richmond-in-Virginia." *Kalki,* 8, no 2 (1983), 216-228.
MacDonald. "A Photographic Essay." Inge & MacDonald, 81-107.
McNeill, Warren A. "JBC in Time's Hourglass." *Cabellian,* 3 (Spring 1971), 64-70.
Scura, Dorothy McInnis. "C & Holt: The Literary Connection." Inge & MacDonald, 40-64.

CRITICAL STUDIES

Books
Canary, Robert H. *The C Scene.* NY: Revisionist, 1977.
Cover, James P. *Notes on Jurgen.* NY: McBride, 1928. Rpt *Kalki,* 3, no 1 (1969), 13-15; 3, no 2 (1969), 70-72; 3, no 3 (1969), 92-97, 104-107; 3, no 4 (1969), 136-142.
Cover & John Philips Cranwell. *Notes on Figures of Earth.* NY: McBride, 1929. Rpt *Kalki,* 2, no 4 (1968), 91-95; 3, no 1 (1969), 22-23.
Davis, Joe Lee. *JBC.* NY: Twayne, 1962.
Duke, Maurice. "JBC's Library: A Catalogue." Dissertation: U Iowa, 1968.
Godshalk, William L. *In Quest of C.* NY: Revisionist, 1975.
Himelick, Raymond. *JBC and the Modern Temper: Three Essays.* NY: Revisionist, 1974.
Holt, Guy, ed. *Jurgen and the Law.* NY: McBride, 1923.
Jurgen and the Censor. NY: Bierstadt, 1920.
McNeill, Warren A. *Cabellian Harmonies,* with introductory note by JBC. NY: Random House, 1928.
Mencken, H L. *JBC.* NY: McBride, 1927. Rpt *JBC: Three Essays.*

Morley-Mower, Geoffrey. *C Under Fire.* NY: Revisionist, 1975.
Rothman, Julius Lawrence. *A Glossarial Index to the "Biography of the Life of Manuel."* NY: Revisionist, 1976.
Schlegel, Dorothy B. *JBC: The Richmond Iconoclast.* NY: Revisionist, 1975.
Tarrant, Desmond. *JBC: The Dream and the Reality.* Norman: U Oklahoma P, 1967.
Untermeyer, Louis. *JBC: The Man and His Masks.* Richmond, Va: npub, 1970.
Van Doren, Carl. *JBC.* NY: Literary Guild, 1932. Rpt *JBC: Three Essays.*
Walpole, Hugh. *The Art of JBC.* NY: McBride, 1920. Rpt *JBC: Three Essays.*
Wells, Arvin R. *Jesting Moses: A Study in Cabellian Comedy.* Gainesville: U Florida P, 1962.

Collections of Essays
Breganzer, Don & Samuel Loveman, eds. *A Round Table in Poictesme: A Symposium.* Cleveland, Ohio: Colophon Club, 1924.
Inge, M Thomas & Edgar E MacDonald, eds. *JBC Centennial Essays.* Baton Rouge: Louisiana State U P, 1983.
JBC: Three Essays. Port Washington, NY: Kennikat, 1967.

Special Journals
Cabellian (quarterly, 1968-1972).
Kalki: Studies in James Branch Cabell (1967-   ).
MissQ, 27 (Fall 1974). JBC issue.

Book Sections & Articles
Allen, Gay Wilson. "Jurgen and Faust." *SR,* 39 (Oct-Dec 1931), 485-492.
Beach, Joseph Warren. "Pedantic Study of Two Critics." *AS,* 1 (Mar 1926), 299-306. Rev as "The Holy Bottle." *VQR,* 2 (Apr 1926), 175-186. Rpt *The Outlook for American Prose* by Beach (Chicago: U Chicago P, 1926).
Blish, James. "The Long Night of a Virginia Author." *JML,* 2, no 3 (1971-1972), 393-405.
Canary, Robert H. "C's Dark Comedies." *MissQ,* 21 (Spring 1968), 83-92.
Collins, Carvel. "Likeness Within Difference: C and Faulkner." *Kalki,* 8, no 4 (1986), 276-283.
Davis, Joe Lee. "Recent C Criticism." *Cabellian,* 1, no 1 (1968), 1-12.
Davis. "C and Santayana in the Neo-Humanist Debate." *Cabellian,* 4 (Spring 1972), 55-67.
Duke, Maurice. "JBC's Personal Library." *SB,* 23 (1970), 207-216.
Duke. "The Ornate Waste Land of JBC." *Kalki,* 6, no 3 (1974), 79-89. Rpt *The Twenties: Fiction, Poetry, Drama,* ed Warren French (De Land, Fla: Everett/Edwards, 1975).

Duke. "C's and Glasgow's Richmond: The Intellectual Background of the City." *MissQ,* 27 (Fall 1974), 375-391.

Duke. " 'C' Rhymes with 'Rabble.' " *Seasoned Authors for a New Season,* ed Louis Filler (Bowling Green, Ohio: Bowling Green U Popular P, 1980), 117-126.

Durham, Frank. "Love as a Literary Exercise: Young JBC Tries His Wings." *MissQ,* 18 (Winter 1964-1965), 26-37.

Edgar, Pelham. "Two Anti-Realists: Willa Cather and C." *The Art of the Novel* (NY: Macmillan, 1933), 255-267.

Fiedler, Leslie A. "The Return of JBC: or, The Cream of the Cream of the Jest." Inge & MacDonald, 131-141.

Flora, Joseph M. "JBC's Tribute to H. L. Mencken and Their Era." *Menckeniana,* 72 (Winter 1979), 1-7.

Flora. "From Richmond to Poictesme: The Early Novels of JBC." *MissQ,* 32 (Spring 1979), 219-239.

Flora. "After the JBC Period." Inge & MacDonald, 65-80.

Godshalk, William L. "*Beyond Life* . . . Introduction." *Kalki,* 4, no 2 (1970), 45-63.

Godshalk. "C and Barth: Our Comic Athletes." *The Comic Imagination in America,* ed Louis D Rubin, Jr (New Brunswick, NJ: Rutgers U P, 1973), 275-283.

Godshalk. "C's *Cream of the Jest* and Recent American Fiction." *SLJ,* 5 (Spring 1973), 18-31.

Godshalk. "JBC: The Life of His Design." Inge & MacDonald, 108-121.

Himelick, Raymond. "C, Shelley and the 'Incorrigible Flesh.' " *SAQ,* 47 (Jan 1948), 88-95.

Himelick. "Figures of C." *MFS,* 2 (Winter 1956-1957), 214-220.

Himelick. "C and the Modern Temper." *SAQ,* 58 (Spring 1959), 176-184.

Hinz, Evelyn J & John J Teunisson. "Life Beyond Life: C's Theory and Practice of Romance." *Genre,* 10 (Fall 1977), 299-327.

Hobson, Fred C, Jr. "JBC, the Last Aristocrat." *Serpent in Eden: H. L. Mencken and the South* (Chapel Hill: U North Carolina P, 1974), 121-146.

Howard, Leon. "Figures of Allegory: A Study of JBC." *SR,* 42 (Jan-Mar 1934), 54-66.

MacDonald, Edgar E. "C's Hero: Cosmic Rebel." *SLJ,* 2 (Fall 1969), 22-42.

MacDonald. "Glasgow, C, and Richmond." *MissQ,* 27 (Fall 1974), 393-413.

MacDonald. "The Ambivalent Heart: Literary Rivalry in Richmond." *The History of Southern Literature,* ed Louis D Rubin, Jr (Baton Rouge: Louisiana State U P, 1985), 264-278.

McIntyre, Clara. "Mr. C's Cosmos." *SR,* 38 (Jul-Sep 1930), 278-285.

Millet, Fred B. "JBC." *Minor American Novelists,* ed Charles A Hoyt (Carbondale: Southern Illinois U P, 1970), 41-66.

Morley-Mower, Geoffrey. "JBC's Flirtation With Clio: The Story of a Collaboration." *Kalki,* 6, no 2 (1972), 39-53.

Morley-Mower. "C's Black Imagination." *Kalki,* 8, no 1 (1980), 179-190.

Parks, Edd Winfield. "JBC." *Southern Renascence,* ed Louis Rubin, Jr & Robert D Jacobs (Baltimore, Md: Johns Hopkins U P, 1953), 251-261.

Parrington, Vernon Louis. "The Incomparable Mr. C." *Main Currents in American Thought,* Vol 3 (NY: Harcourt, Brace, 1930), 335-345.

Pizer, Donald. "The 1920s Fiction of JBC: An Essay in Appreciation." *SoQ,* 23 (Winter 1985), 55-74.

Reimer, James D. "The Innovative Fantasies of JBC." *SoQ,* 23 (Winter 1985), 75-86.

Rubin, Louis D, Jr. "A Southerner in Poictesme." *No Place on Earth: Ellen Glasgow, JBC and Richmond-in-Virginia* (Austin: U Texas P, 1959), 50-81.

Rubin. "Two in Richmond: Ellen Glasgow and JBC." *South: Modern Southern Literature in Its Cultural Setting,* ed Rubin & Robert D Jacobs (Garden City, NY: Doubleday, 1961), 115-141.

Rubin. "A Virginian in Poictesme." Inge & MacDonald, 1-16.

Schlegel, Dorothy B. "C and His Critics." *The Dilemma of the Southern Writer,* ed Richard K Meeker (Farmville, Va: Longwood C, 1961), 119-142.

Spencer, Paul. "C: Fantasist of Reality." *Exploring Fantasy Worlds* (San Bernardino, Calif: Borgo, 1985), 97-106.

Tate, Allen. "Mr. C's Farewell." *NewR,* 41 (8 Jan 1930), 201-202.

Umansky, Harlan L. "Manuel as the Savior of Poictesme." *Kalki,* 8, no 4 (1986), 284-290.

Wagenknecht, Edward. "JBC: The Anatomy of Romanticism." *Cavalcade of the American Novel* (NY: Holt, 1952), 339-353.

Wilson, Edmund. "The JBC Case Reopened." *NYer,* 32 (21 Apr 1956), 140-142, 145-148, 151-158, 161-168.

Arvin R. Wells

GEORGE WASHINGTON CABLE

New Orleans, La, 12 Oct 1844-St Petersburg, Fla, 31 Jan 1925

George Washington Cable was initially admired as a local-color writer whose work offered a charming mixture of romantic plots and characters with authentic depictions of the social and cultural issues of old New Orleans, especially race and caste. Cable's treatment of racial themes in his fiction and his championing the freedman's cause in newspaper articles generated controversy, and while he continued with a variety of reform activities throughout most of his life, his fiction after *The Grandissimes* veered toward the romantic. Cable's greatest popular success came in 1901 with the Civil War romance, *The Cavalier*, but modern critics generally regard his major achievement to be *The Grandissimes* and certain stories in *Old Creole Days*. His themes of ancestral guilt, decaying aristocracy, a tragic past, and the continuing burden of slavery into the present anticipate the work of William Faulkner and other twentieth-century southern writers.

BIBLIOGRAPHIES

Adams, Anthony J & Sara McCaslin. "*The Grandissimes:* An Annotated Bibliography (1880-1979)." *The Grandissimes: Centennial Essays,* ed Thomas J Richardson (Jackson: U P Mississippi, 1981), 81-94. Secondary.

"Bibliography." Butcher (1959), 261-278. Primary & secondary.

Bibliography of American Literature, comp Jacob Blanck. New Haven: Yale U P, 1955-1991. Primary.

"Bibliography." Turner (1956), 358-372. Primary & secondary.

Butcher, Philip. "GWC (1844-1925)." *ALR,* 1 (Fall 1967), 20-25. Secondary.

BOOKS

Old Creole Days. NY: Scribners, 1879. Stories.

The Grandissimes: A Story of Creole Life. NY: Scribners, 1880. Novel.

Madame Delphine. NY: Scribners, 1881. Novel.

The Creoles of Louisiana. NY: Scribners, 1884. History.

Dr. Sevier. 2 vols, Edinburgh: Douglas, 1884; 1 vol, Boston: Osgood, 1885. Novel.

The Silent South, Together With The Freedman's Case in Equity and The Convict Lease System. NY: Scribners, 1885. Augmented ed, 1889. Essays.

Madame Delphine, Carancro . . . Grand Pointe. Edinburgh: Douglas, 1887. Stories.

Bonaventure: A Prose Pastoral of Acadian Louisiana. NY: Scribners, 1888. Novel.

The Negro Question. NY: American Missionary Association, 1888. Augmented ed, NY: Scribners, 1890. Essays.

Strange True Stories of Louisiana. NY: Scribners, 1889.

The Southern Struggle for Pure Government. . . . Boston: Usher, 1890. Address.

What the Negro Must Learn. . . . NY: American Missionary Association, 1890. Address.

The Busy Man's Bible and How to Study and Teach It. Meadville, Pa: Flood & Vincent/Chatauqua-Century, 1891. Essays.

A Memory of Roswell Smith, Born March 30, 1829, Died April 19, 1892. NY: npub, 1892. Memoir.

John March, Southerner. NY: Scribners, 1894. Novel.

Strong Hearts. NY: Scribners, 1899. Stories.

The Cavalier. NY: Scribners, 1901. Novel.

Père Raphaël. NY: Privately printed, 1901. Story.

Bylow Hill. NY: Scribners, 1902. Novel.

Kincaid's Battery. NY: Scribners, 1908. Novel.

"Posson Jone' " and Père Raphaël, With a New Word Setting Forth How and Why the Two Tales Are One. NY: Scribners, 1909. Stories.

Gideon's Band: A Tale of the Mississippi. NY: Scribners, 1914. Novel.

The Amateur Garden. NY: Scribners, 1914. Essays.

The Flower of the Chapdelaines. NY: Scribners, 1918. Novel.

Lovers of Louisiana (To-Day). NY: Scribners, 1918. Novel.

LETTERS

Mark Twain and GWC: The Record of a Literary Friendship by Arlin Turner. East Lansing: Michigan State U P, 1960.

COLLECTION

The C Story Book: Selections for School Reading,

ed Mary E Burt & Lucy Leffingwell Cable. NY: Scribners, 1899.

MANUSCRIPTS & ARCHIVES
Tulane U Library.

BIOGRAPHIES
Books
Bikle, Lucy Leffingwell Cable. *GWC: His Life and Letters*. NY: Scribners, 1928.

Butcher, Philip. *GWC: The Northampton Years*. NY: Columbia U P, 1959.

Cardwell, Guy A. *Twins of Genius*. East Lansing: Michigan State C P, 1953. Includes letters, pp 79-112.

Dennis, Mary Cable. *The Tail of the Comet*. NY: Dutton, 1937.

Turner, Arlin. *GWC: A Biography*. Durham, NC: Duke U P, 1956.

CRITICAL STUDIES
Books
Butcher, Philip. *GWC*. NY: Twayne, 1962.

Ekström, Kjell. *GWC: A Study of His Early Life and Work*. Uppsala: Lundequistska Bokhandeln / Cambridge: Harvard U P, 1950.

Petry, Alice Hall. *A Genius in His Way: The Art of C's Old Creole Days*. Rutherford, NJ: Fairleigh Dickinson U P, 1988.

Rubin, Louis D, Jr. *GWC: The Life and Times of a Southern Heretic*. NY: Pegasus, 1969.

Collection of Essays
Turner, Arlin, ed. *Critical Essays on GWC*. Boston: Hall, 1980.

Special Journal
SoQ, 18 (Summer 1980). GWC issue. Augmented as *The Grandissimes: Centennial Essays*, ed Thomas J Richardson. Jackson: U P Mississippi, 1981.

Book Sections & Articles
Aaron, Daniel. "GWC." *The Unwritten War: American Writers and the Civil War* (NY: Knopf, 1973), 272-282. Rpt Turner (1980).

Arvin, Newton. "Introduction." *The Grandissimes* (NY: Sagamore, 1957), v-xi. Rpt Turner (1980).

Bendixen, Alfred. "C's *The Grandissimes*: A Literary Pioneer Confronts the Southern Tradition." *SoQ*, 18 (Summer 1980), 23-33.

Berkove, Lawrence I. "The Free Man of Color in *The Grandissimes* and Works by Harris and Mark Twain." *SoQ*, 18 (Summer 1980), 60-73.

Bishop, D H. "A Commencement in the Eighties: GWC's First Public Address." *SWR*, 18 (Jan 1933), 108-114.

Bloom, Margaret. "GWC: A New Englander in the South." *Bookman*, 73 (Jun 1931), 401-403.

Butcher, Philip. "GWC: History and Politics." *Phylon*, 9 (Jun 1948), 137-145. Rpt Turner (1980).

Campbell, Michael L. "The Negro in C's *The Grandissimes*." *MissQ*, 27 (Spring 1974), 165-178.

Chase, Richard. "C and His *Grandissimes*." *KR*, 18 (Summer 1956), 373-383. Rpt as "C's *Grandissimes*." *The American Novel and Its Tradition* by Chase (Garden City, NY: Doubleday, 1957).

Clark, William Bedford. "C and the Theme of Miscegenation in *Old Creole Days* and *The Grandissimes*." *MissQ*, 30 (Fall 1977), 597-609.

Clark. "Humor in C's *The Grandissimes*." *SoQ*, 18 (Summer 1980), 51-59.

Clay, Charles M. "GWC." *Critic*, 1 (8 Oct 1881), 270-271. Rpt Turner (1980).

Cleman, John. "The Art of Local Color in GWC's *The Grandissimes*." *AL*, 47 (Nov 1975), 396-410.

Cowie, Alexander. "GWC (1844-1925)." *The Rise of the American Novel* (NY: American Book, 1948), 556-567.

Eaton, Richard Bozman. "GWC and the Historical Romance." *SLJ*, 8 (Fall 1975), 82-94.

Egan, Joseph J. "Lions Rampant: Agricola Fusilier and Bras-Coupé as Antithetical Doubles in *The Grandissimes*." *SoQ*, 18 (Summer 1980), 74-80.

Eidson, J O. "GWC's Philosophy of Progress." *SWR*, 21 (Jan 1936), 211-216.

Ekström, Kjell. "The C-Howells Correspondence." *SN*, 22 (1949-1950), 48-61.

Evans, William. "French-English Literary Dialect in *The Grandissimes*." *AS*, 46 (Fall-Winter 1971), 210-222. Rpt Turner (1980).

Fulweiler, Howard W. "Of Time and the River: 'Ancestral Nonsense' vs. Inherited Guilt in C's 'Belles Demoiselles Plantation.'" *MASJ*, 7 (Fall 1966), 53-59. Rpt Turner (1980).

Hearn, Lafcadio. "The Scenes of C's Romances." *Century*, 27 (Nov 1883), 40-47. Rpt Turner (1980).

Howell, Elmo. "GWC's Creoles: Art and Reform in *The Grandissimes*." *MissQ*, 26 (Winter 1972-1973), 42-53. Rpt Turner (1980).

Hubbell, Jay B. "GWC." *The South in American Literature, 1607-1900* (Durham, NC: Duke U P, 1954), 804-822.

Martin, Jay. "GWC." *Harvests of Change: American Literature, 1865-1914* (Englewood Cliffs, NJ: Prentice-Hall, 1967), 100-105.

Orcutt, W D. "From My Library Walls." *CSM,* 37 (17 Nov 1944), 7.

Pabody, E F. "Mark Twain's Ghost Story." *MinnH,* 18 (Mar 1937), 28-35.

Pattee, Fred Lewis. *A History of American Literature Since 1870* (NY: Century, 1915), 246-253. Rpt Turner (1980).

Richardson, Thomas J. "Honoré Grandissime's Southern Dilemma: Introduction." *SoQ,* 18 (Summer 1980), 1-12.

Ringe, Donald A. "The 'Double Center': Character and Meaning in C's Early Novels." *SNNTS,* 5 (Spring 1973), 52-62.

Ringe. "The Moral World of C's 'Belles Demoiselles Plantation.' " *MissQ,* 29 (Winter 1975-1976), 83-90.

Ringe. "Narrative Voice in C's *The Grandissimes*." *SoQ,* 18 (Summer 1980), 13-22.

Rubin, Louis D, Jr. "The Road to Yoknapatawpha: GWC and *John March, Southerner.*" *VQR,* 35 (Winter 1959), 119-132. Rpt *The Faraway Country: Writers of the Modern South* by Rubin (Seattle: U Washington P, 1963).

Rubin. "The Division of the Heart: C's *The Grandissimes*." *SLJ,* 1 (Spring 1969), 27-47. Rpt Turner (1980).

Rubin. "Politics and the Novel: GWC and the Genteel Tradition." *William Elliott Shoots a Bear: Essays on the Southern Literary Imagination* (Baton Rouge: Louisiana State U P, 1975), 61-81.

Stephens, Robert O. "C's *Grandissimes* and the Comedy of Manners." *AL,* 51 (Jan 1980), 507-519.

Stephens. "C's Grandissime Saga." *ALR,* 20 (Fall 1987), 3-17.

Stone, Edward. "Usher, Poquelin, and Miss Emily: The Progress of Southern Gothic." *GaR,* 14 (Winter 1960), 433-443.

Tinker, E L. "C and the Creoles." *AL,* 5 (Jan 1934), 313-326.

Turner, Arlin. "GWC's Literary Apprenticeship." *LaHQ,* 24 (Jan 1941), 168-185.

Turner. "GWC, Novelist and Reformer." *SAQ,* 48 (Oct 1949), 539-545. Rpt Turner (1980).

Turner. "A Novelist Discovers a Novelist: The Correspondence of H. H. Boyesen and GWC." *WHR,* 5 (Autumn 1951), 343-372.

Warfel, H R. "GWC Amends a Mark Twain Plot." *AL,* 6 (Nov 1934), 328-331.

Wilson, Edmund. "The Ordeal of GWC." *NYer,* 33 (9 Nov 1957), 180, 182-196, 201-208, 211-218, 221-228. Rpt *Patriotic Gore: Studies in the Literature of the American Civil War* by Wilson (NY: Oxford U P, 1962).

Wykoff, G S. "The C Family in Indiana." *AL,* 1 (May 1929), 183-195.

John Lawrence Cleman

ABRAHAM CAHAN

Podberezy, Lithuania, 6 Jul 1860-New York City, NY, 31 Aug 1951

Abraham Cahan holds a pre-eminent position as an ethnic and proletarian American writer. Coming to the United States as a young man, Cahan centered his lengthy career on his editorship of the *Jewish Daily Forward,* an important Yiddish newspaper. Peripheral to his editing work was his activism in the labor movement, socialism, and the ongoing acculturation of immigrants, particularly East European Jews. Cahan began in 1896 to publish his novels and stories, treating both the old world and the new. His most important work of fiction was *The Rise of David Levinsky.* Sometimes called the first American-Jewish novel, its protagonist is an immigrant who in the classic rags-to-riches rise becomes successful, wealthy, and formidably Americanized. Levinsky is the archetype of the man who has turned his back on his past—his European identity, his Jewish heritage. This figure constantly recurs in Cahan's realistic fiction.

BIBLIOGRAPHIES

First Printings of American Authors, Vol 2 (Detroit: Bruccoli Clark/Gale, 1978), 83. Primary.
Marovitz, Sanford E & Lewis Fried. "AC (1860-1951): An Annotated Bibliography." *ALR,* 3 (Summer 1970), 197-241. Primary & secondary.

BOOKS

(This list includes only English-language volumes.)

Social Remedies. NY: New York Labor News, 1889. Nonfiction.
Yekl: A Tale of the New York Ghetto. NY: Appleton, 1896. Novel.
The Imported Bridegroom and Other Stories of the New York Ghetto. Boston & NY: Houghton, Mifflin, 1898. Stories.
The White Terror and the Red: A Novel of Revolutionary Russia. NY: Barnes, 1905.
The Rise of David Levinsky. NY & London: Harper, 1917. Novel.
The Education of AC. Philadelphia: Jewish Publication Society of America, 1969. Autobiography.

OTHER

Arbeiter Zeitung (1891-1894), ed AC. Newspaper.
Jewish Daily Forward (1897, 1902-1951), ed AC. Newspaper.
Hear the Other Side: A Symposium of Democratic Socialist Opinion, ed AC. NY: npub, 1934.

COLLECTIONS

Yekl and The Imported Bridegroom and Other Stories of the New York Ghetto. NY: Dover, 1970.
Grandma Never Lived in America: The New Journalism of AC, ed with intro by Moses Rischin. Bloomington: Indiana U P, 1985.

MANUSCRIPTS & ARCHIVES

YIVA Institute for Jewish Research, New York City, NY.

BIOGRAPHY

Book Section
Sanders, Ronald. *The Downtown Jews: Portraits of an Immigrant Generation* (NY: Harper & Row, 1969), passim.

CRITICAL STUDIES

Book
Chametzky, Jules. *From the Ghetto: The Fiction of AC.* Amherst: U Massachusetts P, 1977.

Book Sections & Articles
Engel, David. "The Discrepancies of the Modern: Reevaluating AC's *The Rise of David Levinsky.*" *SAJL,* 5 (Winter 1979), 68-91.
Fiedler, Leslie A. "Genesis: The American-Jewish Novel Through the Twenties." *Midstream,* 4 (Summer 1958), 21-33.
Hapgood, Hutchins. "A Novelist." *The Spirit of the Ghetto* (NY: Funk & Wagnalls, 1902), 230-253.
Higham, John. "Introduction." *The Rise of David Levinsky* (NY: Harper, 1960), v-xii.
Hindus, Milton. "AC: Early American Realist." *JH,* 7 (Fall 1964), 38-44.
Kirk, Rudolf & Clara M. "AC and William Dean Howells: The Story of a Friendship." *AJHQ,* 52 (Sep 1962), 25-57.

Marovitz, Sanford E. "The Lonely New Americans of AC." *AQ*, 20 (Summer 1968), 196-210.

Marovitz. "*Yekl:* The Ghetto Realism of AC." *ALR*, 2 (Fall 1969), 271-273.

Poole, Ernest. "AC: Socialist-Journalist-Friend of the Ghetto." *Outlook*, 99 (28 Oct 1911), 467-478.

Rosenfeld, Isaac. "America, Land of the Sad Millionaire." *Commentary*, 14 (Aug 1952), 131-135.

Singer, David. "David Levinsky's Fall: A Note on the Liebman Thesis." *AQ*, 19 (Winter 1967), 696-706.

Strout, Cushing. "Personality and Cultural History in the Novel: Two American Examples." *NLH*, 1 (Spring 1970), 423-437.

Vogel, Dan. "C's *Rise of David Levinsky:* Archetype of American Jewish Fiction." *Judaism*, 22 (Summer 1973), 278-287.

Zanger, Jules. "David Levinsky: Master of Pilpul." *PLL*, 13 (Summer 1977), 283-294.

Gerald R. Griffen

GUY WETMORE CARRYL

New York City, NY, 4 Mar 1873-New York City, NY, 1 Apr 1904

Guy Wetmore Carryl, who died at age thirty-one, was perhaps best known as a writer of light verse, particularly parodies of Aesop, Mother Goose, and the Brothers Grimm. Yet during his brief career he also published three novels and one collection of short stories, *Zut and Other Parisians*. *The Lieutenant-Governor*, a novel dealing with labor unions and political intrigue, is considered his most important work of fiction. Carryl's novels and short stories have received almost no critical attention.

BIBLIOGRAPHY

Bibliography of American Literature, comp Jacob Blanck. New Haven: Yale U P, 1955-1991. Primary.

BOOKS

Fables for the Frivolous (With Apologies to La Fontaine). NY & London: Harper, 1898. Poetry.

Mother Goose for Grown-ups. NY & London: Harper, 1900. Poetry.

Grimm Tales Made Gay. Boston & NY: Houghton, Mifflin, 1902. Poetry.

The Lieutenant-Governor: A Novel. Boston & NY: Houghton, Mifflin, 1903.

Zut and Other Parisians. Boston & NY: Houghton, Mifflin, 1903. Stories.

The Transgression of Andrew Vane: A Novel. NY: Holt, 1904.

Far From the Maddening Girls. NY: McClure, Phillips, 1904. Novel.

The Garden of Years and Other Poems. NY & London: Putnam, 1904.

CRITICAL STUDY

Book Section

Stedman, E C. "To the Reader." *The Garden of Years and Other Poems*, ix-xiv.

Gwen L. Nagel

WILLA CATHER

Back Creek Valley, Va, 7 Dec 1873-New York City, NY, 24 Apr 1947

Although Willa Cather was recognized during her lifetime as a major literary figure, her novels were attacked as politically irrelevant by leftist critics during the 1930s. Since her death, attention to her work has increased as critics have identified a wealth of myth, allusion, and symbolism in her fiction. The flourishing of the feminist movement in literature has brought renewed interest in Cather's complex women characters. Her fiction is identified with the Midwest farming frontier as portrayed in *O Pioneers!* and *My Ántonia*; but Cather's material also encompassed the Southwest, French Canada, and Virginia.

BIBLIOGRAPHIES

Arnold, Marilyn. *WC: A Reference Guide.* Boston: Hall, 1986. Secondary.

Crane, Joan. *WC: A Bibliography,* foreword by Frederick B Adams. Lincoln: U Nebraska P, 1982. Primary.

First Printings of American Authors, Vol 4 (Detroit: Bruccoli Clark/Gale, 1979), 69-76. Primary.

McClure, Charlotte S. "WC." *ALR,* 8 (Summer 1975), 209-220. Survey of dissertations.

BOOKS

April Twilights. Boston: Badger, 1903. Augmented as *April Twilights and Other Poems.* NY: Knopf, 1923.

The Troll Garden. NY: McClure, Phillips, 1905. Stories.

Alexander's Bridge. Boston & NY: Houghton Mifflin, 1912; London: Constable / Boston & NY: Houghton Mifflin, 1912; *Alexander's Bridges.* London: Heinemann, 1912. Novel.

O Pioneers! Boston & NY: Houghton Mifflin, 1913. Novel.

My Autobiography by S S McClure. NY: Stokes, 1914. Ghost-written by WC.

The Song of the Lark. Boston & NY: Houghton Mifflin, 1915. Novel.

My Ántonia. Boston & NY: Houghton Mifflin, 1918. Novel.

Youth and the Bright Medusa. NY: Knopf, 1920. Stories.

One of Ours. NY: Knopf, 1922. Novel.

A Lost Lady. NY: Knopf, 1923. Novel.

The Professor's House. NY: Knopf, 1925. Novel.

My Mortal Enemy. NY: Knopf, 1926. Novel.

Death Comes for the Archbishop. NY: Knopf, 1927. Novel.

Shadows on the Rock. NY: Knopf, 1931. Novel.

Obscure Destinies. NY: Knopf, 1932. Stories.

Lucy Gayheart. NY: Knopf, 1935. Novel.

Not Under Forty. NY: Knopf, 1936. Essays.

Sapphira and the Slave Girl. NY: Knopf, 1940. Novel.

The Old Beauty and Others. NY: Knopf, 1948. Stories.

On Writing, foreword by Stephen Tennant. NY: Knopf, 1949. Essays.

Writings From WC's Campus Years, ed James R Shively. Lincoln: U Nebraska P, 1950. Miscellany.

Five Stories, with essay by George N Kates. NY: Vintage/Random House, 1956.

WC in Europe, ed with intro & notes by Kates. NY: Knopf, 1956. Travel letters.

Early Stories of WC, ed with commentary by Mildred R Bennett. NY: Dodd, Mead, 1957.

WC's Collected Short Fiction, 1892-1912, intro by Bennett. Lincoln: U Nebraska P, 1965.

The Kingdom of Art: WC's First Principles and Critical Statements, 1893-1896, ed with commentary by Bernice Slote. Lincoln: U Nebraska P, 1966. Essays & journalism.

The World and the Parish: WC's Articles and Reviews, 1893-1902, 2 vols, ed William M Curtin. Lincoln: U Nebraska P, 1970.

Uncle Valentine and Other Stories: WC's Uncollected Short Fiction, 1915-1929, ed Slote. Lincoln: U Nebraska P, 1973.

WC in Person: Interviews, Speeches, and Letters, ed L Brent Bohlke. Lincoln & London: U Nebraska P, 1986.

OTHER

The Life of Mary Baker G. Eddy and the History of Christian Science by Georgine Milmine; ed WC. NY: Doubleday, Page, 1909.

The Best Stories of Sarah Orne Jewett, 2 vols, selected & arranged with preface by WC. Boston & NY: Houghton Mifflin, 1925.

EDITIONS & COLLECTION

The Novels and Stories of WC, 13 vols. Boston:

Houghton Mifflin, 1937-1941.
The Troll Garden, ed with intro by James
    Woodress. Lincoln: U Nebraska P, 1983.
WC: Early Novels and Stories, ed Sharon O'Brien.
    NY: Library of America, 1987.

MANUSCRIPTS & ARCHIVES

The major collections are at the Willa Cather Pioneer Memorial, Red Cloud, Nebr; Nebraska Historical Society, Lincoln; the Newberry Library, Chicago; U of Virginia Library; U of Vermont Library; the Houghton Library, Harvard U; the Beinecke Library, Yale U; & the Huntington Library, San Marino, Calif.

BIOGRAPHIES
Books
Bennett, Mildred R. *The World of WC.* NY: Dodd,
    Mead, 1951.
Brown, E K. *WC: A Critical Biography,* completed
    by Leon Edel. NY: Knopf, 1953.
Brown, Marion Marsh & Ruth Crone. *WC: The
    Woman and Her Works.* NY: Scribners, 1970.
Brown & Crone. *Only One Point of the Compass:
    WC in the Northeast.* Danbury, Conn: Archer, 1980.
Byrne, Kathleen D & Richard C Snyder. *Chrysalis:
    WC in Pittsburgh, 1896-1906.* Pittsburgh:
    Historical Society of Western Pennsylvania,
    1980.
Lewis, Edith. *WC Living: A Personal Record.* NY:
    Knopf, 1953.
O'Brien, Sharon. *WC: The Emerging Voice.* NY:
    Oxford U P, 1987.
Robinson, Phyllis C. *Willa: The Life of WC.* Garden City, NY: Doubleday, 1983.
Sergeant, Elizabeth Shepley. *WC: A Memoir.* Philadelphia: Lippincott, 1953.
*WC: A Biographical Sketch, an English Opinion,
    and an Abridged Bibliography.* NY: Knopf,
    1927. Probably by WC.
WC: A Pictorial Memoir, photographs by Lucia
    Woods et al; text by Bernice Slote. Lincoln: U
    Nebraska P, 1973.
Woodress, James. *WC: Her Life and Art.* NY: Pegasus, 1970.
Woodress. *WC: A Literary Life.* Lincoln: U Nebraska P, 1987.

Book Sections & Articles
Adams, Frederick B, Jr. "WC, Early Years: Trial
    and Error." *Colophon,* ns 1 (Sep 1939),
    89-100.
Adams. "WC, Middle Years: The Right Road
    Taken." *Colophon,* ns 1 (Feb 1940), 103-108.
Benson, Peter. "WC at *Home Monthly.*" *Biography,* 4 (Summer 1981), 227-248.

Butcher, Fanny. "WC." *Many Lives--One Love*
    (NY: Harper & Row, 1972), 354-368.
Fisher, Dorothy Canfield. "Daughters of the Frontier." *NYHTB* (28 May 1933), 7, 9.
Overton, Grant. "WSC." *The Women Who Make
    Our Novels* (NY: Moffat, Yard, 1918),
    254-266.
Seibel, George. "Miss WC From Nebraska."
    NewCol, 2 (Sep 1949), 195-208.
Slote, Bernice. "Writer in Nebraska." *The Kingdom
    of Art,* 3-29.
Southwick, Helen C. "WC's Early Career: Origins
    of a Legend." *WPaHM,* 65 (Apr 1982), 85-98.
Vermorcken, Elizabeth Moorhead. *These Two Were
    Here: Louise Homes and WC* (Pittsburgh: U
    Pittsburgh P, 1950), 45-62.
Yongue, Patricia Lee. "WC's Aristocrats." *SHR,* 14
    (Winter-Spring 1980), 43-56, 111-125.

CRITICAL STUDIES
Books
Ambrose, Jamie. *WC: Writing at the Frontier.* Oxford, UK: Berg, 1988.
Arnold, Marilyn. *WC's Short Fiction.* Athens: Ohio
    U P, 1984.
Bloom, Edward A & Lillian D. *WC's Gift of Sympathy.* Carbondale: Southern Illinois U P,
    1962.
Daiches, David. *WC: A Critical Introduction.* Ithaca, NY: Cornell U P, 1951.
Edel, Leon. *WC: The Paradox of Success.* Washington: Reference Department, Library of Congress, 1960.
Fryer, Judith. *Felicitous Space: The Imaginative
    Structures of Edith Wharton and WC.* Chapel
    Hill: U North Carolina P, 1986.
Gerber, Philip L. *WC.* Boston: Twayne, 1975.
Giannone, Richard. *Music in WC's Fiction.* Lincoln: U Nebraska P, 1968.
McFarland, Dorothy Tuck. *WC.* NY: Ungar, 1972.
Nelson, Robert J. *WC and France: In Search of the
    Lost Language.* Urbana: U Illinois P, 1988.
Pers, Mona. *WC's Children.* Uppsala, Sweden:
    Uppsala U, 1975.
Randall, John H, III. *The Landscape and the Looking Glass: WC's Search for Value.* Boston:
    Houghton Mifflin, 1960.
Rapin, René. *WC.* NY: McBride, 1930.
Rosowski, Susan J. *The Voyage Perilous: WC's Romanticism.* Lincoln: U Nebraska P, 1986.
Stouck, David. *WC's Imagination.* Lincoln: U Nebraska P, 1975.
Van Ghent, Dorothy. *WC.* Minneapolis: U Minnesota P, 1964.
Welsch, Roger L & Linda K. *C's Kitchens: Foodways in Literature and Life,* Lincoln: U Nebraska P, 1987.

Collections of Essays

Bloom, Harold, ed. *Modern Critical Views: WC.* NY: Chelsea House, 1985.

Bloom, ed. *Modern Critical Interpretations: WC's My Ántonia.* NY: Chelsea House, 1987.

Murphy, John J, ed. *Five Essays on WC: The Merrimack Symposium.* North Andover, Mass: Merrimack C, 1974.

Murphy, ed. *Critical Essays on WC.* Boston: Hall, 1984.

Schroeter, James, ed. *WC and Her Critics.* Ithaca, NY: Cornell U P, 1967.

Slote, Bernice & Virginia Faulkner, eds. *The Art of WC.* Lincoln: Department of English, U Nebraska, 1974.

Special Journals

CLQ, 8 (Jun 1968). WC issue.

CLQ, 10 (Sep 1973). WC issue.

GPQ, 2 (Fall 1982). WC issue.

GPQ, 4 (Fall 1984). WC issue.

L&B, 8 (1988). WC issue.

WAL, 7 (Spring 1972). WC issue.

Willa Cather Pioneer Memorial Newsletter (quarterly, 1957-   ).

WS, 11, no 3 (1984). WC issue.

Book Sections & Articles

Ammons, Elizabeth. "The Engineer as Cultural Hero and WC's First Novel, *Alexander's Bridge.*" *AQ,* 38 (Winter 1986), 746-760.

Arnold, Marilyn. "The Function of Structure in C's *The Professor's House.*" *CLQ,* 11 (Sep 1975), 169-178.

Arnold. "C's Last Stand." *ResearchS,* 43 (Dec 1975), 245-252.

Arnold. "WC's Nostalgia: A Study in Ambivalence." *ResearchS,* 49 (Mar 1981), 23-34.

Arnold. "Coming WC!" *WS,* 11, no 3 (1984), 247-260.

Arnold. " 'Of Human Bondage': C's Subnarrative in *Sapphira and the Slave Girl.*" *MissQ,* 40 (Summer 1987), 323-338.

Arnold. "The Integrating Vision of Bishop Latour in WC's *Death Comes for the Archbishop.*" *L&B,* 8 (1988), 39-57.

Arvin, Newton. "Fiction Mirrors America." *CurrentHist,* 42 (Sep 1935), 610-616.

Auchincloss, Louis. "WC." *Pioneers & Caretakers: A Study of 9 American Women Novelists* (Minneapolis: U Minnesota P, 1965), 92-122.

Bailey, Jennifer. "The Dangers of Femininity in WC's Fiction." *JAmS,* 16 (Dec 1982), 391-406.

Baker, Bruce P, II. "Nebraska Regionalism in Selected Works of WC." *WAL,* 3 (Spring 1968), 19-35.

Baker. "*O Pioneers!*: The Problem of Structure." *GPQ,* 2 (Fall 1982), 218-223.

Baker. "Before the Cruciform Tree: The Failure of Evangelical Protestantism." *L&B,* 8 (1988), 14-26.

Bash, James R. "WC and the Anathema of Materialism." *CLQ,* 10 (Sep 1973), 157-168.

Baum, Bernard. "WC's Waste Land." *SAQ,* 48 (Oct 1949), 589-601.

Beer, Thomas. "Miss C." *The Borzoi 1925* (NY: Knopf, 1925), 23-30.

Bender, Eileen T. "Pioneer or Gadgeteer: Bergsonian Metaphor in the Work of WC." *MQ,* 28 (Autumn 1986), 130-140.

Bennett, Mildred R. "The Childhood Worlds of WC." *GPQ,* 2 (Fall 1982), 204-209.

Bennett. "C and Religion." *L&B,* 8 (1988), 5-13.

Bennett, S M. "Ornament and Environment: Uses of Folklore in WC's Fiction." *TFSB,* 40 (Sep 1974), 95-102.

Bloom, Lillian D. "On Daring to Look Back With Wharton and C." *Novel,* 10 (Winter 1977), 167-178.

Bohlke, L Brent. "Beginnings: WC and 'The Clemency of the Court.' " *PrS,* 48 (Summer 1974), 134-144.

Bohlke. "The Ecstasy of Alexandra Bergson." *CLQ,* 11 (Sep 1975), 139-149.

Borgman, Paul. "The Dialectic of WC's Moral Vision." *Renascence,* 27 (Spring 1975), 145-159.

Boynton, Percy H. "WC." *Some Contemporary Americans* (Chicago: U Chicago P, 1924), 162-177.

Bradford, Curtis. "WC's Uncollected Short Stories." *AL,* 26 (Jan 1955), 537-551.

Brennan, Joseph X. "WC and Music," "Music and WC." *UniversityR,* 31 (Spring-Summer 1965), 175-183, 257-264.

Brown, E K. "WC and the West." *UTQ,* 5 (Oct 1936), 544-566.

Brown. "Homage to WC." *YR,* 36 (Sep 1946), 77-92.

Bruccoli, Matthew J. " 'An Instance of Apparent Plagiarism': F Scott Fitzgerald, WC, and the First *Gatsby* Manuscript." *PULC,* 39 (Spring 1978), 171-178.

Brunauer, Dalma H & June Davis Klamecki. "Myra Henshawe's Mortal Enemy." *C&L,* 25 (Fall 1975), 7-40.

Bush, Sargent, Jr. "*Shadows on the Rock* and WC's View of the Past." *QQ,* 76 (Summer 1969), 269-285.

Celli, Aldo. "Italian Perspectives." Slote & Faulkner, 103-118.

Chaliff, Cynthia. "The Art of WC's Craft." *PLL,* 14 (Winter 1978), 61-73.

Charles, Sister Peter Damian. "*Death Comes for the Archbishop*: A Novel of Love & Death." *NMQ,* 36 (Winter 1966-1967), 389-403.

Charles. "*My Ántonia:* A Dark Dimension." *WAL,* 2 (Summer 1967), 91-108.

Charles. "*The Professor's House:* An Abode of Love and Death." *CLQ,* 8 (Jun 1968), 70-82.

Cherny, Robert W. "WC and the Populists." *GPQ,* 3 (Fall 1983), 206-218.

Comeau, Paul. "The Fool Figure in WC's Fiction." *WAL,* 15 (Winter 1981), 265-278.

Comeau. "WC's *Lucy Gayheart:* A Long Perspective." *PrS,* 55 (Spring-Summer 1981), 199-209.

Comeau. "*The Professor's House* and Anatole France." Murphy (1984), 217-227.

Commager, Henry Steele. "Traditionalism in American Literature." *NCent,* 146 (May 1949), 311-326.

Connolly, Francis X. "WC: Memory as Muse." *Fifty Years of the American Novel: A Christian Appraisal,* ed Harold C Gardiner (NY: Scribners, 1952), 69-87.

Cooperman, Stanley. "The War Lover: Claude (WC)." *World War I and the American Novel* (Baltimore, Md: Johns Hopkins U P, 1967), 129-137. Rpt Murphy (1984).

Cousineau, Diane. "Division and Difference in *A Lost Lady.*" *WS,* 11, no 3 (1984), 305-322.

Crane, Joan St C. "WC's Corrections in the Text of *Death Comes for the Archbishop,* 1927 to 1945." *PBSA,* 74, no 2 (1980), 117-131.

Cunliffe, Marcus. "The Two or More Worlds of WC." Slote & Faulkner, 21-42.

Curtin, William M. "WC: Individualism and Style." *CLQ,* 8 (Jun 1968), 37-55.

Curtin. "WC and the *Varieties of Religious Experience.*" *Renascence,* 27 (Spring 1975), 115-123.

Dahl, Curtis. "An American Georgic: WC's *My Ántonia.*" *CL,* 7 (Winter 1955), 43-51.

Dekker, George. "The Hero and Heroine of Historical Romance." *The American Historical Romance* (Cambridge: Cambridge U P, 1987), 220-271.

Ditsky, John. " 'Listening With Supersensual Ear': Music in the Novels of WC." *JNT,* 13 (Fall 1983), 154-163.

Douglas, Ann. "WC: A Problematic Ideal." *Women, the Arts, and the 1920s in Paris and New York,* ed Kenneth W Wheeler & Virginia Lee Lussier (New Brunswick, NJ: Transaction, 1982), 14-19.

Edel, Leon. "Psychoanalysis." *Literary Biography* (Garden City, NY: Doubleday, 1959), 91-122. Augmented as "A Cave of One's Own." *Stuff of Sleep and Dreams* by Edel (NY: Harper & Row, 1982).

Edel. "Homage to WC." Slote & Faulkner, 185-204.

Edgar, Pelham. "Two Anti-Realists: WC and Cabell." *The Art of the Novel* (NY: Macmillan, 1933), 255-267.

Eichorn, Harry B. "A Falling Out With Love: *My Mortal Enemy.*" Murphy (1984), 230-243.

Fetterley, Judith. "*My Ántonia,* Jim Burden and the Dilemma of the Lesbian Writer." *Gender Studies: New Directions in Feminist Criticism,* ed Judith Spector (Bowling Green, Ohio: Bowling Green State U Popular P, 1986), 43-59.

Footman, Robert H. "The Genius of WC." *AL,* 10 (May 1938), 123-141.

Fox, Maynard. "Symbolic Representation in WC's *O Pioneers!*" *WAL,* 9 (Fall 1974), 187-196.

Fryer, Judith. *Felicitous Space: The Imaginative Structures of Edith Wharton and WC* (Chapel Hill: U North Carolina P, 1986), 201-342.

Gale, Robert L. "WC and the Past." *SA,* 4 (1958), 209-222.

Gelfant, Blanche H. "The Forgotten Reaping-Hook: Sex in *My Ántonia.*" *AL,* 43 (Mar 1971), 60-82. Rpt Murphy (1984), Bloom (1985), Bloom (1987).

Gelfant. "Movement and Melody: The Disembodiment of Lucy Gayheart." *Women Writing in America* (Hanover, NH: U P New England, 1984), 117-143.

Gelfant. " 'Lives' of Women Writers: C, Austin, Porter / Willa, Mary, Katherine Anne." *Novel,* 18 (Fall 1984), 64-80.

George, Benjamin. "The French-Canadian Connection: WC as a Canadian Writer." *WAL,* 11 (Fall 1976), 249-261.

Gervaud, Michel. "WC and France: Elective Affinities." Slote & Faulkner, 65-81.

Giannone, Richard. "WC and the Human Voice." Murphy (1974), 21-49.

Giannone. "WC and the Unfinished Drama of Deliverance." *PrS,* 52 (Spring 1978), 25-46.

Gleason, John B. "The 'Case' of WC." *WAL,* 20 (Winter 1986), 275-299.

Goodman, Charlotte. "The Lost Brother, the Twin: Women Novelists and the Male-Female *Bildungsroman.*" *Novel,* 17 (Fall 1983), 28-43.

Greene, George. "*Death Comes for the Archbishop.*" *NMQ,* 27 (Spring-Summer 1957), 69-82.

Greene. "WC at Mid-Century." *Thought,* 32 (Winter 1957-1958), 577-592.

Griffiths, Frederick T. "The Woman Warrior: WC and *One of Ours.*" *WS,* 11, no 3 (1984), 261-285.

Grumbach, Doris. "A Study of the Small Room in *The Professor's House.*" *WS,* 11, no 3 (1984), 327-345.

Gwin, Minrose C. "Sapphira and Her Slave Women: C and Her Problematic South."

Black and White Women of the Old South (Knoxville: U Tennessee P, 1985), 131-149.

Hamner, Eugénie Lambert. "The Unknown, Well-Known Child in C's Last Novel." *WS*, 11, no 3 (1984), 347-357.

Harrell, David. " 'We Contacted Smithsonian': The Wetherills at Mesa Verde." *NMHistR*, 62 (Jul 1987), 229-248.

Hatcher, Harlan. "WC and the Shifting Moods." *Creating the American Novel* (NY: Farrar & Rinehart, 1935), 58-71.

Havighurst, Walter. "Prairie Life in *My Ántonia*." *My Ántonia* (Boston: Houghton Mifflin, 1949), v-viii.

Helmick, Evelyn Thomas. "The Broken World: Medievalism in *A Lost Lady*." *Renascence*, 28 (Autumn 1975), 39-46. Rpt Murphy (1984).

Helmick. "The Mysteries of Ántonia." *MQ*, 17 (Winter 1976), 173-185. Rpt Bloom (1987).

Hicks, Granville. "The Case Against WC." *EJ*, 22 (Nov 1933), 703-710.

Hinz, John P. "WC--Prairie Spring." *PrS*, 23 (Spring 1949), 82-88.

Hinz. "*A Lost Lady* and *The Professor's House*." *VQR*, 29 (Winter 1953), 70-85.

Huf, Linda. "*The Song of the Lark* (1915): The Exception of WC." *A Portrait of the Artist as a Young Woman* (NY: Ungar, 1983), 80-102.

Jessup, Josephine Lurie. "WC: Tutelary Patroness." *The Faith of Our Feminists: A Study in the Novels of Edith Wharton, Ellen Glasgow, WC* (NY: Smith, 1950), 54-75, passim.

Jones, Howard Mumford. *The Bright Medusa* (Urbana: U Illinois P, 1952), 12-34.

Jones. "WC." *The Frontier in American Fiction* (Jerusalem: Magness, 1956), 75-95.

Kazin, Alfred. "Elegy and Satire: WC and Ellen Glasgow." *On Native Grounds* (NY: Reynal & Hitchcock, 1942), 247-264.

Klein, Marcus. "Introduction." *My Mortal Enemy* (NY: Vintage/Random House, 1961), v-xxii.

Klug, Michael A. "WC: Between Red Cloud and Byzantium." *CRevAS*, 12 (Winter 1981), 287-299.

Knopf, Alfred A. "Miss C." Slote & Faulkner, 205-224.

Kohler, Dayton. "WC: 1876-1947." *CE*, 9 (Oct 1947), 8-18.

Kronenberger, Louis. "WC." *Bookman*, 74 (Oct 1931), 134-140.

Kubitschek, Missy Dehn. "St. Peter and the World All Before Him." *WAL*, 17 (Spring 1982), 13-20.

Lambert, Deborah G. "The Defeat of a Hero: Autonomy and Sexuality in *My Ántonia*." *AL*, 53 (Jan 1982), 676-690. Rpt Bloom (1987).

Lavender, David. "The Tyranny of Facts." *Old Southwest, New Southwest*, ed Judy N

Lensink (Tucson, Ariz: Tucson Public Library, 1987), 62-73.

Lawrence, Margaret. "WC." *The School of Femininity* (NY: Stokes, 1936), 355-364.

Leddy, Michael. "Observation and Narration in WC's *Obscure Destinies*." *SAF*, 16 (Autumn 1988), 141-153.

Lee, Robert Edson. "The Westerners: WC." *From West to East* (Urbana: U Illinois P, 1966), 112-135.

Love, Glen A. "The Cowboy in the Laboratory: WC's Hesitant Moderns." *New Americans: The Westerner and the Modern Experience in the American Novel* (Lewisburg, Pa: Bucknell U P, 1982), 107-169.

Machen, Meredith R. "Carlyle's Presence in *The Professor's House*." *WAL*, 14 (Winter 1980), 273-286.

Martin, Terence. "The Drama of Memory in *My Ántonia*." *PMLA*, 84 (Mar 1969), 304-311. Rpt Bloom (1987).

Maxfield, James F. "Strategies of Self-Deception in WC's *The Professor's House*." *SNNTS*, 16 (Spring 1984), 72-86.

McGill, Robert Alan. "Heartbreak: Western Enchantment and Western Fact in WC's *The Professor's House*." *SDR*, 16 (Autumn 1978), 56-79.

McNamara, Robert. "Phases of American Religion in Thornton Wilder and WC." *CathW*, 135 (Sep 1932), 641-649.

Mencken, H L. "Sunrise on the Prairie." *Smart Set*, 58 (Feb 1919), 138-144. Rpt Schroeter.

Mencken. "WC." *The Borzoi 1920*, ed Alfred Knopf (NY: Knopf, 1920), 28-31.

Miller, James E, Jr. "*My Ántonia*: A Frontier Drama of Time." *AQ*, 10 (Winter 1958), 476-484. Rpt Bloom (1987).

Miller. "*My Ántonia* and the American Dream." *PrS*, 48 (Summer 1974), 112-123.

Miller. "WC and the Art of Fiction." Slote & Faulkner, 121-148.

Monroe, N Elizabeth. "Trends of the Future in WC." *The Novel and Society* (Chapel Hill: U North Carolina P, 1941), 225-245.

Morgan, H Wayne. "WC: The Artist's Quest." *Writers in Transition* (NY: Hill & Wang, 1963), 60-81.

Morris, Lloyd. "WC." *NAR*, 219 (May 1924), 641-652.

Morrow, Nancy. "WC's *A Lost Lady* and the Nineteenth Century Novel of Adultery." *WS*, 11, no 3 (1984), 287-303.

Moseley, Ann. "The Dual Nature of Art in *The Song of the Lark*." *WAL*, 14 (Spring 1979), 19-32.

Moseley. "The Pueblo Emergence Myth in C's *Death Comes for the Archbishop*." *SwAL*, 8 (Fall 1982), 27-35.

Murphy, John J. "WC's Archbishop: A Western and Classical Perspective." *WAL,* 13 (Summer 1978), 141-150. Rpt Bloom (1985).

Murphy. "Euripides' *Hippolytus* and C's *A Lost Lady.*" *AL,* 53 (Mar 1981), 72-86.

Murphy. "A Comprehensive View of C's *O Pioneers!*" Murphy (1984), 113-127.

Murphy. "WC and Religion: Highway to the World and Beyond." *L&B,* 4 (1984), 49-68.

Murphy. "WC." *A Literary History of the American West* (Fort Worth: Texas Christian U P, 1987), 686-715.

Murphy & Kevin A Synnott. "The Recognition of WC's Art." Murphy (1984), 1-28.

Murphy, Michael W. "WC's Mortal Affirmation." *Greyfriar,* 19 (1978), 40-48.

Myers, Walter L. "The Novel Dedicate." *VQR,* 8 (Jul 1932), 410-418.

Nichols, Kathleen L. "The Celibate Male in *A Lost Lady:* The Unreliable Center of Consciousness." Murphy (1984), 186-197.

Nyquist, Edna. "The Significance of the Locale in the Nebraska Fiction of WC, Especially in *My Ántonia.*" *WSL,* 2 (1965), 81-89.

O'Brien, Sharon. "The Unity of WC's 'Two-Part Pastoral': Passion in *O Pioneers!*" *SAF,* 6 (Autumn 1978), 157-171.

O'Brien. "Tomboyism and Adolescent Conflict: Three Nineteenth-Century Case Studies." *Woman's Being, Woman's Place,* ed Mary Kelley (Boston: Hall, 1979), 351-372.

O'Brien. "Mothers, Daughters, and the 'Art Necessity': WC and the Creative Process." *American Novelists Revisited,* ed Fritz Fleischmann (Boston: Hall, 1982), 265-298.

O'Brien. " 'The Thing Not Named': WC as a Lesbian Writer." *Signs,* 9 (Summer 1984), 576-599.

O'Connor, Margaret Anne. "A Guide to the Letters of WC." *RALS,* 4 (Autumn 1974), 145-172.

Oehlschlaeger, Fritz. "WC's 'Consequences' and *Alexander's Bridge:* An Approach Through R. D. Laing and Ernest Becker." *MFS,* 32 (Summer 1986), 191-202.

Olson, Paul A. "The Epic and Great Plains Literature: Rolvaag, C, and Neihardt." *PrS,* 55 (Spring-Summer 1981), 263-285.

Pannill, Linda. "WC's Artist-Heroines." *WS,* 11, no 3 (1984), 223-232.

Pers, Mona. "Repetition in WC's Early Writings: Clues to the Development of an Artist." *AmerSSc,* 8, no 2 (1976), 55-66.

Pers. "Through the Looking-Glass With WC." *SN,* 48, no 1 (1976), 90-96.

Piacentino, Edward J. "Another Angle of WC's Artistic Prism: Impressionistic Character Portraiture in *My Ántonia.*" *Midamerica,* 9 (1982), 53-64.

Popken, Randall L. "From Innocence to Experience in *My Ántonia* and *Boy Life on the Prairie.*" *NDQ,* 46 (Spring 1978), 73-81.

Porter, Katherine Anne. "Critical Reflections on WC." *The Troll Garden* (NY: NAL, 1961), 139-151.

Porterfield, Alexander. "Contemporary American Authors: V: WC." *London Mercury,* 13 (Mar 1926), 516-524.

Priestley, J B. "Introduction." *A Lost Lady* (London: Hamilton, 1961), unpaged.

Priestley. "Introduction." *The Professor's House* (London: Hamilton, 1961), unpaged.

Pulsipher, Jenny Hale. "Expatriation and Reconciliation: The Pilgrimage Tradition in *Sapphira and the Slave Girl.*" *L&B,* 8 (1988), 89-100.

Quirk, Tom. "Fitzgerald and C: *The Great Gatsby.*" *AL,* 54 (Dec 1982), 576-591.

Randall, John H, III. "WC and the Pastoral Tradition." Murphy (1974), 75-96.

Romines, Ann. "After the Christmas Tree: WC and Domestic Ritual." *AL,* 60 (Mar 1988), 61-82.

Rose, Phyllis. "Modernism: The Case of WC." *Modernism Reconsidered,* ed Robert Kiely (Cambridge: Harvard U P, 1983), 123-145.

Rosowski, Susan J. "The Pattern of WC's Novels." *WAL,* 15 (Winter 1981), 243-263.

Rosowski. "WC's *A Lost Lady:* Art Versus the Closing Frontier." *GPQ,* 2 (Fall 1982), 239-248.

Rosowski. "WC's American Gothic: *Sapphira and the Slave Girl.*" *GPQ,* 4 (Fall 1984), 220-230.

Rosowski. "WC's Female Landscapes: *The Song of the Lark* and *Lucy Gayheart.*" *WS,* 11, no 3 (1984), 233-246.

Rosowski. "WC's Magnificat: Matriarchal Christianity in *Shadows on the Rock.*" *L&B,* 8 (1988), 66-75.

Rosowski & Bernice Slote. "WC's 1916 Mesa Verde Essay: The Genesis of *The Professor's House.*" *PrS,* 58 (Winter 1984), 81-92.

Roulston, Robert. "The Contrapuntal Complexity of WC's *The Song of the Lark.*" *MQ,* 17 (Jul 1976), 350-368.

Rucker, Mary E. "Prospective Focus in *My Ántonia.*" *ArQ,* 29 (Winter 1973), 303-316.

Sato, Hiroko. "WC in Japan." Slote & Faulkner, 84-97.

Schach, Paul. "Russian Wolves in Folktales and Literature of the Plains: A Question of Origins." *GPQ,* 3 (Spring 1983), 67-78.

Schneider, Sister Lucy. "Artistry and Instinct: WC's 'Land-Philosophy.' " *CLAJ,* 16 (Jun 1973), 485-504.

Scholes, Robert E. "Hope and Memory in *My Ántonia.*" *Shenandoah,* 14 (Autumn 1962), 24-29. Rpt Bloom (1987).

Schroeter, James. "WC and *The Professor's House*." YR, 54 (Jun 1965), 494-512. Rpt Schroeter.

Schwind, Jean. "The 'Beautiful' War in *One of Ours*." MFS, 30 (Spring 1984), 53-71.

Schwind. "The Benda Illustrations to *My Ántonia*: C's Silent Supplement to Jim Burden's Narrative." PMLA, 100 (Jan 1985), 51-67.

Sherman, Stuart. "WC and the Changing World." *Critical Woodcuts* (NY: Scribners, 1926), 32-48.

Skaggs, Merrill Maguire. "WC's Experimental Southern Novel." MissQ, 35 (Winter 1981-1982), 3-14.

Skaggs. "A Good Girl in Her Place: C's *Shadow on the Rock*." R&L, 17 (Autumn 1985), 27-36.

Skaggs. "*Death Comes for the Archbishop*: C's Mystery and Manners." AL, 57 (Oct 1985), 395-406.

Skaggs. "Death in C Major: WC's Perilous Journey Toward the Ordinary in *Lucy Gayheart*." L&B, 8 (1988), 76-88.

Slote, Bernice. "WC and Her First Book." *April Twilights (1903)* (Lincoln: U Nebraska P, 1968), ix-xlv.

Slote. "WC Reports Chautauqua, 1894." PrS, 43 (Spring 1969), 117-128.

Slote. "WC as a Regional Writer." KQ, 2 (Spring 1970), 7-15.

Slote. "Introduction." *Uncle Valentine and Other Stories*, ix-xxx.

Slote. "WC: The Secret Web." Murphy (1974), 1-19.

Slote. "Introduction." *Alexander's Bridge* (Lincoln: U Nebraska P, 1977), v-xxvi. Rpt Murphy (1984).

Slote. "WC and the Sense of History." *Women, Women Writers, and the West,* ed L L Lee & Lewis Merrill (Troy, NY: Whitston, 1980), 161-171.

Smith, Eleanor M. "The Literary Relationship of Sarah Orne Jewett and WSC." NEQ, 29 (Dec 1956), 472-492.

Snell, George. "Edith Wharton and WC: The James Influence." *The Shapers of American Fiction, 1798-1947* (NY: Dutton, 1947), 140-156.

Sternshein, Mary Kemper. "The Land of Nebraska and Ántonia Shimerda." HGP, 16 (Spring 1983), 34-42.

Stewart, David H. "C's Mortal Comedy." QQ, 73 (Summer 1966), 244-259.

Stineback, David C. "WC's Ironic Masterpiece." ArQ, 29 (Winter 1973), 317-330.

Stineback. "No Stone Unturned: Popular Versus Professional Evaluations of WC." Prospects, 7 (1982), 167-176.

Stouck, David. "Perspective as Structure and Theme in *My Ántonia*." TSLL, 12 (Summer 1970), 285-294. Rpt Bloom (1987).

Stouck. "WC's Unfurnished Novel: Narration in Perspectives." WascanaR, 6, no 2 (1972), 41-51.

Stouck. "*O Pioneers!*: WC and the Epic Imagination." PrS, 46 (Spring 1972), 23-34.

Stouck. "WC and *The Professor's House*: 'Letting Go With the Heart.' " WAL, 7 (Spring 1972), 13-24.

Stouck. "C's Archbishop and Travel Writing." WAL, 17 (Spring 1982), 3-12.

Stouck. "Marriage and Friendship in *My Ántonia*." GPQ, 2 (Fall 1982), 224-231.

Stouck. "WC and the Impressionistic Novel." Murphy (1984), 48-66.

Stouck, Mary-Ann & David. "Hagiographical Style in *Death Comes for the Archbishop*." UTQ, 41 (Summer 1972), 293-307.

Stouck, Mary-Ann & David. "Art and Religion in *Death Comes for the Archbishop*." ArQ, 29 (Winter 1973), 293-302.

Strychacz, Thomas F. "The Ambiguities of Escape in WC's *The Professor's House*." SAF, 14 (Spring 1986), 49-61.

Sutherland, Donald. "WC: The Classic Voice." Slote & Faulkner, 156-179. Rpt Bloom (1985).

Swift, John N. "Memory, Myth, and *The Professor's House*." WAL, 20 (Winter 1986), 301-314.

Tanner, Stephen L. "Seeking and Finding in C's *My Mortal Enemy*." L&B, 8 (1988), 27-38.

Thorberg, Raymond. "WC: From *Alexander's Bridge* to *My Ántonia*." TCL, 7 (Jan 1962), 147-158.

Toler, Sister Colette. "WC's Vision of the Artist." *Personalist*, 45 (Autumn 1964), 503-523.

Trilling, Lionel. "WC." *After the Genteel Tradition,* ed Malcolm Cowley (NY: Norton, 1937), 52-63. Rpt Bloom (1985).

Van Antwerp, Margaret A, ed. "WC." *Dictionary of Literary Biography Documentary Series,* Vol 1 (Detroit: Bruccoli Clark/Gale, 1982), 57-104.

Wagenknecht, Edward. "WC and the Lovely Past." *Cavalcade of the American Novel* (NY: Holt, 1952), 319-338.

Walker, Don D. "The Western Humanism of WC." WAL, 1 (Summer 1966), 75-90.

Wasserman, Loretta. "The Lovely Storm: Sexual Initiation in Two Early WC Novels." SNNTS, 14 (Winter 1982), 348-358.

Wasserman. "The Music of Time: Henri Bergson and WC." AL, 57 (May 1985), 226-239.

Wasserman. "WC's 'The Old Beauty' Reconsidered." SAF, 16 (Autumn 1988), 217-227.

Watkins, Floyd C. "*My Ántonia*: 'Still, All Day Long, Nebraska,' " "*Death Comes for the Archbishop*: Worlds Old and New." *In Time and Place* (Athens: U Georgia P, 1977), 71-

101, 103-130.

Welty, Eudora. "The House of WC." Slote & Faulkner, 3-20. Rpt Murphy (1984), Bloom (1985).

West, Rebecca. "The Classic Artist." *The Strange Necessity* (Garden City, NY: Doubleday, Doran, 1928), 233-248. Rpt Schroeter.

Whaley, Elizabeth Gates. "C's *My Mortal Enemy*." *PrS*, 48 (Summer 1974), 124-133.

Whipple, T K. "WC." *Spokesmen* (NY: Appleton, 1928), 139-160.

Wild, Barbara. " 'The Thing Not Named' in *The Professor's House*." *WAL*, 12 (Winter 1978), 263-274.

Winsten, Archer. "A Defense of WC." *Bookman*, 74 (Mar 1932), 634-640.

Woodress, James. "Sarah Orne Jewett and WC: Anti-Realists." *English Studies Today*, 5th Series, ed Sencer Tonguc (Istanbul: Matbaasi, 1973), 477-488.

Woodress. "WC: American Experience and European Tradition." Slote & Faulkner, 43-62.

Woodress. "WC and History." *ArQ*, 34 (Autumn 1978), 239-254.

Woodress. "The Uses of Biography: The Case of WC." *GPQ*, 2 (Fall 1982), 195-203.

Woodress. "C and Her Friends." Murphy (1984), 81-95.

Woods, Lucia. "Light and Shadow in the C World: A Personal Essay." *GPQ*, 4 (Fall 1984), 245-263.

Work, James C. "WC's Archbishop and the Seven Deadly Sins." *PVR*, 14 (Spring 1986), 93-103.

Yongue, Patricia Lee. "Search and Research: WC in Quest of History." *SwAL*, 5 (1975), 27-39.

Yongue. "WC's *The Professor's House* and Dutch Genre Painting." *Renascence*, 31 (Spring 1979), 155-167.

Zabel, Morton Dauwen. "WC: The Tone of Time." *Craft and Character* (NY: Viking, 1957), 264-275. Rpt Bloom (1985).

James Woodress

MARY HARTWELL CATHERWOOD

Luray, Ohio, 16 Dec 1847-Chicago, Ill, 26 Dec 1902

To modern students of American literature, Mary Hartwell Catherwood is significant for her regional stories recording nineteenth-century life in the Great Lakes region of the Midwest. To her own contemporaries, Catherwood was primarily known as a proponent of the historical romance, a genre that experienced tremendous popularity at the end of the century. Rejecting realism, she wrote novels that were set in the Canadian and American Midwest during the eras of exploration and colonization. Like her regional stories, her historical novels are enriched by careful attention to the details of their time and place. She wrote prolifically for both juvenile and adult journals throughout her career, and much of her regional fiction remains uncollected.

BIBLIOGRAPHIES

Bibliography of American Literature, comp Jacob Blanck. New Haven: Yale U P, 1955-1991. Primary.

Price, Robert. "MHC: A Bibliography." *JISHS*, 33 (Mar 1940), 68-77. Primary.

Price. "MHC's Literary Record of the Great Lakes and French-America." *MichH*, 30 (Oct 1946), 759-763. Primary.

BOOKS

A Woman in Armor. NY: Carleton / London: Low, 1875. Novel.

The Dogberry Bunch. Boston: Lothrop, 1879. Children's novel.

Craque-o'-Doom. Philadelphia: Lippincott, 1881. Novel.

Rocky Fork. Boston: Lothrop, 1882. Children's novel.

Old Caravan Days. Boston: Lothrop, 1884. Children's stories.

The Secrets at Roseladies. Boston: Lothrop, 1888. Children's novel.

The Romance of Dollard. NY: Century, 1889. Novel.

The Story of Tonty. Chicago: McClurg, 1890. Novel.

The Lady of Fort St. John. Boston & NY: Houghton, Mifflin, 1891. Novel.

Old Kaskaskia. Boston & NY: Houghton, Mifflin, 1893. Novel.

The White Islander. NY: Century, 1893. Novel.

The Chase of Saint-Castin and Other Stories of the French in the New World. Boston & NY: Houghton, Mifflin, 1894.

The Days of Jeanne D'Arc. NY: Century, 1897. Novel.

The Spirit of an Illinois Town and The Little Renault: Two Stories of Illinois at Different Periods. Boston & NY: Houghton, Mifflin, 1897.

Bony and Ban: The Story of a Printing Venture. Boston: Lothrop, 1898. Children's novel.

Heroes of the Middle West: The French. Boston: Ginn, 1898. Children's nonfiction.

Mackinac and Lake Stories. NY & London: Harper, 1899.

The Queen of the Swamp and Other Plain Americans. Boston & NY: Houghton, Mifflin, 1899. Stories.

Spanish Peggy: A Story of Young Illinois. Chicago & NY: Stone, 1899. Children's novel.

Lazarre. Indianapolis: Bowen-Merrill, 1901. Novel.

MANUSCRIPTS & ARCHIVES

The Newberry Library, Chicago.

BIOGRAPHY

Books

Price, Robert. "A Critical Biography of Mrs. MHC." Dissertation: Ohio State U, 1943.

Wilson, M L. *Biography of MHC.* Newark, Ohio: American Tribune, 1904.

CRITICAL STUDIES

Book Sections & Articles

Garland, Hamlin. *Roadside Meetings* (NY: Macmillan, 1930), 252-256.

Herron, Ima Honaker. *The Small Town in American Literature* (Durham, NC: Duke U P, 1939), 230-231.

Monaghan, Jay. "*Spanish Peggy,* by MHC." *JISHS,* 40 (Mar 1947), 82-84.

Pattee, Fred Lewis. *The Development of the American Short Story* (NY: Harper, 1923), passim.

Price, Robert. "Mrs. C's Early Experiments With Critical Realism." *AL,* 17 (May 1945), 140-151.

Price. "MHC and Cincinnati." *CHSB,* 22 (Jul 1964), 162-168.

Quinn, Arthur Hobson. "The Romance of History and Politics." *American Fiction* (NY: Appleton-Century, 1936), 484-508.

Simonds, W E. "MHC." *CriticNY,* 42 (Feb 1903), 169-171

Simpson, Claude M. "MHC." *The Local Colorists* (NY: Harper, 1960), 116-128.

Treece, Peggy B. "A Hidden Woman of Local Color: Mrs. MHC." *MMisc,* 3 (1975), 24-31.

Treece. "MHC's Disguised Handbook of Feminism." *MMisc,* 7 (1979), 7-14.

Jane Atteridge Rose

ROBERT W. CHAMBERS

Brooklyn, NY, 26 May 1865-New York City, NY, 16 Dec 1933

A prolific writer of best-selling novels, short stories, and nature books for children, Robert W. Chambers began his career as a magazine illustrator. He worked in many genres, producing more than eighty volumes, including historical novels (dealing with the American Revolution, the Civil War, and the Franco-Prussian War), romances, social satires, problem novels, science fiction, supernatural fiction, and detective stories. Chambers's reputation now rests primarily on his supernatural and fantasy fiction, particularly his classic collection of linked stories, *The King in Yellow*.

BIBLIOGRAPHY

Hornberger, Theodore. "American First Editions at Texas University: V. RWC (1865-1933)." *LCUT*, 2 (Spring 1947), 193-195. Primary.

BOOKS

In the Quarter (Anon). NY & Chicago: Neely, 1894. Novel.

The Red Republic: A Romance of the Commune. NY & London: Putnam, 1895. Novel.

The King in Yellow. NY: Neely, 1895. Stories.

With the Band. NY: Stone & Kimball, 1896. Poetry.

A King and a Few Dukes: A Romance. NY & London: Putnam, 1896. Novel.

The Maker of Moons. NY & c: Putnam, 1896. Stories.

The Mystery of Choice. NY: Appleton, 1897. Stories.

Lorraine: A Romance. NY & London: Harper, 1898. Novel.

The Haunts of Men. NY: Stokes, 1898. Stories.

Ashes of Empire: A Romance. NY: Stokes, 1898. Novel.

Outsiders: An Outline. NY: Stokes, 1899. Novel.

The Cambric Mask: A Romance. NY: Stokes, 1899. Novel.

The Conspirators: A Romance. NY & London: Harper, 1900; *A Gay Conspiracy.* London & NY: Harper, 1900. Novel.

Cardigan: A Novel. NY & London: Harper, 1901.

The Maid-at-Arms. NY & London: Harper, 1902. Novel.

Outdoorland: A Story for Children. NY & London: Harper, 1902.

The Maids of Paradise. NY & London: Harper, 1903. Novel.

Orchard-Land: A Story for Children. NY & London: Harper, 1903.

River-Land: A Story for Children. NY & London: Harper, 1904.

In Search of the Unknown. NY & London: Harper, 1904. Stories.

A Young Man in a Hurry and Other Short Stories. NY & London: Harper, 1904.

Forest-Land. NY: Appleton, 1905. Children's story.

Iole. NY: Appleton, 1905. Novel.

The Reckoning. NY: Appleton, 1905. Novel.

The Fighting Chance. NY: Appleton, 1906. Novel.

The Tracer of Lost Persons. NY: Appleton, 1906. Novel.

Mountain-Land. NY: Appleton, 1906. Children's story.

The Tree of Heaven. NY: Appleton, 1907. Stories.

Garden-Land. NY: Appleton, 1907. Children's story.

The Younger Set. NY: Appleton, 1907. Novel.

The Firing Line. NY: Appleton, 1908. Novel.

Some Ladies in Haste. NY: Appleton, 1908. Stories.

The Danger Mark. NY: Appleton, 1909. Novel.

Hide and Seek in Forest-land. NY & Chicago: Appleton, 1909. Children's story.

Special Messenger. NY: Appleton, 1909. Novel.

Ailsa Paige: A Novel. NY & London: Appleton, 1910.

The Green Mouse. NY & London: Appleton, 1910. Stories.

The Common Law. NY & London: Appleton, 1911. Novel.

The Adventures of a Modest Man. NY & London: Appleton, 1911. Stories.

Blue-Bird Weather. NY & London: Appleton, 1912. Children's story.

The Streets of Ascalon: Episodes in the Unfinished Career of Richard Quarren, Esqre. NY & London: Appleton, 1912. Novel.

Japonette. NY & London: Appleton, 1912. Novel.

The Business of Life. NY & London: Appleton, 1913. Novel.

The Gay Rebellion. NY & London: Appleton, 1913. Novel.

The Hidden Children. NY & London: Appleton, 1914. Novel.

Between Friends. NY & London: Appleton, 1914. Novel.

Anne's Bridge. NY & London: Appleton, 1914. Novel.

Quick Action. NY & London: Appleton, 1914. Novel.

Athalie. NY & London: Appleton, 1915. Novel.

Police!!! NY & London: Appleton, 1915. Stories.

Who Goes There! NY & London: Appleton, 1915. Novel.

The Girl Philippa. NY & London: Appleton, 1916. Novel.

The Better Man. NY & London: Appleton, 1916. Stories.

Barbarians. NY & London: Appleton, 1917. Novel.

The Dark Star. NY & c: Appleton, 1917. Novel.

The Laughing Girl. NY & London: Appleton, 1918. Novel.

The Restless Sex. NY & London: Appleton, 1918. Novel.

The Crimson Tide: A Novel. NY & London: Appleton, 1919.

In Secret. NY: Doran, 1919. Novel.

The Moonlit Way: A Novel. NY & London: Appleton, 1919.

The Slayer of Souls. NY: Doran, 1920. Novel.

The Little Red Foot. NY: Doran, 1921. Novel.

The Flaming Jewel. NY: Doran, 1922. Novel.

Eris. NY: Doran, 1922. Novel.

The Hi-Jackers. NY: Doran, 1923. Novel.

The Talkers. NY: Doran, 1923. Novel.

America; or, The Sacrifice, a Romance of the American Revolution. NY: Grosset & Dunlap, 1924. Novel.

Marie Halkett: A True Story. London: Unwin, 1925; NY & London: Appleton-Century, 1937. Novel.

The Mystery Lady. NY: Grosset & Dunlap, 1925. Novel.

The Man They Hanged. NY & London: Appleton, 1926. Novel.

The Drums of Aulone. NY & London: Appleton, 1927. Novel.

The Rogue's Moon. NY: Appleton, 1928. Novel.

The Sun Hawk. NY: Appleton, 1928. Novel.

The Happy Parrot. NY: Appleton, 1929. Novel.

The Mask and Other Stories. Racine, Wis: Whitman, 1929.

The Painted Minx. NY & London: Appleton, 1930. Novel.

The Rake and the Hussy. NY & London: Appleton, 1930. Novel.

Gitana. NY & London: Appleton, 1931. Novel.

War Paint and Rouge. NY & London: Appleton, 1931. Novel.

Whistling Cat. NY & London: Appleton, 1932. Novel.

Whatever Love Is. NY & London: Appleton-Century, 1933. Novel.

Secret Service Operator 13. NY & London: Appleton-Century, 1934. Novel.

The Young Man's Girl. NY & London: Appleton-Century, 1934. Novel.

The Gold Chase. NY & London: Appleton-Century, 1935. Novel.

Love and the Lieutenant. NY & London: Appleton-Century, 1935. Novel.

Beating Wings. NY & London: Appleton-Century, 1936. Novel.

The Girl in Golden Rags. NY & London: Appleton-Century, 1936. Novel.

The Fifth Horseman. NY & London: Appleton-Century, 1937.

Smoke of Battle. NY & London: Appleton-Century, 1938. Novel.

EDITION & COLLECTION

Works, 40 vols. NY: Putnam, 1895-1917.

The King in Yellow and Other Horror Stories, ed E F Bleiler. NY: Dover, 1970.

MANUSCRIPTS & ARCHIVES

The major collections are at U of Virginia Library; Colgate U Library; the Houghton Library, Harvard U; & the Beinecke Library, Yale U.

CRITICAL STUDIES

Book Sections & Articles

Baldwin, Charles C. "RWC." *The Men Who Make Our Novels* (NY: Moffat, Yard, 1919), 119-123.

Banta, Martha. "Artists, Models, Real Things, and Recognizable Types." *SLitI,* 16 (Fall 1983), 7-34.

Bleiler, E F. "Introduction." *The King in Yellow and Other Horror Stories,* vii-xiii.

Bradley, Marion Zimmer. "The (Bastard) Children of Hastur." *Nyctalops,* 6 (1972), 3-6.

Cooper, Frederic Taber. "Some Representative American Story Tellers: X—RWC." *Bookman,* 30 (Feb 1910), 612-619. Rpt *Some American Story Tellers* by Cooper (NY: Holt, 1911).

Marshall, Marguerite Mooers. "RWC." *Cosmopolitan,* 50 (Apr 1911), 708-709.

Moskowitz, Sam. "The Light Fantastics of RWC." *In Search of the Unknown* (Westport, Conn: Hyperion, 1974), unpaged.

Overton, Grant. "RWC and the Whole Truth." *Authors of the Day* (NY: Doran, 1924), 366-379.

Pendennis. "My Women Types—RWC." *Forum,* 59 (May 1918), 564-569.

Underwood, John Curtis. "RWC and Commercialism." *Literature and Insurgency* (NY: Kennerley, 1914), 447-480.

Weinstein, Lee. "C and *The King in Yellow*." *Romantist*, 3 (1979), 51-57.

Williams, Blanche Colton. "RWC." *Our Short Story Writers* (NY: Moffat, Yard, 1920), 55-72.

Gwen L. Nagel

CHARLES WADDELL CHESNUTT

Cleveland, Ohio, 20 Jun 1858-Cleveland, Ohio, 15 Nov 1932

Charles W. Chesnutt is regarded as the first African-American writer to achieve artistic success in prose fiction. His short story "The Goophered Grapevine," appearing in the *Atlantic Monthly* of August 1887, presented him to a national literary audience. Nevertheless, the book-buying public at the turn of the century was not eager to read fiction of the color line written from an antiracist perspective. The literary career that began so auspiciously lasted less than twenty years as the discouraged Chesnutt turned to more lucrative business activity and to civic affairs. With the sharply increased interest during recent years in African-American literature, Chesnutt has been reassessed and accorded a solid position as a master of the short story, a provocative novelist, a local colorist of fidelity and charm, and a skillful analyst of the social, psychological, and moral results of racism.

BIBLIOGRAPHIES & CATALOGUES

Andrews, William L. "CWC: An Essay in Bibliography." *RALS*, 6 (Spring 1976), 3-22. Secondary.

Ellison, Curtis W & E W Metcalf, Jr. *CWC: A Reference Guide*. Boston: Hall, 1977. Secondary.

First Printings of American Authors, Vol 3 (Detroit: Bruccoli Clark/Gale, 1978), 47-49. Primary.

Freeney, Mildred & Mary T Henry. *A List of Manuscripts, Published Works and Related Items in the CWC Collection of the Erastus Milo Cravath Memorial Library, Fisk University.* Nashville: Fisk U Library, 1954.

House, Beth M. *CWC Collection*. Nashville: Fisk U Library, 1973. Primary.

Martin, Olivia J. *Guide to the Microfilm Edition of the CWC Papers in the Library of the Western Reserve Historical Society*. Cleveland: Ohio Historical Society, 1972.

BOOKS

The Conjure Woman. Boston & NY: Houghton, Mifflin, 1899. Stories.

Frederick Douglass. Boston: Small, Maynard, 1899. Biography.

The Wife of His Youth and Other Stories of the Color Line. Boston & NY: Houghton, Mifflin, 1899.

The House Behind the Cedars. Boston & NY: Houghton, Mifflin, 1900. Novel.

The Marrow of Tradition. Boston & NY: Houghton, Mifflin, 1901. Novel.

The Colonel's Dream. NY: Doubleday, Page, 1905. Novel.

Baxter's Procrustes. Cleveland: Rowfant Club, 1966. Story.

COLLECTION

The Short Fiction of CWC, ed Sylvia Lyons Render. Washington: Howard U P, 1974.

MANUSCRIPTS & ARCHIVES

The major collections are at Fisk U Library & Western Reserve Historical Society, Cleveland, Ohio.

BIOGRAPHIES

Books

Chesnutt, Helen M. *CWC: Pioneer of the Color Line*. Chapel Hill: U North Carolina P, 1952.

Keller, Frances Richardson. *An American Crusade: The Life of CWC*. Provo, Utah: Brigham Young U P, 1978.

Articles

Andrews, William L. "A Reconsideration of *CWC: Pioneer of the Color Line*." *CLAJ*, 19 (Dec 1975), 136-151.

Flusche, Michael. "On the Color Line: CWC." *NCHR*, 53 (Jan 1976), 1-24.

CRITICAL STUDIES

Books

Andrews, William L. *The Literary Career of CWC*. Baton Rouge: Louisiana State U P, 1980.

Heermance, J Noel. *CWC: America's First Great Black Novelist*. Hamden, Conn: Archon, 1974.

Render, Sylvia Lyons. *CWC*. Boston: Twayne, 1980.

Book Sections & Articles

Ames, Russell. "Social Realism in CWC." *Phylon*, 14, no 2 (1953), 199-206.

Andrews, William L. "C's Patesville: The Presence and Influence of the Past in *The House Behind the Cedars*." *CLAJ*, 15 (Mar 1972), 284-294.

Andrews. "William Dean Howells and CWC: Criticism and Race Fiction in the Age of Booker T. Washington." *AL*, 48 (Nov 1976), 327-339.

Babb, Valerie. "Subversion and Repatriation in *The Conjure Woman*." *SoQ*, 25 (Winter 1987), 66-75.

Baldwin, Richard E. "The Art of *The Conjure Woman*." *AL*, 43 (Nov 1971), 385-398.

Bender, Bert. "The Lyrical Short Fiction of Dunbar and C." *A Singer in the Dawn: Reinterpretations of Paul Laurence Dunbar*, ed Jay Martin (NY: Dodd, Mead, 1975), 208-222.

Blake, Susan L. "A Better Mousetrap: Washington's Program and *The Colonel's Dream*." *CLAJ*, 23 (Sep 1979), 49-59.

Bone, Robert. "CC." *Down Home: A History of Afro-American Short Fiction From Its Beginnings to the End of the Harlem Renaissance* (NY: Putnam, 1975), 74-105, 293-295.

Britt, David D. "C's Conjure Tales: What You See Is What You Get." *CLAJ*, 15 (Mar 1972), 269-283.

Burnette, R V. "CWC's *The Conjure Woman* Revisited." *CLAJ*, 30 (Jun 1987), 438-453.

Chametzky, Jules. "Regional Literature and Ethnic Realities." *AR*, 31 (Fall 1971), 385-396.

Condit, John H. "Pulling a C Out of the Fire: 'Hot-Foot Hannibal.' " *CLAJ*, 30 (Jun 1987), 428-437.

Delmar, P Jay. "The Mask as Theme and Structure: CWC's 'The Sheriff 's Children' and 'The Passing of Grandison.' " *AL*, 51 (Nov 1979), 364-375.

Delmar. "Elements of Tragedy in CWC's *The Conjure Woman*." *CLAJ*, 23 (Jun 1980), 451-459.

Delmar. "Character and Structure in CWC's *The Marrow of Tradition* (1901)." *ALR*, 13 (Autumn 1980), 284-289.

Delmar. "Coincidence in CWC's *The House Behind the Cedars*." *ALR*, 15 (Spring 1982), 97-103.

Dixon, Melvin. "The Teller as Folk Trickster in C's *The Conjure Woman*." *CLAJ*, 18 (Dec 1974), 186-197.

Elder, Arlene A. "C on Washington: An Essential Ambivalence." *Phylon*, 38, no 1 (1977), 1-8.

Elder. "CWC: Art or Assimilation?" *The "Hindered Hand": Cultural Implications of Early African-American Fiction* (Westport, Conn: Greenwood, 1978), 147-197.

Farnsworth, Robert M. "Testing the Color Line—Dunbar and C." *The Black American Writer, Vol I: Fiction*, ed C W E Bigsby (De Land, Fla: Everett/Edwards, 1969), 111-124.

Farnsworth. "CC and the Color Line." *Minor American Novelists*, ed Charles A Hoyt (Carbondale: Southern Illinois U P, 1970), 28-40, 139.

Ferguson, SallyAnn H. "C's 'The Conjurer's Revenge': The Economics of Direct Confrontation." *Obsidian*, 7 (Summer-Winter 1981), 37-42.

Ferguson. "Rena Warden: C's Failed 'Future American.' " *SLJ*, 15 (Fall 1982), 74-82.

Ferguson. " 'Frank Fowler': A C Racial Pun." *SoAR*, 50 (May 1985), 47-53.

Fienberg, Lorne. "CWC and Uncle Julius: Black Storytellers at the Crossroads." *SAF*, 15 (Autumn 1987), 161-173.

Fraiman, Susan. "Mother-Daughter Romance in CWC's 'Her Virginia Mammy.' " *SSF*, 22 (Fall 1985), 443-448.

Gayle, Addison. "The Souls of Black Folk." *The Way of the New World: The Black Novel in America* (Garden City, NY: Doubleday, 1975), 25-58, 317-318.

George, Marjorie & Richard S Pressman. "Confronting the Shadow: Psycho-Political Repression in C's *The Marrow of Tradition*." *Phylon*, 48, no 4 (1987), 287-298.

Gibson, Donald B. "CWC: The Anatomy of a Dream." *The Politics of Literary Expression: A Study of Major Black Writers* (Westport, Conn: Greenwood, 1981), 125-154.

Gidden, Nancy Ann. " 'The Gray Wolf 's Ha'nt': CWC's Intrusive Failure." *CLAJ*, 27 (Jun 1984), 406-410.

Giles, James R & Thomas P Lally. "Allegory in C's *The Marrow of Tradition*." *JGE*, 35, no 4 (1984), 259-269.

Hackenberry, Charles. "Meaning and Models: The Uses of Characterization in C's *The Marrow of Tradition* and 'Mandy Oxendine.' " *ALR*, 17 (Autumn 1984), 193-202.

Harris, Trudier. "C's Frank Fowler: A Failure of Purpose?" *CLAJ*, 22 (Mar 1979), 215-228.

Haslam, Gerald W. " 'The Sheriff 's Children': C's Tragic Racial Parable." *NALF*, 2 (Summer 1968), 21-26.

Hemenway, Robert. " 'Baxter's Procrustes': Irony and Protest." *CLAJ*, 18 (Dec 1974), 172-185.

Hemenway. "The Function of Folklore in CC's *The Conjure Woman*." *JFI*, 13, no 3 (1976), 283-309.

Howells, William Dean. "Mr. CWC's Stories." *Atlantic*, 85 (May 1900), 699-701.

Jackson, Wendell. "CWC's Outrageous Fortune." *CLAJ*, 20 (Dec 1976), 195-204.

Lewis, Richard O. "Romanticism in the Fiction of CWC: The Influence of Dickens, Scott, Tourgée, and Douglass." *CLAJ*, 26 (Dec 1982), 145-171.

Mason, Julian D, Jr. "CWC as Southern Author." *MissQ*, 20 (Spring 1967), 77-89.

Mixon, Wayne. "The Unfulfilled Dream: CWC and the New South Movement." *SHR* (Bicentennial Issue 1976), 23-33.

Myers, Karen Magee. "Mythic Patterns in CWC's *The Conjure Woman* and Ovid's *Metamorphoses*." *BALF*, 13 (Spring 1979), 13-17.

Oden, Gloria C. "C's Conjure as African Survival." *MELUS*, 5 (Spring 1978), 38-48.

Ogunyemi, Chikwenye Okonjo. "The Africanness of *The Conjure Woman* and *Feather Woman of the Jungle*." *ArielE*, 8 (Apr 1977), 17-30.

Payne, Ladell. "Trunk and Branch: CWC, 1858-1932." *Black Novelists and the Southern Literary Tradition* (Athens: U Georgia P, 1981), 9-25, 104-106.

Reilly, John M. "The Dilemma in C's *The Marrow of Tradition*." *Phylon*, 32, no 1 (1971), 31-38.

Render, Sylvia Lyons. "Tar Heelia in C." *CLAJ*, 9 (Sep 1965), 39-50.

Render. "Introduction." *The Short Fiction of CWC*, 3-56.

Sedlack, Robert P. "The Evolution of CC's *The House Behind the Cedars*." *CLAJ*, 19 (Dec 1975), 125-135.

Selke, Hartmut K. "CWC: 'The Sheriff 's Children' (1889)." *The Black American Short Story in the 20th Century: A Collection of Critical Essays*, ed Peter Bruck (Amsterdam: Grüner, 1977), 21-38.

Sochen, June. "CWC and the Solution to the Race Problem." *NALF*, 3 (Summer 1969), 52-56.

Sollors, Werner. "The Goopher in CC's Conjure Tales: Superstition, Ethnicity, and Modern Metamorphoses." *LAmer*, 6 (Spring 1985), 107-129.

Stepto, Robert B. " 'The simple but intensely human life of slavery': Storytelling and the Revision of History in CWC's 'Uncle Julius Stories.' " *History and Tradition in Afro-American Culture*, ed Günter H Lenz (Frankfurt: Campus, 1984), 29-55.

Taxel, Joel. "CWC's Sambo: Myth and Reality." *NALF*, 9 (Winter 1975), 105-108.

Terry, Eugene. "CWC: A Victim of the Color Line." *CBS*, 1 (1977), 15-44.

Terry. "The Shadow of Slavery in CC's *The Conjure Woman*." *EthnicG*, 4 (May 1982), 103-125.

Turner, Darwin T. "Introduction." *The House Behind the Cedars* (Riverside, NJ: Collier, 1969), vii-xx.

Whitt, Lena M. "C's Chinquapin County." *SLJ*, 13 (Spring 1981), 41-58.

Wideman, John Edgar. "CWC: *The Marrow of Tradition*." *ASch*, 42 (Winter 1972-1973), 128-134.

Wideman. "CC and the WPA Narratives: The Oral and Literate Roots of Afro-American Literature." *The Slave's Narrative*, ed Charles T Davis & Henry Louis Gates, Jr (NY: Oxford U P, 1985), 59-78.

Wintz, Cary D. "Race and Realism in the Fiction of CWC." *OhH*, 81 (Spring 1972), 122-130.

Keneth Kinnamon

GEORGE RANDOLPH CHESTER

Hamilton County, Ohio, 1869-New York City, NY, 26 Feb 1924

George Randolph Chester began his writing career as a journalist, but his propensities toward humor, satire, and the psychology of human behavior—especially of the American businessman—led him into the short-story genre. The appeal of his early and most popular work was founded in his lively and humorous character studies. He was a canny interpreter of his times and remained critical of the often unscrupulous pursuit of the American dream. Chester rose to the top of his field when his long stories were serialized in such magazines as *Collier's, Cosmopolitan,* and *The Saturday Evening Post,* but his "Get-Rich-Quick Wallingford" stories were primarily responsible for his popular success. One of the most widely read writers of his period, Chester provided an accurate depiction of middle-class America. He has received no critical attention.

BOOKS

Get-Rich-Quick Wallingford: A Cheerful Account of the Rise and Fall of an American Business Buccaneer. Philadelphia: Altemus, 1908. Novel.

The Cash Intrigue: A Fantastic Melodrama of Modern Finance. Indianapolis: Bobbs-Merrill, 1909. Stories.

The Making of Bobby Burnit. Indianapolis: Bobbs-Merrill, 1909. Stories.

Young Wallingford. Indianapolis: Bobbs-Merrill, 1910. Stories.

The Art of Short Story Writing. Cincinnati: Publishers Syndicate, 1910. Repub as *The Art of Writing,* 1910.

The Early Bird: A Business Man's Love Story. Indianapolis: Bobbs-Merrill, 1910. Novel.

The Jingo. Indianapolis: Bobbs-Merrill, 1912. Novel.

Captain Kidd in Wall Street. NY: Hearst's International Library, 1912. Novel.

Five Thousand an Hour: How Johnny Gamble Won the Heiress. Indianapolis: Bobbs-Merrill, 1912. Novel.

Wallingford and Blackie Daw. Indianapolis: Bobbs-Merrill, 1913. Stories.

Wallingford in His Prime. Indianapolis: Bobbs-Merrill, 1913. Stories.

A Tale of Red Roses. Indianapolis: Bobbs-Merrill, 1914. Novel.

The Ball of Fire, with Lillian Chester. NY: Hearst's International Library, 1914. Novel.

Blue Pete's Escape. NY: Winthrop, 1914. Story.

The Honeymoon. NY: Winthrop, 1914. Story.

Cordelia Blossom. NY: Hearst's International Library, 1914. Novel.

The Enemy, with Lillian Chester. NY: Hearst's International Library, 1915. Novel.

Runaway June, with Lillian Chester. NY: Hearst's International Library, 1915. Novel.

The Son of Wallingford, with Lillian Chester. Boston: Small, Maynard, 1921. Stories.

The Wonderful Adventures of Little Prince Toofat. NY: McCann, 1922. Stories.

On the Lot and Off, with Lillian Chester. NY & London: Harper, 1924. Novel.

MANUSCRIPTS & ARCHIVES

Ohioana Library, Columbus, Ohio.

BIOGRAPHY

Article

Corey, Herbert. "The Author of *Wallingford*." *Cosmopolitan,* 50 (May 1911), 790-791.

Martha Bower

KATE CHOPIN

St Louis, Mo, 8 Feb 1851-St Louis, Mo, 22 Aug 1904

During her lifetime, Kate Chopin won national fame as a local colorist for her two short-story collections and gained national infamy for her "immoral" novel *The Awakening*. At the time of her death, Chopin was remembered primarily as a regional writer who characterized Louisiana Creoles and Cajuns in vivid detail. In the late 1960s and early 1970s Per Seyersted's *Critical Biography* and *Complete Works* stirred reassessment of Chopin as an important American writer. Since the 1970s the popularity and critical reputation of her writings have grown. Chopin's works have become the subjects for an array of critical approaches, drawing the interest in particular of students of American literary realism and of feminist critics.

BIBLIOGRAPHIES

"Bibliographic Essay: A Guide to the Literary Works By and About KC." Bonner (1988), 233-245.

Bibliography of American Literature, comp Jacob Blanck. New Haven: Yale U P, 1955-1991. Primary.

Bonner, Thomas, Jr. "KC: An Annotated Bibliography." *BB*, 32 (Jul-Sep 1975), 101-105. Primary & secondary.

Gannon, Barbara C. "KC, a Secondary Bibliography." *ALR*, 17 (Spring 1984), 124-129.

Potter, Richard H. "KC and Her Critics: An Annotated Checklist." *MoHSB*, 26 (Jul 1970), 306-317. Secondary.

Springer, Marlene. *Edith Wharton and KC: A Reference Guide*. Boston: Hall, 1976. Secondary.

Springer. "KC: A Reference Guide Updated." *RALS*, 11 (Autumn 1981), 281-303. Secondary.

BOOKS

At Fault. St Louis: Nixon-Jones, 1890. Novel.

Bayou Folk. Boston & NY: Houghton, Mifflin, 1894. Stories.

A Night in Acadie. Chicago: Way & Williams, 1897. Stories.

The Awakening. Chicago & NY: Stone, 1899. Novel.

A KC Miscellany, ed Per Seyersted & Emily Toth. Oslo: Universitetsforlaget / Natchitoches, La: Northwestern State U P, 1979.

EDITIONS & COLLECTIONS

The Complete Works of KC, 2 vols, ed Per Seyersted. Baton Rouge: Louisiana State U P, 1970.

KC: The Awakening and Other Stories, ed with intro by Lewis Leary. NY: Holt, Rinehart & Winston, 1970.

The Storm and Other Stories by KC With The Awakening, ed with intro by Seyersted. Old Westbury, NY: Feminist, 1974.

The Awakening: An Authoritative Text, Contexts, Criticism, ed with intro by Margaret Culley. NY: Norton, 1976.

MANUSCRIPTS & ARCHIVES

Missouri Historical Society, St Louis.

BIOGRAPHIES

Book

Seyersted, Per. *KC: A Critical Biography*. Oslo: Universitetsforlaget / Baton Rouge: Louisiana State U P, 1969.

Articles

Schuyler, William. "KC." *Writer*, 7 (Aug 1894), 115-117.

Toth, Emily. "The Misdated Death of Oscar Chopin." *KCN*, 1 (Fall 1975), 34.

Toth. "Some Problems in KC Scholarship." *KCN*, 1 (Fall 1975), 30-33.

Toth. "KC Remembered." *KCN*, 1 (Winter 1975-1976), 21-27.

Toth. "The Practical Side of Oscar Chopin's Death." *KCN*, 1 (Winter 1975-1976), 29.

CRITICAL STUDIES

Books

Bonner, Thomas, Jr. "A Critical Study of the Fiction of KC: The Formal Elements." Dissertation: Tulane U, 1975.

Bonner. *The KC Companion*. NY: Greenwood, 1988. Includes KC's translations of French fiction.

Ewell, Barbara C. *KC*. NY: Ungar, 1986.

Rankin, Daniel S. *KC and Her Creole Stories*. Philadelphia: U Pennsylvania P, 1932.
Skaggs, Peggy. *KC*. NY: Twayne, 1985.

Collections of Essays
Bloom, Harold, ed. *KC*. NY: Chelsea House, 1986.
Koloski, Bernard, ed. *Approaches to Teaching KC's The Awakening*. NY: MLA,1988.
Martin, Wendy, ed. *New Essays on The Awakening*. NY: Cambridge U P, 1988.

Special Journals
Kate Chopin Newsletter (triquarterly, 1975—Winter 1976-1977).
LaS, 14 (Spring 1975). KC issue.

Book Sections & Articles
Arms, George. "KC's *The Awakening* in the Perspective of Her Literary Career." *Essays on American Literature in Honor of Jay B. Hubbell,* ed Clarence Gohdes (Durham, NC: Duke U P, 1967), 215-228.
Arner, Robert. "KC." *LaS,* 14 (Spring 1975), 11-139.
Dyer, Joyce Coyne. "Night Images in the Works of KC." *ALR,* 14 (Autumn 1981), 216-230.
Dyer. "Lafcadio Hearn's *Chita* and KC's *The Awakening*: Two Naturalistic Tales of the Gulf Islands." *SoSt,* 23 (Winter 1984), 412-426.
Eble, Kenneth. "A Forgotten Novel: KC's *The Awakening*." *WHR,* 10 (Summer 1956), 261-269. Rpt *The Awakening: An Authoritative Text, Contexts, Criticism.*
Fletcher, Marie. "The Southern Woman in the Fiction of KC." *LaH,* 7 (Spring 1966), 117-132.
Fluck, Winfried. "Tentative Transgressions: KC's Fiction as a Mode of Symbolic Action." *SAF,* 10 (Autumn 1982), 151-171.

Lattin, Patricia Hopkins. "KC's Repeating Characters." *MissQ,* 33 (Winter 1979-1980), 19-37.
Lattin. "The Search for Self in KC's Fiction: Simple Versus Complex Vision." *SoSt,* 21 (Summer 1982), 222-235.
Leary, Lewis. "KC's Other Novel." *SLJ,* 1 (Dec 1968), 60-74.
Ringe, Donald A. "Romantic Imagery in KC's *The Awakening*." *AL,* 43 (Jan 1972), 580-588. Rpt *The Awakening: An Authoritative Text, Contexts, Criticism.*
Ringe. "Cane River World: KC's *At Fault* and Related Stories." *SAF,* 3 (Autumn 1975), 157-166.
Seyersted, Per. "KC: An Important St. Louis Writer Reconsidered." *MoHSB,* 19 (Jan 1963), 89-114.
Showalter, Elaine. "Tradition and the Female Talent: *The Awakening* as a Solitary Book." Martin, 33-58.
Skaggs, Peggy. "Three Tragic Figures in KC's *The Awakening*." *LaS,* 13 (Winter 1974), 345-364.
Toth, Emily. "The Independent Woman and 'Free' Love." *MR,* 16 (Autumn 1975), 647-664.
Toth. "KC's *The Awakening* as Feminist Criticism." *LaS,* 15 (Fall 1976), 241-251.
Toth. "KC and Literary Convention: 'Desiree's Baby.' " *SoSt,* 20 (Summer 1981), 201-208.
Wolff, Cynthia Griffin. "Thanatos and Eros: KC's *The Awakening*." *AQ,* 25 (Oct 1973), 449-471. Rpt *The Awakening: An Authoritative Text, Contexts, Criticism.*
Wolff. "KC and the Fiction of Limits: 'Desiree's Baby.' " *SLJ,* 10 (Spring 1978), 123-133.

Sandra L. Ballard

WINSTON CHURCHILL

St Louis, Mo, 10 Nov 1871-Winter Park, Fla, 12 Mar 1947

A popular American writer of the first quarter of the twentieth century, Winston Churchill was a romanticist with a fondness for American historical settings and for depicting the values of the middle class of his generation. Churchill captured in his works the heady optimism of the Progressive era, but when World War I sent the movement into decline, Churchill began a long withdrawal from writing. *The Uncharted Way,* a nonfiction religio-philosophical treatise, broke the silence but did not find the widespread readership of his early works.

BIBLIOGRAPHY

Steinbaugh, Eric. *WC: A Reference Guide.* Boston: Hall, 1985. Secondary.

BOOKS

The Celebrity: An Episode. NY & London: Macmillan, 1898. Novel.
Richard Carvel. NY & London: Macmillan, 1899. Novel.
The Crisis. NY & London: Macmillan, 1901. Novel.
Mr. Keegan's Elopement. NY & London: Macmillan, 1903. Story.
The Crossing. NY & London: Macmillan, 1904. Novel.
The Title-Mart: A Comedy in Three Acts. NY & London: Macmillan, 1905. Play.
Coniston. NY & London: Macmillan, 1906. Novel.
Mr. Crewe's Career. NY: Macmillan, 1908. Novel.
A Modern Chronicle. NY: Macmillan, 1910. Novel.
The Inside of the Cup. NY: Macmillan, 1913. Novel.
A Far Country. NY: Macmillan, 1915. Novel.
The Dwelling-Place of Light. NY: Macmillan, 1917. Novel.
The Faith of Frances Craniford. NY: npub, 1917. Story.
A Traveller in War-Time; With an Essay on the American Contribution and the Democratic Idea. NY: Macmillan, 1918. Essays.
Dr. Jonathan: A Play in Three Acts. NY: Macmillan, 1919.

The Crisis: A Play in Four Acts. NY & London: French, 1927.
The Uncharted Way: The Psychology of the Gospel Doctrine. Philadelphia: Dorrance, 1940. Nonfiction.

MANUSCRIPTS & ARCHIVES

Dartmouth C Library.

BIOGRAPHIES

Books
Schneider, Robert W. *Novelist to a Generation: The Life and Thought of WC.* Bowling Green, Ohio: Bowling Green U Popular P, 1976.
Titus, Warren I. "WC, American: A Critical Biography." Dissertation: NYU, 1957.

CRITICAL STUDIES

Books
Irvin, Frederick B. "The Didacticism of WC (1871-1947)." Dissertation: U Pittsburgh, 1947.
Titus, Warren I. *WC.* NY: Twayne, 1963.

Book Sections & Articles
Baldwin, Charles C. "WC." *The Men Who Make Our Novels* (NY: Dodd, Mead, rev 1924), 97-106.
Blodgett, Geoffrey. "WC: The Novelist as Reformer." *NEQ,* 47 (Dec 1974), 495-517.
Blotner, Joseph L. "WC and David Graham Phillips: Bosses and Lobbies." *The Political Novel* (Garden City, NY: Doubleday, 1955), 36-37.
Chapman, Eric J. "WC: Popularizer of Progressivism." *DCLB,* 8 (Apr 1968), 43-50.
Chapple, Joe Mitchell. "A Day With the Author of *Richard Carvel.*" *NatM,* 11 (Dec 1899), 247-252.
Cooper, Frederic Taber. "Some Representative American Story Tellers: XII—WC." *Bookman,* 31 (May 1910), 246-253. Rpt as "WC." *Some American Story Tellers* by Cooper (NY: Holt, 1911).
Dixon, James Main. "Some Real Persons and Places in *The Crisis.*" *Bookman,* 14 (Sep 1901), 17-20.
Ellis, J Breckinridge. "Missourians Abroad—No. 11, WC." *MHR,* 16 (Jul 1922), 517-521.

Follett, Wilson. "The Novelist's Use of History." *Bookman,* 68 (Oct 1928), 156-162.

Franklin, Phyllis. "WC." *ALR,* 8 (Summer 1975), 225-256.

Griffin, Lloyd W. "WC, American Novelist." *MB,* 23 (Nov 1948), 331-338.

Hancock, Albert Elmer. "The Historical Fiction of WC." *Outlook,* 77 (30 Jul 1904), 753-755.

Henderson, Brooks. "WC's Country." *Bookman,* 41 (Aug 1915), 607-619.

Hofstadter, Richard & Beatrice. "WC: A Study in the Popular Novel." *AQ,* 2 (Spring 1950), 12-28.

Johnson, Stanley. "A Novelist and His Novels in Politics." *WWork,* 17 (Dec 1908), 11016-11020.

Macfarlane, Peter Clark. "Evolution of a Novelist." *Collier's,* 52 (27 Dec 1913), 5-6, 24.

Milne, Gordon. "In the Vanguard: C and Phillips." *The American Political Novel* (Norman: U Oklahoma P, 1966), 87-103.

Oi, Koji. "The Railroad and the Pastoral Ideal in WC's Political Novels." *SELit,* 43 (Mar 1967), 229-244.

Parsons, Helen V. "*The Tory Lover, Oliver Wiswell,* and *Richard Carvel.*" *CLQ,* 9 (Dec 1970), 220-231.

Remick, James W. "WC and His Campaign." *Outlook,* 84 (1 Sep 1906), 17-22.

Schneider, Robert W. "Novelist to a Generation: The American WC." *MQ,* 3 (Jan 1962), 163-179.

Schneider. "WC: The Conservative Revolution." *Five Novelists of the Progressive Era* (NY: Columbia U P, 1965), 205-251.

Speare, Morris Edmund. "Mr. WC and the Novel of Political Reform." *The Political Novel: Its Development in England and in America* (NY: Oxford U P, 1924), 306-321.

Titus, Warren I. "WC (1871-1947)." *ALR,* 1 (Fall 1967), 26-31.

Underwood, John Curtis. "WC and Civic Righteousness." *Literature and Insurgency* (NY: Kennerley, 1914), 299-345.

Van Doren, Carl. "Contemporary American Novels IV—WC." *Nation,* 112 (27 Apr 1921), 619-621.

Walcutt, Charles Child. "The Romantic Compromise in the Novels of WC." *UMCMP,* no 18 (Nov 1951), 1-53.

Whitelock, William Wallace. "Mr. WC." *CriticNY,* 40 (Feb 1902), 135-141.

"WC's Exposures Are of National Concern." *Arena,* 36 (Oct 1906), 410-414.

Steven P. Ryan

SAMUEL LANGHORNE CLEMENS
(Mark Twain)

Florida, Mo, 30 Nov 1835-Redding, Conn, 21 Apr 1910

Samuel Langhorne Clemens, who wrote under the pseudonym Mark Twain, achieved immense popularity as humorist, novelist, and lecturer. He became a national icon, one of the larger-than-life figures indelibly associated with the history and literature of the United States. Clemens's reputation among his contemporaries was enhanced when, in the 1870s, *Atlantic Monthly* editor William Dean Howells emerged as a strong admirer. Clemens's present-day fame is primarily based on a masterpiece taught in most high schools and colleges, *Adventures of Huckleberry Finn*, but is bolstered by his other novels, including *A Connecticut Yankee in King Arthur's Court*, by travel narratives such as *The Innocents Abroad* and *Roughing It*, and by various dream-tales and fables of his later years, of which *The Mysterious Stranger* is the best known. Clemens's boyhood years in Hannibal, Missouri, and his youthful stint as a steamboat pilot inspired his most evocative works. In the view of a majority of critics his descriptions of small-town life along "the great Mississippi, the majestic, the magnificent Mississippi," chronicled in *The Adventures of Tom Sawyer, Life on the Mississippi, Huckleberry Finn*, and *The Tragedy of Pudd'nhead Wilson*, form the core of his most enduring work. Ernest Hemingway declared, "All modern American literature comes from one book by Mark Twain called *Huckleberry Finn*."

BIBLIOGRAPHIES

American Literary Scholarship: An Annual, 1963- . Durham, NC: Duke U P, 1965- Chapters on Mark Twain.

Beebe, Maurice & John Feaster. "Criticism of Mark Twain: A Selected Checklist." *MFS*, 14 (Spring 1968), 93-139.

Bibliography of American Literature, comp Jacob Blanck. New Haven: Yale U P, 1955-1991. Primary.

Budd, Louis J, ed. "A Listing of and Selection From Newspaper and Magazine Interviews With SLC, 1874-1910." *ALR*, 10 (Winter 1977), ix-100. Separately rpt, Arlington: American Literary Realism, U Texas, 1977.

Dolmetsch, Carl. "*Huck Finn's* First Century: A Bibliographical Survey." *ASInt*, 22 (Oct 1984), 79-121.

Johnson, Merle. *A Bibliography of the Works of Mark Twain, SLC: A List of First Editions in Book Form and of First Printings in Periodicals and Occasional Publications of His Varied Literary Activities*. NY: Harper, rev & augmented, 1935.

Machlis, Paul, ed. *Union Catalogue of C Letters*. Berkeley: U California P, 1986.

McBride, William M. *Mark Twain: A Bibliography of the Collections of the Mark Twain Memorial and the Stowe-Day Foundation*. Hartford, Conn: McBride/Publisher, 1984. Primary & secondary.

Tenney, Thomas Asa. *Mark Twain: A Reference Guide*. Boston: Hall, 1977. Annual supplements in *ALR*, 10-16 (Autumn 1977-Autumn 1983). Additional supplements in the *Mark Twain Circular* (1987-   ). Secondary.

BOOKS

The Celebrated Jumping Frog of Calaveras County, and Other Sketches. NY: Webb, 1867. Stories & sketches.

The Innocents Abroad, or the New Pilgrims' Progress. . . . Hartford, Conn: American Publishing, 1869; *The Innocents Abroad & The New Pilgrims' Progress*, 2 vols. London: Hotten, 1870. Travel.

Mark Twain's (Burlesque) Autobiography and First Romance. NY: Sheldon, 1871. Sketches.

"Roughing It." London: Routledge, 1872. Travel.

The Innocents at Home. London: Routledge, 1872. Travel.

Roughing It, augmented ed. Hartford, Conn: American Publishing, 1872 (*"Roughing It"* & *The Innocents at Home*). Travel.

A Curious Dream; and Other Sketches. . . . London: Routledge, 1872. Stories & sketches.

The Gilded Age: A Tale of Today, with Charles Dudley Warner. Hartford, Conn: American Publishing, 1873. Novel.

Mark Twain's Sketches, New and Old. Hartford, Conn: American Publishing, 1875. Stories & sketches.

The Adventures of Tom Sawyer. Hartford, Conn: American Publishing, 1876. *The Adventures of Tom Sawyer by Mark Twain: A Facsimile of the Author's Holograph Manuscript,* 2 vols. Frederick, Md: U Publications of America / Washington: Georgetown U Library, 1982. Novel.

Old Times on the Mississippi. Toronto: Belford, 1876 (pirated ed); *The Mississippi Pilot.* London: Ward, Lock & Tyler, 1877. Augmented as *Life on the Mississippi.* Boston: Osgood, 1883. Autobiographical sketches & travel.

A True Story, and The Recent Carnival of Crime. Boston: Osgood, 1877. Stories.

An Idle Excursion. Toronto: Rose-Belford, 1878. Augmented as *Punch, Brothers, Punch! and Other Sketches.* NY: Slote, Woodman, 1878. Sketches.

A Tramp Abroad. Hartford, Conn: American Publishing / London: Chatto & Windus, 1880. Travel.

1601: Conversation, as It Was by the Social Fireside, in the Time of the Tudors. Cleveland?: npub, 1880. Bawdy sketch.

The Prince and the Pauper: A Tale for Young People of All Ages. London: Chatto & Windus, 1881; Boston: Osgood, 1882. Novel.

The Stolen White Elephant. London: Chatto & Windus, 1882; *The Stolen White Elephant, Etc.* Boston: Osgood, 1882. Stories.

The Adventures of Huckleberry Finn. . . . London: Chatto & Windus, 1884; *Adventures of Huckleberry Finn. . . .* NY: Webster, 1885. *Adventures of Huckleberry Finn (Tom Sawyer's Comrade) by Mark Twain: A Facsimile of the Manuscript,* 2 vols. Detroit: Bruccoli Clark/Gale, 1983. Novel.

A Connecticut Yankee in King Arthur's Court. NY: Webster, 1889; *A Yankee at the Court of King Arthur.* London: Chatto & Windus, 1889. Novel.

The American Claimant. NY: Webster, 1892. Novel.

Merry Tales. NY: Webster, 1892. Stories.

The £1,000,000 Bank-Note and Other New Stories. NY: Webster, 1893. Stories & sketches.

Tom Sawyer Abroad by Huck Finn. NY: Webster, 1894. Novella.

Pudd'nhead Wilson: A Tale. London: Chatto & Windus, 1894. Augmented as *The Tragedy of Pudd'nhead Wilson and The Comedy of Those Extraordinary Twins.* Hartford, Conn: American Publishing, 1894. Novel & story.

Personal Recollections of Joan of Arc by the Sieur Louis de Conte. . . . NY: Harper, 1896. Historical fiction.

Tom Sawyer Abroad, Tom Sawyer, Detective, and Other Tales. NY: Harper, 1896. Stories.

Tom Sawyer, Detective, as Told by Huck Finn, and Other Stories. London: Chatto & Windus, 1897.

How to Tell a Story and Other Essays. NY: Harper, 1897.

Following the Equator: A Journey Around the World. Hartford, Conn: American Publishing, 1897; *More Tramps Abroad.* London: Chatto & Windus, 1897. Travel.

The Man That Corrupted Hadleyburg and Other Stories and Essays. NY & London: Harper, 1900. Augmented as *The Man That Corrupted Hadleyburg and Other Stories and Sketches.* London: Chatto & Windus, 1900.

A Double Barrelled Detective Story. NY & London: Harper, 1902. Novella.

My Début as a Literary Person, With Other Essays and Stories. Vol 23 of *The Writings of Mark Twain,* Autograph Edition, 1903. Stories & sketches.

A Dog's Tale. NY & London: Harper, 1904. Story.

Extracts From Adam's Diary Translated From the Original MS. NY & London: Harper, 1904. Story.

King Leopold's Soliloquy: A Defense of His Congo Rule. Boston: Warren, 1905. Essay.

Eve's Diary Translated From the Original MS. London & NY: Harper, 1906. Story.

What Is Man? (Anon). NY: De Vinne, 1906. Augmented as *What Is Man? and Other Essays* (as by Mark Twain). NY & London: Harper, 1917. Essays.

The $30,000 Bequest and Other Stories. NY & London: Harper, 1906.

Christian Science With Notes Containing Corrections to Date. NY & London: Harper, 1907. Nonfiction.

A Horse's Tale. NY & London: Harper, 1907. Story.

Is Shakespeare Dead? . . . NY & London: Harper, 1909. Essay.

Extract From Captain Stormfield's Visit to Heaven. NY & London: Harper, 1909. Novella.

Mark Twain's Speeches, comp F A Nast; intro by William Dean Howells. NY & London: Harper, 1910.

The Mysterious Stranger: A Romance, ed Albert Bigelow Paine & Frederick A Duneka. NY & London: Harper, 1916. Augmented as *The Mysterious Stranger and Other Stories,* ed Paine, 1922. Novella.

The Curious Republic of Gondour and Other Whimsical Sketches. NY: Boni & Liveright, 1919.

Mark Twain's Speeches, 2 vols, ed with intro by Paine. NY & London: Harper, 1923.

Europe and Elsewhere, ed with intro by Paine. NY & London: Harper, 1923. Stories & sketches.

Mark Twain's Autobiography, 2 vols, ed with intro by Paine. NY & London: Harper, 1924.

Sketches of the Sixties, with Bret Harte. San Francisco: Howell, 1926.

The Adventures of Thomas Jefferson Snodgrass, ed Charles Honce. Chicago: Covici, 1928. Epistolary fiction.

Mark Twain's Notebook, ed Paine. NY & London: Harper, 1935. Excerpts from notebooks with critical commentary.

Letters From the Sandwich Islands Written for the Sacramento Union, ed G Ezra Dane. San Francisco: Grabhorn, 1937. Travel correspondence.

The Washoe Giant in San Francisco..., ed Franklin Walker. San Francisco: Fields, 1938. Sketches.

Mark Twain's Travels With Mr. Brown..., ed Walker & Dane. NY: Knopf, 1940. Travel correspondence.

Mark Twain in Eruption..., ed with intro by Bernard DeVoto. NY & London: Harper, 1940. Sketches.

Mark Twain at Work, ed DeVoto. Cambridge: Harvard U P, 1942. Sketches with critical commentary.

Mark Twain, Business Man, ed Samuel Charles Webster. Boston: Atlantic Monthly/Little, Brown, 1946. Letters with critical commentary.

Mark Twain of the Enterprise..., ed Henry Nash Smith. Berkeley & Los Angeles: U California P, 1957. Newspaper articles.

Traveling With the Innocents Abroad: Mark Twain's Original Reports From Europe and the Holy Land, ed Daniel Morley McKeithan. Norman: U Oklahoma P, 1958. Travel correspondence.

Contributions to The Galaxy, 1868-1871, by Mark Twain, ed Bruce R McElderry, Jr. Gainesville, Fla: Scholars' Facsimiles & Reprints, 1961. Sketches.

"Ah Sin": A Dramatic Work, with Bret Harte; ed with intro by Frederick Anderson. San Francisco: Book Club of California, 1961. Play.

Letters From the Earth, ed DeVoto. NY & Evanston: Harper & Row, 1962. Stories & sketches.

Mark Twain's San Francisco..., ed Bernard Taper. NY & c: McGraw-Hill, 1963. Newspaper sketches & columns.

Mark Twain's Which Was the Dream and Other Symbolic Writings of the Later Years, ed with intro by John S Tuckey. Berkeley & Los Angeles: U California P, 1967 (The Mark Twain Papers Series). Novellas & stories.

Mark Twain's Satires and Burlesques, ed with intro by Franklin R Rogers. Berkeley & Los Angeles: U California P, 1967 (The Mark Twain Papers Series). Novellas & stories.

Clemens of the Call: Mark Twain in San Francisco, ed with intro by Edgar M Branch. Berkeley & Los Angeles: U California P, 1969. Newspaper sketches & columns.

Mark Twain's Mysterious Stranger Manuscripts, ed with intro by William M Gibson. Berkeley & Los Angeles: U California P, 1969 (The Mark Twain Papers Series). Drafts of novella.

Mark Twain's Hannibal, Huck & Tom, ed with intro by Walter Blair. Berkeley & Los Angeles: U California P, 1969 (The Mark Twain Papers Series). Novellas & stories.

Mark Twain's Fables of Man, ed with intro by Tuckey. Berkeley & c: U California P, 1972 (The Mark Twain Papers Series). Novellas & stories.

Mark Twain Speaking, ed Paul Fatout. Iowa City: U Iowa P, 1976. Speeches.

Mark Twain Speaks for Himself, ed Fatout. West Lafayette, Ind: Purdue U P, 1978. Speeches.

The Devil's Race Track: Mark Twain's Great Dark Writings, ed with intro by Tuckey. Berkeley & c: U California P, 1980. Novellas & stories.

Wapping Alice, Printed for the First Time..., ed Hamlin Hill. Berkeley: Bancroft Library, U California, 1981. Stories, letters & autobiographical dictation.

LETTERS, DIARIES, NOTEBOOKS

Mark Twain's Letters, 2 vols, ed Albert Bigelow Paine. NY & London: Harper, 1917.

Mark Twain's Letters to Will Bowen, ed Theodore Hornberger. Austin: U Texas P, 1941.

Mark Twain to Mrs. Fairbanks, ed Dixon Wecter. San Marino, Calif: Huntington Library, 1949. Letters.

The Love Letters of Mark Twain, ed Wecter. NY: Harper, 1949.

Mark Twain to Uncle Remus, 1881-1885, ed Thomas H English. Atlanta, Ga: Emory U Library, 1953.

Mark Twain-Howells Letters, 2 vols, ed Henry Nash Smith & William M Gibson. Cambridge: Harvard U P, 1960.

Mark Twain's Letters to Mary, ed Lewis Leary. NY: Columbia U P, 1961.

Mark Twain's Letters From Hawaii, ed A Grove Day. NY: Appleton-Century, 1966.

Mark Twain's Letters to His Publishers, 1867-1894, ed Hamlin Hill. Berkeley & Los Angeles: U California P, 1967.

Mark Twain's Correspondence With Henry Huttleston Rogers, 1893-1909, ed Leary. Berkeley & Los Angeles: U California P, 1969.

Mark Twain's Notebooks & Journals. Vol 1, 1855-1873, ed Frederick Anderson, Michael B Frank & Kenneth M Sanderson; Vol 2, 1877-1883, ed Anderson, Lin Salamo & Bernard L Stein; Vol 3, 1883-1891, ed Robert Pack Browning, Frank & Salamo. Berkeley & c: U California P, 1975, 1975, 1979 (The Mark Twain Papers Series).

Mark Twain's Letters, Volume 1, 1853-1866, ed Edgar M Branch, Frank & Sanderson. Berkeley & c: U California P, 1988 (The Mark Twain Papers Series).

OTHER

Mark Twain's Library of Humor, comp Mark Twain, William Dean Howells & Charles Hopkins Clark. NY: Webster, 1888. Rpt NY: Bonanza, 1969. Anthology.

EDITIONS & COLLECTIONS

The Writings of Mark Twain, Autograph Edition, 25 vols. Hartford, Conn: American Publishing, 1899-1907.

The Writings of Mark Twain, Author's National Edition, 25 vols. NY & London: Harper, 1899-1917.

The Writings of Mark Twain, Definitive Edition, 37 vols, ed Albert Bigelow Paine. NY: Wells, 1922-1925.

Concerning Cats: Two Tales by Mark Twain, intro by Frederick Anderson. San Francisco: Book Club of California, 1959.

The Complete Essays of Mark Twain, ed Charles Neider. Garden City, NY: Doubleday, 1963.

On the Poetry of Mark Twain With Selections From His Verse, ed Arthur L Scott. Urbana: U Illinois P, 1966.

A Pen Warmed-up in Hell, ed Anderson. NY & c: Harper & Row, 1972.

Roughing It, ed Franklin R Rogers & Paul Baender. Berkeley & c: U California P, 1972 (The Works of Mark Twain Series).

What Is Man? and Other Philosophical Writings, ed Baender. Berkeley & c: U California P, 1973 (The Works of Mark Twain Series).

The Comic Mark Twain Reader, ed Neider. Garden City, NY: Doubleday, 1977.

A Connecticut Yankee in King Arthur's Court, ed Bernard L Stein. Berkeley & c: U California P, 1979 (The Works of Mark Twain Series).

The Prince and the Pauper, ed Victor Fischer & Lin Salamo. Berkeley & c: U California P, 1979 (The Works of Mark Twain Series).

Early Tales & Sketches, Vol 1 (1851-1864), Vol 2 (1864-1865), ed Edgar M Branch & Robert H Hirst. Berkeley & c: U California P, 1979, 1981 (The Works of Mark Twain Series).

Pudd'nhead Wilson and Those Extraordinary Twins, ed Sidney E Berger. NY & London: Norton, 1980.

The Adventures of Tom Sawyer; Tom Sawyer Abroad; Tom Sawyer, Detective, ed John C Gerber, Baender & Terry Firkins. Berkeley & c: U California P, 1980 (The Works of Mark Twain Series).

The Annotated Huckleberry Finn, ed Michael Patrick Hearn. NY: Potter, 1981.

Mark Twain: Mississippi Writings, ed Guy Cardwell. NY: Library of America, 1982.

Mark Twain: Selected Writings of an American Skeptic, ed Victor Doyno. Buffalo: Prometheus, 1983.

The Innocents Abroad, Roughing It, ed Cardwell. NY: Library of America, 1984.

The Science Fiction of Mark Twain, ed David Ketterer. Hamden, Conn: Archon, 1984.

Adventures of Huckleberry Finn, ed Walter Blair & Fischer. Berkeley & c: U California P, 1988 (The Works of Mark Twain Series).

MANUSCRIPTS & ARCHIVES

The major collections are at the U of California, Berkeley, Library; the Beinecke Library, Yale U; the New York Public Library; Mark Twain Memorial & Stowe-Day Library, Hartford, Conn; the Library of Congress; the Houghton Library, Harvard U; Buffalo & Erie County Public Library; Vassar C Library; the Huntington Library, San Marino, Calif; U of Virginia Library; the Harry Ransom Humanities Research Center, U of Texas, Austin; Mark Twain Home & Museum, Hannibal, Mo; Mark Twain Birthplace Museum, Stoutsville, Mo; & the Center for Mark Twain Studies, Quarry Farm, Elmira C.

BIOGRAPHIES

Books

Andrews, Kenneth R. *Nook Farm: Mark Twain's Hartford Circle.* Cambridge: Harvard U P, 1950.

Baetzhold, Howard G. *Mark Twain and John Bull: The British Connection.* Bloomington: Indiana U P, 1970.

Benson, Ivan. *Mark Twain's Western Years.* Stanford: Stanford U P, 1938.

Brashear, Minnie M. *Mark Twain: Son of Missouri.* Chapel Hill: U North Carolina P, 1934.

Cardwell, Guy A. *Twins of Genius.* East Lansing: Michigan State C P, 1953. Includes letters between George Washington Cable & Mark Twain.

Clemens, Clara. *My Father: Mark Twain.* NY: Harper, 1931.

Clemens, Susy. *Papa: An Intimate Biography of Mark Twain*, ed Charles Neider. Garden City, NY: Doubleday, 1985.

Emerson, Everett. *The Authentic Mark Twain: A Literary Biography of SLC*. Philadelphia: U Pennsylvania P, 1984.

Fatout, Paul. *Mark Twain on the Lecture Circuit*. Bloomington: Indiana U P, 1960.

Fatout. *Mark Twain in Virginia City*. Bloomington: Indiana U P, 1964.

Faude, Wilson H. *The Renaissance of Mark Twain's House: Handbook for Restoration*. Larchmont, NY: Queens House, 1978.

Ferguson, DeLancey. *Mark Twain: Man and Legend*. Indianapolis: Bobbs-Merrill, 1943.

Gillis, William R. *Gold Rush Days With Mark Twain*. NY: Boni, 1930.

Harnsberger, Caroline T. *Mark Twain's Clara, or What Became of the C Family*. Evanston, Ill: P of Ward Schori, 1982.

Hill, Hamlin. *Mark Twain: God's Fool*. NY: Harper & Row, 1973.

Howells, William Dean. *My Mark Twain: Reminiscences and Criticisms*. NY: Harper, 1910.

Jerome, Robert D & Herbert A Wisbey, Jr, eds. *Mark Twain in Elmira*. Elmira, NY: Mark Twain Society, 1977.

Kaplan, Justin. *Mr. C and Mark Twain*. NY: Simon & Schuster, 1966.

Kaplan. *Mark Twain and His World*. NY: Simon & Schuster, 1974.

Lauber, John. *The Making of Mark Twain: A Biography*. NY: American Heritage, 1985.

Lennon, Nigey. *Mark Twain in California: The Turbulent California Years of SC*. San Francisco: Chronicle, 1982.

Mack, Effie M. *Mark Twain in Nevada*. NY: Scribner, 1947.

Meltzer, Milton. *Mark Twain Himself: A Pictorial Biography*. NY: Crowell, 1960.

Mutalik, Keshav. *Mark Twain in India*. Bombay, India: Noble Publishing House, 1978.

Paine, Albert Bigelow. *Mark Twain: A Biography*, 3 vols. NY & London: Harper, 1912.

Salsbury, Edith Colgate, ed. *Susy and Mark Twain*. NY: Harper & Row, 1965.

Shillingsburg, Miriam Jones. *At Home Abroad: Mark Twain in Australasia*. Jackson: U P Mississippi, 1988.

Turner, Arlin. *Mark Twain and George W. Cable: The Record of a Literary Friendship*. East Lansing: Michigan State U P, 1960. Includes letters by Cable about Mark Twain.

Wecter, Dixon. *Sam Clemens of Hannibal*. Boston: Houghton Mifflin, 1952.

Welland, Dennis. *Mark Twain in England*. Atlantic Highland, NJ: Humanities, 1978.

Zall, Paul M, ed. *Mark Twain Laughing: Humorous Anecdotes By and About SLC*. Knoxville: U Tennessee P, 1985.

Article

Lentz, Laurie, ed. "Mark Twain in 1906: An Edition of Selected Extracts From Isabel V. Lyon's Journal." *RALS*, 11 (Spring 1981), 1-36.

CRITICAL STUDIES

Books

Baender, Paul. "Mark Twain's Transcendent Figures." Dissertation: U California, Berkeley, 1956.

Bates, Allan C. "Mark Twain and the Mississippi River." Dissertation: U Chicago, 1968.

Beaver, Harold. *Huckleberry Finn*. London: Allen & Unwin, 1987.

Bellamy, Gladys. *Mark Twain as a Literary Artist*. Norman: U Oklahoma P, 1950.

Blair, Walter. *Mark Twain & Huck Finn*. Berkeley: U California P, 1960.

Blues, Thomas. *Mark Twain and the Community*. Lexington: U P Kentucky, 1970.

Branch, Edgar M. *The Literary Apprenticeship of Mark Twain, With Selections From His Apprentice Writings*. Urbana: U Illinois P, 1950.

Bridgman, Richard. *Traveling in Mark Twain*. Berkeley: U California P, 1987.

Brooks, Van Wyck. *The Ordeal of Mark Twain*. NY: Dutton, rev 1933.

Budd, Louis J. *Mark Twain: Social Philosopher*. Bloomington: Indiana U P, 1962.

Budd. *Our Mark Twain: The Making of His Public Personality*. Philadelphia: U Pennsylvania P, 1983.

Carrington, George C, Jr. *The Dramatic Unity of Huckleberry Finn*. Columbus: Ohio State U P, 1976.

Covici, Pascal, Jr. *Mark Twain's Humor: The Image of a World*. Dallas, Tex: Southern Methodist U P, 1962.

Cox, James M. *Mark Twain: The Fate of Humor*. Princeton: Princeton U P, 1966.

Cummings, Sherwood. *Mark Twain and Science: Adventures of a Mind*. Baton Rouge: Louisiana State U P, 1988.

David, Beverly R. *Mark Twain and His Illustrators*, Vol 1. Troy, NY: Whitston, 1986.

DeVoto, Bernard. *Mark Twain's America*. Boston: Little, Brown, 1932.

Duckett, Margaret. *Mark Twain and Bret Harte*. Norman: U Oklahoma P, 1964.

Egan, Michael. *Mark Twain's Huckleberry Finn: Race, Class and Society*. London: Chatto & Windus, for Sussex U P, 1977.

Ensor, Allison. *Mark Twain and the Bible.* Lexington: U Kentucky P, 1965.

Frear, Walter Francis. *Mark Twain and Hawaii.* Chicago: Lakeside, 1947.

Gale, Robert L. *Plots and Characters in the Works of Mark Twain.* Hamden, Conn: Archon, 1973.

Ganzel, Dewey. *Mark Twain Abroad: The Cruise of the Quaker City.* Chicago: U Chicago P, 1968.

Geismar, Maxwell. *Mark Twain: An American Prophet.* Boston: Houghton Mifflin, 1970.

Gerber, John C. *Mark Twain.* Boston: Twayne, 1988.

Gibson, William M. *The Art of Mark Twain.* NY: Oxford U P, 1976.

Gribben, Alan. *Mark Twain's Library: A Reconstruction*, 2 vols. Boston: Hall, 1980.

Harris, Susan K. *Mark Twain's Escape From Time: A Study of Patterns and Images.* Columbia: U Missouri P, 1982.

Hill, Hamlin. *Mark Twain and Elisha Bliss.* Columbia: U Missouri P, 1964.

Hirst, Robert. "The Making of *The Innocents Abroad:* 1867-1872." Dissertation: U California, Berkeley, 1975.

Hoffman, Andrew Jay. *Twain's Heroes, Twain's Worlds: Mark Twain's Adventures of Huckleberry Finn, A Connecticut Yankee, and Pudd'nhead Wilson.* Philadelphia: U Pennsylvania P, 1988.

Johnson, James L. *Mark Twain and the Limits of Power: Emerson's God in Ruins.* Knoxville: U Tennessee P, 1982.

Kahn, Sholom J. *Mark Twain's Mysterious Stranger: A Study of the Manuscript Texts.* Columbia: U Missouri P, 1978.

Krause, Sydney J. *Mark Twain as Critic.* Baltimore, Md: Johns Hopkins P, 1967.

Kruse, Horst H. *Mark Twain and Life on the Mississippi.* Amherst: U Massachusetts P, 1981.

Long, E Hudson & J R LeMaster. *The New Mark Twain Handbook.* NY: Garland, 1985.

Lorch, Fred W. *The Trouble Begins at Eight: Mark Twain's Lecture Tours.* Ames: Iowa State U P, 1968.

Lynn, Kenneth S. *Mark Twain and Southwestern Humor.* Boston: Little, Brown, 1959.

Macnaughton, William R. *Mark Twain's Last Years as a Writer.* Columbia: U Missouri P, 1979.

Madigan, Francis V, Jr. "Mark Twain's Passage to India: A Genetic Study of *Following the Equator.*" Dissertation: NYU, 1974.

McKeithan, Daniel M. *Court Trials in Mark Twain and Other Essays.* The Hague: Martinus Nijhoff, 1958.

McKeithan. *The Morgan Manuscript of Mark Twain's Pudd'nhead Wilson.* Uppsala, Sweden: American Institute, Uppsala U, 1961.

Pettit, Arthur G. *Mark Twain & the South.* Lexington: U P Kentucky, 1974.

Regan, Robert. *Unpromising Heroes: Mark Twain and His Characters.* Berkeley: U California P, 1966.

Robinson, Forrest G. *In Bad Faith: The Dynamics of Deception in Mark Twain's America.* Cambridge: Harvard U P, 1986.

Rogers, Franklin R. *Mark Twain's Burlesque Patterns as Seen in the Novels and Narratives, 1855-1885.* Dallas, Tex: Southern Methodist U P, 1960.

Rowlette, Robert. *Twain's Pudd'nhead Wilson: The Development and Design.* Bowling Green, Ohio: Bowling Green U Popular P, 1971.

Salomon, Roger F. *Twain and the Image of History.* New Haven: Yale U P, 1961.

Schirer, Thomas. *Mark Twain and the Theatre.* Nurnberg: Verlag Hans Carl, 1984.

Searle, William. *The Saint & the Skeptics: Joan of Arc in the Work of Mark Twain, Anatole France, and Bernard Shaw.* Detroit, Mich: Wayne State U P, 1976.

Seelye, John. *Mark Twain in the Movies: A Meditation With Pictures.* NY: Viking, 1977.

Sewell, David R. *Mark Twain's Languages: Discourse, Dialogue, and Linguistic Variety.* Berkeley: U California P, 1987.

Sloane, David E E. *Mark Twain as a Literary Comedian.* Baton Rouge: Louisiana State U P, 1979.

Sloane. *Adventures of Huckleberry Finn: An American Comic Vision.* Boston: Hall, 1988.

Smith, Harold J. *Women in Mark Twain's World.* NY: Carlton, 1973.

Smith, Henry Nash. *Mark Twain: The Development of a Writer.* Cambridge: Harvard U P, 1962.

Smith. *Mark Twain's Fable of Progress: Political and Economic Ideas in A Connecticut Yankee.* New Brunswick, NJ: Rutgers U P, 1964.

Spengemann, William C. *Mark Twain and the Backwoods Angel: The Matter of Innocence in the Works of SLC.* Kent, Ohio: Kent State U P, 1966.

Stone, Albert E, Jr. *The Innocent Eye: Childhood in Mark Twain's Imagination.* New Haven: Yale U P, 1961.

Tuckey, John S. *Mark Twain and Little Satan: The Writing of The Mysterious Stranger.* West Lafayette, Ind: Purdue U Studies, 1963.

Wagenknecht, Edward. *Mark Twain: The Man and His Work.* Norman: U Oklahoma P, rev 1967.

Walker, Franklin. *Irreverent Pilgrims: Melville, Browne, and Mark Twain in the Holy Land.* Seattle: U Washington P, 1974.

Wiggins, Robert A. *Mark Twain: Jackleg Novelist.* Seattle: U Washington P, 1964.

Collections of Essays

Anderson, Frederick. *Mark Twain: The Critical Heritage*. London: Routledge & Kegan Paul, 1971.

Bloom, Harold, ed. *Mark Twain*. NY: Chelsea House, 1986.

Budd, Louis J, ed. *Critical Essays on Mark Twain, 1867-1910*. Boston: Hall, 1982.

Budd, ed. *Critical Essays on Mark Twain, 1910-1980*. Boston: Hall, 1983.

Budd, ed. *New Essays on Adventures of Huckleberry Finn*. Cambridge: Cambridge U P, 1985.

Budd & Edwin H Cady, eds. *On Mark Twain: The Best From American Literature*. Durham, NC: Duke U P, 1987.

Davis, Sara deSaussure & Philip D Beidler, eds. *The Mythologizing of Mark Twain*. University: U Alabama P, 1984.

Gerber, John. *The Merrill Studies in Huckleberry Finn*. Columbus, Ohio: Merrill, 1971.

Giddings, Robert, ed. *Mark Twain: A Sumptuous Variety*. London: Vision / Totowa, NJ: Barnes & Noble, 1985.

Inge, M Thomas, ed. *Huck Finn Among the Critics*. Frederick, Md: U Publications of America, 1985.

Kesterson, David B, ed. *Critics on Mark Twain: Readings in Literary Criticism*. Coral Gables, Fla: U Miami P, 1973.

McMahan, Elizabeth, ed. *Critical Approaches to Mark Twain's Short Stories*. Port Washington, NY: Kennikat, 1981.

Sattelmeyer, Robert & J Donald Crowley, eds. *One Hundred Years of Huckleberry Finn: The Boy, His Book, & American Culture*. Columbia: U Missouri P, 1985.

Schmitter, Dean Morgan, ed. *Mark Twain: A Collection of Criticism*. NY: McGraw-Hill, 1974.

Scott, Arthur, ed. *Mark Twain: Selected Criticism*. Dallas, Tex: Southern Methodist U P, rev 1967.

Simpson, Claude M, ed. *Twentieth Century Interpretations of Adventures of Huckleberry Finn: A Collection of Critical Essays*. Englewood Cliffs, NJ: Prentice-Hall, 1963.

Smith, Henry Nash, ed. *Mark Twain: A Collection of Critical Essays*. Englewood Cliffs, NJ: Prentice-Hall, 1963.

Special Journals

AQ, 16 (Winter 1964). Mark Twain issue.
Mark Twain Circular (Frequency varies. 1987-   ).
Mark Twain Journal (semi-annually, 1954-   ).
Mark Twain Quarterly (1936-1954).
Mark Twain Society Bulletin (semi-annually, 1978-   ).
MFS, 14 (Spring 1968). Mark Twain issue.
SAF, 13 (Autumn 1985). Mark Twain issue.

SCRev, 5 (Winter 1988). Mark Twain issue.
StAH, 2 (Jan 1976). Mark Twain issue.
Twainian (bimonthly, Jan 1939-   ).

Book Sections & Articles

Anderson, Douglas. "*Huckleberry Finn* and Emerson's 'Concord Hymn.' " *NCF*, 40 (Jun 1985), 43-60.

Arnold, St George Tucker, Jr. "The Twain Bestiary: Mark Twain's Critters and the Tradition of Animal Portraiture in Humor of the Old Southwest." *SFQ*, 41 (1977), 195-211.

Aspiz, Harold. "Lecky's Influence on Mark Twain." *S&S*, 26 (Winter 1962), 15-25.

Austin, James C. "The Age of Twain." *American Humor in France* (Ames: Iowa State U P, 1978), 69-83.

Baender, Paul. "Alias Macfarlane: A Revision of Mark Twain's Biography." *AL*, 38 (May 1966), 187-197.

Baetzhold, Howard G. "Found: Mark Twain's 'Lost Sweetheart.' " *AL*, 44 (Nov 1972), 414-429.

Baetzhold. "Mark Twain and Dickens: Why the Denial?" *DSA*, 16 (1987), 189-219.

Baldanza, Frank. "The Structure of *Huckleberry Finn*." *AL*, 27 (Nov 1955), 347-355.

Bassett, John E. "*The Gilded Age*: Performance, Power, and Authority." *SNNTS*, 17 (Winter 1985), 395-405.

Bassett. "*Life on the Mississippi*: Being Shifty in a New Country." *WAL*, 21 (Spring 1986), 39-45.

Bates, Allan. "Sam Clemens, Pilot Humorist of a Tramp Steamboat." *AL*, 39 (Mar 1967), 102-109.

Beidler, Peter G. "The Raft Episode in *Huckleberry Finn*." *MFS*, 14 (Spring 1968), 11-20.

Beidler, Philip D. "Realistic Style and the Problem of Context in *Innocents Abroad* and *Roughing It*." *AL*, 52 (Mar 1980), 33-49.

Berret, Anthony J, Jr. "Huckleberry Finn and the Minstrel Show." *AmerS*, 27 (Fall 1986), 37-49.

Blair, Walter. "The French Revolution and *Huckleberry Finn*." *MP*, 55 (Aug 1957), 21-35.

Blair. "When Was *Huckleberry Finn* Written?" *AL*, 30 (Mar 1958), 1-25.

Blair. "Mark Twain." *Native American Humor* (San Francisco: Chandler, rev 1960), 147-162.

Blair & Hamlin Hill. "Mark Twain." *America's Humor: From Poor Richard to Doonesbury* (NY: Oxford U P, 1978), 301-363.

Boewe, Mary. "Twain on Lecky: Some Marginalia at Quarry Farm." *MTSB*, 8 (Jan 1985), 1-6.

Branch, Edgar M. " 'My Voice Is Still for Setchell': A Background Study of 'Jim Smiley and His Jumping Frog.' " *PMLA*, 82 (Dec 1967), 591-601.

Branch. " 'The Babes in the Wood': Artemus Ward's 'Double Health' to Mark Twain." *PMLA*, 93 (Oct 1978), 955-972.

Branch. "A New C Footprint: Soleather Steps Forward." *AL*, 54 (Dec 1982), 497-510.

Branch. "Fact and Fiction in the Blind Lead Episode of *Roughing It*." *NevHSQ*, 28 (Winter 1985), 234-248.

Branch. "Mark Twain: The Pilot and the Writer." *MTJ*, 23 (Fall 1985), 28-43.

Branch. "A Proposed Calendar of SC's Steamboats, 15 April 1857 to 8 May 1861, With Commentary." *MTJ*, 24 (Fall 1986), 2-27.

Bray, Robert. "Mark Twain Biography: Entering a New Phase." *MQ*, 15 (Apr 1974), 286-301.

Bray. "*Tom Sawyer* Once and For All." *Rev*, 3 (1981), 75-93.

Briden, Earl F. "Idiots First, Then Juries: Legal Metaphors in Mark Twain's *Pudd'nhead Wilson*." *TSLL*, 20 (Spring 1978), 169-180.

Bridgman, Richard. "Mark Twain and Dan Beard's Clarence: An Anatomy." *CentR*, 31 (Spring 1987), 212-227.

Brodwin, Stanley. "The Humor of the Absurd: Mark Twain's Adamic Diaries." *Criticism*, 14 (Winter 1972), 49-64.

Brodwin. "Blackness and the Adamic Myth in Mark Twain's *Pudd'nhead Wilson*." *TSLL*, 15 (Spring 1973), 167-176.

Brodwin. "Mark Twain's Masks of Satan: The Final Phase." *AL*, 45 (May 1973), 206-227.

Brodwin. "The Useful and Useless River: *Life on the Mississippi* Revisited." *StAH*, 2 (Jan 1976), 196-208.

Brodwin. "The Theology of Mark Twain: Banished Adam and the Bible." *MissQ*, 29 (Spring 1976), 167-189.

Brown, Carolyn S. "Mark Twain: Roughing It on a Tall Frontier," "Mark Twain: Remembering Anything, Whether It Happened or Not," "The Way the Natives Talk: A Note on Colloquial Style." *The Tall Tale in American Folklore and Literature* (Knoxville: U Tennessee P, 1987), 89-107, 108-121, 122-127.

Budd, Isabelle. "Clara Samossoud's Will." *MTJ*, 25 (Spring 1987), 17-30.

Budd, Louis J. "The Southern Currents Under Huckleberry Finn's Raft." *MVHR*, 46 (Sep 1959), 222-237.

Budd. "Mark Twain's Fingerprints in *Pudd'nhead Wilson*." *EA*, 40 (Oct-Dec 1987), 385-399.

Burde, Edgar J. "Mark Twain: The Writer as Pilot." *PMLA*, 93 (Oct 1978), 878-892.

Cardwell, Guy A. "*Life on the Mississippi*: Vulgar Facts and Learned Errors." *ESQ*, 19, no 4 (1973), 283-293.

Cardwell. "SC's Magical Pseudonym." *NEQ*, 48 (Jun 1975), 175-193.

Cardwell. "The Bowdlerizing of Mark Twain." *ESQ*, 21, no 3 (1975), 179-193.

Cardwell. "Mark Twain: The Metaphoric Hero as Battleground." *ESQ*, 23, no 1 (1977), 52-66.

Cardwell. "Mark Twain: A Self-Emasculated Hero." *ESQ*, 23, no 3 (1977), 173-187.

Cardwell. "Retouching Mark Twain's Portrait." *Rev*, 6 (1984), 95-128.

Carter, Everett. "The Meaning of *A Connecticut Yankee*." *AL*, 50 (Nov 1978), 418-440.

Carter, Paul J. "Olivia Clemens Edits *Following the Equator*." *AL*, 30 (May 1958), 194-209.

Carton, Evan. "*Pudd'nhead Wilson* and the Fiction of Law and Custom." *American Realism: New Essays*, ed Eric J Sundquist (Baltimore, Md: Johns Hopkins U P, 1982), 82-94.

Colwell, James L. "Huckleberries and Humans: On the Naming of Huckleberry Finn." *PMLA*, 86 (Jan 1971), 70-76.

Cooley, Thomas. "This Pathetic Drift: Mark Twain." *Educated Lives: The Rise of Modern Autobiography in America* (Columbus: Ohio State U P, 1976), 51-71.

Cummings, Sherwood. "Mark Twain's Acceptance of Science." *CentR*, 6 (Spring 1962), 245-261.

Cummings. "*What Is Man?* The Scientific Sources." *KentSE*, no 1 (1964), 108-116.

David, Beverly R. "The Pictorial *Huck Finn*: Mark Twain and His Illustrator, E. W. Kemble." *AQ*, 26 (Oct 1974), 331-351.

David. "The Unexpurgated *A Connecticut Yankee*: Mark Twain and His Illustrator, Daniel Carter Beard." *Prospects*, 1 (1975), 98-117.

David. "Mark Twain and the Legends for *Huckleberry Finn*." *ALR*, 15 (Autumn 1982), 155-165.

Davis, Thadious M, ed. "Black Writers on *Adventures of Huckleberry Finn* One Hundred Years Later." *MTJ*, 22 (Fall 1984), 1-52.

Delaney, Paul. "The Dissolving Self: The Narrators of Mark Twain's *Mysterious Stranger* Fragments." *JNT*, 6 (Winter 1976), 51-65.

Delaney. "You Can't Go Back to the Raft Ag'in, Huck Honey!: Mark Twain's Western Sequel to *Huckleberry Finn*." *WAL*, 11 (Fall 1976), 215-229.

Doyno, Victor A. "Over Twain's Shoulder: The Composition and Structure of *Huckleberry Finn*." *MFS*, 14 (Spring 1968), 3-9.

Duncan, Jeffrey L. "The Empirical and the Ideal in Mark Twain." *PMLA*, 95 (Mar 1980), 201-212.

Emerson, Everett. "The Strange Disappearance of Mark Twain." *SAF*, 13 (Autumn 1985), 143-155.

Ensor, Allison. "The Contributions of Charles Webster and Albert Bigelow Paine to *Huckleberry Finn*." *AL*, 40 (May 1968), 222-227.

Fender, Stephen. " 'The Prodigal in a Far Country Chawing of Husks': Mark Twain's Search for a Style in the West." *MLR*, 71 (Oct 1976), 737-756.

Fetterley, Judith. "The Sanctioned Rebel." *SNNTS*, 3 (Fall 1971), 293-304.

Fetterley. "Disenchantment: Tom Sawyer in *Huckleberry Finn*." *PMLA*, 87 (Jan 1972), 69-74.

Fetterley. "Yankee Showman and Reformer: The Character of Mark Twain's Hank Morgan." *TSLL*, 14 (Winter 1973), 667-679.

Fiedler, Leslie A. " 'Come Back to the Raft Ag'in, Huck Honey!' " *An End to Innocence: Essays on Culture and Politics* (Boston: Beacon, 1955), 142-151.

Fiedler. *Love and Death in the American Novel* (NY: Stein & Day, rev 1966), 270-296.

Fiedler. "Afterword: 'A Backward Glance O'er Travelled Roads.' " *What Was Literature? Class Culture and Mass Society* (NY: Simon & Schuster, 1982), 232-245.

Fischer, Victor. "Huck Finn Reviewed: The Reception of *Huckleberry Finn* in the United States, 1885-1897." *ALR*, 16 (Spring 1983), 1-57.

Fishkin, Shelley Fisher. "Mark Twain." *From Fact to Fiction: Journalism & Imaginative Writing in America* (Baltimore, Md: Johns Hopkins U P, 1985), 53-84.

Gardner, Joseph H. "Mark Twain and Dickens." *PMLA*, 84 (Jan 1969), 90-101.

Gerber, John C. "Mark Twain's Use of the Comic Pose." *PMLA*, 77 (Jun 1962), 297-304.

Gerber. "*Pudd'nhead Wilson* as Fabulation." *StAH*, 2 (Apr 1975), 21-31.

Gillman, Susan. " 'Dementia Americana': Mark Twain, 'Wapping Alice,' and the Harry K. Thaw Trial." *CritI*, 14 (Winter 1988), 296-314.

Gribben, Alan. "Removing Mark Twain's Mask: A Decade of Criticism and Scholarship." *ESQ*, 26, nos 2 & 3 (1980), 100-108, 149-171.

Gribben. "Mark Twain, Business Man: The Margins of Profit." *StAH*, ns 1 (Jun 1982), 24-43.

Gribben. " 'When Other Amusements Fail': Mark Twain and the Occult." *The Haunted Dusk: American Supernatural Fiction, 1820-1920*, ed Howard Kerr, John W Crowley & Charles L Crow (Athens: U Georgia P, 1983), 169-189.

Gribben. "The Importance of Mark Twain." *American Humor*, ed Arthur Power Dudden (NY: Oxford U P, 1987), 24-49.

Hill, Hamlin. "The Composition and Structure of *Tom Sawyer*." *AL*, 32 (Jan 1961), 379-392.

Hill. "Mark Twain: Audience and Artistry." *AQ*, 15 (Spring 1963), 25-40.

Hill. "Who Killed Mark Twain?" *ALR*, 7 (Spring 1974), 118-124.

Hoffman, Daniel. "Mark Twain." *Form and Fable in American Fiction* (NY: Oxford U P, 1961), 317-350.

Holland, Laurence B. "A 'Raft of Trouble'—Word and Deed in *Huckleberry Finn*." *American Realism: New Essays*, ed Eric J Sundquist (Baltimore, Md: Johns Hopkins U P, 1982), 66-81.

Hook, Andrew. "Reporting Reality: Mark Twain's Short Stories." *The Nineteenth-Century American Short Story*, ed A Robert Lee (London: Vision / Totowa, NJ: Barnes & Noble, 1986), 103-119.

Kerr, Howard. " 'Sperits Couldn't a Done Better': Mark Twain and Spiritualism." *Mediums, and Spirit-Rappers, and Roaring Radicals: Spiritualism in American Literature, 1850-1900* (Urbana: U Illinois P, 1972), 155-189.

Krause, Sydney J. "The Art and Satire of Twain's 'Jumping Frog' Story." *AQ*, 16 (Winter 1964), 562-576.

Krause. "Cooper's Literary Offenses: Mark Twain in Wonderland." *NEQ*, 38 (Sep 1965), 291-311.

Krause. "Olivia Clemens's 'Editing' Reviewed." *AL*, 39 (Nov 1967), 325-351.

Krauth, Leland. "Mark Twain: At Home in the Gilded Age." *GaR*, 28 (Spring 1974), 105-112.

Krauth. "Mark Twain: The Victorian of Southwestern Humor." *AL*, 54 (Oct 1982), 368-384.

Leary, Lewis. *Southern Excursions: Essays on Mark Twain and Others* (Baton Rouge: Louisiana State U P, 1971), 3-110.

Lindborg, Henry J. "A Cosmic Tramp: SC's *Three Thousand Years Among the Microbes*." *AL*, 44 (Jan 1973), 652-657.

Lynn, Kenneth S. "Welcome Back From the Raft, Huck, Honey!" *The Air-Line to Seattle: Studies in Literary and Historical Writing About America* (Chicago: U Chicago P, 1983), 40-49.

Maik, Thomas A. "The Village in *Tom Sawyer*: Myth and Reality." *ArQ*, 42 (Summer 1986), 157-164.

Male, Roy R. *Enter, Mysterious Stranger: American Cloistral Fiction* (Norman: U Oklahoma P, 1979), passim.

Martin, Jay. "Mark Twain: The Dream of Drift and the Dream of Delight." *Harvests of Change: American Literature, 1865-1914* (Englewood Cliffs, NJ: Prentice-Hall, 1967), 165-201.

Marx, Leo. "The Pilot and the Passenger: Landscape Conventions and the Style of *Huckleberry Finn*." *AL*, 28 (May 1956), 129-146.

Marx. *The Pilot and the Passenger: Essays on Literature, Technology, and Culture in the*

United States (NY: Oxford U P, 1988), 11-53, passim.

McKeithan, D M. "Mark Twain's Letters of Thomas Jefferson Snodgrass." *PQ*, 32 (Oct 1953), 353-365.

McNutt, James C. "Mark Twain and the American Indian: Earthly Realism and Heavenly Idealism." *AIQ*, 4 (Aug 1978), 223-242.

Michelson, Bruce. "Mark Twain the Tourist: The Form of *The Innocents Abroad*." *AL*, 49 (Nov 1977), 385-398.

Mills, Barriss. "*Old Times on the Mississippi* as an Initiation Story." *CE*, 25 (Jan 1964), 283-289.

Mills, Nicolaus. "Charles Dickens and Mark Twain." *American and English Fiction in the Nineteenth Century* (Bloomington: Indiana U P, 1973), 92-109.

Monteiro, George. "Narrative Laws and Narrative Lies in *Adventures of Huckleberry Finn*." *SAF*, 13 (Autumn 1985), 227-237.

Parker, Hershel. "*Pudd'nhead Wilson*: Jack-leg Author, Unreadable Text, and Sense-Making Critics." *Flawed Texts and Verbal Icons: Literary Authority in American Fiction* (Evanston, Ill: Northwestern U P, 1984), 115-145.

Poirier, Richard. "Transatlantic Configurations: Mark Twain and Jane Austen." *A World Elsewhere: The Place of Style in American Literature* (NY: Oxford U P, 1966), 144-207.

Pressman, Richard S. "A Connecticut Yankee in Merlin's Cave: The Role of Contradiction in Mark Twain's Novel." *ALR*, 16 (Spring 1983), 58-72.

Quirk, Thomas. " 'Learning a Nigger to Argue': Quitting *Huckleberry Finn*." *ALR*, 20 (Fall 1987), 18-33.

Rees, Robert A. "*Captain Stormfield's Visit to Heaven* and *The Gates Ajar*." *ELN*, 7 (Mar 1970), 197-202.

Rees & Richard Dilworth Rust. "Mark Twain's 'The Turning Point of My Life.' " *AL*, 40 (Jan 1969), 524-535.

Regan, Robert. "The Reprobate Elect in *The Innocents Abroad*." *AL*, 54 (May 1982), 240-257.

Robinson, Forrest G. "Why I Killed My Brother: An Essay on Mark Twain." *L&P*, 30, nos 3 & 4 (1980), 168-181.

Robinson. "The Silences in *Huckleberry Finn*." *NCF*, 37 (Jun 1982), 50-74.

Rodgers, Paul C, Jr. "Artemus Ward and Mark Twain's 'Jumping Frog.' " *NCF*, 28 (Dec 1973), 273-286.

Rogers, Franklin R. "The Road to Reality: Burlesque Travel Literature and *Roughing It*." *BNYPL*, 67 (Mar 1963), 155-168.

Rowe, John Carlos. "Trumping the Trick of Truth: The Extra-Moral Sense of Twain's *Pudd'nhead Wilson*." *Through the Custom-House: Nineteenth-Century American Fiction and Modern Theory* (Baltimore, Md: Johns Hopkins U P, 1982), 139-167.

Rowlette, Robert. " 'Mark Ward on Artemus Twain': Twain's Literary Debt to Ward." *ALR*, 6 (Winter 1973), 13-25.

Rubin, Louis D, Jr. " 'The Begum of Bengal': Mark Twain and the South." *William Elliott Shoots a Bear* (Baton Rouge: Louisiana State U P, 1975), 28-60.

Rucker, Mary E. "Moralism and Determinism in 'The Man That Corrupted Hadleyburg.' " *SSF*, 14 (Winter 1977), 49-54.

Scheick, William J. "Mother Blonay's Curse." *The Half-Blood: A Cultural Symbol in 19th-Century American Fiction* (Lexington: U P Kentucky, 1979), 19-33.

Schmitz, Neil. "The Paradox of Liberation in *Huckleberry Finn*." *TSLL*, 13 (Spring 1971), 125-136.

Schmitz. "Twain, *Huckleberry Finn*, and the Reconstruction." *AmerS*, 12 (Spring 1971), 59-67.

Schmitz. "White Lies, Bluff Reefs," "Huckspeech." *Of Huck and Alice: Humorous Writing in American Literature* (Minneapolis: U Minnesota P, 1983), 65-95, 96-125.

Scott, Arthur L. "The *Century Magazine* Edits *Huckleberry Finn*, 1884-1885." *AL*, 27 (Nov 1955), 356-362.

Scott. "*The Innocents Adrift* Edited by Mark Twain's Official Biographer." *PMLA*, 78 (Jun 1963), 230-237.

Smith, Henry Nash. " 'That Hideous Mistake of Poor C's.' " *HLB*, 9 (Spring 1955), 145-180.

Smith. "Mark Twain's Images of Hannibal: From St. Petersburg to Eseldorf." *TexSE*, 37 (1958), 3-23.

Smith. "The Morals of Power: Business Enterprise as a Theme in Mid-Nineteenth-Century American Fiction." *Essays on American Literature in Honor of Jay B. Hubbell*, ed Clarence Gohdes (Durham, NC: Duke U P, 1967), 90-107.

Smith. "Guilt and Innocence in Mark Twain's Later Fiction." *Democracy and the Novel: Popular Resistance to Classic American Writers* (NY: Oxford U P, 1978), 104-127.

Spengemann, William C. "Mark Twain." *The Adventurous Muse: The Poetics of American Fiction, 1789-1900* (New Haven: Yale U P, 1977), 213-240.

Stein, Allen F. "Return to Phelps Farm: *Huckleberry Finn* and the Old Southwestern Framing Device." *MissQ*, 24 (Spring 1971), 111-116.

Stone, Albert E, Jr. "Mark Twain's *Joan of Arc*: The Child as Goddess." *AL*, 31 (Mar 1959), 1-20.

Tanner, Tony. "The Lost America—The Despair of

Henry Adams and Mark Twain." *ModA*, 5 (Summer 1961), 299-310.

Towers, Tom H. " 'Hateful Reality': The Failure of the Territory in *Roughing It*." *WAL*, 9 (Spring 1974), 3-15.

Towers. " 'I Never Thought We Might Want to Come Back': Strategies of Transcendence in *Tom Sawyer*." *MFS*, 21 (Winter 1975-1976), 509-520.

Towers. "Love and Power in *Huckleberry Finn*." *TSE*, 23 (1978), 17-37.

Towers. "*The Prince and the Pauper:* Mark Twain's Once and Future King." *SAF*, 6 (Autumn 1978), 193-202.

Tuckey, John S. "Mark Twain's Later Dialogue: The 'Me' and the Machine." *AL*, 41 (Jan 1970), 532-542.

Wadlington, Warwick. "Mark Twain: The Authority of the Courtier." *The Confidence Game in American Literature* (Princeton: Princeton U P, 1975), 181-284.

Welland, Dennis. "Mark Twain's Last Travel Book." *BNYPL*, 69 (Jan 1965), 31-48.

Wigger, Anne P. "The Source of Fingerprint Material in Mark Twain's *Pudd'nhead Wilson and Those Extraordinary Twins*." *AL*, 28 (Jan 1957), 517-520.

Wigger. "The Composition of Mark Twain's *Pudd'nhead Wilson and Those Extraordinary Twins:* Chronology and Development." *MP*, 55 (Nov 1957), 93-102.

Williams, James D. "Revision and Intention in Mark Twain's *A Connecticut Yankee*." *AL*, 36 (Nov 1964), 288-297.

Williams. "The Use of History in Mark Twain's *A Connecticut Yankee*." *PMLA*, 80 (Mar 1965), 102-110.

Williams, Murial B. "The Unmasking of Meaning: A Study of the Twins in *Pudd'nhead Wilson*." *MissQ*, 33 (Winter 1979-1980), 39-53.

Wilson, James D. "In Quest of Redemptive Vision: Mark Twain's *Joan of Arc*." *TSLL*, 20 (Spring 1978), 181-198.

Wolff, Cynthia Griffin. "*The Adventures of Tom Sawyer:* A Nightmare Vision of American Boyhood." *MR*, 21 (Winter 1980), 637-652.

Ziff, Larzer. "Literary Absenteeism: Henry James and Mark Twain." *The American 1890s: Life and Times of a Lost Generation* (NY: Viking, 1966), 50-72.

Ziff. "Authorship and Craft: The Example of Mark Twain." *SoR*, ns 12 (Apr 1976), 246-260.

Alan Gribben

IRVIN S. COBB

Paducah, Ky, 23 Jun 1876-New York City, NY, 10 Mar 1944

Irvin S. Cobb was one of the most successful humorists of the 1920s and 1930s. His most popular fictional character was an old-fashioned southern cracker-barrel sage, Judge Priest, about whom Cobb wrote more than seventy tales. Besides being a nostalgic apologist for village life in the South, Cobb wrote horror tales, autobiographical essays, three collections of journalism about World War I, and memorable comic narratives in which he cast himself in the role of a hapless, bumbling figure victimized by a hostile environment. Recent critics note that Cobb was among the first of the humorists to portray the figure of the little guy at the mercy of the modern world.

BIBLIOGRAPHY

"Selected Bibliography." Chatterton, 148-161. Primary & secondary.

BOOKS

C's Anatomy. NY: Doran, 1912. Essays.

Back Home: Being the Narrative Judge Priest and His People. NY: Doran, 1912. Stories.

The Escape of Mr. Trimm: His Plight and Other Plights. NY: Doran, 1913. Stories.

C's Bill-of-Fare. NY: Doran, 1913. Essays.

Europe Revised. NY: Doran, 1914. Travel.

Roughing It De Luxe. NY: Doran, 1914. Travel.

"Speaking of Operations—". NY: Doran, 1915. Essay.

Paths of Glory: Impressions of War Written At and Near the Front. NY: Doran, 1915. Augmented as *The Red Glutton: Impressions of War Written At and Near the Front.* London & NY: Hodder & Stoughton, 1915. Essays.

Fibble, D. D. NY: Doran, 1916. Novel.

Local Color. NY: Doran, 1916. Stories.

Old Judge Priest. NY: Doran, 1916. Stories.

Those Times and These. NY: Doran, 1917. Stories.

"Speaking of Prussians—". NY: Doran, 1917. Essays.

The Glory of the Coming: What Mine Eyes Have Seen of Americans in Action in This Year of Grace and Allied Endeavor. NY: Doran, 1918. Essays.

The Thunders of Silence. NY: Doran, 1918. Story.

Eating in Two or Three Languages. NY: Doran, 1919. Essay.

The Life of the Party. NY: Doran, 1919. Story.

The Abandoned Farmers. NY: Doran, 1920. Essay.

"Oh! Well! You Know How Women Are!" bound with *"Isn't That Just Like a Man!"* by Mary Roberts Rinehart. NY: Doran / London: Hodder & Stoughton, 1920. Essay.

From Place to Place. NY: Doran, 1920. Stories.

A Plea for Old Cap Collier. NY: Doran, 1921. Essay.

One Third Off. NY: Doran, 1921. Essays.

J. Poindexter, Colored. NY: Doran, 1922. Novel.

Sundry Accounts. NY: Doran, 1922. Stories.

Stickfuls: Compositions of a Newspaper Minion. NY: Doran, 1923. Repub as *Stickfuls (Myself—to Date).* NY: Review of Reviews, 1923. Essays.

A Laugh a Day Keeps the Doctor Away. NY: Doran, 1923. Stories.

Snake Doctor, and Other Stories. NY: Doran, 1923.

Goin' on Fourteen: Being Cross-sections Out of a Year in the Life of an Average Boy. NY: Doran, 1924. Novel.

Indiana. NY: Doran, 1924. Essay.

Kansas. NY: Doran, 1924. Essay.

Kentucky. NY: Doran, 1924. Essay.

Maine. NY: Doran, 1924. Essay.

New York. NY: Doran, 1924. Essay.

North Carolina. NY: Doran, 1924. Essay.

Alias Ben Alibi. NY: Doran, 1925. Novel.

"Here Comes the Bride—," and So Forth. NY: Doran, 1925. Stories.

Many Laughs for Many Days. NY: Doran, 1925. Stories.

On an Island That Cost $24.00. NY: Doran, 1926. Stories.

Prose and Cons. NY: Doran, 1926. Stories.

Some United States: A Series of Stops in Various Parts of This Nation With One Excursion Across the Line. NY: Doran, 1926. Travel.

Chivalry Peak. NY: Cosmopolitan, 1927. Novel.

Ladies and Gentlemen. NY: Cosmopolitan, 1927. Stories.

All Aboard: Saga of the Romantic River. NY: Cosmopolitan, 1928. Novel.

Red Likker. NY: Cosmopolitan, 1929. Novel.

This Man's World. NY: Cosmopolitan, 1929. Stories.

Both Sides of the Street. NY: Cosmopolitan, 1930. Travel.

To Be Taken Before Sailing. NY: Cosmopolitan, 1930. Essay.

Incredible Truth. NY: Cosmopolitan, 1931. Essays.

Down Yonder With Judge Priest and ISC. NY: Long & Smith, 1932. Stories.

Murder Day by Day. Indianapolis: Bobbs-Merrill, 1933. Novel.

One Way to Stop a Panic. NY: McBride, 1933. Stories.

Faith, Hope and Charity. Indianapolis & NY: Bobbs-Merrill, 1934. Stories.

ISC's Own Recipe Book. Louisville & Baltimore: Frankfort Distilleries, 1934.

"Who's Who" Plus "Here's How!" NY: Hotel Waldorf-Astoria, 1934. Essay.

Azam: The Story of an Arabian Colt and His Friends. Chicago: Rand McNally, 1937. Legends & stories.

Judge Priest Turns Detective. Indianapolis & NY: Bobbs-Merrill, 1937. Novel.

Favorite Humorous Stories of IC. NY: Triangle, 1940.

Four Useful Pups. Chicago & NY: Rand McNally, 1940. Story.

Exit Laughing. Indianapolis & NY: Bobbs-Merrill, 1941. Autobiography.

Glory, Glory, Hallelujah! Indianapolis & NY: Bobbs-Merrill, 1941. Essay.

Roll Call. Indianapolis & NY: Bobbs-Merrill, 1942. Poetry & essays.

OTHER

The World's Great Humorous Stories, ed ISC. Cleveland: World, 1944.

EDITION & COLLECTIONS

The Works of ISC, 10 vols. NY: Doran, 1912-1920.

IC at His Best. Garden City, NY: Sun Dial, 1923.

C's Cavalcade: A Selection From the Writings of ISC, ed with intro by B D Zevin. Cleveland & NY: World, 1945.

MANUSCRIPTS & ARCHIVES

Free Public Library, Louisville, Kentucky.

BIOGRAPHIES

Books

Chapman, Elisabeth Cobb. *My Wayward Parent: A Book About ISC.* Indianapolis: Bobbs-Merrill, 1945.

Jillson, Willard Rouse. *ISC at Frankfort, Kentucky.* Carrollton, Ky: News-Democrat, 1944.

Lawson, Anita. *ISC.* Bowling Green, Ohio: Bowling Green State U Popular P, 1984.

Neumann, Fred G. *ISC: His Life and Achievements.* NY: Beekman, 1974.

CRITICAL STUDIES

Books

Chatterton, Wayne. *ISC.* Boston: Twayne, 1986.

Davis, Robert H. *ISC: Storyteller.* NY: Doran, 1924.

Book Sections & Articles

"An Attempt to Place ISC Among the Immortals." *Current Opinion,* 54 (Jan 1913), 57.

"Concerning IC." *Bookman,* 37 (Mar 1913), 14-15.

Hoover, Judith D. "Between Times: 19th-Century Values in the 20th Century." *SoQ,* 24 (Spring 1986), 49-57.

Maurice, Arthur Bartlett. "The History of Their Books: VII. ISC." *Bookman,* 69 (Jul 1929), 511-514.

Mencken, H L. "The Heir of Mark Twain." *Prejudices: First Series* (NY: Knopf, 1919), 97-104.

Overton, Grant. "C's Fourth Dimension." *Authors of the Day* (NY: Doran, 1924), 294-311.

Overton. "ISC: Ask Him Another." *Bookman,* 65 (Aug 1927), 673-677.

Pendennis. " 'My Types'—ISC." *Forum,* 58 (Oct 1917), 471-480.

Van Gelder, Robert. "ISC Discusses His Writings." *NYTBR* (2 Nov 1941), 2. Rpt *Writers and Writing* by Van Gelder (NY: Scribners, 1946).

Ward, William S. "ISC." *A Literary History of Kentucky* (Knoxville: U Tennessee P, 1988), 57-61.

Williams, Blanche Colton. "ISC." *Our Short Story Writers* (NY: Moffat, Yard, 1920), 73-84.

Yates, Norris W. "The Crackerbarrel Sage in the West and South: Will Rogers and ISC." *The American Humorist: Conscience of the Twentieth Century* (Ames: Iowa State U P, 1964), 127-133.

Gwen L. Nagel

ROSE TERRY COOKE

Hartford, Conn, 17 Feb 1827-Pittsfield, Mass, 18 Jul 1892

Although she regarded herself primarily as a poet, Rose Terry Cooke achieved her reputation almost exclusively through the more than two hundred short stories she contributed to leading periodicals of her day. Many of these stories, written over a period of almost forty years, were later collected and published in book form. As a New England local colorist, she experimented with Yankee dialect while focusing on the plight of women, both married and single. Personally opposed to divorce, she nonetheless composed tales tacitly critical of a society that condemned women to unfortunate matches. Cooke's work was frequently commented upon in studies of local colorists during the 1930s and is now receiving new attention by students of women's literature.

BIBLIOGRAPHIES

Bibliography of American Literature, comp Jacob Blanck. New Haven: Yale U P, 1955-1991. Primary.

Downey, Jean. "RTC: A Bibliography." *BB*, 21 (May-Aug 1955), 159-163; 21 (Sep-Dec 1955), 191-192. Primary & secondary.

Eppard, Philip B. "*BAL* Addenda: C, Frederic, Freeman and Fuller." *PBSA*, 74, no 2 (1980), 152-153. Primary.

Toth, Susan Allen. "RTC (1827-1892)." *ALR*, 4 (Spring 1971), 170-176. Primary & secondary.

BOOKS

Poems by Rose Terry. Boston: Ticknor & Fields, 1861.

Happy Dodd; or, "She Hath Done What She Could." Boston: Hoyt, 1878. Novel.

Somebody's Neighbors. Boston: Osgood, 1881. Stories.

Groton Massacre Centennial Poem. New London, Conn: Allyn, 1881.

A Lay Preacher. Boston: Congregational Sunday-School & Publishing Society, 1884. Nonfiction.

The Deacon's Week. Boston: Congregational Sunday School & Publishing Society, 1884?

Repub, NY & London: Putnam, 1885. Stories.

Root-Bound and Other Sketches. Boston: Congregational Sunday-School & Publishing Society, 1885.

The Sphinx's Children and Other People's. Boston: Ticknor, 1886. Stories.

No. NY: Phillips & Hunt / Cincinnati: Cranston & Stowe, 1886. Novel.

Poems. NY: Gottsberger, 1888.

The Old Garden. Boston: Prang, 1888. Poetry.

Steadfast: The Story of a Saint and a Sinner. Boston: Ticknor, 1889. Novel.

Huckleberries Gathered From New England Hills. Boston & NY: Houghton, Mifflin, 1891. Stories.

Little Foxes. Philadelphia: Altemus, 1904. Novel.

COLLECTION

How Celia Changed Her Mind and Selected Stories, ed with intro by Elizabeth Ammons. New Brunswick, NJ: Rutgers U P, 1986.

BIOGRAPHIES

Book Sections & Article

Brooks, Van Wyck. *New England: Indian Summer, 1865-1915* (NY: Dutton, 1940), 85-88.

Downey, Jean. "*Atlantic* Friends: Howells and C." *AN&Q*, 1 (May 1963), 132-133.

Spofford, Harriet Prescott. "RTC." *Our Famous Women* (Hartford, Conn: Worthington, 1884), 174-206.

CRITICAL STUDIES

Books

Downey, Jean. "A Biographical and Critical Study of RTC." Dissertation: U Ottawa, 1956.

Smith, Rodney Lee. " 'These Poor Weak Souls': RTC's Presentation of Men and Women Who Were Converts to the Social Gospel in the Gilded Age." Dissertation: U Wisconsin, Milwaukee, 1978.

Book Sections & Articles

Donovan, Josephine. "RTC: Impoverished Wives and Spirited Spinsters." *New England Local Color Literature: A Women's Tradition* (NY: Ungar, 1983), 68-81.

Levy, Babette May. "Mutations in New England Local Color." *NEQ*, 19 (Sep 1946), 338-358.

Makosky, Donald R. "RTC's *Matred and Tamar, a Drama*." *RALS*, 14 (Spring-Autumn 1984), 1-58. Includes text of play.

Martin, Jay. "RTC." *Harvests of Change: American Literature, 1865-1914* (Englewood Cliffs, NJ: Prentice-Hall, 1967), passim.

Newlyn, Evelyn. "RTC and the Children of the Sphinx." *RAFI*, 4 (Winter 1979), 49-57.

Pattee, Fred Lewis. *The Development of the American Short Story* (NY: Harper, 1923), passim.

Rugg, W K. "A Lady Author Comes to Town." *CSM*, 29 (13 May 1937), 11.

Spofford, Harriet Prescott. "RTC." *A Little Book of Friends* (Boston: Little, Brown, 1916), 143-156.

Toth, Susan Allen. "Sarah Orne Jewett and Friends: A Community of Interest." *SSF*, 9 (Summer 1972), 233-241.

Toth. "Character Studies in RTC: New Faces for the Short Story." *KCN*, 2 (Spring 1976), 19-26.

Toth. " 'The Rarest and Most Peculiar Grape': Versions of the New England Woman in Nineteenth-Century Local Color Literature." *Regionalism and the Female Imagination*, ed Emily Toth (NY: Human Sciences, 1985), 15-28.

Wood, Ann Douglas. "The Literature of Impoverishment: The Women Local Colorists in America, 1865-1914." *WS*, 1, no 1 (1972), 3-40.

Cheryl Z. Oreovicz

STEPHEN CRANE

Newark, NJ, 1 Nov 1871-Badenweiler, Germany, 5 Jun 1900

The publication of *The Red Badge of Courage* in 1895 made twenty-four-year-old Stephen Crane famous on both sides of the Atlantic. His impressionistic and naturalistic treatment of the material of his fiction—war and slum life—was highly innovative. Many leading writers and critics of his day acknowledged his keen psychological insights and original narrative and poetic styles. After he died in 1900, his fame declined sharply, and for more than two decades he was almost forgotten. Thomas Beer's 1923 biography helped to revive interest in Crane's work, most of which was out of print; and in the 1920s and 1930s much of it was collected and republished. But not until the early 1950s was his reputation as a major American author fully established. Since then, critics, biographers, and literary historians have examined Crane's styles, themes, and methods and their anticipation of twentieth-century literary modernism.

BIBLIOGRAPHIES & CATALOGUES

Baum, Joan H. *SC (1871-1900)*. NY: Columbia U Libraries, 1956. Catalogue.

Beebe, Maurice & Thomas Gullason. "Criticism of SC: A Selected Checklist." *MFS*, 5 (Autumn 1959), 282-291.

Bibliography of American Literature, comp Jacob Blanck. New Haven: Yale U P, 1955-1991. Primary.

Bruccoli, Matthew J. *SC, 1871-1971: An Exhibition From the Collection of Matthew J. Bruccoli*. Columbia: Department of English, U South Carolina, 1971. Catalogue.

Bruccoli. *The SC Collection From the Library of Prof. Matthew J. Bruccoli*. NY: Swann Galleries, 1974. Auction catalogue.

First Printings of American Authors, Vol 1 (Detroit: Bruccoli Clark/Gale, 1977), 79-82. Primary.

Kibler, James E, Jr. "The Library of S and Cora C." *Proof*, 1 (1971), 199-246.

Monteiro, George. "SC and *Public Opinion:* An Annotated Checklist, an Unrecorded Parody, and a Review of *The O'Ruddy.*" *SCNews,* 5 (Fall 1970), 5-8.

Pizer, Donald. "SC." *Fifteen American Authors Before 1900: Bibliographic Essays on Research and Criticism,* ed Robert A Rees & Earl N Harbert (Madison: U Wisconsin P, 1971), 97-137.

Pizer. "SC: A Review of Scholarship and Criticism Since 1969." *SNNTS,* 10 (Spring 1978), 120-145.

Stallman, R W. *SC: A Critical Bibliography.* Ames: Iowa State U P, 1972. Primary & secondary. Includes Starrett & Williams bibliography.

Starrett, Vincent & Ames W Williams. *SC: A Bibliography.* Glendale, Calif: Valentine, 1948. Primary.

Wertheim, Stanley. "SC." *Hawthorne, Melville, SC: A Critical Bibliography,* ed Theodore L Gross & Wertheim (NY: Free P, 1971), 201-301.

Wertheim. "Guide to Dissertations on American Literary Figures, 1870-1910: Part One—SC." *ALR,* 8 (Summer 1975), 227-241.

BOOKS

Maggie: A Girl of the Streets (A Story of New York) (as by Johnston Smith). NY: Privately printed, 1893. Rev as *Maggie: A Girl of the Streets* (by SC). NY: Appleton, 1896; *Maggie: A Child of the Streets.* London: Heinemann, 1896. Novel.

The Black Riders and Other Lines. Boston: Copeland & Day, 1895. Poetry.

The Red Badge of Courage: An Episode of the American Civil War. NY: Appleton, 1895. *The Red Badge of Courage: A Facsimile Edition of the Manuscript,* 2 vols, ed with intro by Fredson Bowers. Washington: Bruccoli Clark/NCR Microcard Editions, 1973. Novel.

George's Mother. NY & London: Arnold, 1896. Novel.

The Little Regiment and Other Episodes of the American Civil War. NY: Appleton, 1896. Stories.

The Third Violet. NY: Appleton, 1897. Novel.

The Open Boat and Other Tales of Adventure. NY: Doubleday & McClure, 1898. Augmented as *The Open Boat and Other Stories.* London: Heinemann, 1898.

War Is Kind. NY: Stokes, 1899. Poetry.

Active Service: A Novel. NY: Stokes, 1899.

The Monster and Other Stories. NY & London: Harper, 1899. Augmented ed, London & NY: Harper, 1901.

Whilomville Stories. NY & London: Harper, 1900.

Wounds in the Rain: War Stories. NY: Stokes, 1900; *Wounds in the Rain: A Collection of Stories Relating to the Spanish-American War of 1898.* London: Methuen, 1900.

Great Battles of the World. Philadelphia: Lippincott, 1901. Articles.

Last Words. London: Digby, Long, 1902. Stories.

The O'Ruddy: A Romance, with Robert Barr. NY: Stokes, 1903. Novel.

The Sullivan County Sketches of SC, ed with intro by Melvin Schoberlin. Syracuse, NY: Syracuse U P, 1949.

SC: Uncollected Writings, ed with intro by Olov W Fryckstedt. Uppsala, Sweden: Studia Anglistica Upsaliensia, 1963. Stories & sketches.

The War Dispatches of SC, ed R W Stallman & E R Hagemann. NY: NYU P, 1966.

The New York City Sketches of SC and Related Pieces, ed Stallman & Hagemann. NY: NYU P, 1966.

Sullivan County Tales and Sketches, ed with intro by Stallman. Ames: Iowa State U P, 1968.

SC in the West and Mexico, ed Joseph Katz. Kent, Ohio: Kent State U P, 1970. Newspaper articles.

LETTERS, NOTEBOOKS

SC: Letters, ed R W Stallman & Lillian Gilkes. NY: NYU P, 1960.

The Notebook of SC, ed Donald & Ellen Greiner. Charlottesville: Bibliographical Society, U Virginia, 1969.

The Correspondence of SC, 2 vols, ed Stanley Wertheim & Paul Sorrentino. NY: Columbia U P, 1988.

OTHER

Et Cetera: A Collector's Scrap-Book, ed Vincent Starrett. Chicago: Covici, 1924. Miscellany including 2 articles by SC.

"The 'Lost' Newspaper Writings of SC," ed with intro by Thomas A Gullason. *Courier,* 21 (Spring 1986), 57-87.

EDITIONS & COLLECTIONS

Pictures of War. London: Heinemann, 1898.

Men, Women, and Boats, ed with intro by Vincent Starrett. NY: Boni & Liveright, 1921.

The Work of SC, 12 vols, ed Wilson Follett. NY: Knopf, 1925-1926.

The Collected Poems of SC, ed Follett. NY & London: Knopf, 1930.

SC: An Omnibus, ed with intros & notes by R W Stallman. NY: Knopf, 1952.

The Poems of SC, ed Joseph Katz. NY: Cooper Square, 1966.

SC's Maggie: Text and Context, ed Maurice Bassan. Belmont, Calif: Wadsworth, 1966.

The Portable SC, ed with intro by Katz. NY: Viking, 1969.

The Works of SC, 10 vols, ed Fredson Bowers. Charlottesville: U P Virginia, 1969-1976.

SC: Prose and Poetry, ed J C Levenson. NY: Library of America, 1984.

MANUSCRIPTS & ARCHIVES

The major collections are at Columbia U Library; Syracuse U Library; the New York Public Library; & U of Virginia Library.

CONCORDANCES

Baron, Herman. *A Concordance to the Poems of SC,* ed Joseph Katz. Boston: Hall, 1974.

Crosland, Andrew T. *A Concordance to the Complete Poetry of SC.* Detroit: Bruccoli Clark/ Gale, 1975.

BIOGRAPHIES

Books

Beer, Thomas. *SC: A Study in American Letters.* NY: Knopf, 1923.

Berryman, John. *SC.* NY: Sloane, 1950. Augmented ed, NY: World, 1962.

Colvert, James B. *SC.* San Diego: Harcourt Brace Jovanovich, 1984.

Lawrence, Frederic M. *The Real SC,* ed with intro & notes by Joseph Katz. Newark, NJ: Newark Public Library, 1980.

Linson, Corwin Knapp. *My SC,* ed with intro by Edwin H Cady. Syracuse, NY: Syracuse U P, 1958.

Milne, Gordon. *SC at Brede: An Anglo-American Literary Circle of the 1890s.* Lanham, Md: U P America, 1980.

Solomon, Eric. *SC in England: A Portrait of the Artist.* Columbus: Ohio State U P, 1964.

Stallman, R W. *SC: A Biography.* NY: Braziller, 1968.

Book Sections & Articles

Bacheller, Irving. *Coming Up the Road* (Indianapolis: Bobbs-Merrill, 1928), passim.

Bacheller. "Genius." *From Stores of Memory* (NY: Farrar & Rinehart, 1938), 110-112.

Bass, John. "How Novelist C Acts on the Battlefield." *NYJ* (May 1897), 37. Rpt *The War Dispatches of SC.*

Beer, Thomas. "Stephen, Henry, and the Hat." *VanityF,* 18 (Aug 1922), 63, 88.

Beer. "Mrs. SC." *AMercury,* 31 (Mar 1934), 289-295.

Carmichael, Otto. "SC in Havana." *PrS,* 43 (Summer 1969), 200-204.

Cather, Willa (as by Henry Nicklemann). "When I Knew SC." *Library,* 1 (23 Jun 1900), 17-18. Rpt Bassan.

Cazemajou, Jean. "SC: Pennington Seminary:

Étape D'une Éducation Méthodiste." *EA,* 20 (Apr-Jun 1967), 140-148.

Conrad, Mrs Joseph. "Recollections of SC." *Bookman,* 63 (Apr 1926), 134-137.

Conway, John. "The SC-Amy Leslie Affair: A Reconsideration." *JML,* 7 (Feb 1979), 3-14.

Crane, Helen R. "My Uncle, SC." *AMercury,* 31 (Jan 1934), 24-29.

Crane, Mrs George. "SC's Boyhood." *NYWorld* (10 Jun 1900), Sect E, p 3.

Davis, Richard Harding. "Our War Correspondents in Cuba and Puerto Rico." *Harper's,* 98 (May 1899), 938-948.

Ford, Ford Madox. "Henry James, SC and the Main Stream." *Thus To Revisit: Some Reminiscences* (London: Chapman & Hall, 1921), 102-123.

Ford. "SC." *Portraits From Life* (Boston: Houghton Mifflin, 1937), 21-37.

Fryckstedt, Olov W. "SC in the Tenderloin." *SN,* 34 (1962), 135-163.

Garland, Hamlin. "SC as I Knew Him." *YR,* 3 (Apr 1914), 494-506.

Gilkes, Lillian B. *Cora Crane: A Biography of Mrs. SC* (Bloomington: Indiana U P, 1960), passim.

Gilkes. "SC and the Harold Frederics." *Serif,* 6 (Dec 1969), 21-48.

Gullason, Thomas A. "The Cs at Pennington Seminary." *AL,* 39 (Jan 1968), 530-541.

Gullason. "A Family Portfolio." Gullason, 7-50.

Hagemann, E R. "The Death of SC." *PNJHS* (Jul 1959), 173-184.

Jones, Edith R. "SC at Brede." *Atlantic,* 114 (Jul 1954), 57-61.

Leslie, Sir Shane. "SC in Sussex." Bruccoli (1971), 13-17.

Linson, Corwin Knapp. "Little Stories of 'Steve' C." *SatEP,* 177 (11 Apr 1903), 19-20.

Noxon, Frank W. "The Real SC." *Step Ladder,* 14 (Jan 1928), 4-9.

O'Donnell, Thomas F. "John B. Van Petten: SC's History Teacher." *AL,* 27 (May 1955), 196-202.

O'Donnell. "De Forest, Van Petten, and SC." *AL,* 27 (Jan 1956), 578-580.

Oliver, Arthur. "Jersey Memories—SC." *PNJHS,* 16 (Oct 1931), 454-463.

Osborn, Scott C. "SC and Cora Taylor: Some Corrections." *AL,* 26 (Nov 1954), 416-418.

Peaslee, Clarence L. "The College Days of SC." *MoIll,* 13 (Aug 1896), 27-30.

Pizer, Donald. "The Garland-C Relationship." *HLQ,* 24 (Nov 1960), 75-82.

Sidbury, Edna Crane. "My Uncle, SC, As I Knew Him." *LDIBR,* 4 (Mar 1926), 248-250.

Vosburgh, R G. "The Darkest Hour in the Life of SC." *Criterion,* 1 (Feb 1901), 26-27. Rpt *Booklover,* 2 (Summer 1901), 338-339.

Wertheim, Stanley. "SC and the Wrath of Jehova." *LitR*, 7 (Summer 1964), 499-508.

Wertheim. "SC Remembered." *SAF*, 4 (Spring 1976), 45-64.

Wertheim. "SC in the Shadow of the Parthenon." *CLC*, 32 (May 1983), 3-13.

CRITICAL STUDIES

Books

Bergon, Frank. *SC's Artistry.* NY: Columbia U P, 1975.

Cady, Edwin H. *SC.* NY: Twayne, rev 1980.

Cazemajou, Jean. *SC (1871-1900): Écrivain Journaliste.* Paris: Librairie Didier, 1969.

Fried, Michael. *Realism, Writing, Disfiguration: On Thomas Eakins and SC.* Chicago: U Chicago P, 1987.

Gibson, Donald. *The Fiction of SC.* Carbondale: Southern Illinois U P, 1968.

Hoffman, Daniel. *The Poetry of SC.* NY: Columbia U P, 1957.

Holton, Milne. *Cylinder of Vision: The Fiction and Journalistic Writing of SC.* Baton Rouge: Louisiana State U P, 1972.

Knapp, Bettina L. *SC.* NY: Ungar, 1987.

LaFrance, Marston. *A Reading of SC.* Oxford: Clarenden, 1971.

Nagel, James. *SC and Literary Impressionism.* University Park: Pennsylvania State U P, 1980.

O'Donnell, Bernard. *An Analysis of Prose Style to Determine Authorship: The O'Ruddy, a Novel by SC and Robert Barr.* Mouton: The Hague, 1970.

Solomon, Eric. *SC: From Parody to Realism.* Cambridge: Harvard U P, 1966.

Wolford, Chester. *The Anger of SC.* Lincoln: U Nebraska P, 1983.

Collections of Essays

Bassan, Maurice, ed. *SC: A Collection of Critical Essays.* Englewood Cliffs, NJ: Prentice-Hall, 1967.

Gullason, Thomas A, ed. *SC's Career: Perspectives and Evaluations.* NY: NYU P, 1972.

Katz, Joseph, ed. *SC in Transition: Centenary Essays.* DeKalb: Northern Illinois U P, 1972.

Mitchell, Lee Clark, ed. *New Essays on The Red Badge of Courage.* Cambridge: Cambridge U P, 1986.

Weatherford, Richard M, ed. *SC: The Critical Heritage.* London: Routledge & Kegan Paul, 1973.

Wertheim, Stanley, ed. *Studies in Maggie and George's Mother.* Columbus, Ohio: Merrill, 1970.

Special Journals

ArQ, 30 (Summer 1974). SC issue.

Courier, 21 (Spring 1986). SC issue. Includes checklist.

MFS, 5 (Autumn 1959). SC issue. Includes checklist.

Serif, 6 (Dec 1969). SC issue.

SNNTS, 10 (Spring 1978). SC issue. Includes checklists.

Stephen Crane Newsletter (quarterly 1966-1969). Includes checklists.

Book Sections & Articles

Aaron, Daniel. "Howells's 'Maggie.' " *NEQ*, 38 (Mar 1965), 85-90.

Aaron. "SC and Harold Frederic." *The Unwritten War: American Writers and the Civil War* (NY: Knopf, 1973), 210-225.

Adams, Richard P. "Naturalistic Fiction: 'The Open Boat.' " *TSE*, 4 (1954), 137-146. Rpt Gullason.

Ahnebrink, Lars. *The Beginnings of Naturalism in American Fiction* (Uppsala, Sweden: U Uppsala / Cambridge: Harvard U P, 1950), passim.

Anderson, Margaret P. "A Note on 'John Twelve' in SC's 'The Monster.' " *AN&Q*, 15 (Oct 1976), 23-24.

Anderson, Sherwood. "Introduction." *Midnight Sketches,* Vol 11 of *The Work of SC,* ed Follett, xi-xv.

Anderson, Warren D. "Homer and SC." *NCF*, 19 (Jun 1964), 77-86.

Bassan, Maurice. "Misery and Society: Some New Perspectives on SC's Fiction." *SN*, 35 (1963), 104-120.

Bassan. "The Design of SC's Bowery 'Experiment.' " *SSF*, 1 (Winter 1964), 129-132. Rpt Bassan.

Bender, Bert. "Hanging SC in the Impressionistic Museum." *JAAC*, 35 (Fall 1976), 47-55.

Bender. "The Nature and Significance of 'Experience' in 'The Open Boat.' " *JNT*, 9 (Spring 1979), 70-80.

Bernard, Kenneth. " 'The Bride Comes to Yellow Sky': History as Elegy." *EngR*, 17 (Apr 1967), 17-20. Rpt Gullason.

Berryman, John. "SC: *The Red Badge of Courage.*" *The American Novel: From James Fenimore Cooper to William Faulkner,* ed Wallace Stegner (NY: Basic Books, 1965), 86-96. Rpt Gullason.

Berthoff, Warner. "Frank Norris, SC." *The Ferment of Realism: American Literature, 1884-1919* (NY: Free P, 1965), 223-235. Rpt Gullason.

Binder, Henry. "*The Red Badge of Courage* Nobody Knows." *SNNTS*, 10 (Spring 1978), 9-47.

Binder. "Donald Pizer, Ripley Hitchcock, and *The Red Badge of Courage.*" *SNNTS*, 11 (Summer 1979), 216-223.

Brennan, Joseph X. "The Imagery and Art of *George's Mother*." *CLAJ*, 4 (Dec 1960), 106-115. Rpt Gullason, Wertheim (1970).

Brennan. "Ironic and Symbolic Structure in C's *Maggie*." *NCF*, 16 (Mar 1962), 303-315. Rpt Gullason, Wertheim (1970).

Breslin, Paul. "Courage and Convention: *The Red Badge of Courage*." *YR*, 66 (Winter 1977), 209-222.

Brooke-Rose, Christine. "Ill Logics of Irony." Mitchell, 129-146.

Brown, Ellen A. "SC's *Whilomville Stories*: A Backward Glance." *MarkhamR*, 3 (May 1973), 105-109.

Bruccoli, Matthew J. "Maggie's Last Night." *SCNews*, 2 (Fall 1967), 10.

Bruccoli. "SC as a Collector's Item." Katz, 153-173.

Buitenhuis, Peter. "The Essentials of Life: 'The Open Boat' as Existentialist Fiction." *MFS*, 5 (Autumn 1959), 243-250.

Burhans, Clinton S. "Judging Henry Judging: Point of View in *The Red Badge of Courage*." *BSUF*, 15 (Spring 1974), 38-48.

Cady, Edwin H. "Introduction." *Tales, Sketches, and Reports,* Vol 8 of *The Works of SC,* ed Bowers, xxi-xli.

Cazemajou, Jean. "*The Red Badge of Courage*: The 'Religion of Peace' and the War Archetype." Katz, 54-65.

Colvert, James B. "The Origins of SC's Literary Creed." *TexSE*, 34 (1955), 179-188. Rpt Gullason.

Colvert. "Structure and Theme in SC's Fiction." *MFS*, 5 (Autumn 1959), 199-208.

Colvert. "SC's Magic Mountain." Bassan, 95-105.

Colvert. "Introduction." *Bowery Tales: Maggie, George's Mother,* Vol 1 of *The Works of SC,* ed Bowers, xxxiii-lii, 101-108.

Colvert. "Introduction." *Tales of War,* Vol 6 of *The Works of SC,* ed Bowers, xi-xxxvi.

Colvert. "Introduction." *Reports of War,* Vol 9 of *The Works of SC,* ed Bowers, xix-xxix.

Colvert. "SC: Style as Invention." Katz, 127-152.

Colvert. "Introduction." *Poems and Literary Remains,* Vol 10 of *The Works of SC,* ed Bowers, xvii-xxix.

Conrad, Joseph. "Introduction." Beer, 1-33.

Conrad. "His War Book." *Last Essays* (NY: Doubleday, Page, 1926), 119-124. Rpt Bassan.

Cox, James Trammell. "SC as Symbolic Naturalist: An Analysis of 'The Blue Hotel.' " *MFS*, 3 (Summer 1957), 147-158. Rpt Gullason.

Delbanco, Andrew. "The American SC: The Context of *The Red Badge of Courage*." Mitchell, 49-76.

Fryckstedt, Olov W. "Henry Fleming's Tupenny Fury: Cosmic Pessimism in SC's *The Red Badge of Courage*." *SN*, 33 (1961), 265-281.

Garnett, Edward. "SC and His Work." *Friday Nights: Literary Criticisms and Appreciations* (NY: Knopf, 1922), 201-217. Rpt Gullason.

Greenfield, Stanley. "The Unmistakable SC." *PMLA*, 73 (Dec 1958), 562-572.

Hagemann, E R. "Sadder Than the End: Another Look at 'The Open Boat.' " Katz, 66-85.

Hart, John E. "*The Red Badge of Courage* as Myth and Symbol." *UKCR*, 19 (Summer 1953), 249-256.

Horsford, Howard C. " 'He Was a Man.' " Mitchell, 109-127.

Hough, Robert L. "C and Goethe: A Forgotten Relationship." *NCF*, 17 (Sep 1962), 135-148. Rpt Gullason.

Hungerford, Harold R. " 'That Was at Chancellorsville': The Factual Framework of *The Red Badge of Courage*." *AL*, 34 (Jan 1963), 520-531. Rpt Gullason.

Johnson, George W. "SC's Metaphor of Decorum." *PMLA*, 78 (Jun 1963), 250-256. Rpt Bassan.

Kaplan, Amy. "The Spectacle of War in C's Revision of History." Mitchell, 77-108.

Katz, Joseph. "Afterword: Resources for the Study of SC." Katz, 205-231.

Katz. "Theodore Dreiser and SC: Studies in a Literary Relationship." Katz, 174-204.

Knapp, Daniel. "Son of Thunder: SC and the Fourth Evangelist." *NCF*, 24 (Dec 1969), 253-292.

Kwiat, Joseph J. "SC and Painting." *AQ*, 4 (Winter 1952), 331-338. Rpt Gullason.

Kwiat. "The Newspaper Experience: C, Norris, Dreiser." *NCF*, 8 (Sep 1953), 99-117. Rpt Gullason.

LaFrance, Marston. "*George's Mother* and the Other Half of *Maggie*." Katz, 35-53.

LaFrance. "SC Scholarship Today and Tomorrow." *ALR*, 7 (Spring 1974), 125-135.

Lenehan, William T. "The Failure of Naturalistic Techniques in SC's *Maggie*." *SC's Maggie: Text and Context,* 166-173.

Levenson, J C. "Introduction." *Tales of Adventure,* Vol 5 of *The Works of SC,* ed Bowers, xv-cxxxii.

Levenson. "Introduction." *The O'Ruddy,* Vol 4 of *The Works of SC,* ed Bowers, xiii-lxxiv.

Levenson. "Introduction." *The Red Badge of Courage,* Vol 2 of *The Works of SC,* ed Bowers, xiii-xcii.

Levenson. "Introduction." *The Third Violet* and *Active Service,* Vol 3 of *The Works of SC,* ed Bowers, xi-lxii.

Mailloux, Steven. "*The Red Badge of Courage* and Interpretive Conventions: Critical Response to a Maimed Text." *SNNTS*, 10 (Spring 1978), 48-63.

Michelson, Charles. "Introduction." *The Open Boat and Other Tales,* Vol 12 of *The Works of SC,* ed Follett, ix-xxiv.

Monteiro, George. "SC and the Antinomies of Christian Charity." *CentR,* 16 (Winter 1972), 91-104.

Nordloh, David J. "On C Now Edited: The University of Virginia Edition of *The Works of SC.*" *SNNTS,* 10 (Spring 1978), 103-119.

Nye, Russel B. "SC as Social Critic." *ModernQ,* 11 (Summer 1940), 48-54. Rpt Gullason.

Parker, Hershel. "Getting Used to the 'Original Form' of *The Red Badge of Courage.*" Mitchell, 25-47.

Parker & Brian Higgins. "Maggie's 'Last Night': Authorial Design and Editorial Patching." *SNNTS,* 10 (Spring 1978), 64-75.

Perosa, Sergio. "Naturalism and Impressionism in SC's Fiction." Bassan, 80-94.

Pizer, Donald. "SC's *Maggie* and American Naturalism." *Criticism,* 7 (Spring 1965), 168-175. Rpt Bassan, Gullason.

Pizer. "*The Red Badge of Courage* Nobody Knows': A Brief Rejoinder." *SNNTS,* 11 (Spring 1979), 77-81.

Pizer, Donald. "*The Red Badge of Courage:* Text, Theme, and Form." *SAQ,* 84 (Summer 1985), 302-313.

Rogers, Rodney O. "SC and Impressionism." *NCF,* 24 (Dec 1969), 292-304. Rpt Gullason.

Stallman, R W. "Introduction." *The Red Badge of Courage* (NY: Modern Library, 1951), v-xxxvii.

Stallman. "War Tales: *The Red Badge of Courage.*" *SC: An Omnibus,* 175-224.

Stein, William B. "SC's *Homo Absurdus.*" *BuR,* 8 (May 1959), 168-188.

Stone, Edward. "SC." *A Certain Morbidness* (Carbondale: Southern Illinois U P, 1969), 53-69.

Walcutt, Charles Child. "SC: Naturalist and Impressionist." *American Literary Naturalism: A Divided Stream* (Minneapolis: U Minnesota P, 1956), 66-86.

Weinstein, Bernard. "SC: Journalist." Katz, 3-34.

Weiss, Daniel. "*The Red Badge of Courage.*" *PsyR,* 52 (Summer 1965), 32-52.

Wells, H G. "SC From an English Standpoint." *NAR,* 171 (Aug 1900), 233-242.

Westbrook, Max. "SC and the Personal Universal." *MFS,* 8 (Winter 1962-1963), 351-360.

Westbrook. "SC's Poetry: Perspective and Arrogance." *BuR,* 9 (Dec 1963), 24-34. Rpt Gullason.

Westbrook. "Whilomville: The Coherence of Radical Language." Katz, 86-105.

Wyndham, George. "A Remarkable Book." *New Review,* 14 (Jan 1896), 32-40.

Ziff, Larzer. "Outstripping the Event: C's *Maggie.*" *The American 1890s: Life and Times of a Lost Generation* (NY: Viking, 1966), 185-205.

James B. Colvert

F. MARION CRAWFORD

Bagni di Lucca, Italy, 2 Aug 1854-Sorrento, Italy, 9 Apr 1909

F. Marion Crawford embodied sophistication and romance to a generation of American readers. An expatriate living in an Italian villa, author of best-selling novels, plays, histories, and criticism, Crawford was one of the foremost literary celebrities of the turn of the century. Drawn from his exotic travels, his novels of castles and countesses were a product of his belief that fiction must divert and entertain and that it must idealize life. Although realists such as William Dean Howells and Henry James assailed Crawford's romances as socially irrelevant "bad art," Crawford defended his position in *The Novel: What It Is*, claiming that a novelist "must be more than a photographer" and should depict life as "more agreeable and interesting than it ordinarily is." In 1904 he turned his attention to history, attempting to provide the basis for a permanent literary reputation. Following his death Crawford received little critical attention.

BIBLIOGRAPHIES

Bibliography of American Literature, comp Jacob Blanck. New Haven: Yale U P, 1955-1991. Primary.

Moran, John C. "FMC's *An American Politician*: Some BAL Addenda." *PBSA*, 69, no 2 (1975), 267-272. Primary.

Moran. "Recent Interest in FMC—A Bibliographical Account." *Romantist*, 1 (1977), 53-56. Secondary.

Pilkington, John, Jr. "A C Bibliography." *UMSE*, 4 (1963), 1-20. Primary.

BOOKS

Mr. Isaacs: A Tale of Modern India. NY: Macmillan, 1882. Novel.

Doctor Claudius: A True Story. NY: Macmillan, 1883. Novel.

To Leeward. Boston & NY: Houghton, Mifflin, 1884. Novel.

A Roman Singer. Boston & NY: Houghton, Mifflin, 1884. Novel.

An American Politician: A Novel. Boston & NY: Houghton, Mifflin, 1885.

Zoroaster. London & NY: Macmillan, 1885. Novel.

A Tale of a Lonely Parish. London & NY: Macmillan, 1886. Novel.

Saracinesca. NY: Macmillan, 1887. Novel.

Marzio's Crucifix. London & NY: Macmillan, 1887. Novel.

Paul Patoff. Boston & NY: Houghton, Mifflin, 1887. Rev ed, NY & London: Macmillan, 1893. Novel.

With the Immortals. London & NY: Macmillan, 1888. Novel.

Greifenstein. London & NY: Macmillan, 1889. Novel.

Sant' Ilario. London & NY: Macmillan, 1889. Novel.

A Cigarette-Maker's Romance. London & NY: Macmillan, 1890. Novel.

Khaled: A Tale of Arabia. London & NY: Macmillan, 1891. Novel.

The Witch of Prague: A Fantastic Tale. London & NY: Macmillan, 1891. Novel.

The Three Fates. London & NY: Macmillan, 1892. Novel.

Don Orsino. NY & London: Macmillan, 1892. Novel.

The Children of the King: A Tale of Southern Italy. NY & London: Macmillan, 1893. Novel.

The Novel: What It Is. NY & London: Macmillan, 1893. Nonfiction.

Pietro Ghisleri. NY & London: Macmillan, 1893. Novel.

Marion Darche: A Story Without Comment. NY & London: Macmillan, 1893. Novel.

Katherine Lauderdale, 2 vols. NY & London: Macmillan, 1894. Novel.

The Upper Berth. NY & London: Putnam, 1894. Novel.

Love in Idleness: A Tale of Bar Harbour. NY & London: Macmillan, 1894; *Love in Idleness: A Bar Harbour Tale*. London & NY: Macmillan, 1894. Novel.

The Ralstons, 2 vols. NY & London: Macmillan, 1895. Novel.

Constantinople. NY: Scribners, 1895. Travel.

Casa Braccio, 2 vols. NY & London: Macmillan, 1895. Novel.

Adam Johnstone's Son. NY & London: Macmillan, 1896. Novel.

Bar Harbor. NY: Scribners, 1896. Travel.

Taquisara, 2 vols. NY & London: Macmillan, 1896. Novel.

A Rose of Yesterday. NY & London: Macmillan, 1897. Novel.
Corleone: A Tale of Sicily, 2 vols. NY & London: Macmillan, 1897. Novel.
Ave Roma Immortalis: Studies From the Chronicles of Rome, 2 vols. NY & London: Macmillan, 1898. Rev ed, 1902. History.
Via Crucis: A Romance of the Second Crusade. NY & London: Macmillan, 1899. Novel.
The Rulers of the South: Sicily, Calabria, Malta, 2 vols. NY & London: Macmillan, 1900. Repub as *Southern Italy and Sicily and the Rulers of the South,* 1905. History.
In the Palace of the King: A Love Story of Old Madrid. NY & London: Macmillan, 1900. Novel.
Marietta: A Maid of Venice. NY & London: Macmillan, 1901. Novel.
Cecilia: A Story of Modern Rome. NY & London: Macmillan, 1902. Novel.
Man Overboard! NY & London: Macmillan, 1903. Novel.
The Heart of Rome: A Tale of the "Lost Water." NY & London: Macmillan, 1903. Novel.
Whosoever Shall Offend. NY & London: Macmillan, 1904. Novel.
Soprano: A Portrait. London & NY: Macmillan, 1905; *Fair Margaret: A Portrait.* NY & London: Macmillan, 1905. Novel.
Salve Venetia: Gleanings From Venetian History, 2 vols. NY & London: Macmillan, 1905. Repub as *Gleanings From Venetian History,* 2 vols. London & NY: Macmillan, 1905. Repub as *Venice, the Place and the People,* 2 vols. NY: Macmillan, 1909. History.
A Lady of Rome. NY & London: Macmillan, 1906. Novel.
Arethusa. NY & London: Macmillan, 1907. Novel.
The Little City of Hope: A Christmas Story. NY: Macmillan, 1907. Story.
The Primadonna: A Sequel to 'Soprano.' London: Macmillan, 1908; *The Primadonna: A Sequel to "Fair Margaret."* NY & London: Macmillan, 1908. Novel.
The Diva's Ruby: A Sequel of 'Soprano' and 'Primadonna.' London: Macmillan, 1908; *The Diva's Ruby: A Sequel to "Primadonna" and "Fair Margaret."* NY: Macmillan, 1908. Novel.
The White Sister. NY: Macmillan, 1909. Novel.
Stradella. NY: Macmillan, 1909; *Stradella: An Old Italian Love Tale.* London: Macmillan, 1909. Novel.
The Undesirable Governess. NY: Macmillan, 1910. Novel.
Uncanny Tales. London: Unwin, 1911; *Wandering Ghosts.* NY: Macmillan, 1911. Stories.

The White Sister: Romantic Drama in Three Acts, with Walter Hackett. NY: Dramatists Play Service, 1937.

EDITIONS

The Complete Work of FMC, 32 vols. NY: Macmillan, 1911.
The Works of FMC, Sorrento Edition, 25 vols. NY: Macmillan, 1919.

MANUSCRIPTS & ARCHIVES

The Houghton Library, Harvard U.

BIOGRAPHIES

Books
Elliott, Maud Howe. *My Cousin: FMC.* NY: Macmillan, 1934.
Moran, John C. *Seeking Refuge in Torre San Nicola: An Introduction to FMC.* Nashville, Tenn: FMC Memorial Society, 1980.

Book Sections & Article
Chanler, Mrs Winthrop. *Roman Spring: Memoirs* (Boston: Little, Brown, 1934), passim.
Colonna, Vittoria. "Two Literary Friends." *Things Past* (NY: Appleton, 1929), 108-124.
Fraser, Mary Crawford. "Notes of a Romantic Life: The Italian Days of FMC, and the Intimate Side of His Character." *Collier's,* 45 (23 Apr 1910), 22-24.

CRITICAL STUDIES

Books
Moran, John C. *An FMC Companion.* Westport, Conn: Greenwood, 1981.
Pilkington, John, Jr. *FMC.* NY: Twayne, 1964.

Book Section & Articles
Brooks, Van Wyck. *The Dream of Arcadia: American Writers and Artists in Italy, 1760-1915* (NY: Dutton, 1958), 160-163, 206-215.
Cooper, Frederic Taber. "FMC—An Estimate." *Bookman,* 29 (May 1909), 283-292.
Gale, Robert L. " 'My Dear Uncle'—Three Letters From FMC to Samuel Ward." *SA,* 5 (1959), 325-338.
Ouida. "The Italian Novels of MC." *NCent,* 42 (Nov 1897), 719-733.
Pilkington, John, Jr. "FMC: Italy in Fiction." *AQ,* 6 (Spring 1954), 59-65.
Pilkington. "FMC's Lecture Tour, 1897-1898." *UMSE,* 1 (1960), 66-85.
Pilkington. "The Genesis of *Mr. Isaacs.*" *UMSE,* 2 (1961), 29-39.
Walpole, Hugh. "The Stories of FMC." *YR,* 12 (Jul 1923), 673-691.

Randolph Lewis

JAMES OLIVER CURWOOD

Owosso, Mich, 12 Jun 1878-Owosso, Mich, 13 Aug 1927

"Nature is my religion," James Oliver Curwood wrote in 1921. Primarily a writer of romance-adventure and nature fiction set in Western Canada, Curwood was a master of the descriptive nature narrative. Among his best-known novels were *The Grizzly King, Nomads of the North,* and *The Valley of Silent Men.* He also wrote about 150 scenarios, and more than 200 of his stories were made into films. An avid hunter, Curwood gradually turned an about-face to become a conservationist, a conversion that he described in *God's Country, the Trail to Happiness.*

BOOKS

The Courage of Captain Plum. Indianapolis: Bobbs-Merrill, 1908. Novel.

The Wolf Hunters. Indianapolis: Bobbs-Merrill, 1908. Novel.

The Great Lakes: The Vessels That Plough Them.... NY: Putnam, 1909. Nonfiction.

The Gold Hunters. Indianapolis: Bobbs-Merrill, 1909; *The Treasure Hunters.* London: Cassell, 1917. Novel.

The Danger Trail. Indianapolis: Bobbs-Merrill, 1910. Novel.

The Honor of the Big Snows. Indianapolis: Bobbs-Merrill, 1911. Novel.

Philip Steele of the Royal Northwest Mounted Police. Indianapolis: Bobbs-Merrill, 1911. Novel.

Flower of the North. NY & London: Harper, 1912. Novel.

Isobel. NY & London: Harper, 1913; *Ice-Bound Hearts.* London: Everett, 1915. Novel.

Kazan. Indianapolis: Bobbs-Merrill, 1914. Novel.

God's Country—and the Woman. Garden City, NY: Doubleday, Page, 1915. Novel.

The Hunted Woman. Garden City, NY: Doubleday, Page, 1916; *The Valley of Gold.* London: Cassell, 1916. Novel.

The Grizzly King. Garden City, NY: Doubleday, Page, 1916. Novel.

Baree, Son of Kazan. Garden City, NY: Doubleday, Page, 1917; *Son of Kazan.* London: Cassell, 1917. Novel.

The Girl Beyond the Trail. London: Cassell, 1917;

The Courage of Marge O'Doone. Garden City, NY: Doubleday, Page, 1918. Novel.

The Golden Snare. London: Cassell, 1918; NY: Cosmopolitan, 1921. Novel.

Nomads of the North. Garden City, NY: Doubleday, Page, 1919. Novel.

The River's End. NY: Cosmopolitan, 1919. Novel.

Swift Lightning. London: Hodder & Stoughton, 1920; NY: Cosmopolitan, 1926. Novel.

Back to God's Country. NY: Cosmopolitan, 1920. Stories.

The Valley of Silent Men. NY: Cosmopolitan, 1920. Novel.

God's Country, the Trail to Happiness. NY: Cosmopolitan, 1921. Essays.

The Flaming Forest. NY: Cosmopolitan, 1921. Novel.

The Country Beyond. NY: Cosmopolitan, 1922. Novel.

The Alaskan. NY: Cosmopolitan, 1923; *The Last Frontier.* London: Hodder & Stoughton, 1923. Novel.

A Gentleman of Courage. NY: Cosmopolitan, 1924. Novel.

The Ancient Highway. NY: Cosmopolitan, 1925. Novel.

The Black Hunter. NY: Cosmopolitan, 1926. Novel.

The Crippled Lady of Peribonka. London: Hodder & Stoughton, 1927; Garden City, NY: Doubleday, Doran, 1929. Novel.

The Plains of Abraham. Garden City, NY: Doubleday, Doran, 1928. Novel.

The Glory of Living. London: Hodder & Stoughton, 1928. Autobiography.

Green Timber, completed by Dorothea A Bryant. Garden City, NY: Doubleday, Doran, 1930. Novel.

Son of the Forests, completed by Bryant. Garden City, NY: Doubleday, Doran, 1930. Autobiography.

Falkner of the Inland Seas, ed Bryant. Indianapolis: Bobbs-Merrill, 1931. Stories.

MANUSCRIPTS & ARCHIVES

The major collections are at the Bentley Historical Library, U of Michigan & at the Owosso, Mich, Public Library.

BIOGRAPHIES
Book

Swiggett, H D. *JOC: Disciple of the Wilds.* NY: Paebar, 1943.

Articles

Bolin, Donald W. "C's Literary Style." *Book-Mart,* 3 (Dec 1979), 101, 104, 108.

Gamester, Stephen J. "The Man Who Invented God's Country." *Maclean's,* 77 (22 Feb 1964), 19-22, 26.

"JOC Finds the Soul of Nature." *DearbornInd* (6 May 1922), 7, 12.

Kinsey, H C. " 'Jim' C of Owosso." *GoodH,* 75 (Nov 1922), 40-41.

Long, Ray. "JOC and His Far North." *Bookman,* 52 (Feb 1921), 492-495.

Long. "Jim C." *Bookman,* 66 (Nov 1927), 289-291.

Lowe, Kenneth S. "C." *Michigan Out-of-Doors,* 31 (Aug-Sep 1977), 40-41, 81-82.

CRITICAL STUDIES
Special Journal

The Curwood Collector, ed Ivan A Conger (1972-1982).

Judith A. Eldridge

OLIVE TILFORD DARGAN
(Fielding Burke)

Grayson County, Ky, 11 Jan 1869-Asheville, NC, 23 Jan 1968

During her lifetime Olive Tilford Dargan established a critical reputation in several genres. Her works published between 1904 and 1912 were verse dramas, a form that was becoming obsolete even while she was writing in it. Between 1914 and 1922, while modernism was flourishing, she composed lyric poetry in the romantic tradition. She then became known as a regionalist with her publication in 1925 of *Highland Annals,* a collection of sketches about people of the southern Appalachian Mountain region. Because she was deeply affected by the oppression of women and of the poor, most of Dargan's work is to some extent polemical. She is best known today for *Call Home the Heart,* a proletarian novel published under the pseudonym Fielding Burke. Dargan's treatment of interwoven class, gender, and race issues gives her novels an appeal for contemporary readers and critics.

BOOKS

Semiramis and Other Plays. NY: Brentano, 1904.

Repub, NY: Scribners, 1909.

Lords and Lovers and Other Dramas. NY: Scribners, 1906.

The Mortal Gods and Other Plays. NY: Scribners, 1912.

Path Flower and Other Verses. NY: Scribners / London: Dent, 1914.

The Cycle's Rim. NY: Scribners, 1916. Poetry.

The Flutter of the Goldleaf and Other Plays, with Frederick Peterson. NY: Scribners, 1922.

Lute and Furrow. NY: Scribners, 1922. Poetry.

Highland Annals. NY: Scribners, 1925. Rev as *From My Highest Hill: Carolina Mountain Folks.* NY: Lippincott, 1941. Stories.

Call Home the Heart (as by Fielding Burke). NY & c: Longmans, Green, 1932. Novel.

A Stone Came Rolling (as by Burke). NY & Toronto: Longmans, Green, 1935. Novel.

Sons of the Stranger (as by Burke). NY & c: Longmans, Green, 1947. Novel.

The Spotted Hawk. Winston-Salem, NC: Blair, 1958. Poetry.

Innocent Bigamy and Other Stories. Winston-Salem, NC: Blair, 1962.

MANUSCRIPTS & ARCHIVES
U of Kentucky Library.

BIOGRAPHIES
Book Section & Articles
Lathrop, Virginia Terrel. "OTD." *NCarL,* 18 (Spring 1960), 68-76.
Polsky, Jane & Thomas. "The Two Lives of OTD." *Southern Packet,* 4 (Jun 1948), 1-4.
Shannon, Anna W. "Biographical Afterword." *Call Home the Heart* (Old Westbury, NY: Feminist, 1983), 433-446.

CRITICAL STUDIES
Book Sections & Articles
Cook, Sylvia J. *From Tobacco Road to Route 66:*

The Southern Poor White in Fiction (Chapel Hill: U North Carolina P, 1976), passim.
Cook. "Critical Afterword." *Call Home the Heart* (Old Westbury, NY: Feminist, 1983), 447-462.
Lacey, Candida Ann. "Striking Fictions: Women Writers and the Making of a Proletarian Realism." *WSIF,* 9, no 4 (1986), 373-384.
Urgo, Joseph R. "Proletarian Literature and Feminism: The Gastonia Novels and Feminist Protest." *MinnR,* 24 (Spring 1985), 64-84.
Ward, William S. *A Literary History of Kentucky* (Knoxville: U Tennessee P, 1988), 116-117, 290-293.
Wiley, Edwin. "A Glance at the American Stage." *SR,* 13 (Jul 1905), 292-304.

Kathy Cantley Ackerman

REBECCA HARDING DAVIS

Washington, Pa, 26 Jun 1831-Mt Kisco, NY, 29 Sep 1910

Though not widely read in this century, Rebecca Harding Davis commands a place in American literature as an early social realist; several of her novels have been reprinted for their historical interest. Recent attention to her fiction really began when Tillie Olsen reissued Davis's "Life in the Iron Mills" in 1972. With the republication of several more stories since then, readers now can appreciate Davis's imaginative response to the realities of both industrial conditions and female experience in the nineteenth century. Although much of her journalistic fiction suffers from underdevelopment, Davis's best writing has the power of passionate indignation and the clarity of objective insight.

BIBLIOGRAPHIES
First Printings of American Authors, Vol 5, ed

Philip B Eppard (Detroit: Bruccoli Clark Layman/Gale, 1987), 81-83. Primary.
Semple, Ruth M. "RHD, 1831-1910: A Check List." *BB,* 22 (Sep-Dec 1957), 83-85. Primary & secondary.

BOOKS
Margaret Howth: A Story of To-Day. Boston: Ticknor & Fields, 1862. Novel.
Waiting for the Verdict. NY: Sheldon, 1868. Novel.
Dallas Galbraith. Philadelphia: Lippincott, 1868. Novel.
Kitty's Choice: A Story of Berrytown and Other Stories. Philadelphia: Lippincott, 1874.
John Andross. NY: Orange Judd, 1874. Novel.
A Law Unto Herself. Philadelphia: Lippincott, 1878. Novel.
Natasqua. NY: Cassell, 1886. Novel.

Kent Hampden. NY: Scribners, 1892. Children's novel.

Silhouettes of American Life. NY: Scribners, 1892. Stories.

Doctor Warrick's Daughters. NY: Harper, 1896. Novel.

Frances Waldeaux. NY: Harper, 1896. Novel.

Bits of Gossip. Boston & NY: Houghton, Mifflin, 1904. Memoir.

Life in the Iron Mills, or The Korl Woman, with biographical interpretation by Tillie Olsen. Old Westbury, NY: Feminist, 1972. Story.

COLLECTION

Life in the Iron Mills and Other Stories, ed Tillie Olsen. Old Westbury, NY: Feminist, 1985.

MANUSCRIPTS & ARCHIVES

U of Virginia Library.

BIOGRAPHIES

Book Sections & Article

Beer, Thomas. *The Mauve Decade: American Life at the End of the Nineteenth Century* (NY: Knopf, 1926), passim.

Downey, Fairfax. "Portrait of a Pioneer." *Colophon*, no 12 (Dec 1932), unpaged.

Langford, Gerald. "Rebecca." *The Richard Harding Davis Years: A Biography of a Mother and Son* (NY: Holt, Rinehart & Winston, 1961), 3-58.

CRITICAL STUDIES

Book

Sheaffer, Helen Woodward. "RHD: Pioneer Realist." Dissertation: U Pennsylvania, 1948.

Book Sections & Articles

Austin, James C. "Success and Failure of RHD." *MASJ*, 3 (1962), 44-49.

Cohn, Jan. "The Negro Character in Northern Magazine Fiction of the 1860's." *NEQ*, 43 (Dec 1970), 572-592.

Culley, Margaret M. "Vain Dreams: The Dream Convention in Some Nineteenth-Century Women's Fiction." *Frontiers*, 1 (Winter 1976), 94-102.

Duus, Louise. "Neither Saint nor Sinner: Women in Late Nineteenth-Century Fiction." *ALR*, 7 (Summer 1974), 276-278.

Eppard, Philip B. "RHD: A Misattribution." *PBSA*, 69 (Apr-Jun 1975), 265-267.

Fetterley, Judith. "RHD: 'Life in the Iron Mills.'" *Provisions* (Bloomington: Indiana U P, 1985), 306-314.

Goodman, Charlotte. "Portraits of the *Artiste Manqué* by Three Women Novelists." *Frontiers*, 5 (Fall 1980), 57-59.

Harris, Sharon M. "RHD: A Continuing Misattribution." *Legacy*, 5 (Spring 1988), 33-34.

Hesford, Walter. "Literary Contexts of 'Life in the Iron Mills.'" *AL*, 49 (Mar 1977), 70-85.

Holloway, Laura C. "RHD." *The Woman's Story: By Twenty American Women* (NY: Alden, 1889), 69-71.

Malpessi, Frances M. "Sisters in Protest: RHD and Tillie Olsen." *ReAL*, 12 (Spring 1986), 1-9.

Olsen, Tillie. "A Biographical Interpretation." *Life in the Iron Mills, or The Korl Woman*, 67-174.

Pfaelzer, Jean. "RHD: Domesticity, Social Order, and the Industrial Novel." *IJWS*, 4 (May-Jun 1981), 234-244.

Pfaelzer. "Introduction to 'Marcia.'" *Legacy*, 4 (Spring 1987), 3-5.

Quinn, Arthur Hobson. "In Transition to Realism." *American Fiction* (NY: Appleton-Century, 1936), 181-192.

Jane Atteridge Rose

RICHARD HARDING DAVIS

Philadelphia, Pa, 18 Apr 1864-Mount Kisco, NY, 11 Apr 1916

Richard Harding Davis, son of Rebecca Harding Davis, wrote novels, stories, and plays, but he was best known as a journalist who participated in and vividly reported world events. Davis's popular fiction depicted both romantic adventure and a superficial society reflected in illustrations of the Gibson Girl. His best-known character was Courtlandt Van Bibber, a young New York socialite turned Robin Hood, in *Van Bibber and Others*. Davis's literary reputation has declined steadily since his death.

BIBLIOGRAPHIES

Bibliography of American Literature, comp Jacob Blanck. New Haven: Yale U P, 1955-1991. Primary.

Eichelberger, Clayton L & Ann M McDonald. "RHD (1864-1916): A Checklist of Secondary Comment." *ALR*, 4 (Fall 1971), 313-390.

Quinby, Henry Cole. *RHD: A Bibliography*. NY: Dutton, 1924. Primary & secondary.

BOOKS

The Adventures of My Freshman. . . . Bethlehem, Pa: Moravian Print, 1884. Stories.

Gallegher and Other Stories. NY: Scribners, 1891.

Stories for Boys. NY: Scribners, 1891.

Van Bibber and Others. NY: Harper, 1892. Excerpted in *Episodes in Van Bibber's Life*. NY & London: Harper, 1899. One story repub as *Her First Appearance*. NY & London: Harper, 1901. Stories.

The West From a Car-Window. NY: Harper, 1892. Nonfiction.

The Rulers of the Mediterranean. NY: Harper, 1894. Nonfiction.

Our English Cousins. NY: Harper, 1894. Nonfiction.

The Exiles and Other Stories. NY: Harper, 1894.

The Princess Aline. NY: Harper, 1895. Novel.

About Paris. NY: Harper, 1895. Nonfiction.

Three Gringos in Venezuela and Central America. NY: Harper, 1896. Nonfiction.

Cinderella and Other Stories. NY: Scribners, 1896.

Dr. Jameson's Raiders vs. the Johannesburg Reformers. NY: Russell, 1897. Nonfiction.

Cuba in War Time. NY: Russell, 1897. Nonfiction.

Soldiers of Fortune. NY: Scribners, 1897. Novel.

A Year From a Reporter's Note-Book. NY & London: Harper, 1898; *A Year From a Correspondent's Note-Book*. London & NY: Harper, 1898. Nonfiction.

The King's Jackal. NY: Scribners, 1898. Novel.

The Cuban and Porto Rican Campaigns. NY: Scribners, 1898. Nonfiction.

The Lion and the Unicorn. NY: Scribners, 1899. Stories.

With Both Armies in South Africa. NY: Scribners, 1900. Nonfiction.

In the Fog. NY: Russell, 1901. Story.

Ranson's Folly. NY: Scribners, 1902. One story repub as *The Bar Sinister*, 1903. Stories.

Captain Macklin: His Memoirs. NY: Scribners, 1902. Novel.

"Miss Civilization": A Comedy in One Act. NY: Scribners, 1905. Play.

Farces: The Dictator, The Galloper, "Miss Civilization." NY: Scribners, 1906. Both *The Galloper* & *The Dictator* separately published, NY: Scribners/French, 1909. Plays.

Real Soldiers of Fortune. NY: Scribners, 1906. One essay repub as *Baron James Harden-Hickey*, 1906. Nonfiction.

The Scarlet Car. NY: Scribners, 1907. Stories.

The Congo and Coasts of Africa. NY: Scribners, 1907. Nonfiction.

Vera, the Medium. NY: Scribners, 1908. Novel.

The White Mice. NY: Scribners, 1909. Novel.

Once Upon a Time. NY: Scribners, 1910. Stories.

Notes of a War Correspondent. NY: Scribners, 1910. Nonfiction.

The Consul. NY: Scribners, 1911. Story.

The Man Who Could Not Lose. NY: Scribners, 1911. Stories.

The Red Cross Girl. NY: Scribners, 1912. Stories.

The Lost Road. NY: Scribners, 1913. Stories.

Who's Who: A Farce in Three Acts. London: Bickers, 1913.

Peace Manoeuvres: A Play in One Act. NY & London: French, 1914.

The Zone Police: A Play in One Act. NY & London: French, 1914.

The Boy Scout. NY: Scribners, 1914. Story.

With the Allies. NY: Scribners, 1914. Nonfiction.

"Somewhere in France." NY: Scribners, 1914. Stories.

The New Sing Sing. NY: National Committee on Prisons and Prison Reform, 1915. Nonfiction.

With the French in France and Salonika. NY: Scribners, 1916. Nonfiction.

The Deserter. NY: Scribners, 1917. Story repub from *The Novels and Stories of RHD.*

Adventures and Letters of RHD, ed Charles Belmont Davis. NY: Scribners, 1917.

EDITION & COLLECTIONS

The Novels and Stories of RHD, Crossroads Edition, 12 vols. NY: Scribners, 1916.

The Boy Scout and Other Stories for Boys. NY: Scribners, 1917.

From "Gallegher" to "The Deserter": The Best Stories of RHD, ed with intro by Roger Burlingame. NY: Scribners, 1927.

BIOGRAPHIES

Books

Downey, Fairfax. *RHD: His Day.* NY: Scribners, 1933.

Langford, Gerald. *The RHD Years: A Biography of a Mother and Son.* NY: Holt, Rinehart & Winston, 1961.

CRITICAL STUDIES

Book

Osborn, Scott Compton & Robert L Phillips, Jr. *RHD.* Boston: Twayne, 1978.

Collection of Essays

R.H.D.: Appreciations of RHD. NY: Scribners, 1917.

Book Sections & Articles

Beer, Thomas. "RHD." *Liberty,* 1 (11 Oct 1924), 15-21.

Hackett, Francis. "RHD." *NewR,* 14 (2 Mar 1918), 149-150.

Maurice, Arthur Bartlett. "Representative American Story Tellers: I. RHD." *Bookman,* 23 (Apr 1906), 137-145.

"Mr. Van Bibber in 1907." *Bookman,* 25 (Aug 1907), 564-566.

Osborn, Scott C. "The 'Rivalry-Chivalry' of RHD and Stephen Crane." *AL,* 28 (Mar 1956), 50-61.

Osborn. "RHD: Critical Battleground." *AQ,* 12 (Spring 1960), 84-92.

Palmer, Frederick. "RHD." *Scribner's,* 80 (Nov 1926), 472-477.

Scudder, Horace E. "New Figures in Literature and Art: II. RHD." *Atlantic,* 75 (May 1895), 654-658.

Solensten, John M. "The Gibson Boy: A Reassessment." *ALR,* 4 (Fall 1971), 303-312.

Waldron, Robert. "Around the World With Swash and Buckle." *AH,* 18 (Aug 1967), 56-59, 71-74.

Williams, Blanche Colton. "RHD." *Our Short Story Writers* (NY: Moffet, Yard, 1920), 105-128.

Ziff, Larzer. "The Poles of Violence: Ambrose Bierce and RHD." *The American 1890s: Life and Times of a Lost Generation* (NY: Viking, 1966), 166-184.

Gary A. Best

JOHN WILLIAM DE FOREST

Seymour (Humphreysville), Conn, 31 Mar 1826-New Haven, Conn, 17 Jul 1906

More highly regarded in his own time than now, John William De Forest nonetheless continues to receive serious critical attention. This versatile pioneer of American literary realism wrote novels that rivaled in reputation works of his contemporaries William Dean Howells and Henry James. Mixing mordant realism with romantic touches, he wrote about witchcraft and intolerance in late seventeenth-century Salem, slave-holding in the antebellum South, aristocratic excesses in England, and political corruption in Washington during Grant's administration. His best-known novel, *Miss Ravenel's Conversion From Secession to Loyalty,* which described wartime inefficiency and administrative corruption as well as the psychology of frightened troops before battle, is regarded as one of the most important novels about the Civil War.

BIBLIOGRAPHIES

Bibliography of American Literature, comp Jacob Blanck. New Haven: Yale U P, 1955-1991. Primary.

Eichelberger, Clayton L et al. "JWDF (1826-1906): A Critical Bibliography of Secondary Comment." *ALR,* 1 (Fall 1968), 1-56.

Hagemann, E R. "A Checklist of the Writings of JWDF (1826-1906)." *SB,* 8 (1956), 185-194.

Hagemann. "A JWDF Supplement, 1970." *ALR,* 3 (Spring 1970), 148-152. Primary & secondary.

BOOKS

History of the Indians of Connecticut From the Earliest Known Period to 1850. Hartford, Conn: Hamersley, 1851. Nonfiction.

Oriental Acquaintance: Or, Letters From Syria. NY: Dix, Edwards, 1856. Travel.

European Acquaintance: Being Sketches of People in Europe. NY: Harper, 1858. Travel.

Seacliff; or, The Mystery of the Westervelts. Boston: Phillips, Sampson, 1859. Novel.

Miss Ravenel's Conversion From Secession to Loyalty. NY: Harper, 1867. Rev ed, 1939. Novel.

Overland: A Novel. NY: Sheldon, 1871.

Kate Beaumont. Boston: Osgood, 1872. Novel.

The Wetherel Affair. NY: Sheldon, 1873. Novel.

Honest John Vane: A Story. New Haven, Conn: Richmond & Patten, 1875. Novel.

Playing the Mischief: A Novel. NY: Harper, 1875.

Justine's Lovers: A Novel. NY: Harper, 1878.

Irene the Missionary (Anon). Boston: Roberts, 1879. Novel.

The Bloody Chasm: A Novel. NY: Appleton, 1881. Repub as *The Oddest of Courtships; or, The Bloody Chasm: A Novel,* 1882.

A Lover's Revolt. NY & c: Longmans, Green, 1898. Novel.

The De Forests of Avesnes (and of New Netherland): A Huguenot Thread in American Colonial History, 1494 to the Present Time. New Haven, Conn: Tuttle, Morehouse & Taylor, 1900. Genealogy.

The Downing Legends: Stories in Rhyme. . . . New Haven, Conn: Tuttle, Morehouse & Taylor, 1901. Poetry.

Poems: Medley and Palestina. New Haven, Conn: Tuttle, Morehouse & Taylor, 1902.

"The First Time Under Fire" of the 12th Regiment, Connecticut Volunteers, Weitzel's Brigade Georgia Landing, Bayou LaFouche, La. October 27, 1862. Norwich, Conn: npub, 1907. Nonfiction.

A Volunteer's Adventures: A Union Captain's Record of the Civil War. . . , ed James H Croushore. New Haven: Yale U P / London: Cumberlege, Oxford U P, 1946. Nonfiction.

A Union Officer in the Reconstruction, ed Croushore & David Morris Potter. New Haven: Yale U P / London: Cumberlege, Oxford U P, 1948. Nonfiction.

Witching Times, ed Alfred Appel, Jr. New Haven, Conn: College & University P, 1967. Novel.

COLLECTION

"The Complete Short Stories of JWDF: Edited, With Notes and a Critical Introduction" by James Bascom Durham. Dissertation: U Arkansas, 1967.

MANUSCRIPTS & ARCHIVES

The Beinecke Library, Yale U.

CRITICAL STUDIES

Books

Bergmann, Frank. *The Worthy Gentleman of De-*

mocracy: *JWDF and the American Dream.* Heidelberg: Winter, 1971.

Croushore, James H. "JWDF: A Biographical and Critical Study to the Year 1868." Dissertation: Yale U, 1944.

Gargano, James W. "JWDF: A Critical Study of His Novels." Dissertation: Cornell U, 1955.

Geffen, Arthur I. "JWDF's *Miss Ravenel's Conversion From Secession to Loyalty:* Its Sources, Composition, Publication, Reception, Reputation, and Influence." Dissertation: U Chicago, 1968.

Hagemann, E R. "JWDF and the American Scene: An Analysis of His Life and Novels." Dissertation: Indiana U, 1954.

Hijiya, James A. *JWDF and the Rise of American Gentility.* Hanover, NH: Brown U P/U P New England, 1988.

Light, James F. *JWDF.* NY: Twayne, 1965.

Tabor, Carole S. "DF and the South: His Southern Experiences and Their Result in Fiction." Dissertation: Texas Christian U, 1966.

Collection of Essays
Gargano, James W, ed. *Critical Essays on JWDF.* Boston: Hall, 1981.

Special Journal
ALR, 1 (Fall 1968). JWDF issue.

Book Sections & Articles
Antoni, Robert W. "*Miss Ravenel's Conversion:* A Neglected American Novel." *SoQ,* 24 (Spring 1986), 58-63.

Brooks, Van Wyck. *New England: Indian Summer, 1865-1915* (NY: Dutton, 1940), 239-243.

Cecil, L Moffitt. "*Miss Ravenel's Conversion* and *Pilgrim's Progress.*" *CE,* 23 (Feb 1962), 352-357.

Cowie, Alexander. "JWDF (1826-1906)." *The Rise of the American Novel* (NY: American Book, 1948), 505-520.

Falk, Robert. "JWDF: The Panoramic Novel of Realism." *The Victorian Mode in American Fiction, 1865-1885* (East Lansing: Michigan State U P, 1965), 32-42.

Gargano, James W. "A Thematic Analysis of *Miss Ravenel's Conversion.*" *Topic,* 1 (Fall 1961), 40-47.

Gargano. "JWDF and the Critics." *ALR,* 1 (Fall 1968), 57-64.

Gargano. "*Kate Beaumont* and the Omnipresent Narrator." Gargano (1981), 164-172.

Gordon, Clarence. "Mr. DF's Novels." *Atlantic,* 32 (Nov 1873), 611-621. Rpt Gargano (1981).

Habegger, Alfred. "JWDF vs. Elizabeth Stuart Phelps." *Gender, Fantasy, and Realism in American Literature* (NY: Columbia U P, 1982), 38-55, passim.

Hagemann, E R. "JWDF and *The Galaxy,* Some Letters (1867-1872)." *BNYPL,* 59 (Apr 1955), 175-194.

Haight, Gordon S. "Introduction." *Miss Ravenel's Conversion From Secession to Loyalty* (NY: Harper, 1939), ix-xvi. Rpt Gargano (1981).

Hansen, Chadwick. "Introduction." *Witching Times* (State College, Pa: Bald Eagle, 1971), 7-23. Rpt Gargano (1981).

Howells, W D. "The Heroine of *Kate Beaumont.*" *Heroines of Fiction,* Vol 2 (NY: Harper, 1901), 152-163. Rpt Gargano (1981).

Levy, Leo B. "Naturalism in the Making: DF's *Honest John Vane.*" *NEQ,* 37 (Mar 1964), 89-98. Rpt Gargano (1981).

Light, James F. "JWDF (1826-1906)." *ALR,* 1 (Fall 1967), 32-35.

McGill, William J. "The Novelist as Bureaucrat: The Structure of DF's *A Union Officer in the Reconstruction.*" Gargano (1981), 173-181.

McIntyre, Clara F. "JWDF, Pioneer Realist." *UWyP,* 9 (31 Aug 1942), 1-13.

O'Donnell, Thomas F. "DF, Van Petten, and Stephen Crane." *AL,* 27 (Jan 1956), 578-580.

Potter, David M. "JWDF." *New HavenCHSP,* 9 (1951), 188-203.

Robillard, Douglas. "DF Literary Manuscripts in the Yale Library." *ALR,* 1 (Fall 1968), 81-83. Rpt Gargano (1981).

Rogers, Billi M. "JWDF." *ALR,* 8 (Summer 1975), 244-246.

Rubin, Joseph Jay. "Introduction." *Honest John Vane* (State College, Pa: Bald Eagle, 1960), 11-56.

Rubin. "Introduction." *Playing the Mischief* (State College, Pa: Bald Eagle, 1961), 7-33. Rpt Gargano (1981).

Rubin. "Introduction." *Kate Beaumont* (State College, Pa: Bald Eagle, 1963), 7-36.

Simpson, Claude M, Jr. "JWDF: *Miss Ravenel's Conversion.*" *The American Novel From James Fenimore Cooper to William Faulkner,* ed Wallace Stegner (NY: Basic Books, 1965), 35-46.

Solomon, Eric. "The Novelist as Soldier: Cooke and DF." *ALR,* 19 (Spring 1987), 80-88.

Stone, Albert E, Jr. "Best Novel of the Civil War." *AH,* 13 (Jun 1962), 84-88.

Williams, Stanley T. "Introduction." *A Volunteer's Adventures,* v-ix.

Wilson, Edmund. "The Chastening of American Prose Style: JWDF." *Patriotic Gore: Studies in the Literature of the American Civil War* (NY: Oxford U P, 1962), 635-742.

George Monteiro

MARGARET DELAND

Allegheny, Pa, 23 Feb 1857-Boston, Mass, 13 Jan 1945

During a lifetime that spanned the years from the Civil War through World War II, Margaret Deland witnessed social change that is reflected in her literary work. A novelist, short-story writer, and essayist, she examined such issues as adultery, divorce, religious doctrine, suffrage, and changing roles for women. Her fascination with the conflict between conventions and progressive ideas is best manifested in her most noted novel, *John Ward, Preacher,* which was received with both praise and censure. Although Deland championed individual freedom and independent thought, she also upheld such institutions as marriage and motherhood. Rather than being a social reformer, she espoused moderation in an effort to preserve the balance of society.

BIBLIOGRAPHIES

"Bibliography." Reep (1985), 123-130. Primary & secondary.

Humphry, James, III. "The Works of MD." *CLQ,* 8 (Nov 1948), 134-140. Primary.

BOOKS

The Old Garden and Other Verses. Boston & NY: Houghton, Mifflin, 1886.

John Ward, Preacher. Boston & NY: Houghton, Mifflin, 1888. Novel.

Florida Days. Boston: Little, Brown, 1889. Essays.

A Summer Day. Boston: Prang, 1889. Poems.

Sidney. Boston & NY: Houghton, Mifflin, 1890. Novel.

The Story of a Child. Boston: Houghton, Mifflin, 1892. Novel.

Mr. Tommy Dove and Other Stories. Boston & NY: Houghton, Mifflin, 1893.

Philip and His Wife. Boston & NY: Houghton, Mifflin, 1894. Novel.

The Wisdom of Fools. Boston: Houghton, Mifflin, 1897. Stories.

Old Chester Tales. NY & London: Harper, 1899. Stories.

Good for the Soul. NY & London: Harper, 1899. Novel.

Dr. Lavendar's People. NY & London: Harper, 1903. Stories.

The Common Way. NY & London: Harper, 1904. Essays.

The Awakening of Helena Richie. NY & London: Harper, 1906. Novel.

An Encore. NY & London: Harper, 1907. Novel.

R. J.'s Mother and Some Other People. NY & London: Harper, 1908. Stories.

Where the Laborers Are Few. NY & London: Harper, 1909. Novel.

The Way to Peace. NY & London: Harper, 1910. Novel.

The Iron Woman. NY & London: Harper, 1911. Novel.

The Voice. NY & London: Harper, 1912. Novel.

Partners. NY & London: Harper, 1913. Novel.

The Hands of Esau. NY & London: Harper, 1914. Novel.

Around Old Chester. NY & London: Harper, 1915. Stories.

The Rising Tide. NY & London: Harper, 1916. Novel.

The Promises of Alice. NY & London: Harper, 1919. Novel.

Small Things. NY: Appleton, 1919. Essays.

An Old Chester Secret. NY & London: Harper, 1920. Novel.

The Vehement Flame. NY & London: Harper, 1922. Novel.

New Friends in Old Chester. NY & London: Harper, 1924. Stories.

The Kays. NY & London: Harper, 1926. Novel.

Captain Archer's Daughter. NY & London: Harper, 1932. Novel.

If This Be I, As I Suppose It Be. NY & London: Appleton-Century, 1935. Autobiography.

Old Chester Days. NY & London: Harper, 1937. Stories.

Golden Yesterdays. NY & London: Harper, 1941. Autobiography.

MANUSCRIPTS & ARCHIVES

Colby C Library.

BIOGRAPHIES

Book Sections & Articles

Dodd, Loring Holmes. "The Friendliness of MD." *Celebrities at Our Hearthside* (Boston: Dresser, Chapman & Grimes, 1959), 151-156.

McDonald, Donald. "Mrs. D's Childhood." *Outlook,* 64 (17 Feb 1900), 407-410.

Overton, Grant. "MD." *The Women Who Make Our Novels* (NY: Dodd, Mead, rev 1928), 105-107.

Purdy, Lucia. "Mrs. D at Home." *Critic,* 33 (Jul-Aug 1898), 33-39.

Williams, Blanche Colton. "MD." *Our Short Story Writers* (NY: Moffat, Yard, 1920), 129-145.

CRITICAL STUDIES

Books

Preussner, Allana Sue. "The Minister's Wooing." Dissertation: U Colorado, 1979.

Reep, Diana C. *MD.* Boston: Twayne, 1985.

Book Sections & Articles

Alden, Henry Mills. "The Author of *The Iron Woman.*" *Outlook,* 99 (11 Nov 1911), 628-632.

Boynton, Percy H. *America in Contemporary Fiction* (Chicago: U Chicago P, 1940), 38-40.

Brumm, Ursula. "The Motif of the Pastor as an Unsuitable Suitor." *Amst,* 31, no 1 (1986), 61-70.

Chapple, Joe Mitchell. "MD." *NatM,* 9 (Mar 1899), 522-529.

Ford, Mary K. "Some Representative American Story Tellers." *Bookman,* 25 (Jul 1907), 511-519.

Gould, Marjorie D. "Of MD and *Old Chester.*" *CLQ,* series 2, no 10 (May 1949), 167-170.

Howe, M A DeWolfe. "MD: A Study in Influences." *Outlook,* 84 (24 Nov 1906), 730-734.

Kantor, J R K. "*The Damnation of Theron Ware* and *John Ward, Preacher.*" *Serif,* 3 (Mar 1966), 16-21.

McIlvaine, Robert. "Two Awakenings: Edna Pontellier and Helena Richie." *RAFI,* 4 (Winter 1979), 44-48.

Reep, Diana. *The Rescue and Romance: Popular Novels Before World War I* (Bowling Green, Ohio: Bowling Green State U Popular P, 1982), passim.

Smith, Herbert F. *The Popular American Novel, 1865-1920* (Boston: Twayne, 1980), 156-162.

Suderman, Elmer F. "Skepticism and Doubt in the Late Nineteenth-Century American Novels." *BSUF,* 8 (Winter 1967), 63-72.

"T. P. O'Connor Discovers MD." *HarW,* 50 (16 Jun 1906), 859, 861.

Welter, Barbara. *Dimity Convictions: The American Woman in the Nineteenth Century* (Athens: Ohio U P, 1976), 120-129.

Wilson, Albert Frederick. "Can Children Be Taught to Write?" *GoodH,* 61 (Jul 1915), 44-50.

Laraine Missory Olechowski

THOMAS DIXON, JR.

Near the town of Shelby, NC, 11 Jan 1864-Raleigh, NC, 3 Apr 1946

Thomas Dixon first came to national prominence as a dynamic preacher of the social gospel in Baptist churches in Boston and New York City. When he turned to fiction he gained fame for his portrayals of life in the South during Reconstruction. These chronicles, beginning with *The Leopard's Spots,* took the side of white southerners against the assertion of rights by newly freed black slaves. When *The Clansman,* with its glorification of the role of the Ku Klux Klan during Reconstruction, was made into the film *The Birth of a Nation,* Dixon's name was forever linked with white supremacy in the South. Dixon's other novels dealt with a host of issues, including socialism and the new woman. His fiction was never praised for its literary qualities but is of continuing interest for its vivid presentation of his social and political views.

BOOKS

Living Problems in Religion and Social Science. NY: Dillingham, 1889.
What Is Religion? An Outline of Vital Ritualism. NY: Scott, 1891.
D on Ingersoll: Ten Discourses. NY: Ogilvie, 1892.
The Failure of Protestantism in New York and Its Causes. NY: Strauss, 1896.
D's Sermons, Delivered in the Grand Opera House, New York, 1898-1899. NY: Bussey, 1899?
The Leopard's Spots: A Romance of the White Man's Burden—1865-1900. NY: Doubleday, Page, 1902. Novel.
The One Woman: A Story of Modern Utopia. NY: Doubleday, Page, 1903. Novel.
The Life Worth Living: A Personal Experience. NY: Doubleday, Page, 1905. Essays.
The Clansman: An Historical Romance of the Ku Klux Klan. NY: Doubleday, Page, 1905. Repub with intro by Thomas D Clark, Lexington: U P Kentucky, 1970. Novel.
The Traitor: A Story of the Fall of the Invisible Empire. NY: Doubleday, Page, 1907. Novel.
Comrades: A Story of Social Adventure in California. NY: Doubleday, Page, 1909. Novel.
The Root of Evil. Garden City, NY: Doubleday, Page, 1911. Novel.

The Sins of the Father: A Romance of the South. NY & London: Appleton, 1912. Novel.
The Southerner: A Romance of the Real Lincoln. NY & London: Appleton, 1913. Novel.
The Victim: A Romance of the Real Jefferson Davis. NY & London: Appleton, 1914. Novel.
The Foolish Virgin: A Romance of Today. NY & London: Appleton, 1915. Novel.
The Fall of a Nation: A Sequel to The Birth of a Nation. NY & London: Appleton, 1916. Novel.
The Way of a Man: A Story of the New Woman. NY & London: Appleton, 1919. Novel.
A Man of the People: A Drama of Abraham Lincoln. NY & London: Appleton, 1920. Play.
The Man in Gray: A Romance of North and South. NY & London: Appleton, 1921. Novel.
The Black Hood. NY & London: Appleton, 1924. Novel.
The Love Complex. NY: Boni & Liveright, 1925. Novel.
The Hope of the World: A Story of the Coming War. NY: Author, 1925.
The Torch: A Story of the Paranoiac Who Caused a Great War. NY: Author, 1927. Scenario.
The Sun Virgin. NY: Liveright, 1929. Novel.
Companions. NY & Cleveland: Otis, 1931.
The Inside Story of the Harding Tragedy, with Harry M Daugherty. NY: Churchill, 1932.
A Dreamer in Portugal: The Story of Bernarr Macfadden's Mission to Continental Europe. NY: Covici-Friede, 1934.
The Flaming Sword. Atlanta: Monarch, 1939. Novel.

MANUSCRIPTS & ARCHIVES

Duke U Library.

BIOGRAPHIES

Books
Cook, Raymond A. *Fire From the Flint: The Amazing Careers of TD.* Winston-Salem, NC: Blair, 1968.
Crowe, M Karen, ed. "Southern Horizons: The Autobiography of TD: A Critical Edition." Dissertation: NYU, 1982.

CRITICAL STUDIES

Books

Cook, Raymond A. *TD.* NY: Twayne, 1974.

Karina, Stephen Joseph. "With Flaming Sword: The Reactionary Rhetoric of TD." Dissertation: U Georgia, 1978.

Wright, James Zebulon. "TD: The Mind of a Southern Apologist." Dissertation: George Peabody C for Teachers, 1966.

Articles

Allen, A R. "TD, Jr. and Political Religion: From Social Reformer to Racist." *Foundations,* 14 (Apr-Jun 1971), 136-152.

Bloomfield, Maxwell. "D's *The Leopard's Spots:* A Study in Popular Racism." *AQ,* 16 (Fall 1964), 387-401.

Carter, Everett. "Cultural History Written With Lightning: The Significance of *The Birth of a Nation.*" *AQ,* 12 (Fall 1960), 347-357.

Cook, Raymond A. "The Versatile Career of TD." *EUQ,* 11 (Jun 1955), 103-112.

Cook. "The Literary Principles of TD." *GaR,* 13 (Spring 1959), 97-102.

Cook. "The Man Behind *The Birth of a Nation.*" *NCHR,* 39 (Autumn 1962), 519-540.

Da Ponte, Durant. "The Greatest Play of the South." *TSL,* 2 (1957), 15-24.

Davenport, F Garvin, Jr. "TD's Mythology of Southern History." *JSoH,* 36 (Aug 1970), 350-367.

Kinney, James. "The Rhetoric of Racism: TD and the 'Damned Black Beast.' " *ALR,* 15 (Autumn 1982), 145-154.

Oakes, Frances. "Whitman and D: A Strange Case of Borrowing." *GaR,* 11 (Fall 1957), 333-340.

Riggio, Thomas P. "*Uncle Tom* Reconstructed: A Neglected Chapter in the History of a Book." *AQ,* 28 (Spring 1976), 56-70.

Roberts, Samuel K. "Kelly Miller and TD, Jr. on Blacks in American Civilization." *Phylon,* 41 (Jun 1980), 202-209.

Philip B. Eppard

MARY MAPES DODGE

New York City, NY, 26 Jan 1831?-Onteora Park, NY, 21 Aug 1905

Mary Mapes Dodge's reputation rests primarily on her work as editor of *St. Nicholas,* considered the finest children's magazine published in the United States, and as author of *Hans Brinker; or, The Silver Skates,* a children's novel that remains a steady seller in several languages more than one hundred years after its publication. Initially praised for its attention to detail, *Hans Brinker* has more recently been hailed as an early example of psychological realism in American children's literature. Scholarly attention has focused on Dodge's use of humor and on her strong influence as editor of *St. Nicholas* on children aspiring to be writers, many of whom began their literary careers in the magazine.

BIBLIOGRAPHY

Bibliography of American Literature, comp Jacob Blanck. New Haven: Yale U P, 1955-1991. Primary.

BOOKS

The Irvington Stories. NY: O'Kane / San Francisco: Bancroft, 1865. Augmented ed, NY: Allison, 1898.

Hans Brinker; or, The Silver Skates. A Story of Life in Holland. NY: O'Kane, 1866; *The Silver Skates.* London: Low, 1867. Children's novel.

A Few Friends and How They Amused Themselves: A Tale in Nine Chapters Containing Descriptions of Twenty Pastimes and Games, and a

Fancy-Dress Party. Philadelphia: Lippincott, 1869. Story.

Rhymes and Jingles. NY: Scribner, Armstrong, 1875. Augmented ed, NY: Scribners, 1904.

Theophilus and Others. NY: Scribner, Armstrong, 1876. Novel.

Along the Way. NY: Scribners, 1879. Augmented as *Poems and Verses.* NY: Century, 1904.

Donald and Dorothy. Boston: Roberts, 1883. Children's novel.

The Land of Pluck: Stories and Sketches for Young Folk. NY: Century, 1894.

When Life Is Young: A Collection of Verse for Boys and Girls. NY: Century, 1894.

OTHER

St. Nicholas (1873-1905), ed MMD. Children's magazine.

Baby Days: A Selection of Songs, Stories, and Pictures, for Very Little Folks, comp MMD. NY: Scribner, 1877. Augmented as *Baby World: Stories, Rhymes, and Pictures for Little Folks.* NY: Century, 1884. Augmented again as *A New Baby World: Stories, Rhymes, and Pictures for Little Folks.* NY: Century, 1897.

The Children's Book of Recitations, comp MMD. NY: De Witt, 1898.

BIOGRAPHIES

Books

Howard, Alice B. *MMD of St. Nicholas.* NY: Messner, 1943.

Mason, Miriam E. *MMD, Jolly Girl.* Indianapolis: Bobbs-Merrill, 1949.

Wright, Catherine Morris. *Lady of the Silver Skates: The Life and Correspondence of MMD.* Jamestown, RI: Clingstone, 1979.

Book Sections & Article

Clarke, William Fayal. "In Memory of MMD." *St. Nicholas,* 32 (Oct 1905), 1059-1071.

Runkle, Lucia Gilbert. "MMD." *Our Famous Women* (Hartford, Conn: Worthington, 1884), 276-294.

Tutwiler, Julia R. "MMD in New York City." *Women Authors of Our Day in Their Homes: Personal Descriptions and Interviews,* ed

Francis Whiting Halsey (NY: Pott, 1903), 257-268.

CRITICAL STUDIES

Books

Erisman, Fred R. " 'There Was a Child Went Forth': A Study of *St. Nicholas Magazine* and Selected Children's Authors, 1890-1915." Dissertation: U Minnesota, 1966.

Roggenbuck, Mary Jane. "*St. Nicholas Magazine:* A Study of the Impact and Historical Influence of the Editorship of MMD." Dissertation: U Michigan, 1976.

Book Sections & Articles

Brack, O M, Jr. "Mark Twain in Knee Pants: The Expurgation of *Tom Sawyer Abroad.*" *Proof,* 2 (1972), 145-151.

Darling, Richard L. "The Genesis of a Classic: *Hans Brinker.*" *The Rise of Children's Book Reviewing in America, 1865-1881* (NY: Bowker, 1968), 228-237.

Fargeon, Eleanor. "A Comedy in Wax or Lucy and Their Majesties." *Horn Book,* 41 (Aug 1965), 358-363.

Griswold, Jerome. "*Hans Brinker:* Sunny World, Angry Waters." *ChildL,* 12 (1984), 47-60.

Kelly, Robert Gordon. *Mother Was a Lady: Self and Society in Selected American Children's Periodicals, 1865-1890* (Westport, Conn: Greenwood, 1974), passim.

Mayes, Herbert R. "Reminiscences of *St. Nicholas.*" *PW,* 222 (23 Jul 1982), 74-77.

Moore, Anne C. "The Creation and Criticism of Children's Books: A Retrospect and a Forecast." *ALA Bulletin,* 28 (Sep 1934), 693-701.

Sturges, Florence M. "The *St. Nicholas* Bequest." *Horn Book,* 36 (Oct 1960), 365-377.

Targ, William. "A Hundred for Hans." *NYTBR* (7 Nov 1965), 53.

White, E B. "Onward and Upward With the Arts: The St. Nicholas League." *NYer,* 10 (8 Dec 1934), 38, 40, 42, 44, 47-48, 50, 52.

Wright, Catherine Morris. "How *St. Nicholas* Got Rudyard Kipling and What Happened Then." *PULC,* 35 (Spring 1974), 259-289.

Carol Acree & Jerome Griswold

IGNATIUS DONNELLY

Philadelphia, Pa, 3 Nov 1831-Minneapolis, Minn, 1 Jan 1901

Ignatius Donnelly was best known as a reform politician and father of the People's Party. He earned his greatest literary renown from such pseudoscientific nonfiction as *Atlantis: The Antediluvian World* and his controversial arguments for Francis Bacon's authorship of Shakespeare's plays. His novels largely went unread; only the dystopian *Caesar's Column*, which exploited populist fears of a capitalist conspiracy, became a popular success. Because of its didacticism, pedantry, and sentimentalism, Donnelly's fiction is usually considered to have scant literary value, though his depiction of urban suffering and totalitarianism in *Caesar's Column* links him with the American literary naturalists. In recent years readers have begun to find merit in the novel's powerful symbolism and its nightmarish evocation of social cataclysm.

BIBLIOGRAPHIES

Bibliography of American Literature, comp Jacob Blanck. New Haven: Yale U P, 1955-1991. Primary.
"Selected Bibliography." Ridge, 402-414. Primary & secondary.

BOOKS

The Mourner's Vision. A Poem. Philadelphia: npub, 1850.
Ninninger City: A Pamphlet. Philadelphia: Duross, 1856. Nonfiction.
Minnesota. Address Delivered at the Broadway House. . . . NY: Folger & Turner, 1857.
The Sonnets of Shakspeare: An Essay. St Paul, Minn: Privately printed, 1859.
Atlantis: The Antediluvian World. NY: Harper, 1882. Rev ed, ed Egerton Sykes, 1949. Nonfiction.
Ragnarok: The Age of Fire and Gravel. NY: Appleton, 1883. Nonfiction.
The Great Cryptogram: Francis Bacon's Cipher in the So-called Shakespeare Plays. Chicago & c: Peale, 1888. Nonfiction.
Caesar's Column: A Story of the Twentieth Century (as by Edmund Boisgilbert, M.D.). Chicago: Schulte, 1890. Novel.
Doctor Huguet: A Novel. Chicago: Schulte, 1891.

The Golden Bottle or the Story of Ephraim Benezet of Kansas. NY & St Paul: Merrill, 1892. Novel.
The American People's Money. Chicago: Laird & Lee, 1895. Augmented as *The Bryan Campaign for the American People's Money,* 1896. Nonfiction.
The Cipher in the Plays and on the Tombstone. Minneapolis: Verulam, 1899. Nonfiction.
A Tribute to Abraham Lincoln. Washington: Burdick, 1942.

DIARY

"The Diary of ID, 1859-1884," ed Theodore L Nydahl. Dissertation: U Minnesota, 1942.

OTHER

"National Platform of the People's Party." *The Political Text-Book and Voter's Guide Compiled by the New York World* (NY: Press Publishing, 1892), 6-7.
Representative (1893-1901), ed & published by ID. Newspaper.

COLLECTION

Donnelliana: An Appendix to "Caesar's Column." Excerpts From the Wit, Wisdom, Poetry and Eloquence of ID, ed Everett W Fish. Chicago: Schulte, 1892.

MANUSCRIPTS & ARCHIVES

Minnesota Historical Society, St Paul.

BIOGRAPHIES

Books
Fish, Everett W. *Biography of ID.* Chicago: Schulte, 1892. Rpt from *Donnelliana.*
Ridge, Martin. *ID: Portrait of a Politician.* Chicago: U Chicago P, 1962.
Sullivan, Oscar M. *North Star Sage: The Story of ID.* NY: Vantage, 1953.
Wack, Henry Wellington. *Personal Recollections of a Great Baconian, Hon. ID.* NY: Bacon Society, nd.

Book Section
Hicks, John D. *The Populist Revolt: A History of*

the *Farmer's Alliance and the People's Party* (Minneapolis: U Minnesota P, 1931), passim.

CRITICAL STUDIES

Books

Anderson, David D. *ID*. Boston: Twayne, 1980.

O'Connor, William D. *Mr. D's Reviewers*. Chicago: Belford, Clark, 1889.

Pyle, J Gilpin. *The Little Cryptogram*. St Paul: Pioneer, 1888.

Book Sections & Articles

Anderson, David D. "Minnesota's Seven-Storied Mountaineer." *MMisc*, 2 (1975), 27-32.

Anderson. "ID in Retrospect." *MMisc*, 6 (1978), 30-34.

Axelrad, Allan M. "Ideology and Utopia in the Works of ID." *AmS*, 12 (Fall 1971), 47-65.

Baker, J Wayne. "Populist Themes in the Fiction of ID." *AmS*, 14 (Fall 1973), 65-83.

Bovee, John R. "*Doctor Huguet*: D on Being Black." *MinnH*, 41 (Summer 1969), 286-294.

DeMeules, Donald H. "ID: A Don Quixote in the World of Science." *MinnH*, 37 (Jun 1961), 229-234.

Flanagan, John T. "Dr. Holmes Advises Young ID." *AL*, 13 (Mar 1941), 59-61.

Friedman, William F & Elizabeth S. "ID and 'The Great Cryptogram.' " *The Shakespearean Ciphers Examined* (Cambridge: Cambridge U P, 1957), 27-50.

Handlin, Oscar. "American Views of the Jew at the Opening of the Twentieth Century." *PAJHS*, 40 (Jun 1951), 323-344.

Hofstadter, Richard. "The Folklore of Populism." *The Age of Reform* (NY: Knopf, 1955), 67-70.

Jaher, Frederic Cople. "ID." *Doubters and Dissenters* (London: Free P, 1964), 96-123.

Martin, Jay. "Paradises (To Be) Regained." *Harvests of Change: American Literature, 1865-1914* (Englewood Cliffs, NJ: Prentice-Hall, 1967), 231-233.

Patterson, John S. "Alliance and Antipathy: ID's Ambivalent Vision in *Doctor Huguet*." *AQ*, 22 (Winter 1970), 824-845.

Patterson. "From Yeoman to Beast: Images of Blackness in *Caesar's Column*." *AmS*, 12 (Fall 1971), 21-31.

Pollack, Norman. "Handlin on Anti-Semitism: A Critique of American Views of the Jew." *JAH*, 51 (Dec 1964), 391-403.

Pollack. "ID on Human Rights: A Study of Two Novels." *Mid-America*, 47 (Apr 1965), 99-112.

Pollack. "Epilogue: A Transformation of Social Values." *The Populist Mind*, ed Pollack (Indianapolis: Bobbs-Merrill, 1967), 469-496.

Rideout, Walter B. "Introduction." *Caesar's Column* (Cambridge: Harvard U P, 1960), vii-xxxii.

Ridge, Martin. "The Humor of ID." *MinnH*, 33 (Winter 1953), 326-330.

Robertson, John M. *The Baconian Heresy* (NY: Dutton, 1913), passim.

Saxton, Alexander. "*Caesar's Column*: The Dialogue of Utopia and Catastrophe." *AQ*, 19 (Summer 1967), 224-238.

Ueda, Reed T. "Economic and Technological Evil in the Modern Apocalypse: D's *Caesar's Column* and *The Golden Bottle*." *JPC*, 14 (Summer 1980), 1-9.

Ziff, Larzer. "The Midwestern Imagination." *The American 1890s: Life and Times of a Lost Generation* (NY: Viking, 1966), 82-85.

Stephen C. Brennan

THEODORE DREISER

Terre Haute, Ind, 27 Aug 1871-Los Angeles, Calif, 28 Dec 1945

Born into a poor midwestern German-American family, Theodore Dreiser began his career as a journalist and wrote little fiction before his first novel, *Sister Carrie*, was published in 1900. *Carrie* was weakly supported by its publisher because of Dreiser's amoral depiction of its heroine's transgressions, and Dreiser did not return to fiction until 1911, with *Jennie Gerhardt*. By the mid-1920s Dreiser was considered one of the major forces in modern American literature, and his *An American Tragedy* was almost universally regarded as a twentieth-century masterpiece. Many readers remained critical of his seeming clumsiness as a novelist and of his limitations as a speculative thinker, but few denied the power of his dramatizations of the gap between desire and reality and between myth and circumstance in American life. An entire generation of young American writers who came of age between the two world wars viewed Dreiser's work and career as examples of the possibility of pursuing a truthful examination of American life. Although Dreiser turned from fiction to political and philosophical issues during the last two decades of his career, his novels continue to attract much critical attention both as the fullest expression of naturalistic fiction in America and as major works of art.

BIBLIOGRAPHIES

Boswell, Jeanetta. *TD and the Critics, 1911-1982: A Bibliography With Selective Annotations.* Metuchen, NJ: Scarecrow, 1986. Secondary.

Elias, Robert H. "TD." *Sixteen Modern American Authors: A Survey of Research and Criticism*, ed Jackson R Bryer (Durham, NC: Duke U P, 1974), 123-179. Essay on secondary sources.

First Printings of American Authors, Vol 4. Detroit: Bruccoli Clark/Gale, 1979. Primary.

Pizer, Donald, Richard W Dowell & Frederic W Rusch. *TD: A Primary and Secondary Bibliography*. Boston: Hall, 1975.

BOOKS

Sister Carrie. NY: Doubleday, Page, 1900. Abridged ed, London: Heinemann, 1901. Novel.

Jennie Gerhardt. NY & London: Harper, 1911. Novel.

The Financier. NY & London: Harper, 1912. Rev ed, NY: Boni & Liveright, 1927. Novel.

A Traveler at Forty. NY: Century, 1913. Travel.

The Titan. NY: Lane / London: Lane, Bodley Head / Toronto: Bell & Cockburn, 1914. Novel.

The "Genius." NY: Lane / London: Lane, Bodley Head / Toronto: Gundy, 1915. Novel.

Plays of the Natural and the Supernatural. NY: Lane / London: Lane, Bodley Head, 1916. Rev as *Plays, Natural and Supernatural*. London: Constable, 1930.

A Hoosier Holiday. NY: Lane / London: Lane, Bodley Head, 1916. Travel.

Free and Other Stories. NY: Boni & Liveright, 1918.

The Hand of the Potter. NY: Boni & Liveright, 1918. Rev ed, 1927. Play.

Twelve Men. NY: Boni & Liveright, 1919. Sketches.

Hey Rub-a-Dub-Dub. . . . NY: Boni & Liveright, 1920. Essays.

A Book About Myself. NY: Boni & Liveright, 1922. Repub as *Newspaper Days*. NY: Liveright, 1931. Autobiography.

The Color of a Great City. NY: Boni & Liveright, 1923. Sketches.

An American Tragedy. 2 vols, NY: Boni & Liveright, 1925; 1 vol, London: Constable, 1926. Novel.

Moods: Cadenced and Declaimed. NY: Boni & Liveright, 1926. Rev ed, 1928. Rev again as *Moods: Philosophic and Emotional, Cadenced and Declaimed*. NY: Simon & Schuster, 1935. Poems.

Chains: Lesser Novels and Stories. NY: Boni & Liveright, 1927.

D Looks at Russia. NY: Liveright, 1928. Travel.

A Gallery of Women, 2 vols. NY: Liveright, 1929. Biographical sketches.

A History of Myself: Dawn. NY: Liveright, 1931. Autobiography.

Tragic America. NY: Liveright, 1931. Essays.

America Is Worth Saving. NY: Modern Age, 1941. Essays.

The Bulwark. Garden City, NY: Doubleday, 1946. Novel.

The Stoic. Garden City, NY: Doubleday, 1947.
Novel.

Notes on Life, ed Marguerite Tjader & John J
McAleer. University: U Alabama P, 1974. Essays.

TD: A Selection of Uncollected Prose, ed with intro
by Donald Pizer. Detroit: Wayne State U P,
1977. Essays.

An Amateur Laborer, ed with intro by Richard W
Dowell. Philadelphia: U Pennsylvania P, 1983.
Autobiography.

Selected Magazine Articles of TD, 2 vols, ed with
intro by Yoshinobu Hakutani. Rutherford,
NJ: Fairleigh Dickinson U P, 1985, 1987. Essays.

*TD's "Heard in the Corridors": Articles and Re-
lated Writings*, ed with intro by T D
Nostwich. Ames: Iowa State U P, 1988. Essays.

*TD: Journalism: Volume One, Newspaper Writ-
ings, 1892-1895*, ed with intro by Nostwich.
Philadelphia: U Pennsylvania P, 1988. Essays.

LETTERS & DIARIES

Letters of TD, 3 vols, ed Robert H Elias. Philadelphia: U Pennsylvania P, 1959.

Letters to Louise, ed Louise Campbell. Philadelphia: U Pennsylvania P, 1959.

TD: American Diaries, 1902-1926, ed with intro
by Thomas P Riggio. Philadelphia: U Pennsylvania P, 1982.

*Dreiser-Mencken Letters: The Correspondence of
TD & H. L. Mencken, 1907-1945*, 2 vols, ed
with intro by Riggio. Philadelphia: U Pennsylvania P, 1986.

OTHER

*Harlan Miners Speak: Report on Terrorism in the
Kentucky Coal Fields. . . .* NY: Harcourt,
Brace, 1932. Intro & much of the questioning
in the testimony by TD.

The Living Thoughts of Thoreau, ed with intro by
TD. NY: Longmans, Green, 1939.

EDITION & COLLECTIONS

The Best Short Stories of TD, ed with intro by
Howard Fast. Cleveland & NY: World, 1947.
Rpt with intro by James T Farrell, 1956.

TD, ed with intro by Farrell. NY: Dell, 1962. Stories, essays & poetry.

Selected Poems (From Moods) by TD, ed with intro
by Robert P Saalbach. Jericho, NY: Exposition, 1969.

*Sister Carrie: An Authoritative Text, Backgrounds
and Sources, Criticism*, ed Donald Pizer. NY:
Norton, 1970.

A Trilogy of Desire, ed with intro by Philip L
Gerber. Cleveland & NY: World, 1972.
Cowperwood novels.

TD: Sister Carrie, Jennie Gerhardt, Twelve Men, ed
Richard Lehan. NY: Library of America,
1987.

MANUSCRIPTS & ARCHIVES

The major collections are at the U of Pennsylvania
Library; the Lilly Library, Indiana U; the New
York Public Library; & U of Virginia Library.

BIOGRAPHIES

Books

Dreiser, Helen. *My Life With D*. Cleveland: World,
1951.

Dreiser, Vera, with Brett Howard. *My Uncle Theodore*. NY: Nash, 1976.

Dudley, Dorothy. *Forgotten Frontiers: D and the
Land of the Free*. NY: Harrison Smith, 1931.
Repub as *D and the Land of the Free*. NY:
Beechhurst, 1946.

Elias, Robert H. *TD: Apostle of Nature*. Ithaca,
NY: Cornell U P, rev 1970.

Kennell, Ruth E. *TD and the Soviet Union, 1927-
1945: A First-Hand Chronicle*. NY: International, 1969.

Lingeman, Richard. *TD: At the Gates of the City,
1871-1907*. NY: Putnam, 1986.

Swanberg, W A. *Dreiser*. NY: Scribners, 1965.

Tjader, Marguerite. *TD: A New Dimension*. Nor-
walk, Conn: Silvermine, 1965.

Book Sections & Articles

Aaron, Daniel. *Writers on the Left* (NY: Harcourt,
Brace & World, 1961), passim.

Burke, John J. "Season of Despair: TD in Philadelphia, 1902-1903." *PaEng*, 12 (Spring 1986),
31-38.

Epstein, Joseph. "The Mystery of TD." *NewC*, 5
(Nov 1986), 33-43.

Gerber, Philip L. "D: The Great Sloth of the Thirties." *ON*, 11 (Spring-Summer 1985), 7-23.

Gilmer, Walker. *Horace Liveright: Publisher of the
Twenties* (NY: Lewis, 1970), passim.

Kramer, Dale. *Chicago Renaissance* (NY: Appleton-
Century, 1966), passim.

Manchester, William R. *Disturber of the Peace:
The Life of H. L. Mencken* (NY: Harper,
1951), passim.

CRITICAL STUDIES

Books

Gerber, Philip L. *TD*. NY: Twayne, 1964.

Gerber. *Plots and Characters in the Fiction of TD*.
Hamden, Conn: Archon, 1977.

Griffin, Joseph. *The Small Canvas: An Introduction to D's Short Stories*. Rutherford, NJ: Fairleigh Dickinson U P, 1985.

Hakutani, Yoshinobu. *Young D: A Critical Study*. Rutherford, NJ: Fairleigh Dickinson U P, 1980.

Hussman, Lawrence E, Jr. *D and His Fiction*. Philadelphia: U Pennsylvania P, 1983.

Lehan, Richard. *TD: His World and His Novels*. Carbondale: Southern Illinois U P, 1969.

Lundén, Rolf. *The Inevitable Equation: The Antithetic Pattern of TD's Thought and Art*. Uppsala, Sweden: Studia Anglistica Upsaliensia, 1973.

Lundén. *Dreiser Looks at Scandinavia*. Uppsala, Sweden: Studia Anglistica Upsaliensia, 1977.

Lundquist, James. *TD*. NY: Ungar, 1974.

Matthiessen, F O. *TD*. NY: Sloane, 1951.

McAleer, John J. *TD: An Introduction and Interpretation*. NY: Holt, Rinehart & Winston, 1968.

Moers, Ellen. *Two Ds*. NY: Viking, 1969.

Mookerjee, R N. *TD: His Thought and Social Criticism*. Delhi, India: National, 1974.

Pizer, Donald. *The Novels of TD: A Critical Study*. Minneapolis: U Minnesota P, 1976.

Shapiro, Charles. *TD: Our Bitter Patriot*. Carbondale: Southern Illinois U P, 1962.

Warren, Robert Penn. *Homage to TD*. NY: Random House, 1971.

West, James L W, III, ed. *A Sister Carrie Portfolio*. Charlottesville: U P Virginia, 1985.

Collections of Essays

Bloom, Harold, ed. *TD's An American Tragedy*. NY: Chelsea House, 1988.

Kazin, Alfred & Charles Shapiro, eds. *The Stature of TD*. Bloomington: Indiana U P, 1955.

Lydenberg, John, ed. *D: A Collection of Critical Essays*. Englewood Cliffs, NJ: Prentice-Hall, 1971.

Pizer, Donald, ed. *Critical Essays on TD*. Boston: Hall, 1981.

Raja, L J, ed. *TD: The Man and His Message*. Annamalainagar, India: Kathy, 1984.

Salzman, Jack, ed. *The Merrill Studies in An American Tragedy*. Columbus, Ohio: Merrill, 1971.

Salzman, ed. *TD: The Critical Reception*. NY: Lewis, 1972.

Special Journals

Dreiser Newsletter (semiannually, 1970-1986). Includes checklists.

Dreiser Studies (semiannually, 1987-   ). Includes checklists.

LibraryC, 38 (Winter 1972). TD issue.

LibraryC, 44 (Spring 1979). *Sister Carrie* issue.

MFS, 23 (Autumn 1977). TD issue. Includes checklist.

Book Sections & Articles

Bellow, Saul. "D and the Triumph of Art." *Commentary*, 11 (May 1951), 502-503. Rpt Kazin & Shapiro.

Block, Haskell. "D's *An American Tragedy*." *Naturalistic Triptych* (NY: Random House, 1970), 54-77.

Bourne, Randolph. "The Art of TD." *Dial*, 62 (14 Jun 1917), 507-509. Rpt Kazin & Shapiro, Lydenberg, Pizer (1981).

Bowlby, Rachel. "Starring: D's *Sister Carrie*," "The Artist as Adman: D's *The 'Genius.'* " *Just Looking: Consumer Culture in D, Gissing and Zola* (London: Methuen, 1985), 52-65, 118-133.

Brennan, Stephen C. "TD's *An Amateur Laborer*: A Myth in the Making." *ALR*, 19 (Winter 1987), 66-84.

Burgan, Mary A. "*Sister Carrie* and the Pathos of Naturalism." *Criticism*, 15 (Fall 1973), 336-349.

Conder, John J. "D's Trilogy and the Dilemma of Determinism." *Naturalism in American Fiction* (Lexington: U P Kentucky, 1984), 86-117.

Farrell, James T. "TD." *ChiR*, 1 (Summer 1946), 127-144.

Fisher, Philip. "The Life History of Objects: The Naturalist Novel and the City." *Hard Facts: Setting and Form in the American Novel* (Oxford: Oxford U P, 1985), 128-178.

Fishkin, Shelley Fisher. "TD." *From Fact to Fiction: Journalism & Imaginative Writing in America* (Baltimore, Md: Johns Hopkins U P, 1985), 85-134. Rpt Bloom.

Forrey, Robert. "D and the Prophetic Tradition." *AmerS*, 15 (Fall 1974), 21-35.

Geismar, Maxwell. "TD: The Double Soul." *Rebels and Ancestors: The American Novel, 1890-1915* (Boston: Houghton Mifflin, 1953), 287-379.

Gelfant, Blanche H. "TD: The Portrait Novel." *The American City Novel* (Norman: U Oklahoma P, 1954), 42-94.

Gerber, Philip L. "D's *Financier*: A Genesis." *JML*, 1 (Mar 1971), 354-374.

Gerber. "The Financier Himself: D and C. T. Yerkes." *PMLA*, 88 (Jan 1973), 112-121.

Gerber. "Frank Cowperwood: Boy Financier." *SAF*, 2 (Autumn 1974), 165-174.

Gerber. "D's *Stoic*: A Study in Literary Frustration." *LMonog*, 7 (1975), 85-144.

Grebstein, Sheldon N. "*An American Tragedy*: Theme and Structure." *The Twenties*, ed Richard Langford (De Land, Fla: Everett/Edwards, 1966), 62-66. Rpt Pizer (1981).

Hoffman, Frederick J. "The Scene of Violence: Dostoevsky and D." *MFS*, 6 (Summer 1960), 91-105. Rpt Salzman (1971).

Howe, Irving. "The Stature of TD." *NewR*, 151 (25 Jul 1964), 19-21. Rpt Lydenberg, Salzman (1971), Pizer (1981).

Hughson, Lois. "Biography as a Model for the Novel: TD." *From Biography to History: The Historical Imagination and American Fiction, 1880-1940* (Charlottesville: U P Virginia, 1988), 122-159.

Kaplan, Amy. "The Sentimental Revolt of *Sister Carrie*." *The Social Construction of American Realism* (Chicago: U Chicago P, 1988), 140-160.

Katz, Joseph. "TD's *Ev'ry Month*." *LibraryC*, 38 (Winter 1972), 46-66.

Katz. "TD and Stephen Crane: Studies in a Literary Relationship." *Stephen Crane in Transition: Centenary Essays,* ed Katz (DeKalb: Northern Illinois U P, 1972), 174-204.

Kazin, Alfred. *On Native Grounds* (NY: Reynal & Hitchcock, 1942), 73-90. Rpt Kazin & Shapiro.

Kazin. "D: The Esthetic of Realism." *Contemporaries* (Boston: Little, Brown, 1962), 87-99.

Kwiat, Joseph J. "D's *The 'Genius'* and Everett Shinn, the 'Ash-Can' Painter." *PMLA*, 67 (Mar 1952), 15-31.

Kwiat. "The Newspaper Experience: Crane, Norris, D." *NCF,* 8 (Sep 1953), 99-117.

Lynn, Kenneth S. "TD: The Man of Ice." *The Dream of Success: A Study of the Modern American Imagination* (Boston: Atlantic/ Little, Brown, 1955), 13-74.

Mailer, Norman. "Modes and Mutations: Quick Comments on the Modern American Novel." *Commentary*, 41 (Mar 1966), 37-40.

Marcus, Mordecai. "Loneliness, Death, and Fulfillment in *Jennie Gerhardt*." *SAF,* 7 (Spring 1979), 61-73.

Markels, Julian. "D and the Plotting of Inarticulate Experience." *MR*, 2 (Spring 1961), 431-448. Rpt *Sister Carrie: An Authoritative Text, Backgrounds and Sources, Criticism;* Salzman (1971); Pizer (1981).

Martin, Ronald E. "TD: At Home in the Universe of Force." *American Literature and the Universe of Force* (Durham, NC: Duke U P, 1981), 215-255.

Mencken, H L. "TD." *A Book of Prefaces* (NY: Knopf, 1917), 67-148.

Michaels, Walter Benn. "*Sister Carrie's* Popular Economy," "D's *Financier*: The Man of Business as a Man of Letters." *The Gold Standard and the Logic of Naturalism* (Berkeley: U California P, 1987), 29-83.

Millgate, Michael. "TD." *American Social Fiction* (NY: Barnes & Noble, 1964), 67-86.

Mitchell, Lee Clark. " 'And Then Rose for the First Time': Repetition and Doubling in *An American Tragedy*." *Novel*, 19 (Fall 1985), 39-56.

Moers, Ellen. "Reappraisals: The Finesse of D." *ASch*, 33 (Winter 1963-1964), 109-114. Rpt *Sister Carrie: An Authoritative Text, Backgrounds and Sources, Criticism;* Lydenberg; Pizer (1981).

More, Paul Elmer. *The Demon of the Absolute* (Princeton: Princeton U P, 1928), 64-69. Rpt Pizer (1981).

Orlov, Paul A. "The Subversion of the Self: Anti-Naturalistic Crux in *An American Tragedy*." *MFS*, 23 (Autumn 1977), 457-472.

Orlov. "Technique as Theme in *An American Tragedy*." *JNT*, 14 (Spring 1984), 75-93. Rpt Bloom.

Parrington, Vernon Louis. "TD: Chief of American Naturalists." *Main Currents in American Thought*, Vol 3 (NY: Harcourt, Brace, 1930), 354-359.

Petrey, Sandy. "The Language of Realism, the Language of False Consciousness: A Reading of *Sister Carrie*." *Novel*, 10 (Winter 1977), 101-113.

Phillips, William L. "The Imagery of D's Novels." *PMLA*, 78 (Dec 1963), 572-585. Rpt Pizer (1981).

Pizer, Donald. "Late Nineteenth-Century American Naturalism," "Nineteenth-Century American Naturalism: An Approach Through Form," "American Literary Naturalism: The Example of D," "The Problem of Philosophy in the Naturalistic Novel," "TD's 'Nigger Jeff': The Development of an Aesthetic." *Realism and Naturalism in Nineteenth-Century American Literature* (Carbondale: Southern Illinois U P, rev 1984), 9-69, 180-193.

Poirier, Richard. "Panoramic Environment and the Anonymity of the Self." *A World Elsewhere: The Place of Style in American Literature* (NY: Oxford U P, 1966), 235-252. Rpt Pizer (1981).

Richman, Sidney. "TD's *The Bulwark*: A Final Resolution." *AL*, 34 (May 1962), 229-245. Rpt Pizer (1981).

Riggio, Thomas P. "Another Two Ds: The Artist as 'Genius.' " *SNNTS*, 9 (Summer 1977), 119-136.

Riggio. "American Gothic: Poe and *An American Tragedy*." *AL*, 49 (Jan 1978), 515-532.

Salzman, Jack. "The Curious History of D's *The Bulwark*." *Proof*, 3 (1973), 21-61.

Samuels, Charles T. "Mr. Trilling, Mr. Warren, and *An American Tragedy*." *YR*, 53 (Summer 1964), 629-640. Rpt Lydenberg, Pizer (1981).

See, Fred G. "D's Lost Language of the Heart." *Desire and the Sign: Nineteenth-Century American Fiction* (Baton Rouge: Louisiana State U P, 1987), 122-145.

Sherman, Stuart P. "The Naturalism of Mr. D." *Nation*, 101 (2 Dec 1915), 648-650. Rpt Kazin & Shapiro, Lydenberg, Pizer (1981).

Shulman, Robert. "D and the Dynamics of American Capitalism: *Sister Carrie* and *The Financier*." *Social Criticism & Nineteenth-Century American Fictions* (Columbia: U Missouri P, 1987), 284-316.

Smith, Carl S. "D's *Trilogy of Desire*: The Financier as Artist." *CRevAS*, 7 (Fall 1976), 151-162.

Trilling, Lionel. "Reality in America." *The Liberal Imagination* (NY: Viking, 1950), 3-21. Rpt Kazin & Shapiro, Lydenberg, Pizer (1981).

Van Antwerp, Margaret A, ed. "TD." *Dictionary of Literary Biography Documentary Series*, Vol 1 (Detroit: Bruccoli Clark/Gale, 1982), 165-238.

Vivas, Eliseo. "D, an Inconsistent Mechanist." *Ethics*, 48 (Jul 1938), 498-508. Rpt Kazin & Shapiro, Pizer (1981).

Wadlington, Warwick. "Pathos and D." *SoR*, 7 (Spring 1971), 411-429. Rpt Pizer (1981).

Walcutt, Charles Child. "TD: The Wonder and Terror of Life." *American Literary Naturalism: A Divided Stream* (Minneapolis: U Minnesota P, 1956), 180-221. Rpt Kazin & Shapiro; *Sister Carrie: An Authoritative Text, Backgrounds and Sources, Criticism*; Lydenberg; Pizer (1981).

Weimer, David R. "Heathen Catacombs: TD." *The City as Metaphor* (NY: Random House, 1966), 65-77.

Westbrook, Max. "D's Defense of Carrie Meeber." *MFS*, 23 (Autumn 1977), 381-393.

Witemeyer, Hugh. "Gaslight and Magic Lamp in *Sister Carrie*." *PMLA*, 86 (Mar 1971), 236-240.

Donald Pizer

ALICE MOORE DUNBAR-NELSON

New Orleans, La, 19 Jul 1875-Philadelphia, Pa, 18 Sep 1935

Alice Moore Dunbar-Nelson was born into the upper-class black Creole society of New Orleans. Although her literary achievements were overshadowed by those of her first husband, Paul Laurence Dunbar, Dunbar-Nelson was a versatile author of plays, poetry, short stories, and essays. A solid female presence in the Harlem Renaissance, Dunbar-Nelson created literary works that represent early examples of African-American feminist discourse. Her fiction and poetry treat the "ordinary" African-American woman at a time when the upper-class mulatto of privilege was the dominant subject of fiction about black life. Dunbar-Nelson's innovative focus secures her position as one of the first African-American writers to dismantle traditional stereotypes of minstrel and plantation African-American characters that prevailed at the time.

BIBLIOGRAPHY

Williams, Ora. "Works By and About AR(M)D-N: A Bibliography." *CLAJ*, 19 (Mar 1976), 322-326.

BOOKS

Violets and Other Tales. Boston: Monthly Review, 1895. Poetry, essays & stories.

The Goodness of St. Rocque and Other Stories. NY: Dodd, Mead, 1899.

DIARY

Give Us Each Day: The Diary of AD-N, ed Gloria T Hull. NY & London: Norton, 1984.

OTHER

Masterpieces of Negro Eloquence: The Best Speeches Delivered by the Negro From the Days of Slavery to the Present Time, ed AD-N. NY: Bookery, 1914.

The Dunbar Speaker and Entertainer, ed AD-N; intro by Leslie Pinckney Hill. Naperville, Ill: Nichols, 1920. Speeches.

"Une Femme Dit." *PittsburghC* (Feb-Sep 1926). Column.

"As in a Looking Glass." *Washington Eagle* (1926-1930). Column.

EDITION & COLLECTION

An AD-N Reader, ed Ora Williams. Washington: U P America, 1979.

The Works of AD-N, 3 vols; ed Gloria T Hull. NY & Oxford: Oxford U P, 1988.

MANUSCRIPTS & ARCHIVES

U of Delaware, Newark, Library.

BIOGRAPHIES

Articles

"AD-N." *JNH,* 21 (Jan 1936), 95-96.

Holly, Allie Miller. "Thy Vision Has Lighted the World." *Delta,* 60 (Nov 1972), 46-47.

CRITICAL STUDIES

Book Sections & Article

Bryan, Violet Harrington. "Creating and Re-Creating the Myth of New Orleans: Grace King and AD-N." *POMPA* (1987), 185-196.

Hull, Gloria T. "Researching AD-N: A Personal and Literary Perspective." *All the Women Are White, All the Blacks Are Men, But Some of Us Are Brave: Black Women's Studies,* ed Hull, Patricia Bell Scott & Barbara Smith (Old Westbury, NY: Feminist, 1982), 189-195.

Hull. "AD-N." *Color, Sex, and Poetry: Three Women Writers of the Harlem Renaissance* (Bloomington: Indiana U P, 1987), 33-104.

Hull. "Introduction." *The Works of AD-N,* Vols 1-3, xxix-liv.

Joyce Hope Scott

FINLEY PETER DUNNE

Chicago, Ill, 10 Jul 1867-New York City, NY, 24 Apr 1936

Finley Peter Dunne is best known for the fictional character he created, Mr. Dooley, an Irish-American from Chicago, who first appeared in Chicago newspapers in 1893 and, later, in such periodicals as *Collier's* and *Harper's Weekly.* Through Mr. Dooley, Dunne commented on politics of the day and became widely acclaimed as a humorist. The Irish-American dialect of Mr. Dooley placed him in a growing category of vernacular-speaking characters popular at the turn of the century. From the Spanish-American War to Theodore Roosevelt (referred to as "Tiddy Rosenfelt" by Dooley), nothing was too sacred to escape Mr. Dooley's satiric monologues. Mr. Dooley's dialect speech and straightforward manner added to the movement towards realism in American art early in the 1900s.

BOOKS

Mr. Dooley in Peace and in War. Boston: Small, Maynard, 1898. Sketches.

Mr. Dooley in the Hearts of His Countrymen. Boston: Small, Maynard, 1899. Sketches.

Mr. Dooley's Philosophy. NY: Russell, 1900. Sketches.

Mr. Dooley's Opinions. NY: Russell, 1901. Sketches.

Observations by Mr. Dooley. NY: Russell, 1902. Sketches.

Mr. Dooley on Timely Topics of the Day—On Life Insurance Investigation, On Business and Political Honesty, On National Housecleaning. NY: Colliers, 1905. Sketches.

Dissertations by Mr. Dooley. NY & London: Harper, 1906. Sketches.

Mr. Dooley Says. NY: Scribners, 1910. Sketches.
Mr. Dooley on Making a Will and Other Necessary Evils. NY: Scribners, 1919. Sketches.

DIARIES

Mr. Dooley Remembers: The Informal Memoirs of FPD, ed Philip Dunne. Boston & Toronto: Little, Brown/Atlantic Monthly, 1963.

COLLECTIONS

What Dooley Says. . . . Chicago: Kazmar, 1899.
Mr. Dooley at His Best, ed Elmer Ellis; foreword by Franklin P Adams. NY: Scribners, 1938.
Mr. Dooley Now and Forever, ed Louis Filler. Stanford, Calif: Academic Reprints, 1954.
The World of Mr. Dooley, ed Filler. NY: Collier, 1962.
Mr. Dooley on the Choice of Law, ed Edward J Bander. Charlottesville, Va: Michie, 1963.
Mr. Dooley on Ivrything and Ivrybody, ed Robert Hutchinson. NY: Dover, 1963.
Mr. Dooley—Wise & Funny—We Need Him Now, ed Barbara C Schaaf. Springfield, Ill: Herndon, 1988.

MANUSCRIPTS & ARCHIVES

The major collections are at Princeton U Library & the Library of Congress.

BIOGRAPHY

Book
Ellis, Elmer. *Mr. Dooley's America: A Life of FPD.* NY: Knopf, 1941.

CRITICAL STUDIES

Books
Bander, Edward J. *Mr. Dooley and Mr. Dunne: The Literary Life of a Chicago Catholic.* Charlottesville, Va: Michie, 1981.
DeMuth, James. *Small Town Chicago: The Comic Perspective of FPD, George Ade, and Ring Lardner.* Port Washington, NY: Kennikat, 1980.
Eckley, Grace. *FPD.* Boston: Twayne, 1981.
Fanning, Charles. *FPD and Mr. Dooley: The Chicago Years.* Lexington: U P Kentucky, 1978.
Schaaf, Barbara C. *Mr. Dooley's Chicago.* Garden City, NY: Anchor/Doubleday, 1977.

Articles
DeMuth, James. "Hard Times in the Sixth Ward: Mr. Dooley on the Depression of the 1890's." *StAH,* ns 3 (Summer-Fall 1984), 123-137.
Harrison, John M. "FPD and the Progressive Movement." *JQ,* 44 (Autumn 1967), 475-481.
Kelleher, John V. "Mr. Dooley and the Same Old World." *Atlantic,* 177 (Jun 1946), 119-125.
Schaaf, Barbara C. "The Man Who Invented Mr. Dooley." *ChiM,* 26 (Mar 1977), 116-217.
St. Clair, Janet. "Chicago's Tutors: The Humorous Columnists of the 1880's and 90's." *ATQ,* 2 (Sep 1988), 237-248.
Thogmartin, Clyde. "Mr. Dooley's Brogue: The Literary Dialect of FPD." *VLang,* 16 (Spring 1982), 184-198.

William C. Hill

EDWARD EGGLESTON

Vevay, Ind, 10 Dec 1837-Lake George, NY, 4 Sep 1902

Edward Eggleston's best-known work is *The Hoosier School-Master*, a novel of life in Indiana. An early literary realist, he also won acclaim as a social historian. Eggleston's novels depict the customs of the Middle West as a separate and valid culture and realistically convey Hoosier speech. Eggleston spent time as a Methodist circuit rider (1856-1857) and as a Methodist pastor (1864-1866). In 1875 he founded the nondenominational Church of the Christian Endeavor in Brooklyn, NY, where he served as pastor until 1879. Working for a time as a lobbyist in Washington, Eggleston promoted more effective copyright laws for American authors.

BIBLIOGRAPHIES

Bibliography of American Literature, comp Jacob Blanck. New Haven: Yale U P, 1955-1991. Primary.

Randel, William. "EE (1837-1902)." *ALR*, 1 (Fall 1967), 36-38. Secondary.

BOOKS

Sunday School Conventions and Institutes, With Suggestions on County and Township Organization. Chicago: Adams, Blackmer & Lyon, 1867.

The Manual: A Practical Guide to the Sunday-School Work. Chicago: Adams, Blackmer & Lyon, 1869.

Mr. Blake's Walking-Stick: A Christmas Story for Boys and Girls. Chicago: Adams, Blackmer & Lyon / NY: Randolph, 1870.

The Book of Queer Stories, and Stories Told on a Cellar Door. Chicago: Adams, Blackmer & Lyon / NY: Randolph / Boston: Shute, 1871.

The Hoosier School-Master: A Novel. NY: Orange Judd, 1871. Rev ed, with intro and notes on the dialect, 1892.

The End of the World: A Love Story. NY: Orange Judd, 1872. Novel.

Tracts for Sunday School Teachers. Chicago: Adams, Blackmer & Lyon, 1872?

The Mystery of Metropolisville. NY: Orange Judd, 1873. Novel.

The Circuit Rider: A Tale of the Heroic Age. NY: Ford, 1874. Novel.

The Schoolmaster's Stories, for Boys and Girls. Boston: Shepard, 1874. Rev as *Queer Stories for Boys and Girls*. NY: Scribners, 1884.

Roxy. NY: Scribners, 1878. Novel.

Tecumseh and the Shawnee Prophet. . ., with Lillie Eggleston Seelye. NY: Dodd, Mead, 1878. History.

Pocahontas. . ., with Lillie Eggleston Seelye. NY: Dodd, Mead, 1879; *The Indian Princess. . . .* London: Ward, Lock, 1881. History.

Brant and Red Jacket. . ., with Lillie Eggleston Seelye. NY: Dodd, Mead, 1879; *The Rival Warriors, Chiefs of the Five Nations*. London: Ward, Lock, 1881. History.

Montezuma and the Conquest of Mexico, with Lillie Eggleston Seelye. NY: Dodd, Mead, 1880; *The Mexican Prince*. London: Ward, Lock, 1881. History.

The Hoosier School-Boy. London: Warne, 1882; NY: Scribners, 1883. Novel.

The Graysons: A Story of Illinois. NY: Century, 1887. Novel.

A History of the United States and Its People for the Use of Schools. NY: Appleton, 1888. Rev as *The Household History of the United States and Its People for Young Americans*, 1889.

A First Book in American History. . . . NY: Appleton, 1889.

The Faith Doctor: A Story of New York. NY: Appleton, 1891. Novel.

Duffels. NY: Appleton, 1893. Stories.

Stories of Great Americans for Little Americans: Second Reader Grade. NY & c: American Book, 1895. History.

Stories of American Life and Adventure: Third Reader Grade. NY & c: American Book, 1895. History.

The Beginners of a Nation. . . . NY: Appleton, 1896. History.

The Transit of Civilization From England to America in the Seventeenth Century. NY: Appleton, 1901. History.

The New Century History of the United States. NY & c: American Book, 1904.

The Ultimate Solution of the American Negro Problem. Boston: Badger, 1913. History.

LETTERS, DIARIES

"An Unpublished Journal of EE's With Supplementary Letters" by Harlan DeBaun Logan. Thesis: Indiana U, 1932.

OTHER

The Infant Class: Hints on Primary Religious Instruction by Sara J Timanus; ed with intro by EE. Chicago: Adams, Blackmer & Lyon, 1870.

Christ in Literature: Being a Treasury of Choice Readings. . . , ed EE. NY: Ford, 1875.

The Story of Columbus by Elizabeth Eggleston Seelye; ed with intro by EE. NY: Appleton, 1892.

The Story of Washington by Elizabeth Eggleston Seelye; ed with intro by EE. NY: Appleton, 1893.

MANUSCRIPTS & ARCHIVES

Cornell U Library.

BIOGRAPHIES

Books

Auringer, O C. *Friendship's Crown of Verses; Being Memorials of EE.* Clinton, NY: Browning, 1907.

Eggleston, Frances Goode. *EE: Authors' Club Biography.* NY: Authors' Club, 1885.

Eggleston, George Cary. *The First of the Hoosiers: Reminiscences of EE.* Philadelphia: Drexel Biddle, 1903.

Randel, William. *EE: Author of The Hoosier School-Master.* NY: King's Crown, 1946.

Book Section & Article

Auringer, O C. "Dr. EE at Lake George." *Authors at Home,* ed J L & J B Gilder (NY: Wessels, 1902), 85-96.

Rawley, James A. "Some New Light on EE." *AL,* 11 (Jan 1940), 453-458.

CRITICAL STUDIES

Books

Paine, Stephen. "A Critical Study of the Writings of EE." Dissertation: Duke U, 1961.

Randel, William. *EE.* NY: Twayne, 1963.

Book Sections & Articles

Ahnebrink, Lars. "Realism in the Middle West: EE, Edgar Watson Howe, and Joseph Kirkland." *The Beginnings of Naturalism in American*

Fiction (Uppsala, Sweden: U Uppsala / Cambridge: Harvard U P, 1950), 50-59.

Benson, Ronald M. "Ignoble Savage: EE and the American Indian." *IllQ,* 35 (Feb 1973), 41-51.

Bloom, Margaret. "E's Notes on Hoosier Dialect." *AS,* 9 (Dec 1934), 319-320.

Bray, Robert. "Camp-Meeting Revivalism and the Idea of Western Community: Three Generations of Ohio Valley Writers." *ON,* 10 (Fall 1984), 257-284.

"EE: An Interview." *Outlook,* 55 (6 Feb 1897), 431-437.

Flanagan, John T. "The Hoosier Schoolmaster in Minnesota." *MinnH,* 18 (Dec 1937), 347-370.

Flanagan. "The Novels of EE." *CE,* 5 (Feb 1944), 250-254.

Haller, J M. "EE, Linguist." *PQ,* 24 (Apr 1945), 175-186.

Hirschfeld, Charles. "EE: Pioneer in Social History." *Historiography and Urbanization: Essays in American History in Honor of W. Stull Holt,* ed Eric F Goldman (Baltimore, Md: Johns Hopkins P, 1941), 189-210.

Nicholson, Meredith. "EE." *The Provincial American and Other Papers* (Boston: Houghton Mifflin, 1912), 33-53.

Randel, William. "EE's Library at Traverse de Sioux." *MinnH,* 26 (Sep 1945), 242-247.

Randel. "Zoroaster Higgins: EE as a Political Satirist in Verse." *AL,* 17 (Nov 1945), 255-260.

Randel. "EE on Dialect." *AS,* 30 (May 1955), 111-114.

Rawley, J A. "Some New Light on EE." *AL,* 11 (Jan 1940), 453-458.

Rawley. "EE: Historian." *IMH,* 40 (Dec 1944), 341-352.

Spencer, Benjamin T. "The New Realism and a National Literature." *PMLA,* 56 (Dec 1941), 1116-1132.

Stone, Edward. "EE's Religious Transit." *UTSE,* 19 (1939), 210-218.

Stone. "EE." *Voices of Despair: Four Motifs in American Literature* (Athens: Ohio U P, 1966), 137-178.

Underwood, Gary N. "Toward a Reassessment of EE's Literary Dialects." *BRMMLA,* 28 (Dec 1974), 109-120.

Wilson, Jack H. "E's Indebtedness to George Eliot in *Roxy.*" *AL,* 42 (Mar 1970), 38-49.

Tony Trigilio

EDGAR FAWCETT

New York City, NY, 26 May 1847-London, England, 2 May 1904

Although his career encompassed verse and drama as well as fiction, Edgar Fawcett was best known as a novelist who satirized the social pretensions of New York society. Born to a wealthy family and educated at Columbia College, he moved easily in the aristocratic circles he ridiculed. From his first novel, *Purple and Fine Linen* in 1873, to *An Ambitious Woman* and *Rutherford* in 1884 and *New York* in 1898, his fiction was characterized by realistic portrayals and amusing satire but amateurish plots and static characters. An expatriate in his later years, Fawcett also addressed the international theme of innocent Americans in the rich culture of Europe.

BIBLIOGRAPHY

Bibliography of American Literature, comp Jacob Blanck. New Haven: Yale U P, 1955-1991. Primary.

BOOKS

Short Poems for Short People. NY: Felt, 1872.
Purple and Fine Linen: A Novel. NY: Carleton / London: Low, 1873.
Ellen Story: A Novel. NY: Hale, 1876.
Fantasy and Passion. Boston: Roberts, 1878. Poetry.
A Hopeless Case. Boston: Houghton, Mifflin, 1880. Novel.
A Gentleman of Leisure: A Novel. Boston: Houghton, Mifflin, 1881.
An Ambitious Woman: A Novel. Boston: Houghton, Mifflin, 1884.
Tinkling Cymbals: A Novel. Boston: Osgood, 1884.
Song and Story: Later Poems. Boston: Osgood, 1884.
Rutherford. NY & London: Funk & Wagnalls, 1884. Novel.
The Adventures of a Widow: A Novel. Boston: Osgood, 1884.
The Buntling Ball: A Graeco-American Play, Being a Poetical Satire on New York Society. NY & London: Funk & Wagnalls, 1884.
Social Silhouettes (Being the Impressions of Mr. Mark Manhattan). . . . Boston: Ticknor, 1885. Essays.

The New King Arthur: An Opera Without Music . . . (Anon). NY & London: Funk & Wagnalls, 1885. Play.
Romance and Revery: Poems. Boston: Ticknor, 1886.
The House at High Bridge: A Novel. Boston: Ticknor, 1887.
The Confessions of Claud: A Romance. Boston: Ticknor, 1887.
A Man's Will: A Novel. NY & London: Funk & Wagnalls, 1888.
Olivia Delaplaine: A Novel. Boston: Ticknor, 1888.
Divided Lives: A Novel. Chicago & c: Belford, Clarke, 1888.
Miriam Balestier: A Novel. Chicago & c: Belford, Clarke, 1888.
A Demoralizing Marriage. Philadelphia: Lippincott, 1889. Novel.
Agnosticism and Other Essays. NY & c: Belford, Clarke / London: Drane, 1889.
Solarion: A Romance. Philadelphia: Lippincott, 1889.
The Evil That Men Do: A Novel. NY: Belford, 1889.
A Daughter of Silence: A Novel. NY: Belford, 1890.
Fabian Dimitry: A Novel. Chicago & NY: Rand, McNally, 1890.
How a Husband Forgave: A Novel. NY: Belford, 1890.
A New York Family: A Novel. NY: Cassell, 1891.
Songs of Doubt and Dream (Poems). NY & c: Funk & Wagnalls, 1891.
A Romance of Two Brothers. NY: Minerva, 1891. Novel.
Women Must Weep: A Novel. Chicago: Laird & Lee, 1891. Repub as *A Story of Three Girls (Women Must Weep)*, 1895.
An Heir to Millions. Chicago: Schulte, 1892. Novel.
The Adopted Daughter. Chicago & NY: Neely, 1892. Novel.
American Push. Chicago: Schulte, 1892. Novel.
Loaded Dice: A Novel. NY: Tait, 1893.
The New Nero: A Realistic Romance. NY: Collier, 1893.
A Martyr of Destiny. NY: Collier, 1894. Repub as *Outrageous Fortune: A Novel*. NY: Dillingham, 1894.

Her Fair Fame: A Novel. NY: Merrill & Baker, 1894.

A Mild Barbarian: A Novel. NY: Appleton, 1894.

The Ghost of Guy Thyrle. NY: Collier, 1895. Novel.

Life's Fitful Fever, Being the Memoirs of Clemence Disosway Torrington..., 2 vols. NY: Collier, 1896. Fiction.

A Romance of Old New York. Philadelphia & London: Lippincott, 1897. Novel.

New York: A Novel. London & NY: Neely, 1898.

The Vulgarians. NY & London: Smart Set, 1903. Novel.

Voices and Visions: Later Verses. London: Nash, 1903.

COLLECTION

Brooms and Brambles: A Book of Verses. London: Stock, 1889.

MANUSCRIPTS & ARCHIVES

U Virginia Library.

CRITICAL STUDIES

Book

Harrison, Stanley R. *EF.* NY: Twayne, 1972.

Articles

Browar, Lisa M. "The Discovery of a Ghost in EF's Canon." *PBSA*, 72 (Jul-Sep 1978), 350-353.

Harrison, Stanley R. "Through a Nineteenth-Century Looking Glass: The Letters of EF." *TSE*, 15 (1967), 107-157.

Howells, William Dean. "Recent American Fiction." *Atlantic*, 46 (Sep 1880), 412-424.

Howells. "Recent Fiction: A Review of *A Gentleman of Leisure*." *Atlantic*, 48 (Oct 1881), 561-564.

Howells. "Recent American Fiction." *Atlantic*, 53 (May 1884), 707-713.

Kevin S. Best

DOROTHY CANFIELD FISHER

Lawrence, Kans, 17 Feb 1879-Arlington, Vt, 9 Nov 1958

Dorothy Canfield Fisher is best remembered for her treatment of small-town Vermont in short stories and novels. As a writer on education, she was influential in introducing the theories of Maria Montessori to the United States. Fisher, who published her fiction under her maiden name Canfield, was genteel in her literary tastes, a fact that made her fiction seem increasingly obsolete by the 1920s. Consequently, she has not received much critical attention. Her Vermont writings place her in the tradition of the late nineteenth-century local colorists. She was in all of her writings an upholder of liberal, democratic ideals.

BOOKS

Corneille and Racine in England. NY: Columbia U P, 1904. Nonfiction.

Elementary Composition, with George R Carpenter. NY & London: Macmillan, 1906. Nonfiction.

Gunhild: A Norwegian-American Episode. NY: Holt, 1907. Novel.

What Shall We Do Now? Five Hundred Games and Pastimes, with others. NY: Stokes, 1907.

The Squirrel-Cage. NY: Holt, 1912. Novel.

A Montessori Mother. NY: Holt, 1912. Repub as *Montessori for Parents.* Cambridge, Mass: Bentley, 1965. Nonfiction.

The Montessori Manual for Teachers and Parents. Npl: Richardson, 1913.

Mothers and Children. NY: Holt, 1914. Nonfiction.

A Peep into the Educational Future. Buffalo, NY: Park School, 1915. Nonfiction.

Hillsboro People, with verses by Sarah N Cleghorn. NY: Holt, 1915. Stories.

The Bent Twig. NY: Holt, 1915. Novel.

The Real Motive. NY: Holt, 1916. Stories.

Self-Reliance. Indianapolis: Bobbs-Merrill, 1916. Nonfiction.

Fellow Captains, with Cleghorn. NY: Holt, 1916. Miscellany.

Understood Betsy. NY: Holt, 1917. Novel.

Home Fires in France. NY: Holt, 1918. Stories.

The Day of Glory. NY: Holt, 1919. Stories.

The Brimming Cup. NY: Harcourt, Brace, 1921. Novel.

What Grandmother Did Not Know. Boston & Chicago: Pilgrim, 1922. Nonfiction.

Rough-Hewn. NY: Harcourt, Brace, 1922. Novel.

Raw Material. NY: Harcourt, Brace, 1923. Stories.

The French School at Middlebury. Middlebury, Vt: Middlebury C, 1923. Nonfiction.

The Home-Maker. NY: Harcourt, Brace, 1924. Novel.

Made-to-Order Stories. NY: Harcourt, Brace, 1925.

Her Son's Wife. NY: Harcourt, Brace, 1926. Novel.

Why Stop Learning? NY: Harcourt, Brace, 1927. Nonfiction.

Learn or Perish. NY: Liveright, 1930. Nonfiction.

The Deepening Stream. NY: Harcourt, Brace, 1930. Novel.

Basque People. NY: Harcourt, Brace, 1931. Stories.

Vermont Summer Homes. Montpelier: Vermont Bureau of Publicity, 1932. Nonfiction.

Moral Pushing and Pulling. Brattleboro, Vt: Hildreth, 1933. Address.

Bonfire. NY: Harcourt, Brace, 1933. Novel.

Tourists Accommodated: Some Scenes From Present-Day Summer Life in Vermont. NY: Harcourt, Brace, 1934. Play.

Wells College Phi Beta Kappa Address. Aurora, NY: Wells C, 1936.

Fables for Parents. NY: Harcourt, Brace, 1937. Stories.

On a Rainy Day, with Sarah Fisher Scott. NY: Barnes, 1938. Nonfiction.

Seasoned Timber. NY: Harcourt, Brace, 1939. Excerpted in *The Election on Academy Hill. . . .* NY & Chicago: Harcourt, Brace, 1939. Novel.

Tell Me a Story: A Book of Stories to Tell to Children. Lincoln & c: University Publishing, 1940.

Nothing Ever Happens and How It Does, with Cleghorn. Boston: Beacon, 1940. Stories.

Liberty and Union, with Cleghorn. NY: Book-of-the-Month Club, 1940. Play.

A Family Talk About War. NY: Children's Crusade for Children, 1940. Play.

Our Young Folks. NY: Harcourt, Brace, 1943. Nonfiction.

American Portraits. NY: Holt, 1946. Biography.

Book-Clubs. NY: New York Public Library, 1947. Lecture.

Four-Square. NY: Harcourt, Brace, 1949. Stories.

Something Old, Something New: Stories of People Who Are America. NY: Scott, 1949.

Paul Revere and the Minute Men. NY: Random House, 1950. Children's history.

Our Independence and the Constitution. NY: Random House, 1950. Children's history.

A Fair World for All: The Meaning of the Declaration of Human Rights. NY: Whittlesey House, 1952.

Vermont Tradition: The Biography of an Outlook on Life. Boston: Little, Brown, 1953.

Memories of My Home Town. Arlington, Vt: Arlington Historical Society, 1955. Augmented as *Memories of Arlington, Vermont.* NY: Duell, Sloan & Pearce, 1957.

A Harvest of Stories. NY: Harcourt, Brace, 1956.

And Long Remember: Some Great Americans Who Have Helped Me. NY: Whittlesey House, 1959.

OTHER

Life of Christ by Giovanni Papini; trans DCF. NY: Harcourt, Brace, 1923.

Work: What It Has Meant to Men Through the Ages by Adriano Tilgher; trans DCF. NY: Harcourt, Brace, 1930.

MANUSCRIPTS & ARCHIVES

U of Vermont Library.

BIOGRAPHIES

Books

Washington, Ida H. *DCF: A Biography.* Shelburne, Vt: New England, 1982.

Yates, Elizabeth. *Pebble in a Pool: The Widening Circles of DCF's Life.* NY: Dutton, 1958. Repub as *The Lady From Vermont: DCF's Life and World.* Brattleboro, Vt: Greene, 1971.

CRITICAL STUDIES

Books

Lovering, Joseph P. "The Contribution of DCF to the Development of Realism in the American Novel." Dissertation: U Ottawa, 1956.

McAllister, Lois. "DCF: A Critical Study." Dissertation: Case Western Reserve U, 1969.

Articles

Boynton, Percy H. "Two New England Regionalists." *CE,* 1 (Jan 1940), 291-299.

Firebaugh, Joseph J. "DC and the Moral Bent." *EdForum,* 15 (Mar 1951), 283-294.

Lovering, Joseph P. "DCF." *VtH*, ns 29 (Oct 1961), 234-238.
Phelps, William Lyon. "DCF." *EJ*, 22 (Jan 1933), 1-8.
Smith, Bradford. "DCF: The Deepening Stream." *VtH*, ns 27 (Jul 1959), 228-239.

Smith. "DCF." *Atlantic*, 204 (Aug 1959), 73-77.
Wyckoff, Elizabeth. "DC: A Neglected Best Seller." *Bookman*, 74 (Sep 1931), 40-44.

Philip B. Eppard

MARY HALLOCK FOOTE

Milton, NY, 19 Nov 1847-Hingham, Mass, 25 Jun 1938

Though she was born and educated in the East, Mary Hallock Foote became one of the leading western writers of her time. When she moved to the West, she was already a well-known illustrator. Her early works were marred by melodramatic plots and the romance formula, but their strong characterization, felicitous style, detailed descriptions of frontier life, and portrayal of the conflict between East and West attracted a reading public and earned her the praise of critics and other writers. By the time Foote published her last two novels, considered her best work by modern critics, public taste had changed and she lost much of her readership. Both Wallace Stegner's Pulitzer Prize-winning novel *Angle of Repose* (1971), based on Foote's life and correspondence, and a 1972 edition of her reminiscences helped rescue her from obscurity.

BIBLIOGRAPHIES

Etulain, Richard W. "MHF (1847-1938)." *ALR*, 5 (Spring 1972), 144-150. Secondary.
Etulain. "MHF: A Checklist." *WAL*, 10 (Spring 1975), 59-65. Primary & secondary.

BOOKS

The Led-Horse Claim: A Romance of a Mining Camp. Boston: Osgood, 1883. Novel.
John Bodewin's Testimony. Boston: Ticknor, 1886. Novel.

The Last Assembly Ball, and The Fate of a Voice. Boston & NY: Houghton, Mifflin, 1889. Novel & story.
The Chosen Valley. Boston & NY: Houghton, Mifflin, 1892. Novel.
Coeur d'Alene. Boston & NY: Houghton, Mifflin, 1894. Novel.
In Exile and Other Stories. Boston & NY: Houghton, Mifflin, 1894.
The Cup of Trembling and Other Stories. Boston & NY: Houghton, Mifflin, 1895.
The Little Fig-Tree Stories. Boston & NY: Houghton, Mifflin, 1899. Children's stories.
The Prodigal. Boston & NY: Houghton, Mifflin, 1900. Novel.
The Desert and the Sown. Boston & NY: Houghton, Mifflin, 1902. Novel.
A Touch of Sun and Other Stories. Boston & NY: Houghton, Mifflin, 1903.
The Royal Americans. Boston & NY: Houghton Mifflin, 1910. Novel.
A Picked Company. Boston & NY: Houghton Mifflin, 1912. Novel.
The Valley Road. Boston & NY: Houghton Mifflin, 1915. Novel.
Edith Bonham. Boston & NY: Houghton Mifflin, 1917. Novel.
The Ground-Swell. Boston & NY: Houghton Mifflin, 1919. Novel.
A Victorian Gentlewoman in the Far West: The Reminiscences of MHF, ed Rodman W Paul. San Marino, Calif: Huntington Library, 1972. Autobiography.

COLLECTION

The Idaho Stories and Far West Illustrations of MHF, ed Barbara Cragg, Dennis M Walsh & Mary Ellen Walsh. Pocatello: Idaho State U P, 1988.

MANUSCRIPTS & ARCHIVES

The major collections are at Stanford U Library & the Huntington Library, San Marino, Calif.

BIOGRAPHIES
Book Section & Articles
Foote, Arthur B. "Memoir of Arthur DeWint Foote." *TASCE,* 99 (1934), 1449-1452.
Paul, Rodman W. "Introduction." *A Victorian Gentlewoman in the Far West: The Reminiscences of MHF,* 1-44.
Paul. "When Culture Came to Boise: MHF in Idaho." *IY,* 20 (Summer 1976), 2-12.

CRITICAL STUDIES

Books
Johnson, Lee Ann. *MHF.* Boston: Twayne, 1980.
Maguire, James H. *MHF.* Boise, Idaho: Boise State C, 1972.

Book Sections & Articles
Armitage, Shelley. "The Illustrator as Writer: MHF and the Myth of the West." *Under the Sun: Myth and Realism in Western American Liter-ature,* ed Barbara H Meldrum (Troy, NY: Whitston, 1985), 150-174.
Armstrong, Regina. "Representative American Women Illustrators: The Character Workers—II." *Critic,* 37 (Aug 1900), 131-141.
Benn, Mary Lou. "MHF: Early Leadville Writer." *ColMag,* 33 (Apr 1956), 93-108.
Benn. "MHF in Idaho." *UWyP,* 20 (15 Jul 1956), 157-178.
Cragg, Barbara. "MHF's Images of the Old West." *Landscape,* 24, no 3 (1980), 42-47.
Davidson, Levette Jay. "Letters From Authors." *ColMag,* 19 (Jul 1942), 122-125.
Donaldson, Thomas. *Idaho of Yesterday* (Caldwell, Idaho: Caxton, 1941), 358-363.
Gilder, Helena de Kay. "Author Illustrators, II: MHF." *Book Buyer,* 11 (Aug 1894), 338-342.
Graulich, Melody. "MHF (1847-1938)." *Legacy,* 3 (Fall 1986), 43-52.
Schopf, Bill. "The Image of the West in *The Century,* 1881-1889." *Possible Sack,* 3 (Mar 1972), 8-13.
Smith-Rosenberg, Carroll. "The Female World of Love and Ritual: Relations Between Women in Nineteenth-Century America." *Signs,* 1 (Autumn 1975), 1-29.
Walsh, Mary Ellen Williams. "*Angle of Repose* and the Writings of MHF: A Source Study." *Critical Essays on Wallace Stegner,* ed Anthony Arthur (Boston: Hall, 1982), 184-209.

Gwen L. Nagel

PAUL LEICESTER FORD

Brooklyn, NY, 23 Mar 1865-New York City, NY, 8 May 1902

Paul Leicester Ford was an editor and bibliographer of Americana as well as a historian, biographer, and novelist. He devoted the first part of his career to reprinting documents from the early national period and compiling bibliographical guides to historical and political writings. Ford was active in the founding of the American Historical Society and in the early 1890s served as coeditor of the *Library Journal.* He published many magazine articles, edited important scholarly collections of John Dickinson's and Thomas Jefferson's writings, and wrote best-selling biographies that humanized George Washington and Benjamin Franklin. Ford also was the author of such popular novels as *The Honorable Peter Stirling and What People Thought of Him,* which treated politics in New York City, and *Janice Meredith,* a romance set during the American Revolution.

BIBLIOGRAPHIES

"Bibliography." DuBois, 191-203. Primary & secondary.

Bibliography of American Literature, comp Jacob Blanck. New Haven: Yale U P, 1955-1991. Primary.

BOOKS

"The Best Laid Plans": As Enacted in Two Social Cups of Tea, Two Social Jokes, and One Social Agony (Anon). Npl: Privately printed, 1889. Rev ed, 1889. Essay.

Who Was the Mother of Franklin's Son? An Historical Conundrum, Hitherto Given Up—Now Partly Answered. Brooklyn, NY: npub, 1889. Repub with afterword by John Clyde Oswald, New Rochelle, NY: npub, 1932. Essay.

The Origin, Purpose and Result of the Harrisburg Convention of 1788: A Study in Popular Government. Brooklyn, NY: npub, 1890. Essay.

Some Notes Towards an Essay on the Beginnings of American Dramatic Literature, 1606-1789. Npl: npub, 1893. Essay.

Josiah Tucker and His Writings: An Eighteenth Century Pamphleteer on America. Chicago: U P Chicago, 1894. Essay.

The Honorable Peter Stirling and What People Thought of Him. NY: Holt, 1894. Novel.

The True George Washington. Philadelphia: Lippincott, 1896. Biography.

The Great K. & A. Robbery. NY: Dodd, Mead, 1897. Repub as *The Great K. & A. Train-Robbery,* 1897. Novel.

The Story of an Untold Love. Boston & NY: Houghton, Mifflin, 1897. Novel.

Tattle-Tales of Cupid. NY: Dodd, Mead, 1898. Stories & plays.

Washington and the Theatre. NY: Dunlap Society, 1899. Nonfiction.

The Many-Sided Franklin. NY: Century, 1899. Biography.

Janice Meredith: A Story of the American Revolution. NY: Dodd, Mead, 1899. Novel.

Wanted: A Match Maker. NY: Dodd, Mead, 1900. Novel.

Wanted—A Chaperon. NY: Dodd, Mead, 1902. Novel.

A Checked Love Affair and "The Cortelyou Feud." NY: Dodd, Mead, 1903. Stories.

Love Finds the Way. NY: Dodd, Mead, 1904. Story.

Janice Meredith: A Play in Four Acts, with Edward E Rose. NY: French, 1927.

OTHER

Webster Genealogy. Compiled and Printed for Presentation Only by Noah Webster. New Haven: 1836. With Notes and Corrections by His Great-Grandson, PLF. Brooklyn, NY: Privately printed, 1876.

Bibliotheca Hamiltoniana: A List of Books Written by, or Relating to Alexander Hamilton, comp PLF. NY: Knickerbocker, 1886.

Bibliography and Reference List of the History and Literature Relating to the Adoption of the Constitution of the United States, 1787-8, comp PLF. Brooklyn, NY: npub, 1888.

Pamphlets on the Constitution of the United States, Published During Its Discussion by the People, 1787-1788, ed PLF. Brooklyn, NY: npub, 1888.

A List of the Members of the Federal Convention of 1787, comp PLF. Brooklyn, NY: npub, 1888.

Some Materials for a Bibliography of the Official Publications of the Continental Congress,

1774-1789, comp & annotated by PLF. Brooklyn, NY: npub, 1888.

Check-List of American Magazines Printed in the Eighteenth Century, comp PLF. Brooklyn, NY: npub, 1889.

Checklist of Bibliographies, Catalogues, Reference-Lists, and Lists of Authorities of American Books and Subjects, comp PLF. Brooklyn, NY: npub, 1889.

Franklin Bibliography. A List of Books Written by, or Relating to Benjamin Franklin, comp PLF. Brooklyn, NY: npub, 1889.

The Ideals of the Republic: or, Great Words From Great Americans, ed PLF. NY & London: Putnam, 1889. Augmented as *Great Words From Great Americans,* 1890?

The Prefaces, Proverbs, and Poems of Benjamin Franklin Originally Printed in Poor Richard's Almanacs for 1733-1758, ed PLF. NY & London: Putnam, 1890.

Winnowings in American History, 15 vols; ed PLF & Worthington Ford. Brooklyn, NY: Historical Printing Club, 1890-1891.

Essays on the Constitution of the United States, Published During Its Discussion by the People, 1787-1788, ed PLF. Brooklyn, NY: Historical Printing Club, 1892.

Writings of Christopher Columbus Descriptive of the Discovery and Occupation of the New World, ed PLF. NY: Webster, 1892.

The Writings of Thomas Jefferson, 10 vols; ed PLF. NY & London: Putnam, 1892-1899.

Notes on the State of Virginia by Thomas Jefferson; ed PLF. Brooklyn, NY: Historical Printing Club, 1894.

The Writings of John Dickinson. Political Writings 1764-1774, Vol 1; ed PLF. Philadelphia: Historical Society of Pennsylvania, 1895.

The New-England Primer: A History of Its Origin and Development. . . , ed PLF. NY: Dodd, Mead, 1897.

The Federalist, ed PLF. NY: Holt, 1898.

A House Party: An Account of the Stories Told at a Gathering of Famous American Authors, ed with intros & story by PLF. Boston: Small, Maynard, 1901.

The Journals of Hugh Gaine, Printer, 2 vols; ed PLF. NY: Dodd, Mead, 1902.

Mason Locke Weems: His Works and Ways . . . a Bibliography Left Unfinished by PLF, 3 vols; ed Emily Ellsworth Ford Skeel. NY: npub, 1929.

MANUSCRIPTS & ARCHIVES

The major collections are at the New York Public Library & the Beinecke Library, Yale U.

BIOGRAPHIES

Book
DuBois, Paul Z. *PLF: An American Man of Letters, 1865-1902.* NY: Franklin, 1977.

CRITICAL STUDIES

Book Sections & Articles
Eames, Wilberforce. "PLF." *Bibliographer,* 1 (May 1902), 197.

Kammen, Michael G. *A Season of Youth: The American Revolution and the Historical Imagination* (NY: Knopf, 1978), passim.

Kane, Patricia. "PLF: An Unrealistic Realist." *JPC,* 7 (Winter 1973), 569-581.

Loewenberg, Bert James. *American History in American Thought: Christopher Columbus to Henry Adams* (NY: Simon & Schuster, 1972), 343-344.

Maurice, Arthur Bartlett. "New York in Fiction." *Bookman,* 10 (Sep 1899), 33-49.

Maurice. "PLF." *Bookman,* 10 (Feb 1900), 563-566.

Paltsits, Victor Hugo. "PLF as Bibliographer and Historian." *Bookman,* 15 (Jul 1902), 427-429.

Speare, Morris Edmund. "PLF and the Industry of Politics." *The Political Novel* (NY: Oxford U P, 1924), 322-333.

Swift, Lindsay. "PLF at Home: The Man of Affairs and the Man of Letters." *Critic,* 33 (Nov 1898), 343-349.

"Two American Writers." *Outlook,* 71 (17 May 1902), 157-158.

William F. Cash

JOHN FOX, JR.

Stony Point, Ky, 16 Dec 1862 or 1863-Big Stone Gap, Va, 8 Jul 1919

A native of the region about which he wrote, John Fox, Jr., recorded authentic descriptions of the customs, dialect, and daily lives of the Cumberland mountain people of Kentucky, Tennessee, Virginia, and West Virginia. Fox became one of the most popular novelists in the nation with *The Little Shepherd of Kingdom Come*, reputedly the first novel printed in the United States to sell one million copies. *The Trail of the Lonesome Pine*, another novel that enjoyed enormous popularity and remains in print today, dramatizes a central conflict in much of Fox's fiction: cultural distinctions between mountain natives and outsiders.

BIBLIOGRAPHIES

Bibliography of American Literature, comp Jacob Blanck. New Haven: Yale U P, 1955-1991. Primary.

Boger, Lorise C. "JWF, 1862-1919." *The Southern Mountaineer in Literature: An Annotated Bibliography* (Morgantown: West Virginia U Library, 1964), 26-28. Primary.

Thompson, Lawrence S & Algernon D. "JF, Jr." *The Kentucky Novel* (Lexington: U P Kentucky, 1953), 54-56. Primary.

Titus, Warren I. "JF, Jr. (1862-1919)." *ALR*, 1 (Summer 1968), 5-8. Secondary.

BOOKS

A Cumberland Vendetta and Other Stories. NY: Harper, 1896.

"Hell fer Sartain" and Other Stories. NY: Harper, 1897.

The Kentuckians: A Novel. NY & London: Harper, 1897.

A Mountain Europa. NY & London: Harper, 1899. Novel.

Crittenden: A Kentucky Story of Love and War. NY: Scribners, 1900. Novel.

Blue-grass and Rhododendron: Out-Doors in Old Kentucky. NY: Scribners, 1901. Stories.

The Little Shepherd of Kingdom Come. NY: Scribners, 1903. Novel.

Christmas Eve on Lonesome and Other Stories. NY: Scribners, 1904.

Following the Sun-Flag: A Vain Pursuit Through Manchuria. NY: Scribners, 1905. Nonfiction.

A Knight of the Cumberland. NY: Scribners, 1906. Novel.

The Trail of the Lonesome Pine. NY: Scribners, 1908. Novel.

The Heart of the Hills. NY: Scribners, 1913. Novel.

In Happy Valley. NY: Scribners, 1917. Stories.

Erskine Dale, Pioneer. NY: Scribners, 1920. Novel.

LETTERS

JF, Jr.: Personal and Family Letters, comp Elizabeth Fox Moore. Lexington: U Kentucky Library Associates, 1955.

OTHER

Introduction. *The White Mice*, Vol 7 of *The Novels and Stories of Richard Harding Davis*, Crossroads Edition (NY: Scribners, 1916), v-viii. Rpt *R.H.D.: Appreciations of Richard Harding Davis* (NY: Scribners, 1917).

COLLECTION

A Purple Rhododendron and Other Stories by JF, Jr. Appalachia, Va: Young, 1967.

MANUSCRIPTS & ARCHIVES

The major collections are at the U of Kentucky Library and the Duncan Tavern Historic Center, Paris, Ky.

BIOGRAPHIES

Book

Green, Harold Everett. *Towering Pines: The Life of JF, Jr*. Boston: Meador, 1943 (Unreliable; confuses JF, Jr, with another John Fox).

Article

Page, Thomas Nelson. "JF." *Scribner's*, 66 (Dec 1919), 674-683.

CRITICAL STUDIES

Books

Kruger, Arthur N. "The Life and Works of JF, Jr." Dissertation: Louisiana State U & Agricultural & Mechanical C, 1941.

Titus, Warren I. *JF, Jr.* NY: Twayne, 1971.

Book Sections & Articles

Dunlap, Mary M. "JF, Jr." *ALR,* 8 (Summer 1975), 249-250.

Holman, Harriet R. "JF, Jr.: Appraisal and Self-Appraisal: 'Personal Sketch of JF, Jr. (1908).'" *SLJ,* 3 (Spring 1971), 18-38. Includes autobiographical sketch.

Holman. "Interlude: Scenes From JF's Courtship of Fritzi Sheff, as Reported by Richard Harding Davis." *SLJ,* 7 (Spring 1975), 77-87.

"JF, Jr. and His Kentucky." *Nation,* 109 (19 Jul 1919), 72-73.

Marcosson, Isaac F. "The JF Country." *Bookman,* 32 (Dec 1910), 363-369.

Shapiro, Henry D. *Appalachia on Our Mind* (Chapel Hill: U North Carolina P, 1978), 70-76, passim.

Townsend, John Wilson. "JF, Jr." *Kentucky in American Letters, 1784-1912,* Vol 2 (Cedar Rapids, Iowa: Torch, 1913), 172-176.

Tucker, Edward L. "JF, Jr.: Bon Vivant and Mountain Chronicler." *VC,* 21 (Spring 1972), 18-29.

Ward, William S. "JF, Jr." *A Literary History of Kentucky* (Knoxville: U Tennessee P, 1988), 76-83.

Sandra L. Ballard

HAROLD FREDERIC

Utica, NY, 19 Aug 1856-Surrey, England, 19 Oct 1898

Harold Frederic's rapid rise to journalistic eminence and his emergence as a force in American fiction constituted a classic American success story. However, following his death in mid-life and mid-career, the revelation of his scandalous marital arrangements and the perception that his fiction was no more than a byproduct of his journalism dampened the critical recognition that he had begun to receive. Nevertheless, he has retained an admiring readership and has inspired periodic attempts at a reappraisal, focused, for the most part, on *The Damnation of Theron Ware.* His other novels of similar interest have received relatively little attention. Although his contemporary reputation rested on his perceived religious iconoclasm, most of the early twentieth-century criticism attempted to categorize him as a regionalist, a realist, or a naturalist. More recently, criticism, noting his affinities to Nathaniel Hawthorne and William James, has tended to locate his works in the historical mainstream of American fiction.

BIBLIOGRAPHIES & CATALOGUE

Bibliography of American Literature, comp Jacob Blanck. New Haven: Yale U P, 1955-1991. Primary.

O'Donnell, Thomas F, Stanton Garner & Robert H Woodward. *A Bibliography of Writings By and About HF.* Boston: Hall, 1975.

Polk, Noel. *The Literary Manuscripts of HF: A Catalogue.* NY: Garland, 1979.

BOOKS

Seth's Brother's Wife: A Study of Life in the Greater New York. NY: Scribners, 1887. Novel.

The Lawton Girl. NY: Scribners, 1890. Novel.

In the Valley. NY: Scribners, 1890. Novel.

The Young Emperor William II of Germany: A Study in Character Development on a Throne. NY: Putnam, 1891. Nonfiction.

The New Exodus: A Study of Israel in Russia. NY: Putnam / London: Heinemann, 1892. Nonfiction.

The Return of the O'Mahony: A Novel. NY: Bonner, 1892.

The Copperhead. NY: Scribners, 1893. Augmented as *The Copperhead and Other Stories of the North During the American War.* London: Heinemann, 1894.

Marsena, and Other Stories of the Wartime. NY: Scribners, 1894. *Marsena* separately published, London: Unwin, 1896.

The Damnation of Theron Ware. Chicago: Stone & Kimball, 1896; *Illumination.* London: Heinemann, 1896. Novel.

Mrs. Albert Grundy: Observations in Philistia. London: Lane / NY: Merriam, 1896. Satire.

March Hares (as by George Forth). London: Lane / NY: Appleton, 1896; (as by HF). NY: Appleton, 1896. Novel.

The Deserter and Other Stories: A Book of Two Wars. Boston: Lothrop, 1898.

Gloria Mundi: A Novel. Chicago & NY: Stone, 1898. Abridged as *Pomps and Vanities.* London: Heinemann, 1913.

The Market-Place. NY: Stokes, 1899. Novel.

LETTERS

The Correspondence of HF, ed George E Fortenberry, Stanton Garner & Robert H Woodward; text established by Charlyne Dodge. *The HF Edition,* Vol 1.

EDITIONS & COLLECTIONS

In the Sixties, preface by HF. NY: Scribners, 1897. Stories.

HF's Stories of York State, ed Thomas F O'Donnell. Syracuse: Syracuse U P, 1966.

The Major Works of HF, 5 vols. NY: Greenwood, 1969.

The HF Edition, Vols 1 & 2. Fort Worth: Texas Christian U P, 1977-1981; Vols 3 & 4. Lincoln & London: U Nebraska P, 1985-1986.

MANUSCRIPTS & ARCHIVES

The major collections are at the Library of Congress, the New York Public Library & Princeton U Library.

BIOGRAPHIES

Book

O'Donnell, Thomas F. *F in the Mohawk Valley.* Utica, NY: O'Donnell, 1968.

Article

Sherard, Robert H. "HF." *Idler,* 12 (Nov 1897), 531-540.

CRITICAL STUDIES

Books

Briggs, Austin, Jr. *The Novels of HF.* Ithaca, NY: Cornell U P, 1969.

Garner, Stanton. *HF.* Minneapolis: U Minnesota P, 1969.

Haines, Paul. "HF." Dissertation: NYU, 1945.

O'Donnell, Thomas F & Hoyt C Franchere. *HF.* NY: Twayne, 1961.

Special Journals

ALR, 1 (Spring 1968). HF issue.

Frederic Herald (triquarterly, 1967-1970).

Book Sections & Articles

Aaron, Daniel. "Stephen Crane and HF." *The Unwritten War: American Writers and the Civil War* (NY: Knopf, 1973), 210-225.

Blackall, Jean Frantz. "Perspectives on HF's *The Market-Place.*" *PMLA,* 86 (May 1971), 388-405.

Blackall. "F's *Gloria Mundi* as a Novel of Education." *MarkhamR,* 3 (May 1972), 41-46.

Bredahl, A Carl, Jr. "The Artist in *The Damnation of Theron Ware.*" *SNNTS,* 4 (Fall 1972), 432-441.

Bromley, Larry. "History of the Text." *Gloria Mundi* (Lincoln: U Nebraska P, 1986), 345-370.

Carrington, George C, Jr. "HF's Clear Farcical Vision: *The Damnation of Theron Ware.*" *ALR,* 19 (Spring 1987), 3-26.

Carter, Everett. "HF." *Howells and the Age of Realism* (Philadelphia: Lippincott, 1954), 239-245.

Carter. "Introduction." *The Damnation of Theron Ware* (Cambridge: Harvard U P, 1960), vii-xxiv.

Coale, Samuel Chase. "HF: Naturalism as Romantic Snarl." *In Hawthorne's Shadow: American Romance From Melville to Mailer* (Lexington: U P Kentucky, 1985), 46-62.

Crane, Stephen. "HF." *ChaB,* 8 (15 Mar 1898), 358-359.

Crowley, John W. "The Nude and the Madonna in *The Damnation of Theron Ware.*" *AL,* 45 (Nov 1973), 379-389.

Donaldson, Scott. "The Seduction of Theron Ware." *NCF,* 29 (Mar 1975), 441-452.

Donaldson. "Introduction." *The Damnation of Theron Ware, or Illumination* (NY: Penguin, 1986), vii-xxx.

Earnest, Ernest. "The Flamboyant American: HF." *Expatriates and Patriots: American Artists, Scholars, and Writers in Europe* (Durham, NC: Duke U P, 1968), 220-236.

Eichelberger, Clayton L. "Philanthropy in F's *The*

Market-Place." *AQ,* 20 (Spring 1968), 111-116.

Garner, Stanton. "Some Notes on HF in Ireland." *AL,* 39 (Mar 1967), 60-74.

Garner. "The Publishing History of HF: A Correction." *BBr,* 22 (1968), 95-101.

Garner. "More Notes on HF in Ireland." *AL,* 39 (Jan 1968), 560-562.

Garner. "HF and Swinburne's *Locrine:* A Matter of Clubs, Copyrights, and Character." *AL,* 45 (May 1973), 285-292.

Garner. "History of the Text." *The Market-Place* (Fort Worth: Texas Christian U P, 1981), 357-407.

Garner. "History of the Text." *The Damnation of Theron Ware or Illumination* (Lincoln: U Nebraska P, 1985), 353-415.

Johnson, George W. "HF's Young Goodman Ware: The Ambiguities of a Realistic Romance." *MFS,* 8 (Winter 1962-1963), 361-374.

Kantor, J R K. "*The Damnation of Theron Ware* and *John Ward, Preacher.*" *Serif,* 3 (Mar 1966), 16-21.

Krause, Sydney J. "HF and the Failure Motif." *SAF,* 15 (Spring 1987), 55-69.

LeClair, Thomas. "The Ascendant Eye: A Reading of *The Damnation of Theron Ware.*" *SAF,* 3 (Spring 1975), 95-102.

Lovett, Robert Morss. "HF." *The Damnation of Theron Ware* (NY: Boni, 1924), i-xii.

Luedtke, Luther S. "HF's Satanic Soulsby: Interpretation and Sources." *NCF,* 30 (Jun 1975), 82-104.

Lyons, John O. "Hebraism, Hellenism, and HF's

Theron Ware." *Arnoldian,* 6 (Winter 1979), 7-15.

O'Donnell, Thomas F. "Oriskany, 1877: The Centennial and the Birth of F's *In the Valley.*" *NYH,* 57 (Apr 1976), 139-164.

Oehlschlaeger, Fritz. "Passion, Authority, and Faith in *The Damnation of Theron Ware.*" *AL,* 58 (May 1986), 238-255.

Raleigh, John Henry. "*The Damnation of Theron Ware.*" *AL,* 30 (May 1958), 210-227.

Stein, Allen F. "Evasions of an American Adam: Structure and Theme in *The Damnation of Theron Ware.*" *ALR,* 5 (Winter 1972), 23-36.

Suderman, Elmer F. "*The Damnation of Theron Ware* as a Criticism of American Religious Thought." *HLQ,* 33 (Nov 1969), 61-75.

Towers, Tom H. "The Problem of Determinism in F's First Novel." *CE,* 26 (Feb 1965), 361-366.

Walcutt, Charles Child. "HF and American Naturalism." *AL,* 11 (Mar 1939), 11-22.

Walcutt. "Adumbrations: HF and Hamlin Garland." *American Literary Naturalism: A Divided Stream* (Minneapolis: U Minnesota P, 1956), 45-65.

Wilson, Edmund. "Introduction." *HF's Stories of York State,* xi-xvi.

Wilson. "Two Neglected American Novelists, II—HF, the Expanding Upstater." *NYer,* 46 (6 Jun 1970), 112-134.

Wüstenhagen, Heinz. "HF's *The Lawton Girl:* Ein Beitrag zur Erforschung des realistischen amerikanischen Romans in den 90er Jahren." *ZAA,* 12 (1964), 32-53.

Stanton Garner

MARY E. WILKINS FREEMAN

Randolph, Mass, 31 Oct 1852-Metuchen, NJ, 15 Mar 1930

Mary E. Wilkins Freeman, who wrote stories, novels, and one play, achieved both popular and critical success and in 1926 was awarded the Howells Medal for fiction by the American Academy of Letters. Even before her death, however, her popularity ebbed, and for years her work was virtually ignored. Her contemporaries labeled her a local-color realist whose subjects were the last remnants of New England Puritanism. Critics agree that her early short stories of life in rural New England were her best work. A revival of interest in Freeman has been generated by the recent increase in attention to women's writing.

BIBLIOGRAPHIES

"Bibliography." Foster, 210-222. Primary & secondary.

Bibliography of American Literature, comp Jacob Blanck. New Haven: Yale U P, 1955-1991. Primary.

"Selected Bibliography." *Selected Stories of MEWF*, 343-344. Secondary.

BOOKS

Decorative Plaques: Designs by George F. Barnes, Poems by Mary E. Wilkins. Boston: Lothrop, 1883.

Goody Two-Shoes and Other Famous Nursery Tales, with Clara Doty Bates. Boston: Lothrop, 1883.

The Cow With Golden Horns and Other Stories. Boston: Lothrop, 1884? Children's stories.

The Adventures of Ann: Stories of Colonial Times. Boston: Lothrop, 1886.

A Humble Romance and Other Stories. NY & London: Harper, 1887. Repub in 2 vols as *A Humble Romance and Other Stories & A Far-Away Melody and Other Stories.* Edinburgh: Douglas, 1890.

A New England Nun and Other Stories. NY: Harper, 1891.

The Pot of Gold and Other Stories. Boston: Lothrop, 1892. Children's stories.

Young Lucretia and Other Stories. NY: Harper, 1892.

Jane Field: A Novel. London: Osgood, McIlvaine, 1892; NY: Harper, 1893.

Giles Corey, Yeoman: A Play. NY: Harper, 1893.

Pembroke: A Novel. NY: Harper, 1894.

Comfort Pease and Her Gold Ring. NY & c: Revell, 1895. Story.

Madelon: A Novel. NY: Harper, 1896.

Once Upon a Time and Other Child-Verses. Boston: Lothrop, 1897.

Jerome, a Poor Man: A Novel. NY & London: Harper, 1897.

Silence and Other Stories. NY & London: Harper, 1898.

The People of Our Neighborhood. Philadelphia: Curtis / NY: Doubleday & McClure, 1898; *Some of Our Neighbours.* London: Dent, 1898. Stories.

The Jamesons. Philadelphia: Curtis / NY: Doubleday & McClure, 1899. Novel.

The Love of Parson Lord and Other Stories. NY & London: Harper, 1900.

The Heart's Highway: A Romance of Virginia in the Seventeenth Century. NY: Doubleday, Page, 1900. Novel.

Understudies. NY & London: Harper, 1901. Stories.

The Portion of Labor. NY & London: Harper, 1901. Novel.

Six Trees. NY & London: Harper, 1903. Stories.

The Wind in the Rose-Bush and Other Stories of the Supernatural. NY: Doubleday, Page, 1903.

The Givers. NY & London: Harper, 1904. Stories.

The Debtor: A Novel. NY & London: Harper, 1905.

"Doc." Gordon. NY & London: Authors & Newspapers Association, 1906. Novel.

By the Light of the Soul: A Novel. NY & London: Harper, 1906.

The Fair Lavinia and Others. NY & London: Harper, 1907. Stories.

Why Miss Ann Maria Simmons Never Married. Franklin, Ohio & Denver, Colo: Eldridge Entertainment House, nd. Monologue.

The Shoulders of Atlas: A Novel. NY & London: Harper, 1908.

The Winning Lady and Others. NY & London: Harper, 1909. Stories.

The Green Door. NY: Moffat, Yard, 1910. Children's story.

The Butterfly House. NY: Dodd, Mead, 1912. Novel.

The Yates Pride: A Romance. NY & London: Harper, 1912. Novella.

The Copy-Cat & Other Stories. NY & London: Harper, 1914.

An Alabaster Box, with Florence Morse Kingsley. NY & London: Appleton, 1917. Novel.

Edgewater People. NY & London: Harper, 1918. Stories.

LETTERS

The Infant Sphinx: Collected Letters of MEWF, ed with intro by Brent L Kendrick. Metuchen, NJ & London: Scarecrow, 1985.

OTHER

"The Long Arm." *The Long Arm and Other Detective Stories* (London: Chapman & Hall, 1895), 1-66.

"The Old-Maid Aunt." *The Whole Family: A Novel by Twelve Authors* (NY & London: Harper, 1908), 30-59.

COLLECTIONS

The Best Stories of Mary E. Wilkins, ed with intro by Henry Wysham Lanier. NY & London: Harper, 1927.

Collected Ghost Stories, ed with intro by Edward Wagenknecht. Sauk City, Wis: Arkham House, 1974.

The Revolt of Mother and Other Stories, ed Michele Clark. Old Westbury, NY: Feminist, 1974.

Selected Stories of MEWF, ed with intro & afterword by Marjorie Pryse. NY & London: Norton, 1983.

MANUSCRIPTS & ARCHIVES

The major collections are at the New York Public Library; Columbia U Library; Princeton U Library; & U of Virginia Library.

BIOGRAPHY

Book

Foster, Edward. *MEWF.* NY: Hendricks House, 1956.

CRITICAL STUDIES

Books

Hamblen, Abigail Ann. *The New England Art of MWF.* Amherst, Mass: Green Knight, 1966.

Westbrook, Perry D. *MWF.* Boston: Twayne, rev 1988.

Book Sections & Articles

Bader, Julia. "The Dissolving Vision: Realism in Jewett, F and Gilman." *American Realism: New Essays,* ed Eric J Sundquist (Baltimore, Md: Johns Hopkins U P, 1982), 176-198.

Barnstone, Aliki. "Houses Within Houses: Emily Dickinson and MWF's 'A New England Nun.' " *CentR,* 28 (Spring 1984), 129-145.

Clark, Michele. "Afterword." *The Revolt of Mother and Other Stories,* 163-201.

DeEulis, Marilyn Davis. " 'Her Box of a House': Spatial Restriction as Psychic Signpost in MWF's 'The Revolt of Mother.' " *MarkhamR,* 8 (Fall 1978), 51-52.

Donovan, Josephine. "MEWF and the Tree of Knowledge." *New England Local Color Literature: A Women's Tradition* (NY: Ungar, 1983), 119-138.

Donovan. "Silence or Capitulation: Prepatriarchal 'Mothers' Gardens' in Jewett and F." *SSF,* 23 (Winter 1986), 43-48.

Fisken, Beth Wynne. " 'Unusual' People in a 'Usual Place': 'The Balking of Christopher,' by MWF." *CLQ,* 21 (Jun 1985), 99-103.

Glasser, Leah Blatt. "MEWF: The Stranger in the Mirror." *MR,* 25 (Summer 1984), 323-339.

Hirsch, David H. "Subdued Meaning in 'A New England Nun.' " *SSF,* 2 (Winter 1965), 124-136.

Howells, William Dean. "Puritanism in American Fiction." *Literature and Life: Studies* (NY: Harper, 1902), 278-283.

Johns, Barbara A. "Love-Cracked: Spinsters as Subversives in 'Anna Malann,' 'Christmas Jenny,' and 'An Object of Love.' " *CLQ,* 23 (Mar 1987), 4-15.

Kendrick, Brent L. "MEWF." *ALR,* 8 (Summer 1975), 255-257.

Levy, Babette May. "Mutations in New England Local Color." *NEQ,* 19 (Sep 1946), 338-358.

Machen, Arthur. *Hieroglyphics: A Note Upon Ecstasy in Literature* (NY: Knopf, 1923), 151-160.

Matthiessen, F O. "New England Stories." *American Writers on American Literature,* ed John Macy (NY: Liveright, 1931), 399-413.

McElrath, Joseph R, Jr. "The Artistry of MEWF's 'The Revolt.' " *SSF,* 17 (Summer 1980), 255-261.

Meese, Elizabeth A. "Signs of Undecidability: Reconsidering the Stories of MWF." *Crossing the Double-Cross: The Practice of Feminist Criticism* (Chapel Hill: U North Carolina P, 1986), 21-38.

More, Paul Elmer. "Hawthorne: Looking Before and After." *The Shelburne Essays, Second Series* (NY: Putnam, 1905), 173-187.

Morey, Ann-Janine. "American Myth and Biblical Interpretation in the Fiction of Harriet Beecher Stowe and MEWF." *JART,* 55 (Winter 1987), 741-763.

Moss, Mary. "Some Representative American Story Tellers II—Mary E. Wilkins." *Bookman,* 24 (Sep 1906), 20-29.

Oaks, Susan. "The Haunting Will: The Ghost Stories of MWF." *CLQ,* 21 (Dec 1985), 208-220.

Pattee, Fred Lewis. "On the Terminal Moraine of New England Puritanism." *Side Lights on American Literature* (NY: Century, 1922), 175-209.

Pryse, Marjorie. "The Humanity of Women in F's 'A Village Singer.' " *CLQ,* 19 (Jun 1983), 69-77.

Pryse. "An Uncloistered 'New England Nun.' " *SSF,* 20 (Fall 1983), 289-295.

Reichardt, Mary R. "MWF: One Hundred Years of Criticism." *Legacy,* 4 (Fall 1987), 31-44.

Thompson, Charles Miner. "Miss Wilkins: An Idealist in Masquerade." *Atlantic,* 83 (May 1899), 665-675.

Toth, Susan Allen. "MWF's Parable of a Wasted Life." *AL,* 42 (Jan 1971), 564-567.

Toth. "Defiant Light: A Positive View of MWF." *NEQ,* 46 (Mar 1973), 82-93.

Tutwiler, J R. "Two New England Writers—In Relation to Their Art and to Each Other." *Gunton's,* 25 (Nov 1903), 419-425.

Warner, Sylvia Townsend. "Item, One Empty House." *NYer,* 42 (26 Mar 1966), 131-138.

Wood, Ann Douglas. "The Literature of Impoverishment: The Women Local Colorists in America, 1865-1914." *WS,* 1, no 1 (1972), 3-45.

Shirley Marchalonis

ALICE FRENCH
(Octave Thanet)

Andover, Mass, 19 Mar 1850-Davenport, Iowa, 9 Jan 1934

The daughter of a wealthy manufacturer, Alice French divided her time between Davenport, Iowa, and a plantation in Arkansas, the locales for most of her fiction. Writing in the local-color tradition, French, who published all of her work under the pseudonym Octave Thanet, portrayed the social customs, dialects, and conflicts facing people in midwestern industrial towns and the rural South. Her fiction dealt with labor problems, social structures, domestic conflicts, and female relationships. Though her works were popular in the 1890s and she was praised for her humor and contributions to regionalism, she has received little recent attention.

BIBLIOGRAPHY

"AF's Writings," "Bibliography." McMichael, 222-245. Primary & secondary.

BOOKS

Knitters in the Sun. Boston & NY: Houghton, Mifflin, 1887. Stories.

Expiation. NY: Scribners, 1890. Novel.

Otto the Knight and Other Trans-Mississippi Stories. Boston & NY: Houghton, Mifflin, 1891.

We All. NY: Appleton, 1891. Children's novel.

An Adventure in Photography. NY: Scribners, 1893. Essay & photographs.

Stories of a Western Town. NY: Scribners, 1893.

The Missionary Sheriff: Being Incidents in the Life of a Plain Man Who Tried to Do His Duty. NY: Harper, 1897. Stories.

A Book of True Lovers. Chicago: Way & Williams, 1897. Stories.

A Slave to Duty & Other Women. Chicago & NY: Stone, 1898. Stories.

The Heart of Toil. NY: Scribners, 1898. Stories.

The Captured Dream and Other Stories. NY &
London: Harper, 1899.
The Man of the Hour. Indianapolis: Bobbs-Merrill,
1905. Novel.
The Lion's Share. Indianapolis: Bobbs-Merrill,
1907. Novel.
By Inheritance. Indianapolis: Bobbs-Merrill, 1910.
Novel.
Stories That End Well. Indianapolis: Bobbs-Merrill,
1911.
A Step on the Stair. Indianapolis: Bobbs-Merrill,
1913. Novel.
And the Captain Answered. Indianapolis: Bobbs-
Merrill, 1917. Novel.

OTHER

The Best Letters of Lady Mary Wortley Montagu,
ed AF (as by Octave Thanet). Chicago:
McClurg, 1890.

MANUSCRIPTS & ARCHIVES

Newberry Library, Chicago.

BIOGRAPHY

Book
McMichael, George. *Journey to Obscurity: The
Life of Octave Thanet.* Lincoln: U Nebraska
P, 1965.

CRITICAL STUDIES

Books
Rushton, Linda E. "The Arkansas Fiction of AF."
Dissertation: U Arkansas, 1982.

Tigges, Sandra Ann Healey. "AF: A Noble Anachronism." Dissertation: U Iowa, 1981.

Book Sections & Articles
Bentzon, Th (Marie Thérèse Blanc). "In Arkansas
Apropos of Octave Thanet's Romances,"
trans Evelyn S Schaeffer. *MidlandM,* 6 (Jul
1896), 37-47; 6 (Aug 1896), 136-145.
Bush, Robert. "The Literary Paternalism of Octave
Thanet." *NewberryLB,* 6 (Nov 1962), 24-28.
Dougan, Michael B. "When Fiction Is Reality: Ar-
kansas Fiction of Octave Thanet." *PAPA,* 2
(Summer 1976), 29-36.
Dougan. "Local Colorists and the Race Question:
Opie Read and Octave Thanet." *PAPA,* 9 (Fall
1983), 26-34.
Faderman, Lillian. *Surpassing the Love of Men: Ro-
mantic Friendship and Love Between Women
From the Renaissance to the Present* (NY:
Morrow, 1981), 215-216.
McQuin, Susan C. "AF's View of Women." *BI,* 20
(Apr 1974), 34-42.
Reid, Mary J. "Four Women Writers of the West."
Overland, 24 (Aug 1894), 138-144.
Reid. "The Theories of Octave Thanet and Other
Western Realists." *MidlandM,* 9 (Feb 1898),
99-108.
Sewell, Rebecca. "Clover Bend Plantation." *SWR,*
21 (Apr 1936), 312-318.
Shinn, Josiah H. "Miss AF of Clover Bend." *Publi-
cations of the Arkansas Historical Associa-
tion,* Vol 1, ed John Hugh Reynolds (Fayette-
ville: Arkansas Historical Association, 1906),
344-351.

Gwen L. Nagel

HENRY BLAKE FULLER

Chicago, Ill, 9 Jan 1857-Chicago, Ill, 28 Jul 1929

Henry Blake Fuller's life and writing career were shaped by Chicago, but after his first pilgrimage to Italy in 1879, he spent the remainder of his life comparing the Chicago he knew with the Italy of his dreams. In novel after novel, article after article, even satirical verse, he compared the "uncivilized" Chicagoans to the civilized Italians and other Europeans. He pictured the city as inhabited by primitive cliff-dwellers madly in love with money and possessing only the most rudimentary taste for the arts. From first to last, the problem of the artist in America versus his counterpart in Europe remained Fuller's overriding subject.

BIBLIOGRAPHIES

Bibliography of American Literature, comp Jacob Blanck. New Haven: Yale U P, 1955-1991. Primary.

Silet, Charles L P. *HBF and Hamlin Garland: A Reference Guide.* Boston: Hall, 1977. Secondary.

BOOKS

The Chevalier of Pensieri-Vani Together With Frequent References to the Prorege of Arcopia (as by Stanton Page). Boston: Cupples, 1890. Augmented as *The Chevalier of Pensieri-Vani* (as by HBF). NY: Century, 1892. Novel.

The Chatelaine of La Trinité. NY: Century, 1892. Novel.

The Cliff-Dwellers: A Novel. NY: Harper, 1893.

With the Procession: A Novel. NY: Harper, 1895.

The Puppet-Booth: Twelve Plays. NY: Century, 1896.

From the Other Side: Stories of Transatlantic Travel. Boston & NY: Houghton, Mifflin, 1898.

The New Flag: Satires. Chicago: npub, 1899.

The Last Refuge: A Sicilian Romance. Boston & NY: Houghton, Mifflin, 1900. Novel.

Under the Skylights. NY: Appleton, 1901. Novel.

Waldo Trench and Others: Stories of Americans in Italy. NY: Scribners, 1908.

Lines Long and Short: Biographical Sketches in Various Rhythms. Boston & NY: Houghton Mifflin, 1917.

On the Stairs. Boston & NY: Houghton Mifflin, 1918. Novel.

Bertram Cope's Year: A Novel. Chicago: Seymour/Alderbrink, 1919.

Gardens of This World. NY: Knopf, 1929. Novel.

Not on the Screen. NY & London: Knopf, 1930. Novel.

OTHER

The Coffee-House: A Comedy in Three Acts by Carlo Goldoni; trans HBF. NY & London: French, 1925.

The Fan: A Comedy in Three Acts by Goldoni; trans HBF. NY & London: French, 1925.

"Howells or James?—An Essay by HBF," ed Darrel Abel. *MFS,* 3 (Summer 1957), 159-164.

MANUSCRIPTS & ARCHIVES

The major collections are at the Newberry Library, Chicago; U of Southern California Library; the Huntington Library, San Marino, Calif; the Houghton Library, Harvard U; & the Chicago Historical Society Library.

BIOGRAPHIES

Books

Bowron, Bernard R, Jr. *HBF of Chicago: The Ordeal of a Genteel Realist in Ungenteel America.* Westport, Conn: Greenwood, 1974.

Griffin, Constance M. *HBF.* Philadelphia: U Pennsylvania P, 1939.

Book Sections

Garland, Hamlin. *Back-Trailers From the Middle Border* (NY: Macmillan, 1928), passim.

Garland. *Roadside Meetings* (NY: Macmillan, 1930), passim.

Garland. *My Friendly Contemporaries: A Literary Log* (NY: Macmillan, 1932), passim.

Garland. *Afternoon Neighbors: Further Excerpts From a Literary Log* (NY: Macmillan, 1934), passim.

Seymour, Ralph Fletcher. *Some Went This Way* (Chicago: Seymour, 1945), passim.

CRITICAL STUDIES

Books

Jackson, Kenny. "An Evolution of the New Chicago From the Old: A Study of HBF's Chicago Novels." Dissertation: U Pennsylvania, 1961.

Mitchum, Jeremiah Lewis. "HBF's Social and Esthetic Commentary." Dissertation: Michigan State U, 1973.

Morton, Sue. "The Fiction of HBF." Dissertation: U Wisconsin, Madison, 1978.

Pearce, Richard A. "Chicago in the Fiction of the 1890s as Illustrated in the Novels of HBF and Robert Herrick." Dissertation: Columbia U, 1963.

Pilkington, John, Jr. *HBF.* NY: Twayne, 1970.

Rosenblatt, Paul. "The Image of Civilization in the Novels of HBF." Dissertation: Columbia U, 1960.

Collection of Essays

Morgan, Anna, ed. *Tributes to Henry B.* Chicago: Seymour, 1929.

Book Sections & Articles

Brooks, Van Wyck. "Painters and Scholars: HBF." *The Dream of Arcadia: American Writers and Artists in Italy, 1760-1915* (NY: Dutton, 1958), 216-226.

Dell, Floyd. "Chicago in Fiction." *Bookman,* 38 (Nov 1913), 270-277.

Dreiser, Theodore. "The Great American Novel." *The American Spectator Yearbook,* ed George Jean Nathan et al (NY: Stokes, 1934), 16-25.

Duffey, Bernard I. "HF." *The Chicago Renaissance in American Letters* (East Lansing: Michigan State C P, 1954), 27-50.

Gelfant, Blanche H. *The American City Novel* (Norman: U Oklahoma P, 1954), passim.

Howells, Mildred, ed. *Life in Letters of William Dean Howells,* Vol 2 (Garden City, NY: Doubleday, Doran, 1928), passim.

Huneker, James. "The Seven Arts: Mr. F's Masterpiece." *Puck,* 78 (11 Sep 1915), 10, 21.

Lawrence, Elwood P. "F of Chicago: A Study in Frustration." *AQ,* 6 (Summer 1954), 137-146.

Lovett, Robert Morss. "F of Chicago." *NewR,* 60 (21 Aug 1929), 16-18.

Monroe, Harriet. "HBF." *Poetry,* 35 (Oct 1929), 34-41.

Monroe. *A Poet's Life* (NY: Macmillan, 1938), passim.

Murray, Donald M. "HBF, Friend of Howells." *SAQ,* 52 (Jul 1953), 431-444.

Oppenheim, J H. "Autopsy on Chicago." *AMercury,* 40 (Apr 1937), 454-461.

Repplier, Agnes. "A By-Way in Fiction." *Lippincott's,* 47 (Jun 1891), 760-765. Rpt *Essays in Miniature* by Repplier (Boston: Houghton, Mifflin, 1895).

Shultz, Victor. "HBF: Civilized Chicagoan." *Bookman,* 70 (Sep 1929), 34-38.

Smith, Carl S. *Chicago and the American Literary Imagination, 1880-1920* (Chicago: U Chicago P, 1984), passim

Turner, Susan J. *A History of the Freeman* (NY: Columbia U P, 1963), passim.

Van Vechten, Carl. "HBF." *Excavations: A Book of Advocacies* (NY: Knopf, 1926), 129-147.

John Pilkington, Jr.

ZONA GALE

Portage, Wis, 26 Aug 1874-Portage, Wis, 27 Dec 1938

Zona Gale produced twenty-two volumes of fiction, seven plays, five books of nonfiction, and one collection of poetry. Her fiction ranges from short stories in the local-color tradition, for which she is best known, to political tracts advocating civic improvements and women's rights. Her dramatization of her novel *Miss Lulu Bett* won a Pulitzer Prize. Its theme, the woman oppressed by life in small-town middle America, reflects a concern running throughout her work. Gale's sentimental early novels and her later mystical writings are largely ignored today.

BIBLIOGRAPHY

"Selected Bibliography." Simonson, 147-150. Primary & secondary.

BOOKS

Romance Island. Indianapolis: Bobbs-Merrill, 1906. Novel.
The Loves of Pelleas and Etarre. NY & London: Macmillan, 1907. Stories.
Friendship Village. NY: Macmillan, 1908. Stories.
Friendship Village: Love Stories. NY: Macmillan, 1909. Stories.
Mothers to Men. NY: Macmillan, 1911. Novel.
Christmas. NY: Macmillan, 1912. Novella.
Civic Improvement in the Little Towns. Washington: American Civic Association, 1913. Essay.
When I Was a Little Girl. NY: Macmillan, 1913. Novel.
Neighborhood Stories. NY: Macmillan, 1914. Stories.
Heart's Kindred. NY: Macmillan, 1915. Novel.
A Daughter of the Morning. Indianapolis: Bobbs-Merrill, 1917. Novel.
Birth. NY: Macmillan, 1918. Novel.
Peace in Friendship Village. NY: Macmillan, 1919. Stories.
The Neighbours. NY: Huebsch, 1920. Play.
Miss Lulu Bett. NY & London: Appleton, 1920. Novel.
Miss Lulu Bett: An American Comedy of Manners. NY: Appleton, 1921. Play.
The Secret Way. NY: Macmillan, 1921. Poetry.
Uncle Jimmy. Boston: Baker, 1922. Play.

What Women Won in Wisconsin. Washington: National Women's Party, 1922. Essay.
Why I Shall Vote for Senator Robert M. La Follette. Madison, Wis: npub, 1922. Essay.
Faint Perfume. NY: Appleton, 1923. Novel.
Mister Pitt. NY & London: Appleton, 1925. Play.
Preface to a Life. NY & London: Appleton, 1926. Novel.
Yellow Gentians and Blue. NY & London: Appleton, 1927. Stories.
Portage, Wisconsin and Other Essays. NY: Knopf, 1928.
Borgia. NY: Knopf, 1929. Novel.
Bridal Pond. NY: Knopf, 1930. Stories.
Evening Clothes. Boston: Baker, 1932. Play.
Papa La Fleur. NY & London: Appleton, 1933. Novel.
Old Fashioned Tales. NY & London: Appleton-Century, 1933. Stories.
Faint Perfume. NY & c: French, 1934. Play.
The Clouds. NY & c: French, 1936. Play.
Light Woman. NY & London: Appleton-Century, 1937. Novel.
Frank Miller of Mission Inn. NY & London: Appleton-Century, 1938. Biography.
Magna. NY & London: Appleton-Century, 1939. Novel.

MANUSCRIPTS & ARCHIVES

The major collections are at the State Historical Society of Wisconsin, Madison, & at Princeton U Library.

BIOGRAPHY

Book
Derleth, August. *Still Small Voice: The Biography of ZG.* NY: Appleton-Century, 1940.

CRITICAL STUDIES

Books
Follett, Wilson. *ZG: An Artist in Fiction.* NY: Appleton, 1923.
Simonson, Harold P. *ZG.* NY: Twayne, 1962.

Book Sections & Articles
Forman, Henry James. "ZG: A Touch of Greatness." *WMH,* 46 (Autumn 1962), 32-37.

Gard, Robert. *Grassroots Theatre: A Search for Regional Arts in America* (Madison: U Wisconsin P, 1955), 15-17, 87-89, passim.

Herron, Ima Honaker. *The Small Town in American Literature* (Durham, NC: Duke U P, 1939), 345-349, 364-365.

Maxwell, William. "ZG." *YR,* 76 (Mar 1987), 221-225.

Monteiro, George. "ZG and Ridgely Torrence." *ALR,* 3 (Winter 1970), 77-79.

Simonson, Harold P. "ZG's Acquaintance With Francis Grierson." *HSSCQ,* 41 (Mar 1959), 11-16.

Simonson. "ZG (1874-1938)." *ALR,* 1 (Summer 1968), 14-17.

Sochen, June. *Movers and Shakers: American Women Thinkers and Activists, 1900-1970* (NY: Quadrangle, 1973), 123-127.

Sutherland, Cynthia. "American Women Playwrights as Mediators of the 'Woman Problem.' " *MD,* 21 (Sep 1978), 319-336.

White, Katherine A. "*Miss Lulu Bett* Revived." *TCW,* 1 (Winter 1984), 38-40.

Vern L. Lindquist

HAMLIN GARLAND

New Salem, Wis, 14 Sep 1860-Los Angeles, Calif, 4 Mar 1940

Hamlin Garland's major contributions to American literature are his naturalistic stories of midwestern agrarian life in *Main-Travelled Roads,* his early portrayal of the New Woman in *Rose of Dutcher's Coolly,* and his nine volumes of autobiographical sketches, including *Boy Life on the Prairie* and *A Daughter of the Middle Border,* for which he won the Pulitzer Prize in 1921. For financial reasons, he devoted two decades of his life to writing popular romances such as *The Captain of the Gray-Horse Troop,* but even these volumes contain much of value, such as his positive depiction of Native Americans and his fascination with the American West. His early endorsement of Impressionism in art and literature, the profoundly democratic aesthetic he outlined in *Crumbling Idols,* his social dedication in *The Book of the American Indian,* as well as his early stories, all merit the attention of modern readers.

BIBLIOGRAPHIES

Arvidson, Lloyd A. "A Bibliography of the Published Writings of HG." Thesis: U Southern California, 1952. Primary.

Arvidson. *HG: Centennial Tributes and a Checklist of the HG Papers in the University of Southern California Library.* Los Angeles: U Southern California, 1962. Primary.

Bryer, Jackson R, Eugene Harding & Robert A Rees. *HG and the Critics: An Annotated Bibliography.* Troy, NY: Whitston, 1973. Secondary.

Pizer, Donald. "HG: A Bibliography of Newspaper and Periodical Publications (1885-1895)." *BB,* 22 (Jan-Apr 1957), 41-44. Primary.

Pizer. "HG (1890-1940)." *ALR,* 1 (Fall 1967), 45-51. Secondary.

Silet, Charles L P. *Henry Blake Fuller and HG: A Reference Guide.* Boston: Hall, 1977. Secondary.

Silet & Robert E Welch. "Further Additions to *HG and the Critics.*" *ALR,* 9 (Summer 1976), 268-275. Secondary.

Silet & Welch. "Corrections to *HG and the Critics.*" *PBSA,* 72 (Jan-Mar 1978), 106-109. Secondary.

Stronks, James. "A Supplement to Bryer and Harding's *HG and the Critics: An Annotated Bibliography*." *ALR*, 9 (Summer 1976), 261-267. Secondary.

BOOKS

Under the Wheel: A Modern Play in Six Scenes. Boston: Barta, 1890.

Main-Travelled Roads. Boston: Arena, 1891. Augmented ed, NY & London: Macmillan, 1899. Augmented again, NY & London: Harper, 1922. Augmented again, NY & London: Harper, 1930. Stories.

Jason Edwards, an Average Man. Boston: Arena, 1892. Novel.

A Member of the Third House. Chicago: Schulte, 1892. Novel.

A Spoil of Office: A Story of the Modern West. Boston: Arena, 1892. Rev ed, NY: Appleton, 1897. Novel.

A Little Norsk; or Ol' Pap's Flaxen. NY: Appleton, 1892. Novel.

Prairie Songs. . . . Cambridge, Mass & Chicago: Stone & Kimball, 1893. Verse.

Prairie Folks. Cambridge, Mass & Chicago: Stone & Kimball, 1893. Stories.

Crumbling Idols: Twelve Essays on Art. . . . Chicago & Cambridge, Mass: Stone & Kimball, 1894.

Rose of Dutcher's Coolly. Chicago: Stone & Kimball, 1895. Rev ed, NY & London: Macmillan, 1899.

Wayside Courtships. NY: Appleton, 1897. Novel.

The Spirit of Sweetwater. Philadelphia: Curtis / NY: Doubleday & McClure, 1898. Augmented as *Witch's Gold*. NY: Doubleday, Page, 1906. Novel.

Ulysses S. Grant: His Life and Character. NY: Doubleday & McClure, 1898. Biography.

Boy Life on the Prairie. NY & London: Macmillan, 1899. Rev ed, 1908. Autobiography.

The Trail of the Goldseekers: A Record of Travel in Prose and Verse. NY & London: Macmillan, 1899.

The Eagle's Heart. NY: Appleton, 1900. Novel.

Her Mountain Lover. NY: Century, 1901. Novel.

The Captain of the Gray-Horse Troop. NY & London: Harper, 1902. Novel.

Hesper. NY & London: Harper, 1903. Novel.

The Light of the Star. NY & London: Harper, 1904. Novel.

The Tyranny of the Dark. NY & London: Harper, 1905. Novel.

Money Magic. NY & London: Harper, 1907. Novel.

The Long Trail: A Story of the Northwest Wilderness. NY & London: Harper, 1907. Novel.

The Shadow World. NY & London: Harper, 1908. Novel.

The Moccasin Ranch: A Story of Dakota. NY & London: Harper, 1909. Novel.

Cavanagh, Forest Ranger. NY & London: Harper, 1910. Novel.

Other Main-Travelled Roads. NY & London: Harper, 1910. Stories.

Victor Ollnee's Discipline. NY & London: Harper, 1911. Novel.

The Forester's Daughter: A Romance of the Bear-Tooth Range. NY & London: Harper, 1914. Novel.

They of the High Trails. NY & London: Harper, 1916. Novel.

A Son of the Middle Border. NY: Macmillan, 1917. Autobiography.

A Daughter of the Middle Border. NY: Macmillan, 1921. Autobiography.

A Pioneer Mother. Chicago: Bookfellows, 1922. Autobiography.

The Book of the American Indian. NY & London: Harper, 1923. Stories.

Trail-Makers of the Middle Border. NY: Macmillan, 1926. Autobiography.

The Westward March of American Settlement. Chicago: American Library Association, 1927. Essay.

Back-Trailers From the Middle Border. NY: Macmillan, 1928. Autobiography.

Prairie Song and Western Story. Boston & NY: Allyn & Bacon, 1928. Stories.

Roadside Meetings. NY: Macmillan, 1930. Autobiography.

Companions on the Trail. NY: Macmillan, 1931. Autobiography.

My Friendly Contemporaries: A Literary Log. NY: Macmillan, 1932. Autobiography.

Afternoon Neighbors: Further Excerpts From a Literary Log. NY: Macmillan, 1934. Autobiography.

Iowa, O Iowa! Iowa City: Clio, 1935. Verse.

Joys of the Trail. Chicago: Bookfellows, 1935.

The Long Trail. NY & London: Harper, 1935. Children's stories.

Forty Years of Psychic Research: A Plain Narrative of Fact. NY: Macmillan, 1936. Autobiography.

The Mystery of the Buried Crosses: A Narrative of Psychic Exploration. NY: Dutton, 1939. Essay.

HG's Observations on the American Indian, 1895-1905, ed Lonnie E Underhill & Daniel F Littlefield. Tucson: U Arizona P, 1976.

DIARIES

HG's Diaries, ed Donald Pizer. San Marino, Calif: Huntington Library, 1968.

MANUSCRIPTS & ARCHIVES

The major collections are at the U of Southern California Library, the New York Public Library & the Huntington Library, San Marino, Calif.

BIOGRAPHY

Books

Holloway, Jean. *HG: A Biography*. Austin: U Texas P, 1960.

Mane, Robert. *HG: L'homme et l'oeuvre (1860-1940)*. Paris: Didier, 1968.

Pizer, Donald. *HG's Early Work and Career*. Berkeley: U California P, 1960.

CRITICAL STUDIES

Books

Borchers, Hans. *HG (1860-1940): Die Entwicklung eines amerikanischen Realisten*. Bern: H Lang/ Frankfurt am Main: P Lang, 1975.

Crouch, Lora. *HG: Dakota Homesteader*. Sioux Falls, S Dak: Dakota Territory Centennial Commission, 1961.

Gish, Robert. *HG: The Far West*. Boise: Boise State U, 1976.

McCullough, Joseph B. *HG*. Boston: Twayne, 1978.

Collections of Essays

Nagel, James, ed. *Critical Essays on HG*. Boston: Hall, 1982.

Silet, Charles L P, Robert E Welch & Richard Boudreau, eds. *The Critical Reception of HG: 1891-1978*. Troy, NY: Whitston, 1985.

Book Sections & Articles

Ahnebrink, Lars. *The Beginnings of Naturalism in American Fiction* (Uppsala, Sweden: U Uppsala / Cambridge: Harvard U P, 1950), 63-89.

Alsen, Eberhard. "HG's First Novel: *A Spoil of Office*." *WAL*, 4 (Summer 1969), 91-105.

Bowen, Edwin W. "HG: The Middle-West Short-Story Writer." *SR*, 27 (Oct 1919), 411-422.

Boynton, Percy H. *The Rediscovery of the Frontier* (Chicago: U Chicago P, 1931), 80-85.

Browne, Ray B. " 'Popular' and Folk Songs: Unifying Force in G's Autobiographical Works." *SFQ*, 25 (Sep 1961), 153-166.

Carter, J L. "HG's Liberated Women." *ALR*, 6 (Summer 1973), 255-258.

Clark, Michael. "Herbert Spencer, HG, and *Rose of Dutcher's Coolly*." *ALR*, 17 (Autumn 1984), 203-208.

Hazard, Lucy Lockwood. "HG." *The Frontier in American Literature* (NY: Barnes & Noble, 1941), 261-267.

Herron, Ima Honaker. *The Small Town in American Literature* (Durham, NC: Duke U P, 1939), 218-226.

Herrscher, Walter. "The Natural Environment in HG's *Main-Travelled Roads*." *ON*, 11 (Spring-Summer 1985), 35-50.

Hicks, Granville. *The Great Tradition* (NY: Macmillan, 1933), 142-148.

Jacobson, Marcia. "The Flood of Remembrance and the Stream of Time: HG's *Boy Life on the Prairie*." *WAL*, 17 (Nov 1982), 227-242.

Kaye, Frances W. "HG: A Closer Look at the Later Fiction." *NDQ*, 43 (Summer 1975), 45-56.

Krauth, Leland. "*Boy Life on the Prairie*: Portrait of the Artist as a Young American." *MarkhamR*, 11 (Winter 1982), 25-29.

McCullough, Joseph B. "HG's Romantic Fiction." Nagel, 349-362.

Miller, Charles T. "HG's Retreat From Realism." *WAL*, 1 (Summer 1966), 119-129.

Parrington, Vernon Louis. "HG and the Middle Border." *Main Currents in American Thought*, Vol 3 (NY: Harcourt, Brace, 1930), 288-300.

Pizer, Donald. "Romantic Individualism in G, Norris and Crane." *AQ*, 10 (Winter 1958), 463-475.

Pizer. "The Radical Drama in Boston, 1889-1891." *NEQ*, 31 (Sep 1958), 361-374.

Pizer. "HG's *A Son of the Middle Border*: An Appreciation." *SAQ*, 65 (Autumn 1966), 448-459.

Popken, Randall L. "From Innocence to Experience in *My Ántonia* and *Boy Life on the Prairie*." *NDQ*, 46 (Spring 1978), 73-81.

Raw, Ruth M. "HG, the Romanticist." *SR*, 36 (Apr 1928), 202-210.

Reamer, Owen J. "G and the Indians." *NMQ*, 34 (Autumn 1964), 257-280.

Rocha, Mark William. "HG's Temperance Play." *ALR*, 21 (Spring 1989), 67-71.

Stronks, James B. "A Realist Experiments With Impressionism: HG's 'Chicago Studies.' " *AL*, 36 (Mar 1964), 38-52.

James Nagel

KATHARINE FULLERTON GEROULD

Brockton, Mass, 6 Feb 1879-Princeton, NJ, 27 Jul 1944

Katharine Fullerton Gerould was regarded during her lifetime as a foremost author of the short story. Her publishing career began in 1902 and spanned thirty-seven years, during which she wrote nearly fifty stories for the *Atlantic Monthly, Harper's, Century,* and *Scribner's Magazine.* Gerould often treated educated, upper-class New Englanders forced to preserve themselves—or their self-esteem—in crises. Although her stories have received little significant critical attention, they are notable for their style and subtle characterization.

BOOKS

Vain Oblations. NY: Scribners, 1914. Stories.

The Great Tradition and Other Stories. NY: Scribners, 1915.

Hawaii: Scenes and Impressions. NY: Scribners, 1916. Essays.

A Change of Air. NY: Scribners, 1917. Novel.

Modes and Morals. NY: Scribners, 1920. Essays.

Lost Valley: A Novel. NY & London: Harper, 1922.

Valiant Dust. NY: Scribners, 1922. Stories.

Conquistador. NY: Scribners, 1923. Novel.

The Aristocratic West. NY & London: Harper, 1925. Stories.

The Light That Never Was. NY: Scribners, 1931. Novel.

Ringside Seats. NY: Dodd, Mead, 1937. Essays.

MANUSCRIPTS & ARCHIVES

The major collections are at the Beinecke Library, Yale U & Princeton U Library.

BIOGRAPHIES

Book Sections

Lewis, R W B. *Edith Wharton: A Biography* (NY: Harper & Row, 1975), passim.

Sherman, Stuart P. "The Superior Class." *The Genius of America* (NY: Scribners, 1923), 125-143.

CRITICAL STUDIES

Book Section & Articles

Brooks, Cleanth, Jr & Robert Penn Warren. "Dixie Looks at Mrs. G." *AmR,* 6 (Mar 1936), 585-595.

Gillman, Lawrence. "The Book of the Month: The Strange Case of Mrs. G." *NAR,* 211 (Apr 1920), 564-568.

Kilmer, Joyce. "Is O. Henry a Pernicious Literary Influence? Mrs. KFG Says That He Wrote Expanded Anecdotes, Not Short Stories, With Nothing but Climax." *NYTM* (23 Jul 1916), 12.

Wright, Austin McGiffert. *The American Short Story in the Twenties* (Chicago: U Chicago P, 1961), passim.

Traci L. Hulsey

CHARLOTTE PERKINS GILMAN

Hartford, Conn, 3 Jul 1860-Pasadena, Calif, 17 Aug 1935

Magazine editor and lecturer Charlotte Perkins Gilman wrote poetry, essays, nearly two hundred short stories, and several novels. Her major nonfiction work *Women and Economics* brought her renown as a feminist. She examined the confinement that was often the price women, especially women artists, paid to fit the nineteenth-century domestic model, and her fiction and nonfiction explored possible solutions to the problems she saw women facing. Although better known in her own time for her theoretical books, Gilman is primarily remembered today for her short story "The Yellow Wall-paper" and her utopian novel *Herland.*

BIBLIOGRAPHY

Scharnhorst, Gary. *CPG: A Bibliography.* Metuchen, NJ: Scarecrow, 1985. Primary & secondary.

BOOKS

Gems of Art for the Home and Fireside (as by Charlotte Perkins Stetson). Providence, RI: Reid, 1888. Nonfiction.
In This Our World (as by Stetson). Oakland, Calif: McCombs & Vaughn, 1893. Augmented ed, London: Unwin, 1895. Augmented again, San Francisco: Barry, 1895. Augmented again, Boston: Small, Maynard, 1898. Poetry.
Women and Economics: A Study of the Economic Relation Between Men and Women as a Factor in Social Evolution (as by Stetson). Boston: Small, Maynard, 1898. Nonfiction.
The Yellow Wall-paper (as by Stetson). Boston: Small, Maynard, 1899. Story.
Concerning Children. Boston: Small, Maynard, 1900. Nonfiction.
The Home: Its Work and Influence. NY: McClure, Phillips, 1903. Nonfiction.
Human Work. NY: McClure, Phillips, 1904. Nonfiction.
Women and Social Service. Warren, Ohio: National American Woman Suffrage Association, 1907. Address.
What Diantha Did. NY: Charlton, 1910. Novel.
The Man-Made World; or, Our Androcentric Culture. NY: Charlton, 1911. Nonfiction.

The Crux. NY: Carlton, 1911. Novel.
Suffrage Songs and Verses. NY: Charlton, 1911. Poetry.
Moving the Mountain. NY: Charlton, 1911. Novel.
His Religion and Hers: A Study of the Faith of Our Fathers and the Work of Our Mothers. NY & London: Century, 1923. Nonfiction.
The Living of CPG: An Autobiography. NY & London: Appleton-Century, 1935.
Herland. NY: Pantheon, 1979. Novel.

OTHER

Impress (Nov 1893-Feb 1895), ed CPG (as by Charlotte Perkins Stetson). Magazine.
Forerunner (Nov 1909-Dec 1916), ed CPG. Repub NY: Greenwood, 1968. Magazine.
Mag-Marjorie. Forerunner, 3 (Jan-Dec 1912). Novel.
Won-Over. Forerunner, 4 (Jan-Dec 1913). Novel.
Benigna Machiavelli. Forerunner, 5 (Jan-Dec 1914). Novel.
With Her in Ourland. Forerunner, 7 (Jan-Dec 1916). Novel.

COLLECTION

The CPG Reader, ed Ann J Lane. NY: Pantheon, 1980.

MANUSCRIPTS & ARCHIVES

Radcliffe C Library, Harvard U.

BIOGRAPHIES

Books
Hill, Mary A. *CPG: The Making of a Radical Feminist, 1860-1896.* Philadelphia: Temple U P, 1980.
Winkler, Barbara Scott. *Victorian Daughters: The Lives and Feminism of CPG and Olive Schreiner.* Ann Arbor: U Michigan P, 1980.

Book Sections & Articles
Berkin, Carol Ruth. "Private Woman, Public Woman: The Contradictions of CPG." *Women in America: A History,* ed Berkin & Mary Beth Norton (Boston: Houghton Mifflin, 1979), 150-173.

"Charlotte Perkins Stetson: A Daring Humorist of Reform." *American Fabian,* 3 (Jan 1897), 1-3.

Gale, Zona. "Foreword." *The Living of CPG,* xiii-xxxviii.

Hill, Mary A. "CPG: A Feminist Struggle With Womanhood." *MR,* 21 (Fall 1980), 503-526.

Hill, ed. *Endure: The Diaries of Charles Walter Stetson* (Philadelphia: Temple U P, 1985), passim.

Hough, Eugene. "The Work and Influence of Charlotte Perkins Stetson in the Labor Movement." *American Fabian,* 3 (Jan 1897), 12.

Howe, Harriet. "CPG—As I Knew Her." *Equal Rights,* 5 (Sep 1936), 211-216.

Hughes, James L. "World Leaders I Have Known/ CPG." *CanadianM,* 61 (Aug 1923), 335-338.

Nies, Judith. "CPG." *Seven Women* (NY: Viking, 1977), 126-145.

Wellington, Amy. *Women Have Told: Studies in the Feminist Tradition* (Boston: Little, Brown, 1930), 115-131.

CRITICAL STUDIES

Books
Allen, Polly Wynn. *Building Domestic Liberty: CPG's Architectural Feminism.* Amherst: U Massachusetts P, 1988.

Doyle, William T. "CG and the Cycle of Feminist Reform." Dissertation: U California, Berkeley, 1960.

Porter, Mary A. "CPG: A Feminist Paradox." Dissertation: McGill U, 1975.

Potts, Helen Jo. "CPG: A Humanist Approach to Feminism." Dissertation: North Texas State U, 1975.

Scharnhorst, Gary. *CPG.* Boston: Twayne, 1985.

Book Sections & Articles
Bader, Julia. "The Dissolving Vision: Realism in Jewett, Freeman and G." *American Realism: New Essays,* ed Eric J Sundquist (Baltimore, Md: Johns Hopkins U P, 1982), 176-198.

Black, Alexander. "The Woman Who Saw It First." *Century,* 107 (Nov 1923), 33-42.

Degler, Carl N. "CPG on the Theory and Practice of Feminism." *AQ,* 8 (Spring 1956), 21-39.

Degler. "Introduction." *Women and Economics* (NY: Harper & Row, 1966), vi-xxxv.

DeLamotte, Eugenia C. "Male and Female Mysteries in 'The Yellow Wallpaper.' " *Legacy,* 5 (Spring 1988), 3-14.

Fetterley, Judith. "Reading About Reading: 'A Jury of Her Peers,' 'The Murders of the Rue Morgue,' and 'The Yellow Wallpaper.' " *Gender and Reading,* ed Elizabeth A Flynn & Patrocinio P Schweickart (Baltimore, Md: Johns Hopkins U P, 1986), 147-164.

Fleenor, Julian. "The Gothic Prism: CPG's Gothic Stories and Her Autobiography." *The Female Gothic,* ed Fleenor (Montreal: Eden, 1983), 227-241.

Friedman, Susan Stanford. "Women's Autobiographical Selves: Theory and Practice." *The Private Self: Theory and Practice of Women's Autobiographical Writings,* ed Shari Benstock (Chapel Hill: U North Carolina P, 1988), 34-62.

Gubar, Susan. "She and *Herland.*" *Coordinates: Placing Science Fiction and Fantasy,* ed George E Slusser, Eric S Rabkin & Robert Scholes (Carbondale: Southern Illinois U P, 1983), 139-149.

Haney-Peritz, Janice. "Monumental Feminism and Literature's Ancestral House: Another Look at 'The Yellow Wallpaper.' " *WS,* 12, no 2 (1986), 113-128.

Hayden, Dolores. "CPG and the Kitchenless House." *RHR,* 21 (Fall 1979), 224-247.

Hedges, Elaine R. "Afterword." *The Yellow Wallpaper* (Old Westbury, NY: Feminist, 1973), 37-63.

Kennard, Jean E. "Convention Coverage; or, How to Read Your Own Life." *NLH,* 13 (Autumn 1981), 69-88.

Kessler, Carol Farley. "Brittle Jars and Bitter Jangles: Light Verse by CPG." *RAFI,* 4 (Winter 1979), 35-43.

Keyser, Elizabeth. "Looking Backward: *Herland* to *Gulliver's Travels.*" *SAF,* 11 (Spring 1983), 31-46.

Krieg, Joann P. "CPG and the Whitman Connection." *WWR,* 1 (Mar 1984), 21-25.

Lane, Ann J. "Introduction." *Herland,* v-xxiii.

Lane. "The Fictional World of CPG." *The CPG Reader,* ix-xlii.

MacPike, Loralee. "Environment as Psychopathological Symbolism in 'The Yellow Wallpaper.' " *ALR,* 8 (Summer 1975), 286-288.

Matossian, Lou Ann. "A Woman-made Language: CPG and *Herland.*" *W&Lang,* 10 (Spring 1987), 16-20.

Miller, Margaret. "The Ideal Woman in Two Feminist Science-Fiction Utopias." *SFS,* 10 (Jul 1983), 191-198.

O'Neill, William. *Everyone Was Brave: The Rise and Fall of Feminism in America* (NY: Quadrangle, 1969), 38-48, 130-133, passim.

Scharnhorst, Gary. "Making Her Fame: CPG in California." *CalH,* 64 (Summer 1985), 192-201.

Schöpp-Schilling, Bette. " 'The Yellow Wallpaper': A Rediscovered 'Realistic' Story." *ALR,* 8 (Summer 1975), 284-286.

Schumaker, Conrad. "Too Terribly Good to Be Printed: CPG's 'The Yellow Wallpaper.' " *AL,* 57 (Dec 1985), 588-599.

Stern, Madeleine B. "Introduction." *Forerunner*, Vol 1 (NY: Greenwood, 1968), iii-x.

Treichler, Paula A. "Escaping the Sentence: Diagnosis and Discourse in 'The Yellow Wallpaper.' " *TSWL*, 3 (Spring-Fall 1981), 61-77.

Veeder, William. "Who Is Jane? The Intricate Feminism of CPG." *ArQ*, 44 (Autumn 1988), 40-79.

Weinstein, Lee. " 'The Yellow Wallpaper': A Supernatural Interpretation." *StWF*, 4 (Fall 1988), 23-35.

Wilson, Christopher P. "CPG's Steady Burghers:

The Terrain of *Herland*." *WS*, 12, no 3 (1986), 271-292.

Wood, Ann Douglas. " 'Fashionable Diseases': Women's Complaints and Their Treatment in Nineteenth-Century America." *JIH*, 4 (Summer 1973), 25-52. Rpt *The Private Side of American History: Readings in Everyday Life*, ed Thomas R Frazier (NY: Harcourt Brace Jovanovich, 1979).

Sonja Launspach

ELLEN GLASGOW

Richmond, Va, 22 Apr 1873-Richmond, Va, 21 Nov 1945

When Ellen Glasgow published her first novel anonymously in March 1897, she launched a writing career that spanned more than forty-five years. Her novels were often critically acclaimed during her lifetime, especially beginning in 1925 with *Barren Ground*, still regarded by many as her masterpiece. In 1938 Glasgow was elected a member of the American Academy of Arts and Letters, which in 1940 awarded her its prestigious Howells Medal. She received the Pulitzer Prize in 1942 for her novel *In This Our Life*. Following her death, however, her novels were criticized for the very "evasive idealism" that she fought against, and critics relegated her to the position of "social historian." At that time she was regarded primarily as a regional novelist and a transitional figure between sentimental southern romancers and later writers such as Faulkner. Glasgow recently has regained some of the critical status she enjoyed during the latter part of her career. Scholars have focused on her use of history, her narrative control, her sophisticated philosophical background, and her place as a woman writer.

BIBLIOGRAPHIES & CATALOGUE

First Printings of American Authors, Vol 2 (Detroit:

Bruccoli Clark/Gale, 1978), 175-185. Primary.

Kelly, William W. *EG: A Bibliography*. Charlottesville: Bibliographical Society of the U of Virginia/U P Virginia, 1964. Primary & secondary.

MacDonald, Edgar E & Tonette Bond Inge. *EG: A Reference Guide*. Boston: Hall, 1986. Secondary.

Schmidt, Jan Zlotnik. "EG: An Annotated Checklist, 1973-Present." *EGN*, 9 (Oct 1978), 1-14. Primary & secondary.

Tutwiler, Carrington C, Jr. *EG's Library*. Charlottesville: Bibliographical Society of the U of Virginia, 1967.

BOOKS

The Descendant (Anon). NY: Harper, 1897. Novel.

Phases of an Inferior Planet. NY & London: Harper, 1898. Novel.

The Voice of the People. NY: Doubleday, Page, 1900. Novel.

The Battle-Ground. NY: Doubleday, Page, 1902. Novel.

The Freeman and Other Poems. NY: Doubleday, Page, 1902.

The Deliverance. NY: Doubleday, Page, 1904. Novel.

The Wheel of Life. NY: Doubleday, Page, 1906.
Novel.

The Ancient Law. NY: Doubleday, Page, 1908.
Novel.

The Romance of a Plain Man. NY: Macmillan,
1909. Novel.

The Miller of Old Church. Garden City, NY: Doubleday, Page, 1911. Novel.

Virginia. Garden City, NY: Doubleday, Page, 1913.
Novel.

Life and Gabriella: The Story of a Woman's Courage. Garden City, NY: Doubleday, Page,
1916. Novel.

The Builders. Garden City, NY: Doubleday, Page,
1919. Novel.

One Man in His Time. Garden City, NY & Toronto: Doubleday, Page, 1922. Novel.

The Shadowy Third and Other Stories. Garden
City, NY: Doubleday, Page, 1923; *Dare's Gift
and Other Stories.* London: Murray, 1924.

Barren Ground. Garden City, NY: Doubleday,
Page, 1925. Novel.

The Romantic Comedians. Garden City, NY: Doubleday, Page, 1926. Novel.

They Stooped to Folly. NY: Literary Guild, 1929;
Garden City, NY: Doubleday, Doran, 1929.
Novel.

The Sheltered Life. Garden City, NY: Doubleday,
Doran, 1932. Novel.

Vein of Iron. NY: Harcourt, Brace, 1935. Novel.

Of Ellen Glasgow: An Inscribed Portrait, with
Branch Cabell. NY: Maverick, 1938.

In This Our Life. NY: Harcourt, Brace, 1941.
Novel.

A Certain Measure. NY: Harcourt, Brace, 1943.
Essays.

The Woman Within. NY: Harcourt, Brace, 1954.
Autobiography.

Beyond Defeat: An Epilogue to an Era, ed with
intro by Luther Y Gore. Charlottesville: U P
Virginia, 1966. Novel.

*EG's Reasonable Doubts: A Collection of Her
Writings,* ed Julius Rowan Raper. Baton
Rouge: Louisiana State U P, 1988. Miscellany.

LETTERS

Letters of EG, ed with intro & commentary by
Blair Rouse. NY: Harcourt, Brace, 1958.

"Agent and Author: EG's Letters to Paul Revere
Reynolds" by James B Colvert. *SB,* 14 (1961),
177-196.

Five Letters From EG Concerning Censorship...,
intro by Louis D Rubin, Jr. Richmond, Va:
Friends of the Richmond Public Library,
1962.

"EG's *Virginia:* Preliminary Notes" by Oliver
Steele. *SB,* 27 (1974), 265-289.

EDITIONS & COLLECTION

The Old Dominion Edition of the Works of EG, 8
vols, rev with new prefaces by EG. Garden
City, NY: Doubleday, Doran, 1929-1933.

The Virginia Edition of the Works of EG, 12 vols,
new prefaces by EG. NY: Scribners, 1938.

The Collected Stories of EG, ed with intro by Richard K Meeker. Baton Rouge: Louisiana State
U P, 1963.

MANUSCRIPTS & ARCHIVES

U of Virginia Library.

BIOGRAPHIES

Books

Godbold, E Stanly, Jr. *EG and the Woman Within.*
Baton Rouge: Louisiana State U P, 1972.

Parent, Monique. *EG, Romancière.* Paris: Nizet,
1962.

Book Sections & Articles

de Graffenried, Thomas P. *The de Graffenried Family Scrap Book* (Charlottesville: U P Virginia,
1958), 206-221, 258, 265.

Duke, Maurice. "Cabell's and G's Richmond: The
Intellectual Background of the City." *MissQ,*
27 (Fall 1974), 375-391.

Kellner, Bruce. "EG and Gertrude Stein." *EGN,* 2
(Mar 1975), 13-16.

MacDonald, Edgar E. "The G-Cabell Entente." *AL,*
41 (Mar 1969), 76-91.

MacDonald. "EG: An Essay in Bibliography."
RALS, 2 (Autumn 1972), 131-156. Rev as
"EG." *American Women Writers: Bibliographical Essays,* ed Maurice Duke, Jackson R
Bryer & Thomas Inge (Westport, Conn:
Greenwood, 1983).

MacDonald. "Biographical Notes on EG." *RALS,* 3
(Autumn 1973), 249-253. Rev as "An Essay
in Bibliography," Inge.

MacDonald. "G, Cabell, and Richmond." *MissQ,*
27 (Fall 1974), 393-413. Rpt Inge.

MacDonald. "The Ambivalent Heart: Literary Revival in Richmond." *The History of Southern
Literature,* ed Louis D Rubin, Jr (Baton
Rouge: Louisiana State U P, 1985), 264-278.

Raper, Julius Rowan. "The Man EG Could Respect." *EGN,* 2 (Mar 1975), 4-8. Rev Raper
(1971).

Scura, Dorothy. "G and the Southern Renaissance:
The Conference at Charlottesville." *MissQ,*
27 (Fall 1974), 415-434. Rpt Inge.

Steele, Oliver L, Jr. "Gertrude Stein and EG: Memoir of a Meeting." *AL,* 33 (Mar 1961), 76-77.

CRITICAL STUDIES

Books

Allsup, Judith Louise. "Feminism in the Novels of

EG." Dissertation: Southern Illinois U, 1974.

Ekman, Barbro. *The End of a Legend: EG's History of Southern Women*. Uppsala, Sweden: Studia Anglistica Upsaliensia, 1979.

Lebedun, Frances Jean. "Mature Artistry: Textual Variants in the Collected Novels of EG." Dissertation: U Missouri, Columbia, 1978.

Matthews, Pamela R. " 'Two Women Blended': EG and Her Fictions." Dissertation: Duke U, 1988.

McDowell, Frederick P W. *EG and the Ironic Art of Fiction*. Madison: U Wisconsin P, 1960.

Raper, Julius Rowan. *Without Shelter: The Early Career of EG*. Baton Rouge: Louisiana State U P, 1971.

Raper. *From the Sunken Garden: The Fiction of EG, 1916-1945*. Baton Rouge: Louisiana State U P, 1980.

Richards, Marion K. *EG's Development as a Novelist*. The Hague: Mouton, 1971.

Rouse, Blair. *EG*. NY: Twayne, 1962.

Santas, Joan Foster. *EG's American Dream*. Charlottesville: U P Virginia, 1965.

Thiébaux, Marcelle. *EG*. NY: Ungar, 1982.

Wagner, Linda W. *EG: Beyond Convention*. Austin: U Texas P, 1982.

Collection of Essays

Inge, M Thomas, ed. *EG: Centennial Essays*. Charlottesville: U P Virginia, 1976.

Special Journals

Ellen Glasgow Newsletter (semiannually, 1974-   ). Includes checklists.

MissQ, 31 (Winter 1977-1978). Special section, "The Apprenticeship of EG," 3-56.

MissQ, 32 (Fall 1979). Special section, "*Barren Ground*: EG's Critical Arrival," 549-609.

Book Sections & Articles

Anderson, Mary Castiglie. "Cultural Archetype and the Female Hero: Nature and Will in EG's *Barren Ground*." *MFS*, 28 (Autumn 1982), 383-393.

Atteberry, Phillip D. "EG and the Sentimental Novel of Virginia." *SoQ*, 23 (Summer 1985), 5-14.

Bunselmeyer, J E. "EG's 'Flexible' Style." *CentR*, 28 (Spring 1984), 112-128.

Caldwell, Ellen M. "EG and the Southern Agrarians." *AL*, 56 (May 1984), 203-213.

Frazee, Monique Parent. "EG as Feminist." Inge, 167-187.

Geismar, Maxwell. "EG: The Armor of the Legend." *Rebels and Ancestors* (Boston: Houghton Mifflin, 1953), 217-283.

Gore, Luther Y, ed. " 'Literary Realism or Nominalism' by EG: An Unpublished Essay." *AL*, 34 (Mar 1962), 72-79.

Holland, Robert. "Miss G's 'Prufrock.' " *AQ*, 9 (Winter 1957), 435-440.

Holman, C Hugh. "April in Queenborough: EG's Comedies of Manners." *SR*, 82 (Spring 1974), 263-283. Rpt as "The Comedies of Manners," Inge. Rpt *Windows on the World: Essays on American Social Fiction* by Holman (Knoxville: U Tennessee P, 1979).

Holman. "*Barren Ground* and the Shape of History." *SAQ*, 77 (Spring 1978), 137-145. Rpt *Windows on the World: Essays on American Social Fiction* by Holman (Knoxville: U Tennessee P, 1979).

Jessup, Josephine Lurie. "EG: Evangel Militant." *The Faith of Our Feminists: A Study in the Novels of Edith Wharton, EG, Willa Cather* (NY: Smith, 1950), 34-53, passim.

Jones, Anne Goodwyn. "EG: The Perfect Mould." *Tomorrow Is Another Day: The Woman Writer in the South, 1859-1936* (Baton Rouge: Louisiana State U P, 1981), 225-270.

Kazin, Alfred. "Elegy and Satire: Willa Cather and EG." *On Native Grounds* (NY: Reynal & Hitchcock, 1942), 247-264.

McDowell, Frederick P W. "EG and the Art of the Novel." *PQ*, 30 (Jul 1951), 328-347.

Murr, Judy Smith. "History in *Barren Ground* and in *Vein of Iron*: Theory, Structure and Symbol." *SLJ*, 8 (Fall 1975), 39-54.

Pannill, Linda. "EG's Allegory of Love and Death: 'The Greatest Good.' " *RALS*, 14 (Spring-Autumn 1984), 161-166.

Raper, Julius Rowan. "Invisible Things: The Short Stories of EG." *SLJ*, 9 (Spring 1977), 66-90. Rev Raper (1980).

Raper. "Ambivalence Toward Authority: A Look at G's Library, 1890-1906." *MissQ*, 31 (Winter 1977-1978), 5-16.

Rubin, Louis D, Jr. "Miss Ellen." *No Place on Earth: EG, James Branch Cabell and Richmond-in-Virginia* (Austin: U Texas P, 1959), 3-49.

Rubin. "Two in Richmond: EG and James Branch Cabell." *South: Modern Southern Literature and Its Cultural Setting*, ed Rubin & Robert D Jacobs (Garden City, NY: Doubleday, 1961), 115-141.

Schmidt, Jan Zlotnik. "EG's Heroic Legends: A Study of *Life and Gabriella, Barren Ground, and Vein of Iron*." *TSL*, 26 (1981), 117-141.

Seidel, Kathryn Lee. "The Comic Male: Satire in EG's Queenborough Trilogy." *SoQ*, 23 (Summer 1985), 15-26.

Steele, Oliver L. "EG, Social History, and the 'Virginia Edition.' " *MFS*, 7 (Summer 1961), 173-176.

Wagner, Linda W. "*Barren Ground*'s Vein of Iron: Dorinda Oakley and Some Concepts of the Heroine in 1925." *MissQ*, 32 (Fall 1979), 553-564. Rpt *American Modern* by Wagner (Port Washington, NY: Kennikat, 1980), 56-66.

Wagner. "EG: Daughters as Justified." *The Lost Tradition,* ed Cathy N Davidson & E M Broner (NY: Ungar, 1980), 139-146.

Walker, Nancy. "Women Writers and Literary Naturalism: The Case of EG." *ALR,* 18 (Spring-Autumn 1985), 133-146.

Wittenberg, Judith B. "The Critical Fortunes of *Barren Ground*." *MissQ,* 32 (Fall 1979), 591-609.

Pamela R. Matthews

SUSAN GLASPELL

Davenport, Iowa, 1 Jul 1876?-Provincetown, Mass, 27 Jul 1948

Susan Glaspell wrote novels, plays, a biography, and many short stories, essays, and articles. Her novels, which were set in the Midwest, present idealistic women characters struggling with changes in American society. During her lifetime, Glaspell's work attracted critical attention, and some of her books were best-sellers. In 1913 she married George Cram Cook, and together they founded the Provincetown Players, an experimental theater group. In 1931 she won a Pulitzer Prize for her play *Alison's House.* The popularity of her writing declined during the 1930s, but in recent years critics have focused on feminist themes in Glaspell's work.

BIBLIOGRAPHIES

Bach, Gerhard. "SG (1876-1948): A Bibliography of Dramatic Criticism." *GrLR,* 3 (Winter 1977), 1-34. Secondary.

Noe, Marcia. "A SG Checklist." *BI,* 27 (Nov 1977), 14-20. Primary.

BOOKS

The Glory of the Conquered: The Story of a Great Love. NY: Stokes, 1909. Novel.

The Visioning: A Novel. NY: Stokes, 1911.

Lifted Masks: Stories. NY: Stokes, 1912.

Fidelity: A Novel. Boston: Small, Maynard, 1915.

Trifles. NY: Shay/Washington Square Players, 1916. Play.

Suppressed Desires, with George Cram Cook. NY: Shay, 1917. Play.

The People and Close the Book: Two One-Act Plays. NY: Shay, 1918.

Plays. Boston: Small, Maynard, 1920.

Inheritors: A Play in Three Acts. Boston: Small, Maynard, 1921.

The Verge: A Play in Three Acts. Boston: Small, Maynard, 1922.

Bernice: A Play in Three Acts. London: Benn, 1924.

Tickless Time: A Comedy in One Act, with Cook. Boston: Baker, 1925.

The Road to the Temple. London: Benn, 1926; NY: Stokes, 1927. Biography.

The Comic Artist: A Play in Three Acts, with Norman Häghejm Matson. NY: Stokes, 1927.

A Jury of Her Peers. London: Benn, 1927. Story.

Brook Evans. NY: Stokes, 1928. Novel.

Fugitive's Return. NY: Stokes, 1929. Novel.

Alison's House: A Play in Three Acts. NY & c: French, 1930. Play.

Ambrose Holt and Family. NY: Stokes, 1931. Novel.

The Morning Is Near Us: A Novel. NY: Stokes, 1940.

Cherished and Shared of Old. NY: Messner, 1940. Children's story.

Norma Ashe: A Novel. Philadelphia & NY: Lippincott, 1942.

Judd Rankin's Daughter. Philadelphia & NY: Lippincott, 1945; *Prodigal Giver.* London: Gollancz, 1946. Novel.

COLLECTION

Plays by SG, ed with intro by C W E Bigsby; notes by Christine Dymkowski. Cambridge & c: Cambridge U P, 1987.

MANUSCRIPTS & ARCHIVES

The New York Public Library.

BIOGRAPHIES

Book

Noe, Marcia. *SG: Voice From the Heartland.* Macomb: Western Illinois U P, 1983.

Book Sections

Dell, Floyd. *Homecoming: An Autobiography* (NY: Farrar & Rinehart, 1933), passim.

Deutsch, Helen & Stella Hanau. *The Provincetown: A Story of the Theatre* (NY: Farrar & Rinehart, 1931), passim.

CRITICAL STUDIES

Book

Waterman, Arthur E. *SG.* NY: Twayne, 1966.

Book Sections & Articles

Alkalay-Gut, Karen. " 'Jury of Her Peers': The Importance of Trifles." *SSF,* 21 (Winter 1984), 1-9.

Bach, Gerhard. "SG—Provincetown Playwright." *GrLR,* 4 (Winter 1978), 31-43.

Ben-Zvi, Linda. "SG and Eugene O'Neill." *EON,* 6 (Summer-Fall 1982), 21-29.

Ben-Zvi. "SG and Eugene O'Neill: The Imagery of Gender." *EON,* 10 (Spring 1986), 22-27.

Dymkowski, Christine. "On the Edge: The Plays of SG." *MD,* 31 (Mar 1988), 91-105.

Fetterley, Judith. "Reading About Reading: 'A Jury of Her Peers,' 'The Murders in the Rue Morgue,' and 'The Yellow Wallpaper.' " *Gender and Reading,* ed Elizabeth A Flynn & Patrocinio P Schweickart (Baltimore, Md: Johns Hopkins U P, 1986), 147-164.

Gubar, Susan & Anne Hedin. "A Jury of Our Peers: Teaching and Learning in the Indiana Women's Prison." *CE,* 43 (Dec 1981), 779-789.

Hedges, Elaine. "Small Things Reconsidered: SG's 'A Jury of Her Peers.' " *WS,* 12, no 1 (1986), 89-110.

Kolodny, Annette. "A Map for Rereading; or, Gender and the Interpretation of Literary Texts." *NLH,* 11 (Spring 1980), 451-467.

Larabee, Ann. "Death in Delphi: SG and the Companionate Marriage." *MARev,* 7, no 2 (1987), 93-106.

Noe, Marcia. "SG's Analysis of the Midwestern Character." *BI,* 27 (Nov 1977), 3-14.

Noe. "Region as Metaphor in the Plays of SG." *WIRS,* 4 (Spring 1981), 77-85.

Smith, Beverly A. "Women's Work—*Trifles?* The Skill and Insights of Playwright SG." *IJWS,* 5 (Mar-Apr 1982), 172-184.

Stein, Karen F. "The Women's World of G's *Trifles.*" *Women in American Theatre,* ed Helen Krich Chinoy & Linda Walsh Jenkins (NY: Theatre Communications Group, rev 1987), 253-256.

Sutherland, Cynthia. "American Women Playwrights as Mediators of the 'Woman Problem.' " *MD,* 21 (Sep 1978), 319-336.

Waterman, Arthur E. "SG (1882?-1948)." *ALR,* 4 (Spring 1971), 183-191.

Waterman. "SG's *The Verge*: An Experiment in Feminism." *GrLR,* 6 (Summer 1979), 17-23.

Lori J. Williams

ANNA KATHARINE GREEN

Brooklyn, NY, 11 Nov 1846-Buffalo, NY, 11 Apr 1935

Anna Katharine Green was one of the originators of the modern detective novel. Her best-seller *The Leavenworth Case* was the first detective novel written by an American woman. Setting her novels in America and using an American policeman as a main character were innovations in the genre. Her sharp detectives were also the first to reappear in subsequent novels. Ebeneezer Gryce, who solves the Leavenworth mystery, is perhaps the best known, but Green's Amelia Butterworth and Violet Strange—literature's first female sleuths—are impressive. Both characters manage to balance traditional feminine intuition with strong-willed, keen-minded detection. Although her work includes melodramatic flourishes, Green's strength lies in her carefully structured plots and her innovative characterization—both of which helped establish the popularity of detective fiction in America.

BIBLIOGRAPHIES

First Printings of American Authors, Vol 4 (Detroit: Bruccoli Clark/Gale, 1979), 203-209. Primary.

Giffuni, Cathy. "A Bibliography of AKG." *Clues,* 8 (Fall-Winter 1980), 113-133. Secondary.

BOOKS

The Leavenworth Case: A Lawyer's Story. NY: Putnam, 1878. Novel.

A Strange Disappearance. NY: Putnam, 1880. Novel.

The Sword of Damocles: A Story of New York Life. NY: Putnam, 1881. Novel.

The Defence of the Bride and Other Poems. NY & London: Putnam, 1882.

Hand and Ring. NY & London: Putnam, 1883. Novel.

X Y Z: A Detective Story. NY: Putnam, 1883. Novel.

The Mill Mystery. NY & London: Putnam, 1886. Novel.

7 to 12: A Detective Story. NY & London: Putnam, 1887. Novel.

Risifi's Daughter. NY & London: Putnam, 1887. Verse drama.

Behind Closed Doors. NY & London: Putnam, 1888. Novel.

The Forsaken Inn. NY: Bonner, 1890. Novel.

A Matter of Millions. NY: Bonner, 1890. Novel.

The Old Stone House and Other Stories. NY & London: Putnam, 1891.

Cynthia Wakeham's Money. NY & London: Putnam, 1892. Novel.

Marked "Personal." NY & London: Putnam, 1893. Novel.

Miss Hurd: An Enigma. NY & London: Putnam, 1894. Novel.

The Doctor, His Wife and the Clock. NY & London: Putnam, 1895. Novel.

Doctor Izard. NY & London: Putnam, 1895. Novel.

That Affair Next Door. NY & London: Putnam, 1897. Novel.

Lost Man's Lane. . . . NY & London: Putnam, 1898. Novel.

Agatha Webb. NY & London: Putnam, 1899. Novel.

The Circular Study. NY: McClure, Phillips, 1900. Novel.

A Difficult Problem, The Staircase at the Heart's Delight, and Other Stories. NY: Lupton, 1900.

One of My Sons. NY & London: Putnam, 1901. Novel.

Three Women and a Mystery. NY: Lovell, 1902. Stories.

The Filigree Ball. . . . Indianapolis: Bobbs-Merrill, 1903. Novel.

The House in the Mist. Indianapolis: Bobbs-Merrill, 1905. Novel & stories.

The Millionaire Baby. Indianapolis: Bobbs-Merrill, 1905. Novel.

The Amethyst Box. Indianapolis: Bobbs-Merrill, 1905. Novel.

The Woman in the Alcove. Indianapolis: Bobbs-Merrill, 1906. Novel.

The Chief Legatee. NY & London: Authors & Newspapers Association, 1906; *A Woman of Mystery.* London: Collier, 1909. Novel.

The Mayor's Wife. Indianapolis: Bobbs-Merrill, 1907. Novel.

The House of the Whispering Pines. NY & London: Putnam, 1910. Novel.

Three Thousand Dollars. Boston: Badger/Gorham, 1910. Novel.

Initials Only. NY: Dodd, Mead, 1911. Novel.

Masterpieces of Mystery. NY: Dodd, Mead, 1913. Repub as *Room Number 3 and Other Detective Stories.* NY: Dodd, Mead, 1919.

Dark Hollow. NY: Dodd, Mead, 1914. Novel.

The Golden Slipper and Other Problems for Violet Strange. NY & London: Putnam, 1915. Stories.

To the Minute, Scarlet and Black: Two Tales of Life's Perplexities. NY & London: Putnam, 1916. Stories.

The Mystery of the Hasty Arrow. NY: Dodd, Mead, 1917. Novel.

The Step on the Stair. NY: Dodd, Mead, 1923. Novel.

MANUSCRIPTS & ARCHIVES

The Harry Ransom Humanities Research Center, University of Texas, Austin.

CRITICAL STUDIES

Book Sections & Articles

Hayne, Barrie. "AKG." *10 Women of Mystery,* ed Earl F Bargainnier (Bowling Green, Ohio: Bowling Green State U Popular P, 1981), 150-178.

LaCour, Tage. "Founding Mothers." *Murderess Ink,* ed Dilys Winn (NY: Workman, 1979), 43-46.

LaCour & Harald Mogensen. "Lady Detectives." *The Murder Book* (NY: McGraw-Hill, 1971), 72-73.

Maida, Patricia D. "AKG, 1846-1935." *Legacy,* 3 (Fall 1986), 53-59.

Overton, Grant. "AKG." *The Women Who Make Our Novels* (NY: Dodd, Mead, rev 1928), 167- 173.

Welter, Barbara. "Murder Most Genteel: The Mystery Novels of AKG." *Dimity Convictions: The American Woman in the Nineteenth Century* (Athens: Ohio U P, 1976), 130-144.

Woodward, Kathleen. "AKG." *Bookman,* 70 (Oct 1929), 168-170.

Laura Plummer

ZANE GREY

Zanesville, Ohio, 31 Jan 1872-Los Angeles, Calif, 23 Oct 1939

During his productive years and for a couple of decades after his death, Zane Grey was the most popular Western novelist in American literary history. With the advent of Western fiction containing more accurate historical detail, the emergence of Louis L'Amour (the best-selling Western writer of all time), and the appearance of the so-called "adult" Western, Grey sales began to taper off. But his loyal readers number in the tens of thousands today. Typically, his cowboy heroes are arrow-straight, tough, and chivalrous; his heroines, often naive Easterners, are improved by contact with Grey's men and other virtuous western influences; his villains are relentlessly evil; and the varied landscape of the West is colorfully depicted. In fiction set in the South Seas, Grey revealed a Melvillean love of the ocean, respect for the natives (comparable to his earlier championing of Native American rights), and distrust of missionaries. His works are weakened by melodrama, verbosity, and repetition but perhaps actually strengthened by unresolved tensions between idealism and Darwinism.

BIBLIOGRAPHIES

First Printings of American Authors, Vol 5, ed Philip B Eppard (Detroit: Bruccoli Clark/Gale, 1987), 121-140. Primary.

Meyers, Edward A. *A Bibliographical Check List of the Writings of ZG.* Collinsville, Conn: Country Lane, 1983.

Scott, Kenneth W. *ZG: Born to the West: A Reference Guide.* Boston: Hall, 1979. Secondary.

BOOKS

Betty Zane. NY: Francis, 1903. Novel.

The Spirit of the Border. NY: Burt, 1906. Novel.

Tarpon, the Silver King. NY: New York & Cuba Mail Steamship Co, 1906. Nonfiction.

The Last of the Plainsmen. NY: Outing, 1908. Autobiography.

The Last Trail. NY: Burt, 1909. Novel.

The Short-Stop. Chicago: McClurg, 1909. Children's novel.

Nassau, Cuba, Yucatan, Mexico: A Personal Note of Appreciation of These Nearby Foreign Lands. NY: New York & Cuba Mail S S Co, 1909. Travel.

The Heritage of the Desert. NY & London: Harper, 1910. Abridged as *Desert Heritage.* London: World, 1965. Novel.

The Young Forester. NY & London: Harper, 1910. Children's novel.

The Young Pitcher. NY & London: Harper, 1911. Children's novel.

The Young Lion Hunter. NY & London: Harper, 1911. Children's novel.

Riders of the Purple Sage. NY & London: Harper, 1912. Abridged as *Riders of Vengeance.* London: World, 1965. Novel.

Ken Ward in the Jungle. NY & London: Harper, 1912. Children's novel.

Desert Gold. NY & London: Harper, 1913. Abridged as *Prairie Gold.* London: World, 1965. Novel.

The Light of Western Stars. NY & London: Harper, 1914. Novel.

The Rustlers of Pecos County. NY: Munsey, 1914. Repub in *The Rustlers of Pecos County & Silvermane,* ed Loren Grey. NY: Belmont Tower, 1979. Stories.

The Lone Star Ranger. NY & London: Harper, 1915. Novel.

The Rainbow Trail. NY & London: Harper, 1915. Novel.

The Border Legion. NY & London: Harper, 1916. Novel.

Wildfire. NY & London: Harper, 1917. Novel.

The U.P. Trail. NY & London: Harper, 1918; *The Roaring U.P. Trail.* London: Hodder & Stoughton, 1918. Novel.

The Desert of Wheat. NY & London: Harper, 1919. Novel.

Tales of Fishes. NY & London: Harper, 1919. Excerpted in *Great Game Fishing at Catalina.* Avalon, Calif: Santa Catalina Island, 1919. Nonfiction.

The Man of the Forest. NY & London: Harper, 1920. Novel.

The Redheaded Outfield and Other Baseball Stories. NY: Grosset & Dunlap, 1920. Children's stories.

The Mysterious Rider. NY & London: Harper, 1921. Novel.

To the Last Man. NY & London: Harper, 1922. Novel.

The Day of the Beast. NY & London: Harper, 1922. Novel.

Tales of Lonely Trails. NY & London: Harper, 1922. Autobiography.

Wanderer of the Wasteland. NY & London: Harper, 1923. Novel.

Tappan's Burro and Other Stories. NY & London: Harper, 1923. Children's stories.

The Call of the Canyon. NY & London: Harper, 1924. Novel.

Roping Lions in the Grand Canyon. NY & London: Harper, 1924. Children's novel.

Tales of Southern Rivers. NY & London: Harper, 1924. Nonfiction.

Tales of Fishing Virgin Seas. NY & London: Harper, 1925. Nonfiction.

The Thundering Herd. NY & London: Harper, 1925. Novel.

The Vanishing American. NY & London: Harper, 1925; *The Vanishing Indian.* London: Hodder & Stoughton, 1926. Novel.

Under the Tonto Rim. NY & London: Harper, 1926. Novel.

Tales of the Angler's Eldorado: New Zealand. NY & London: Harper, 1926. Nonfiction.

Forlorn River. NY & London: Harper, 1927. Novel.

Tales of Swordfish and Tuna. NY & London: Harper, 1927. Nonfiction.

"Nevada." NY & London: Harper, 1928. Novel.

Wild Horse Mesa. NY & London: Harper, 1928. Novel.

Don: The Story of a Lion Dog. NY & London: Harper, 1928. Children's novella.

Tales of Fresh-Water Fishing. NY & London: Harper, 1928. Nonfiction.

Fighting Caravans. NY & London: Harper, 1929. Novel.

The Wolf-Tracker. NY & London: Harper, 1930. Children's novel.

The Shepherd of Guadaloupe. NY & London: Harper, 1930. Novel.

Sunset Pass. NY & London: Harper, 1931. Novel.

Tales of Tahitian Waters. NY & London: Harper, 1931. Nonfiction.

ZG's Book of Camps and Trails. NY & London: Harper, 1931. Essays.

Arizona Ames. NY & London: Harper, 1932. Novel.

Robbers' Roost. NY & London: Harper, 1932. Abridged as *Thieves' Canyon.* London: World, 1965. Novel.

The Drift Fence. NY & London: Harper, 1932. Novel.

The Hash Knife Outfit. NY & London: Harper, 1933. Novel.

Code of the West. NY & London: Harper, 1934. Novel.

Thunder Mountain. NY & London: Harper, 1935. Novel.

The Trail Driver. NY & London: Harper, 1936. Novel.

The Lost Wagon Train. NY & London: Harper, 1936. Novel.

An American Angler in Australia. NY & London: Harper, 1937. Nonfiction.

West of the Pecos. NY & London: Harper, 1937. Novel.

Raiders of Spanish Peaks. NY & London: Harper, 1938. Novel.

Western Union. NY & London: Harper, 1939. Novel.

Knights of the Range. NY & London: Harper, 1939. Novel.

30,000 on the Hoof. NY & London: Harper, 1940. Novel.

Twin Sombreros. NY & London: Harper, 1941. Novel.

Majesty's Rancho. NY & London: Harper, 1942. Novel.

Stairs of Sand. NY & London: Harper, 1943. Novel.

Wilderness Trek. NY & London: Harper, 1944. Novel.

Shadow on the Trail. NY & London: Harper, 1946. Novel.

Valley of Wild Horses. NY & London: Harper, 1947. Novel.

Rogue River Feud. NY & London: Harper, 1948. Novel.

The Deer Stalker. NY: Harper, 1949. Novel.

The Maverick Queen. NY: Harper, 1950. Novel.

The Dude Ranger. NY: Harper, 1951. Novel.

Captives of the Desert. NY: Harper, 1952. Novel.

Wyoming. NY: Harper, 1953. Novel.

Lost Pueblo. NY: Harper, 1954. Novel.

Black Mesa. NY: Harper, 1955. Novel.

Stranger From the Tonto. NY: Harper, 1956. Novel.

The Fugitive Trail. NY: Harper, 1957. Novel.

The Arizona Clan. NY: Harper, 1958. Novel.

Horse Heaven Hill. NY: Harper, 1959. Novel.

The Ranger and Other Stories. NY: Harper, 1960. Children's stories.

Blue Feather and Other Stories. NY: Harper, 1961. Children's stories.

Boulder Dam. NY & c: Harper & Row, 1963. Novel.

Adventures of Finspot, ed G M Farley & Betty Zane Grosso. San Bernardino, Calif: D-J Books, 1974.

ZG's Savage Kingdom, ed Loren Grey. NY: Belmont Tower, 1975. Stories.

Shark: The Killer of the Deep. NY: Belmont Tower, 1976. Repub in *Shark! ZG's Tales of Man-Eating Sharks,* ed Loren Grey. NY: Belmont Tower, 1976. Nonfiction.

The Trail of the Jaguar, ed Farley. Williamsport, Md: ZG Collector, 1976. Novel.

The Reef Girl. NY & c: Harper & Row, 1977. Novel.

The Tenderfoot. NY: Belmont Tower, 1977. Unfinished novella.

The Westerner, ed Loren Grey. NY: Belmont Tower, 1977. Novel.

The Buffalo Hunter, ed Loren Grey. NY: Belmont Tower, 1978. Biography.

Tales From a Fisherman's Log. London & c: Hodder & Stoughton, 1978. Nonfiction.

The Camp Robber and Other Stories, ed Loren Grey. Roslyn, NY: Black, 1979.

The Lord of Lackawaxen Creek. Salisbury, Conn: Lime Rock, 1981. Novel.

Amber's Mirage and Other Stories. NY: Pocket Books, 1983.

The Secret of Quaking Asp Cabin. NY: Pocket Books, 1983. Novella.

The Undiscovered ZG Fishing Stories, ed George Reiger; foreword by James A Michener. Piscataway, NJ: Winchester, 1983.

OTHER

Last of the Great Scouts (Buffalo Bill), with Helen Cody Wetmore. NY: Grosset & Dunlap, 1918. Foreword & final chapter by ZG.

ZG's King of the Royal Mounted. Racine, Wis: Whitman, 1936. Big Little Book written by Romer Grey from a story line by ZG.

ZG's King of the Royal Mounted and the Northern Treasure. Racine, Wis: Whitman, 1937. Big Little Book written by Romer Grey from a story line by ZG.

ZG's Tex Thorne Comes Out of the West. Racine, Wis: Whitman, 1937. Big Little Book written by Romer Grey from a story line by ZG.

ZG's King of the Royal Mounted in Arctic Law. Racine, Wis: Whitman, 1937. Big Little Book written by Romer Grey from a story line by ZG.

ZG's King of the Royal Mounted Gets His Man. Racine, Wis: Whitman, 1938. Big Little Book written by Romer Grey from a story line by ZG.

ZG's King of the Royal Mounted in the Far North. Racine, Wis: Whitman, 1938. Big Little Book written by Romer Grey from a story line by ZG.

ZG's King of the Royal Mounted Policing the Frozen North. Racine, Wis: Whitman, 1938. Big Little Book written by Romer Grey from a story line by ZG.

ZG's King of the Royal Mounted and the Long Arm of the Law. Racine, Wis: Whitman, 1938. Big Little Book written by Romer Grey from a story line by ZG.

ZG's King of the Royal Mounted and the Great Jewel Mystery. Racine, Wis: Whitman, 1939. Big Little Book written by Romer Grey from a story line by ZG.

King of the Royal Mounted and the Ghost Guns of Roaring River. Racine, Wis: Whitman, 1946. Based on a comic strip written by Romer Grey from a story line by ZG.

COLLECTIONS

The ZG Ominbus, ed Ruth G Gentles. NY & London: Harper, 1943. Repub as *ZG Roundup.* NY: Grosset & Dunlap, 1943.

ZG's Adventures in Fishing, ed Ed Zern. NY: Harper, 1952.

ZG: Outdoorsman: ZG's Best Hunting and Fishing Tales, ed George Reiger. Englewood Cliffs, NJ: Prentice-Hall, 1972.

ZG's Greatest Animal Stories, ed Loren Grey. NY: Belmont Tower, 1975.

ZG's Greatest Western Stories, ed Loren Grey. NY: Belmont Tower, 1975.

ZG's Greatest Indian Stories, ed Loren Grey. NY: Belmont Tower, 1975.

Round-Up, ed Loren Grey. NY: Manor Books, 1976.

Yaqui and Other Great Indian Stories, ed Loren Grey. NY: Belmont Tower, 1976.

The Big Land, ed Loren Grey. NY: Belmont Tower, 1976.

Five Complete Novels: Riders of the Purple Sage, To the Last Man, The Thundering Herd, The Hash Knife Outfit, West of the Pecos. NY: Avenel, 1980.

The Wolf Tracker and Other Animal Tales, foreword by Loren Grey. Santa Barbara, Calif: Santa Barbara, 1984.

MANUSCRIPTS & ARCHIVES

The major collections are at the Library of Congress; the New York Public Library; the Harry Ransom Humanities Research Center, U of Texas, Austin; & Wagner C Library.

BIOGRAPHY

Books

Farley, G M. *ZG: A Documented Portrait.* Tuscaloosa, Ala: Portals, 1986.

Gay, Carol. *ZG: Story Teller.* Columbus: State Library of Ohio, 1979.

Grey, Loren. *ZG, a Photographic Odyssey.* Dallas, Tex: Taylor, 1985.

Gruber, Frank. *ZG: A Biography.* NY: World, 1970.

CRITICAL STUDIES

Books

Jackson, Carlton. *ZG.* NY: Twayne, 1973.

Kant, Candace C. *ZG's Arizona*. Flagstaff, Ariz: Northland, 1984.

Karr, Jean. *ZG: Man of the West*. NY: Greenberg, 1949.

Ronald, Ann. *ZG*. Boise, Idaho: Boise State U, 1975.

Schneider, Norris F. *ZG, "The Man Whose Books Made the West Famous."* Zanesville, Ohio: Schneider, 1967.

Topping, Gary. "ZG's West: Essays in Intellectual History and Criticism." Dissertation: U Utah, 1977.

Wheeler, Joseph Lawrence. "ZG's Impact on American Life and Letters: A Study in the Popular Novel." Dissertation: George Peabody C for Teachers, 1975.

Collection of Essays
ZG: The Man and His Work. NY & London: Harper, 1928.

Special Journal
The Zane Grey Collector (quarterly, 1968-1976).

Book Sections & Articles
Ball, Lee, Jr. "ZG's Novels as History: A Review Essay." *RRVHR*, 1 (Winter 1974), 421-428.

Bauer, Erwin A. "ZG: Ohio's Writer of the Purple Sage." *Blue Feather and Other Stories*, 229-234.

Bloodworth, William. "ZG's Western Eroticism." *SDR*, 23 (Autumn 1985), 5-14.

Bold, Christine. *Selling the Wild West: Popular Western Fiction* (Bloomington: Indiana U P, 1987), 79-91.

Boyle, Robert H. "The Man Who Lived Two Lives in One." *SportsIllus*, 28 (29 Apr 1968), 68-70, 75-76, 79-80, 82.

Branch, Douglas. *The Cowboy and His Interpreters* (NY: Appleton, 1926), passim.

Cawelti, John G. *The Six-Gun Mystique* (Bowling Green, Ohio: Bowling Green U Popular P, 1971), passim.

Cawelti. *Adventure, Mystery, and Romance: Formula Stories as Art and Popular Culture* (Chicago: U Chicago P, 1976), passim.

Easton, Robert & MacKenzie Brown. *Lord of Beasts: The Life of Buffalo Jones* (Tucson: U Arizona P, 1961), passim.

Estleman, Loren D. "*Riders of the Purple Sage* (1912)." *The Wister Trace: Classic Novels of the American Frontier* (Ottawa, Ill: Jameson, 1987), 31-34.

Etulain, Richard W. "A Dedication to the Memory of ZG, 1872-1939." *Ar&W*, 12 (Autumn 1970), 217-220.

Folsom, James K. *The American Western Novel* (New Haven, Conn: College & University P, 1966), passim.

Frantz, Joe B & Julian E Choate, Jr. *The American Cowboy: The Myth & the Reality* (Norman: U Oklahoma P, 1955), passim.

Goble, Danney. " 'The Days That Were No More': A Look at ZG's West." *JArH*, 14 (Spring 1973), 62-75.

Hamilton, Cynthia. "ZG." *Western and Hard-Boiled Detective Fiction in America* (Iowa City: U Iowa P, 1987), 71-93.

Hart, James D. *The Popular Book* (NY: Oxford U P, 1950), passim.

Horn, Maurice. *Comics of the American West* (NY: Winchester, 1977), 31-35.

Kimball, Arthur. "Silent Walls: 'Nature' in G's *The Vanishing American*." *SDR*, 26 (Spring 1988), 78-90.

Loomis, Edward. "History and Fiction: *To the Last Man*." *SDR*, 23 (Autumn 1985), 28-32.

Nesbitt, John D. "Uncertain Sex in the Sagebrush." *SDR*, 23 (Autumn 1985), 15-27.

Oehlschlaeger, Fritz H. "Civilization as Emasculation: The Threatening Role of Women in the Frontier Fiction of Harold Bell Wright and ZG." *MQ*, 22 (Summer 1981), 346-360.

Olafson, Robert B. "ZG's Washington: *The Desert of Wheat* (1919)." *PacNWF*, 9 (Winter 1984), 26-33.

Olsen, Theodore Victor. "ZG. . . ." *Roundup*, 14 (Sep 1966), 4, 6, 20; 14 (Oct 1966), 4, 6; 14 (Nov 1966), 4, 6; 14 (Dec 1966), 8, 10, 19.

Patrick, Arnold. "Getting into Six Figures: ZG." *Bookman*, 60 (Dec 1924), 424-429.

Peebles, Samuel. "Notes on ZG." *ZGCollector*, 5, no 3 (1973), 11.

Powell, Lawrence Clark. "Books Determine." *WilsonLB*, 30 (Sep 1955), 62-65.

Powell. "Southwest Classics Reread: Writer of the Purple Page." *Westways*, 64 (Aug 1972), 50-55, 69.

Rascoe, Burton. "Opie Read and ZG." *SatRL*, 21 (11 Nov 1939), 8.

Richeson, Cena Golder. "Wild Horses and Purple Sage: Falling in Love With ZG." *Roundup*, 37 (Apr 1988), 6-7, 10.

Scott, K W. "*The Heritage of the Desert*: ZG Discovers the West." *MarkhamR*, 2 (Feb 1970), 10-14.

Stott, Graham St John. "ZG and James Simpson Emmett." *BYUS*, 18 (Summer 1978), 491-503.

Taylor, J Golden. "The Western Short Story." *SDR*, 2 (Autumn 1964), 37-55.

Topping, Gary. "ZG's West." *JPC*, 7 (Winter 1973), 681-689. Rpt *The Popular Western*, ed Richard W Etulain & Michael T Marsden

(Bowling Green, Ohio: Bowling Green U Popular P, 1974).

Topping. "The Pastoral Ideal in Popular American Literature: ZG and Edgar Rice Burroughs." *Rendezvous*, 12 (Fall 1977), 11-25.

Topping. "ZG: A Literary Reassessment." *WAL*, 13 (Spring 1978), 51-64.

Topping. "ZG in Zion: An Examination of His Supposed Anti-Mormonism." *BYUS*, 18 (Summer 1978), 483-490.

Whipple, T K. "American Sagas." *Study Out the Land* (Berkeley: U California P, 1943), 19-29.

Whitford, Kathryn. "Shades of Grey! The Border and the Buffalo." *ZGCollector*, 7, no 2 (1976), 8-10.

Wilson, Daniel J. "Nature in Western Popular Literature From the Dime Novel to ZG." *NDQ*, 44 (Spring 1976), 41-50.

Wilson, Maggie. "The Wonderful World of ZG." *Arizona Highways*, 60 (Aug 1984), 30-37.

Robert L. Gale

SUTTON ELBERT GRIGGS

Chatfield, Tex, 1872-Houston, Tex, 1930

The novels and political tracts of Sutton Elbert Griggs espouse black nationalism, black pride, and black militancy. One of the most neglected African-American writers of the period between the Spanish-American War and World War I, Griggs was the author of five novels and many tracts. *Imperium in Imperio*, his best-known novel, is a propagandistic work that describes a black government within the United States and portrays a determined race of black people. With his melodramatic style, fantastic episodes, and graphic scenes of brutality, Griggs sought to awaken the general American public to atrocities against blacks and to provide his own people a guide to a better way of life in America.

BOOKS

Imperium in Imperio. Cincinnati, Ohio: Editor, 1899. Novel.

Overshadowed. Nashville, Tenn: Orion, 1901. Novel.

Unfettered. Nashville, Tenn: Orion, 1902. Novel.

The Hindered Hand; or, The Reign of the Repressionist. Nashville, Tenn: Orion, 1905. Novel.

The One Great Question. . . . Nashville, Tenn: Orion, 1907. Nonfiction.

Pointing the Way. Nashville, Tenn: Orion, 1908. Novel.

Needs of the South. Nashville, Tenn: Orion, 1909. Nonfiction.

The Race Question in a New Light. Nashville, Tenn: Orion, 1909. Augmented as *Wisdom's Call*, 1911. Nonfiction.

The Story of My Struggles. Memphis, Tenn: National Public Welfare League, 1914. Nonfiction.

How to Rise. Memphis, Tenn: National Public Welfare League, 1915. Nonfiction.

Life's Demands; or, According to Law. Memphis, Tenn: National Public Welfare League, 1916. Nonfiction.

The Reconstruction of a Race. Memphis, Tenn: National Public Welfare League, 1917. Nonfiction.

Light on Racial Issues. Memphis, Tenn: National Public Welfare League, 1921. Nonfiction.

Science of Collective Efficiency. Memphis, Tenn: National Public Welfare League, 1921. Augmented as *Guide to Racial Greatness; or, The Science of Collective Efficiency*, 1923. Nonfiction.

The Negro's Next Step. Memphis, Tenn: National

Public Welfare League, 1923. Nonfiction.

Kingdom Builders' Manual: Companion Book to Guide to Racial Greatness. Memphis, Tenn: National Public Welfare League, 1924. Nonfiction.

Paths of Progress; or, Co-operation Between the Races. Memphis, Tenn: National Public Welfare League, 1925. Nonfiction.

Triumph of the Simple Virtues; or, The Life Story of John L. Webb. Hot Springs, Ark: Messenger, 1926. Nonfiction.

The Winning Policy. Memphis, Tenn: National Public Welfare League, 1927. Nonfiction.

CRITICAL STUDIES

Book Sections & Articles

Bone, Robert. *The Negro Novel in America* (New Haven: Yale U P, rev 1965), passim.

Elder, Arlene A. "SG: The Dilemma of the Black Bourgeoisie." *The "Hindered Hand": Cultural Implications of Early African-American Fiction* (Westport, Conn: Greenwood, 1978), 69-103, passim.

Fleming, Robert E. "SEG: Militant Black Novelist." *Phylon*, 34 (Mar 1973), 73-77.

Gloster, Hugh M. "SEG, Novelist of the New Negro." *Phylon*, 4 (Fourth Quarter 1943), 335-345.

Gloster. *Negro Voices in American Fiction* (NY: Russell & Russell, rev 1965), 56-67, passim.

Gloster. Introduction. *Imperium in Imperio* (NY: Arno & New York Times, 1969), i-vi.

Tatham, Campbell. "Reflections: SG's *Imperium in Imperio*." *StBL*, 5 (Spring 1974), 7-15.

Betty E. Taylor Thompson

EDWARD EVERETT HALE

Boston, Mass, 3 Apr 1822-Boston, Mass, 10 Jun 1909

Edward Everett Hale published more than one hundred books and pamphlets, edited several influential magazines, was a Unitarian minister, and at the end of his life served as the chaplain for the United States Senate. Hale made his literary reputation with themes of patriotism. His story "The Man Without a Country," which portrays the anguish of a young man exiled from his homeland, was greeted with enthusiasm by a country engrossed in the Civil War. Although Hale's work was respected in his lifetime, it has never enjoyed wide critical investigation.

BIBLIOGRAPHY

Holloway, Jean. "A Checklist of the Writings of EEH." *BB*, 21 (May-Aug 1954), 90-92; 21 (Sep-Dec 1954), 114-120; 21 (Jan-Apr 1955), 140-143.

BOOKS

(This list omits separately published individual sermons.)

Jenny's Journey. Boston: Carter, Hendee, 1840? Novel.

How to Conquer Texas Before Texas Conquers Us. Boston: Redding, 1845. Essay.

Margaret Percival in America: A Tale . . . (Anon, with Lucretia Peabody Hale). Boston: Phillips, Sampson, 1850. Novel.

Sketches of Christian History. Boston: npub, 1850. Repub as *Scenes From Christian History*. Boston: Crosby, Nichols, 1852. Stories.

Letters on Irish Emigration. Boston: Phillips, Sampson, 1852.

*Kanzas and Nebraska: The History, Geographical and Physical Characteristics, and Political Po-

sition of Those Territories. . . . Boston: Phillips, Sampson, 1854. Nonfiction.

The Elements of Christian Doctrine, and Its Development: Five Sermons. Boston: Walker, Wise, 1860.

Ninety Days' Worth of Europe. Boston: Walker, Wise, 1861. Travel.

The Man Without a Country (Anon). Boston: Ticknor & Fields, 1865. Story.

If, Yes, and Perhaps: Four Possibilities and Six Exaggerations, With Some Bits of Fact. Boston: Ticknor & Fields, 1868. Stories.

The Ingham Papers: Some Memories of the Life of Capt. Frederic Ingham, U.S.N. . . . Boston: Fields, Osgood, 1869. Stories.

Sybaris and Other Homes. Boston: Fields, Osgood, 1869. Novel.

How To Do It. Boston: Osgood, 1871. Addresses.

Ten Times One Is Ten: The Possible Reformation (as by Col. Frederic Ingham). Boston: Roberts, 1871. Novel.

His Level Best and Other Stories. Boston: Roberts, 1872.

Six of One by Half a Dozen of the Other: An Every Day Novel, with Harriet Beecher Stowe, Adeline D T Whitney, Lucretia P Hale, Frederic B Perkins & Frederick W Loring. Boston: Roberts, 1872.

Christmas Eve and Christmas Day: Ten Christmas Stories. Boston: Roberts, 1873.

Ups and Downs: An Every-day Novel. Boston: Roberts, 1873.

In His Name: A Christmas Story. Boston: Proprietors of Old and New, 1873.

Workingmen's Homes: Essays and Stories. . . , with others. Boston: Osgood, 1874.

The Good Time Coming: or, Our New Crusade. Boston: Roberts, 1875. Repub as *Our New Crusade: A Temperance Story,* 1875. Novel.

One Hundred Years Ago: How the War Began. Boston: Lockwood, Brooks, 1875. History.

Philip Nolan's Friends: A Story of the Change of Western Empire. NY: Scribner, Armstrong, 1877. Novel.

Biographical Sketch of James Edward Root. Albany: Munsell, 1877.

G.T.T.; or, The Wonderful Adventures of a Pullman. Boston: Roberts, 1877. Novel.

Back to Back: A Story of Today. NY: Harper, 1878. Novel.

Mrs. Merriam's Scholars: A Story of the "Original Ten." Boston: Roberts, 1878. Novel.

Sketches of the Lives of the Brothers Everett. Boston: Little, Brown, 1878. Essay.

What Career? Ten Papers on the Choice of a Vocation and the Use of Time. Boston: Roberts, 1878.

The Wolf at the Door. Boston: Roberts, 1878. Novel.

From Thanksgiving to Fast: Fifteen Sermons. . . . Boston: Ellis, 1879.

Stories of War, Told by Soldiers. Boston: Roberts, 1879.

Crusoe in New York and Other Tales. Boston: Roberts, 1880.

The Kingdom of God and Twenty Other Sermons. . . . Boston: Roberts, 1880.

The Life in Common and Twenty Other Sermons. Boston: Roberts, 1880.

Stories of the Sea Told by Sailors. Boston: Roberts, 1880.

A Family Flight Through France, Germany, Norway and Switzerland, with Susan Hale. Boston: Lothrop, 1881. Travel.

June to May: The Sermons of the Year. . . . Boston: Roberts, 1881.

Stories of Adventure Told by Adventurers. Boston: Roberts, 1881.

A Family Flight Over Egypt and Syria, with Susan Hale. Boston: Lothrop, 1882. Travel.

Stories of Discovery Told by Discoverers. Boston: Roberts, 1883.

Our Christmas in a Palace: A Traveller's Story. NY: Funk & Wagnalls, 1883.

Seven Spanish Cities and the Way to Them. Boston: Roberts, 1883. Travel.

Christmas in Narragansett. NY & London: Funk & Wagnalls, 1884. Stories.

A Family Flight Around Home, with Susan Hale. Boston: Lothrop, 1884. Travel.

A Family Flight Through Spain, with Susan Hale. Boston: Lothrop, 1884. Travel.

The Fortunes of Rachel. NY: Funk & Wagnalls, 1884. Novel.

Stories of the Wadsworth Club. Boston: Smith, 1884.

Boys' Heroes. Boston: Lothrop, 1885. Stories.

Stories of Invention Told by Inventors and Their Friends. Boston: Roberts, 1885.

What Is the American People? Boston: Smith, 1885. Address.

Easter: A Collection for a Hundred Friends. Boston: Smith, 1886. Sermons & poetry.

A Family Flight Through Mexico, with Susan Hale. Boston: Lothrop, 1886. Travel.

The Story of Spain, with Susan Hale. NY & London: Putnam, 1886. Repub as *Spain,* 1899. History.

History of the United States: Written for the Chautauqua Reading Circles. NY: Chautauqua, 1887.

Red and White: A Christmas Story. Boston: Smith, 1887. Story.

Franklin in France. . . , 2 vols, with Edward Everett Hale, Jr. Boston: Roberts, 1888. Biography.

Daily Bread: A Story of the Snow Blockade. Boston: Smith, 1888. Story.

How They Lived in Hampton: A Study of Practical Christianity Applied in the Manufacture of Woollens. Boston: Smith, 1888. Nonfiction.

The Life of George Washington, Studied Anew. NY & London: Putnam, 1888.

Mr. Tangier's Vacations: A Novel. Boston: Roberts, 1888.

My Friend the Boss: A Story of To-day. Boston: Smith, 1888. Novel.

The Ten Times One Is Ten and Lend a Hand Clubs: How to Begin. Boston: Smith, 1888. Essay.

Tom Torrey's Tariff Talks. Boston: Stilman, 1888. Stories.

Afloat and Ashore. Chicago: Searle & Gorton, 1891. Story.

Four and Five: A Story of a Lend-a-Hand Club. Boston: Roberts, 1891. Novel.

The Life of Christopher Columbus, From His Own Letters and Journals and Other Documents of His Times. Chicago: Howe, 1891. Repub as *The Story of Columbus as He Told It Himself.* Boston: Smith, 1893. Nonfiction.

The Story of Massachusetts. Boston: Lothrop, 1891. History.

The New Harry and Lucy: A Story of Boston in the Summer of 1891, with Lucretia Peabody Hale. Boston: Roberts, 1892. Novel.

East and West: A Story of New-Born Ohio. NY: Cassell, 1892; *The New Ohio: A Story of East and West.* London: Cassell, 1892. Novel.

Every-day Sermons. Boston: Smith, 1892.

Sybil Knox; or, Home Again: A Story of To-day. NY: Cassell, 1892. Novel.

For Fifty Years: Verses Written on Occasion in the Course of the Nineteenth Century. Boston: Roberts, 1893.

One Good Turn: A Story. Boston: Smith, 1893.

A New England Boyhood. NY: Cassell, 1893. Augmented as *A New England Boyhood, and Other Bits of Autobiography,* Vol 6 of *The Works of EEH.*

Ralph Waldo Emerson. . . . Boston: Smith, 1893. Biography.

Sermons of the Winter. Boston: Smith, 1893.

Aunt Caroline's Present. Boston: Smith, 1895. Story.

Colonel Clipsham's Calendar. Boston: Smith, 1895. Story.

Hands Off. Boston: Smith, 1895. Story.

If Jesus Came to Boston. Boston: Lamson, Wolffe, 1895. Story.

A Safe Deposit. Boston: Smith, 1895. Story.

Studies in American Colonial Life. Meadville, Pa: Flood & Vincent, 1895. Essays.

Susan's Escort. Boston: Smith, 1895. Repub in *Susan's Escort and Others.* NY: Harper, 1897. Story.

The Foundation of the Nation. Boston: Smith, 1896. Address.

Independence Day: An Address. Philadelphia: Altemus, 1896.

Historic Boston and Its Neighborhood: An Historical Pilgrimage Personally Conducted by EEH. NY: Appleton, 1898.

Young Americans Abroad, with Susan Hale. Boston: Lothrop, 1898. Travel.

The Brick Moon and Other Stories, Vol 4 of *The Works of EEH,* 1899.

James Russell Lowell and His Friends. Boston & NY: Houghton, Mifflin, 1899. Biography.

A Permanent Tribunal: The Emperor of Russia and His Circular Regarding Permanent Peace. Boston: Ellis, 1899. Essay.

Picturesque Massachusetts, Vol 2 of *Picturesque and Architectural New England,* ed D H Hurd. Boston: Hurd, 1899.

Young Americans in the Orient. Boston: Lothrop, 1900. Travel.

Addresses and Essays on Subjects of History, Education, and Government, Vol 8 of *The Works of EEH,* 1900.

How to Do It; to Which Is Added, How To Live, Vol 7 of *The Works of EEH,* 1900. Essays.

Sunday Afternoon Stories for Home and School: Written or Revised by EEH, 2 vols. Boston: Lend a Hand Record, 1901.

Memories of a Hundred Years, 2 vols. NY & London: Macmillan, 1902. Rev & augmented ed, 1904. Autobiography.

New England History in Ballads, by EEH and His Children, With a Few Additions by Other People. Boston: Little & Brown, 1903.

"We, the People": A Series of Papers on Topics of To-day. NY: Dodd, Mead, 1903.

The Ideas of the Founders: An Address. . . . Boston: Lend a Hand Record, 1904.

Prayers in the Senate. . . . Boston: Little, Brown, 1904.

The Foundations of the Republic. NY: Pott, 1906. Addresses.

Tarry at Home Travels. NY & London: Macmillan, 1906. Travel.

Prospero's Island. NY: Printed for the Dramatic Museum of Columbia U, 1919. Essay.

LETTERS

The Life and Letters of EEH, 2 vols, ed Edward Everett Hale, Jr. Boston: Little, Brown, 1917.

OTHER

(This list omits the many volumes for which EEH provided introductions and for most of which he received title-page credit as editor.)

Christian Examiner (1857-1861), ed EEH & Frederic H Hedge. Magazine.

Old and New (1870-1875), ed EEH. Magazine.
Lend a Hand Record (1886-1897), ed EEH et al. Magazine.
New England Magazine (1889), ed EEH.
Peace Crusade (1899), ed EEH. Newspaper.

EDITION

The Works of EEH, Library Edition, 10 vols. Boston: Little, Brown, 1898-1901.

MANUSCRIPTS & ARCHIVES

New York State Library, Albany.

BIOGRAPHIES

Book
Holloway, Jean. *EEH.* Austin: U Texas P, 1956.

Book Section & Articles
Abbott, Lyman. "EEH: An American Abou Ben Adhem." *Silhouettes of My Contemporaries* (Garden City, NY: Doubleday, Page, 1921), 100-125.
Bingham, M T & G F Whicher. "Notes and Queries: 'Emily Dickinson's Earliest Friend.' " *AL,* 6 (Apr 1934), 191-193.
Bowen, E W. "EEH." *SAQ,* 17 (Jul 1918), 231-242.
DeNormandie, James. "Tribute to EEH." *PMHS,* 43 (Oct 1909), 4-16.
Frothingham, Paul Revere. "Memoir of EEH." *PMHS,* 55 (Apr 1922), 307-318.
Garver, Austin S. "EEH." *PAAS,* 20 (20 Oct 1909), 60-69.

Hale, Edward Everett, Jr. "EEH: A Practical Idealist." *Outlook,* 85 (6 Apr 1907), 801-805.
Higginson, Thomas Wentworth. "EEH." *Outlook,* 92 (19 Jun 1909), 403-406. Rpt *Carlyle's Laugh and Other Surprises* by Higginson (Boston: Houghton Mifflin, 1909).
Mead, Edwin D. "EEH." *NEMag,* 40 (Jul 1909), 520-529.
Merriam, George S. "Reminiscences of EEH." *Outlook,* 96 (12 Nov 1910), 581-588.

CRITICAL STUDIES

Books
Adams, John R. *EEH.* Boston: Twayne, 1977.
James, Nancy Esther. "Realism in Romance: A Critical Study of the Short Stories of EEH." Dissertation: Pennsylvania State U, 1969.

Book Section & Articles
Bellman, Samuel I. "Riding on Wishes: Ritual Make-Believe Patterns in Three 19th-Century American Authors: Aldrich, H, Bunner." *Ritual in the United States,* ed Don Harkness (Tampa, Fla: American Studies, 1985), 15-20.
Coleman, Earle. "EEH: Preacher as Publisher." *PBSA,* 46 (First Quarter 1952), 139-150.
Kennedy, William Sloane. "EEH." *Century,* 29 (Jan 1885), 338-343.
Monteiro, George. "The Full Particulars of the Minister's Behavior—According to H." *NHJ 1972* (1973), 173-182.

James L. Pettibone

LUCRETIA PEABODY HALE

Boston, Mass, 2 Sep 1820-Boston, Mass, 12 Jun 1900

Lucretia Peabody Hale, who was born into a prominent literary family, began publishing stories in the *Atlantic* in 1858. A collection appearing as *The Peterkin Papers* more than twenty years later brought her fame and popularity that continued well into the twentieth century. Hale's gently satiric stories emphasize the trials of ordinary people dealing with everyday events raised to the level of crises. At the same time, they record the manners, mores, and foibles of the society she depicts. In addition to writing fiction, religious tracts, and needlecraft manuals, Hale composed fillers and editorials for journals edited by her brothers.

BOOKS

Margaret Percival in America: A Tale . . . (Anon, with Edward Everett Hale). Boston: Phillips, Sampson, 1850. Novel.

Seven Stormy Sundays. Boston: American Unitarian Association, 1859. Sermons & hymns.

Struggle for Life. Boston: Walker, Wise, 1861. Stories.

The Lord's Supper and Its Observance. Boston: Walker, Fuller, 1866. Nonfiction.

The Service of Sorrow. Boston: American Unitarian Association, 1867. Nonfiction.

Six of One by Half a Dozen of the Other: An Every Day Novel, with Edward Everett Hale, Harriet Beecher Stowe, Adeline D T Whitney, Frederic B Perkins & Frederick W Loring. Boston: Roberts, 1872.

Designs in Outline for Art-Needlework. Boston: Tilton, 1879.

More Stitches for Decorative Embroidery. Boston: Tilton, 1879.

Point-Lace: A Guide to Lace Work. Boston: Tilton, 1879.

The Peterkin Papers. Boston: Osgood, 1880. Stories.

The Art of Knitting. Boston: Tilton, 1881.

The Last of the Peterkins, With Others of Their Kin. Boston: Roberts, 1886. Novel.

An Uncloseted Skeleton, with Edward Lassetter Bynner. Boston: Ticknor, 1888. Novel.

Fagots for the Fireside. . . . Boston: Ticknor, 1889. Augmented ed, Boston & NY: Houghton, Mifflin, 1895. Games.

Sunday-School Stories for Little Children on the Golden Texts of the International Lessons of 1889, with Mrs Bernard Whitman. Boston: Roberts, 1889.

Stories for Children, Containing Simple Lessons in Morals: A Supplementary Reader for Schools, or for Use at Home. Boston & NY: Leach, Shewell & Sanborn, 1892.

The New Harry and Lucy: A Story of Boston in the Summer of 1891, with Edward Everett Hale. Boston: Roberts, 1892. Novel.

MANUSCRIPTS & ARCHIVES

Smith C Library.

BIOGRAPHY

Book Section

Hale, Edward Everett. *A New England Boyhood* (NY: Cassell, 1893), passim.

CRITICAL STUDIES

Articles

Wankmiller, Madelyn C. "LPH and *The Peterkin Papers.*" *Horn Book,* 34 (Apr 1958), 95-103, 137-147.

White, Eliza Orne. "LPH." *Horn Book,* 16 (Sep-Oct 1940), 317-322.

Cheryl Z. Oreovicz

HENRY HARLAND
(Sidney Luska)

Brooklyn, NY, 1 Mar 1861-San Remo, Italy, 20 Dec 1905

Henry Harland is remembered today primarily as the cofounder and editor (from 1894-1897) of *The Yellow Book,* for which Aubrey Beardsley acted as artistic director. With E. C. Stedman as his literary mentor Harland began his career as a realist and a self-proclaimed student of William Dean Howells. He wrote his first six novels under the pseudonym Sidney Luska, suggesting that the name would lend credibility to these works about Jewish life in New York City. In 1898 he moved to London and came under the influence of Henry James. While living abroad Harland continued to write novels and publish collections of short stories.

BIBLIOGRAPHY

Bibliography of American Literature, comp Jacob Blanck. New Haven: Yale U P, 1955-1991. Primary.

BOOKS

As It Was Written: A Jewish Musician's Story (as by Sidney Luska). NY: Cassell, 1885. Novel.

Mrs Pexeida (as by Luska). NY: Cassell, 1886. Novel.

The Yoke of the Thorah (as by Luska). NY: Cassell, 1887. Novel.

My Uncle Florimond (as by Luska/HH). Boston: Lothrop, 1888. Novel.

A Latin-Quarter Courtship and Other Stories (as by Luska/HH). NY: Cassell, 1889.

Grandison Mather; or, An Account of the Fortunes of Mr. and Mrs. Thomas Gardiner (as by Luska/HH). NY: Cassell, 1889. Novel.

Two Voices. NY: Cassell, 1890. Stories.

Two Women or One? From the Mss. of Dr. Leonard Benary. NY: Cassell, 1890. Novel.

Mea Culpa: A Woman's Last Word. NY: Lovell, 1891. Novel.

Mademoiselle Miss and Other Stories. London: Heinemann, 1893; *Mademoiselle Miss to Which Is Added: The Funeral March of a Marionette. The Prodigal Father. A Sleeveless Errand. A Light Sovereign.* NY: Lovell, Coryell, 1893.

Grey Roses. London: Lane / Boston: Roberts, 1895; *Gray Roses.* Boston: Roberts / London: Lane, 1895. Stories.

Comedies & Errors. London & NY: Lane, Bodley Head, 1898. Stories.

The Cardinal's Snuff-Box. London & NY: Lane, Bodley Head, 1900. Novel.

The Lady Paramount. London & NY: Lane, Bodley Head, 1902. Novel.

My Friend Prospero: A Novel. NY: McClure, Phillips, 1904.

The Royal End: A Romance. NY: Dodd, Mead, 1909. Novel.

MANUSCRIPTS & ARCHIVES

The major collections are at Columbia U Library, the Library of Congress & the New York Public Library.

BIOGRAPHY

Book

Clarke, John J. "HH, a Critical Biography." Dissertation: Brown U, 1957.

Article

Glastonbury, G. "The Life and Writings of HH." *IM,* 39 (Apr 1911), 210-219.

CRITICAL STUDIES

Book

Beckson, Karl. *HH: His Life and Work.* London: Eighteen Nineties Society, 1978.

Book Sections & Articles

Cheshire, David & Malcolm Bradbury. "American Realism and the Romance of Europe: Fuller, Frederic, H." *PAH,* 4 (1970), 283-310.

Harap, Louis. "The Strange Case of HH." *The Image of the Jew in American Literature* (Philadelphia: Jewish Publication Society of America, 1974), 455-471.

Howells, William Dean. "Editor's Study." *Harper's,* 73 (Jul 1886), 314-319.

Howells. "Editor's Study." *Harper's,* 78 (May 1898), 987.

James, Henry. "The Story-Teller at Large: Mr. HH." *FoR*, ns 63 (1 Apr 1898), 650-654.

Mix, Katherine Lyon. *A Study in Yellow: The "Yellow Book" and Its Contributors* (Lawrence: U Kansas P, 1960), passim.

O'Brien, Justin. "HH, an American Forerunner of Proust." *MLN*, 65 (Jun 1939), 420-428.

Jean Kowaleski

JOEL CHANDLER HARRIS

Eatonton, Ga, 9 Dec 1848?-Atlanta, Ga, 3 Jul 1908

Joel Chandler Harris's first two books, *Uncle Remus: His Songs and His Sayings* and *Nights With Uncle Remus,* have never been out of print, and his short stories have been regularly anthologized. Harris earned five reputations: as a regional humorist, a major New South journalist, the recreator of the Uncle Remus folktales, a children's author, and a writer of local-color short fiction and novels. An accomplished dialect-writer and portrayer of southern rural blacks and poor whites, Harris was widely respected. The Uncle Remus tales have been recognized as both entertaining folk stories and socio-economic allegories that reflect the complex relationships of blacks and whites before and following the Civil War. "Free Joe," "Mingo," and other local-color stories are admired for Harris's sensitivity to racial interrelationships. Harris's major public theme as New South journalist and literary recreator of the Old South was the promotion of "neighborliness," mutual understanding, and reconciliation between blacks and whites and between North and South.

BIBLIOGRAPHIES

Bibliography of American Literature, comp Jacob Blanck. New Haven: Yale U P, 1955-1991. Primary.

Bickley, R Bruce, Jr, with Karen L Bickley & Thomas H English. *JCH: A Reference Guide.* Boston: Hall, 1978. Secondary.

Bickley, R Bruce, Jr & Hugh T Keenan. "JCH: An Annotated Secondary Bibliography." *AtlantaHJ,* 30 (Fall-Winter 1986-1987), 141-148.

Blanck, Jacob. "*BAL* Addendum: JCH—Entry No. 7115." *PBSA,* 61 (Third Quarter 1967), 266. Primary.

Strickland, William Bradley. "JCH: A Bibliographical Study." Dissertation: U Georgia, 1976. Primary.

Strickland. "A Check List of the Periodical Contributions of JCH (1848-1908)." *ALR,* 9 (Summer 1976), 207-229. Primary.

Strickland & R Bruce Bickley, Jr. "A Checklist of the Periodical Contributions of JCH: Part 2." *ALR,* 11 (Spring 1978), 139-140. Primary.

BOOKS

Uncle Remus: His Songs and His Sayings. . . . NY: Appleton, 1881; *Uncle Remus and His Legends of the Old Plantation.* London: Bogue, 1881. Rev ed, NY: Appleton, 1895. Folktales, sketches, songs & proverbs.

Nights With Uncle Remus: Myths and Legends of the Old Plantation. Boston: Osgood, 1883. Folktales.

Mingo and Other Sketches in Black and White. Boston: Osgood, 1884. Stories.

Free Joe and Other Georgian Sketches. NY: Scribners, 1887. Stories.

Daddy Jake the Runaway and Short Stories Told After Dark. NY: Century, 1889.

Balaam and His Master and Other Sketches and Stories. Boston & NY: Houghton, Mifflin, 1891.

On the Plantation: A Story of a Georgia Boy's Adventures During the War. NY: Appleton, 1892; *A Plantation Printer: The Adventures of a Georgia Boy During the War.* London: Osgood, McIlvaine, 1892. Novel.

Uncle Remus and His Friends: Old Plantation Stories, Songs, and Ballads With Sketches of Negro Character. Boston & NY: Houghton, Mifflin, 1892.

Little Mr. Thimblefinger and His Queer Country: What the Children Saw and Heard There. Boston & NY: Houghton, Mifflin, 1894. Children's stories.

Mr. Rabbit at Home: A Sequel to Little Mr. Thimblefinger and His Queer Country. Boston & NY: Houghton, Mifflin, 1895. Children's stories.

The Story of Aaron (So Named), The Son of Ben Ali, Told by His Friends and Acquaintances. Boston & NY: Houghton, Mifflin, 1896. Children's novel.

Stories of Georgia. NY & c: American Book, 1896. Rev ed, 1910? Textbook.

Sister Jane, Her Friends and Acquaintances: A Narrative of Certain Events and Episodes Transcribed From the Papers of the Late William Wornum. Boston & NY: Houghton, Mifflin, 1896. Novel.

Aaron in the Wildwoods. Boston & NY: Houghton, Mifflin, 1897. Children's novel.

Tales of the Home Folks in Peace and War. Boston & NY: Houghton, Mifflin, 1898. Stories.

Plantation Pageants. Boston & NY: Houghton, Mifflin, 1899. Children's novel.

The Chronicles of Aunt Minervy Ann. NY: Scribners, 1899. Stories.

On the Wing of Occasions. . . . NY: Doubleday, Page, 1900. Stories & novella.

The Making of a Statesman and Other Stories. NY: McClure, Phillips, 1902.

Gabriel Tolliver: A Story of Reconstruction. NY: McClure, Phillips, 1902. Novel.

Wally Wanderoon and His Story-Telling Machine. NY: McClure, Phillips, 1903. Children's novel.

A Little Union Scout. NY: McClure, Phillips, 1904. Novel.

The Tar-Baby and Other Rhymes of Uncle Remus. NY: Appleton, 1904. Poems & songs.

Told by Uncle Remus: New Stories of the Old Plantation. NY: McClure, Phillips, 1905. Folktales.

Uncle Remus and Brer Rabbit. NY: Stokes, 1907. Folktales.

The Bishop and the Boogerman. . . . NY: Doubleday, Page, 1909. *The Bishop and the Bogie-Man.* London: Murray, 1909. Children's novel.

The Shadow Between His Shoulder-Blades. Boston: Small, Maynard, 1909. Novel.

Uncle Remus and the Little Boy. Boston: Small, Maynard, 1910. Folktales.

Uncle Remus Returns. Boston & NY: Houghton Mifflin, 1918. Folktales.

The Witch Wolf: An Uncle Remus Story. Cambridge, Mass: Bacon & Brown, 1921. Folktale.

JCH, Editor and Essayist: Miscellaneous Literary, Political, and Social Writings, ed Julia Collier Harris. Chapel Hill: U North Carolina P, 1931.

Qua: A Romance of the Revolution, ed Thomas H English. Atlanta, Ga: Emory U Library, 1946. Novel.

Seven Tales of Uncle Remus, ed English. Atlanta, Ga: Emory U Library, 1948. Folktales.

LETTERS

"Selected Letters of JCH, 1863-1885," ed Joseph M Griska, Jr. Dissertation: Texas A&M U, 1976.

OTHER

JCH's Life of Henry W. Grady, Including His Writings and Speeches. . . , ed JCH. NY: Cassell, 1890.

Evening Tales Done into English From the French of Frédéric Ortoli, trans JCH. NY: Scribners, 1893. Folktales.

Mark Twain to Uncle Remus, 1881-1885, ed Thomas H English. Atlanta, Ga: Emory U Library, 1953. Includes 1 letter by JCH.

COLLECTIONS

The Complete Tales of Uncle Remus, comp Richard Chase. Boston: Houghton Mifflin, 1955.

Free Joe: Stories by JCH, ed John Tumlin. Savannah, Ga: Beehive, 1975.

MANUSCRIPTS & ARCHIVES

Emory U Library.

BIOGRAPHIES

Books

Cousins, Paul M. *JCH: A Biography.* Baton Rouge: Louisiana State U P, 1968.

Harris, Julia Collier. *The Life and Letters of JCH.* Boston & NY: Houghton Mifflin, 1918.

Wiggins, Robert Lemuel. *The Life of JCH: From Obscurity in Boyhood to Fame in Early Manhood.* Nashville, Tenn & c: Methodist Episcopal Church, South, 1918.

Book Sections & Articles

Bell, William R. "The Relationship of JCH and Mark Twain." *AtlantaHJ,* 30 (Fall-Winter 1986-1987), 97-111.

Griska, Joseph M, Jr. " 'In Stead of a "Gift of Gab" ': Some New Perspectives on JCH Biography." Bickley (1981), 210-225.

Griska. "JCH: 'Accidental Author' or 'Aggressive Businessman'?" *AtlantaHJ*, 30 (Fall-Winter 1986-1987), 71-78.

Kelly, Karen M. "The Early Days of the Uncle Remus Memorial Association." *AtlantaHJ*, 30 (Fall-Winter 1986-1987), 113-127.

Rorabaugh, W J. "When Was JCH Born? Some New Evidence." *SLJ*, 17 (Fall 1984), 92-95.

Thomas, Kenneth H, Jr. "Roots and Environment: The Family Background of JCH." *AtlantaHJ*, 30 (Fall-Winter 1986-1987), 37-56.

Wade, John Donald. "Profits and Losses in the Life of JCH." *AmR*, 1 (Apr 1933), 17-35.

Weaks, Mary Louise. "A Meeting of Southerners: JCH, Mark Twain, and George Washington Cable." *AtlantaHJ*, 30 (Fall-Winter 1986-1987), 89-96.

CRITICAL STUDIES

Books

Baer, Florence E. *Sources and Analogues of the Uncle Remus Tales*. Helsinki: Folklore Fellows Communications, 1981.

Bickley, R Bruce, Jr. *JCH*. Boston: Twayne, 1978. Rev ed, Athens: U Georgia P, 1987.

Brooks, Stella Brewer. *JCH—Folklorist*. Athens: U Georgia P, 1950.

Ives, Sumner. *The Phonology of the Uncle Remus Stories*. Gainesville, Fla: American Dialect Society, 1954.

Collection of Essays

Bickley, R Bruce, Jr, ed. *Critical Essays on JCH*. Boston: Hall, 1981.

Special Journals

AtlantaHJ, 30 (Fall-Winter 1986-1987). JCH issue.
Wren's NestN (1984-   ). Includes checklists. Frequency varies.

Book Sections & Articles

Baer, Florence E. "JCH: An 'Accidental' Folklorist." Bickley (1981), 185-195.

Berkove, Lawrence I. "The Free Man of Color in *The Grandissimes* and Works by H and Mark Twain." *SoQ*, 18 (Summer 1980), 60-73.

Bickley, R Bruce, Jr. "Two Allusions to JCH in *Ulysses*: 'Wusser Scared' and 'Corporosity' Redux." *ELN*, 17 (Sep 1979), 42-45.

Bickley. "JCH's *Boogerman* Frightens Mrs. Grundy." *ELN*, 23 (Sep 1985), 61-63.

Bickley. "JCH and the Old and New South: Paradoxes of Perception." *AtlantaHJ*, 30 (Fall-Winter 1986-1987), 9-31.

Bone, Robert. "The Oral Tradition." *Down Home: A History of Afro-American Short Fiction From Its Beginnings to the End of the Harlem Renaissance* (NY: Putnam, 1975), 19-41. Rpt Bickley (1981).

Brooks, Van Wyck. "The South: Lanier and JCH." *The Times of Melville and Whitman* (NY: Dutton, 1947), 351-377.

Budd, Louis J. "JCH and the Genteeling of Native American Humor." Bickley (1981), 196-209.

Carkeet, David. "The Source for the Arkansas Gossips in *Huckleberry Finn*." *ALR*, 14 (Spring 1981), 90-92.

Dauner, Louise. "Myth and Humor in the Uncle Remus Fables." *AL*, 20 (May 1948), 129-143.

David, Beverly R. "Visions of the South: JCH and His Illustrators." *ALR*, 9 (Summer 1976), 189-206.

English, Thomas H. "In Memory of Uncle Remus." *SLM*, 2 (Feb 1940), 77-83. Rpt Bickley (1981).

English. "The Other Uncle Remus." *GaR*, 21 (Summer 1967), 210-217.

Flusche, Michael. "JCH and the Folklore of Slavery." *JAS*, 9 (Dec 1975), 347-363.

Flusche. "Underlying Despair in the Fiction of JCH." *MissQ*, 29 (Winter 1975-1976), 91-103. Rpt Bickley (1981).

Goldthwaite, John. "The Black Rabbit: Part One." *Signal*, no 47 (May 1985), 86-111; "Part Two." *Signal*, no 48 (Sep 1985), 148-167.

Griska, Joseph M, Jr. "Uncle Remus Correspondence: The Development and Reception of JCH's Writing, 1880-1885." *ALR*, 14 (Spring 1981), 26-37.

Hedin, Raymond. "Uncle Remus: Puttin' On Ole Massa's Son." *SLJ*, 15 (Fall 1982), 83-90.

Hemenway, Robert. "Introduction: Author, Teller, and Hero." *Uncle Remus: His Songs and His Sayings*, ed Hemenway (NY: Penguin, 1982), 7-31.

Horowitz, Floyd R. "Ralph Ellison's Modern Version of Brer Bear and Brer Rabbit in *Invisible Man*." *MASJ*, 4 (Fall 1963), 21-27.

Howell, Marcella. "Will the Authentic *Hare* Please Stand Up: An Analysis of JCH's Uncle Remus Tales." *Afro-American Folklore: A Unique American Experience*, ed George E Carter & James R Parker (La Crosse: Institute for Minority Studies, U Wisconsin, 1977), 23-30.

Hubbell, Jay B. "JCH." *The South in American Literature* (Durham, NC: Duke U P, 1954), 782-795.

Ives, Sumner. "A Theory of Literary Dialect." *TSE*, 2 (1950), 137-182.

Ives. "Dialect Differentiation in the Stories of JCH." *AL*, 27 (Mar 1955), 88-96.

Jones, George Fenwick. "Reineke Fuchs and Brer Rabbit: Oral or Written Tradition?" *Vistas and Vectors: Essays Honoring the Memory of Helmut Rehder,* ed Lee B Jennings & George Schulz-Behrend (Austin: U Texas P, 1979), 44-53.

Keenan, Hugh T. "Twisted Tales: Propaganda in the Tar-Baby Stories." *SoQ,* 22 (Winter 1984), 54-69.

Lester, Julius. "Foreword." *The Tales of Uncle Remus: The Adventures of Brer Rabbit* (NY: Dial, 1987), xiii-xxi.

Leyburn, Ellen Douglas. "Animal Stories." *Satiric Allegory: Mirror of Man* (New Haven: Yale U P, 1956), 57-70. Rpt Bickley (1981).

Light, Kathleen. "Uncle Remus and the Folklorists." *SLJ,* 7 (Spring 1975), 88-104. Rpt Bickley (1981).

MacKethan, Lucinda Hardwick. "JCH: Speculating on the Past." *The Dream of Arcady: Place and Time in Southern Literature* (Baton Rouge: Louisiana State U P, 1980), 61-85.

Martin, Jay. "JCH and the Cornfield Journalist." *Harvests of Change: American Literature, 1865-1914* (Englewood Cliffs, NJ: Prentice-Hall, 1967), 96-100. Rpt Bickley (1981).

Mikkelsen, Nina. "When the Animals Talked—A Hundred Years of Uncle Remus." *CLAQ,* 8 (Spring 1983), 3-5, 31.

Mixon, Wayne. "JCH and the Yeoman Tradition." *Southern Writers and the New South Movement, 1865-1913* (Chapel Hill: U North Carolina P, 1980), 73-84.

Montenyohl, Eric L. "The Origins of Uncle Remus." *FForum,* 18 (Spring 1986), 136-167.

Montenyohl. "JCH's Revision of Uncle Remus: The First Version of 'A Story of the War.'" *ALR,* 19 (Fall 1986), 65-72.

Montenyohl. "JCH and American Folklore." *AtlantaHJ,* 30 (Fall-Winter 1986-1987), 79-88.

Moore, Opal & Donnarae MacCann. "The Uncle Remus Travesty." *CLAQ,* 11 (Summer 1986), 96-99.

Muffett, D J M. "Uncle Remus Was a Hausaman?" *SFQ,* 39 (Jun 1975), 151-166.

Page, Thomas Nelson. "Immortal Uncle Remus." *Book Buyer,* 12 (Dec 1895), 642-645. Rpt Bickley (1981).

Pederson, Lee. "Language in the Uncle Remus Tales." *MP,* 82 (Feb 1985), 292-298.

Pederson. "Rewriting Dialect Literature: 'The Wonderful Tar-Baby Story.'" *AtlantaHJ,* 30 (Fall-Winter 1986-1987), 57-70.

Piacentino, Edward J. "Another Chapter in the Literary Relationship of Mark Twain and JCH." *MissQ,* 38 (Winter 1984-1985), 73-85.

Rubin, Louis D, Jr. "Uncle Remus and the Ubiquitous Rabbit." *SoR,* 10 (Oct 1974), 787-804. Rpt *William Elliott Shoots a Bear* by Rubin (Baton Rouge: Louisiana State U P, 1975). Rpt Bickley (1981).

Smith, Herbert F. "JCH's Contributions to *Scribner's Monthly* and *Century Magazine.*" *GaHQ,* 47 (Jun 1963), 169-179.

Stafford, John. "Patterns of Meaning in *Nights With Uncle Remus.*" *AL,* 18 (May 1946), 89-108.

Strickland, William Bradley. "Stereotypes and Subversion in *The Chronicles of Aunt Minervy Ann.*" *AtlantaHJ,* 30 (Fall-Winter 1986-1987), 129-139.

Sullivan, Philip E. "Buh Rabbit: Going through the Changes." *StBL,* 4 (Summer 1973), 28-32.

Tate, Allen. "The Cornfield Journalist." *NewR* (3 Aug 1932), 320-321. Rpt Bickley (1981).

Turner, Arlin. "JCH in the Currents of Change." *SLJ,* 1 (Autumn 1968), 105-111. Rpt Bickley (1981).

Turner, Darwin T. "Daddy Joel Harris and His Old-Time Darkies." *SLJ,* 1 (Autumn 1968), 20-41. Rpt Bickley (1981).

Twain, Mark. "Uncle Remus and Mr. Cable." *Life on the Mississippi* (Boston: Osgood, 1883), 471-472. Rpt Bickley (1951).

Walker, Alice. "Uncle Remus: No Friend of Mine." *Southern Exposure,* 9 (Summer 1981), 29-31.

Walton, David A. "JCH as Folklorist: A Reassessment." *KFQ,* 11 (Spring 1966), 21-26.

Wolfe, Bernard. "Uncle Remus and the Malevolent Rabbit: 'Takes a Limber-Toe Gemmun fer ter Jump Jim Crow.'" *Commentary,* 8 (Jul 1949), 31-41. Rpt *Mother Wit From the Laughing Barrel,* ed Alan Dundes (Englewood Cliffs, NJ: Prentice-Hall, 1973). Rpt Bickley (1981).

R. Bruce Bickley, Jr.

CONSTANCE CARY HARRISON

Lexington, Ky, 25 Apr 1843-Washington, DC, 21 Nov 1920

Though little known today, the novels and stories of Constance Cary Harrison, depicting both northern and southern life, were once widely read in America and Great Britain. Harrison lived in Richmond, Virginia, during the Civil War, which she recorded in sketches of wartime life. Her autobiography, *Recollections Grave and Gay*, remains an important document for the study of southern life and manners during that period. Moving to New York, she turned her observations of polite society into novels such as *The Anglomaniacs*, a satire of the American pursuit of European sophistication. Harrison's essays on etiquette and her book *The Well-Bred Girl in Society* provide accounts of the strictures of late-nineteenth-century society.

BIBLIOGRAPHY

Bibliography of American Literature, comp Jacob Blanck. New Haven: Yale U P, 1955-1991. Primary.

BOOKS

Golden-Rod: An Idyl of Mount Desert. NY: Harper, 1880. Novella.

Woman's Handiwork in Modern Homes. NY: Scribners, 1881. Text by CCH.

The Story of Helen Troy. NY: Harper, 1881. Novel.

The Old-Fashioned Fairy Book. NY: Scribners, 1884. Stories.

Bric-a-Brac Stories. NY: Scribners, 1885; *Folk and Fairy Tales.* London: Ward & Downey, 1885.

Bar Harbor Days. NY: Harper, 1887. Novel.

The Anglomaniacs. NY: Cassell, 1890. Novel.

Flower de Hundred: The Story of a Virginia Plantation. NY: Cassell, 1890. Novel.

Alice in Wonderland: A Play for Children in Three Acts. NY: De Witt, 1890.

A Daughter of the South and Shorter Stories. NY: Cassell, 1892.

An Edelweiss of the Sierras, Golden-Rod, and Other Tales. NY: Harper, 1892.

Belhaven Tales, Crow's Nest, Una and King David. NY: Century, 1892. Stories.

Sweet Bells Out of Tune. NY: Century, 1893. Novel.

A Bachelor Maid. NY: Century, 1894. Novel.

An Errant Wooing. NY: Century, 1895. Novel.

A Virginia Cousin & Bar Harbor Tales. Boston & NY: Lamson, Wolffe, 1895. Stories.

The Merry Maid of Arcady, His Lordship, and Other Stories. Boston & c: Lamson, Wolffe, 1897.

A Son of the Old Dominion. Boston & c: Lamson, Wolffe, 1897. Novel.

Good Americans. NY: Century, 1898. Novel.

The Well-Bred Girl in Society. Philadelphia: Curtis / NY: Doubleday & McClure, 1898. Nonfiction.

A Triple Entanglement. London: Unwin, 1898; Philadelphia: Lippincott, 1899. Novel.

The Carcellini Emerald With Other Tales. Chicago & NY: Stone, 1899. Stories.

The Circle of a Century. NY: Century, 1899. Novel.

A Princess of the Hills: An Italian Romance. Boston: Lothrop, 1901. Novel.

The Unwelcome Mrs. Hatch: A Drama of Every Day. NY: Burgoyne, 1901. Play.

The Unwelcome Mrs. Hatch. NY: Appleton, 1903. Novel.

Sylvia's Husband. NY: Appleton, 1904. Novel.

The Carlyles: A Story of the Fall of the Confederacy. NY: Appleton, 1905. Novel.

Latter-Day Sweethearts. London: Unwin, 1906; NY & London: Authors & Newspapers Association, 1907. Novel.

The Count and the Congressman. NY: Cupples & Leon, 1908. Novel.

Transplanted Daughters. London: Unwin, 1909. Novel.

Recollections Grave and Gay. NY: Scribners, 1911. Autobiography.

OTHER

Short Comedies for Amateur Players. . . , adapted & arranged by CCH. NY: De Witt, 1889.

A Russian Honeymoon . . . by Eugène Augustin Scribe; adapted by CCH. NY: De Witt, 1890. Play.

Short Stories, ed CCH. NY: Harper, 1893.

MANUSCRIPTS & ARCHIVES

The major collections are at the Library of Congress, Columbia U Library, U of Virginia Library & the Virginia Historical Society, Richmond.

CRITICAL STUDIES
Book
Maxwell, Sherrolyn. "CCH: American Woman of Letters." Dissertation: U North Carolina, Chapel Hill, 1977.

Book Section & Article
Scura, Dorothy M. "Homage to CCH." *SHR*, 10 (Bicentennial Issue 1976), 35-46.
Snyder, Henry N. "Mrs. Burton H." *Southern Writers: Biographical and Critical Studies*, Vol 2 (Nashville, Tenn: M E Church, South, 1903), 244-271.

Joe Essid

BRET HARTE
Albany, NY, 25 Aug 1836-Surrey, England, 5 May 1902

Bret Harte was once regarded as one of the most talented writers in the United States. He earned a national reputation with a comic poem "Plain Language From Truthful James" and stories that seemed to capture the vitality of life on the California frontier, perhaps most notably "The Luck of Roaring Camp" and "The Outcasts of Poker Flat." Harte's stories were recognized as original and distinguished contributions to American fiction; critics admired his craftsmanship, and readers applauded his special blend of humor and sentimentality, vivid characterization and colorful dialogue. Harte moved to the East and eventually to Europe, where he continued to write prolifically. He failed, however, to find new material or new methods of treatment. His works increasingly appeared to be imitations of his earliest successes, and his reputation declined sharply. A handful of Harte's western stories are still anthologized and cited as important contributions to the American local-color movement, but today his works rarely receive attention from literary critics.

BIBLIOGRAPHIES & CATALOGUE
Barnett, Linda Diz. *BH: A Reference Guide*. Boston: Hall, 1980. Secondary.

Bibliography of American Literature, comp Jacob Blanck. New Haven: Yale U P, 1955-1991. Primary.
Clark, Lucy Trimble. *BH: A Checklist of Printed and Manuscript Works of FBH in the Library of the University of Virginia*. Charlottesville: U Virginia P, 1957. Catalogue.
Gaer, Joseph, ed. *BH: Bibliography and Biographical Data*. San Francisco: State Emergency Relief Administration, California Library Research, 1935. Rpt NY: Franklin, 1968.
Stewart, George R. *A Bibliography of the Writings of BH in the Magazines and Newspapers of California, 1857-1871*. Berkeley: U California P, 1933. Rpt Norwood, Pa: Norwood Editions, 1977.

BOOKS
Condensed Novels and Other Papers. NY: Carleton / London: Low, 1867. Augmented ed, Boston: Osgood, 1871. Parodies.
The Lost Galleon and Other Tales. San Francisco: Towne & Bacon, 1867. Poetry.
The Luck of Roaring Camp and Other Sketches. Boston: Fields, Osgood, 1870. Augmented ed, 1870. Stories.

Poems. Boston: Fields, Osgood, 1871; *That Heathen Chinee and Other Poems, Mostly Humorous*. London: Hotten, 1871.

East and West Poems. Boston: Osgood, 1871.

The Little Drummer; or, The Christmas Gift That Came to Rupert: A Story for Children. London: Hotten, 1872.

Mrs. Skaggs's Husbands and Other Sketches. London: Hotten, 1872; Boston: Osgood, 1873. Stories.

An Episode of Fiddletown and Other Sketches. London: Routledge 1873. Stories.

MLiss, an Idyl of Red Mountain: A Story of California in 1863. NY: De Witt, 1873. Novel (Piracy with 50 added chapters by R G Densmore).

Idyls of the Foothills. Leipzig: Tauchnitz, 1874. Stories & poetry.

Echoes of the Foot-hills. Boston: Osgood, 1875. Poetry.

Tales of the Argonauts and Other Sketches. Boston: Osgood, 1875. Stories.

Gabriel Conroy: A Novel. Hartford, Conn: American Publishing, 1876.

Two Men of Sandy Bar: A Drama. Boston: Osgood, 1876. Play.

Thankful Blossom, a Romance of the Jerseys, 1779. Boston: Osgood, 1877. Augmented as *Thankful Blossom and Other Tales*. Leipzig: Tauchnitz, 1877. Novella.

The Story of a Mine. London: Routledge, 1877; Boston: Osgood, 1878. Novel.

The Man on the Beach. London: Routledge, 1878. Stories.

"Jinny." London: Routledge, 1878. Stories & poetry.

Drift From Two Shores. Boston: Houghton, Osgood, 1878. Stories.

The Twins of Table Mountain and Other Stories. Boston: Houghton, Osgood, 1879.

Flip and Other Stories. London: Chatto & Windus, 1882. 2 novellas & story; 2 novellas repub as *Flip and Found at Blazing Star*. Boston & NY: Houghton, Mifflin, 1882.

In the Carquinez Woods. London: Longmans, Green, 1883; Boston & NY: Houghton, Mifflin, 1884. Novella.

On the Frontier. Boston & NY: Houghton, Mifflin, 1884. Stories.

By Shore and Sedge. Boston & NY: Houghton, Mifflin, 1885. Stories.

Maruja. Boston & NY: Houghton, Mifflin, 1885. Novella.

Snow-Bound at Eagle's. Boston & NY: Houghton, Mifflin, 1886. Novella.

The Queen of the Pirate Isle. London: Chatto & Windus, 1886; Boston & NY: Houghton, Mifflin, 1887. Novella.

A Millionaire of Rough-and-Ready and Devil's Ford. Boston & NY: Houghton, Mifflin, 1887. Each separately published, London: White, 1887. Novellas.

The Crusade of the Excelsior. Boston & NY: Houghton, Mifflin, 1887. Novel.

A Phyllis of the Sierras and A Drift From Redwood Camp. Boston & NY: Houghton, Mifflin, 1888. Novellas.

The Argonauts of North Liberty. Boston & NY: Houghton, Mifflin, 1888. Novel.

Cressy. Boston & NY: Houghton, Mifflin, 1889. Novel.

The Heritage of Dedlow Marsh and Other Tales. Boston & NY: Houghton, Mifflin, 1889.

A Waif of the Plains. Boston & NY: Houghton, Mifflin, 1890. Novel.

A Ward of the Golden Gate. Boston & NY: Houghton, Mifflin, 1890. Novel.

A Sappho of Green Springs and Other Stories. Boston & NY: Houghton, Mifflin, 1891.

A First Family of Tasajara. 2 vols, London & NY: Macmillan, 1891; 1 vol, Boston & NY: Houghton, Mifflin, 1892. Novel.

Colonel Starbottle's Client and Some Other People. Boston & NY: Houghton, Mifflin, 1892. Stories.

Susy: A Story of the Plains. Boston & NY: Houghton, Mifflin, 1893. Novel.

Sally Dows, Etc. London: Chatto & Windus, 1893; *Sally Dows and Other Stories*. Boston & NY: Houghton, Mifflin, 1893.

A Protégée of Jack Hamlin's and Other Stories. Boston & NY: Houghton, Mifflin, 1894. Augmented ed, London: Chatto & Windus, 1894.

The Bell-Ringer of Angel's and Other Stories. Boston & NY: Houghton, Mifflin, 1894.

Clarence. Boston & NY: Houghton, Mifflin, 1895. Novel.

In a Hollow of the Hills. Boston & NY: Houghton, Mifflin, 1895. Novel.

Barker's Luck and Other Stories. Boston & NY: Houghton, Mifflin, 1896.

Three Partners; or, The Big Strike on Heavy Tree Hill. Boston & NY: Houghton, Mifflin, 1897. Novel.

Tales of Trail and Town. Boston & NY: Houghton, Mifflin, 1898. Stories.

Stories in Light and Shadow. Boston & NY: Houghton, Mifflin, 1898.

Mr. Jack Hamlin's Mediation and Other Stories. Boston & NY: Houghton, Mifflin, 1899.

From Sand Hill to Pine. Boston & NY: Houghton, Mifflin, 1900. Stories.

Under the Redwoods. Boston & NY: Houghton, Mifflin, 1901. Stories.

On the Old Trail. London: Pearson, 1902; *Openings in the Old Trail*. Boston & NY: Houghton, Mifflin, 1902. Stories.

Condensed Novels, Second Series: New Burlesques. Boston & NY: Houghton, Mifflin, 1902. Parodies.

Sue: A Play in Three Acts, with T Edgar Pemberton. London: Greening, 1902.

Trent's Trust and Other Stories. Boston & NY: Houghton, Mifflin, 1903.

The Lectures of BH, comp Charles Meeker Kozlay. Brooklyn, NY: Kozlay, 1909.

Stories and Poems and Other Uncollected Writings, comp Kozlay. Boston & NY: Houghton Mifflin, 1914.

Sketches of the Sixties, with Mark Twain. San Francisco: Howell, 1926.

"Ah Sin": A Dramatic Work, with Mark Twain; ed with intro by Frederick Anderson. San Francisco: Book Club of California, 1961. Play.

LETTERS

The Letters of BH, ed Geoffrey Bret Harte. Boston & NY: Houghton Mifflin, 1926.

"BH Goes East: Some Unpublished Letters" by Bradford A Booth. *AL*, 19 (May 1948), 318-335.

San Francisco in 1886 . . . Being Letters to the Springfield Republican, ed George R Stewart & Edwin S Fussell. San Francisco: Book Club of California, 1951.

"The Unpublished Letters of BH to John Hay" by Brenda Murphy & George Monteiro. *ALR*, 12 (Spring 1979), 77-126.

COLLECTION

The Writings of BH, 20 vols. Boston: Houghton, Mifflin, 1896-1914.

MANUSCRIPTS & ARCHIVES

The major collections are at UCLA Library; U of California, Berkeley, Library; U of Virginia Library; & the Huntington Library, San Marino, Calif.

BIOGRAPHIES

Boynton, Henry W. *BH*. NY: McClure, Phillips, 1903.

Merwin, Henry Childs. *The Life of BH*. Boston: Houghton Mifflin, 1911.

O'Connor, Richard. *BH: A Biography*. Boston: Little, Brown, 1966.

Pemberton, T Edgar. *Life of BH*. NY: Dodd, Mead, 1903.

Stewart, George R. *BH, Argonaut and Exile*. Boston: Houghton Mifflin, 1931.

CRITICAL STUDIES

Books

Duckett, Margaret. *Mark Twain and BH*. Norman: U Oklahoma P, 1964.

Morrow, Patrick D. *BH*. Boise, Idaho: Boise State C, 1972.

Morrow. *BH: Literary Critic*. Bowling Green, Ohio: Bowling Green U Popular P, 1979.

Special Journal

WAL, 8 (Fall 1973). BH issue.

Book Sections & Articles

Buckland, Roscoe L. "Jack Hamlin: BH's Romantic Rogue." *WAL*, 8 (Fall 1973), 111-122.

Burton, Linda. "For Better or Worse, Tennessee and His Partner: A New Approach to BH." *ArQ*, 36 (Autumn 1980), 211-216.

Conner, William F. "The Euchring of Tennessee: A Reexamination of BH's 'Tennessee's Partner.'" *SSF*, 17 (Spring 1980), 113-120.

Duckett, Margaret. "BH's Portrayal of Half-Breeds." *AL*, 25 (May 1953), 193-212.

Duckett. "BH and the Indians of Northern California." *HLQ*, 18 (Nov 1954), 59-83.

Duckett. "Plain Language From BH." *NCF*, 11 (Mar 1957), 241-260.

Erskine, John. "BH." *Leading American Novelists* (NY: Holt, 1910), 324-369. Rpt Freeport, NY: Books for Libraries, 1966.

Fenn, William Purviance. *Ah Sin and His Brethren in American Literature* (Peking: California C in China, 1933), passim.

Gardner, Joseph H. "BH and the Dickensian Mode in America." *CRevAS*, 2 (Fall 1971), 89-101.

Gates, W B. "BH and Shakespeare." *SCB*, 20 (Winter 1960), 29-33.

Glover, Donald E. "A Reconsideration of BH's Later Work." *WAL*, 8 (Fall 1973), 143-151.

Kuhlman, Susan. *Knave, Fool, and Genius: The Confidence Man as He Appears in Nineteenth-Century American Fiction* (Chapel Hill: U North Carolina P, 1973), 34-48.

May, Ernest R. "BH and the *Overland Monthly*." *AL*, 22 (Nov 1950), 260-271.

Morrow, Patrick D. "BH, Popular Fiction, and the Local Color Movement." *WAL*, 8 (Fall 1973), 123-131.

Quinn, Arthur Hobson. "BH and the Fiction of Moral Contrast." *American Fiction* (NY: Appleton-Century, 1936), 232-242.

Starr, Kevin. *Americans and the California Dream, 1850-1915* (NY: Oxford U P, 1973), passim.

Stegner, Wallace. "Introduction." *The Outcasts of*

Poker Flat and Other Tales (NY: NAL, 1961), vii-xvi. Rpt as "The West Synthetic: BH." *The Sound of Mountain Water* by Stegner (Garden City, NY: Doubleday, 1969).

Thomas, Jeffrey F. "BH and the Power of Sex." *WAL*, 8 (Fall 1973), 91-109.

Thomas. "BH." *ALR*, 8 (Summer 1975), 266-270.

Walker, Franklin. *San Francisco's Literary Frontier* (NY: Knopf, 1939), passim.

Williams, S T. "Ambrose Bierce and BH." *AL*, 17 (May 1945), 179-180.

Alfred Bendixen

LAFCADIO HEARN

Santa Maura, Greece, 27 Jun 1850-Yokohama, Japan, 26 Sep 1904

Lafcadio Hearn began his writing career as a journalist whose articles were known for their attention to minute, frequently morbid detail. His first national recognition came with *Chita*, a journalistic novel about a storm-wracked island off New Orleans. His translations of French realists were well received and remain in print. Hearn is best remembered, however, for his descriptions and interpretations of Japanese culture. In the 1890s he moved to Yokohama, married a daughter of a samurai family, became a Japanese citizen, changed his name to Koizumi Yokumo, and delivered in Japanese universities a series of influential, posthumously published lectures on English and American literature. Much of Hearn's best fiction draws upon Japanese legend and folklore, fusing exotic subject matter with polished, lyrical style.

BIBLIOGRAPHIES & CATALOGUES

Bibliography of American Literature, comp Jacob Blanck. New Haven: Yale U P, 1955-1991. Primary.

A Catalog of First Editions of LH. Beverly Hills, Calif: Penguin, 1933.

Gwyn, Ann S. *LH: A Catalogue of the Collection at the Howard-Tilton Memorial Library, Tulane University*. New Orleans: Friends of the Tulane U Library, 1977.

Perkins, P D & Ione. *LH: A Bibliography of His Writings*, intro by Sanki Ichikawa. Boston: Houghton Mifflin, 1934. Rpt NY: Franklin, 1968. Primary & secondary.

Targ, William. *LH: First Editions and Values: A Checklist for Collectors*. Chicago: Black Archer, 1935.

BOOKS

Stray Leaves From Strange Literature: Stories Reconstructed From the Anvari-Soheïli, Baitál Paehísí, Mahabharta, Pantchatantra, Gulistan, Talmud, Kalewala, Etc. Boston: Osgood, 1884. Stories & essays.

Some Chinese Ghosts. Boston: Roberts, 1887. Stories.

Chita: A Memory of Last Island. NY: Harper, 1889. Novel.

Two Years in the French West Indies. NY: Harper, 1890. Essays.

Youma: The Story of a West-Indian Slave. NY: Harper, 1890. Novel.

Glimpses of Unfamiliar Japan, 2 vols. Boston & NY: Houghton, Mifflin, 1894. Essays & sketches.

"Out of the East": Reveries and Studies in New Japan. Boston & NY: Houghton, Mifflin, 1895. Essays.

Kokoro: Hints and Echoes of Japanese Inner Life. Boston & NY: Houghton, Mifflin, 1896. Essays.

Gleanings in Buddha-Fields: Studies of Hand and Soul in the Far East. Boston & NY: Houghton, Mifflin, 1897. Essays.

Exotics and Retrospectives. Boston: Little, Brown, 1898. Essays.

In Ghostly Japan. Boston: Little, Brown, 1899. Essays.

Shadowings. Boston: Little, Brown, 1900. Stories & essays.

A Japanese Miscellany. Boston: Little, Brown, 1901. Stories & essays.

Kottō: Being Japanese Curios, With Sundry Cobwebs. NY & London: Macmillan, 1902. Stories.

Kwaidan: Stories and Studies of Strange Things. Boston & NY: Houghton, Mifflin, 1904. Stories & essays.

Japan: An Attempt at Interpretation. NY & London: Macmillan, 1904. Augmented ed, 1904. Essays.

The Romance of the Milky Way and Other Studies & Stories. Boston & NY: Houghton Mifflin, 1905.

Leaves From the Diary of an Impressionist: Early Writings, intro by Ferris Greenslet. Boston & NY: Houghton Mifflin, 1911.

Editorials From the Kobe Chronicle. NY: Privately printed, 1913.

Fantastics and Other Fancies, ed Charles Woodward Hutson. Boston & NY: Houghton Mifflin, 1914. Stories.

Interpretations of Literature, 2 vols, ed with intro by John Erskine. NY: Dodd, Mead, 1915. Lectures.

Appreciations of Poetry, ed with intro by Erskine. NY: Dodd, Mead, 1916. Lectures.

Life and Literature, ed with intro by Erskine. NY: Dodd, Mead, 1917. Lectures.

Karma. NY: Boni & Liveright, 1918. Stories & essays.

Leaves From the Diary of an Impressionist, Creole Sketches, and Some Chinese Ghosts. Boston & NY: Houghton Mifflin, 1922 (Vol 1 of *The Writings of LH*). Separately published & augmented as *Creole Sketches,* ed Hutson, 1924. Essays & sketches.

Essays in European and Oriental Literature, ed Albert Mordell. NY: Dodd, Mead, 1923.

An American Miscellany: Articles and Stories Now First Collected by Albert Mordell, 2 vols. NY: Dodd, Mead, 1924; *Miscellanies...,* 2 vols. London: Heinemann, 1924.

Occidental Gleanings: Sketches and Essays Now First Collected by Albert Mordell, 2 vols. NY: Dodd, Mead, 1925.

Editorials, ed Hutson. Boston & NY: Houghton Mifflin, 1926.

Insects and Greek Poetry. NY: Rudge, 1926. Lecture.

A History of English Literature in a Series of Lectures, 2 vols. Tokyo: Hokuseido, 1927. Rev ed, 1 vol, 1930.

Supplement to A History of English Literature... Vol. I (From Ben Jonson to Restoration Drama). Tokyo: Hokuseido, 1927. Lectures.

Some Strange English Literary Figures of the Eighteenth and Nineteenth Centuries in a Series of Lectures, ed R Tanabé. Tokyo: Hokuseido, 1927.

Lectures on Shakespeare, ed Iwao Inagaki. Tokyo: Hokuseido, 1928.

Essays on American Literature, ed Sanki Ichikawa; intro by Mordell. Tokyo: Hokuseido, 1929.

Lectures on Prosody. Tokyo: Hokuseido, 1929.

Victorian Philosophy. Tokyo: Hokuseido, 1930. Lectures.

Gibbeted: Execution of a Youthful Murderer, Shocking Tragedy at Dayton, a Broken Rope and a Double Hanging, Sickening Scenes Behind the Scaffold-Screen. Los Angeles: Murray, 1933. Sketches.

Barbarous Barbers and Other Stories, ed Ichiro Nishizaki. Tokyo: Hokuseido, 1939.

Buying Christmas Toys and Other Essays, ed Ichiro Nishizaki. Tokyo: Hokuseido, 1939.

Literary Essays, ed Ichiro Nishizaki. Tokyo: Hokuseido, 1939.

The New Radiance and Other Scientific Sketches, ed Ichiro Nishizaki. Tokyo: Hokuseido, 1939.

Oriental Articles, ed Ichiro Nishizaki. Tokyo: Hokuseido, 1939.

Children of the Levee, ed O W Frost; intro by John Ball. Lexington: U Kentucky P, 1957. Sketches.

Earless Ho-Ichi: A Classic Japanese Tale of Mystery by LH, intro by Donald Keene. Tokyo: Kodansha, 1966. Story.

LETTERS

Letters From the Raven: Being the Correspondence of LH With Henry Watkin, ed with intro & commentary by Milton Bronner. NY: Brentano, 1907.

The Japanese Letters of LH, ed with intro by Elizabeth Bisland. Boston & NY: Houghton Mifflin, 1910.

Some New Letters and Writings of LH, ed Sanki Ichikawa. Tokyo: Kenkyusha, 1925.

Letters From Shimane and Kyūshū. Kyoto: Sunward, 1934.

"Newly Discovered Letters From LH to Dr. Rudolph Matas," ed Ichiro Nishizaki. *OUSAC,* 8 (Mar 1956), 85-118.

"New H Letters From the French West Indies," ed Ichiro Nishizaki. *OUSAC,* 12 (Jun 1959), 59-110.

OTHER

One of Cleopatra's Nights and Other Fantastic Romances by Théophile Gautier; trans LH. NY: Worthington, 1882.

La Cuisine Creole: A Collection of Culinary Recipes From Leading Chefs and Noted Creole

Housewives, Who Have Made New Orleans Famous for Its Cuisine (Anon), comp LH. NY: Coleman, 1885.

"Gombo Zhèbes": Little Dictionary of Creole Proverbs, Selected From Six Creole Dialects, Translated into French and into English, With Notes, Complete Index to Subjects and Some Brief Remarks Upon the Creole Idioms of Louisiana, comp LH. NY: Coleman, 1885.

The Crime of Sylvestre Bonnard by Anatole France; trans with intro by LH. NY: Harper, 1890. Novel.

The Boy Who Drew Cats, trans LH. Tokyo: Hasegawa, 1896. Japanese fairy tale.

The Goblin Spider, trans LH. Tokyo: Hasegawa, 1899. Japanese fairy tale.

The Old Woman Who Lost Her Dumpling, trans LH. Tokyo: Hasegawa, 1902. Japanese fairy tale.

Chin Chin Kobakama, trans LH. Tokyo: Hasegawa, 1903. Japanese fairy tale.

The Temptation of St. Anthony by Gustave Flaubert; trans LH. NY: Harriman, 1910. Novel.

Japanese Lyrics, trans LH. Boston & NY: Houghton Mifflin, 1915.

The Fountain of Youth, trans LH. Tokyo: Hasegawa, 1922. Japanese fairy tale.

Saint Anthony and Other Stories by Guy de Maupassant, trans LH; ed Albert Mordell. NY: Boni, 1924.

The Adventures of Walter Schnaffs and Other Stories by Guy de Maupassant, trans LH; intro by Mordell. Tokyo: Hokuseido, 1931.

Stories From Pierre Loti, trans LH; intro by Mordell. Tokyo: Hokuseido, 1933.

Japanese Goblin Poetry Rendered into English by LH, comp Kazuo Koizumi. Tokyo: Oyama, 1934.

Sketches and Tales From the French, trans LH; ed Mordell. Tokyo: Hokuseido, 1935.

Stories From Emile Zola, trans LH; ed Mordell. Tokyo: Hokuseido, 1935.

Re-Echo by Kazuo Hearn Koizumi; ed Nancy Jane Fellers; photos & original pen & watercolor sketches by LH. Caldwell, Idaho: Caxton, 1957.

EDITIONS & COLLECTIONS

Books and Habits: From the Lectures of LH, ed with intro by John Erskine. NY: Dodd, Mead, 1921.

The Writings of LH, 16 vols. Boston & NY: Houghton Mifflin, 1922.

Pre-Raphaelite and Other Poets: Lectures, ed Erskine. NY: Dodd, Mead, 1922.

Kimiko and Other Japanese Sketches. Boston & NY: Houghton Mifflin, 1923.

Stories and Sketches, comp with notes by

R Tanabé. Tokyo: Hokuseido, 1925.

Poets and Poems, comp with notes by R Tanabé. Tokyo: Hokuseido, 1926.

Romance and Reason, comp with notes by R Tanabé. Tokyo: Hokuseido, 1928.

Facts and Fancies, ed with notes by R Tanabé. Tokyo: Hokuseido, 1929.

Complete Lectures on Art, Literature and Philosophy, ed Ryuji Tanabé, Teisaburo Ochiai & Ichiro Nishizaki. Tokyo: Hokuseido, 1932.

Complete Lectures on Poets, ed Ryuji Tanabé, Teisaburo Ochiai & Ichiro Nishizaki. Tokyo: Hokuseido, 1934.

Complete Lectures on Poetry, ed Ryuji Tanabé, Teisaburo Ochiai & Ichiro Nishizaki. Tokyo: Hokuseido, 1934.

Japan's Religions: Shinto and Buddhism, ed Kazumitsu Kato. New Hyde Park, NY: University Books, 1966.

The Buddhist Writings of LH, ed with intro by Kenneth Rexroth. Santa Barbara, Calif: Ross-Erickson, 1977.

LH: Writings From Japan, ed with intro by Francis King. Harmondsworth, UK: Penguin, 1984.

MANUSCRIPTS & ARCHIVES

Tulane U Library.

BIOGRAPHIES

Books

Barel, Leona Queyrouze. *The Idyl: My Personal Reminiscences of LH*. Tokyo: Hokuseido, 1933.

Bisland, Elizabeth. *The Life and Lectures of LH*, 2 vols. Boston & NY: Houghton, Mifflin, 1906.

Frost, O W. *Young H*. Tokyo: Hokuseido, 1958.

Gould, George M. *Concerning LH*, with bibliography by Laura Stedman. Philadelphia: Jacobs, 1908.

Kennard, Nina H. *LH: Containing Some Letters From LH to His Half-Sister, Mrs. Atkinson*. London: Nash, 1912.

Kirkwood, Kenneth P. *Unfamiliar LH*. Tokyo: Hokuseido, 1936.

Kirkwood. *LH's Ancestry*. Tokyo: Nippon, 1938.

Koizumi, Kazuo. *Father and I: Memories of LH*. Boston: Houghton Mifflin, 1935.

Koizumi, Setsuko. *Reminiscences of LH*. Boston: Houghton Mifflin, 1918.

McWilliams, Vera. *LH*. Boston: Houghton Mifflin, 1946.

Noguchi, Yone. *LH in Japan*, with reminiscences by Mrs LH & sketches by LH. Yokohama: Kelly & Walsh, 1910.

Stevenson, Elizabeth. *LH*. NY: Macmillan, 1961.

Temple, Jean. *Blue Ghost: A Study of LH*. NY: Cape & Smith, 1931.

Thomas, Edward. *LH*. Boston: Houghton Mifflin, 1912.

Tinker, Edward Larocque. *LH's American Days*. NY: Dodd, 1924.

Articles

Eber, Robert. "LH: A Biographical Sketch." *Romantist*, 3 (1979), 73-75.

Hakutani, Yoshinobu. "LH." *ALR*, 8 (Summer 1975), 271-274.

Yu, Beongcheon. "LH (or Koizumi Yakumo) (1850-1904)." *ALR*, 1 (Fall 1967), 52-55.

CRITICAL STUDIES

Books

Coyne, Robert F. "LH's Criticism of English Literature." Dissertation: Florida State U, 1969.

Hylland, Marilyn Gail. "Ghost/Goblins, Dreams, and the Divinity of Art: Three Major Themes of Dimension. A Study of LH's Japanese Period." Dissertation: Southern Illinois U, 1973.

Kunst, Arthur E. *LH*. NY: Twayne, 1969.

Lazar, Margaret Ann McAdow. "The Art of LH: A Study of His Literary Development." Dissertation: Texas Christian U, 1977.

Lewis, Oscar. *H and His Biographers: The Record of a Literary Controversy, Together With a Group of Letters From LH to Joseph Tunison*. San Francisco: Westgate, 1930.

Mordell, Albert. *Discoveries: Essays on LH*. Tokyo: Orient/West, 1964.

Rosenstone, Robert A. *Mirror in the Shrine*. Cambridge: Harvard U P, 1988.

Vincent, Mary Louise. "LH and Late Romanticism." Dissertation: U Minnesota, 1967.

Webb, Kathleen M. *LH and His German Critics: An Examination of His Appeal*. NY: Lang, 1984.

Yu, Beongcheon. *An Ape of Gods: The Art and Thought of LH*. Detroit: Wayne State U P, 1964.

Book Section & Articles

Blunden, Edmund. "LH, Teacher." *Orient/West*, 10 (1966), 299-301.

Dyer, Joyce Coyne. "LH's *Chita* and Kate Chopin's *The Awakening*: Two Naturalistic Tales of the Gulf Islands." *SoSt*, 23 (Winter 1984), 412-426.

Erwin, Jahn. "LH's Image of Japan." *Orient/West*, 8 (1963), 33-40.

Hughes, Jon Christopher. "*Ye Giglampz* and the Apprenticeship of LH." *ALR*, 15 (Autumn 1982), 182-194.

Kunst, Arthur E. "LH's Use of Japanese Sources." *LE&W*, 10 (Sep 1966), 245-263.

Kunst. "LH vis-a-vis French Literature." *CLS*, 4, no 3 (1967), 307-317.

Leary, Lewis. "LH, 'One of Our Southern Writers': A Footnote to Southern Literary History." *Essays on American Literature in Honor of Jay B. Hubbell*, ed Clarence Gohdes (Durham, NC: Duke U P, 1967), 202-214.

McNeil, W K. "LH: American Folklorist." *JAF*, 91 (Oct-Dec 1978), 947-967.

Kristi Kibbe

JOSEPH HERGESHEIMER

Germantown, Pa, 15 Feb 1880-Sea Isle, NJ, 25 Apr 1954

Joseph Hergesheimer's reputation peaked in the early 1930s, when most of his peers and their critics agreed that he was among America's principal authors. Fortunate in such publishers as Alfred A. Knopf for his books and George Horace Lorimer for his profitable stories in *The Saturday Evening Post,* he had a very wide audience. But by the time the Depression had set in, he was dismissed as an esthete concerned only with surfaces, and in another ten years he was largely forgotten. Hergesheimer's career is now analyzed more often than his fiction: he is viewed either as a victim of changing taste or as an author whose narrow vision justified the collapse of his reputation. However, his best work, taken for what it is—for instance, *Java Head* as an historical novel showing painstaking research and considerable technical skill—has always commanded respect.

BIBLIOGRAPHIES & CATALOGUE

Napier, James J. "JH: A Selected Bibliography, 1913-1945." *BB,* 24 (Sep-Dec 1963), 46-48; 24 (Jan-Apr 1964), 52, 69-70. Primary & secondary.

Stappenbeck, Herb. *A Catalogue of the JH Collection at the University of Texas.* Austin: U Texas P, 1974. Primary.

Swire, H L R. *A Bibliography of the Works of JH.* Philadelphia: Centaur Book Shop, 1922.

BOOKS

The Lay Anthony. NY & London: Kennerley, 1914. Rev ed, NY: Knopf, 1919. Novel.

Mountain Blood. NY & London: Kennerley, 1915. Rev ed, NY: Knopf, 1930. Novel.

The Three Black Pennys. NY: Knopf, 1917. Repub with intro by JH, 1930. Novel.

Gold and Iron. NY: Knopf, 1918. Repub separately as *Wild Oranges* & *The Dark Fleece* & *Tubal Cain,* 1922. Novellas.

Java Head. NY: Knopf, 1919. Novel.

The Happy End. NY: Knopf, 1919. One story separately repub as *Tol'able David,* 1923. Stories.

Hugh Walpole: An Appreciation. NY: Doran, 1919. Essay.

Linda Condon. NY: Knopf, 1919. Novel.

San Cristóbal de la Habana. NY: Knopf, 1920. Travel.

Cytherea. NY: Knopf, 1922. Novel.

The Bright Shawl. NY: Knopf, 1922. Novel.

The Presbyterian Child. NY: Knopf, 1923. Autobiography.

Balisand. NY: Knopf, 1924. Novel.

From an Old House. NY: Knopf, 1925. Autobiography.

Tampico. NY: Knopf, 1926. Novel.

Quiet Cities. NY: Knopf, 1928. Stories.

Swords and Roses. NY & London: Knopf, 1929. Essays.

Triall by Armes. London: Mathews & Marrot, 1929. Story.

The Party Dress. NY & London: Knopf, 1930. Novel.

The Limestone Tree. NY: Knopf, 1931. Novel.

Sheridan: A Military Narrative. Boston & NY: Houghton Mifflin, 1931. Biography.

Berlin. NY: Knopf, 1932. Travel.

Love in the United States and The Big Shot. London: Benn, 1932. Novellas.

Tropical Winter. NY: Knopf, 1933. Stories.

The Foolscap Rose. NY: Knopf, 1934. Novel.

LETTERS

Between Friends: Letters of James Branch Cabell and Others, ed Padraic Colum & Margaret Freeman Cabell (NY: Harcourt, Brace & World, 1962), passim. Contains 21 letters from JH to Cabell.

MANUSCRIPTS & ARCHIVES

The Harry Ransom Humanities Research Center, U of Texas, Austin.

BIOGRAPHIES
Book Sections & Articles

Bode, Carl, ed. *The New Mencken Letters* (NY: Dial, 1977), passim.

Clark, Emily. "JH." *Innocence Abroad* (NY: Knopf, 1931), 87-106.

Forgue, Guy J, ed. *Letters of H L Mencken* (NY: Knopf, 1961), passim.

Gray, Jerome B. "An Author and His Town." *Bookman,* 67 (Apr 1928), 159-164.

Knopf, Alfred A. "Reminiscences of H, Van Vechten, and Mencken." *YULG,* 24 (Apr 1950), 145-164.

Langford, Gerald, ed. *Ingénue Among the Lions: The Letters of Emily Clark to JH* (Austin: U Texas P, 1965), passim.

Napier, James J. "Letters of Sinclair Lewis to JH, 1915-1922." *AL,* 38 (May 1966), 236-246.

Van Vechten, Carl. "How I Remember JH." *YULG,* 22 (Jan 1948), 87-93.

Wagenknecht, Edward, ed. *The Letters of James Branch Cabell* (Norman: U Oklahoma P, 1975), passim.

CRITICAL STUDIES

Books

Cabell, James Branch. *JH: An Essay in Interpretation.* Chicago: Bookfellows, 1921.

Gimmestad, Victor E. *JH.* Boston: Twayne, 1984.

Jones, Llewellyn. *JH: The Man and His Books.* NY: Knopf, 1920.

Martin, Ronald E. *The Fiction of JH.* Philadelphia: U Pennsylvania P, 1965.

Book Sections & Articles

Cabell, James Branch. "Diversions of the Anchorite." *Straws and Prayer-Books* (NY: McBride, 1924), 191-221.

Fain, John Tyree. "H's Use of Historical Sources." *JSoH,* 18 (Nov 1952), 497-504.

Hicks, Granville. "Two Roads." *The Great Tradition* (NY: Macmillan, rev 1935), 207-256.

Hubbell, Jay B. *Who Are the Major American Writers?* (Durham, NC: Duke U P, 1972), passim.

Justus, James H. "JH's Germany: A Radical Art of Surfaces." *JAmS,* 7 (Apr 1973), 47-66.

Kejzlarová, Ingeborg. "JH: A 'Lost' Writer of American Twentieth Century Fiction?" *PP,* 19, no 2 (1976), 73-86.

Kelley, Leon. "America and Mr. H." *SR,* 40 (Apr-Jun 1932), 171-193.

Mencken, H L. "H." *Prejudices: Fifth Series* (NY: Knopf, 1926), 42-49.

Priestley, J B. "JH: An English View." *Bookman,* 63 (May 1926), 272-280.

Sinclair, Upton. "The Ivory Tower." *Money Writes!* (NY: Boni, 1927), 92-99.

Slate, Joseph E. "The JH Collection." *LCUT,* 7 (Fall 1961), 24-31.

Tucker, Edward L. "JH to Mr. Gordon: A Letter." *SAF,* 6 (Autumn 1978), 218-227.

Van Gelder, Robert. "The Curious Retirement of Mr. H." *Writers and Writing* (NY: Scribners, 1946), 149-151.

West, Geoffrey. "JH: An Appreciation." *EngRev,* 53 (Oct 1931), 556-564.

Richard J. Schrader

ROBERT HERRICK

Cambridge, Mass, 26 Apr 1868-St Thomas, Virgin Islands, 23 Dec 1938

In the early years of the twentieth century Robert Herrick was regarded as an important successor to the realist tradition in America and as a serious critic of American society. His many novels, stories, and essays exposed the destructive effects of contemporary life and attacked a system of competition that, he believed, resulted in the corruption of the individual. While his adopted city of Chicago often provided the economic and cultural setting for his novels, his moral voice owed much to the Puritan and Transcendentalist traditions of his New England heritage. In novels concerned with capitalism, radical politics, sexual mores, social pressure, and individual choice, Herrick offered hope for redemption through personal decision rather than public policy. Early assessments of his fiction focused on his social protest, but later critics viewed Herrick as an idealist concerned with exploring individual integrity in an industrial age.

BIBLIOGRAPHIES

Carlson, Douglas O. "RH: An Addendum." *ALR,* 3 (Summer 1968), 67-68. Secondary.

Franklin, Phyllis. "A Handlist of the RH Papers at the University of Chicago." *ALR,* 8 (Spring 1975), 108-154.

Franklin. "RH." *ALR,* 8 (Summer 1975), 276-279. Secondary.

Genthe, Charles V. "RH (1868-1938)." *ALR,* 1 (Fall 1967), 56-60. Primary & secondary.

BOOKS

Literary Love-Letters and Other Stories. NY: Scribners, 1897.

The Man Who Wins. NY: Scribners, 1897. Novel.

The Gospel of Freedom. NY & London: Macmillan, 1898. Novel.

Love's Dilemmas. Chicago: Stone, 1898. Stories.

Composition and Rhetoric for Schools, with Lindsay Todd Damon. Chicago: Scott, Foresman, 1899.

Teaching English, with others. Chicago: Scott, Foresman, 1899.

Methods of Teaching Rhetoric. Chicago: Scott, Foresman, 1899.

The Web of Life. NY & London: Macmillan, 1900. Novel.

The Real World. NY & London: Macmillan, 1901. Novel.

Their Child. NY & London: Macmillan, 1903. Novel.

The Common Lot. NY & London: Macmillan, 1904. Novel.

The Memoirs of an American Citizen. NY & London: Macmillan, 1905. Novel.

The Master of the Inn. NY: Scribners, 1908. Novel.

Together. NY & London: Macmillan, 1908. Novel.

A Life for a Life. NY: Macmillan, 1910. Novel.

The Healer. NY: Macmillan, 1911. Novel.

One Woman's Life. NY: Macmillan, 1913. Novel.

His Great Adventure. NY: Macmillan, 1913. Novel.

Clark's Field. Boston & NY: Houghton Mifflin, 1914. Novel.

The World Decision. Boston & NY: Houghton Mifflin, 1916. Essays.

The Conscript Mother. NY: Scribners, 1916. Novel.

Homely Lilla. NY: Harcourt, Brace, 1923. Novel.

Waste. NY: Harcourt, Brace, 1924. Novel.

Wanderings. NY: Harcourt, Brace, 1925. Stories

Chimes. NY: Macmillan, 1926. Novel.

Little Black Dog. Chicago: Rockwell, 1931. Novel.

The End of Desire. NY: Farrar & Rinehart, 1932. Novel.

Sometime. NY: Farrar & Rinehart, 1933. Novel.

OTHER

Silas Marner by George Eliot; ed with preface by RH. NY: Longmans, Green, 1895.

Twice-Told Tales by Nathaniel Hawthorne; ed RH & Robert W Bruère. Chicago: Scott, Foresman, 1903.

The House of the Seven Gables by Hawthorne; ed with preface by RH. Chicago: Scott, Foresman, 1904.

MANUSCRIPTS & ARCHIVES

U of Chicago Library.

BIOGRAPHY

Book

Nevius, Blake. *RH: The Development of a Novelist.* Berkeley: U California P, 1962.

CRITICAL STUDIES

Books

Budd, Louis J. *RH*. NY: Twayne, 1971.

Pearce, Richard A. "Chicago in the Fiction of the 1890s as Illustrated in the Novels of Henry Blake Fuller and RH." Dissertation: Columbia U, 1963.

Book Sections & Articles

Arvin, Newton. "Homage to RH." *NewR*, 82 (6 Mar 1935), 93-95.

Baldwin, Charles C. "RH." *The Men Who Make Our Novels* (NY: Dodd, Mead, rev 1924), 243-250.

Björkman, Edwin. "Two Studies of RH." *Voices of To-Morrow* (NY: Kennerley, 1913), 260-289.

Cargill, Oscar. *Intellectual America: Ideas on the March* (NY: Macmillan, 1941), passim.

Cooper, Frederic Taber. "RH." *Some American Story Tellers* (NY: Holt, 1911), 140-167.

Dessner, Lawrence Jay. "RH, American Novelist." *MarkhamR*, 3 (Oct 1971), 10-14.

Duffey, Bernard. "RH." *The Chicago Renaissance in American Letters* (East Lansing: Michigan State C P, 1954), 113-123.

Franklin, Phyllis. "RH as Novelist and Journalist." *ALR*, 3 (Fall 1970), 393-395.

Franklin. "The Influence of William James on RH's Early Fiction." *ALR*, 7 (Autumn 1974), 395-402.

Franklin. "RH's Postwar Literary Theories and *Waste*." *ALR*, 11 (Autumn 1978), 275-283.

Hale, Swinburne. "Mr. RH and His Realism." *HMo*, 36 (May 1903), 105-114.

Hicks, Granville. *The Great Tradition* (NY: Macmillan, 1933), 182-186.

Holland, Robert A. "*Together*: A Nietzschean Novel." *SR*, 16 (Oct 1908), 495-504.

Horlacher, Friedrich W. "Economics and the Novel: Henry George and RH." *NEQ*, 55 (Sep 1982), 416-431.

Howells, W D. "The Novels of RH." *NAR*, 189 (Jun 1909), 812-820.

Jackson, Kenny A. "RH's Use of Chicago." *MASJ*, 5 (Spring 1964), 24-32.

Kazin, Alfred. *On Native Grounds* (NY: Reynal & Hitchcock, 1942), 121-126, passim.

Krutch, Joseph Wood. "The Long Journey." *Nation*, 121 (7 Oct 1925), 388-389.

Lüdeke, H. "RH: Novelist of American Democracy." *ES*, 18 (Apr 1936), 49-57.

Lynn, Kenneth S. "The Passion of RH." *The Dream of Success: A Study of the Modern American Imagination* (Boston: Atlantic/ Little, Brown, 1955), 208-240.

Nielsen, Harald. "RH." *PoetL*, 19 (Autumn 1908), 337-363.

Simms, L Moody, Jr. "RH and the Race Question." *NDQ*, 39 (Autumn 1971), 34-38.

Taylor, Walter Fuller. "The Humanism of RH." *AL*, 28 (Nov 1956), 287-301.

Towers, Tom. "Self and Society in the Novels of RH." *JPC*, 1 (Fall 1967), 141-157.

Wagenknecht, Edward. "RH, Idealist." *Cavalcade of the American Novel* (NY: Holt, 1952), 235-244.

Jim Weber

MARIETTA HOLLEY
(Josiah Allen's Wife)

Jefferson County, NY, 16 Jul 1836-Jefferson County, NY, 1 Mar 1926

Under the pseudonym Josiah Allen's Wife, Marietta Holley created the character of Samantha Allen, who has been called the first female comic protagonist of the American humorist tradition. Samantha's vernacular dialect and down-home philosophy provided Holley with the perfect vehicle for treatment of such issues as women's rights, temperance, race, war, and imperialism. Two of Holley's twenty-five books, *My Opinions and Betsy Bobbet's* and *Samantha at Saratoga*, were best-sellers, and most of her books were widely read in America and abroad. In her coverage of women's issues, Holley always countered Samantha's views with the arguments of another character (often her husband, Josiah); Samantha's practical and commonsensical reason invariably exposed her opponent's views as foolish. As her last few novels became repetitive and formulaic, Holley's popularity declined; her work was virtually forgotten in the years following her death.

BIBLIOGRAPHY

First Printings of American Authors, Vol 5, ed Philip B Eppard (Detroit: Bruccoli Clark Layman/Gale, 1987), 145-151. Primary.

BOOKS

My Opinions and Betsy Bobbet's. . . . Hartford, Conn: American Publishing / Toledo, Ohio: Bliss / Chicago: Gilman / Cincinnati: Nettleton, 1873. Novel.

Josiah Allen's Wife as a P.A. and P.L.: Samantha at the Centennial. . . . Hartford, Conn: American Publishing, 1877. Novel.

Betsy Bobbett: A Drama. . . . Adams, NY: Allen, 1880.

The Lament of the Mormon Wife: A Poem. Hartford, Conn: American Publishing, 1880.

My Wayward Pardner; or, My Trials With Josiah, America, the Widow Bump, and Etcetery. Hartford, Conn: American Publishing, 1880. Novel.

Miss Richards' Boy and Other Stories. Hartford, Conn: American Publishing, 1883.

Sweet Cicely; or, Josiah Allen as a Politician. NY & London: Funk & Wagnalls, 1885. Novel.

Miss Jones' Quilting and Other Stories. NY: Ogilvie, 1887. *Other Stories* by Ella Wheeler Wilcox.

Samantha at Saratoga; or, "Flirtin' With Fashion." Philadelphia: Hubbard, 1887. Novel.

Poems. NY & London: Funk & Wagnalls, 1887.

Samantha Among the Brethren. NY & London: Funk & Wagnalls, 1890. Novel.

The Widder Doodle's Courtship and Other Sketches. NY: Ogilvie, 1890. Repub as *The Widder Doodle's Love Affair and Other Stories.* NY: Lupton, 1893.

Samantha on the Race Problem. NY: Dodd, Mead, 1892. Repub as *Samantha Among the Colored Folks: "My Ideas on the Race Problem,"* 1894. Novel.

Tirzah Ann's Summer Trip and Other Sketches. NY: Lupton, 1892.

Samantha at the World's Fair. NY & c : Funk & Wagnalls, 1893. Novel.

Josiah's Alarm and Abel Perry's Funeral. Philadelphia: Lippincott, 1895. Stories.

Samantha in Europe. NY & c: Funk & Wagnalls, 1896. Novel.

Samantha at the St. Louis Exposition. NY: Dillingham, 1904. Novel.

Around the World With Josiah Allen's Wife. NY: Dillingham, 1905. Novel.

Samantha vs. Josiah, Being the Story of a Borrowed Automobile and What Came of It. NY & London: Funk & Wagnalls, 1906. Repub as *Samatha versus Josiah: Discussions of the Natural and the Supernatural,* 1911. Stories.

Samantha on Children's Rights. NY: Dillingham, 1909. Novel.

Josiah's Secret: A Play. Watertown, NY: Hungerford-Holbrook, 1910.

Samantha at Coney Island and a Thousand Other Islands. NY: Christian Herald, 1911. Novel.

Samantha on the Woman Question. NY & c: Revell, 1913. Novel.

Josiah Allen on the Woman Question. NY & c: Revell, 1914. Novel.

The Story of My Life. Watertown, NY: Times Publishing, 1931. Autobiography.

COLLECTION

Samantha Rastles the Woman Question, ed with
   intro by Jane Curry. Urbana & c: U Illinois P,
   1983.

MANUSCRIPTS & ARCHIVES

The major collections are at the Historical Society
of Pennsylvania; the Houghton Library, Harvard U;
Radcliffe C Library, Harvard U; Smith C Library;
St Lawrence U Library; & U of Illinois Library.

BIOGRAPHIES

Book

Winter, Kate H. *MH: Life With "Josiah Allen's
   Wife."* Syracuse, NY: Syracuse U P, 1984.

Article

Wagnalls, Mabel. "A Glimpse of MH." *LadiesHJ*,
   20 (Nov 1903), 61.

CRITICAL STUDIES

Book

Blyley, Katherine G. "MH." Dissertation: U Pittsburgh, 1937.

Book Sections & Articles

Armitage, Shelley. "MH: The Humorist as Propagandist." *RMR*, 34 (Fall 1980), 193-201.

Blair, Walter. "Josh and Samantha." *Horse Sense in
   American Humor* (Chicago: U Chicago P,
   1942), 231-239.

Butler, Ellis Parker. "MH." *MTQ*, 2 (Fall 1937),
   13.

Butler. "The Uniqueness of MH." *MTJ*, 10 (Spring-
   Summer 1958), 11.

Curry, Jane. "Samantha 'Rastles' the Woman Question." *JPC*, 8 (Spring 1975), 805-824.

Ericson, Eston Everett. "An American Indebtedness
   to Carlyle." *N&Q*, 6 (Dec 1959), 456-457.

Graulich, Melody, " 'Wimmen is my theme, and
   also Josiah': The Forgotten Humor of MH."
   ATQ, 47-48 (Summer-Fall 1980), 187-198.

Sloane, David E E. "MH: 'Josiah Allen's Wife.' "
   ALR, 8 (Summer 1975), 279-280.

Toth, Emily. "A Laughter of Their Own: Women's
   Humor in the United States." *Critical Essays
   on American Humor*, ed William Bedford
   Clark & W Craig Turner (Boston: Hall,
   1984), 199-215.

Williams, Patricia. "The Crackerbox Philosopher as
   Feminist: The Novels of MH." *AHumor*, 7,
   no 1 (1980), 16-21.

Winter, Kate H. "*Legacy* Profile: MH 'Josiah
   Allen's Wife' (1836-1926)." *Legacy*, 2 (Spring
   1985), 3-5.

Kelly West

PAULINE ELIZABETH HOPKINS

Portland, Maine, 1859-Boston, Mass, 13 Aug 1930

Pauline Elizabeth Hopkins's novels and short stories have only recently begun to attract critical recognition. Hopkins sought to intensify her readers' awareness of racial discrimination and to celebrate African-Americans' courage, perseverance, and intelligence, as well as their achievements. Previously known solely for her historical romance *Contending Forces*, Hopkins is now recognized as a formative voice in African-American literature. Her use of popular fictional techniques, such as the romance form, enabled her to reach a wide audience. Although Hopkins focused on and decried injustices suffered by African-American women, her overriding purpose in her writings was to further the cause of racial equality.

BOOKS

Contending Forces: A Romance Illustrative of Negro Life North and South. Boston: Colored Co-operative, 1900. Novel.

A Primer of Facts Pertaining to the Greatness of Africa. Cambridge, Mass: Hopkins, 1905. Nonfiction.

The Magazine Novels of PH, foreword by Henry Louis Gates, Jr; intro by Hazel V Carby. NY & Oxford: Oxford U P, 1988 (*Hagar's Daughter: A Story of Southern Caste Prejudice*; *Winona: A Tale of Negro Life in the South and Southwest*; & *Of One Blood; or, The Hidden Self*).

OTHER

"George Washington: A Christmas Story." *ColoredAM*, 2 (Dec 1900), 95-104.

"Bro'r Abr'm Jimson's Wedding: A Christmas Story." *ColoredAM*, 4 (Dec 1901), 103-112. Rpt *Invented Lives: Narratives of Black Women, 1860-1960*, ed Mary Helen Washington (Garden City, NY: Doubleday, 1987).

"Famous Men of the Negro Race." *ColoredAM*, 2 (Feb 1901)-3 (Oct 1901). Essays.

"Famous Women of the Negro Race." *ColoredAM*, 4 (Nov 1901)-5 (Oct 1902). Essays.

"Topsy Templeton." *New Era* (1916). Novella.

EDITIONS

Contending Forces: A Romance Illustrative of Negro Life North and South, afterword by Gwendolyn Brooks. Carbondale & Edwardsville: Southern Illinois U P / London & Amsterdam: Feffer & Simons, 1978.

Contending Forces: A Romance Illustrative of Negro Life North and South, foreword by Henry Louis Gates, Jr; intro by Richard Yarborough. NY & Oxford: Oxford U P, 1988.

MANUSCRIPTS & ARCHIVES

Fisk U Library.

BIOGRAPHIES

Articles

Johnson, Abby Arthur & Ronald M. "Away From Accommodation: Radical Editors and Protest Journalism, 1900-1910." *JNH*, 62 (Oct 1977), 325-338.

Shockley, Ann Allen. "PEH: A Biographical Excursion into Obscurity." *Phylon*, 33 (1972), 22-26.

CRITICAL STUDIES

Book Sections

Campbell, Jane. "Female Paradigms in Frances Harper's *Iola Leroy* and PH's *Contending Forces*." *Mythic Black Fiction: The Transformation of History* (Knoxville: U Tennessee P, 1986), 18-41.

Carby, Hazel. " 'Of What Use Is Fiction?': PEH," " 'All the Fire and Romance': The Magazine Fiction of PEH." *Reconstructing Womanhood: The Emergence of the Afro-American Woman Novelist* (NY: Oxford U P, 1987), 121-144, 145-162.

Tate, Claudia. "PH: Our Literary Foremother." *Conjuring: Black Women, Fiction, and Literary Tradition*, ed Marjorie Pryse & Hortense J Spillers (Bloomington: Indiana U P, 1985), 53-66.

Washington, Mary Helen. "Uplifting the Women and the Race: The Forerunners—Harper & H." *Invented Lives: Narratives of Black Women, 1860-1960* (Garden City, NY: Doubleday, 1987), 73-86.

Jane Campbell

EMERSON HOUGH

Newton, Iowa, 28 Jun 1857-Evanston, Ill, 30 Apr 1923

Emerson Hough worked on newspapers in Des Moines and in Sandusky, Ohio, and later managed a branch of *Field and Stream* in Chicago. Not until 1902, with the publication of *The Mississippi Bubble,* was Hough able to support himself solely as an author. He then became a prolific writer of frontier novels and articles on conservation and preservation. Hough had an intense concern for accuracy of detail, yet his work was often criticized for being conventional. Although Hough's historical and cultural contributions are recognized by scholars, his writings have been mostly forgotten by modern readers.

BIBLIOGRAPHY

Bibliography of American Literature, comp Jacob Blanck. New Haven: Yale U P, 1955-1991. Primary.

BOOKS

Madre D'Oro: A Four-Act Spectacular Drama. Chicago: Hough, 1888.

The Singing Mouse Stories. NY: Forest & Stream, 1895. Augmented ed, Indianapolis: Bobbs-Merrill, 1910.

The Story of the Cowboy. NY: Appleton, 1897. Repub as *The Cowboy,* 2 vols. NY: America of the Americans Society, 1920? Novel.

The Girl at the Halfway House: A Story of the Plains. NY: Appleton, 1900. Novel.

The Mississippi Bubble. . . . Indianapolis: Bowen-Merrill, 1902. Novel.

The Way to the West and the Lives of Three Early Americans, Boone—Crockett—Carson. Indianapolis: Bobbs-Merrill, 1903. History.

The Law of the Land. . . . Indianapolis: Bobbs-Merrill, 1904. Novel.

Heart's Desire: The Story of a Contented Town. . . . NY: Macmillan, 1905. Novel.

The King of Gee-Whiz, lyrics by Wilbur D Nesbitt. Indianapolis: Bobbs-Merrill, 1906. Play.

The Story of the Outlaw. . . . NY: Outing, 1907. Novel.

The Way of Man. NY: Outing, 1907. Novel.

The Young Alaskans. NY & London: Harper, 1908. Novel.

54-40 or Fight. Indianapolis: Bobbs-Merrill, 1909. Novel.

The Sowing: A "Yankee's" View of England's Duty to Herself and Canada. Chicago & c: Vanderhoof-Gunn, 1909. Nonfiction.

The Purchase Price; or, The Cause of Compromise. Indianapolis: Bobbs-Merrill, 1910. Novel.

The Young Alaskans on the Trail. NY & London: Harper, 1911. Novel.

John Rawn, Prominent Citizen. Indianapolis: Bobbs-Merrill, 1912. Novel.

The Lady and the Pirate. . . . Indianapolis: Bobbs-Merrill, 1913. Novel.

The Young Alaskans in the Rockies. NY & London: Harper, 1913. Novel.

Getting a Wrong Start, a Truthful Autobiography (Anon). NY: Macmillan, 1915. Novel.

Out of Doors. NY & London: Appleton, 1915. Nonfiction.

Let Us Go Afield. NY & London: Appleton, 1916. Nonfiction.

The Magnificent Adventure. . . . NY & London: Appleton, 1916. Novel.

The Firefly's Light. NY: Trow, 1916. Nonfiction.

The Man Next Door. NY & London: Appleton, 1917. Novel.

The Broken Gate. NY & London: Appleton, 1917. Novel.

The Way Out: A Story of the Cumberlands To-day. NY & London: Appleton, 1918. Novel.

The Passing of the Frontier: A Chronicle of the Old West. New Haven: Yale U P / Toronto: Glasgow, Brook / London: Humphrey Milford, Oxford U P, 1918. Nonfiction.

The Young Alaskans in the Far North. NY & London: Harper, 1918. Novel.

The Indefinite Attitude Toward the War and When Shall It Change? NY: American Defence Society, 1918. Nonfiction.

The Sagebrusher: A Story of the West. NY & London: Appleton, 1919. Novel.

The Web: The Authorized History of the American Protective League. Chicago: Reilly & Lee, 1919.

Maw's Vacation: The Story of a Human Being in Yellowstone. St Paul, Minn: Haynes, 1921. Repub as *Maw's Vacation: The Yellowstone Story.* Yellowstone Park: Haynes Picture Shops, 1929. Story.

The Covered Wagon. NY & London: Appleton, 1922. Novel.

The Young Alaskans on the Missouri. NY & London: Harper, 1922. Novel.

North of 36. NY & London: Appleton, 1923. Novel.

Mother of Gold. NY & London: Appleton, 1924. Novel.

The Ship of Souls. NY & London: Appleton, 1925. Novel.

COLLECTION

The Frontier Omnibus: Three Complete Novels by EH. NY: Grosset & Dunlap, 1936.

MANUSCRIPTS & ARCHIVES

The major collections are at the Iowa State Department of History & Archives, Des Moines, & the U of Iowa Library.

BIOGRAPHIES

Book Sections

Adams, Ramon F. *Burrs Under the Saddle* (Norman: U Oklahoma P, 1964), 265-272.

Baldwin, Charles C. "EH." *The Men Who Make Our Novels* (NY: Dodd, Mead, rev 1924), 251-259.

Henry, Stuart. "Early Women Settlers on the Plains." *Conquering Our Great American Plains* (NY: Dutton, 1930), 253-281.

Hutchinson, W H. *A Bar Cross Man: The Life and Personal Writings of Eugene Manlove Rhodes* (Norman: U Oklahoma P, 1956), passim.

CRITICAL STUDIES

Books

Johnson, Carole M. "EH and the American West: A Biographical and Critical Study." Dissertation: U Texas, Austin, 1975.

Stone, Lee Alexander. *EH: His Place in American Letters.* Chicago: Privately printed, 1925.

Wylder, Delbert E. *EH.* Austin, Tex: Steck-Vaughn, 1969.

Wylder. *EH.* Boston: Twayne, 1981.

Book Section & Articles

Daher, Michael. "EH and Daniel Boone." *SSMLN,* 4 (Fall 1974), 15-16.

Gaston, Edwin W, Jr. *The Early Novel of the Southwest* (Albuquerque: U New Mexico P, 1961), passim.

Grahame, Pauline. "A Novelist of the Unsung." *Palimpsest,* 11 (Feb 1930), 67-77.

Gray, Richard Hopkins. "A Dedication to the Memory of EH, 1857-1923." *Ar&W,* 17 (Spring 1975), 1-4.

Grover, Dorys Crow. "EH: Midwestern Novelist of the Frontier." *SSMLN,* 4 (Spring 1974), 2-3.

Grover. "W. H. D. Koerner and EH: A Western Collaboration." *Montana,* 29 (Apr 1979), 2-15.

Hutchinson, W H. "The Mythic West of W. H. D. Koerner." *AWest,* 4 (May 1967), 54-60.

Johnson, Carole M. "EH's American West." *BI,* 21 (Nov 1974), 26-42.

Johnson. "EH's *The Story of the Outlaw:* A Critique and a Judgment." *Ar&W,* 17 (Winter 1975), 309-326.

Miller, John H. "EH: 'Merry Christmas. Sued You Today.'" *IUB,* 8 (Mar 1967), 23-35.

Wylder, Delbert E. "EH's *Heart's Desire:* Revisit to Eden." *WAL,* 1 (Spring 1966), 44-54.

Wylder. "EH and the Popular Novel." *SwAL,* 2 (Fall 1972), 83-89.

Wylder. "EH as Conservationist and Muckraker." *WAL,* 12 (Summer 1977), 93-109.

Michael J. Sandle

E. W. HOWE

Treaty, Ind, 3 May 1853-Atchison, Kans, 3 Oct 1937

E. W. Howe is best known as the author of the realistic novel *The Story of a Country Town.* Samuel Clemens gave the novel a favorable review and wrote to Howe that "your style is so simple, sincere, and direct, and at the same time so strong, that I think it must have been born to you, not made." Although Howe did not enjoy great popular success with his subsequent novels, he continued to be a household name through the maxims and perceptive commentary on world and local issues that appeared in his newspapers, the *Atchison Globe* and *E. W. Howe's Monthly.* Quoted for such witticisms as "a good scare is worth more to a man than good advice," the editor-novelist became commonly known as the "Sage of Potato Hill."

BIBLIOGRAPHIES

Eichelberger, Clayton L. "EWH: Critical Bibliography of Secondary Comment." *ALR,* 2 (Spring 1969), 1-49.

Eichelberger. "EWH and Joseph Kirkland: More Critical Comment." *ALR,* 4 (Summer 1971), 279-290.

First Printings of American Authors, Vol 2 (Detroit: Bruccoli Clark/Gale, 1978), 211-215. Primary.

BOOKS

The Story of a Country Town. Atchison, Kans: Howe, 1883. Novel.

The Mystery of the Locks. Boston: Osgood, 1885. Novel.

A Moonlight Boy. Boston: Ticknor, 1886. Novel.

A Man Story. Boston: Ticknor, 1889. Novel.

An Ante-Mortem Statement. Atchison, Kans: Globe, 1891. Novel.

The Confession of John Whitlock, Late Preacher of the Gospel. Atchison, Kans: Globe, 1891. Novel.

Daily Notes of a Trip Around the World. Topeka, Kans: Crane, 1907. Travel.

The Trip to the West Indies. Topeka, Kans: Crane, 1910. Travel.

Country Town Sayings. Topeka, Kans: Crane, 1911. Newspaper columns.

Travel Letters From New Zealand, Australia and Africa. Topeka, Kans: Crane, 1913.

Success Easier Than Failure. Topeka, Kans: Crane, 1917. Maxims.

The Blessing of Business. Topeka, Kans: Crane, 1918. Maxims.

Ventures in Common Sense. Topeka, Kans: Crane, 1919; *Adventures in Common Sense.* London: Melrose, 1922. Extracts from *E. W. Howe's Monthly.*

The Anthology of Another Town. NY: Knopf, 1920. Sketches.

Dying Like a Gentleman and Other Stories. Girard, Kans: Haldeman-Julius, 1926.

Notes for My Biographer. Girard, Kans: Haldeman-Julius, 1926. Autobiography & letters.

Preaching From the Audience. Girard, Kans: Haldeman-Julius, 1926. Essays.

Sinner Sermons. Girard, Kans: Haldeman-Julius, 1926.

The Covered Wagon and the West (With Other Stories). Girard, Kans: Haldeman-Julius, 1928.

Her Fifth Marriage and Other Stories. Girard, Kans: Haldeman-Julius, 1928.

When a Woman Enjoys Herself and Other Tales of a Small Town. Girard, Kans: Haldeman-Julius, 1928. Stories.

Plain People. NY: Dodd, Mead, 1929. Autobiography.

The Indignations of EWH. Girard, Kans: Haldeman-Julius, 1933. Essays & quotations.

OTHER

Atchison Globe (1877-1910), ed & published by EWH. Newspaper.

E.W. Howe's Monthly (Mar 1911-Nov 1933), written by EWH. Newspaper.

MANUSCRIPTS & ARCHIVES

The major collections are at the Houghton Library, Harvard U; U of Kansas Library; the Lilly Library, Indiana U; & U of Southern California Library.

BIOGRAPHIES

Book

Pickett, Calder M. *Ed Howe: Country Town Philosopher.* Lawrence: U P Kansas, 1968.

Article

Howe, Eugene A. "My Father Was the Most Wretchedly Unhappy Man I Ever Knew." *SatEP,* 214 (25 Oct 1941), 25, 44-46, 49.

CRITICAL STUDIES

Books

Bucco, Martin. *EWH.* Boise, Idaho: Boise State U, 1977.

Ropp, Philip Hortestine. "EWH." Dissertation: U Virginia, 1949.

Sackett, S J. *EWH.* NY: Twayne, 1972.

Book Section & Articles

Ahnebrink, Lars. "Realism in the Middle West: Edward Eggleston, EWH, and Joseph Kirkland." *The Beginnings of Naturalism in American Fiction* (Uppsala, Sweden: U Uppsala / Cambridge: Harvard U P, 1950), 50-59.

Albertini, Virgil. "EWH and *The Story of a Country Town.*" *NMoSUS,* 35 (Fall 1975), 19-29.

Boyd, Ernest. "The Sage of Potato Hill." *Nation,* 139 (29 Aug 1934), 247-248.

Boynton, Percy H. "Some Expounders of the Middle Border." *EJ,* 19 (Jun 1930), 431-440.

Brune, R E. "Found: EH's Golden *Globe.*" *WHR,* 6 (Winter 1951-1952), 99-102.

Carson, Gerald. "The Village Atheist: EWH, Purveyor of Plain Thought for Plain People." *Scribner's,* 84 (Dec 1928), 733-739.

Clymer, Rolla A. "A Golden Era of Kansas Journalism." *KHQ,* 24 (Spring 1958), 97-111.

Cooper, Kenneth S. "EWH—A Self-Educated Educator." *EdForum,* 26 (Jan 1962), 233-237.

Hall, Grover C. "EWH and H. L. Mencken." *HJM,* (Jul 1925), 163-167.

Howells, William Dean. "Two Notable Novels." *Century,* 28 (Aug 1884), 632-634.

Lord, Russell. "The Indignant Kansan." *Country Home,* 57 (Sep 1934), 7-9, 30-31.

Pickett, Calder M. "EWH: Legend and Truth." *ALR,* 2 (Spring 1969), 70-73.

Pickett. "EWH and the Kansas Scene." *KQ,* 2 (Spring 1970), 39-45.

Sackett, S J. "EWH as Proverb Maker." *JAFict,* 85 (Jan-Mar 1972), 73-77.

Schorer, C E. "Growing Up With the Country." *MidwestJ,* 6 (Fall 1954), 12-26.

Schorer. "Mark Twain's Criticism of *The Story of a Country Town.*" *AL,* 27 (Mar 1955), 109-112.

Schramm, Wilbur L. "EH Versus Time." *SatRL,* 17 (5 Feb 1938), 10-11.

Stronks, James B. "William Dean Howells, EH, and *The Story of a Country Town.*" *AL,* 29 (Jan 1958), 473-478.

Van Doren, Carl. "Prudence Militant: EWH, Village Sage." *Century,* 106 (May 1923), 151-156.

Stephen E. Hopkins

WILLIAM DEAN HOWELLS

Martin's Ferry, Ohio, 1 Mar 1837-New York City, NY, 11 May 1920

In a sixty-year career as novelist, travel writer, magazine editor and columnist, and literary and social critic, William Dean Howells was an intellectual force. He was controversial for championing fictional realism and advanced the cause in such novels as *A Modern Instance* and *The Rise of Silas Lapham,* the best known of his many books, and in *Criticism and Fiction,* a distillation of his critical positions. He was equally controversial for championing social and economic justice, particularly in *A Hazard of New Fortunes* and in "The Editor's Study" and "The Editor's Easy Chair," his long-running columns for the Harper periodicals. His reputation began to fail before his death, but his stature improved as part of the anti-modernist reaction of the 1950s. Howells now holds a modest place through the combined interests of apologists for realism, psychological critics emphasizing the honesty and subtlety of his depiction of his characters and himself, and students of American culture acknowledging the accuracy of his account of the American scene.

BIBLIOGRAPHIES & CATALOGUES

Ballinger, Richard H. "A Calendar of the WDH Collection in the Library of Harvard University." Dissertation: Harvard U, 1952.

The Barrett Library: WDH: A Checklist of Printed and Manuscript Works in the Library of the University of Virginia, comp Fannie Mae Elliott & Lucy Clark. Charlottesville: U Virginia P, 1959.

Beebe, Maurice. "Criticism of WDH: A Selected Checklist." *MFS,* 16 (Autumn 1970), 395-419.

Bibliography of American Literature, comp Jacob Blanck. New Haven: Yale U P, 1955-1991. Primary.

Eichelberger, Clayton L. *Published Comment on WDH Through 1920: A Research Bibliography.* Boston: Hall, 1976.

Gibson, William M & George Arms. *A Bibliography of WDH.* NY: New York Public Library, 1948. Primary.

Halfmann, Ulrich. "Addenda to Gibson and Arms: Twenty-three New H Items." *PBSA,* 66 (Second Quarter 1972), 174-177. Primary.

Halfmann & Don R Smith. "WDH: A Revised and Annotated Bibliography of Secondary Comment in Periodicals and Newspapers, 1868-1919." *ALR,* 5 (Spring 1972), 91-121.

Merrill, Ginette de B. "Two H Collections." *RALS,* 11 (Spring 1981), 81-90. Manuscripts.

Nordloh, David J. "WDH." *Fifteen American Authors Before 1900,* ed Earl N Harbert & Robert A Rees (Madison: U Wisconsin P, 1984), 306-329. Essay on secondary sources.

Reeves, John K. "The Literary Manuscripts of WDH." *BNYPL,* 62 (Jun 1958), 267-278; 62 (Jul 1958), 350-363.

Woodress, James & Stanley P Anderson. "A Bibliography of Writing About WDH." *ALR,* 2 (Special Number 1969), 1-139.

BOOKS

Poems of Two Friends, with John J Piatt. Columbus, Ohio: Follett, Foster, 1860.

Lives and Speeches of Abraham Lincoln and Hannibal Hamlin, life of Lincoln by WDH, life of Hamlin by J L Hayes. Columbus, Ohio: Follett, Foster, 1860. Augmented ed, 1860.

Venetian Life. London: Trübner, 1866; NY: Hurd & Houghton, 1866. Rev & augmented ed, 1867. Augmented again, Boston: Osgood, 1872. Rev & augmented again, Boston & NY: Houghton, Mifflin, 1907. Travel.

Italian Journeys. NY: Hurd & Houghton, 1867. Augmented ed, Boston: Osgood, 1872. Rev & augmented again, Boston & NY: Houghton, Mifflin, 1901. Travel.

No Love Lost: A Romance of Travel. NY: Putnam, 1869. Story in verse.

Suburban Sketches. NY: Hurd & Houghton, 1871. Augmented ed, Boston: Osgood, 1872. Excerpted in *A Day's Pleasure.* Boston: Osgood, 1876. Essays.

Their Wedding Journey. Boston: Osgood, 1872. Augmented ed, Boston: Houghton, Mifflin, 1887. Novel.

A Chance Acquaintance. Boston: Osgood, 1873. Novel.

Poems. Boston: Osgood, 1873. Augmented ed, Boston: Ticknor, 1886.

A Foregone Conclusion. Boston: Osgood, 1875. Novel.

Sketch of the Life and Character of Rutherford B. Hayes. . . . NY: Hurd & Houghton / Boston: Houghton, 1876.

The Parlor Car: Farce. Boston: Osgood, 1876. Play.

Out of the Question: A Comedy. Boston: Osgood, 1877. Play.

A Counterfeit Presentment: Comedy. Boston: Osgood, 1877. Play.

The Lady of the Aroostook. Boston: Houghton, Osgood, 1879. Novel.

The Undiscovered Country. Boston: Houghton, Mifflin, 1880. Novel.

A Fearful Responsibility and Other Stories. Boston: Osgood, 1881; *A Fearful Responsibility and Tonelli's Marriage.* Edinburgh: Douglas, 1882. Stories.

Doctor Breen's Practice: A Novel. Edinburgh: Douglas, 1881; Boston: Osgood, 1881.

A Modern Instance: A Novel. 2 vols, Edinburgh: Douglas, 1882; 1 vol, Boston: Osgood, 1882.

The Sleeping-Car: A Farce. Boston: Osgood, 1883. Play.

A Woman's Reason: A Novel. Edinburgh: Douglas, 1883; Boston: Osgood, 1883.

The Register: Farce. Boston: Osgood, 1884. Play.

Three Villages. Boston: Osgood, 1884. Essays.

The Elevator: Farce. Boston: Osgood, 1885. Play.

The Rise of Silas Lapham. Edinburgh: Douglas, 1885; Boston: Ticknor, 1885. Novel.

Tuscan Cities. Boston: Ticknor, 1886. Travel.

The Garroters: Farce. NY: Harper, 1886. Play.

Indian Summer. Edinburgh: Douglas, 1886; Boston: Ticknor, 1886. Novel.

The Minister's Charge; or, The Apprenticeship of Lemuel Barker. Edinburgh: Douglas, 1886; Boston: Ticknor, 1887. Novel.

Modern Italian Poets: Essays & Versions. Edinburgh: Douglas, 1887; NY: Harper, 1887. Criticism & translations.

April Hopes: A Novel. Edinburgh: Douglas, 1887; *April Hopes.* NY: Harper, 1888.

A Sea-Change; or, Love's Stowaway: A Lyricated Farce in Two Acts and an Epilogue. Boston: Ticknor, 1888. Play.

Annie Kilburn: A Novel. Edinburgh: Douglas, 1888; NY: Harper, 1889.

The Mouse-Trap and Other Farces. NY: Harper, 1889. Rpt in 3 vols as *The Mouse-Trap & A Likely Story & Five O'Clock Tea,* 1894. Plays.

A Hazard of New Fortunes. 2 vols, Edinburgh: Douglas, 1889; 1 vol, NY: Harper, 1890. Novel.

The Shadow of a Dream: A Novel. Edinburgh: Douglas, 1890; *The Shadow of a Dream: A Story.* NY: Harper, 1890. Novel.

A Boy's Town Described for "Harper's Young People." NY: Harper, 1890. Memoir.

Criticism and Fiction. NY: Harper, 1891. Criticism.

The Albany Depot: Farce. NY: Harper, 1892. Play.

An Imperative Duty: A Novel. NY: Harper, 1892.

Mercy: A Novel. Edinburgh: Douglas, 1892; *The Quality of Mercy: A Novel.* NY: Harper, 1892.

A Letter of Introduction: Farce. NY: Harper, 1892. Play.

A Little Swiss Sojourn. NY: Harper, 1892. Travel.

Christmas Every Day and Other Stories Told for Children. NY: Harper, 1893.

The World of Chance: A Novel. NY: Harper, 1893.

The Unexpected Guests: A Farce. NY: Harper, 1893. Play.

My Year in a Log Cabin. NY: Harper, 1893. Essay.

Evening Dress: Farce. NY: Harper, 1893. Play.

The Coast of Bohemia: A Novel. NY: Harper, 1893.

A Traveler From Altruria: Romance. NY: Harper, 1894. Novel.

My Literary Passions. NY: Harper, 1895. Criticism.

Stops of Various Quills. NY: Harper, 1895. Poetry.

The Day of Their Wedding: A Novel. NY: Harper, 1896. Repub in *Idyls in Drab.* Edinburgh: Douglas, 1896. Novella.

A Parting and a Meeting: Story. NY: Harper, 1896. Repub in *Idyls in Drab.* Edinburgh: Douglas, 1896. Novella.

Impressions and Experiences. NY: Harper, 1896. Essays.

A Previous Engagement: Comedy. NY: Harper, 1897. Play.

The Landlord at Lion's Head: A Novel. NY: Harper, 1897.

An Open-Eyed Conspiracy: An Idyl of Saratoga. NY & London: Harper, 1897. Novella.

Stories of Ohio. NY & c: American Book, 1897. History textbook.

The Story of a Play: A Novel. NY & London: Harper, 1898.

Ragged Lady: A Novel. NY & London: Harper, 1899.

Their Silver Wedding Journey, 2 vols. NY & London: Harper, 1899. Abridged as *Hither and Thither in Germany,* 1920. Novel.

Bride Roses: A Scene. Boston & NY: Houghton, Mifflin, 1900. Play.

Room Forty-Five: A Farce. Boston & NY: Houghton, Mifflin, 1900. Play.

An Indian Giver: A Comedy. Boston & NY: Houghton, Mifflin, 1900. Play.

The Smoking Car: A Farce. Boston & NY: Houghton, Mifflin, 1900. Play.

Literary Friends and Acquaintance: A Personal Retrospect of American Authorship. NY & London: Harper, 1900. Reminiscences.

A Pair of Patient Lovers. NY & London: Harper, 1901. Stories.

Heroines of Fiction, 2 vols. NY & London: Harper, 1901. Criticism.

The Kentons: A Novel. NY & London: Harper, 1902.

The Flight of Pony Baker: A Boy's Town Story. NY & London: Harper, 1902. Stories.

Literature and Life: Studies. NY & London: Harper, 1902. Criticism.

Questionable Shapes. NY & London: Harper, 1903. Stories.

Letters Home. NY & London: Harper, 1903. Novel.

The Son of Royal Langbrith: A Novel. NY & London: Harper, 1904.

Miss Bellard's Inspiration: A Novel. NY & London: Harper, 1905.

London Films. NY & London: Harper, 1905. Travel.

Certain Delightful English Towns, With Glimpses of the Pleasant Country Between. NY & London: Harper, 1906. Travel.

Through the Eye of the Needle: A Romance. NY & London: Harper, 1907. Novel.

Between the Dark and the Daylight: Romances. NY & London: Harper, 1907. Stories.

Fennel and Rue: A Novel. NY & London: Harper, 1908.

Roman Holidays and Others. NY & London: Harper, 1908. Travel.

The Mother and the Father: Dramatic Passages. NY & London: Harper, 1909. Stories.

Seven English Cities. NY & London: Harper, 1909. Travel.

My Mark Twain: Reminiscences and Criticisms. NY & London: Harper, 1910.

Imaginary Interviews. NY & London: Harper, 1910. Essays.

Parting Friends: A Farce. NY & London: Harper, 1911. Play.

New Leaf Mills: A Chronicle. NY & London: Harper, 1913. Novel.

Familiar Spanish Travels. NY & London: Harper, 1913. Travel.

The Seen and Unseen at Stratford-on-Avon: A Fantasy. NY & London: Harper, 1914. Story.

The Daughter of the Storage and Other Things in Prose and Verse. NY & London: Harper, 1916. Essays & poetry.

The Leatherwood God. NY: Century, 1916. Novel.

Years of My Youth. NY & London: Harper, 1916. Autobiography.

The Vacation of the Kelwyns: An Idyl of the Middle Eighteen-Seventies. NY & London: Harper, 1920. Novel.

Mrs. Farrell: A Novel, intro by Mildred Howells. NY & London: Harper, 1921.

Howells and James: A Double Billing. Includes *Novel-Writing and Novel-Reading: An Impersonal Explanation* by WDH, ed William M Gibson; *Henry James and the Bazar Letters,* ed Leon Edel & Lyall H Powers. NY: New York Public Library, 1958. Essay.

Criticism and Fiction and Other Essays, ed with intros and notes by Clara Marburg Kirk & Rudolf Kirk. NY: NYU P, 1959.

The Complete Plays of WDH, ed Walter J Meserve. NY: NYU P, 1960.

Letters of an Altrurian Traveller (1893-94): A Facsimile Reproduction, with intro by Clara M & Rudolf Kirk. Gainesville, Fla: Scholars' Facsimiles & Reprints, 1961. Essays.

Discovery of a Genius: WDH and Henry James, ed Albert Mordell. NY: Twayne, 1961. Articles about Henry James.

WDH as Critic, ed Edwin H Cady. London & Boston: Routledge & Kegan Paul, 1973.

Editor's Study, ed with intro by James W Simpson. Troy, NY: Whitston, 1983. Columns.

LETTERS & DIARY

Life in Letters of WDH, 2 vols, ed Mildred Howells. Garden City, NY: Doubleday, Doran, 1928.

Mark Twain-H Letters, 2 vols, ed Henry Nash Smith & William M Gibson. Cambridge: Belknap/Harvard U P, 1960.

WDH: Selected Letters, 6 vols, ed George Arms et al. Boston: Twayne, 1979-1983.

John Hay-H Letters: The Correspondence of John Milton Hay and WDH, 1861-1905, ed with intro & annotations by George Monteiro & Brenda Murphy. Boston: Twayne, 1980.

" 'The Real Diary of a Boy': H in Ohio, 1852-1853," ed Thomas Wortham. *ON,* 10 (Spring 1984), 3-40.

OTHER

Three Years in Chili. By a Lady of Ohio, ed WDH. Columbus, Ohio: Follett, Foster, 1861.

Atlantic Monthly (1871-1881), ed WDH. Magazine.

A Little Girl Among the Old Masters, with intro & comment by WDH. Boston: Osgood, 1884. Drawings by Mildred Howells.

"Sketch of George Fuller's Life." *George Fuller: His Life and Works* (Boston & NY: Houghton, Mifflin, 1886), 1-52.

Mark Twain's Library of Humor, comp Mark Twain, WDH & Charles Hopkins Clark. NY: Webster, 1888. Rpt NY: Bonanza, 1969. Anthology.

Samson . . . by Ippolito d'Aste, trans WDH. NY: Koppel, 1889. Play.

The Poems of George Pellew, ed WDH. Boston: Clarke, 1892.

Recollections of Life in Ohio, From 1813 to 1840 by William Cooper Howells; ed with intro & conclusion by WDH. Cincinnati, Ohio: Clarke, 1895.

"The Father." *The Whole Family: A Novel by Twelve Authors* (NY & London: Harper, 1908), 3-29.

The Great Modern American Stories: An Anthology, ed with intro by WDH. NY: Boni & Liveright, 1920.

Don Quixote, ed WDH; intro by Mildred Howells. NY & London: Harper, 1923.

EDITIONS & COLLECTIONS

The Writings of WDH: Library Edition, 6 vols. NY & London: Harper, 1908-1911.

Selected Writings of WDH, ed Henry Steele Commager. NY: Random House, 1950.

Prefaces to Contemporaries (1882-1920), ed George Arms, William M Gibson & Frederic C Marston, Jr. Gainesville, Fla: Scholars' Facsimiles & Reprints, 1957.

WDH: Representative Selections, ed Clara Marburg Kirk & Rudolf Kirk. NY: Hill & Wang, rev 1961.

A Selected Edition of WDH, 23 vols to date, ed Edwin H Cady et al. Bloomington: Indiana U P, 1968- .

MANUSCRIPTS & ARCHIVES

The Houghton Library, Harvard U.

BIOGRAPHIES

Books

Cady, Edwin H. *The Road to Realism: The Early Years, 1837-1885, of WDH.* Syracuse, NY: Syracuse U P, 1956.

Cady. *The Realist at War: The Mature Years, 1885-1920, of WDH.* Syracuse, NY: Syracuse U P, 1958.

Howells, Elinor Mead. *If Not Literature: Letters of Elinor Mead Howells,* ed Ginette de B Merrill & George Arms. Columbus: Miami U/Ohio State U P, 1988.

Lynn, Kenneth S. *WDH: An American Life.* NY: Harcourt Brace Jovanovich, 1971.

Book Sections & Articles

Bolton, Sarah K. "WDH." *Famous American Authors* (NY: Crowell, 1887), 258-285.

Brooks, Van Wyck. "H in Venice." *The Dream of Arcadia: American Writers and Artists in Italy, 1760-1915* (NY: Dutton, 1958), 145-154.

Fertig, Walter L. "Maurice Thompson and *A Modern Instance.*" *AL,* 38 (Mar 1966), 103-111.

Fryckstedt, Olov W. "H and Conway in Venice." *SN,* 30 (1958), 165-174.

Kirk, Clara M & Rudolf. " 'The H Family' by Richard J Hinton." *JRUL,* 14 (Dec 1950), 14-23.

Kirk, Rudolf & Clara M. "H and the Church of the Carpenter." *NEQ,* 32 (Jun 1959), 185-206.

Merrill, Ginette de B. "Redtop and the Belmont Years of WDH and His Family." *HLB,* 28 (Jan 1980), 33-57.

Meserole, Harrison T. "The Dean in Person: H's Lecture Tour." *WHR,* 10 (Autumn 1956), 337-347.

Nordloh, David J. "WDH at Kittery Point." *HLB,* 28 (Oct 1980), 431-437.

Rowlette, Robert. "WDH's 1899 Midwest Lecture Tour." *ALR,* 9 (Winter 1976), 1-31; 10 (Spring 1977), 125-167.

INTERVIEWS

Halfmann, Ulrich, ed. "Interviews With WDH." *ALR,* 6 (Fall 1973). Rpt separately, Arlington: American Literary Realism, U Texas at Arlington, 1973.

CRITICAL STUDIES

Books

Alexander, William. *WDH: The Realist as Humanist.* NY: Franklin, 1981.

Bennett, George N. *WDH: The Development of a Novelist.* Norman: U Oklahoma P, 1959.

Bennett. *The Realism of WDH, 1889-1920.* Nashville, Tenn: Vanderbilt U P, 1973.

Brooks, Van Wyck. *H: His Life and His World.* NY: Dutton, 1959.

Cady, Edwin H. *Young H & John Brown: Episodes in a Radical Education.* Columbus: Ohio State U P, 1985.

Carrington, George C, Jr. *The Immense Complex Drama: The World and Art of the H Novel.* Columbus: Ohio State U P, 1966.

Carrington & Ildikó de Papp Carrington. *Plots and Characters in the Fiction of WDH.* Hamden, Conn: Shoe String, 1976.

Carter, Everett. *H and the Age of Realism.* Philadelphia: Lippincott, 1954.

Cooke, Delmar Gross. *WDH: A Critical Study.* NY: Dutton, 1922.

Crowley, John W. *The Black Heart's Truth: The Early Career of WDH.* Chapel Hill: U North Carolina P, 1985.

Dean, James L. *H's Travels Toward Art.* Albuquerque: U New Mexico P, 1970.

Eble, Kenneth E. *WDH.* Boston: Twayne, 1982.

Firkins, Oscar W. *WDH: A Study.* Cambridge: Harvard U P, 1924.

Fryckstedt, Olov W. *In Quest of America: A Study*

of *H's Early Development as a Novelist.*
Cambridge: Harvard U P, 1958.

Gibson, William M. "Mark Twain and H: Anti-Imperialists." Dissertation: U Chicago, 1940.

Gibson. *WDH.* Minneapolis: U Minnesota P, 1967. Rpt *Six American Novelists of the Nineteenth Century,* ed Richard Foster (Minneapolis: U Minnesota P, 1968), 155-190.

Harvey, Alexander. *WDH: A Study of the Achievement of a Literary Artist.* NY: Huebsch, 1917.

Hough, Robert L. *The Quiet Rebel: WDH as Social Commentator.* Lincoln: U Nebraska P, 1959.

Kirk, Clara Marburg. *WDH: Traveler From Altruria.* New Brunswick, NJ: Rutgers U P, 1962.

Kirk. *WDH and Art in His Time.* New Brunswick, NJ: Rutgers U P, 1965.

Kirk & Rudolf Kirk. *WDH.* NY: Twayne, 1962.

McMurray, William. *The Literary Realism of WDH.* Carbondale: Southern Illinois U P, 1967.

Nettels, Elsa. *Language, Race, and Social Class in H's America.* Lexington: U P Kentucky, 1988.

Olsen, Rodney Donald. "Identity and Doubt: The Youth of WDH." Dissertation: U Missouri, 1981.

Prioleau, Elizabeth Stevens. *The Circle of Eros: Sexuality in the Work of WDH.* Durham, NC: Duke U P, 1983.

Vanderbilt, Kermit. *The Achievement of WDH: A Reinterpretation.* Princeton: Princeton U P, 1968.

Wagenknecht, Edward. *WDH, the Friendly Eye.* NY: Oxford U P, 1969.

Woodress, James L, Jr. *H & Italy.* Durham, NC: Duke U P, 1952.

Collections of Essays

Cady, Edwin H & David L Frazier, eds. *The War of the Critics Over WDH.* Evanston, Ill: Row, Peterson, 1962.

Cady & Norma W Cady, eds. *Critical Essays on WDH, 1866-1920.* Boston: Hall, 1983.

Eble, Kenneth E, ed. *H: A Century of Criticism.* Dallas, Tex: Southern Methodist U P, 1962.

Eschholz, Paul A, ed. *Critics on WDH: Readings in Literary Criticism.* Coral Gables, Fla: U Miami P, 1975.

Special Journals

MFS, 16 (Autumn 1970). WDH issue.

ON, 8 (Spring 1982); 8 (Summer 1982); 10 (Spring 1984). WDH issues.

Book Sections & Articles

Aaron, Daniel. "WDH: The Gentleman From Altruria." *Men of Good Hope* (NY: Oxford U P, 1951), 172-207.

Amacher, Anne Ward. "The Genteel Primitivist and the Semi-Tragic Octoroon." *NEQ,* 29 (Jun 1956), 216-227.

Andrews, William L. "WDH and Charles W. Chesnutt: Criticism and Race Fiction in the Age of Booker T. Washington." *AL,* 48 (Nov 1976), 327-339.

Arms, George. "The Literary Background of H's Social Criticism." *AL,* 14 (Nov 1942), 260-276.

Arms. " 'Ever Devotedly Yours': The Whitlock-H Correspondence." *JRUL,* 10 (Dec 1946), 1-19.

Arms. "H's New York Novel: Comedy and Belief." *NEQ,* 21 (Sep 1948), 313-325. Rpt Eschholz.

Arms. "H's English Travel Books: Problems in Technique." *PMLA,* 82 (Mar 1967), 104-116.

Arms & William M Gibson. "*Silas Lapham, Daisy Miller,* and the Jews." *NEQ,* 16 (Mar 1943), 118-122.

Arvin, Newton. "The Usableness of H." *NewR,* 91 (30 Jun 1937), 227-228. Rpt Cady & Frazier, Eble (1962).

Baldwin, Marilyn. "The Transcendental Phase of WDH." *ESQ,* 57 (Fourth Quarter 1969), 57-61.

Baxter, Sylvester. "H's Boston." *NEMag,* ns 9 (Oct 1893), 129-152.

Becker, George J. "WDH: The Awakening of Conscience." *CE,* 19 (Apr 1958), 283-291.

Bell, Michael Davitt. "The Sin of Art and the Problem of American Realism: WDH." *Prospects,* 9 (1984), 115-142.

Bennett, Scott. "David Douglas and the British Publication of WDH's Works." *SB,* 25 (1972), 107-124.

Berces, Francis Albert. "Mimesis, Morality and *The Rise of Silas Lapham.*" *AQ,* 22 (Summer 1970), 190-202.

Boardman, Arthur. "Social Point of View in the Novels of WDH." *AL,* 39 (Mar 1967), 42-59.

Bremer, Sidney H. "Invalids and Actresses: H's Duplex Imagery for American Women." *AL,* 47 (Jan 1976), 599-614.

Brooks, Van Wyck. "H in Cambridge," "H and James," "H in New York." *New England: Indian Summer, 1865-1915* (NY: Dutton, 1940), 204-223, 224-249, 373-394.

Budd, Louis J. "WDH's Defense of the Romance." *PMLA,* 67 (Mar 1952), 32-42.

Budd. "H, the *Atlantic Monthly,* and Republicanism." *AL,* 24 (May 1952), 139-156.

Cady, Edwin H. "The Neuroticism of WDH." *PMLA,* 61 (Mar 1946), 229-238. Rpt Eble (1962).

Cady. "The H Nobody Knows." *Mad River Review,* 1 (Winter 1964-1965), 3-25.

Cargill, Oscar. "Henry James's 'Moral Policeman': WDH." *AL,* 29 (Jan 1958), 371-398. Rpt as "WDH as Henry James's 'Moral Policeman.' " *Toward a Pluralistic Criticism* by Cargill (Carbondale: Southern Illinois U P, 1965).

Carrington, George C, Jr. "H and the Dramatic Essay." *ALR,* 17 (Spring 1984), 44-66.

Carter, Everett S. "The Palpitating Divan." *EJ,* 39 (May 1950), 237-242. Rpt Cady & Frazier, Eble (1962).

Carter. "The Haymarket Affair in Literature." *AQ,* 2 (Fall 1950), 270-278.

Cohn, Jan. "The Houses of Fiction: Domestic Architecture in H and Edith Wharton." *TSLL,* 15 (Fall 1973), 537-549.

Cooley, Thomas. "The Wilderness Within: H's *A Boy's Town.*" *AL,* 47 (Jan 1976), 583-598.

Cronkhite, G Ferris. "H Turns to the Inner Life." *NEQ,* 30 (Dec 1957), 474-485.

Crowley, John W. "An Interoceanic Episode: *The Lady of the Aroostook.*" *AL,* 49 (May 1977), 180-191.

Crowley. "Winifred Howells and the Economy of Pain." *ON,* 10 (Spring 1984), 41-75.

Crowley & Charles L Crow. "Psychic and Psychological Themes in H's 'A Sleep and a Forgetting.' " *ESQ,* 23 (First Quarter 1977), 41-51.

Cumpiano, Marion W. "The Dark Side of *Their Wedding Journey.*" *AL,* 40 (Jan 1969), 472-486.

Delbanco, Andrew. "H and the Suppression of Knowledge." *SoR,* 19 (Oct 1983), 765-784.

Dennis, Scott A. "*The World of Chance:* H's Hawthornian Self-Parody." *AL,* 52 (May 1980), 279-293.

Dove, John Roland. "H's Irrational Heroines." *UTSE,* 35 (1956), 64-80.

Dowling, Joseph A. "WDH's Literary Reputation in England, 1882-1897." *DR,* 45 (Autumn 1965), 277-288.

Dowling. "H and the English: A Democrat Looks at English Civilization." *BNYPL,* 76 (1972), 251-264.

Eakin, Paul John. "The H Heroine: From *The Lady of the Aroostook* to *April Hopes.*" *The New England Girl: Cultural Ideals in Hawthorne, Stowe, H and James* (Athens: U Georgia P, 1976), 83-130.

Eble, Kenneth E. "H's Kisses." *AQ,* 9 (Winter 1957), 441-447. Rpt Eble (1962).

Eichelberger, Clayton L. "WDH: Perception and Ambivalence." *The Chief Glory of Every People: Essays on Classic American Writers,* ed Matthew J Bruccoli (Carbondale: Southern Illinois U P, 1973), 119-140.

Ekström, Kjell. "The Cable-H Correspondence." *SN,* 22 (1949-1950), 48-61.

Ekstrom, William F. "The Equalitarian Principle in the Fiction of WDH." *AL,* 24 (Mar 1952), 40-50.

Engel, Bernard F. "WDH and the Verse Drama." *ELWIU,* 7 (Spring 1980), 67-78.

Erickson, C A. "The Tough- and Tender-Minded: WDH's *The Landlord at Lion's Head.*" *SNNTS,* 17 (Winter 1985), 383-394.

Eschholz, Paul A. "H's *A Modern Instance:* A Realist's Moralistic Vision of America." *SDR,* 10 (Spring 1972), 91-102. Rpt Eschholz.

Fischer, William C, Jr. "WDH: Reverie and the Nonsymbolic Aesthetic." *NCF,* 25 (Jun 1970), 1-30.

Ford, Thomas W. "H and the American Negro." *TSLL,* 5 (Winter 1964), 530-537.

Fox, Arnold B. "H's Doctrine of Complicity." *MLQ,* 13 (Mar 1952), 56-60. Rpt Eble (1962).

Frazier, David L. "Time and the Theme of *Indian Summer.*" *ArQ,* 16 (Autumn 1960), 260-267.

Gargano, James W. "*A Modern Instance:* The Twin Evils of Society." *TSLL,* 4 (Autumn 1962), 399-407.

Garland, Hamlin. "Sanity in Fiction." *NAR,* 176 (Mar 1903), 336-348. Rpt Cady & Frazier.

Gibson, William M. "Materials and Form in H's First Novels." *AL,* 19 (May 1947), 158-166. Rpt Eschholz.

Gifford, Henry. "WDH: His Moral Conservatism." *KR,* 20 (Winter 1958), 124-133. Rpt Cady & Frazier.

Gillespie, Robert. "The Fictions of Basil March." *CLQ,* 12 (Mar 1976), 14-28.

Girgus, Sam B. "H and Marcuse: A Forecast of the One-Dimensional Age." *AQ,* 25 (Mar 1973), 108-118.

Goldman, Laurel T. "A Different View of the Iron Madonna: WDH and His Magazine Readers." *NEQ,* 50 (Dec 1977), 563-586.

Graham, John. "Struggling Upward: *The Minister's Charge* and *A Cool Million.*" *CRevAS,* 4 (Fall 1973), 184-196.

Gullason, Thomas A. "New Light on the Crane-H Relationship." *NEQ,* 30 (Sep 1957), 389-392.

Habegger, Alfred. *Gender, Fantasy, and Realism in American Literature* (NY: Columbia U P, 1982), passim.

Hoffman, Frederick J. "Henry James, WDH and the Art of Fiction." *The Modern Novel in America, 1900-1950* (Chicago: Regnery, 1951), 1-27.

Hunt, Gary A. " 'A Reality That Can't Be Quite Definitely Spoken': Sexuality in *Their Wedding Journey.*" *SNNTS,* 9 (Spring 1977), 17-32.

Jackson, Fleda Brown. "A Sermon Without Exegesis: The Achievement of Stasis in *The Rise of Silas Lapham.*" *JNT,* 16 (Spring 1986), 131-

147.

Jacobson, Marcia. "The Mask of Fiction: WDH's Experiments in Autobiography." *Biography*, 10 (Winter 1987), 55-67.

Kaplan, Amy. " 'The Knowledge of the Line': Realism and the City in H's *A Hazard of New Fortunes*." *PMLA*, 101 (Jan 1986), 69-81.

Kar, Annette. "Archetypes of American Innocence: Lydia Blood and Daisy Miller." *AQ*, 5 (Spring 1953), 31-38.

Kazin, Alfred. "H the Bostonian." *ClioI*, 3 (Feb 1974), 219-234.

Kirk, Clara M. "Reality and Actuality in the March Family Narratives of WDH." *PMLA*, 74 (Mar 1959), 137-152.

Kirk & Rudolf Kirk. "WDH, George William Curtis, and the 'Haymarket Affair.' " *AL*, 40 (Jan 1969), 487-498.

Kirk, Rudolf & Clara M. "Abraham Cahan and WDH: The Story of a Friendship." *AJHQ*, 52 (Sep 1962), 25-57.

Long, Robert Emmet. "Transformations: *The Blithedale Romance* to H and James." *AL*, 47 (Jan 1976), 552-571.

Lydenberg, John & Edwin H Cady. "The H Revival: Rounds Two and Three." *NEQ*, 32 (Sep 1959), 394-407.

Marston, Jane. "Evolution and Howellsian Realism in *The Undiscovered Country*." *ALR*, 14 (Autumn 1981), 231-241.

Mathews, James W. "Toward Naturalism: Three Late Novels of WDH." *Genre*, 6 (Dec 1973), 362-375.

Matthews, Brander. "Mr. H as a Critic." *Forum*, 32 (Jan 1902), 629-638. Rpt Cady & Frazier, Eble (1962).

Morby, Edwin S. "WDH and Spain." *HispR*, 14 (Jul 1946), 187-212.

Murphy, Brenda. "Realistic Dramatic Theory," "The Literary Realists as Playwrights." *American Realism and American Drama* (Cambridge: Cambridge U P, 1987), 24-49, 50-85.

Parker, Barbara L. "H's *Oresteia*: The Union of Theme and Structure in *The Shadow of a Dream*." *AL*, 49 (Mar 1977), 57-69.

Parker, Gail Thain. "WDH: Realism and Feminism." *Uses of Literature*, ed Monroe Engel (Cambridge: Harvard U P, 1973), 133-161.

Parks, Edd Winfield. "H and the Gentle Reader." *SAQ*, 50 (Apr 1951), 239-247.

Parrington, Vernon Louis. "WDH and the Realism of the Commonplace." *Main Currents in American Thought*, Vol 3 (NY: Harcourt, Brace, 1930), 241-253. Rpt Cady & Frazier.

Pattee, Fred Lewis. "The Classical Reaction." *A History of American Literature Since 1870* (NY: Century, 1915), 186-219.

Payne, Alma J. "The Family in the Utopia of WDH." *GaR*, 15 (Summer 1961), 217-229.

Payne, James Robert. "Psychological and Supernatural Themes in H's *The Flight of Pony Baker*." *MarkhamR*, 9 (Spring 1980), 52-56.

Perkins, George. "*A Modern Instance*: H's Transition to Artistic Maturity." *NEQ*, 47 (Sep 1974), 427-439.

Phelps, William Lyon. "WDH." *Essays on Modern Novelists* (NY: Macmillan, 1910), 56-81.

Piacentino, Edward J. "Arms in Love and War in H's 'Editha.' " *SSF*, 24 (Fall 1987), 425-432.

Pizer, Donald. "The Evolutionary Foundation of WDH's *Criticism and Fiction*." *PQ*, 40 (Jan 1961), 91-103. Rpt *Realism and Naturalism in Nineteenth-Century American Literature* by Pizer (Carbondale: Southern Illinois U P, 1966).

Reeves, John K. "The Limited Realism of H's *Their Wedding Journey*." *PMLA*, 77 (Dec 1962), 617-628.

Schneider, Robert W. "WDH: The Mugwump Rebellion." *Five Novelists of the Progressive Era* (NY: Columbia U P, 1965), 19-55.

See, Fred G. "The Demystification of Style: Metaphoric and Metonymic Language in *A Modern Instance*." *NCF*, 28 (Mar 1974), 379-403.

Seib, Kenneth. "Uneasiness at Niagara: H's *Their Wedding Journey*." *SAF*, 4 (Spring 1976), 15-25.

Sokoloff, B A. "WDH and the Ohio Village: A Study in Environment and Art." *AQ*, 11 (Spring 1959), 58-75.

Spangler, George. "*The Shadow of a Dream*: H's Homosexual Tragedy." *AQ*, 23 (Spring 1971), 110-119.

Springer, Haskell S. "*The Leatherwood God*: From Narrative to Novel." *OhH*, 74 (Summer 1965), 191-202, 212.

Stein, Allen F. "WDH." *After the Vows Were Spoken: Marriage in American Literary Realism* (Columbus: Ohio State U P, 1984), 19-53.

Tanselle, G Thomas. "The Boston Seasons of Silas Lapham." *SNNTS*, 1 (Spring 1969), 60-66.

Tavernier-Courbin, Jacqueline. "Towards the City: H's Characterization in *A Modern Instance*." *MFS*, 24 (Spring 1978), 111-127.

Toth, Susan Allen. "Character and Focus in *The Landlord at Lion's Head*." *CLQ*, Series 11 (Jun 1975), 116-128.

Towers, Tom H. "Savagery and Civilization: The Moral Dimensions of H's *A Boy's Town*." *AL*, 40 (Jan 1969), 499-509.

Trilling, Lionel. "WDH and the Roots of Modern Taste." *PR*, 18 (Sep-Oct 1951), 516-536. Rpt Cady & Frazier.

Turaj, Frank. "The Social Gospel in H's Novels." *SAQ*, 66 (Summer 1967), 449-464.

Twain, Mark. "WDH." *What Is Man? and Other Essays* (NY: Harper, 1917), 228-239. Rpt Eble (1962).

Uba, George R. "H and the Practicable Utopia: The Allegorical Structure of the Altrurian Romances." *JNT*, 13 (Fall 1983), 118-130.

Updike, John. "A Critic at Large: H as Antinovelist." *NYer*, 63 (13 Jul 1987), 78-88.

Vanderbilt, Kermit. *The Undiscovered Country:* H's Version of American Pastoral." *AQ*, 17 (Winter 1965), 634-655.

Walts, Robert W. "H's Plans for Two Travel Books." *PBSA*, 57 (Fourth Quarter 1963), 453-459.

Wasserstrom, William. "WDH: The Indelible Stain." *NEQ*, 32 (Dec 1959), 486-495.

Westbrook, Max. "The Critical Implications of H's Realism." *UTSE*, 36 (1957), 71-79.

Wilson, Jack H. "H's Use of George Eliot's *Romola* in *April Hopes*." *PMLA*, 84 (Oct 1969), 1620-1627.

Woodress, James. "The Dean's Comeback: Four Decades of H Scholarship." *TSLL*, 2 (Spring 1960), 115-123. Rpt Cady & Frazier, Eble (1962).

Wright, Ellen F. "WDH and the Irrational." *NCF*, 38 (Dec 1983), 304-323.

Ziff, Larzer. "Literary Hospitality: WDH." *The American 1890s: Life and Times of a Lost Generation* (NY: Viking, 1966), 24-49.

David J. Nordloh

HELEN HUNT JACKSON
(H. H., Saxe Holm)

Amherst, Mass, 15 Oct 1830-San Francisco, Calif, 12 Aug 1885

Helen Hunt Jackson, who often used the pseudonyms H. H. and Saxe Holm, was a highly popular writer of verse, juvenilia, adult fiction, and essays as well as a prolific journalist. She also wrote two treatises for the United States government on the effects of its policies on the American Indian; her findings were published in *A Century of Dishonor* and *Report on the Conditions and Needs of the Mission Indians of California*, the latter of which was written with Abbot Kinney. Her novel *Ramona*, which was her most widely read work, is a romance that treats issues of race, economics, and politics among Southern Californians of Native American, Spanish, and Anglo descent. Although Jackson has been labeled a writer of sentimental fiction and poetry, her work has recently attracted critical interest in the areas of cultural, historical, and women's studies.

BIBLIOGRAPHIES

Bibliography of American Literature, comp Jacob Blanck. New Haven: Yale U P, 1955-1991. Primary.

Byers, John R, Jr & Elizabeth S. "HHJ (1830-1885): A Critical Bibliography of Secondary Comment." *ALR*, 6 (Summer 1973), 196-241.

"Selected Books About HHJ and Her Times," "Selected Books by HHJ," "Selected List of HHJ's Publications in Periodicals." Banning, 233-240.

BOOKS

Verses (as by H. H.). Boston: Fields, Osgood, 1870. Augmented ed, Boston: Osgood, 1871. Augmented again, Boston: Roberts, 1874.

Bits of Travel (as by H. H.). Boston: Osgood, 1872. Essays.

Bits of Talk About Home Matters (as by H. H.). Boston: Roberts, 1873. Essays.

Saxe Holm's Stories (as by Saxe Holm). NY: Scribner, Armstrong, 1874. Children's stories.

The Story of Boon (as by H. H.). Boston: Roberts, 1874. Poetry.

Mercy Philbrick's Choice (Anon). Boston: Roberts, 1876. Novel.

Bits of Talk, in Verse and Prose, for Young Folks (as by H. H.). Boston: Roberts, 1876.

Hetty's Strange History (Anon). Boston: Roberts, 1877. Novel.

Bits of Travel at Home (as by H. H.). Boston: Roberts, 1878. Essays.

Saxe Holm's Stories, Second Series (as by Holm). NY: Scribners, 1878. Children's stories.

Nelly's Silver Mine: A Story of Colorado Life (as by H. H.). Boston: Roberts, 1878. Children's novel.

A Century of Dishonor: A Sketch of the United States Government's Dealings With Some of the Indian Tribes (as by H. H.). NY: Harper, 1881. Nonfiction.

Mammy Tittleback and Her Family: A True Story of Seventeen Cats (as by H. H.). Boston: Roberts, 1881. Children's novel.

The Training of Children (as by H. H.). NY: N. Y. & Brooklyn Publishing, 1882. Essays.

Report on the Conditions and Needs of the Mission Indians of California . . . to the Commissioner of Indian Affairs, with Abbot Kinney. Washington: Government Printing Office, 1883.

The Hunter Cats of Connorloa. Boston: Roberts, 1884. Children's novel.

Ramona: A Story. Boston: Roberts, 1884. Novel.

Easter Bells: An Original Poem. NY: White, Stokes, & Allen, 1884.

Zeph: A Posthumous Story. Boston: Roberts, 1885. Children's novel.

Glimpses of Three Coasts. Boston: Roberts, 1886. Essays.

Sonnets and Lyrics. Boston: Roberts, 1886.

Between Whiles. Boston: Roberts, 1887. Stories.

Pansy Billings and Popsy: Two Stories of Girl Life. Boston: Lothrop, 1898. Children's stories.

OTHER

Bathmendi: A Persian Tale by Jean-Pierre Claris de Florian; trans HHJ (as by H. H.). Boston: Loring, 1867. Children's story.

Letters From a Cat, Published by Her Mistress for the Benefit of All Cats and the Amusement of Little Children, ed HHJ (as by H. H.). Boston: Roberts, 1879.

COLLECTIONS

The HJ Year-Book, comp Harriet T Perry. Boston: Roberts, 1895.

Cat Stories. Boston: Roberts, 1898.

MANUSCRIPTS & ARCHIVES

The major collections are at the Huntington Library, San Marino, Calif; the Jones Library, Amherst, Mass; the Pasadena Public Library; the New York Public Library; & the Sterling Memorial Library, Yale U.

BIOGRAPHIES

Books

Banning, Evelyn I. *HHJ*. NY: Vanguard, 1973.

Odell, Ruth. *HHJ*. NY: Appleton-Century, 1939.

Book Sections

Dillon, Richard. "HHJ." *Humbugs and Heroes: A Gallery of California Pioneers* (Garden City, NY: Doubleday, 1970), 171-176.

Pierce, Frederick Clifton. *Fiske and Fisk Family* (Chicago: Conkey, 1896), passim.

Reynolds, Moira Davison. "HHJ." *Nine American Women of the Nineteenth Century: Leaders into the Twentieth* (Jefferson, NC: McFarland, 1988), 99-117.

CRITICAL STUDIES

Books

Allen, Margaret V. *Ramona's Homeland*. Chula Vista, Calif: Denrich, 1914.

Clough, Edwin H. *Ramona's Marriage Place: The House of Estudillo*. Chula Vista, Calif: Denrich, 1910.

Davis, Carlyle Channing & William A Alderson. *The True Story of "Ramona": Its Facts and Fictions, Inspiration and Purpose*. NY: Dodge, 1914.

James, George Wharton. *Through Ramona's Country*. Boston: Little, Brown, 1909.

Vroman, Adam Clark & T F Barnes. *The Genesis of the Story of Ramona, Why the Book Was Written, Explanatory Text of Points of Interest Mentioned in the Story*. Los Angeles: Kingsley-Barnes & Neuner, 1899.

Whitaker, Rosemary. *HHJ*. Boise, Idaho: Boise State U, 1987.

Book Sections & Articles

Bianchi, Martha Dickinson. *The Life and Letters of Emily Dickinson* (Boston: Houghton Mifflin, 1924), passim.

Byers, John R, Jr. "HHJ (1830-1885)." *ALR*, 2 (Summer 1969), 143-148.

Byers. "The Indian Matter of HHJ's *Ramona*: From Fact to Fiction." *AIQ*, 2 (Winter 1975-1976), 331-346.

Dobie, J Frank. "HHJ and *Ramona*." *SWR*, 44 (Spring 1959), 93-98.

Hamblen, Abigail Ann. "*Ramona*: A Story of Passion." *WestR*, 8, no 1 (1971), 21-25.

Harsha, W J. "How *Ramona* Wrote Itself." *SW*, 59 (Aug 1930), 370-375.

Higginson, Thomas Wentworth. "HJ (H. H.)." *Contemporaries*, Vol 2 (Boston: Houghton, Mifflin, 1899), 142-167.

Hubbard, Sara A. "HHJ." *Dial*, 6 (Sep 1885), 109-110.

Keller, Karl. "HHJ: Pioneer Activist of Southern California." *Seacoast*, 2 (Mar 1981), 60-65.

Kime, Wayne R. "HHJ." *ALR*, 8 (Autumn 1975), 291-292.

Lubbers, Klaus. *Emily Dickinson: The Critical Revolution* (Ann Arbor: U Michigan P, 1968), passim.

Marsden, Michael T. "HHJ: Docudramatist of the American Indian." *MarkhamR*, 10 (Fall-Winter 1981-1982), 15-19.

Mathes, Valerie Sherer. "HHJ: Official Agent to the California Mission Indians." *SCQ*, 63 (Spring 1981) 63-77.

McConnell, Virginia. " 'H. H.,' Colorado, and the Indian Problem." *JW*, 12 (Apr 1973), 272-280.

McWilliams, Carey. "Southern California: Ersatz Mythology." *CommonG*, 6 (Winter 1946), 29-38.

Nevins, Allan. "HHJ: Sentimentalist vs. Realist." *ASch*, 10 (Summer 1941), 269-285.

Patterson, Rebecca. *The Riddle of Emily Dickinson* (Boston: Houghton Mifflin, 1951), passim.

Pound, Louise. "Biographical Accuracy and 'H. H.' " *AL*, 2 (Mar 1930-Jan 1931), 418-421.

Rolle, Andrew F. "Introduction to the Torchbook Edition." *A Century of Dishonor* (NY: Harper & Row, 1965), vii-xxii.

Scheick, William J. *The Half-Blood: A Cultural Symbol in Nineteenth-Century American Fiction* (Lexington: U P Kentucky, 1979), passim.

Sewall, Richard B. *The Life of Emily Dickinson*, Vol 2 (NY: Farrar, Straus & Giroux, 1974), passim.

Shinn, Milicent W. "The Verse and Prose of 'H. H.' " *Overland*, 2nd series, 6 (Sep 1885), 315-323.

Staub, Michael E. "Friendship of Emily Dickinson With HHJ." *DicS*, 68 (Dec 1988), 17-25.

Stellman, Louis J. "The Man Who Inspired *Ramona*." *Overland*, 50 (Sep 1907), 252-255.

Walker, Cheryl. "Tradition and the Individual Talent: HHJ and Emily Dickinson." *The Nightingale's Burden: Women Poets and American Culture Before 1900* (Bloomington: Indiana U P, 1982), 87-116.

Wells, Anna Mary. *Dear Preceptor: The Life and Times of Thomas Wentworth Higginson* (Boston: Houghton Mifflin, 1963), passim.

Whitaker, Rosemary. "*Legacy* Profile: HHJ (1830-1885)." *Legacy*, 3 (Spring 1986), 56-62.

Alice Shukalo

HENRY JAMES

New York City, NY, 15 Apr 1843-London, England, 28 Feb 1916

Henry James's early work indicates a debt to Hawthorne, Balzac, and the romanticists; his mature writing both reflects and surpasses the achievement of the French and Russian realists; and his later novels provide a bridge to the stream-of-consciousness prose of such modernists as Virginia Woolf, James Joyce, and William Faulkner. Throughout, James focused on a group of sheltered, affluent characters whose fates are nonetheless common to everyone. His themes are failed love, sexual betrayal, untimely death, loneliness; more often than not, the works that examine these themes are set in a Europe where expatriate Americans discover great art, grand passion, and bitter disappointment. James not only lived the highly mannered life that his characters enjoyed but also paralleled it in an elaborately stylized prose. He championed the cause of psychological realism and either pioneered new techniques or refined existing ones; his critical writings cover such general topics as the treatment of ideas and the place of morality in fiction as well as such specific ones as point of view and character type. No other author has contributed so intelligently to the discussion of literary theory and practice.

BIBLIOGRAPHIES

*American Literary Scholarship: An Annual, 1963- *. Durham, NC: Duke U P, 1965- . Chapters on HJ.

Bibliography of American Literature, comp Jacob Blanck. New Haven: Yale U P, 1955-1991. Primary.

Bradbury, Nicola. *An Annotated Critical Bibliography of HJ*. NY: St Martin, 1987. Includes topical index. Secondary.

Budd, John. *HJ: A Bibliography of Criticism, 1975-1981*. Westport, Conn: Greenwood, 1983.

Edel, Leon & Dan H Laurence, with James Rambeau. *A Bibliography of HJ*. Oxford: Clarendon, rev 1982. Primary.

Foley, Richard N. *Criticism in American Periodicals of the Works of HJ From 1866 to 1916*. Washington: Catholic U of America P, 1944.

Gale, Robert L. "HJ." *Eight American Authors: A Review of Research and Criticism*, ed James Woodress (NY: Norton, rev 1971), 321-375.

Hamilton, Eunice C. "Biographical and Critical Studies of HJ." *AL*, 20 (Jan 1949), 424-435.

Holman, C Hugh. "J, H (1943-1916)." *The American Novel Through HJ* (Arlington Heights, Ill: AHM, rev 1979), 78-96. Primary & secondary.

McColgan, Kristin Pruitt. *HJ, 1917-1959: A Reference Guide*. Boston: Hall, 1979. Secondary.

Ricks, Beatrice. *HJ: A Bibliography of Secondary Works*. Metuchen, NJ: Scarecrow, 1975.

Scura, Dorothy McInnis. *HJ, 1960-1974: A Reference Guide*. Boston: Hall, 1979. Secondary.

Taylor, Linda J. *HJ, 1866-1916: A Reference Guide*. Boston: Hall, 1982. Secondary.

BOOKS

A Passionate Pilgrim and Other Tales. Boston: Osgood, 1875. Stories.

Transatlantic Sketches. Boston: Osgood, 1875. Travel essays.

Roderick Hudson. Boston: Osgood, 1876. Rev ed, 3 vols, London: Macmillan, 1879. Novel.

The American. Boston: Osgood, 1877. *HJ, The American: The Version of 1877 . . . Reproduced in Facsimile*, intro by Rodney G Davis. Npl: Scolar, 1976. Novel.

French Poets and Novelists. London: Macmillan, 1878; NY: Grosset & Dunlap, 1964. Essays.

Watch and Ward. Boston: Houghton, Osgood, 1878. Novel.

The Europeans: A Sketch. 2 vols, London: Macmillan, 1878; 1 vol, Boston: Houghton, Osgood, 1879. *HJ, The Europeans: A Facsimile of the Manuscript*, intro by Leon Edel. NY: Fertig, 1979. Novel.

Daisy Miller: A Study. NY: Harper, 1879. Novella.

An International Episode. NY: Harper, 1879. Novella.

Daisy Miller: A Study, An International Episode, Four Meetings. London: Macmillan, 1879. Novellas.

The Madonna of the Future and Other Tales, 2 vols. London: Macmillan, 1879. Stories.

Confidence. 2 vols, London: Chatto & Windus, 1879; 1 vol, Boston: Houghton, Osgood, 1880. Novel.

Hawthorne. London: Macmillan, 1879; NY: Harper, 1880. Literary criticism.

The Diary of a Man of Fifty and A Bundle of Letters. NY: Harper, 1880. Novellas.

Washington Square. NY: Harper, 1881. Novel.

Washington Square, The Pension Beaurepas, A Bundle of Letters, 2 vols. London: Macmillan, 1881. Novel & novellas.

The Portrait of a Lady. 3 vols, London: Macmillan, 1881; 1 vol, Boston & NY: Houghton, Mifflin, 1882. Novel.

The Siege of London, The Pension Beaurepas, and The Point of View. Boston: Osgood, 1883. Novellas.

Daisy Miller: A Comedy in Three Acts. Boston: Osgood, 1883. Play.

Portraits of Places. London: Macmillan, 1883; Boston: Osgood, 1884. Travel essays.

Tales of Three Cities. Boston: Osgood, 1884. Novellas.

A Little Tour in France. Boston: Osgood, 1885. Travel essays.

The Author of Beltraffio, Pandora, Georgina's Reasons, The Path of Duty, Four Meetings. Boston: Osgood, 1885. Stories.

Stories Revived, 3 vols. London: Macmillan, 1885. Stories.

The Bostonians. London & NY: Macmillan, 1886. Novel.

The Princess Casamassima. London & NY: Macmillan, 1886. Novel.

Partial Portraits. London & NY: Macmillan, 1888. Essays.

The Reverberator. London & NY: Macmillan, 1888. Novel.

The Aspern Papers, Louisa Pallant, The Modern Warning. London & NY: Macmillan, 1888. Novellas.

A London Life, The Patagonia, The Liar, Mrs. Temperly. London & NY: Macmillan, 1889. Novellas.

The Tragic Muse, 2 vols. Boston & NY: Houghton, Mifflin, 1890. Novel.

The American: A Comedy in Four Acts. London: Heinemann, 1891. Play.

The Lesson of the Master, The Marriages, The Pupil, Brooksmith, The Solution, Sir Edmund Orme. NY & London: Macmillan, 1892. Stories.

The Real Thing and Other Tales. NY & London: Macmillan, 1893. Stories.

Picture and Text. NY: Harper, 1893. Essays.

The Private Life, The Wheel of Time, Lord Beaupre, The Visits, Collaboration, Owen Wingrave. London: Osgood, McIlvaine, 1893. Rpt in 2 vols as *The Private Life, Lord Beaupre, The Visits & The Wheel of Time, Collaboration, Owen Wingrave*. NY: Harper, 1893. Stories.

Essays in London and Elsewhere. NY: Harper, 1893.

Theatricals, Two Comedies: Tenants, Disengaged. NY: Harper, 1894. Plays.

Theatricals, Second Series: The Album, The Reprobate. NY: Harper, 1895. Plays.

Terminations: The Death of the Lion, The Coxon Fund, The Middle Years, The Altar of the Dead. NY: Harper, 1895. Stories.

Embarrassments: The Figure in the Carpet, Glasses, The Next Time, The Way It Came. NY & London: Macmillan, 1896. Stories.

The Other House. NY & London: Macmillan, 1896. Novel.

The Spoils of Poynton. Boston & NY: Houghton, Mifflin, 1897. Novel.

What Maisie Knew. Chicago & NY: Stone, 1897. Novel.

In the Cage. Chicago & NY: Stone, 1897. Novella.

The Two Magics: The Turn of the Screw, Covering End. NY & London: Macmillan, 1898. Novellas.

The Awkward Age. NY & London: Harper, 1899. Novel.

The Soft Side. NY & London: Macmillan, 1900. Stories.

The Sacred Fount. NY: Scribners, 1901. Novel.

The Wings of the Dove. NY: Scribners, 1902. Novel.

The Better Sort. NY: Scribners, 1903. Stories.

The Ambassadors. NY & London: Harper, 1903. Novel.

William Wetmore Story and His Friends, 2 vols. Boston: Houghton, Mifflin, 1903. Biography.

The Golden Bowl, 2 vols. NY: Scribners, 1904. Novel.

The Question of Our Speech, The Lesson of Balzac: Two Lectures. Boston & NY: Houghton, Mifflin, 1905.

English Hours. Boston & NY: Houghton, Mifflin, 1905. Travel essays.

The American Scene. NY & London: Harper, 1907. Travel essays.

Views and Reviews. Boston: Ball, 1908. Essays.

Julia Bride. NY & London: Harper, 1909. Story.

Italian Hours. Boston & NY: Houghton Mifflin, 1909. Travel essays.

The Finer Grain. NY: Scribners, 1910. Stories.

The Outcry. NY: Scribners, 1911. Novel.

A Small Boy and Others. NY: Scribners, 1913. Autobiography.

Notes of a Son and Brother. NY: Scribners, 1914. Autobiography.

Notes on Novelists With Some Other Notes. NY: Scribners, 1914. Essays.

The Ivory Tower, ed Percy Lubbock. NY: Scribners, 1917. Unfinished novel.

The Sense of the Past, ed Lubbock. NY: Scribners, 1917. Unfinished novel.

The Middle Years, ed Lubbock. NY: Scribners, 1917. Unfinished autobiography.

Within the Rim and Other Essays, 1914-15. London: Collins, 1918.

Gabrielle de Bergerac, ed Albert Mordell. NY: Boni & Liveright, 1919. Story.

Travelling Companions, ed Mordell. NY: Boni & Liveright, 1919. Stories.

A Landscape Painter, ed Mordell. NY: Scott & Seltzer, 1919. Stories.

Master Eustace. NY: Seltzer, 1920. Stories.

Notes and Reviews. Cambridge, Mass: Dunster House, 1921. Essays.

The Art of the Novel: Critical Prefaces, intro by Richard P Blackmur. NY: Scribners, 1934.

The Scenic Art: Notes on Acting & the Drama: 1872-1901, ed with intro & notes by Allan Wade. New Brunswick, NJ: Rutgers U P, 1948. Essays.

The Ghostly Tales of HJ, ed with intro by Leon Edel. New Brunswick, NJ: Rutgers U P, 1949. Stories.

The Complete Plays of HJ, ed with foreword by Edel. Philadelphia & NY: Lippincott, 1949.

Eight Uncollected Tales, ed with intro by Edna Kenton. New Brunswick, NJ: Rutgers U P, 1950. Stories.

The American Essays, ed with intro by Edel. NY: Vintage, 1956.

The Future of the Novel: Essays on the Art of Fiction, ed with intro by Edel. NY: Vintage, 1956.

The Painter's Eye: Notes and Essays on the Pictorial Arts, ed with intro by John L Sweeney. Cambridge: Harvard U P, 1956.

Parisian Sketches: Letters to the New York Tribune, 1875-1876, ed with intro by Edel & Ilse Dusoir Lind. NY: NYU P, 1957. Travel essays.

The House of Fiction: Essays on the Novel by HJ, ed with intro by Edel. London: Hart-Davis, 1957.

Literary Reviews and Essays by HJ on American, English, and French Literature, ed Mordell. NY: Twayne, 1957.

French Writers and American Women: Essays by HJ, ed with intro by Peter Buitenhuis. Branford, Conn: Compass, 1960.

Theory of Fiction: HJ, ed with intro by James E Miller, Jr. Lincoln: U Nebraska P, 1972.

LETTERS, DIARIES, NOTEBOOKS

The Letters of HJ, 2 vols, ed with intro by Percy Lubbock. NY: Scribners, 1920.

HJ: Letters to A. C. Benson and Auguste Monod, ed with intro by E F Benson. London: Mathews & Marrot / NY: Scribners, 1930.

Theatre and Friendship: Some HJ Letters With a Commentary by Elizabeth Robins. NY: Putnam, 1932.

The Notebooks of HJ, ed with notes by F O Matthiessen & Kenneth B Murdock. NY: Oxford U P, 1947.

HJ and Robert Louis Stevenson: A Record of Friendship and Criticism, ed with intro by Janet Adam Smith. London: Hart-Davis, 1948; NY: Macmillan, 1949.

Thomas Sergeant Perry: A Biography and Letters to Perry From William, Henry, and Garth Wilkinson James, by Virginia Harlow. Durham, NC: Duke U P, 1950.

The Selected Letters of HJ, ed with intro by Leon Edel. NY: Farrar, Straus & Cudahy, 1955.

HJ and H. G. Wells: A Record of Their Friendship, Their Debate on the Art of Fiction, and Their Quarrel, ed with intro by Edel & Gordon N Ray. Urbana: U Illinois P, 1958.

Howells and James: A Double Billing. Includes *Novel-Writing and Novel-Reading: An Impersonal Explanation* by William Dean Howells, ed William M Gibson; *HJ and the Bazar Letters*, ed Edel & Lyall H Powers. NY: New York Public Library, 1958.

HJ and John Hay: The Record of a Friendship, ed with intro by George Monteiro. Providence, RI: Brown U P, 1965.

HJ: Letters, Vol. 1, 1843-1875, ed with intro by Edel. Cambridge: Harvard U P, 1974.

HJ: Letters, Vol. 2, 1875-1883, ed with intro by Edel. Cambridge: Harvard U P, 1975.

HJ: Letters, Vol. 3, 1883-1895, ed with intro by Edel. Cambridge: Harvard U P, 1980.

HJ: Letters, Vol. 4, 1895-1916, ed with intro by Edel. Cambridge: Harvard U P, 1984.

HJ: Selected Letters, ed with intro by Edel. Cambridge: Harvard U P, 1987.

The Complete Notebooks of HJ, ed with intro & notes by Edel & Powers. NY & Oxford: Oxford U P, 1987.

Selected Letters of HJ to Edmund Gosse, 1882-1915: A Literary Friendship, ed with intro by Rayburn S Moore. Baton Rouge & London: Louisiana State U P, 1988.

OTHER

"The Married Son." *The Whole Family: A Novel by Twelve Authors* (NY & London: Harper, 1908), 144-184.

EDITIONS & COLLECTIONS

Novels and Tales of HJ, 14 vols. London: Macmillan, 1883.

The Novels and Tales of HJ, New York Edition, 26 vols, selected & rev by HJ. NY: Scribners, 1907-1918.

The Novels and Stories of HJ, 35 vols, ed Percy Lubbock. London: Macmillan, 1921-1923.

The American Novels and Stories of HJ, ed F O Matthiessen. NY: Knopf, 1947.

The Complete Tales of HJ, 12 vols, ed with intros by Leon Edel. Philadelphia & NY: Lippincott, 1962-1964.

The Bodley Head HJ, ed with intros by Edel. London: Bodley Head, 1967-

The Tales of HJ, ed Maqbool Aziz. Oxford: Oxford U P, 1973-

MANUSCRIPTS & ARCHIVES

The major collections are at the Houghton Library, Harvard U; the Beinecke Library, Yale U; & the Library of Congress.

CONCORDANCES

Bender, Claire E & Todd K. *A Concordance to HJ's The Turn of the Screw*. NY: Garland, 1988.

Bender, Todd K. *A Concordance to HJ's Daisy Miller*. NY: Garland, 1987.

Bender, Todd K & D Leon Higdon. *A Concordance to HJ's The Spoils of Poynton*. NY: Garland, 1988.

Higdon, D Leon & Todd K Bender. *A Concordance to HJ's The American*. NY: Garland, 1985.

BIOGRAPHIES

Books

Bosanquet, Theodora. *HJ at Work*. London: Hogarth, 1924.

Dupee, F W. *HJ*. NY: Sloane, 1951.

Edel, Leon. *HJ: The Untried Years, 1843-1870*. Philadelphia: Lippincott, 1953.

Edel. *HJ: The Conquest of London, 1870-1881*. Philadelphia: Lippincott, 1962.

Edel. *HJ: The Middle Years, 1882-1895*. Philadelphia: Lippincott, 1962.

Edel. *HJ: The Treacherous Years, 1895-1901*. Philadelphia: Lippincott, 1969.

Edel. *HJ: The Master, 1901-1916*. Philadelphia: Lippincott, 1972.

Edel. *HJ: A Life*. NY: Harper & Row, 1985.

Edgar, Pelham. *HJ: Man and Author*. London: Richards, 1927.

Grattan, C Hartley. *The Three James: A Family of Minds: HJ, Sr., William James, and HJ*. NY: Longmans, Green, 1932.

Hyde, H Montgomery. *HJ at Home*. NY: Farrar, Straus & Giroux, 1969.

LeClair, Robert Charles. *The Young HJ: 1843-1870*. NY: Bookman, 1955.

Matthiessen, F O. *The James Family. Including Selections From the Writings of HJ, Senior, William, H, & Alice James*. NY: Knopf, 1947.

Moore, Harry T. *HJ*. NY: Viking, 1974.

Nowell-Smith, Simon, ed. *The Legend of the Master*. NY: Scribners, 1948.

Page, Norman, ed. *HJ: Interviews and Recollections*. NY: St Martin, 1984.

Seymour, Miranda. *A Ring of Conspirators: HJ and His Literary Circle, 1895-1915*. London: Hodder & Stoughton, 1988.

Book Sections & Articles

Allen, Gay Wilson. *William James* (NY: Viking, 1967), passim.

Edel, Leon. "The Exile of HJ." *UTQ*, 2 (Jul 1933), 520-532.

Edel. "Time and the Biographer." *Listener*, 54 (22 Sep 1955), 461-462.

Edel. "To the Poet of Prose." *MFS*, 12 (Spring 1966), 3-6.

Garis, Robert. "Anti-Literary Biography." *HudR*, 23 (Spring 1970), 143-153.

Gass, William H. "A Spirit in Search of Itself." *Fiction and the Figures of Life* (NY: Knopf, 1970), 157-163.

Hampshire, Stuart. "A Son and Brother." *NYRB*, 8 (29 Jun 1967), 3-4.

Hoffman, Frederick J. "The Expense and Power of Greatness: An Essay on Leon Edel's *J*." *VQR*, 39 (Summer 1963), 518-528.

Kirby, David. "The Sex Lives of the J Family." *VQR*, 64 (Winter 1988), 56-73.

LeClair, Robert C. "HJ and Minny Temple." *AL*, 21 (Mar 1949), 35-48.

Maher, Jane. *Biography of Broken Fortunes: Wilkie and Bob, Brothers of William, H, and Alice James* (Hamden, Conn: Archon, 1986), passim.

Moore, Rayburn S. "The Full Light of a Higher Criticism: Edel's Biography and Other Recent Studies of HJ." *SAQ*, 63 (Winter 1964), 104-114.

Strouse, Jean. *Alice James: A Biography* (Boston: Houghton Mifflin, 1980), passim.

Trilling, Lionel. "The Jameses." *TLS* (20 Oct 1972), 1257.

Wegelin, Christof. "Jamesian Biography." *NCF*, 18 (Dec 1963), 283-287.

CRITICAL STUDIES

Books

Allen, Elizabeth. *A Woman's Place in the Novels of HJ*. London: Macmillan, 1984.

Anderson, Charles R. *Person, Place, and Thing in HJ's Novels*. Durham, NC: Duke U P, 1977.

Anderson, Quentin. *The American HJ*. New Brunswick, NJ: Rutgers U P, 1957.

Andreas, Osborn. *HJ and the Expanding Horizon: A Study of the Meaning and Basic Themes of J's Fiction*. Seattle: U Washington P, 1948.

Anesko, Michael. *"Friction With the Market": HJ and the Profession of Authorship*. NY: Oxford U P, 1986.

Armstrong, Paul B. *The Phenomenology of HJ*. Chapel Hill: U North Carolina P, 1983.

Auchincloss, Louis. *Reading HJ*. Minneapolis: U Minnesota P, 1975.

Beach, Joseph Warren. *The Method of HJ*. New Haven: Yale U P, 1918.

Bell, Millicent. *Edith Wharton and HJ: The Story of Their Friendship*. NY: Braziller, 1965.

Blackmur, R P. *Studies in HJ*, ed with intro by Veronica A Makowsky. NY: New Directions, 1983.

Bowden, Edwin T. *The Themes of HJ*. New Haven: Yale U P, 1956.

Bradbury, Nicola. *HJ: The Later Novels*. Oxford: Clarendon, 1979.

Brooks, Peter. *The Melodramatic Imagination: Balzac, HJ, Melodrama, and the Mode of Excess*. New Haven: Yale U P, 1976.

Buitenhuis, Peter. *The Grasping Imagination: The American Writings of HJ*. Toronto: U Toronto P, 1970.

Cargill, Oscar. *The Novels of HJ*. NY: Macmillan, 1961.

Cary, Elizabeth Luther. *The Novels of HJ*. NY: Putnam, 1905.

Crews, Frederick C. *The Tragedy of Manners: Moral Drama in the Later Novels of HJ*. New Haven: Yale U P, 1957.

Donadio, Stephen. *Nietzsche, HJ, and the Artistic Will*. NY: Oxford U P, 1978.

Edel, Leon. *HJ*. Minneapolis: U Minnesota P, 1960.

Edel & Adeline R Tintner. *The Library of HJ*. Ann Arbor, Mich: UMI, 1987.

Egan, Michael. *HJ: The Ibsen Years*. London: Vision, 1972.

Fogel, Daniel Mark. *HJ and the Structure of the Romantic Imagination*. Baton Rouge: Louisiana State U P, 1981.

Ford, Ford Madox. *HJ: A Critical Study*. NY: Boni, 1915.

Fowler, Virginia C. *HJ's American Girl: The Embroidery on the Canvas*. Madison: U Wisconsin P, 1984.

Franklin, Rosemary F. *An Index to HJ's Prefaces to the New York Edition*. Charlottesville: Bibliographical Society, U Virginia, 1966.

Gale, Robert L. *The Caught Image: Figurative Language in the Fiction of HJ*. Chapel Hill: U North Carolina P, 1964.

Gale. *Plots and Characters in the Fiction of HJ*. Hamden, Conn: Archon, 1965.

Geismar, Maxwell. *HJ and the Jacobites*. Boston: Houghton Mifflin, 1963.

Grover, Philip. *HJ and the French Novel: A Study in Inspiration*. NY: Barnes & Noble, 1973.

Hocks, Richard A. *HJ and Pragmatistic Thought*. Chapel Hill: U North Carolina P, 1974.

Holder-Barell, Alexander. *The Development of Imagery and Its Functional Significance in HJ's Novels*. NY: Haskell House, 1966.

Holland, Laurence Bedwell. *The Expense of Vision: Essays on the Craft of HJ*. Princeton: Princeton U P, 1964.

Howells, W D. *Discovery of a Genius: William Dean Howells and HJ*, ed Albert Mordell. NY: Twayne, 1961.

Hutchinson, Stuart. *HJ: An American as Modernist*. London: Vision / Totowa, NJ: Barnes & Noble, 1982.

Isle, Walter. *Experiments in Form*. Cambridge: Harvard U P, 1968.

Jacobson, Marcia. *HJ and the Mass Market*. University: U Alabama P, 1983.

Johnson, Courtney, Jr. *HJ and the Evolution of Consciousness: A Study of The Ambassadors*. East Lansing: Michigan State U P, 1987.

Jones, Vivien. *J the Critic*. NY: St Martin, 1985.

Kelley, Cornelia Pulsifer. *The Early Development of HJ*. Carbondale: Southern Illinois U P, rev 1969.

Krook, Dorothea. *The Ordeal of Consciousness in HJ*. NY: Cambridge U P, 1962.

Leavis, F R. *The Great Tradition: George Eliot, HJ, Joseph Conrad*. London: Chatto & Windus, 1948.

Lebowitz, Naomi. *The Imagination of Loving: HJ's Legacy to the Novel*. Detroit, Mich: Wayne State U P, 1965.

Leeming, Glenda. *Who's Who in HJ*. NY: Taplinger, 1976.

Levy, Leo B. *Versions of Melodrama: A Study of the Fiction and Drama of HJ, 1865-1897*. Berkeley: U California P, 1957.

Long, Robert Emmet. *The Great Succession: HJ and the Legacy of Hawthorne*. Pittsburgh: U Pittsburgh P, 1979.

Lubbock, Percy. *The Craft of Fiction*. London: Cape, 1921.

Margolis, Anne T. *HJ and the Problem of Audience*. Ann Arbor: UMI, 1985.

Matthiessen, F O. *HJ: The Major Phase*. NY: Oxford U P, 1944.

Maves, Carl. *Sensuous Pessimism: Italy in the Work of HJ*. Bloomington: Indiana U P, 1973.

McCarthy, Harold T. *HJ: The Creative Process*. NY: Yoseloff, 1958.

McElderry, Bruce R, Jr. *HJ*. NY: Twayne, 1965.

Mull, Donald L. *HJ's "Sublime Economy": Money as Symbolic Center in the Fiction*. Middletown, Conn: Wesleyan U P, 1973.

Nettels, Elsa. *J and Conrad*. Athens: U Georgia P, 1977.

Perosa, Sergio. *HJ and the Experimental Novel*. Charlottesville: U Virginia P, 1978.

Peterson, Dale E. *The Clement Vision: Poetic Realism in Turgenev and J*. Port Washington, NY: Kennikat, 1975.

Pirie, Gordon. *HJ*. London: Evans, 1974.

Poirier, Richard. *The Comic Sense of HJ: A Study of the Early Novels*. NY: Oxford U P, 1960.

Posnock, Ross. *HJ and the Problem of Robert Browning*. Athens: U Georgia P, 1985.

Powers, Lyall H. *HJ: An Introduction and Interpretation*. NY: Holt, Rinehart & Winston, 1970.

Powers. *HJ and the Naturalist Movement*. East Lansing: Michigan State U P, 1971.

Purdy, Strother B. *The Hole in the Fabric: Science, Contemporary Literature, and HJ*. Pittsburgh: U Pittsburgh P, 1977.

Putt, S Gorley. *A Reader's Guide to HJ*. Ithaca, NY: Cornell U P, 1966.

Roberts, Morris. *HJ's Criticism*. Cambridge: Harvard U P, 1929.

Rowe, John Carlos. *The Theoretical Dimensions of HJ*. Madison: U Wisconsin P, 1984.

Samuels, Charles Thomas. *The Ambiguity of HJ*. Urbana: U Illinois P, 1971.

Schneider, Daniel J. *The Crystal Cage: Adventures of the Imagination in the Fiction of HJ*. Lawrence: Regents P of Kansas, 1978.

Seltzer, Mark. *HJ & the Art of Power*. Ithaca, NY: Cornell U P, 1984.

Shine, Muriel G. *The Fictional Children of HJ*. Chapel Hill: U North Carolina P, 1969.

Sicker, Philip. *Love and the Quest for Identity in the Fiction of HJ*. Princeton: Princeton U P, 1980.

Smit, David W. *The Language of a Master: Theories of Style and the Late Writings of HJ*. Carbondale: Southern Illinois U P, 1988.

Springer, Mary Doyle. *A Rhetoric of Literary Characters: Some Women of HJ*. Chicago: U Chicago P, 1978.

Stafford, William T. *A Name, Title, and Place Index to the Critical Writings of HJ*. Englewood, Colo: Microcard Editions, 1975.

Stallman, Robert W. *The Houses That J Built and Other Literary Studies*. East Lansing: Michigan State U P, 1961.

Stowell, H Peter. *Literary Impressionism, J and Chekhov*. Athens: U Georgia P, 1980.

Tintner, Adeline R. *The Museum World of HJ*. Ann Arbor, Mich: UMI, 1986.

Tintner. *The Book World of HJ: Appropriating the Classics*. Ann Arbor, Mich: UMI, 1987.

Vaid, Krishna Baldev. *Technique in the Tales of HJ*. Cambridge: Harvard U P, 1964.

Veeder, William. *HJ—The Lessons of the Master: Popular Fiction and Personal Style in the Nineteenth Century*. Chicago: U Chicago P, 1975.

Wagenknecht, Edward. *Eve and HJ: Portraits of Women and Girls in His Fiction*. Norman: U Oklahoma P, 1978.

Wallace, Ronald. *HJ and the Comic Form*. Ann Arbor: U Michigan P, 1975.

Ward, J A. *The Search for Form: Studies in the Structure of J's Fiction*. Chapel Hill: U North Carolina P, 1967.

Wegelin, Christof. *The Image of Europe in HJ*. Dallas, Tex: Southern Methodist U P, 1958.

Weinstein, Philip M. *HJ and the Requirements of the Imagination*. Cambridge: Harvard U P, 1971.

Wiesenfarth, Joseph. *HJ and the Dramatic Analogy*. NY: Fordham U P, 1963.

Winner, Viola Hopkins. *HJ and the Visual Arts*. Charlottesville: U P Virginia, 1970.

Wright, Walter J. *The Madness of Art: A Study of HJ*. Lincoln: U Nebraska P, 1962.

Yeazell, Ruth Bernard. *Language and Knowledge in the Late Novels of HJ*. Chicago: U Chicago P, 1976.

Collections of Essays

Banta, Martha, ed. *New Essays on The American*. NY: Cambridge U P, 1987.

Bloom, Harold, ed. *HJ*. NY: Chelsea House, 1987.

Bloom, ed. *HJ's Daisy Miller, The Turn of the Screw, and Other Tales*. NY: Chelsea House, 1987.

Bloom, ed. *HJ's The Portrait of a Lady*. NY: Chelsea House, 1987.

Buitenhuis, Peter, ed. *Twentieth Century Interpretations of The Portrait of a Lady*. Englewood Cliffs, NJ: Prentice-Hall, 1968.

Dupee, F W, ed. *The Question of HJ*. NY: Holt, 1945.

Edel, Leon, ed. *HJ: A Collection of Critical Essays*. Englewood Cliffs, NJ: Prentice-Hall, 1963.

Gard, Roger, ed. *HJ: The Critical Heritage*. London: Routledge & Kegan Paul / NY: Barnes & Noble, 1968.

Gargano, James W, ed. *Critical Essays on HJ: The Early Novels*. Boston: Hall, 1987.

Gargano, ed. *Critical Essays on HJ: The Late Novels*. Boston: Hall, 1987.

Goode, John, ed. *The Air of Reality: New Essays on HJ*. London: Methuen, 1972.

Lebowitz, Naomi, ed. *Discussions of HJ*. Boston: Heath, 1962.

Powers, Lyall H, ed. *The Merrill Studies in The Portrait of a Lady*. Columbus, Ohio: Merrill, 1970.

Powers, ed. *HJ's Major Novels: Essays in Criticism*. East Lansing: Michigan State U P, 1973.

Stafford, William T, ed. *J's Daisy Miller: The Story, the Play, the Critics*. NY: Scribners, 1963.

Stafford, ed. *Perspectives on J's The Portrait of a Lady*. NY: NYU P, 1967.

Stafford, ed. *The Merrill Studies in The American*. Columbus, Ohio: Merrill, 1971.

Stone, Albert E, ed. *Twentieth Century Interpretations of The Ambassadors*. Englewood Cliffs, NJ: Prentice-Hall, 1969.

Tanner, Tony, ed. *HJ: Modern Judgements*. London: Macmillan, 1968.

Tompkins, Jane P, ed. *Twentieth Century Interpretations of The Turn of the Screw and Other Tales*. Englewood Cliffs, NJ: Prentice-Hall, 1970.

Vann, J Don, ed. *Critics on HJ*. Coral Gables: U Miami P, 1972.

Willen, Gerald, ed. *A Casebook on HJ's The Turn of the Screw*. NY: Crowell, rev 1969.

Special Journals

H&H, 7 (Apr-May 1934). HJ issue.
Henry James Review (1979-). Includes checklists.
KR, 5 (Autumn 1943). HJ issue.
LRev, 5 (August 1918). HJ issue.
MFS, 3 (Spring 1957). HJ issue.
MFS, 12 (Spring 1966). HJ issue.
MLS, 13 (Fall 1983). HJ issue.
MTQ, 5 (Spring 1943). HJ issue.

Book Sections & Articles

Adams, Percy G. "Young HJ and the Lesson of His Master Balzac." *RLC*, 35 (Jul-Sep 1961), 458-467.

Arms, George & William M Gibson. "*Silas Lapham, Daisy Miller,* and the Jews." *NEQ*, 16 (Mar 1943), 118-122.

Auchincloss, Louis. "A Strategy for J Readers." *Nation*, 190 (23 Apr 1960), 364-367.

Banta, Martha. "Beyond Post-Modernism: The Sense of History in *The Princess Casamassima*." *HJR*, 3 (Winter 1982), 96-107.

Barnett, Louise K. "Speech in *The Ambassadors*: Woolett and Paris as Linguistic Communities." *Novel*, 16 (Spring 1983), 215-229.

Bayley, John. "Formalist Games and Real Life." *EIC*, 31 (Oct 1981), 271-281.

Bell, Millicent. "The Bostonian Story." *PR*, 52, no 2 (1985), 109-119.

Bender, Eileen T. " 'The Question of His Own French': Dialect and Dialectic in *The Ambassadors*." *HJR*, 5 (Winter 1984), 128-134.

Berland, Alwyn. "HJ and the Aesthetic Tradition." *JHI*, 23 (Jul-Sep 1962), 407-419.

Blackall, Jean Frantz. "Literary Allusion as Imaginative Event in *The Awkward Age*." *MFS*, 26 (Summer 1980), 179-197.

Blackmur, R P. "The Loose and Baggy Monsters of HJ: Notes on the Underlying Classic Form in the Novel." *Accent*, 11 (Summer 1951), 129-146. Rpt Stone.

Booth, Wayne. "The Price of Impersonal Narration, II: HJ and the Unreliable Narrator." *The Rhetoric of Fiction* (Chicago: U Chicago P, 1961), 339-374.

Cargill, Oscar. "HJ's 'Moral Policeman': William Dean Howells." *AL*, 29 (Jan 1958), 371-398. Rpt as "William Dean Howells as HJ's 'Moral Policeman.' " *Toward a Pluralistic Criticism* by Cargill (Carbondale: Southern Illinois U P, 1965).

Clark, Harry Hayden. "HJ and Science: *The Wings of the Dove*." *TWA*, 52 (1963), 1-15.

Cox, C B. "HJ and Stoicism." *E&S*, ns 8 (1955), 76-88.

Cromer, Viris. "J and Ibsen." *CL*, 25 (Spring 1973), 114-127.

Culver, Stuart. "Representing the Author: HJ, Intellectual Property and the Work of Writing." *HJ: Fiction as History*, ed Ian F A Bell (London: Vision / NY: Barnes & Noble, 1984), 114-136.

Daiches, David. "Sensibility and Technique (Preface to a Critique)." *KR*, 5 (Autumn 1943), 569-579.

Deakin, Motley F. "Daisy Miller, Tradition, and the European Heroine." *CLS*, 6 (Mar 1969), 45-59.

Dean, Sharon. "Constance Fenimore Woolson and HJ: The Literary Relationship." *MSE*, 7, no 3 (1980), 1-9.

Eakin, Paul John. *The New England Girl: Cultural Ideals in Hawthorne, Stowe, Howells, and J* (Athens: U Georgia P, 1976), passim.

Edel, Leon. "The Architecture of HJ's 'New York Edition.' " *NEQ*, 24 (Jun 1951), 169-178.

Edel. "The Point of View." *The Modern Psychological Novel* (NY: Grosset & Dunlap, rev 1964), 35-52.

Edel. "HJ: The Americano-European Legend." *UTQ*, 36, no 4 (1967), 321-334.

Edwards, Herbert. "HJ and Ibsen." *AL*, 24 (May 1952), 208-223.

Fay, Eliot G. "Balzac and HJ." *FR*, 24 (Feb 1951), 325-330.

Felman, Shoshana. "Turning the Screw of Interpretation." *YFS*, nos 55-56 (1977), 94-207.

Fergusson, Francis. "J's Idea of Dramatic Form." *KR*, 5 (Autumn 1943), 495-507.

Finn, C M. "Commitment and Identity in *The Ambassadors*." *MLR*, 66 (Jul 1971), 522-531.

Gilmore, Michael T. "The Commodity World of *The Portrait of a Lady*." *NEQ*, 59 (Mar 1986), 51-74.

Greenslade, William. "The Power of Advertising: Chad Newsome and the Meaning of Paris in *The Ambassadors*." *ELH*, 49 (Spring 1982), 99-122.

Guedalla, Philip. "The Crowner's Quest." *New Statesman*, 12 (15 Feb 1919), 421-422.

Habegger, Alfred. "Reciprocity and the Market Place in *The Wings of the Dove* and *What Maisie Knew*." NCF, 25 (Mar 1971), 455-473.

Habegger. *Gender, Fantasy and Realism in American Literature* (NY: Columbia U P, 1982), passim.

Hoffman, Frederick J. "HJ, William Dean Howells and the Art of Fiction." *The Modern Novel in America, 1900-1950* (Chicago: Regnery, 1951), 1-27.

Ian, Marcia. "The Elaboration of Privacy in *The Wings of the Dove*." ELH, 51 (Spring 1984), 107-136.

Kimball, Jean. "A Classified Subject Index to HJ's Critical Prefaces to the New York Edition (Collected in *The Art of the Novel*)." HJR, 6 (Winter 1985), 89-133.

Kirby, David K. "HJ: Art and Autobiography." DR, 52 (Winter 1972-1973), 637-644.

Leitch, Thomas M. "The Editor as Hero: HJ and the New York Edition." HJR, 3 (Fall 1981), 24-32.

Lerner, Daniel. "The Influence of Turgenev on HJ." SLAVR, 20 (Dec 1941), 28-54.

Levy, Leo B. "*The Golden Bowl* and 'The Voice of Blood.' " HJR, 1 (Winter 1980), 154-163.

Long, Robert Emmet. "Transformations: *The Blithesdale Romance* to Howells and J." AL, 47 (Jan 1976), 552-571.

Malmgren, Carl. "HJ's Major Phase: Making Room for the Reader." HJR, 3 (Fall 1981), 17-23.

Mansell, Darrel. "The Ghost of Language in *The Turn of the Screw*." MLQ, 46 (Mar 1985), 48-63.

Monteiro, George. "Hawthorne, J, and the Destructive Self." TSLL, 4 (Spring 1962), 58-71.

Moore, Rayburn S. "The Strange Irregular Rhythm of Life: J's Late Tales and Constance Woolson." SAB, 41 (Nov 1976), 86-93.

Morris, Wright. "Use of the Past: HJ," "Objects and Places." *The Territory Ahead* (NY: Harcourt, Brace, 1958), 93-112, 187-214.

Mulqueen, James E. "Perfection of a Pattern: The Structure of *The Ambassadors, The Wings of the Dove*, and *The Golden Bowl*." ArQ, 27 (Summer 1971), 133-142.

Murphy, Kevin. "The Unfixable Text: Bewilderment of Vision in *The Turn of the Screw*." TSLL, 20 (Winter 1978), 538-551.

Pacey, W C D. "HJ and His French Contemporaries." AL, 13 (Nov 1941), 240-256.

Poulet, Georges. "Appendix: Time and American Writers." *Studies in Human Time*, trans Elliott Coleman (Baltimore, Md: Johns Hopkins U P, 1956), 350-354.

Pound, Ezra. "HJ." *Literary Essays of Ezra Pound*, ed T S Eliot (Norfolk, Conn: New Directions, 1954), 295-338.

Rahv, Philip. "Attitudes to HJ." NewR, 108 (15 Feb 1943), 220-224.

Rahv. "The Heiress of All the Ages." PR, 10 (May-Jun 1943), 227-247.

Reid, Stephen. "Moral Passion in *The Portrait of a Lady* and *The Spoils of Poynton*." MFS, 12 (Spring 1966), 24-43.

Reilly, Robert J. "HJ and the Morality of Fiction." AL, 39 (Mar 1967), 1-30.

Robbins, Bruce. "Shooting Off J's Blanks: Theory, Politics, and *The Turn of the Screw*." HJR, 5 (Spring 1984), 192-199.

Rourke, Constance. "The American." *American Humor: A Study of the National Character* (Tallahassee: Florida State U P, rpt 1986), 235-265.

Rowe, Joyce A. "Strether Unbound: The Selective Vision of HJ's Ambassador." *Equivocal Endings in Classic American Novels* (Cambridge: Cambridge U P, 1988), 75-99.

Siebers, Tobin. "Hesitation, History, and Reading: HJ's *The Turn of the Screw*." TSLL, 25 (Winter 1983), 558-573.

Simon, Irène. "Jane Austen and *The Art of the Novel*." ES, 43 (Jun 1962), 225-239.

Snow, Lotus. "The Disconcerting Poetry of Mary Temple: A Comparison of the Imagery of *The Portrait of a Lady* and *The Wings of the Dove*." NEQ, 31 (Sep 1958), 312-339.

Spender, Stephen. "HJ," "HJ and the Contemporary Subject." *The Destructive Element: A Study of Modern Writers and Beliefs* (London: Cape, 1935), 11-110, 189-200.

Sutherland, Judith L. "J: More Than Melody." *The Problematic Fictions of Poe, J & Hawthorne* (Columbia: U Missouri P, 1984), 38-70.

Tanner, Tony. "HJ." *The Reign of Wonder: Naivety and Reality in American Literature* (Cambridge: Cambridge U P, 1965), 259-335.

Tintner, Adeline R. " 'High Melancholy and Sweet': J and the Arcadian Tradition." CLQ, 12 (Sep 1976), 109-121.

Tuttleton, James W. "HJ: The Superstitious Valuation of Europe." *The Novel of Manners in America* (Chapel Hill: U North Carolina P, 1972), 48-85.

Van Ghent, Dorothy. "On *The Portrait of a Lady*." *The English Novel: Form and Function* (NY: Rinehart, 1953), 211-228.

Wagner, Vern. "HJ: Money and Sex." SR, 93 (Apr-Jun 1985), 216-231.

Waldmeir, Joseph J. "Miss Tina Did It: A Fresh Look at *The Aspern Papers*." CentR, 26 (Summer 1982), 256-267.

Warren, Austin. "HJ: Symbolic Imagery in the Later Novels." *Rage for Order: Essays in*

Criticism (Chicago: U Chicago P, 1948), 142-161. Rpt Lebowitz, Edel (1963).

Watt, Ian. "The First Paragraph in *The Ambassadors*: An Explication." *EIC*, 10 (Jul 1960), 250-274. See responses by J C Maxwell & Watt, *EIC*, 11 (Jan 1961), 116-119. Rpt Tanner, Stone.

Weissman, Judith. "Antique Secrets in HJ." *SR*, 93 (Apr-Jun 1985), 196-215.

Wellek, René. "HJ's Literary Theory and Criticism." *AL*, 30 (Nov 1958), 293-321.

Wessel, Catherine Cox. "Strategies for Survival in J's *The Golden Bowl*." *AL*, 55 (Dec 1983), 576-590.

Willett, Maurita. "HJ's Indebtedness to Balzac." *RLC*, 41 (Apr-Jun 1967), 204-227.

Winters, Yvor. "Maule's Well or HJ and the Relation of Morals to Manners." *In Defense of Reason* (Denver, Colo: Swallow/U Denver P, 1947), 300-343.

Young, Robert E. "An Error in *The Ambassadors*." *AL*, 22 (Nov 1950), 245-253. See responses by Leon Edel, *AL*, 23 (Mar 1951), 128-130; by Young, *AL*, 23 (Jan 1952), 487-490; & by Edel, *AL*, 24 (Nov 1952), 370-372.

Ziff, Larzer. "Literary Absenteeism: HJ and Mark Twain." *The American 1890s: Life and Times of a Lost Generation* (NY: Viking, 1966), 50-72.

David Kirby

SARAH ORNE JEWETT

South Berwick, Maine, 3 Sep 1849-South Berwick, Maine, 24 Jun 1909

Although Sarah Orne Jewett wrote poetry, several volumes of short stories, many works of fiction for children, and a historical romance, she is best known for her novel *The Country of the Pointed Firs,* considered one of the best examples of regional literature published in the nineteenth century. In this and in most of her short fiction, Jewett portrayed village and rural life in New England, especially her native Maine. Early commentators focused on her subtlety of characterization, her skill at rendering dialect, her genial humor, and her nostalgia for the heritage of her region. Though Jewett was praised for her artistry, contemporary reviewers also criticized her for the apparent weakness of her plots; more recent commentators have identified unifying structural devices in her fiction. During the past two decades scholarly activity on Jewett has been spurred by critical interest in women's studies.

BIBLIOGRAPHIES

Bibliography of American Literature, comp Jacob Blanck. New Haven: Yale U P, 1955-1991. Primary.

Nagel, Gwen L. "*SOJ: A Reference Guide:* An Update." *ALR,* 17 (Autumn 1984), 228-263. Secondary.

Nagel, Gwen L & James. *SOJ: A Reference Guide.* Boston: Hall, 1978. Secondary.

Weber, Clara C & Carl J. *A Bibliography of the Published Writings of SOJ.* Waterville, Maine: Colby C P, 1949. Primary & secondary.

BOOKS

Deephaven. Boston: Osgood, 1877. Novel.

Play Days: A Book of Stories for Children. Boston: Houghton, Osgood, 1878.

Old Friends and New. Boston: Houghton, Osgood, 1879. Stories.

Country By-Ways. Boston: Houghton, Mifflin, 1881. Stories & sketches.

The Mate of the Daylight, and Friends Ashore. Boston & NY: Houghton, Mifflin, 1884. Stories.

A Country Doctor. Boston & NY: Houghton, Mifflin, 1884. Novel.

A Marsh Island. Boston & NY: Houghton, Mifflin, 1885. Novel.

A White Heron and Other Stories. Boston & NY: Houghton, Mifflin, 1886.

The Story of the Normans, Told Chiefly in Relation to Their Conquest of England. NY & London: Putnam, 1887. History.

The King of Folly Island and Other People. Boston & NY: Houghton, Mifflin, 1888. Stories.

Betty Leicester: A Story for Girls. Boston & NY: Houghton, Mifflin, 1890.

Strangers and Wayfarers. Boston & NY: Houghton, Mifflin, 1890. Stories.

A Native of Winby and Other Tales. Boston & NY: Houghton, Mifflin, 1893. Stories.

Betty Leicester's English Xmas: A New Chapter of an Old Story. Baltimore: Privately printed, 1894. Rev as *Betty Leicester's Christmas.* Boston & NY: Houghton, Mifflin, 1899. Children's story.

The Life of Nancy. Boston & NY: Houghton, Mifflin, 1895. Stories.

The Country of the Pointed Firs. Boston & NY: Houghton, Mifflin, 1896. Novel.

The Queen's Twin and Other Stories. Boston & NY: Houghton, Mifflin, 1899.

The Tory Lover. Boston & NY: Houghton, Mifflin, 1901. Novel.

An Empty Purse: A Christmas Story. Boston: Privately printed, 1905.

Verses, ed M A DeWolfe Howe. Boston: Privately printed, 1916.

The Uncollected Short Stories of SOJ, ed Richard Cary. Waterville, Maine: Colby C P, 1971.

LETTERS

Letters of SOJ, ed Annie Fields. Boston & NY: Houghton, Mifflin, 1911.

Letters of SOJ Now in the Colby College Library, with explanatory notes by Carl J Weber. Waterville, Maine: Colby C P, 1947.

SOJ Letters, ed with intro by Richard Cary. Waterville, Maine: Colby C P, 1956. Augmented ed, 1967.

OTHER

Stories and Poems for Children by Celia Thaxter; ed SOJ. Boston & NY: Houghton, Mifflin, 1895.

The Poems of Celia Thaxter, ed SOJ. Boston & NY: Houghton, Mifflin, 1896.

Letters of Sarah Wyman Whitman, ed SOJ. Boston & NY: Houghton, Mifflin, 1907.

COLLECTIONS

Tales of New England. Boston & NY: Houghton, Mifflin, 1890.

Stories and Tales, 7 vols. Boston & NY: Houghton Mifflin, 1910.

The Best Stories of SOJ, 2 vols, selected & arranged with preface by Willa Cather. Boston & NY: Houghton Mifflin, 1925.

The World of Dunnet Landing: A SOJ Collection, ed David Bonnell Green. Lincoln: U Nebraska P, 1962. Part II, pp 351-420, contains critical essays on SOJ.

MANUSCRIPTS & ARCHIVES

The major collections are at the Houghton Library, Harvard U; Colby C Library; & the Boston Public Library.

BIOGRAPHIES

Books

Frost, John Eldridge. *SOJ.* Kittery Point, Maine: Gundalow Club, 1960.

Matthiessen, F O. *SOJ.* Boston: Houghton Mifflin, 1929.

CRITICAL STUDIES

Books

Cary, Richard. *SOJ.* NY: Twayne, 1962.

Donovan, Josephine. *SOJ.* NY: Ungar, 1980.

Renza, Louis A. *"A White Heron" and the Question of Minor Literature.* Madison: U Wisconsin P, 1984.

Sougnac, Jean. *SOJ.* Paris: Jouve et Cie, 1937.

Thorp, Margaret Farrand. *SOJ.* Minneapolis: U Minnesota P, 1966.

Collections of Essays

Cary, Richard, ed. *Appreciation of SOJ: 29 Interpretive Essays.* Waterville, Maine: Colby C P, 1973.

Nagel, Gwen L, ed. *Critical Essays on SOJ.* Boston: Hall, 1984.

Special Journal

CLQ, 22 (Mar 1986). SOJ issue.

Book Sections & Articles

Ammons, Elizabeth. "Going in Circles: The Female Geography of *The Country of the Pointed Firs.*" *SLitI,* 16 (Fall 1983), 83-92.

Ammons. "J's Witches." Nagel (1984), 165-184.

Atkinson, Michael. "The Necessary Extravagance of SOJ: Voices of Authority in 'A White Heron.'" *SSF,* 19 (Winter 1982), 71-74.

Bader, Julia. "The Dissolving Vision: Realism in J, Freeman and Gilman." *American Realism: New Essays,* ed Eric J Sundquist (Baltimore, Md: Johns Hopkins U P, 1982), 176-198.

Berthoff, Warner. "The Art of J's *Pointed Firs.*" *NEQ,* 32 (Mar 1959), 31-53.

Bishop, Ferman. "The Sense of the Past in SOJ." *UWB*, no 41 (Feb 1959), 3-10. Rpt Cary (1973).

Blanc-Bentzon, Marie Thérèse. "Le roman de la femme-medecin." *RdM*, 67 (1 Feb 1885), 598-632. Rpt, in trans, Cary (1973).

Cary, Richard. "J, Tarkington, and the Maine Line." *CLQ*, Series 4 (Feb 1956), 89-95.

Cary. "Introduction." *Deephaven and Other Stories* (New Haven: College & University P, 1966), 7-23.

Cary. "The Literary Rubrics of SOJ." Nagel (1984), 198-211.

Cather, Willa. "Preface." *The Best Stories of SOJ*, Vol 1, ix-xix.

Cather. "Miss J." *Not Under Forty* (NY: Knopf, 1936), 76-95.

Donovan, Josephine. "The Unpublished Love Poems of SOJ." *Frontiers*, 4 (Jan 1979), 26-31. Rpt Nagel (1984).

Donovan. "A Woman's Vision of Transcendence: A New Interpretation of the Works of SOJ." *MR*, 21 (Summer 1980), 365-380.

Donovan. "SOJ and the World of the Mothers." *New England Local Color Literature: A Women's Tradition* (NY: Ungar, 1983), 99-118.

Donovan. "SOJ's Critical Theory: Notes Toward a Feminine Literary Mode." Nagel (1984), 212-225.

Eakin, Paul John. "SOJ and the Meaning of Country Life." *AL*, 38 (Jan 1967), 508-531. Rpt Cary (1973).

Folsom, Marcia McClintock. " 'Tact is a Kind of Mind-Reading': Empathic Style in SOJ's *The Country of the Pointed Firs*." *CLQ*, 18 (1982), 66-78. Rpt Nagel (1984).

Hobbs, Glenda. "Pure and Passionate: Female Friendship in SOJ's 'Martha's Lady.' " *SSF*, 17 (Winter 1980), 21-29. Rpt Nagel (1984).

Holstein, Michael. "Writing as a Healing Art in SOJ's *The Country of the Pointed Firs*." *SAF*, 16 (Spring 1988), 39-49.

Magowan, Robin. "Pastoral and the Art of Landscape in *The Country of the Pointed Firs*." *NEQ*, 36 (Jun 1963), 229-240. Rpt Cary (1973).

Masteller, Jean Carwile. "The Women Doctors of Howells, Phelps, and J: The Conflict of Marriage and Career." Nagel (1984), 135-147.

Nagel, Gwen. " 'This prim corner of land where she was queen': SOJ's New England Gardens." *CLQ*, 22 (Mar 1986), 43-62.

Piacentino, Edward J. "Local Color and Beyond: The Artistic Dimension of SOJ's 'The Foreigner.' " *CLQ*, 21 (Jun 1985), 92-98.

Pryse, Marjorie. "Introduction to the Norton Edition." *The Country of the Pointed Firs and Other Stories*, selected by Mary Ellen Chase (NY: Norton, 1982), v-xx.

Pryse. "Women 'at Sea': Feminist Realism in SOJ's 'The Foreigner.' " *ALR*, 15 (Autumn 1982), 244-252. Rpt Nagel (1984).

Smith, Eleanor M. "The Literary Relationship of SOJ and Willa S. Cather." *NEQ*, 29 (Dec 1956), 472-492.

Stouck, David. "*The Country of the Pointed Firs*: A Pastoral of Innocence." *CLQ*, 9 (Dec 1970), 213-220. Rpt Cary (1973).

Thompson, Charles Miner. "The Art of Miss J." *Atlantic*, 94 (Oct 1904), 485-497.

Toth, Susan Allen. "SOJ and Friends: A Community of Interest." *SSF*, 9 (Summer 1972), 233-241.

Voelker, Paul D. "*The Country of the Pointed Firs*: A Novel by SOJ." *CLQ*, 9 (Dec 1970), 201-213. Rpt Cary (1973).

Waggoner, Hyatt H. "The Unity of *The Country of the Pointed Firs*." *TCL*, 5 (Jul 1959), 67-73. Rpt *The World of Dunnet Landing*; Cary (1973).

Westbrook, Perry. *Acres of Flint: SOJ and Her Contemporaries* (Metuchen, NJ: Scarecrow, rev 1981), 42-77.

Woodress, James. "SOJ and Willa Cather: Anti-Realists." *English Studies Today*, 5th Series, ed Sencer Tonguc (Istanbul: Matbaasi, 1973), 477-488.

Zagarell, Sandra A. "Narrative of Community: The Identification of a Genre." *Signs*, 13 (Spring 1988), 498-527.

Gwen L. Nagel

JAMES WELDON JOHNSON

Jacksonville, Fla, 17 Jun 1871-Wiscasset, Maine, 26 Jun 1938

James Weldon Johnson achieved distinction in several careers: education, journalism, law, music, diplomacy, civil rights, and literature. His literary endeavors included pioneer work in collecting and preserving both folk and formal literature in the African-American tradition as well as original contributions in fiction, poetry, autobiography, and social commentary. Although the novel *The Autobiography of an Ex-Colored Man* was little noticed when it first appeared anonymously in 1912, its republication in 1927, when its author was the crusading leader of the National Association for the Advancement of Colored People, attracted much interest, and the book now occupies a central position in the canon of African-American fiction. *God's Trombones,* a powerful verse rendition of traditional black pulpit oratory, is one of the major achievements of African-American poetry. Closely attuned to the new literary developments following World War I, Johnson was the key figure in the transition from the work of his contemporaries Charles Waddell Chesnutt, W. E. B. Du Bois, and Paul Laurence Dunbar at the turn of the century to the writers of the Harlem Renaissance.

BIBLIOGRAPHY

Fleming, Robert. *JWJ and Arna Wendell Bontemps: A Reference Guide.* Boston: Hall, 1978. Secondary.

BOOKS

The Autobiography of an Ex-Colored Man (Anon). Boston: Sherman, French, 1912. Repub as *The Autobiography of an Ex-Coloured Man.* NY: Knopf, 1927. Novel.

Fifty Years and Other Poems. Boston: Cornhill, 1917.

God's Trombones. NY: Viking, 1927. Poetry.

Black Manhattan. NY: Knopf, 1930. Nonfiction.

Saint Peter Relates an Incident of the Resurrection Day. NY: Viking, 1930. Poem.

Along This Way: The Autobiography of JWJ. NY: Viking, 1933.

Negro Americans, What Now? NY: Viking, 1934. Nonfiction.

Saint Peter Relates an Incident: Selected Poems. NY: Viking, 1935.

OTHER

The Book of American Negro Poetry, ed JWJ. NY: Harcourt, Brace, 1922. Augmented ed, 1931.

The Book of American Negro Spirituals, ed JWJ. NY: Viking, 1925.

The Second Book of Negro Spirituals, ed JWJ. NY: Viking, 1926.

MANUSCRIPTS & ARCHIVES

The Beinecke Library, Yale U.

BIOGRAPHIES

Book

Levy, Eugene. *JWJ: Black Leader, Black Voice.* Chicago: U Chicago P, 1973.

Book Section & Articles

Bacote, Clarence A. "JWJ and Atlanta University." *Phylon,* 32 (Winter 1971), 333-343.

Logan, Rayford W. "JWJ and Haiti." *Phylon,* 32 (Winter 1971), 396-402.

Ovington, Mary White. "JWJ, 1920-1931: We Meet the Nation." *The Walls Came Tumbling Down* (NY: Harcourt, Brace, 1947), 176-243.

CRITICAL STUDIES

Books

Fleming, Robert E. *JWJ.* Boston: Twayne, 1987.

Tolbert-Rouchaleau, Jane. *JWJ.* NY: Chelsea House, 1988.

Special Journal

Phylon, 32 (Winter 1971). JWJ issue.

Book Sections & Articles

Baker, Houston A, Jr. "A Forgotten Prototype: *The Autobiography of an Ex-Colored Man* and *Invisible Man.*" *Singers of Daybreak: Studies in Black American Literature* (Washington: Howard U P, 1974), 17-31.

Bell, Bernard W. "JWJ (1871-1938)." *The Afro-American Novel and Its Tradition* (Amherst: U Massachusetts P, 1987), 86-92.

Carroll, Richard A. "Black Racial Spirit: An Analysis of JWJ's Critical Perspective." *Phylon,* 32 (Winter 1971), 344-364.

Collier, Eugenia. "JWJ: Mirror of Change." *Phylon,* 21 (Winter 1960), 351-359.

Collier. "The Endless Journey of an Ex-Coloured Man." *Phylon,* 32 (Winter 1971), 365-373.

Cooke, Michael G. "Self-Veiling: JWJ, Charles Chesnutt, and Nella Larsen." *Afro-American Literature in the Twentieth Century: The Achievement of Intimacy* (New Haven: Yale U P, 1984), 43-70.

Daniel, Walter C. "JWJ: 'The Turpentined Imagination.' " *Images of the Preacher in Afro-American Literature* (Washington: U P America, 1981), 39-67.

Davis, Arthur P. "JWJ." *From the Dark Tower: Afro-American Writers, 1900 to 1960* (Washington: Howard U P, 1974), 28-32.

Faulkner, Howard. "JWJ's Portrait of the Artist as Invisible Man." *BALF,* 19 (Winter 1985), 147-151.

Fleming, Robert E. "Contemporary Themes in J's *Autobiography of an Ex-Coloured Man.*" *NALF,* 4 (Winter 1970), 120-124, 141.

Fleming. "Irony as a Key to J's *The Autobiography of an Ex-Coloured Man.*" *AL,* 43 (Mar 1971), 83-96.

Fleming. "The Composition of JWJ's 'Fifty Years.' " *AmerP,* 4 (Winter 1987), 51-56.

Garrett, Marvin P. "Early Recollections and Structural Irony in *The Autobiography of an Ex-Colored Man.*" *Crit,* 13, no 2 (1971), 5-14.

Gates, Henry Louis, Jr. "Dis and Dat: Dialect and the Descent." *Figures in Black: Words, Signs, and the "Racial" Self* (NY: Oxford U P, 1987), 167-195.

Ikonne, Chidi. "JWJ." *From Du Bois to Van Vechten: The Early New Negro Literature, 1903-1926* (Westport, Conn: Greenwood, 1981), 66-73.

Levy, Eugene. "Ragtime and Race Pride: The Career of JWJ." *JPC,* 1 (Spring 1968), 357-370.

Long, Richard A. "A Weapon of My Song: The Poetry of JWJ." *Phylon,* 32 (Winter 1971), 374-382.

MacKethan, Lucinda H. "*Black Boy* and *Ex-Coloured Man:* Version and Inversion of the Slave Narrator's Quest for Voice." *CLAJ,* 32 (Dec 1988), 123-147.

Mason, Julian. "JWJ: A Southern Writer Resists the South." *CLAJ,* 31 (Dec 1987), 154-169.

O'Sullivan, Maurice J, Jr. "Of Souls and Pottage: JWJ's *The Autobiography of an Ex-Coloured Man.*" *CLAJ,* 23 (Sep 1979), 60-70.

Payne, Ladell. "Themes and Cadences: JWJ, 1871-1938." *Black Novelists and the Southern Literary Tradition* (Athens: U Georgia P, 1981), 26-37.

Portelli, Alessandro. "*The Autobiography of an Ex-Coloured Man* di JWJ." *SA,* 18 (1972), 241-267.

Redding, Saunders. "JWJ and the Pastoral Tradition." *MissQ,* 28 (Fall 1975), 417-421.

Rosenblatt, Roger. "*The Autobiography of an Ex-Colored Man.*" *Black Fiction* (Cambridge: Harvard U P, 1974), 173-184.

Ross, Stephen M. "Audience and Irony in J's *The Autobiography of an Ex-Coloured Man.*" *CLAJ,* 18 (Dec 1974), 198-210.

Scruggs, Charles. "H. L. Mencken and JWJ: Two Men Who Helped Shape a Renaissance." *Critical Essays on H. L. Mencken,* ed Douglas C Stenerson (Boston: Hall, 1987), 186-203.

Skerrett, Joseph T, Jr. "Irony and Symbolic Action in JWJ's *The Autobiography of an Ex-Coloured Man.*" *AQ,* 32 (Winter 1980), 540-558.

Smith, Valerie. "Privilege and Evasion in *The Autobiography of an Ex-Colored Man.*" *Self-Discovery and Authority in Afro-American Narrative* (Cambridge: Harvard U P, 1987), 44-64.

Stepto, Robert B. "Lost in a Quest: JWJ's *The Autobiography of an Ex-Coloured Man.*" *From Behind the Veil: A Study of Afro-American Narrative* (Urbana: U Illinois P, 1979), 95-127.

Vauthier, Simone. "The Interplay of Narrative Modes in JWJ's *The Autobiography of an Ex-Colored Man.*" *JA,* 18 (1973), 173-181.

Wagner, Jean. "JWJ." *Black Poets of the United States,* trans Kenneth Douglas (Urbana: U Illinois P, 1973), 351-384.

Whalum, Wendell P. "JWJ's Theories and Performance Practices of Afro-American Folksong." *Phylon,* 32 (Winter 1971), 383-395.

Keneth Kinnamon

OWEN JOHNSON

New York City, NY, 27 Aug 1878-Vineyard Haven, Mass, 27 Jan 1952

Although Owen Johnson wrote historical novels and novels of high and low society during the first third of this century, he is best remembered as the author of a handful of books about life in an elite boys' prep school and at Yale during the 1890s. A close observer of the flexible social mores among the privileged class in the eastern seaboard area, Johnson wrote candidly about the effects of divorce and marital instability and about the young women he called "salamanders"—alluring and designing flirts who got the most they could out of their wealthy suitors without "getting burned." Johnson's adult novels were not generally well-received by reviewers; but his stories of Lawrenceville Prep and *Stover at Yale* conveyed a sense of immediacy and displayed an artistic skill that were lacking in the other books.

BIBLIOGRAPHY

First Printings of American Authors, Vol 5, ed Philip B Eppard (Detroit: Bruccoli Clark Layman/Gale, 1987), 161-165. Primary.

BOOKS

Arrows of the Almighty. NY & London: Macmillan, 1901. Novel.
In the Name of Liberty: A Story of the Terror. NY: Century, 1905. Repub as *Nicole; or, In the Name of Liberty: A Story of the Terror*. London: Macmillan, 1905. Novel.
Max Fargus. NY: Baker & Taylor, 1906. Novel.
The Eternal Boy: Being the Story of the Prodigious Hickey. NY: Dodd, Mead, 1909. Repub as *The Prodigious Hickey*. NY: Baker & Taylor, 1910. Novel.
The Humming Bird. NY: Baker & Taylor, 1910. Novel.
The Varmint. NY: Baker & Taylor, 1910. Novel.
The Tennessee Shad, Chronicling the Rise and Fall of the Firm of Doc Macnooder and the Tennessee Shad. NY: Baker & Taylor, 1911. Novel.
Stover at Yale. NY: Stokes, 1912. Novel.
The Sixty-First Second. NY: Stokes, 1913. Novel.
Murder in Any Degree. . . . NY: Century, 1913. Novel.
The Salamander. Indianapolis: Bobbs-Merrill, 1914. Repub as *The Enemy Sex*. NY: Grosset & Dunlap, 1914. Novel.
Making Money. NY: Stokes, 1915. Novel.
The Spirit of France. Boston: Little, Brown, 1916. Nonfiction.
The Woman Gives: A Story of Regeneration. Boston: Little, Brown, 1916. Novel.
Virtuous Wives. Boston: Little, Brown, 1918. Novel.
The Wasted Generation. Boston: Little, Brown, 1921. Novel.
Skippy Bedelle: His Sentimental Progress From the Urchin to the Complete Man of the World. Boston: Little, Brown, 1922. Novel.
Blue Blood: A Dramatic Interlude. Boston: Little, Brown, 1924. Novel.
Children of Divorce. Boston: Little, Brown, 1927. Novel.
Sacrifice. NY & c: Longmans, Green, 1929. Novel.
The Coming of the Amazons: A Satiristic Speculation on the Scientific Future of Civilization. NY & Toronto: Longmans, Green, 1931. Novel.

COLLECTIONS

Lawrenceville Stories. NY: Baker & Taylor, 1910.
The Lawrenceville Stories, intro by Cleveland Amory. NY: Simon & Schuster, 1967.

MANUSCRIPTS & ARCHIVES

The Lawrenceville School, Lawrenceville, NJ.

BIOGRAPHIES

Articles
Maurice, Arthur Bartlett. "OJ." *Bookman*, 39 (Jun 1914), 416-420.
Maurice. "The History of Their Books X: OJ." *Bookman*, 70 (Dec 1929), 414-416.
Tunis, John R. "A Man of Distinction." *NYTBR* (24 Sep 1967), 8.

CRITICAL STUDIES

Book Sections & Articles
Hooker, Brian. "OJ's *Stover at Yale*." *Bookman*, 35 (May 1912), 309-312.
Lamoreaux, David. "*Stover at Yale* and the Grid-

iron Metaphor." *JPC*, 11 (Fall 1977), 330-344.

Lyons, John O. *The College Novel in America* (Carbondale: Southern Illinois U P, 1962), passim.

Messenger, Christian K. *Sport and the Spirit of Play in American Fiction: Hawthorne to Faulkner* (NY: Columbia U P, 1981), passim.

Samuel I. Bellman

MARY JOHNSTON

Buchanan, Va, 21 Nov 1870-Warm Springs, Va, 9 May 1936

A popular Virginia author, Mary Johnston is remembered for her historical romances, of which *To Have and To Hold* was her best known and commercially most successful. Fifteen of her twenty-three novels, including her two epic tales of the Civil War, *The Long Roll* and *Cease Firing,* depict heroic characters from Virginia. Though popular during her early career, Johnston lost much of her reading audience when she turned to spiritualism. By the time she returned to the historical novel, literary tastes had changed. During her lifetime Johnston was praised for her skillful creation of setting and atmosphere, her use of history, and her depiction of antebellum life, but since her death she has received little critical attention.

BIBLIOGRAPHIES

Longest, George C. *Three Virginia Writers: MJ, Thomas Nelson Page and Amélie Rives Troubetzkoy: A Reference Guide.* Boston: Hall, 1978. Secondary.

"Selected Bibliography." Cella, 156-160. Primary & secondary.

Woodbridge, Annie. "Textual Note and Short Story Bibliography." *The Collected Short Stories of MJ,* xix-xxi. Primary.

BOOKS

Prisoners of Hope. Boston & NY: Houghton, Mifflin, 1898; *The Old Dominion.* London: Constable, 1899. Novel.

To Have and To Hold. Boston & NY: Houghton, Mifflin, 1900; *By Order of the Company.* London: Constable, 1900. Novel.

Audrey. Boston & NY: Houghton, Mifflin, 1902. Novel.

Sir Mortimer. NY & London: Harper, 1904. Novel.

The Goddess of Reason. Boston & NY: Houghton, Mifflin, 1907. Play.

Lewis Rand. Boston & NY: Houghton Mifflin, 1908. Novel.

The Long Roll. Boston & NY: Houghton Mifflin, 1911. Novel.

Cease Firing. Boston & NY: Houghton Mifflin, 1912. Novel.

Hagar. Boston & NY: Houghton Mifflin, 1913. Novel.

The Witch. Boston & NY: Houghton Mifflin, 1914. Novel.

The Fortunes of Garin. Boston & NY: Houghton Mifflin, 1915. Novel.

The Wanderers. Boston & NY: Houghton Mifflin, 1917. Stories.

Pioneers of the Old South: A Chronicle of English Colonial Beginnings. New Haven: Yale U P / Toronto: Glasgow, Brook / London: Humphrey Milford, Oxford U P, 1918. Nonfiction.

Foes. NY & London: Harper, 1918; *The Laird of Glenfernie.* London: Constable, 1919. Novel.

Michael Forth. NY & London: Harper, 1919. Novel.

Sweet Rocket. NY & London: Harper, 1920. Novel.

Silver Cross. Boston: Little, Brown, 1922. Novel.

1492. Boston: Little, Brown, 1922; *Admiral of the Ocean-Sea.* London: Butterworth, 1923. Novel.

Croatan. Boston: Little, Brown, 1923. Novel.

The Slave Ship. Boston: Little, Brown, 1924. Novel.

The Great Valley. Boston: Little, Brown, 1926. Novel.

The Exile. Boston: Little, Brown, 1927. Novel.

Hunting Shirt. Boston: Little, Brown, 1931. Novel.

Miss Delicia Allen. Boston: Little, Brown, 1933. Novel.

Drury Randall. Boston: Little, Brown, 1934. Novel.

The Collected Short Stories of MJ, ed Annie & Hensley C Woodbridge. Troy, NY: Whitston, 1982.

MANUSCRIPTS & ARCHIVES

U of Virginia Library.

CRITICAL STUDIES

Books

Cella, C Ronald. *MJ.* Boston: Twayne, 1981.

Hartley, Gayle Melton. "The Novels of MJ: A Critical Study." Dissertation: U South Carolina, 1972.

Book Sections & Articles

Coleman, E D. "Penwoman of Virginia's Feminists." *VC,* 6 (Winter 1956), 8-11.

Edwards, Mary P. "Tea and Metaphysics: Excerpts From MJ's Diary." *EGN,* 19 (Oct 1983), 2-9.

MacDonald, Edgar. "MJ and Henry Sydnor Harrison." *EGN,* 20 (Apr 1984), 3-5.

Nelson, Lawrence G. "MJ and the Historic Imagination." *Southern Writers: Appraisals in Our Time,* ed R C Simonini, Jr (Charlottesville: U P Virginia, 1964), 71-102.

Overton, Grant. "MJ's Adventure." *Cargoes for Crusoes* (NY: Appleton / NY: Doran / Boston: Little, Brown, 1924), 375-387.

Overton. "MJ." *The Women Who Make Our Novels* (NY: Dodd, Mead, rev 1928), 189-201.

Roberson, John R, ed. "Two Virginia Novelists on Women's Suffrage: An Exchange of Letters Between MJ and Thomas Nelson Page." *VMHB,* 64 (Jul 1956), 286-290.

Sadler, Lynn. "The West Indies as a Symbol of Freedom in J's *Prisoners of Hope* and *The Slave Ship,* and in Bontemps's *Black Thunder.*" *JLN,* 15 (Jan-Apr 1982), 42-48, inside back cover.

Sadler. "Women and Freedom in Selected Novels of MJ and Frances Gaither." *JLN,* 16 (Sep-Dec 1983), 115-124.

Sherman, Caroline B. "The Rediscovery of MJ (1870-1936)." *SLM,* 4 (Sep 1942), 431-432.

Wagenknecht, Edward. "The World and MJ." *SR,* 44 (Apr-Jun 1936), 188-206.

Wagenknecht. "Allotropes and MJ." *Cavalcade of the American Novel* (NY: Holt, 1952), 197-203.

Watson, Ritchie Devon, Jr. "MJ." *The Cavalier in Virginia Fiction* (Baton Rouge: Louisiana State U P, 1985), 197-212.

Woodbridge, Annie. "MJ on War: An Unpublished Letter and a Comment." *JLN,* 11 (Jan-Apr 1978), 31-32.

Woodbridge. "Two Virginia Utopias: MJ's *Sweet Rocket,* Ellen Glasgow's 'Hunter's Fare.'" *JLN,* 11 (May-Dec 1978), 102-104.

Woodbridge. "Preface." *The Collected Short Stories of MJ,* v-xvi.

Gwen L. Nagel

RICHARD MALCOLM JOHNSTON

Hancock County, Ga, 8 Mar 1822-Baltimore, Md, 23 Sep 1898

Although in his own time Richard Malcolm Johnston enjoyed popular and critical success, his works are now neglected. Once labeled by critics the "dean of southern writers," Johnston was a transitional figure in southern fiction. Admired for his effective characterizations, Johnston provided a lighthearted yet detailed portrait of the white middle class of nineteenth-century Middle Georgia. His early tales and sketches demonstrate the rough but vigorous artistry of the writers of the Old Southwest; his later fiction more closely resembles the local colorists with their refined style and tighter narratives. The four editions of his best-known work, *Dukesborough Tales,* show this evolution through the raw vitality in the earlier editions and the more polished but sentimental style in the later editions.

BIBLIOGRAPHY

Bibliography of American Literature, comp Jacob Blanck. New Haven: Yale U P, 1955-1991. Primary.

BOOKS

The English Classics: A Historical Sketch of the Literature of England From the Earliest Times to the Accession of King George III. Philadelphia: Lippincott, 1860. Augmented as *English Literature: A Historical Sketch of English Literature From the Earliest Times,* with William Hand Browne. NY & Baltimore, Md: University Publishing, 1873. Textbook.

Georgia Sketches. . . (as by Philemon Perch). Augusta, Ga: Stockton, 1864.

Dukesborough Tales (as by Perch). Baltimore: Turnbull, 1871. Augmented ed, 1874. Augmented again, NY: Harper, 1883. Rev as *Dukesborough Tales: The Chronicles of Mr. Bill Williams.* NY: Appleton, 1892.

Life of Alexander H. Stephens, with Browne. Philadelphia: Lippincott, 1878. Rev ed, 1883. Augmented ed, 1884.

Old Mark Langston: A Tale of Duke's Creek. NY: Harper, 1884. Novel.

Two Gray Tourists: From Papers of Mr. Philemon Perch. . . . Baltimore, Md: Baltimore Publishing, 1885. Travel.

Mr. Absalom Billingslea and Other Georgia Folk. NY: Harper, 1888. Sketches.

Ogeechee Cross-Firings: A Novel. NY: Harper, 1889.

Widow Guthrie: A Novel. NY: Appleton, 1890.

The Primes and Their Neighbors: Ten Tales of Middle Georgia. . . . NY: Appleton, 1891.

Studies, Literary and Social. . . First Series. Indianapolis: Bowen-Merrill, 1891. Essays.

Mr. Fortner's Marital Claims and Other Stories. NY: Appleton, 1892.

Mr. Billy Downs and His Likes. NY: Webster, 1892. Stories.

Studies, Literary and Social . . . Second Series. Indianapolis: Bowen-Merrill, 1892. Essays.

Little Ike Templin and Other Stories. Boston: Lothrop, 1894.

Lectures on Literature: English, French and Spanish. Akron, Ohio: McBride, 1897.

Old Times in Middle Georgia. NY & London: Macmillan, 1897. Stories.

Pearce Amerson's Will. Chicago: Way & Williams, 1898. Novel.

Autobiography of Col. RMJ. Washington: Neale, 1900.

MANUSCRIPTS & ARCHIVES

The major collections are at the Enoch Pratt Free Library, Baltimore, Md; the Georgia Historical Society, Savannah; & the Library of Congress.

BIOGRAPHIES

Book Sections & Articles

Armstrong, Regina. "RMJ, Gentleman and Man-of-Letters." *CathW,* 68 (Nov 1898), 261-270.

Gavigan, Walter V. "Two Gentlemen of Georgia." *CathW,* 145 (Aug 1937), 584-589.

Herrick, Sophie Bledsoe. "RMJ." *Century,* 36 (Jun 1888), 276-280.

Long, Francis Taylor. "The Life of RMJ in Maryland, 1867-1898." *MHM,* 34 (Dec 1939), 305-324; 35 (Sep 1940), 270-286; 36 (Mar 1941), 54-69.

Parks, Edd Winfield. "RMJ." *Segments of Southern Thought* (Athens: U Georgia P, 1938), 223-244.

Parks. "Professor RMJ." *GaHQ,* 25 (Mar 1941), 1-15.

"RMJ." *Dial,* 25 (1 Oct 1898), 213-215.

Smith, Charles Forster. "RMJ." *Reminiscences and Sketches* (Nashville, Tenn: Methodist Episcopal Church, South, 1908), 164-188.

Steiner, Bernard M. "Colonel RMJ." *ConservativeR,* 1 (Feb 1899), 74-77.

CRITICAL STUDIES

Books

Brinson, Lessie Brannen. "A Study of the Life and Works of RMJ." Dissertation: George Peabody C for Teachers, 1938.

Hitchcock, Bert. *RMJ.* Boston: Twayne, 1978.

Voyles, Jimmy Ponder. "RMJ: A Biographical and Critical Study." Dissertation: U Georgia, 1971.

Wood, Clara Ruth Coleman. "The Fiction of RMJ." Dissertation: U North Carolina, Chapel Hill, 1973.

Zeigler, Mary Elizabeth Brown. "The Lexicon of RMJ's Middle Georgia Dialect." Dissertation: U Georgia, 1983.

Book Sections & Articles

Bickley, R Bruce, Jr. "RMJ." *ALR,* 8 (Autumn 1975), 293-294.

Bush, Robert. "RMJ's Marriage Group." *GaR,* 18 (Winter 1964), 429-436.

Coleman, Charles W, Jr. "The Recent Movement in Southern Literature." *Harper's,* 74 (May 1887), 837-855.

Eaton, Clement. *The Waning of the Old South Civilization, 1860-1880's* (Athens: U Georgia P, 1968), passim.

Edwards, Corliss Hines, Jr. "RMJ's View of the Old-Field School." *GaHQ,* 50 (Dec 1966), 382-390.

Hubbell, Jay B. "RMJ." *The South in American Literature, 1607-1900* (Durham, NC: Duke U P, 1954), 777-782, 940-941.

Skaggs, Merrill Maguire. *The Folk of Southern Fiction* (Athens: U Georgia P, 1972), passim.

Voyles, Jimmy Ponder. "RMJ's Literary Career: An Estimate." *MarkhamR,* 4 (Feb 1974), 29-34.

Webb, William A. "RMJ." *Southern Writers: Biographical and Critical Studies,* Vol 2 (Nashville, Tenn: M E Church, South, 1903), 46-81.

J. Arthur Bond

CLARENCE BUDINGTON KELLAND

Portland, Mich, 11 Jul 1881-Scottsdale, Ariz, 18 Feb 1964

Clarence Budington Kelland was a prolific and extremely popular short-story writer, novelist, and essayist. His more than seventy novels include twenty adult mysteries as well as two juvenile series featuring Mark Tidd and Catty Atkins. An admitted formula writer, Kelland nevertheless varied his characters to include an eccentric scientist, Old West pioneers, and a tuba-playing poet. Many of his novels were serialized in mass-circulation magazines, and his works inspired more than a dozen motion pictures. Kelland has received almost no critical attention.

BOOKS

Mark Tidd: His Adventures and Strategies. NY & London: Harper, 1913. Children's novel.

Thirty Pieces of Silver. NY & London: Harper, 1913. Novel.

Mark Tidd in the Backwoods. NY & London: Harper, 1914. Children's novel.

Mark Tidd in Business. NY & London: Harper, 1915. Children's novel.

Into His Own: The Story of an Airedale. Philadelphia: McKay, 1915. Children's stories.

The Hidden Spring: A Novel. NY & London: Harper, 1916.

Mark Tidd's Citadel. NY & London: Harper, 1916. Children's novel.

Mark Tidd, Editor. NY & London: Harper, 1917. Children's novel.

Sudden Jim: A Novel. NY & London: Harper, 1917.

The Source: A Novel. NY & London: Harper, 1918.

Mark Tidd: Manufacturer. NY & London: Harper, 1918. Children's novel.

The Highflyers. NY & London: Harper, 1919. Novel.

The Little Moment of Happiness. NY & London: Harper, 1919. Novel.

Catty Atkins. NY & London: Harper, 1920. Children's novel.

Efficiency Edgar. NY & London: Harper, 1920. Novel.

Youth Challenges. NY & London: Harper, 1920. Novel.

Catty Atkins: Riverman. NY & London: Harper, 1921. Children's novel.

Scattergood Baines. NY & London: Harper, 1921. Stories.

Conflict. NY & London: Harper, 1922. Novel.

Catty Atkins: Sailorman. NY & London: Harper, 1922. Children's novel.

Catty Atkins: Financier. NY & London: Harper, 1923. Children's novel.

Contraband. NY & London: Harper, 1923. Novel.

Catty Atkins: Bandmaster. NY & London: Harper, 1924. Children's novel.

The Steadfast Heart. NY & London: Harper, 1924. Novel.

Mark Tidd in Italy. NY & London: Harper, 1925. Children's novel.

Miracle. NY: Harper, 1925. Novel.

Mark Tidd in Egypt. NY & London: Harper, 1926. Children's novel.

Rhoda Fair. NY: Harper, 1926. Novel.

Dance Magic. NY: Harper, 1927. Novel.

Knuckles. NY & London: Harper, 1928. Novel.

Mark Tidd in Sicily. NY & London: Harper, 1928. Children's novel.

Dynasty. NY & London: Harper, 1929. Novel.

Hard Money. NY & London: Harper, 1930. Novel.

Gold. NY & London: Harper, 1931. Novel.

Speak Easily. NY & London: Harper, 1932. Novel.

The Great Crooner. NY & London: Harper, 1933. Novel.

The Cat's-Paw. NY & London: Harper, 1934. Novel.

The Jealous House. NY & London: Harper, 1934. Novel.

Dreamland. NY & London: Harper, 1935. Novel.

Roxana. NY & London: Harper, 1936. Novel.

Spotlight. NY & London: Harper, 1937. Novel.

Star Rising. NY & London: Harper, 1938. Novel.

Skin Deep. NY & London: Harper, 1939. Novel.

Arizona. NY & London: Harper, 1939. Novel.

Scattergood Baines Pulls the Strings. NY & London: Harper, 1939. Stories.

Scattergood Baines Returns. NY & London: Harper, 1940. Stories.

Valley of the Sun. NY & London: Harper, 1940. Novel.

Silver Spoon. NY & London: Harper, 1941. Novel.

Archibald the Great. NY & London: Harper, 1942. Novel.

Sugarfoot. NY & London: Harper, 1942. Novel.

Heart on Her Sleeve. NY & London: Harper, 1943. Novel.

Alias Jane Smith. NY & London: Harper, 1944. Novel.

Land of the Torreones. NY & London: Harper, 1946. Novel.

Double Treasure. NY: Harper, 1946. Novel.

Merchant of Valor. NY & London: Harper, 1947. Novel.

Murder for a Million. Kingswood, Surrey, UK: World's Work, 1947. Novel.

This Is My Son. NY: Harper, 1948. Novel.

The Cosmic Jest, music by Frank R Denke. San Francisco: Bohemian Club, 1949. Play.

Desert Law. NY: Bantam, 1949. Novel.

Stolen Goods. NY: Harper, 1950. Novel.

The Great Mail Robbery. NY: Harper, 1951. Novel.

No Escape. London: Museum, 1951. Novel.

The Key Man. NY: Harper, 1952. Novel.

Tombstone. NY: Harper, 1953. Novel.

Dangerous Angel. NY: Harper, 1953. Novel.

Death Keeps a Secret. NY: Harper, 1953. Novel.

Murder Makes an Entrance. NY: Harper, 1955. Novel.

The Case of the Nameless Corpse. NY: Harper, 1956. Novel.

West of the Law. NY: Harper, 1958. Novel.

Where There's Smoke. NY: Harper, 1959. Novel.

The Lady and the Giant. NY: Dodd, Mead, 1959. Novel.

The Monitor Affair: A Novel of the Civil War. NY: Dodd, Mead, 1960. Novel.

Counterfeit Gentleman. NY: Dodd, Mead, 1960. Novel.

Mark of Treachery. NY: Dodd, Mead, 1961. Novel.

The Sinister Strangers. NY: Dodd, Mead, 1961. Novel.

Party Man. NY: Dodd, Mead, 1962. Novel.

The Artless Heiress. NY: Dodd, Mead, 1962. Novel.

OTHER

Quizzer No. 20: Being Questions and Answers on Insurance for Students Preparing for Examination for Admission to the Bar. . . . Detroit: Sprague, 1911. Textbook.

The American Boy's Workshop: Each Subject by an Expert, ed & rewritten by CBK. Philadelphia: McKay, 1914. Children's nonfiction.

BIOGRAPHIES

Articles

Arnold, Oren. "Fifty Thousand Years of K." *RDi*, 45 (Nov 1944), 60-63.

"Durable Bud." *Time*, 63 (22 Mar 1954), 116.
Van Gelder, Robert. "A Talk With CBK." *NYTBR* (27 Apr 1941), 2, 20.

Beverly Brummett Klatt

GRACE KING

New Orleans, La, 29 Nov 1852-New Orleans, La, 12 Jan 1932

A Southerner and an aristocrat, Grace King wrote several histories of her native region, but she is best known for her short stories and novels about New Orleans. A realist, King took as her central subject the lives of Southerners during Reconstruction, their strength in the face of suffering and altered fortunes, the relationship between blacks and whites, and the changing roles of women in the postwar South. Her first novel, *Monsieur Motte,* was inspired in part by her wish to counter the portrait of Creole life that appeared in the works of George Washington Cable. Her most substantial novel, *The Pleasant Ways of St. Médard,* was based on her own family's experience during Reconstruction. In both her novels and short fiction, particularly her *Balcony Stories,* King conveyed the rich detail and texture that during her lifetime earned her critical acclaim as a local colorist. King is receiving renewed attention as a regionalist who focused on the lives of women.

BIBLIOGRAPHIES

Beer, Wm. "List of Writings of GK." *LaHQ,* 6 (Jul 1923), 378-379. Primary.
Bush, Robert. "GK (1852-1932)." *ALR,* 8 (Winter 1975), 43-51. Primary & secondary.
Muhlenfeld, Elisabeth S. "GK." *ALR,* 8 (Autumn 1975), 295-296. Secondary.
Vaughan, Bess. "A Bio-Bibliography of GEK."

LaHQ, 17 (Oct 1934), 752-770. Primary & secondary.

BOOKS

Monsieur Motte. NY: Armstrong, 1888. Novel.
Tales of a Time and Place. NY: Harper, 1892. Stories.
Jean Baptiste le Moyne, Sieur de Bienville. NY: Dodd, Mead, 1892. Biography.
Balcony Stories. NY: Century, 1893.
A History of Louisiana, with John R Ficklen. New Orleans: Graham, 1893. Rev ed, 1905.
New Orleans: The Place and the People. NY & London: Macmillan, 1895. History.
De Soto and His Men in the Land of Florida. NY & London: Macmillan, 1898. History.
The Pleasant Ways of St. Médard. NY: Holt, 1916. Novel.
Creole Families of New Orleans. NY: Macmillan, 1921. History.
La Dame de Sainte Hermine. NY: Macmillan, 1924. Novel.
Mount Vernon on the Potomac: History of the Mount Vernon Ladies' Association of the Union. NY: Macmillan, 1929.
Memories of a Southern Woman of Letters. NY: Macmillan, 1932. Autobiography.

LETTERS

"Charles Gayarré and GK: Letters of a Louisiana Friendship" by Robert Bush. *SLJ,* 7 (Fall 1974), 100-131.

COLLECTION

GK of New Orleans: A Selection of Her Writings,
ed with intro by Robert Bush. Baton Rouge:
Louisiana State U P, 1973.

MANUSCRIPTS & ARCHIVES

Louisiana State U Library.

BIOGRAPHIES

Articles

Snyder, Henry N. "Miss GEK." *Southern Writers:
Biographical and Critical Studies,* Vol 2
(Nashville, Tenn: M E Church, South, 1903),
272-291.

Taylor, Helen. "The Case of GK." *SoR,* 18 (Oct
1982), 685-702.

CRITICAL STUDIES

Books

Bush, Robert. *GK: A Southern Destiny.* Baton
Rouge: Louisiana State U P, 1983.

Kirby, David. *GK.* Boston: Twayne, 1980.

Book Sections & Articles

Bryan, Violet Harrington. "Creating and Re-
Creating the Myth of New Orleans: GK and
Alice Dunbar-Nelson." *POMPA* (1987),
185-196.

Bush, Robert. "GK and Mark Twain." *AL,* 44
(Mar 1972), 31-51.

Bush. "GK: The Emergence of a Southern Intellectual Woman." *SoR,* 13 (Spring 1977), 272-
288.

Cocks, Reginald S. "The Fiction of GK." *LaHQ,* 6
(Jul 1923), 353-359.

Fletcher, Marie. "GEK: Her Delineation of the
Southern Heroine." *LaS,* 5 (Spring 1966), 50-
60.

Guyol, Louise Hubert. "A Southern Author in Her
New Orleans Home." *LaHQ,* 6 (Jul 1923),
365-374.

Juncker, Clara. "GK: Woman-as-Artist." *SLJ,* 20
(Fall 1987), 37-44.

Kendall, John S. "A New Orleans Lady of Letters."
LaHQ, 19 (Apr 1936), 436-465.

Lochhead, Marion. "Stars and Striplings: American
Youth in the Nineteenth Century." *QRL,* 297
(Apr 1959), 180-188.

McReynolds, Douglas J. "Passion Repressed: The
Short Fiction of GK." *RMR,* 37, no 4 (1983),
207-216.

Piacentino, Edward J. "The Enigma of Black Identity in GK's 'Joe.' " *SLJ,* 19 (Fall 1986), 56-
67.

Anne Pizziferri

JOSEPH KIRKLAND

Geneva, NY, 7 Jan 1830-Chicago, Ill, 28 Apr 1893

Joseph Kirkland's literary reputation rests almost entirely on one novel, *Zury: The Meanest Man in Spring County,* which he published at the age of fifty-seven. *Zury* has been praised for its vivid portrayal of midwestern life; its meticulous rendering of dialect; its graphic depictions of toil, poverty, and greed; and its honest treatment of sexuality. The novel details the central character's rise to wealth through hard work and merciless business practices as well as his ultimate reformation at the hands of the schoolteacher with whom he falls in love. *Zury,* a milestone in American fiction, charted a direction for later writers of midwestern realistic fiction, including Hamlin Garland, Sherwood Anderson, and Sinclair Lewis.

BIBLIOGRAPHIES

Bibliography of American Literature, comp Jacob Blanck. New Haven: Yale U P, 1955-1991. Primary.

Eichelberger, Clayton L & F L Stallings. "JK (1830-1893): A Critical Bibliography of Secondary Comment." *ALR,* 2 (Spring 1969), 51-69.

Eichelberger. "Edgar Watson Howe and JK: More Critical Comment." *ALR,* 4 (Summer 1971), 279-290.

BOOKS

Zury: The Meanest Man in Spring County. . . . Boston & NY: Houghton, Mifflin, 1887. Rev ed, 1888. Novel.

The McVeys (An Episode). Boston & NY: Houghton, Mifflin, 1888. Novel.

The Captain of Company K. Chicago: Dibble, 1891. Novel.

The Story of Chicago, Vol 1. Chicago: Dibble, 1892. Augmented ed, 1892. Vol 2, with Caroline Kirkland. Chicago: Dibble, 1894. Nonfiction.

OTHER

History of Chicago, Illinois, 2 vols, ed with contributions by JK & John Moses. Chicago & NY: Munsell, 1895.

MANUSCRIPTS & ARCHIVES

The Newberry Library, Chicago.

CRITICAL STUDIES

Book

Henson, Clyde E. *JK.* NY: Twayne, 1962.

Book Sections & Articles

Ahnebrink, Lars. "Realism in the Middle West: Edward Eggleston, Edward Watson Howe, and JK." *The Beginnings of Naturalism in American Fiction* (Uppsala, Sweden: U Uppsala / Cambridge: Harvard U P, 1950), 50-59.

Blair, Walter. "Roots of American Realism." *UniversityR,* 6 (Jun 1940), 275-281.

Bowron, Bernard. "Realism in America." *CL,* 3 (Summer 1951), 268-285.

Duffey, Bernard. "The Real World." *The Chicago Renaissance in American Letters* (East Lansing: Michigan State U P, 1954), 90-111.

Flanagan, John T. "JK, Pioneer Realist." *AL,* 11 (Nov 1939), 273-284.

Flanagan. "A Note on JK." *AL,* 12 (Mar 1940), 107.

Flanagan. "Folklore in Five Middlewestern Novelists." *GrLR,* 1 (Winter 1975), 43-57.

Henson, Clyde E. "JK's Novels." *JISHS,* 44 (Summer 1951), 142-146.

Henson. "JK's Influence on Hamlin Garland." *AL,* 23 (Jan 1952), 458-463.

Henson. "JK (1830-1894)." *ALR,* 1 (Fall 1967), 67-70.

Holaday, Clayton A. "JK's *Captain of Company K:* A Twice-Told Tale." *AL,* 25 (Mar 1953), 62-68.

Holaday. "JK's Company K." *JISHS,* 49 (Autumn 1956), 295-307.

Holaday. "A Note on K's Autobiographical Writing." *ALR,* 2 (Spring 1969), 75-77.

LaBudde, Kenneth. "A Note on the Text of JK's *Zury.*" *AL,* 20 (Jan 1949), 452-455.

Lease, Benjamin. "Realism and JK's *Zury.*" *AL,* 23 (Jan 1952), 464-466.

Lease. "The JK Papers." *ALR,* 2 (Spring 1969), 73-75.

"Letters of a Pioneer Realist." *NewberryLB,* 3 (Dec 1945), 3-7.

Mabbott, Thomas Ollive & Phillip D Jordan. "*The Prairie Chicken:* Notes on Lincoln and Mrs. K." *JISHS,* 25 (Oct 1932), 154-166.

Monteiro, George. "A Note on the Realism of JK." *ALR,* 2 (Spring 1969), 77-78.

"*The Prairie Chicken:* A Rarity." *JISHS,* 47 (Spring 1954), 84-88.

Roberts, Audrey J. " 'Word Murder': An Early JK Essay Published Anonymously." *ALR,* 6 (Winter 1973), 73-79.

Roberts. "Two Additions to the JK Canon." *ALR,* 6 (Summer 1973), 252-254.

Soloman, Eric. "Another Analogue for *The Red Badge of Courage.*" *NCF,* 13 (Jun 1958), 63-67.

Stronks, James B. "A Note on Realism in Civil War Fiction." *CWH,* 2 (Sep 1956), 144-145.

Stronks. "JK Writes Lincoln for a Job." *JISHS,* 50 (Winter 1957), 416-417.

Stronks. "From Atlanta to the Sea: Verse by a Soldier Poet." *CWH,* 4 (Mar 1958), 23-25.

Calvin Gibson

PETER B. KYNE

San Francisco, Calif, 12 Oct 1880-San Francisco, Calif, 25 Nov 1957

Largely forgotten now, Peter B. Kyne produced novels and short stories that appealed to wide popular interest by portraying admirable American businessmen. Characters like his Cappy Ricks—sea captain turned shrewd capitalist—were honest, hardworking entrepreneurs who thrived on the California coast as soldiers or as masters of the lumber, shipping, or mining industries. His protagonists believed in a work ethic that combined virtue and rich rewards. Kyne's romantic adventure stories were particularly popular during the boom years of the 1920s.

CATALOGUE

Two San Francisco Writers: Inventory of the Papers of Dean S. Jennings and Inventory of the Papers of PBK. Eugene: U Oregon Library, 1974.

BOOKS

The Three Godfathers. NY: Doran, 1913. Novel.

The Long Chance. NY: Fly, 1914. Novel.

Cappy Ricks; or, The Subjugation of Matt Peasley. NY: Fly, 1916. Novel.

Ireland über Alles: A Tale of the Sea. London: Nash, 1917. Repub as *The Stolen Ship.* London: Hodder & Stoughton, 1919. Novel.

Webster—Man's Man. Garden City, NY: Doubleday, Page, 1917. Novel.

The Valley of the Giants. Garden City, NY: Doubleday, Page, 1918. Novel.

The Green-Pea Pirates. Garden City, NY: Doubleday, Page, 1919. Repub as *Captain Scraggs; or, The Green-Pea Pirates.* NY: Grosset & Dunlap, 1921. Novel.

PBK: An Autobiography, by Request. Npl: International Magazine, 1919.

Kindred of the Dust. NY: Cosmopolitan, 1920. Novel.

The Go-Getter: A Story That Tells You How to Be One. NY: Cosmopolitan, 1921. Novella.

The Pride of Palomar. NY: Cosmopolitan, 1921. Novel.

Cappy Ricks Retires. NY: Cosmopolitan, 1922. Novel.

Never the Twain Shall Meet. NY: Cosmopolitan, 1923. Novel.

The Enchanted Hill. NY: Cosmopolitan, 1924. Novel.

The Understanding Heart. NY: Cosmopolitan, 1926. Novel.

They Also Serve. NY: Cosmopolitan, 1927. Novel.

Made of Money. London: Hodder & Stoughton, 1927. Novel.

Money to Burn. NY: Grosset & Dunlap, 1928. Novel.

The Silent Comrade. London: Hodder & Stoughton, 1928. Novel.

Tide of Empire. NY: Cosmopolitan, 1928. Novel.

Jim the Conqueror. NY: Cosmopolitan, 1929. Novel.

The Parson of Panamint and Other Stories. NY: Cosmopolitan, 1929.

The Thunder God: A Romantic Story of Love, Hatred and Adventure. NY: Grosset & Dunlap, 1930. Novel.

Outlaws of Eden. NY: Cosmopolitan, 1930. Novel.

Golden Dawn. NY: Cosmopolitan, 1930. Novel.

The Gringo Privateer and Island of Desire. NY: Cosmopolitan, 1931. *The Gringo Privateer & Island of Desire* separately published, London: Hodder & Stoughton, 1932. Novels.

Two Make a World. NY: Kinsey, 1932. Novel.

Lord of Lonely Valley. NY: Kinsey, 1932. Novel.

Comrades of the Storm. NY: Kinsey, 1933. Novel.

Cappy Ricks Comes Back. NY: Kinsey, 1934. Novel.

The Cappy Ricks Special. NY: Kinsey, 1935. Novel.

Soldiers, Sailors and Dogs. NY: Kinsey, 1936. Stories.

Dude Woman. NY: Kinsey, 1940. Novel.

The Book I Never Wrote. San Francisco, Calif: Privately printed, 1942. Memoir.

COLLECTIONS

The PBK Omnibus. NY: Grosset & Dunlap, 1935.

The Golden West: Three Novels by PBK. NY: Farrar & Rinehart, 1935.

MANUSCRIPTS & ARCHIVES

U of Oregon Library.

BIOGRAPHY

Book Section

Baldwin, Charles C. "PBK." *The Men Who Make Our Novels* (NY: Dodd, Mead, rev 1924), 317-320.

CRITICAL STUDIES

Articles

Barrick, Mac E. "The Hat Ranch: Fact, Fiction, or Folklore?" *WF*, 34 (Apr 1975), 149-153.

Bode, Carl. "Cappy Ricks and the Monk in the Garden." *PMLA*, 64 (Mar 1949), 59-69.

Robert T. Kelley

ALFRED HENRY LEWIS

Cleveland, Ohio, 20 Jan 1857-New York City, NY, 23 Dec 1914

Like many of his literary contemporaries, Alfred Henry Lewis worked as a journalist. He is best known, however, for creating Wolfville—a fictional town based loosely on Tombstone, Arizona. In all seven Wolfville books, the town is populated by a gallery of colorful figures. The Old Cattleman, who narrates many of the tales, is a philosophical, tolerant, and individualistic cowboy who drolly recounts Lewis's experience of the American West: a mixture of lively frontier chaos and oppressive determinism; religious fervor and rugged practical jokes; the deification of womanhood and the violence of western gunfighters. Lewis's Wolfville creations were popular successes and influential contributions to the humorous dialect tradition in American literature and to the lore of the Old West.

BIBLIOGRAPHY

Bibliography of American Literature, comp Jacob Blanck. New Haven: Yale U P, 1955-1991. Primary.

BOOKS

Wolfville. NY: Stokes, 1897. Stories.
Sandburrs. NY: Stokes, 1900. Stories.
Richard Croker. NY: Life, 1901. Biography.
Wolfville Days. NY: Stokes, 1902. Stories.
Wolfville Nights. NY: Stokes, 1902. Novel.
Peggy O'Neal. Philadelphia: Biddle, 1903. Novel.
The Black Lion Inn. NY: Russell, 1903. Stories.
The Boss and How He Came to Rule New York. NY: Barnes, 1903. Novel.
The President: A Novel. NY: Barnes, 1904.
The Sunset Trail. NY: Barnes, 1905. Novel.
The Throwback: A Romance of the Southwest. NY: Outing, 1906. Novel.
The Story of Paul Jones: An Historical Romance. NY: Dillingham, 1906. Novel.
Confessions of a Detective. NY: Barnes, 1906. Stories.
When Men Grew Tall; or, The Story of Andrew Jackson. NY: Appleton, 1907. Biography.

An American Patrician; or, The Story of Aaron Burr. NY: Appleton, 1908. Biography.
Wolfville Folks. NY: Appleton, 1908. Novel.
The Apaches of New York. NY: Dillingham, 1912. Novel.
Faro Nell and Her Friends: Wolfville Stories. NY: Dillingham, 1913.
Nation-Famous New York Murders. NY: Dillingham, 1914. Stories.

OTHER

Verdict (19 Dec 1898-12 Nov 1900), ed AHL. Newspaper.
The Mormon Menace, Being the Confessions of John Doyle Lee, ed with intro by AHL. NY: Home Protection, 1905.
A Compilation of the Messages and Speeches of Theodore Roosevelt, 1901-1905, ed with intro by AHL. Washington: Bureau of National Literature & Art, 1906.

COLLECTIONS

Old Wolfville: Chapters From the Fiction of AHL, ed with intro & commentary by Louis Filler. Yellow Springs, Ohio: Antioch P, 1968.
Wolfville Yarns, ed Rolfe & John Humphries. Kent, Ohio: Kent State U P, 1968.

CRITICAL STUDIES

Book
Ravitz, Abe C. *AHL.* Boise, Idaho: Boise State U, 1978.

Book Section & Articles
Filler, Louis. "Wolfville." *NMQR,* 13 (Spring 1943), 35-47.
Humphries, Rolfe. "Tall-Tale Americana." *Nation,* 205 (28 Aug 1967), 153-157.
Humphries. "Introduction." *Wolfville Yarns,* v-xvii.
Manzo, Flournoy D. "AHL: Western Storyteller." *Ar&W,* 10 (Spring 1968), 5-24.
Mehl, R F, Jr. "Jack London, AHL, and the Primitive Woman." *JLN,* 6 (May-Aug 1973), 66-70.

Laura Plummer

JOSEPH C. LINCOLN

Brewster, Mass, 13 Feb 1870-Winter Park, Fla, 10 Mar 1944

A writer of popular novels set on Cape Cod, Joseph C. Lincoln came from a seafaring family. His first novel, *Cap'n Eri,* marked the beginning of a long career as a writer of best-selling novels about sea captains, fishermen, and other characters of the New England village scene. His romantic and humorous works focus on the eccentricities of his characters as well as the atmosphere of Cape Cod. Some contemporary commentators criticized his books for their sentimentality, lack of intellectual content, formulaic and simple plots. Others, including Hamlin Garland, lauded his characterizations, humor, and treatment of the Cape Cod setting.

BIBLIOGRAPHY

Sullwold, Stephen W. "A Descriptive Bibliography of JCL First Editions." Rex, 181-312. Primary.

BOOKS

Cape Cod Ballads and Other Verse. Trenton, NJ: Brandt, 1902.

Cap'n Eri: A Story of the Coast. NY: Barnes, 1904. Novel.

Partners of the Tide. NY: Barnes, 1905. Novel.

Mr. Pratt: A Novel. NY: Barnes, 1906.

The "Old Home House." NY: Barnes, 1907. Repub as *Cape Cod Stories.* NY: Burt, 1912. Stories.

Cy Whittaker's Place. NY: Appleton, 1908. Novel.

Our Village. NY: Appleton, 1909. Sketches.

Keziah Coffin. NY & London: Appleton, 1909. Novel.

The Depot Master. NY & London: Appleton, 1910. Novel.

Cap'n Warren's Wards. NY & London: Appleton, 1911. Novel.

The Woman-Haters: A Yarn of Eastboro Twin-Lights. NY & London: Appleton, 1911. Novel.

The Postmaster. NY & London: Appleton, 1912. Novel.

The Rise of Roscoe Paine. NY & London: Appleton, 1912. Novel.

Mr. Pratt's Patients. NY & London: Appleton, 1913. Novel.

Kent Knowles: Quahaug. NY & London: Appleton, 1914. Novel.

Cap'n Dan's Daughter. NY & London: Appleton, 1914. Novel.

Thankful's Inheritance. NY & London: Appleton, 1915. Novel.

Mary-'Gusta. NY & London: Appleton, 1916. Novel.

Extricating Obadiah. NY & London: Appleton, 1917. Novel.

"Shavings": A Novel. NY & London: Appleton, 1918.

The Portygee: A Novel. NY & London: Appleton, 1920.

Galusha the Magnificent: A Novel. NY & London: Appleton, 1921.

Fair Harbor: A Novel. NY & London: Appleton, 1922.

Doctor Nye of North Ostable: A Novel. NY & London: Appleton, 1923.

Rugged Water. NY & London: Appleton, 1924. Novel.

Queer Judson. NY & London: Appleton, 1925. Novel.

The Managers: A Comedy of Cape Cod. NY & London: Appleton, 1925. Play.

The Big Mogul. NY & London: Appleton, 1926. Novel.

The Aristocratic Miss Brewster. NY & London: Appleton, 1927. Novel.

Silas Bradford's Boy. NY & London: Appleton, 1928. Novel.

Blair's Attic, with Freeman Lincoln. NY: Coward-McCann, 1929. Novel.

Blowing Clear. NY & London: Appleton, 1930. Novel.

All Alongshore. NY: Coward-McCann, 1931. Repub as *All Alongshore: Cape Cod Characters.* NY: Blue Ribbon, 1941. Stories.

Payment Deferred. NY: Printed for the Booksellers of America by Coward-McCann, 1931. Story.

Head Tide. NY & London: Appleton, 1932. Novel.

Back Numbers. NY: Coward-McCann, 1933. Stories.

The Peel Trait. NY & London: Appleton-Century, 1934. Novel.

Storm Signals. NY & London: Appleton-Century, 1935. Novel.

Cape Cod Yesterdays. Boston: Little, Brown, 1935. Reminiscences.

Great-Aunt Lavinia. NY & London: Appleton-Century, 1936. Novel.

Storm Girl. NY & London: Appleton-Century, 1937. Novel.

A. Hall & Co. NY & London: Appleton-Century, 1938. Novel.

Christmas Days. NY: Coward-McCann, 1938. Stories.

The Ownley Inn, with Freeman Lincoln. NY: Coward-McCann, 1939. Novel.

Rhymes of the Old Cape. NY & London: Appleton-Century, 1939. Poetry.

Out of the Fog. NY & London: Appleton-Century, 1940. Novel.

The New Hope, with Freeman Lincoln. NY: Coward-McCann, 1941. Novel.

The Bradshaws of Harniss. NY & London: Appleton-Century, 1943. Novel.

COLLECTION

The JCL Reader, ed with intro by Freeman Lincoln. NY: Appleton-Century-Crofts, 1959.

BIOGRAPHY

Books

McCue, James Westaway. *Joe Lincoln of Cape Cod.* Silver Lake, Mass: Cape Cod, 1949.

Rex, Percy Fielitz. *The Prolific Pencil: A Biography of JCL, Litt.D.,* ed Fredrika A Burrow. Taunton, Mass: Sullwold, 1980.

Article

Haeselbarth, Adam C. "JCL." *BookNM* (1 May 1914), 417-420.

CRITICAL STUDIES

Book Sections & Articles

Baldwin, Charles C. "JCL." *The Men Who Make Our Novels* (NY: Dodd, Mead, rev 1924), 335-341.

"Books: *The Ownley Inn.*" *Time,* 34 (14 Aug 1939), 63-64.

Garland, Hamlin. "Cape Cod's Genial Chronicler." *PW,* 97 (17 Apr 1920), 1286.

Greene, Burton. "JCL and the Triumph of the Little Man: A Defense of Popular Culture." *JOFS,* 4 (Summer 1969), 90-102.

Orcutt, William Dana. "JL—Interpreter of Cape Cod." *From My Library Walls: A Kaleidoscope of Memories* (NY: Longmans, Green, 1945), 190-194.

Overton, Grant. *American Nights Entertainment* (NY: Appleton/Doran/Doubleday, Page/Scribners, 1923), 321-344. Rpt *Authors of the Day* by Overton (NY: Doran, 1924).

Gwen L. Nagel

DAVID ROSS LOCKE
(Petroleum V. Nasby)

Vestal, NY, 20 Sep 1833-Toledo, Ohio, 15 Feb 1888

David Ross Locke was one of the group of enormously popular vernacular writers, including Charles Farrar Browne, Henry Wheeler Shaw, and Charles Henry Smith, who gained prominence during and just after the Civil War. Locke's persona Petroleum Vesuvius Nasby promoted Republican politics through hundreds of comically misspelled, racist, satirical letters ostensibly advocating the Confederate cause or Democratic interests. The Toledo, Ohio, *Weekly Blade*, which Locke edited from 1865 to 1888, became nationally known as "Nasby's paper." Locke's poetry, novels, short fiction, and temperance propaganda—minor even in their day—retain interest primarily to complete the portrait of this influential nineteenth-century journalist.

BIBLIOGRAPHIES

Bibliography of American Literature, comp Jacob Blanck. New Haven: Yale U P, 1955-1991. Primary.

"Selected Bibliography." Austin, 148-154. Primary & secondary.

BOOKS

(This list omits the many political and temperance pamphlets by DRL).

The Nasby Papers. Letters and Sermons Containing the Views on the Topics of the Day, of Petroleum V. Nasby. Indianapolis: Perrine, 1864. Comic letters.

Nasby. Divers Views, Opinions, and Prophecies of Yoors Trooly Petroleum V Nasby. Cincinnati, Ohio: Carroll, 1866. Miscellany.

Swinging Round the Circle; or, Andy's Trip to the West, Together With a Life of Its Hero. By Petroleum V. Nasby. NY: Haney, 1866. Repub as *Andy's Trip to the West.* . . . NY: American News, 1866. Repub as *Nasby's Life of Andy Jonsun.* NY: Haney, 1869. Captioned cartoons & burlesque biography.

"Swingin Round the Cirkle." By Petroleum V. Nasby . . . His Ideas of Men, Politics, and Things, as Set Forth in His Letters to the Public Press, During the Year 1866. Boston: Lee & Shepard, 1867. Comic letters.

Ekkoes From Kentucky. By Petroleum V. Nasby . . . Bein a Perfect Record uv the Ups, Downs, and Experiences uv the Dimocrisy. . . . Boston: Lee & Shepard, 1868. Comic letters.

The Struggles (Social, Financial and Political) of Petroleum V. Nasby. . . . Boston: Richardson, 1872. Repub as *The Moral History of America's Life-Struggle.* Boston: Richardson / St Louis: Etna, 1874. Abridged as *The Struggles of Petroleum V. Nasby,* ed with intro by Joseph Jones; notes by Gunther Barth. Boston: Beacon, 1963. Comic letters.

Eastern Fruit on Western Dishes: The Morals of Abou Ben Adhem. Edited by D. R. Locke. Boston: Lee & Shepard / NY: Lee, Shepard & Dillingham, 1875. Sketches.

A Paper City. Boston: Lee & Shepard / NY: Dillingham, 1879. Novel.

Hannah Jane. Boston: Lee & Shepard / NY: Dillingham, 1882. Poetry.

Nasby in Exile; or, Six Months of Travel. . . . Toledo, Ohio & Boston: Locke, 1882. Travel sketches.

The Demagogue: A Political Novel. Boston: Lee & Shepard / NY: Dillingham, 1891.

OTHER

Hancock [Ohio] *Jeffersonian* (1861-1865), ed DRL. Newspaper.

[Toledo, Ohio] *Weekly Blade* (1865-1888), ed DRL. Newspaper.

Strong Heart and Steady Hand. Weekly Blade (17 May-2 Aug 1888). Novel.

COLLECTIONS

The Nasby Letters. Being the Original Nasby Letters, as Written During His Lifetime. Toledo, Ohio: Toledo Blade, 1893.

Civil War Letters of Petroleum V. Nasby, comp with intro by Harvey S Ford. Columbus: Ohio State U P for the Ohio Historical Society, 1962.

MANUSCRIPTS & ARCHIVES

Rutherford B Hayes Memorial Center, Fremont, Ohio.

BIOGRAPHIES

Books

Clemens, Cyril. *Petroleum Vesuvius Nasby*. Webster Groves, Mo: International Mark Twain Society, 1936.

Harrison, John M. *The Man Who Made Nasby, DRL*. Chapel Hill: U North Carolina P, 1969.

Articles

Marchman, Watt P. "DRL." *Museum Echoes*, 30 (May 1957), 35-38.

Ransome, Jack Clifford. "DRL, Civil War Propagandist." *NOQ*, 20 (Jan 1948), 5-19.

Ransome. "DRL: The Post War Years." *NOQ*, 20 (Summer 1948), 144-158.

CRITICAL STUDIES

Book

Austin, James C. *Petroleum V. Nasby (DRL)*. NY: Twayne, 1965.

Book Sections & Articles

Anderson, David D. "The Odyssey of Petroleum Vesuvius Nasby." *OhH*, 74 (1965), 232-246.

Austin, J C. "Petroleum Vesuvius Nasby to Gen Ullissis S. Grant." *YULG*, 39 (Jul 1964), 46-50.

Bier, Jesse. " 'Literary Comedians': The Civil War and Reconstruction." *The Rise and Fall of American Humor* (NY: Holt, Rinehart & Winston, 1968), 77-116.

Blair, Walter. "Literary Comedians (1855-1900)." *Native American Humor, 1800-1900* (NY: American Book, 1937), 102-124.

Blair & Hamlin Hill. "Phunny Phellows: Shaw, L, and Smith." *America's Humor: From Poor Richard to Doonesbury* (NY: Oxford U P, 1978), 284-299.

Grosh, Ronald M. "Civil War Politics in the Novels of DRL." *Midamerica*, 13 (1986), 19-30.

Harrison, J M. "DRL and the Fight on Reconstruction." *JQ*, 39 (Autumn 1962), 491-499.

Jones, Joseph. "Petroleum V. Nasby Tries the Novel: DRL's Excursions into Political and Social Fiction." *UTSE*, 30 (1951), 202-218.

Kesterson, David B. "The Literary Comedians and the Language of Humor." *StAH*, 1 (Jun 1982), 44-51.

Minor, Dennis E. "The Many Roles of Nasby." *MarkhamR*, 4 (Oct 1973), 16-20.

Pond, J B. *Eccentricities of Genius* (NY: Dillingham, 1900), 192-195.

Taft, W H. "DRL: Forgotten Editor." *JQ*, 34 (Spring 1957), 202-207.

Judith Yaross Lee

JACK LONDON

San Francisco, Calif, 12 Jan 1876-Glen Ellen, Calif, 22 Nov 1916

Despite his considerable reputation abroad, Jack London initially was scorned by American critics, who tended to dismiss him as a socialist crusader of minor literary importance and as a hack who somehow managed to produce a handful of perennially popular dog stories and Klondike adventure tales. During the past two decades, however, critical interest in London has risen steadily, revealing the scope of his creative genius. In a literary career lasting only eighteen years he produced more than two hundred short stories, twenty novels, and four hundred nonfiction pieces on such wide-ranging subjects as agronomy, astral projection, prizefighting, psychology, war, and zoology. London's sociological study of the slums of the East End of London (*The People of the Abyss*), his acclaimed dystopian novel (*The Iron Heel*), his sympathetic dramatization of the world of the feeble-minded ("Told in the Drooling Ward"), his speculative fiction on extraterrestrial intelligences ("The Red One"), and his pioneering use of Jung's theories of the unconscious ("The Water Baby") reveal the dimensions of his work and suggest directions for the ongoing reassessment of London's contribution to American literature.

BIBLIOGRAPHIES

"Bibliographical Update." Tavernier-Courbin, 281-291. Secondary.

Bibliography of American Literature, comp Jacob Blanck. New Haven: Yale U P, 1955-1991. Primary.

Hamilton, David Mike. *"The Tools of My Trade": Annotated Books in JL's Library*. Seattle: U Washington P, 1986.

Kingman, Russ. "JL, Playwright." *PacH*, 24 (Summer 1980), 135-140. Primary.

Lachtman, Howard. "Criticism of JL: A Selected Checklist." *MFS*, 22 (Spring 1976), 107-125.

Sherman, Joan R. *JL: A Reference Guide*. Boston: Hall, 1977. Secondary.

Sisson, James E. "JL's Published Poems: A Chronological Bibliography." *London Collector*, 1 (Jul 1970), 20-21. Primary.

Sisson. "JL's Plays: A Chronological Bibliography." *Daughters of the Rich*, 17-20. Primary.

Walker, Dale L & James E Sisson, III. *The Fiction of JL: A Chronological Bibliography*. El Paso: Texas Western P, 1972. Primary.

Woodbridge, Hensley C, John London & George H Tweney. *JL: A Bibliography*. Georgetown, Calif: Talisman, 1966. Augmented ed, Millwood, NY: Kraus, 1973. Primary & secondary.

BOOKS

The Son of the Wolf: Tales of the Far North. Boston & NY: Houghton, Mifflin, 1900. Stories.

The God of His Fathers & Other Stories. NY: McClure, Phillips, 1901.

Children of the Frost. NY & London: Macmillan, 1902. Stories.

The Cruise of the Dazzler. NY: Century, 1902. Stories.

A Daughter of the Snows. Philadelphia: Lippincott, 1902. Novel.

The Kempton-Wace Letters, with Anna Strunsky. NY & London: Macmillan, 1903. Fictional letters.

The Call of the Wild. NY & London: Macmillan, 1903. Novel.

The People of the Abyss. NY & London: Macmillan, 1903. Nonfiction.

The Faith of Men and Other Stories. NY & London: Macmillan, 1904.

The Sea-Wolf. NY & London: Macmillan, 1904. Novel.

War of the Classes. NY & London: Macmillan, 1905. Essays.

The Game. NY & London: Macmillan, 1905. Novel.

Tales of the Fish Patrol. NY & London: Macmillan, 1905. Stories.

Moon-Face and Other Stories. NY & London: Macmillan, 1906.

White Fang. NY & London: Macmillan, 1906. Novel.

Scorn of Women in Three Acts. NY & London: Macmillan, 1906. Play.

Before Adam. NY & London: Macmillan, 1907. Novel.

Love of Life and Other Stories. NY & London: Macmillan, 1907.

The Road. NY: Macmillan, 1907. Travel.

The Iron Heel. NY & London: Macmillan, 1908. Novel.

Martin Eden. NY: Macmillan, 1909. Novel.

Lost Face. NY: Macmillan, 1910. Stories.

Revolution and Other Essays. NY: Macmillan, 1910.

Burning Daylight. NY: Macmillan, 1910. Novel.

Theft: A Play in Four Acts. NY & London: Macmillan, 1910.

When God Laughs and Other Stories. NY: Macmillan, 1911.

Adventure. NY: Macmillan, 1911. Novel.

The Cruise of the Snark. NY: Macmillan, 1911. Travel.

South Sea Tales. NY: Macmillan, 1911. Stories.

The House of Pride and Other Tales of Hawaii. NY: Macmillan, 1912.

A Son of the Sun. Garden City, NY: Doubleday, Page, 1912. Stories.

Smoke Bellew. NY: Century, 1912. Abridged ed, London: Mills & Boon, 1913. Abridged again as *Smoke and Shorty.* London: Mills & Boon, 1920. Stories.

The Night-Born. . . . NY: Century, 1913. Stories.

The Abysmal Brute. NY: Century, 1913. Novel.

John Barleycorn. NY: Century, 1913. Nonfiction.

The Valley of the Moon. NY: Macmillan, 1913. Novel.

The Strength of the Strong. NY: Macmillan, 1914. Stories.

The Mutiny of the Elsinore. NY: Macmillan, 1914. Novel.

The Scarlet Plague. NY: Macmillan, 1915. Novel.

The Jacket. London: Mills & Boon, 1915; *The Star Rover.* NY: Macmillan, 1915. Novel.

The Acorn-Planter: A California Forest Play. . . . NY: Macmillan, 1916.

The Little Lady of the Big House. NY: Macmillan, 1916. Novel.

The Turtles of Tasman. NY: Macmillan, 1916. Stories.

The Human Drift. NY: Macmillan, 1917. Essays & miscellany.

Jerry of the Islands. NY: Macmillan, 1917. Novel.

Michael, Brother of Jerry. NY: Macmillan, 1917. Novel.

The Red One. NY: Macmillan, 1918. Stories.

Hearts of Three, with Charles Goddard. London: Mills & Boon, 1918; NY: Macmillan, 1920. Novel/film scenario.

On the Makaloa Mat. NY: Macmillan, 1919; *Island Tales.* London: Mills & Boon, 1920. Stories.

Dutch Courage and Other Stories. NY: Macmillan, 1922.

The Assassination Bureau, Ltd., completed by Robert L Fish. NY & c: McGraw-Hill, 1963. Novel.

JL Reports: War Correspondence, Sports Articles, and Miscellaneous Writings, ed King Hendricks & Irving Shepard. Garden City, NY: Doubleday, 1970.

No Mentor But Myself: A Collection of Articles, Essays, Reviews, and Letters, by JL, on Writing and Writers, ed Dale L Walker. Port Washington, NY: Kennikat, 1979.

A Klondike Trilogy: Three Uncollected Stories, ed Earle Labor. Santa Barbara, Calif: Neville, 1983.

LETTERS

Letters From JL, Containing an Unpublished Correspondence Between L and Sinclair Lewis, ed King Hendricks & Irving Shepard. NY: Odyssey, 1965.

The Letters of JL, 3 vols, ed Earle Labor, Robert C Leitz, III & I Milo Shepard. Stanford, Calif: Stanford U P, 1988.

OTHER

Daughters of the Rich by Hilda Gilbert (as by JL), ed James E Sisson. Oakland, Calif: Holmes, 1972. Play.

Gold by Herbert Heron (as by Heron & JL), ed Sisson. Oakland, Calif: Holmes, 1979. Play.

Dearest Greek: J & Charmian L's Presentation Inscriptions to George Sterling, ed Stanley Wertheim & Sal Noto. Cupertino, Calif: Eureka, 1983.

With a Heart Full of Love: JL's Presentation Inscriptions to the Women in His Life, ed Noto. Berkeley, Calif: Twowindows, 1986.

EDITIONS & COLLECTIONS

JL, American Rebel: A Collection of His Social Writings Together With an Extensive Study of the Man and His Times, ed Philip S Foner. NY: Citadel, 1947.

JL's Tales of Adventure, ed Irving Shepard. Garden City, NY: Hanover House, 1956.

The Bodley Head JL, 4 vols, ed Arthur Calder-Marshall. London: Bodley Head, 1963-1966.

Curious Fragments: JL's Tales of Fantasy Fiction, ed Dale L Walker. Port Washington, NY: Kennikat, 1975.

Tales of the North by JL: The Complete Novels of White Fang, The Sea-Wolf, The Call of the Wild, The Cruise of the Dazzler, Plus Fifteen Stories Including Son of the Wolf, In the Forest of the North, In a Far Country, The White Silence, ed Russ Kingman. Secaucus, NJ: Castle, 1979.

Stories of Adventure by JL: The Complete Novel of The Game, Plus 46 Short Stories, Including An Odyssey of the North, Brown Wolf, Love of Life, The Sun-Dog Trail, The Death of Ligoun, and Seven Tales of the Fish Patrol, ed Kingman. Secaucus, NJ: Castle, 1980.

The Call of the Wild by JL: A Casebook With Text, Background Sources, Reviews, Critical Essays, and Bibliography, ed Earl J Wilcox. Chicago: Nelson-Hall, 1981.

JL: Novels & Social Writings, ed Donald Pizer. NY: Library of America, 1982.

JL: Novels & Stories, ed Pizer. NY: Library of America, 1982.

Sporting Blood: Selections From JL's Greatest Sports Writing, ed Howard Lachtman. Novato, Calif: Capra, 1984.

Young Wolf: The Early Adventure Stories of JL, ed Lachtman. Santa Barbara, Calif: Capra, 1984.

The Best of JL: Martin Eden, Before Adam, The Call of the Wild, White Fang, The Sea-Wolf, and 25 Short Stories, ed Kingman. Secaucus, NJ: Castle, 1985.

JL's California: The Golden Poppy & Other Writings, ed Sal Noto. NY: Beaufort, 1986.

In a Far Country: JL's Tales of the West, ed Walker. Ottawa, Ill: Jameson, 1987.

MANUSCRIPTS & ARCHIVES

The major collections are at the Huntington Library, San Marino, Calif & Utah State U Library.

BIOGRAPHIES

Books

Bamford, Georgia Loring. *The Mystery of JL: Some of His Friends, Also a Few Letters—A Reminiscence*. Oakland, Calif: Bamford, 1931.

Haughey, Homer L & Connie Kale Johnson. *JL Ranch Album*. Stockton, Calif: Heritage, 1985.

Haughey & Johnson. *JL Homes Album*. Stockton, Calif: Heritage, 1987.

Kingman, Russ. *A Pictorial Life of JL*. NY: Crown, 1979.

London, Charmian Kittredge. *The Log of the Snark*. NY: Macmillan, 1915.

London. *Our Hawaii: Islands and Islanders*. NY: Macmillan, 1917. Rev ed, 1922.

London. *The Book of JL*, 2 vols. NY: Century, 1921.

London, Joan. *JL and His Times: An Unconventional Biography*. NY: Doubleday, Doran, 1939. Repub with new intro by the author, Seattle: U Washington P, 1968.

O'Connor, Richard. *JL: A Biography*. Boston: Little, Brown, 1964.

Sinclair, Andrew. *Jack: A Biography of JL*. NY: Harper & Row, 1977.

Stasz, Clarice. *American Dreamers: Charmian and JL*. NY: St Martin, 1988.

Stone, Irving. *Sailor on Horseback: The Biography of JL*. Boston: Houghton Mifflin, 1938.

Walker, Franklin. *JL and the Klondike: The Genesis of an American Writer*. San Marino, Calif: Huntington Library, 1966.

Book Sections & Articles

Etulain, Richard W. "The Lives of JL." *WAL*, 11 (Summer 1976), 149-164.

Fleming, Becky London. "Memories of My Father, JL." *PacH*, 18 (Fall 1974), 5-10.

Hueffer, Oliver Madox. "JL: A Personal Sketch." *Living Age*, 8th series, Vol 5 (13 Jan 1917), 124-126. Rpt Tavernier-Courbin.

Lachtman, Howard. "Four Horses, a Wife, and a Valet: Up the California Coast With JL." *PacH*, 21 (Summer 1977), 103-134.

Peterson, C T. "The JL Legend." *ABC*, 8 (Jan 1958), 13-17.

Sandburg, Charles A. "JL: A Common Man." *Tomorrow*, 2 (Apr 1906), 35-39. Rpt Tavernier-Courbin.

Shivers, Alfred S. "JL: Not a Suicide." *DR*, 49 (Spring 1969), 43-57.

Shivers, Samuel A. "JL: Author in Search of a Biographer." *ABC*, 12 (Mar 1962), 25-27.

Starr, Kevin. "The Sonoma Finale of JL, Rancher." *Americans and the California Dream: 1850-1915* (NY: Oxford U P, 1973), 210-238.

Stasz, Clarice. "The Social Construction of Biography: The Case for JL." *MFS*, 22 (Spring 1976), 51-71.

Walker, Franklin. *The Seacoast of Bohemia: An Account of Early Carmel* (San Francisco: Book Club of California, 1966), passim.

Walling, Anna Strunsky. "Memoirs of JL." *Masses*, 9 (Jul 1917), 13-17.

Waters, Hal. "Anna Strunsky and JL." *ABC*, 17 (Nov 1966), 28-30.

CRITICAL STUDIES

Books

Beauchamp, Gorman. *JL*. Mercer Island, Wash: Starmont House, 1984.

Hedrick, Joan D. *Solitary Comrade: JL and His Work*. Chapel Hill: U North Carolina P, 1982.

Hendricks, King, ed. *Creator and Critic: A Controversy Between JL and Philo M. Buck, Jr*. Logan: Utah State U, 1961.

Hendricks. *JL: Master Craftsman of the Short Story*. Logan: Utah State U, 1966. Rpt Ownbey.

Johnston, Carolyn. *JL—An American Radical?* Westport, Conn: Greenwood, 1984.

Lundquist, James. *JL: Adventures, Ideas, and Fiction*. NY: Ungar, 1987.

McClintock, James I. *White Logic: JL's Short Stories*. Grand Rapids, Mich: Wolf House, 1975.

Nakada, Sachiko. *JL and the Japanese: An Interplay Between the West and the East.* Yamanashi-ken, Japan: Central Institute Jorinji Zen Monastery, 1986.

Walcutt, Charles Child. *JL.* Minneapolis: U Minnesota P, 1966.

Walker, Dale L. *The Alien Worlds of JL.* Grand Rapids, Mich: Wolf House, 1973.

Watson, Charles, Jr. *The Novels of JL: A Reappraisal.* Madison: U Wisconsin P, 1983.

Woodward, Robert H. *JL and the Amateur Press.* Grand Rapids, Mich: Wolf House, 1983.

Collections of Essays

Ownbey, Ray Wilson, ed. *JL: Essays in Criticism.* Santa Barbara, Calif: Smith, 1978.

Tavernier-Courbin, Jacqueline, ed. *Critical Essays on JL.* Boston: Hall, 1983.

Special Journals

ABC, 17 (Nov 1966). JL issue.

Jack London Echoes (1981-1984).

Jack London Newsletter (annually, 1967-).

The London Collector (1970-1973).

MFS, 22 (Spring 1976). JL issue.

PacH, 21 (Summer 1977). JL issue.

WAL, 11 (Summer 1976). JL issue.

What's New About London, Jack? (annually, 1971-).

Book Sections & Articles

Ahearn, Marie L. "*The People of the Abyss*: JL as New Journalist." *MFS,* 22 (Spring 1976), 73-83.

Baskett, Sam S. "JL on the Oakland Waterfront." *AL,* 27 (Nov 1955), 363-371.

Baskett. "JL's Heart of Darkness." *AQ,* 10 (Spring 1958), 66-77. Rpt Ownbey.

Baskett. "*Martin Eden*: JL's Poem of the Mind." *MFS,* 22 (Spring 1976), 23-36.

Baskett. "*Martin Eden*: JL's Splendid Dream." *WAL,* 12 (Fall 1977), 199-214.

Beauchamp, Gorman. "*The Iron Heel* and *Looking Backward.*" *ALR,* 9 (Autumn 1976), 307-314.

Bender, Bert. "JL in the Tradition of American Sea Fiction." *AmNeptune,* 46 (Summer 1986), 188-199. Rpt *Sea-Brothers: The Tradition of American Sea Fiction From Moby-Dick to the Present* by Bender (Philadelphia: U Pennsylvania P, 1988).

Birchard, Robert S. "JL and the Movies." *FilmH,* 1 (1987), 15-37.

Blackman, Gordon N, Jr. "JL: Visionary Realist." *JLN,* 13 (Sep-Dec 1980), 82-95; 14 (Jan-Apr 1981), 1-12.

Brazil, John R. "Ambrose Bierce, JL and George Sterling: Victorians Between Two Worlds." *SJS,* 4 (Feb 1978), 19-38.

Brown, Ellen. "A Perfect Sphere: JL's 'The Red One.' " *JLN,* 11 (May-Dec 1978), 81-85.

Bruccoli, Matthew J. "Introduction." *The Sea-Wolf* (Boston: Houghton Mifflin, 1964), v-xv.

Bykov, Vil. "JL in the Soviet Union." *BClubCalQNL,* 24 (Summer 1959), 52-58.

Campbell, Jeanne. "Falling Stars: Myth in 'The Red One.' " *JLN,* 11 (May-Dec 1978), 86-101.

Conlon, Stephen. "Some Aspects of JL in Australia." *JLEchoes,* 4 (1984), 24-29.

Conn, Peter. *The Divided Mind: Ideology and Imagination in America, 1898-1917* (Cambridge: Cambridge U P, 1983), 104-109.

Cooper, James Glennon. "The Womb of Time: Archetypal Patterns in the Novels of JL." *JLN,* 8 (Jan-Apr 1975), 1-5; 9 (Jan-Apr 1976), 16-28; 12, nos 1-3 (1979), 12-23.

Cooper. "The Summit and the Abyss: JL's Moral Philosophy." *JLN,* 12, nos 1-3 (1979), 24-27.

Courbin, Jacqueline M. "JL's Portrayal of the Natives in His First Four Collections of Arctic Tales." *JLN,* 10 (Sep-Dec 1978), 127-137.

Dhondt, Steven T. " 'There Is a Good Time Coming': JL's Spirit of Proletarian Revolt." *JLN,* 3 (Jan-Apr 1970), 25-34.

Ellis, James. "A New Reading of *The Sea-Wolf.*" *WAL,* 2 (Summer 1967), 127-134. Rpt Ownbey.

Feied, Frederick. *No Pie in the Sky: The Hobo as American Cultural Hero in the Works of JL, John Dos Passos, and Jack Kerouac* (NY: Citadel, 1964), passim.

Flink, Andrew. "*Call of the Wild*: JL's Catharsis." *JLN,* 11 (Jan-Apr 1978), 12-19.

Foner, Philip S. "JL: American Rebel." *JL, American Rebel: A Collection. . . ,* 3-130.

Geismar, Maxwell. "JL: The Short Cut." *Rebels and Ancestors: The American Novel, 1890-1915* (Boston: Houghton Mifflin, 1953), 139-216.

Giles, James R. "Beneficial Atavism in Frank Norris and JL." *WAL,* 4 (Spring 1969), 15-27.

Giles. "JL 'Down and Out' in England: The Relevance of the Sociological Study *People of the Abyss* to L's Fiction." *JLN,* 2 (Sep-Dec 1969), 79-83.

Giles. "Some Notes on the Red-Blooded Reading of Kipling by JL and Frank Norris." *JLN,* 3 (May-Aug 1970), 56-62.

Graham, Don. "JL's Tale Told by a High-Grade Feeb." *SSF,* 15 (Fall 1978), 429-433. Rev as "Madness and Comedy: A Neglected JL Vein," Tavernier-Courbin.

Hendricks, King. "Determination and Courage." *Eleusis,* 56 (May 1964), 305-313.

Hendricks. "JL: Master Craftsman of the Short Story." Ownbey, 13-30.

Hensley, Dennis E. "JL's Use of the Linguistic Style of the King James Bible." *JLEchoes*, 3 (Jul 1983), 4-11.

Howard, June. *Form and History in American Literary Naturalism* (Chapel Hill: U North Carolina P, 1985), passim.

Jorgenson, Jens Peter. " 'The Red One': A Freudian Approach." *JLN*, 8 (Sep-Dec 1975), 101-103.

Labor, Earle. "JL's Symbolic Wilderness: Four Versions." *NCF*, 17 (Sep 1962), 149-161. Rpt Ownbey.

Labor. "Portrait of the Artist as Professional." *JLN*, 6 (Sep-Dec 1973), 93-98.

Labor. "From 'All Gold Canyon' to *The Acorn Planter*: JL's Agrarian Vision." *WAL*, 11 (Summer 1976), 83-101.

Labor. "JL's 'Planchette': The Road Not Taken." *PacH*, 21 (Summer 1977), 138-146.

Labor. "JL's *Mondo Cane*: 'Bâtard,' *The Call of the Wild*, and *White Fang*." Tavernier-Courbin, 114-130.

Labor. "JL's Pacific World." Tavernier-Courbin, 205-222.

Labor. "The Making of a Major Author: JL and the Politics of Literary Reputation." *JLN*, 19 (Sep-Dec 1986), 100-104.

Labor & King Hendricks. "JL's Twice-Told Tale." *SSF*, 4 (Summer 1967), 334-347.

Lacassin, Francis. "JL Between the Challenge of the Supernatural and the Last Judgment." *JLN*, 8 (May-Aug 1975), 59-65.

Lacassin. "On the Roads of the Night: A Search for the Origin of *The Star Rover*." Tavernier-Courbin, 180-194.

Lachtman, Howard. "Man and Superwoman in JL's 'The Kanaka Surf.' " *WAL*, 7 (Summer 1972), 101-110.

Lachtman. "Revisiting JL's Valley of the Moon." *PacH*, 24 (Summer 1980), 141-156.

Lampkin, Loretta M. "JL and the Reluctant Reader—Another Dimension." *JLN*, 10 (Sep-Dec 1978), 146-150.

Li, Shuyan. "JL in China." *JLN*, 19 (Jan-Apr 1986), 42-46.

Littel, Katherine M. "The 'Nietzschean' and the Individualist in JL's Socialist Writings." *JLN*, 15 (May-Aug 1982), 76-91.

Lynn, Kenneth S. "JL: The Brain Merchant." *The Dream of Success: A Study of the Modern American Imagination* (Boston: Atlantic/ Little, Brown, 1955), 75-118.

Maffi, Mario. "JL in Italy: On Some Recent Editions of *Martin Eden*." *JLN*, 13 (Jan-Apr 1980), 12-19.

Mansfield, Katherine. "Hearts Are Trumps." *Athenaeum* (27 Aug 1920), 272. Rpt *Novels and Novelists* by Mansfield (NY: Knopf, 1930). Rpt Tavernier-Courbin.

Martin, Jay. *Harvests of Change: American Literature, 1865-1914* (Englewood Cliffs, NJ: Prentice-Hall, 1967), passim.

Martin, Ronald E. "JL: Radical Individualism and Social Justice in the Universe of Force." *American Literature and the Universe of Force* (Durham, NC: Duke U P, 1981), 184-214.

Martin, Stoddard. "JL." *California Writers* (NY: St Martin, 1983), 17-66.

May, Charles E. " 'To Build a Fire': Physical Fiction and Metaphysical Critics." *SSF*, 15 (Winter 1978), 19-24.

McClintock, James I. "JL's Use of Carl Jung's *Psychology of the Unconscious*." *AL*, 42 (Nov 1970), 336-347. Rpt Ownbey.

McClintock. "JL: Finding the Proper Trend of Literary Art." *CEA*, 34 (May 1972), 25-28.

Mills, Gordon. "JL's Quest for Salvation." *AQ*, 7 (Spring 1955), 3-14.

Mills. "The Symbolic Wilderness: James Fenimore Cooper and JL." *NCF*, 13 (Mar 1959), 329-340.

Mills. "The Transformation of Material in a Mimetic Fiction." *MFS*, 22 (Spring 1976), 9-22. Rpt Ownbey.

Mitchell, Lee Clark. " 'Keeping His Head': Repetition and Responsibility in L's 'To Build a Fire.' " *JML*, 13 (Mar 1986), 76-96.

Mohan, Chandra. "JL's Humanism." *JLN*, 8 (May-Aug 1975), 40-49.

Moreland, David A. "The Author as Hero: JL's *The Cruise of the Snark*." *JLN*, 15 (Jan-Apr 1982), 57-75.

Moreland. "Violence in the South Sea Fiction of JL." *JLN*, 16 (Jan-Apr 1983), 1-35.

Moreland. "The Quest That Failed: JL's Last Tales of the South Seas." *PacificS*, 8 (Fall 1984), 48-70.

Newlin, Keith. "Portrait of a Professional: The Plays of JL." *ALR*, 20 (Winter 1988), 65-84.

Oriard, Michael. "JL: The Father of American Sports Fiction." *JLN*, 11 (Jan-Apr 1978), 1-11.

Orwell, George. "Introduction." *Love of Life and Other Stories by JL* (London: Elek, 1946), 7-15.

Pankake, John. "JL's Wild Man: The Broken Myths of *Before Adam*." *MFS*, 22 (Spring 1976), 37-49.

Pattee, Fred Lewis. *The Development of the American Short Story* (NY: Harper, 1923), 347-353.

Pearsall, Robert Brainard. "Elizabeth Barrett Meets Wolf Larsen." *WAL*, 4 (Spring 1969), 3-13.

Petersen, Per Serritslev. "Science-Fictionalizing the Paradox of Living: JL's 'The Red One' and the Ecstasy of Regression." *Dolphin*, 11 (Apr 1985), 38-58.

Peterson, Clell T. "JL's Sonoma Novels." *ABC*, 9 (Oct 1958), 15-20.

Peterson. "JL's Alaskan Stories." *ABC*, 9 (Apr 1959), 15-22.

Peterson. "The Theme of JL's 'To Build a Fire.'" *ABC*, 17 (Nov 1966), 15-18.

Pizer, Donald. "JL: The Problem of Form." *SLitI*, 16 (Fall 1983), 107-115.

Qualtiere, Michael. "Nietzschean Psychology in L's *The Sea-Wolf*." *WAL*, 16 (Winter 1982), 261-278.

Reesman, Jeanne C. "The Problem of Knowledge in JL's 'The Water Baby.'" *WAL*, 23 (Fall 1988), 201-215.

Riber, Jorgen. "Archetypal Patterns in 'The Red One.'" *JLN*, 8 (Sep-Dec 1975), 104-106.

Schriber, Mary Sue. "L in France, 1905-1939." *ALR*, 9 (Spring 1976), 171-177.

Shivers, Alfred S. "JL's Mate-Women." *ABC*, 15 (Oct 1964), 17-21.

Shivers, Samuel A. "The Demoniacs in JL." *ABC*, 12 (Sep 1961), 11-14.

Simpson, Claude M, Jr. "JL: Proletarian or Plutocrat?" *StanfordT*, Series 1, no 13 (Jul 1965), 2-6.

Spangler, George M. "Divided Self and World in *Martin Eden*." *JLN*, 9 (Sep-Dec 1976), 118-126. Rpt Tavernier-Courbin.

Spinner, Jonathan Harold. "JL's *Martin Eden*: The Development of the Existential Hero." *MichA*, 3 (Summer 1970), 43-48. Rpt Ownbey.

Stasz, Clarice. "Androgyny in the Novels of JL." *WAL*, 11 (Summer 1976), 121-133. Rpt Ownbey.

Tavernier-Courbin, Jacqueline. "The Many Facets of JL's Humor." *Thalia*, 2, no 3 (1979), 3-9. Rpt Tavernier-Courbin.

Tavernier-Courbin. "California and After: JL's Quest for the West." *JLN*, 13 (May-Aug 1980), 41-54.

Tavernier-Courbin. "JL's Science Fiction." *JLN*, 17 (Sept-Dec 1984). 71-78.

Walker, Dale L. "JL's War." *JLEchoes*, 3 (Oct 1983), 22-33.

Walker, Franklin. "Afterword." *The Sea-Wolf and Selected Stories* (NY: NAL, 1964), 337-348.

Walker. "JL: *Martin Eden*." *The American Novel From James Fenimore Cooper to William Faulkner*, ed Wallace Stegner (NY: Basic Books, 1965), 133-143.

Walker. "Ideas and Action in JL's Fiction." *Essays on American Literature in Honor of Jay B. Hubbell*, ed Clarence Gohdes (Durham, NC: Duke U P, 1967), 259-272.

Ward, Susan. "JL's Women: Civilization vs. the Frontier." *JLN*, 9 (May-Aug 1976), 81-85.

Ward. "Toward a Simpler Style: JL's Stylistic Development." *JLN*, 11 (May-Dec 1978), 71-80.

Ward. "JL and the Blue Pencil: L's Correspondence With Popular Editors." *ALR*, 14 (Spring 1981), 16-25.

Ward. "Ideology for the Masses: JL's *The Iron Heel*." Tavernier-Courbin, 166-179.

Ward. "Social Philosophy as Best-Seller: JL's *The Sea-Wolf*." *WAL*, 17 (Winter 1983), 321-332.

Watson, Charles N, Jr. "JL's Yokohama Swim and His First Tall Tale." *StAH*, 3 (Nov 1976), 84-95.

Watson. "JL: Up From Spiritualism." *The Haunted Dusk: American Supernatural Fiction, 1820-1920*, ed Howard Kerr, John W Crowley & Charles L Crow (Athens: U Georgia P, 1983), 191-207.

Westbrook, Wayne W. *Wall Street in the American Novel* (NY: New York U P, 1980), passim.

Wilcox, Earl J. "JL's Naturalism: The Example of *The Call of the Wild*." *JLN*, 2 (Sep-Dec 1969), 91-101.

Wilcox. "'The Kipling of the Klondike': Naturalism in L's Early Fiction." *JLN*, 6 (Jan-Apr 1973), 1-12. Rpt Ownbey.

Wilcox. "Overtures of Literary Naturalism in *The Son of the Wolf* and *The God of His Fathers*." Tavernier-Courbin, 105-113.

Williams, Tony. "*Jerry of the Islands* and *Michael, Brother of Jerry*." *JLN*, 17 (May-Aug 1984), 28-60.

Williams. "*The Mutiny of the Elsinore*—A Re-evaluation." *JLN*, 19 (Jan-Apr 1986), 13-41.

Wilson, Christopher P. "The Brain Worker: JL." *The Labor of Words: Literary Professionalism in the Progressive Era* (Athens: U Georgia P, 1985), 92-112.

Woodbridge, Hensley C. "JL's Current Reputation Abroad." *PacH*, 21 (Summer 1977), 166-177.

Zirkle, Conway. *Evolution, Marxian Biology, and the Social Scene* (Philadelphia: U Pennsylvania P, 1959), passim.

Earle Labor

HARRIETT M. LOTHROP
(Margaret Sidney)

New Haven, Conn, 22 Jun 1844-San Francisco, Calif, 2 Aug 1924

Harriett M. Lothrop's reputation as an author, both in her own time and posthumously, rests on her creation of the irrepressibly cheerful Pepper family. Writing under the pseudonym Margaret Sidney, she turned out more than fifty books, almost all of which were intended for young readers. Twelve of these chronicled the adventures of the Peppers. The most famous book in the series, and the one for which she is remembered today, is *Five Little Peppers and How They Grew*. In this novel Lothrop presents an idealized version of rural poverty, as five plucky children help their widowed mother make a home. Those few critics who have assessed her work agree that Lothrop tapped into a nostalgia for an Edenic childhood that continues to shape American family stories to this day.

BOOKS

Five Little Peppers and How They Grew. Boston: Lothrop, 1880. Children's novel.

Half Year at Broncton. Boston: Lothrop, 1881. Children's novel.

So as by Fire. Boston: Lothrop, 1881. Children's novel.

What the Seven Did; or, The Doings of the Wordsworth Club. Boston: Lothrop, 1882. Children's novel.

Ballad of the Lost Hare. Boston: Lothrop, 1882. Poetry.

The Pettibone Name: A New England Story. Boston: Lothrop, 1882. Children's novel.

Who Told It to Me. Boston: Lothrop, 1883. Children's novel.

How They Went to Europe. Boston: Lothrop, 1884. Children's novel.

Ringing Words and Other Sketches. Boston: Lothrop, 1885.

On Easter Day. Boston: Lothrop, 1886. Poetry.

The Golden West as Seen by the Ridgeway Club. Boston: Lothrop, 1886. Children's novel.

Hester and Other New England Stories. Boston: Lothrop, 1886.

The Minute Man: A Ballad of "The Shot Heard Round the World." Boston: Lothrop, 1886. Poetry.

Two Modern Little Princes and Other Stories. Boston: Lothrop, 1886. Children's stories.

A New Departure for Girls. Boston: Lothrop, 1886. Children's novel.

Dilly and the Captain. Boston: Lothrop, 1887. Children's novel.

How Tom and Dorothy Made and Kept a Christian Home. Boston: Lothrop, 1888. Children's novel.

Old Concord: Her Highways and Byways. Boston: Lothrop, 1888. Rev ed, 1892. Adult nonfiction.

St. George and the Dragon: A Story of Boy Life, and Kensington Junior. Boston: Lothrop, 1888. Children's novel.

The Little Red Shop. Boston: Lothrop, 1889. Children's novel.

Our Town: Dedicated to All Members of the Y.P.S.C.E. Boston: Lothrop, 1889. Children's novel.

An Adirondack Cabin: A Family Story. . . . Boston: Lothrop, 1890. Children's novel.

Five Little Peppers Midway. Boston: Lothrop, 1890. Children's novel.

Rob: A Story for Boys. Boston: Lothrop, 1891.

Five Litte Peppers Grown Up. Boston: Lothrop, 1892. Children's novel.

Little Paul and the Frisbie School. Boston: Lothrop, 1893. Children's novel.

Whittier With the Children. Boston: Lothrop, 1893. Adult nonfiction.

The Old Town Pump: A Story of East and West. Boston: Lothrop, 1895. Children's novel.

The Gingham Bag: The Tale of an Heirloom. Boston: Lothrop, 1896. Children's novel.

Phronsie Pepper: The Last of the Five Little Peppers. Boston: Lothrop, 1897. Repub as *Phronsie Pepper: The Youngest of the Five Little Peppers*, 1897. Children's novel.

A Little Maid of Concord Town: A Romance of the American Revolution. Boston: Lothrop, 1898. Children's novel.

The Stories Polly Pepper Told to the Five Little Peppers in the Little Brown House. Boston: Lothrop, 1899. Repub as *Polly Pepper's Book*. NY: Grosset & Dunlap, 1947. Children's stories.

The Judge's Cave, Being a Romance of the New

*Haven Colony in the Days of the Regicides,
1661.* Boston: Lothrop, 1900. Novel.
The Adventures of Joel Pepper. Boston: Lothrop,
1900. Children's novel.
Five Little Peppers Abroad. Boston: Lothrop, 1902.
Children's novel.
Sally, Mrs. Tubbs. Boston: Lothrop, 1903. Chil-
dren's novel.
Five Little Peppers at School. Boston: Lothrop,
1903. Children's novel.
Five Little Peppers and Their Friends. Boston:
Lothrop, 1904. Children's novel.
Ben Pepper. Boston: Lothrop, 1905. Children's
novel.
Two Little Friends in Norway. Boston: Lothrop,
Lee & Shepard, 1906. Children's novel.
Five Little Peppers in the Little Brown House. Bos-
ton: Lothrop, Lee & Shepard, 1907. Chil-
dren's novel.
A Little Maid of Boston Town. Boston: Lothrop,
Lee & Shepard, 1910. Children's novel.
Our Davie Pepper. Boston: Lothrop, Lee &
Shepard, 1916. Children's novel.

OTHER

Young Folks' Cyclopaedia of Stories, comp HML.
Boston: Lothrop, 1885.
Lullabies and Jingles, comp HML. Boston: Loth-
rop, 1893.
The Child's Day Book, With Helps Toward the Joy

of Living and the Beautiful Heaven Above,
comp HML. Boston: Lothrop, 1893.

EDITION

Five Little Peppers and How They Grew, 12 vols.
Boston: Houghton Mifflin, 1936-1937. (Complete Peppers novels).

BIOGRAPHIES

Book Section & Articles
Carson, Norma Bright. " 'Margaret Sidney': The
Writer of the Famous Polly Pepper Books."
BookNM, 28 (Feb 1910), 407-414.
Johnson, Elizabeth. "Margaret Sidney vs. HL."
Horn Book, 47 (Apr 1971), 139-146; 47
(Jun 1971), 313-320.
Lothrop, Margaret M. "The Lothrops and the Five
Little Peppers." *The Wayside: Home of Au-
thors* (NY: American Book, 1940), 151-197.

CRITICAL STUDIES

Book Section & Article
Jordan, Alice M. *From Rollo to Tom Sawyer and
Other Papers* (Boston: Horn Book, 1948),
143.
Levin, Betty. "Peppers' Progress: One Hundred
Years of the Five Little Peppers." *Horn Book,*
57 (Apr 1981), 161-173.

Janice M. Alberghene

CHARLES MAJOR

Indianapolis, Ind, 25 Jul 1856-Shelbyville, Ind, 13 Feb 1913

Charles Major achieved great popular success with his first novel, *When Knighthood Was in Flower.* Set in sixteenth-century European courts, this historical romance embroidered exotic intrigue with realistic details to overshadow its sometimes cumbersome plotting. The novel found enthusiastic readers in the United States and England. Both it and Major's second book in the genre, *Dorothy Vernon of Haddon Hall,* had sustained appearances on best-seller lists and were successfully adapted for the stage as well as silent films. Although he published four more historical romances (a fifth was released posthumously), none of them achieved the impact of his early work, as tastes in popular fiction shifted after the Spanish-American War. Major did retain a more enduring regional reputation, however, through adventure novels and stories recalling the Indiana frontier and his childhood, especially in *The Bears of Blue River.*

BIBLIOGRAPHIES

Bibliography of American Literature, comp Jacob Blanck. New Haven: Yale U P, 1955-1991. Primary.

Hepburn, William M. "The CM Manuscripts in the Purdue University Libraries." *IQB,* 2 (Jul 1946), 71-81.

BOOKS

When Knighthood Was in Flower; or, The Love Story of Charles Brandon and Mary Tudor . . . Rewritten and Rendered into Modern English From Sir Edwin Caskoden's Memoir by Edwin Caskoden. Indianapolis & Kansas City: Bowen-Merrill, 1898. Novel.

The Bears of Blue River. NY: Doubleday & McClure, 1901. Novel.

Dorothy Vernon of Haddon Hall. NY & London: Macmillan, 1902. Novel.

A Forest Hearth: A Romance of Indiana in the Thirties. NY & London: Macmillan, 1903. Novel.

Yolanda, Maid of Burgundy. NY & London: Macmillan, 1905. Novel.

Uncle Tom Andy Bill: A Story of Bears and Indian Treasure. NY: Macmillan, 1908. Novel.

A Gentle Knight of Old Brandenburg. NY: Macmillan, 1909. Novel.

The Little King: A Story of the Childhood of King Louis XIV, King of France. NY: Macmillan, 1910. Novel.

Sweet Alyssum. Indianapolis: Bobbs-Merrill, 1911. Stories.

The Touchstone of Fortune, Being the Memoir of Baron Clyde. . . . NY: Macmillan, 1912. Novel.

Rosalie. NY: Macmillan, 1925. Novel.

MANUSCRIPTS & ARCHIVES

Purdue U Library.

CRITICAL STUDIES

Articles

Baetzhold, Howard G. "CM: Hoosier Romancer." *IMH,* 51 (Mar 1955), 31-42.

Scherrer, Anton. "CM." *IMH,* 45 (Sep 1949), 265-267.

William Burriss

DON MARQUIS

Walnut, Ill, 29 Jul 1878-Forest Hills, Long Island, NY, 29 Dec 1937

Don Marquis wrote novels, stories, plays, poetry, and humorous essays, but during his lifetime he was best known as the columnist for the *New York Evening Sun* who, in the "Sun Dial" columns, introduced the figures of Archy the cockroach and Mehitabel the cat. Marquis created other popular characters, including the pretentious Hermione of Greenwich Village and Clem Hawley, "the Old Soak," a hard-drinking philosopher who railed against Prohibition. Marquis's wit, use of colloquial idiom, and social satire won for him a large audience. What continued popularity he enjoys today is due primarily to Archy and Mehitabel.

BIBLIOGRAPHY

"Selected Bibliography." Lee, 155-161. Primary & secondary.

BOOKS

Danny's Own Story. Garden City, NY: Doubleday, Page, 1912. Novel.

Dreams & Dust. NY & London: Harper, 1915. Poetry.

The Cruise of the Jasper B. NY & London: Appleton, 1916. Novel.

Hermione and Her Little Group of Serious Thinkers. NY & London: Appleton, 1916. Sketches.

Prefaces. NY & London: Appleton, 1919. Essays.

Carter and Other People. NY & London: Appleton, 1921. Stories.

Noah an' Jonah an' Cap'n John Smith: A Book of Humorous Verse. NY & London: Appleton, 1921.

The Old Soak and Hail and Farewell. Garden City, NY & Toronto: Doubleday, Page, 1921. Sketches & poetry.

Poems and Portraits. Garden City, NY & Toronto: Doubleday, Page, 1922. Poetry.

The Revolt of the Oyster. Garden City, NY: Doubleday, Page, 1922. Stories.

Sonnets to a Red-Haired Lady (by a Gentleman With a Blue Beard) and Famous Love Affairs. Garden City, NY & Toronto: Doubleday, Page, 1922. Poetry.

The Old Soak's History of the World. . . . Garden City, NY: Doubleday, Page, 1924. Sketches.

The Dark Hours: Five Scenes From a History. Garden City, NY: Doubleday, Page, 1924. Play.

Pandora Lifts the Lid, with Christopher Morley. NY: Doran, 1924. Novel.

Words and Thoughts: A Play in One Act. NY & London: Appleton, 1924.

The Awakening and Other Poems. London: Heinemann, 1924; Garden City, NY: Doubleday, Page, 1925.

The Old Soak: A Comedy in Three Acts. NY & London: French, 1926. Play.

The Almost Perfect State. Garden City, NY: Doubleday, Page, 1927. Essays.

Out of the Sea: A Play in Four Acts. Garden City, NY: Doubleday, Page, 1927.

Archy and Mehitabel. Garden City, NY: Doubleday, Page, 1927. Poetry.

Love Sonnets of a Cave Man and Other Verses. Garden City, NY: Doubleday, Doran, 1928.

When the Turtles Sing and Other Unusual Tales. Garden City, NY: Doubleday, Doran, 1928. Stories.

A Variety of People. Garden City, NY: Doubleday, Doran, 1929. Stories.

Off the Arm. Garden City, NY: Doubleday, Doran, 1930. Novel.

Archys Life of Mehitabel. Garden City, NY: Doubleday, Doran, 1933. Poetry.

Chapters for the Orthodox. Garden City, NY: Doubleday, Doran, 1934. Stories.

Master of the Revels: A Comedy in Four Acts. Garden City, NY: Doubleday, Doran, 1934.

Archy Does His Part. Garden City, NY: Doubleday, Doran, 1935. Poetry.

Her Foot Is on the Brass Rail. NY: Privately printed, 1935. Essay.

Sun Dial Time. Garden City, NY: Doubleday, Doran, 1936. Stories.

Sons of the Puritans, preface by Christopher Morley. NY: Doubleday, Doran, 1939. Novel.

LETTERS

Selected Letters of DM, ed William McCollum, Jr. Stafford, Va: Northwoods, 1982.

COLLECTIONS

the lives and times of archy & mehitabel. NY: Doubleday, Doran, 1940.

The Best of DM, intro by Christopher Morley. Garden City, NY: Doubleday, 1946.

MANUSCRIPTS & ARCHIVES

The major collections are at Columbia U Library; U of Oregon Library; the New York Public Library; & the Walter Hampden-Edwin Booth Theatre Collection & Library, New York City.

BIOGRAPHY

Book

Anthony, Edward. *O Rare DM: A Biography.* Garden City, NY: Doubleday, 1962.

CRITICAL STUDIES

Book

Lee, Lynn. *DM.* Boston: Twayne, 1981.

Special Journal

The Don Marquis Letter (1980-   ).

Book Sections & Articles

Arnold, St George Tucker, Jr. "DM, *archy and mehitabel,* and the Triumph of Comic Vitality: Cats and Cockroaches on the Darkling Plain." *Thalia,* 5 (Fall-Winter 1982-1983), 3-13.

Blair, Walter & Hamlin Hill. *America's Humor: From Poor Richard to Doonesbury* (NY: Oxford U P, 1978), passim.

Crowell, Chester T. "The Fun of DM." *Atlantic,* 178 (Nov 1946), 129-131.

De Casseres, Benjamin. "Portraits En Brochette: DM." *Bookman,* 73 (Jul 1931), 487-491.

DeVoto, Bernard. "Almost Toujours Gai." *The Easy Chair* (Boston: Houghton Mifflin, 1955), 65-73.

Ford, Corey. *The Time of Laughter* (Boston: Little, Brown, 1967), 63-70.

Hasley, Louis. "DM: Ambivalent Humorist." *PrS,* 45 (Spring 1971), 59-73.

Hill, Hamlin. "Archy and Uncle Remus: DM's Debt to Joel Chandler Harris." *GaR,* 15 (Spring 1961), 78-87.

Jaffe, Dan. "Archy Jumps Over the Moon." *The Twenties: Fiction, Poetry, Drama,* ed Warren French (De Land, Fla: Everett/Edwards, 1975), 427-437.

"The Literary Spotlight XXXI: DM." *Bookman,* 59 (Jul 1924), 539-543.

Masson, Thomas. "DM." *Our American Humorists* (NY: Dodd, Mead, 1922), 247-260.

Morley, Christopher. "DM." *Shandygaff* (Garden City, NY: Doubleday, Page, 1918), 22-42.

Morley. "A Successor to Mark Twain," "O Rare DM." *Letters of Askance* (Philadelphia: Lippincott, 1939), 81-113, 114-121.

Pinsker, Sanford. "On or About December 1910: When Human Character—and American Humor—Changed." *Critical Essays on American Humor,* ed William Bedford Clark & W Craig Turner (Boston: Hall, 1984), 184-199.

Sherman, Stuart P. "DM—What Is He?" *NYHTB* (8 Feb 1925), 1-3.

Van Doren, Carl. "Day In and Day Out: Adams, Morley, M, and Broun, Manhattan Wits." *Century,* 107 (Dec 1923), 308-315.

White, E B. "DM." *The Second Tree From the Corner* (NY: Harper, 1954), 182-189.

Yates, Norris W. "The Many Masks of DM." *The American Humorist: Conscience of the Twentieth Century* (Ames: Iowa State U P, 1964), 194-216.

Gwen L. Nagel

BRANDER MATTHEWS

New Orleans, La, 21 Feb 1852-New York City, NY, 31 Mar 1929

Critic, journalist, fiction writer, playwright, and professor of dramatic literature at Columbia University from 1892-1924, Brander Matthews was arguably the most distinguished American scholar of the drama during the late nineteenth and early twentieth centuries. His defenses of literary realism earned him the respect of Mark Twain and William Dean Howells, and his essays promoting literary "Americanism" were enthusiastically received by Theodore Roosevelt, Henry Cabot Lodge, and their fellow cultural nationalists. Matthews's *An Introduction to the Study of American Literature* was among the earliest textbooks in the discipline, and his *Philosophy of the Short-Story* has been cited as the first extended treatment of the short story as a distinct genre. Matthews became a frequent target of H. L. Mencken, Randolph Bourne, and the younger critics who rebelled against the "Genteel Tradition" during the 1910s and 1920s. Matthews's name faded into obscurity after his death, but he has recently begun receiving some scholarly attention.

CATALOGUE

The Bookshelf of BM. NY: Columbia U P, 1931. Repub, NY: AMS, 1966. Catalogue of BM's papers, books & pamphlets at Columbia U Library.

BOOKS

Edged Tools: A Play in Four Acts. NY & London: French, 1873.

Too Much Smith; or, Heredity, a Physiological and Psychological Absurdity in One Act (as by Arthur Penn), adapted from *La Postérité d'arun Bourgmestre* by Mario Uchard. NY: Werner, 1879. Play.

The Theaters of Paris. NY: Scribners, 1880. Criticism.

French Dramatists of the Nineteenth Century. NY: Scribners, 1881. Rev & augmented ed, 1891. Rev & augmented again, 1901. Criticism.

The Home Library (as by Penn). NY: Appleton, 1883. Catalogue.

In Partnership: Studies in Story-Telling, with H C Bunner. NY: Scribners, 1884. Criticism & stories.

The Last Meeting: A Story. NY: Scribners, 1885. Novella.

A Secret of the Sea. NY: Scribners, 1886. Augmented ed, London: Chatto & Windus, 1886. Stories.

Cheap Books and Good Books. NY: American Copyright League, 1888. Essay.

Check and Counter-Check: A Tale of Twenty-five Hours, with George H Jessop. Bristol, Conn: Arrowsmith, 1888. Repub as *A Tale of Twenty-five Hours*. NY: Appleton, 1892. Novel.

Pen and Ink: Papers on Subjects of More or Less Importance. NY & London: Longmans, Green, 1888. Rev & augmented ed, NY: Scribners, 1902. Essays.

American Authors and British Pirates. NY: American Copyright League, 1889. Essays.

A Family Tree and Other Stories. London & NY: Longmans, Green, 1889. Stories.

With My Friends: Tales Told in Partnership, with others. NY: Longmans, Green, 1891. Stories.

Americanisms and Briticisms, With Other Essays on Other Isms. NY: Harper, 1892.

In the Vestibule Limited. NY & London: Harper, 1892. Stories.

Tom Paulding: The Story of a Search for Buried Treasure in the Streets of New York. NY: Century, 1892. Children's novel.

The Decision of the Court: A Comedy. NY: Harper, 1893. Play.

The Story of a Story and Other Stories. NY: Harper, 1893.

The Royal Marine: An Idyl of Narragansett Pier. NY: Harper, 1894. Novella.

Studies of the Stage. NY: Harper, 1894. Essays.

This Picture and That: A Comedy. NY & London: Harper, 1894. Play.

Vignettes of Manhattan. NY: Harper, 1894.

Bookbindings Old and New: Notes of a Booklover, With an Account of the Grolier Club of New York. NY & London: Macmillan, 1895.

Books and Play-books: Essays on Literature and Drama. London: Osgood, McIlvane, 1895.

His Father's Son: A Novel of New York. NY: Harper, 1895.

Aspects of Fiction and Other Ventures in Criticism. NY: Harper, 1896. Augmented ed, NY: Scribners, 1902. Essays.

An Introduction to the Study of American Literature. NY & c: American Book, 1896. Augmented ed, 1911. Augmented again, 1918. Textbook.

Tales of Fantasy and Fact. NY: Harper, 1896. Stories.

Outlines in Local Color. NY & London: Harper, 1898. Stories.

The Action and the Word: A Novel of New York. NY & London: Harper, 1900.

A Confident To-morrow: A Novel of New York. NY & London: Harper, 1900.

The Historical Novel and Other Essays. NY: Scribners, 1901.

Notes on Speech-making. NY & c: Longmans, Green, 1901. Essays.

Parts of Speech: Essays on English. NY: Scribners, 1901.

The Philosophy of the Short-Story. NY & c: Longmans, Green, 1901. Criticism.

Cuttyback's Thunder; or, Frank Wylde. A Comedy in One Act, adapted from *Le Serment d'Horace* by Henry Mürger. Boston: Baker, 1902.

The Development of the Drama. NY: Scribners, 1903. Criticism.

Recreations of an Anthologist. NY: Dodd, Mead, 1904. Essays.

American Character. NY: Crowell, 1906. Essays.

Inquiries and Opinions. NY: Scribners, 1907. Essays.

A Gold Mind: A Play in Three Acts, with Jessop. NY & London: French, 1908.

The American of the Future and Other Essays. NY: Scribners, 1909.

Molière: His Life and His Works. NY: Scribners, 1910.

A Study of the Drama. Boston & NY: Houghton Mifflin, 1910. Criticism.

A Study of Versification. Boston & c: Houghton Mifflin, 1911. Criticism.

Fugitives From Justice. NY: Corlies, Macy, 1912. Poetry.

Gateways to Literature and Other Essays. NY: Scribners, 1912.

Vistas of New York. NY & London: Harper, 1912. Stories.

Shakspere as a Playwright. NY: Scribners, 1913. Criticism.

On Acting. NY: Scribners, 1914. Essays.

A Book About the Theater. NY: Scribners, 1916. Criticism.

These Many Years: Recollections of a New Yorker. NY: Scribners, 1917. Autobiography.

The Principles of Playmaking and Other Discussions of the Drama. NY & London: Scribners, 1919. Essays.

Essays on English. NY & London: Scribners, 1921.

The Tocsin of Revolt and Other Essays. NY: Scribners, 1922.

Playwrights on Playmaking and Other Studies of the Stage. NY & London: Scribners, 1923. Essays.

The Clown: In History, Romance and Drama. Springfield, Ohio: Crowell, 1924. Essays.

Suggestions for Teachers of American Fiction. NY: American Book, 1925.

Rip Van Winkle Goes to the Play and Other Essays on Plays and Players. NY & London: Scribners, 1926.

OTHER

Comedies for Amateur Acting, ed BM. NY: Appleton, 1880.

Poems of American Patriotism, ed BM. NY: Scribners, 1882. Rev & augmented ed, 1898.

Sheridan's Comedies: "The Rivals" and "The School for Scandal," ed BM. Boston: Osgood, 1885.

Actors and Actresses of Great Britain and the United States, From the Days of David Garrick to the Present Time, 5 vols, ed BM & Laurence Hutton. NY: Cassell, 1886.

André: A Tragedy in Five Acts by William Dunlap; ed BM. NY: Dunlap Society, 1887.

Ballads of Books, ed BM. NY: Coombes, 1887.

Bunker Hill; or, The Death of General Warren by John Daly Burk; ed with intro by BM. NY: Dunlap Society, 1891.

The Dramatic Essays of Charles Lamb, ed with intro by BM. NY: Dodd, Mead, 1891.

Washington Irving's Tales of a Traveller, ed BM. NY & London: Longmans, Green, 1895.

Great Plays (French and German) by Corneille, Molière, Racine, Lessing, Schiller, and Hugo, ed with intro by BM. NY: Appleton, 1901.

American Familiar Verse, ed BM. NY & London: Longmans, Green, 1904.

The Short-Story: Specimens Illustrating Its Development, ed BM. NY & c: American Book, 1907.

The Oxford Book of American Essays, ed BM. NY: Oxford U P, 1914.

The Chief European Dramatists: Twenty-one Plays From the Drama of Greece, Rome, Spain, France, Italy, Germany, Denmark, and Norway, From 500 BC to 1879 AD, ed BM. Boston & NY: Houghton Mifflin, 1916.

Autobiography and Essays by Thomas Henry Huxley, ed with intro by BM. NY & c: Gregg, 1919.

The Chief British Dramatists, Excluding Shake-
speare: Twenty-five Plays From the Middle of
the Fifteenth Century to the End of the Nine-
teenth, ed BM. Boston & NY: Houghton
Mifflin, 1924.
Papers on Playmaking, ed BM; preface by Henry W
Wells. NY: Hill & Wang, 1957.
Papers on Acting, ed BM; preface by Wells. NY:
Hill & Wang, 1958.

MANUSCRIPTS & ARCHIVES

Columbia U Library.

BIOGRAPHIES

Book Section & Articles
Butler, Nicholas Murray. "BM." Commemorative
Tributes of the American Academy of Arts
and Letters, 1905-1941 (Freeport, NY: Books
for Libraries, 1968), 234-238.
Hamilton, Clayton. "B (February 21, 1852-March
31, 1929)." Scribner's, 86 (Jul-Dec 1929),
82-87.
Kleinfield, H L. "The Tutelage of a Young American: BM in Europe, 1866." CLC, 13 (Feb
1964), 35-42.

CRITICAL STUDIES

Book Section & Articles
Bender, Jack E. "BM: Critic of the Theatre." EThJ,
12 (Oct 1960), 169-176.
Bourne, Randolph. "A Vanishing World of Gentil-
ity." Dial, 64 (14 Mar 1918), 234-235.
"The Literary Spotlight XX: BM." Bookman, 57
(Jun 1923), 432-436.
Phelps, William Lyon. "A Cosmopolitan Critic."
Forum, 39 (Jan-Mar 1908), 377-380.
Rascoe, Burton. "Three American Critics." Book-
man, 56 (Oct 1922), 222-224.
Sherman, Stuart P. "BM and the Mohawks." Points
of View (NY: Scribners, 1924), 251-260.
Trent, William P. "Mr. BM as a Critic." SR, 3
(May 1895), 373-384.
Trent. "BM as a Dramatic Critic." IntlM, 4 (Aug
1901), 289-293.

Lawrence J. Oliver

GEORGE BARR McCUTCHEON

Tippecanoe County, Ind, 26 Jul 1866-New York City, NY, 23 Oct 1928

George Barr McCutcheon was known during his lifetime for his popular romances, the most prominent
of which were the tales of Graustark, an imaginary
Balkan country. The first of these swashbuckling
novels, published in 1901, won him a large audience. McCutcheon's most enduring work has been
Brewster's Millions, a comic fantasy about an unexpectedly inherited fortune. Several of his novels
were adapted by others for the stage and movies.
McCutcheon's own plays were realistic and satiric
rather than melodramatic, and he also experimented with realism in Mary Midthorne, a novel
set in Indiana.

BIBLIOGRAPHY

Bibliography of American Literature, comp Jacob
Blanck. New Haven: Yale U P, 1955-1991.
Primary.

BOOKS

Graustark: The Story of a Love Behind a Throne.
Chicago: Stone, 1901. Novel.
Castle Craneycrow. Chicago: Stone, 1902. Novel.
Brewster's Millions (as by Richard Greaves). Chi-
cago: Stone, 1903; (as by GBM). London:
Collier, 1907. Novel.
The Sherrods. NY: Dodd, Mead, 1903. Novel.

The Day of the Dog. NY: Dodd, Mead, 1904. Novel.

Beverly of Graustark. NY: Dodd, Mead, 1904. Novel.

The Purple Parasol. NY: Dodd, Mead, 1905. Novel.

Nedra. NY: Dodd, Mead, 1905. Novel.

Cowardice Court. NY: Dodd, Mead, 1906. Novel.

Jane Cable. NY: Dodd, Mead, 1906. Novel.

The Flyers. NY: Dodd, Mead, 1907. Novel.

The Daughter of Anderson Crow. NY: Dodd, Mead, 1907. Novel.

The Husbands of Edith. NY: Dodd, Mead, 1908. Novel.

The Man From Brodney's. NY: Dodd, Mead, 1908. Novel.

The Alternative. NY: Dodd, Mead, 1909. Novel.

Truxton King: A Story of Graustark. NY: Dodd, Mead, 1909. Novel.

The Butterfly Man. NY: Dodd, Mead, 1910. Novel.

The Rose in the Ring. NY: Dodd, Mead, 1910. Novel.

Brood House: A Play in Four Acts. NY: Privately printed, 1910.

What's-His-Name. NY: Dodd, Mead, 1911. Novel.

Mary Midthorne. NY: Dodd, Mead, 1911. Novel.

Her Weight In Gold. NY: Dodd, Mead, 1912. Augmented ed, 1914. Stories.

The Hollow of Her Hand. NY: Dodd, Mead, 1912. Novel.

A Fool and His Money. NY: Dodd, Mead, 1913. Novel.

Black Is White. NY: Dodd, Mead, 1914. Novel.

The Prince of Graustark. NY: Dodd, Mead, 1914. Novel.

Mr. Bingle. NY: Dodd, Mead, 1915. Novel.

The Light That Lies. NY: Dodd, Mead, 1916. Novel.

From the Housetops. NY: Dodd, Mead, 1916. Novel.

Green Fancy. NY: Dodd, Mead, 1917. Novel.

Shot With Crimson. NY: Dodd, Mead, 1918. Novel.

The City of Masks. NY: Dodd, Mead, 1918; *The Court of New York.* London: Melrose, 1919. Novel.

One Score and Ten: A Comedy in Four Acts. NY: npub, 1919. Play.

Sherry. NY: Dodd, Mead, 1919. Novel.

Anderson Crow, Detective. NY: Dodd, Mead, 1920. Novel.

West Wind Drift. NY: Dodd, Mead, 1920. Novel.

Quill's Window. NY: Dodd, Mead, 1921. Novel.

Yollop. NY: Dodd, Mead, 1922. Novel.

Viola Gwyn. NY: Dodd, Mead, 1922. Novel.

Oliver October. NY: Dodd, Mead, 1923. Novel.

East of the Setting Sun: A Story of Graustark. NY: Dodd, Mead, 1924. Novel.

Romeo in Moon Village. NY: Dodd, Mead, 1925. Novel.

Kindling and Ashes; or, The Heart of Barbara Wayne. NY: Dodd, Mead, 1926. Novel.

The Inn of the Hawk and Raven: A Tale of Old Graustark. NY: Dodd, Mead, 1927. Novel.

Blades. NY: Dodd, Mead, 1928. Novel.

The Merivales. NY: Dodd, Mead, 1929. Novel.

Books Were Once Men: An Essay For Booklovers, intro by William Dana Orcutt. NY: Dodd, Mead, 1931. Essay.

OTHER

"The Double Doctor: A Farce." *The Indiana Experience,* ed Arnold Leslie Lazarus (Bloomington & London: Indiana U P, 1979), 299-322. Play.

MANUSCRIPTS & ARCHIVES

The major collections are at Purdue University Library; the New York Public Library; the Beinecke Library, Yale U; & the Harry Ransom Humanities Research Center, U of Texas, Austin.

CRITICAL STUDIES

Book

Lazarus, Arnold Leslie & Victor H Jones. *Beyond Graustark: GBM, Playwright Discovered.* Port Washington, NY: Kennikat, 1981.

Articles

Jones, Victor H. "Why Richard Greaves?" *MMisc,* 5 (1977), 12.

Jones. "Footnotes to *Brewster's Millions.*" *JPC,* 21 (Summer 1987), 103-120.

Kopka, James. "GBM and the Graustark Legacy." *IndEJ,* 6 (Winter 1972), 3-10.

Lazarus, Arnold Leslie. "GBM: Youth and Drama." *Biography,* 4 (Summer 1981), 208-226.

Wallace, Raymond P. "Cardboard Kingdoms." *SJS,* 13 (Spring 1987), 23-34.

West, James L W, III. "GBM's Literary Ledger." *YULG,* 59 (Apr 1985), 155-161.

John Cavin

WILLIAM McFEE

At sea, 15 Jun 1881-New Milford, Conn, 2 Jul 1966

The works of William McFee were widely popular in their own day and were frequently compared to those of Joseph Conrad in subject and style. British by birth, McFee spent roughly seventeen years at sea before settling in America and becoming a United States citizen. Almost all of his novels and essays deal with the sea, which comes to represent escape from life's burdens but which also makes wanderers and aliens of those who choose the nautical life. Through the adventures of characters disconnected from their native lands, McFee explored the individual's relationship to the world. The psychological conflicts in the novels are set against a backdrop of cultures and traditions at odds with one another. Although McFee's novels were often criticized as too subjective, too filled with the author's opinions on social issues, his essays were praised for their autobiographical tone and content.

BIBLIOGRAPHY

Babb, James T. *A Bibliography of the Writings of WM,* intro & notes by WM. Garden City, NY: Doubleday, Doran, 1931. Primary.

BOOKS

Letters From an Ocean Tramp. London & c: Cassell, 1908. Rev as *An Ocean Tramp.* Garden City, NY & Toronto: Doubleday, Page, 1921. Novel.

Aliens. NY: Longmans, Green / London: Arnold, 1914. Rev ed, Garden City, NY: Doubleday, Page, 1918. Novel.

Casuals of the Sea: The Voyage of A Soul. Garden City, NY: Doubleday, Page, 1916. Novel.

A Port Said Miscellany. Boston: Atlantic Monthly, 1918. Essay.

Captain Macedoine's Daughter. Garden City, NY: Doubleday, Page, 1920. Novel.

A Six-Hour Shift. Garden City, NY: Doubleday, Page, 1920. Story.

Harbours of Memory. Garden City, NY & Toronto: Doubleday, Page, 1921. Essays & stories.

An Engineer's Notebook: Essays on Life and Letters. NY: Shay, 1921.

Command. Garden City, NY: Doubleday, Page, 1922. Novel.

The Gates of the Caribbean: The Story of a Great White Fleet Caribbean Cruise. Npl: United Fruit Co Steamship Service, 1922. Essay.

Race. Garden City, NY: Doubleday, Page, 1924. Novel.

Swallowing the Anchor. Garden City, NY: Doubleday, Page, 1925. Essays.

Sunlight in New Granada. Garden City, NY: Doubleday, Page, 1925. Essays.

The Life of Sir Martin Frobisher. NY: Harper, 1928; *Sir Martin Frobisher.* London: Lane, Bodley Head, 1928. Biography.

Pilgrims of Adversity. Garden City, NY: Doubleday, Doran, 1928. Novel.

Sailors of Fortune. Garden City, NY: Doubleday, Doran, 1929. Stories.

North of Suez. Garden City, NY: Doubleday, Doran, 1930. Novel.

Born to Be Hanged. Gaylordsville, Conn: Slide Mountain, 1930. Story.

The Harbourmaster: A Novel. Garden City, NY: Doubleday, Doran, 1931.

No Castle in Spain. Garden City, NY: Doubleday, Doran, 1933. Novel.

The Reflections of Marsyas. Gaylordsville, Conn: Slide Mountain, 1933. Autobiography & poetry.

More Harbours of Memory. Garden City, NY: Doubleday, Doran, 1934. Essays.

The Beachcomber: A Novel. Garden City, NY: Doubleday, Doran, 1935.

Sailor's Wisdom. London: Cape, 1935. Story.

Sailor's Bane. Philadelphia: Ritten House, 1936. Story.

Derelicts: A Novel. NY: Doubleday, Doran, 1938.

Watch Below. NY: Random House, 1940. Novel.

Spenlove in Arcady. NY: Random House, 1941. Novel.

Ship to Shore. NY: Random House, 1944. Novel.

In the First Watch. NY: Random House, 1946. Autobiography.

Family Trouble. NY: Random House, 1949. Novel.

The Law of the Sea. Philadelphia & NY: Lippincott, 1950. Maritime history & law.

The Adopted. London: Faber & Faber, 1952. Novel.

MANUSCRIPTS & ARCHIVES
The Beinecke Library, Yale U.

BIOGRAPHIES
Book
Maule, Harry E. *WM: Author-Engineer.* Garden City, NY: Doubleday, Page, 1923.

Articles
Elder, Arthur J. "WM—Engineer and Author." *Bookman,* 44 (Sep 1916), 57-62.
Leatherby, James Norman. "WM: Writing Engineer." *PrS,* 23 (Summer 1949), 171-180.

Jean Kowaleski

OSCAR MICHEAUX

Near the town of Metropolis, Ill, 2 Jan 1884-Charlotte, NC, 26 Mar 1951

Novelist and filmmaker Oscar Micheaux intended to inspire and entertain his audience. The inspiration, derived from Booker T. Washington's ideas, carried a message that black Americans could, through diligence and dedication to practical goals, better their own condition; the entertainment was provided by melodramatic plots and sympathetic protagonists. Micheaux's early books, which drew on his own experiences as a homesteader and as a book salesman, led to a career as a producer and distributor of movies for black audiences. These films, like his novels, often depicted a prosperous and successful black middle class. Some critics argue that Micheaux's subject matter marks a retreat from racial concerns and from black culture and embodies oppressive myths of his time.

BOOKS

The Conquest: The Story of a Negro Pioneer, by the Pioneer. Lincoln, Nebr: Woodruff, 1913. Novel.
The Forged Note: A Romance of the Darker Races. Lincoln, Nebr: Western Book Supply, 1915. Novel.
The Homesteader. Sioux City, Iowa: Western Book Supply, 1917. Novel.
The Wind From Nowhere. NY: New York Book Supply, 1944. Novel.
The Case of Mrs. Wingate. NY: New York Book Supply, 1945. Novel.
The Story of Dorothy Stanfield, Based on a Great Insurance Swindle—and a Woman! NY: New York Book Supply, 1946. Novel.
The Masquerade: An Historical Novel. NY: New York Book Supply, 1947.

CRITICAL STUDIES

Book
Young, Joseph A. "OM's Novels: Black Apologies for White Oppression." Dissertation: U Nebraska, Lincoln, 1984.

Book Sections & Article
Bogle, Donald. "OM." *Toms, Coons, Mulattoes, Mammies, and Bucks: An Interpretive History of Blacks in American Films* (NY: Viking, 1973), 109-116.
Cripps, Thomas. *Slow Fade to Black: The Negro in American Film, 1900-1942* (NY: Oxford U P, 1977), 183-193, 342-346.
Fontenot, Chester J, Jr. "OM: Black Novelist and Film Maker." *Vision and Refuge: Essays on the Literature of the Great Plains,* ed Virginia Faulkner (Lincoln: U Nebraska P, 1982), 109-125.
Gloster, Hugh M. "OM." *Negro Voices in American Fiction* (Chapel Hill: U North Carolina P, 1948), 84-89.
Herbert, Janis. "OM: A Black Pioneer." *SDR,* 11 (Winter 1973-1974), 62-69.
Sampson, Henry T. "The Micheaux Film Corporation: OM." *Blacks in Black and White: A Source Book on Black Films* (Metuchen, NJ: Scarecrow, 1977), 42-55.

J. Randal Woodland

S. WEIR MITCHELL

Philadelphia, Pa, 15 Feb 1829-Philadelphia, Pa, 4 Jan 1914

S. Weir Mitchell combined careers as scientist and man of letters. As a scientist, he contributed to early research in medicine and neuroscience, published more than 170 technical papers, served as a surgeon in the Civil War, and was active in medical education and several Philadelphia hospitals throughout his life. As a writer, he displayed the scientist's intellectual rigor and critical turn of mind. Mitchell's novels and short stories provide psychological insights on the medical quack, spiritualism, and the abnormal personality; he also wrote in the more familiar genres of historical romance, picaresque novel, fantasy, and children's fiction. His most popular novels were *Hugh Wynne* and *The Adventures of François*. Since his death, Mitchell's fiction and poetry have received only occasional scholarly attention.

BIBLIOGRAPHIES & CATALOGUES

"Bibliography." Burr (1929), 397-413. Primary.

"Bibliography." Lovering, 169-173. Primary & secondary.

Bibliography of American Literature, comp Jacob Blanck. New Haven: Yale U P, 1955-1991. Primary.

A Catalogue of the Scientific and Literary Work of SWM. Philadelphia: npub, 1894. Primary.

A List of the Original Memoirs of SWM. Philadelphia: Lippincott, 1868. Primary.

BOOKS

(This list omits the many works by SWM on scientific or medical subjects.)

The Children's Hour, with Elizabeth W Sherman. Philadelphia: Published for the Sanitary Commission, 1864. Children's stories.

The Wonderful Stories of Fuz-Buz the Fly and Mother Grabem the Spider. Philadelphia: Lippincott, 1867. Children's stories.

Hephzibah Guinness; Thee and You; and A Draft on the Bank of Spain. Philadelphia: Lippincott, 1880. Stories.

The Hill of Stones and Other Poems. Boston & NY: Houghton, Mifflin, 1883.

In War Time. Boston & NY: Houghton, Mifflin, 1884. Novel.

Roland Blake. Boston & NY: Houghton, Mifflin, 1886. Novel.

A Masque and Other Poems. Boston & NY: Houghton, Mifflin, 1887.

Prince Little Boy and Other Tales Out of Fairyland. Philadelphia: Lippincott, 1888. Children's stories.

Far in the Forest: A Story. Philadelphia: Lippincott, 1889. Novel.

The Cup of Youth and Other Poems. Boston & NY: Houghton, Mifflin, 1889.

A Psalm of Deaths and Other Poems. Boston & NY: Houghton, Mifflin, 1890.

Characteristics. NY: Century, 1892. Novel.

The Mother and Other Poems. Boston & NY: Houghton, Mifflin, 1893.

Francis Drake: A Tragedy of the Sea. Boston & NY: Houghton, Mifflin, 1893. Verse drama.

Mr. Kris Kringle: A Christmas Tale. Philadelphia: Jacobs, 1893. Children's story.

When All the Woods Are Green: A Novel. NY: Century, 1894.

Philip Vernon: A Tale in Prose and Verse. NY: Century, 1895.

A Madeira Party. NY: Century, 1895. Stories.

Hugh Wynne: Free Quaker. . ., 2 vols. NY: Century, 1897. Rev ed, 1897. Novel.

The Adventures of François: Foundling, Thief, Juggler, and Fencing-Master During the French Revolution. NY: Century, 1898. Novel.

Ode on a Lycian Tomb. NY: Privately printed, 1899. Poem.

The Wager and Other Poems. NY: Century, 1900.

The Autobiography of a Quack and The Case of George Dedlow. NY: Century, 1900. Rpt in *The Autobiography of a Quack and Other Stories*, 1901. Stories.

Dr. North and His Friends. NY: Century, 1900. Novel.

Circumstance. NY: Century, 1901. Novel.

A Comedy of Conscience. NY: Century, 1903. Novel.

Little Stories. NY: Century, 1903.

New Samaria and The Summer of St. Martin. Philadelphia & London: Lippincott, 1904. Stories.

The Youth of Washington Told in the Form of an Autobiography. NY: Century, 1904. Rev ed, 1910. Novel.

Constance Trescot: A Novel. NY: Century, 1905.

A Diplomatic Adventure. NY: Century, 1906. Novel.

A Venture in 1777. Philadelphia: Jacobs, 1908. Novel.

The Red City: A Novel of the Second Administration of President Washington. NY: Century, 1908.

The Comfort of the Hills and Other Poems. NY: Century, 1910.

The Guillotine Club and Other Stories. NY: Century, 1910.

John Sherwood, Ironmaster. NY: Century, 1911. Novel.

Westways: A Village Chronicle. NY: Century, 1913. Novel.

OTHER

Pearl: Rendered into Modern English Verse by SWM. NY: Century, 1906. Augmented ed, Portland, Maine: Mosher, 1908.

COLLECTIONS

The Collected Poems. NY: Century, 1896.

The Complete Poems of SWM. NY: Century, 1914.

MANUSCRIPTS & ARCHIVES

The major collections are at the Library of Congress, U of Pennsylvania Library & the C of Physicians Library, Philadelphia.

BIOGRAPHIES

Books

Burr, Anna Robeson. *Weir Mitchell: His Life and Letters.* NY: Duffield, 1929.

Burr, Charles Walts. *SWM: Physician, Man of Science, Man of Letters, Man of Affairs.* Philadelphia: College of Physicians, 1920.

Walter, Richard D. *SWM, M.D., Neurologist: A Medical Biography.* Springfield, Ill: Thomas, 1970.

Book Section & Articles

Hinsdale, Guy. "SWM: Poet, Novelist, Friend, Physician." *GMHCUP,* 38 (Apr 1936), 303-313.

Hinsdale. "Recollections of Weir Mitchell." *GMHCUP,* 50 (Summer 1948), 248-254.

Oberholtzer, Ellis P. "Personal Memories of Weir Mitchell." *Bookman,* 39 (Apr 1914), 132-138.

Quinn, Arthur Hobson. "Weir Mitchell: Artist, Pioneer, and Patrician." *Century,* 120 (Winter 1930), 139-148.

Schauffler, R H. "Versatility and Dr. SWM." *Century,* 87 (Nov 1913), 267-269.

Taylor, J M. "Personal Glimpses of SWM." *AnMH,* ns 1 (Sep 1929), 583-598.

CRITICAL STUDIES

Books

Earnest, Ernest P. *SWM: Novelist and Physician.* Philadelphia: U Pennsylvania P, 1950.

Lovering, Joseph P. *SWM.* NY: Twayne, 1971.

Rein, David. *SWM as a Psychiatric Novelist.* NY: International Universities P, 1952.

Articles

Earnest, Ernest P. "Weir Mitchell as Novelist." *ASch,* 17 (Summer 1948), 314-322.

Earnest. "SWM as Man of Letters." *TSCPP,* 22 (Feb 1955), 100-104.

Farrand, Max. "*Hugh Wynne*: A Historical Novel." *WashHQ,* 1 (Apr 1907), 101-108.

Griffith, Kelley, Jr. "Weir Mitchell and the Genteel Romance." *AL,* 44 (May 1972), 247-261.

Richardson, Lyon N. "SWM at Work." *AL,* 11 (Mar 1939), 58-65.

Schelling, F E. "SWM, Poet and Novelist." *GMHCUP,* 32 (Apr 1930), 323-337.

Paul Leslie Ross

CLARENCE E. MULFORD

Streator, Ill, 3 Feb 1883-Portland, Maine, 11 May 1956

Author of romantic novels about the West, Clarence E. Mulford is best known as the creator of the cowboy hero Hopalong Cassidy, who also became an extremely popular figure in movies and in radio and television series. (After Mulford's retirement, his publisher hired the young Louis L'Amour to write four additional Cassidy novels.) Despite the great popularity of their hero, Mulford's works received mixed reviews. His sprawling plots and his mere competence at creating dialogue and characters (especially women) are balanced by his skillful depiction of action scenes and his meticulous attention to authentic details of the West. Mulford left, in the more than two dozen interlocking novels that he wrote, a vast tale of western life.

BIBLIOGRAPHY

"CEM." *Encyclopedia of Frontier and Western Fiction,* ed Jon Tuska & Vicki Piekarski (NY: McGraw-Hill, 1983), 242-247. Primary & filmography.

BOOKS

Bar-20. NY: Outing, 1907. Stories.
The Orphan. NY: Outing, 1908. Novel.
Hopalong Cassidy. Chicago: McClurg, 1910. Novel.
Bar-20 Days. Chicago: McClurg, 1911. Novel.
Buck Peters, Ranchman, with John Wood Clay. Chicago: McClurg, 1912. Novel.
The Coming of Cassidy and the Others. Chicago: McClurg, 1913. Novel.
The Man From Bar-20. Chicago: McClurg, 1918. Novel.
Johnny Nelson. Chicago: McClurg, 1920. Novel.
The Bar-20 Three. Chicago: McClurg, 1921. Novel.
"Tex." Chicago: McClurg, 1922. Novel.
"Bring Me His Ears." Chicago: McClurg, 1922; *Beckoning Trails.* London: Hodder & Stoughton, 1922. Novel.
Black Buttes. Garden City, NY: Doubleday, Page, 1923. Novel.
Rustlers' Valley. Garden City, NY: Doubleday, Page, 1924. Novel.
Hopalong Cassidy Returns. Garden City, NY: Doubleday, Page, 1924. Novel.
Cottonwood Gulch. Garden City, NY: Doubleday, Page, 1925. Novel.
Hopalong Cassidy's Protege. Garden City, NY: Doubleday, Page, 1926. Repub as *Hopalong Cassidy's Saddlemate.* NY: Popular Library, 1950? Novel.
The Bar 20 Rides Again. Garden City, NY: Doubleday, Page, 1926. Novel.
Corson of the JC. Garden City, NY: Doubleday, Page, 1927. Novel.
Mesquite Jenkins. Garden City, NY: Doubleday, Doran, 1928. Novel.
Me an' Shorty. Garden City, NY: Doubleday, Doran, 1929. Novel.
The Deputy Sheriff. Garden City, NY: Doubleday, Doran, 1930. Novel.
Hopalong Cassidy and the Eagle's Brood. Garden City, NY: Doubleday, Doran, 1931. Novel.
Mesquite Jenkins, Tumbleweed. Garden City, NY: Doubleday, Doran, 1932. Novel.
The Round-Up. Garden City, NY: Doubleday, Doran, 1933. Novel.
Trail Dust. Garden City, NY: Doubleday, Doran, 1934. Novel.
On the Trail of the Tumbling T. Garden City, NY: Doubleday, Doran, 1935. Novel.
Hopalong Cassidy Takes Cards. Garden City, NY: Doubleday, Doran, 1937. Novel.
Hopalong Cassidy Serves a Writ. Garden City, NY: Doubleday, Doran, 1941. Novel.

MANUSCRIPTS & ARCHIVES

The major collections are at the Library of Congress & the Fryeburg Public Library, Fryeburg, Maine.

BIOGRAPHIES

Book Section & Article

Barnes, Jack C. "Cowboys in Fryeburg: CM." *Bittersweet* (Jun 1982), 5-8, 22-24.
Nevins, Francis M, Jr. *The Films of Hopalong Cassidy* (Waynesville, NC: World of Yesterday, 1988), 9-17.

CRITICAL STUDIES

Book

Perham, Joseph A. "Reflections on Hopalong

Cassidy: A Study of CM." Thesis: U Maine, 1966.

Book Section & Articles

Bloodworth, William A, Jr. "M and Bower: Myth and History in the Early Western." *GPQ*, 1 (Spring 1981), 95-104.

Davison, Richard Allan. "*The Great Gatsby* and *Hopalong Cassidy*, Fitzgerald's Anachronism?" *FHA* (1979), 155-157.

Felchner, William J. "CEM—Creator of Hopalong Cassidy." *IllM*, 24 (Sep-Oct 1985), 24-27.

Nevins, Francis M, Jr. "Hopalong Cassidy: Knight of the Frontier." *CLC*, 36 (Feb 1987), 25-36.

Sonnichsen, C L. *From Hopalong to Hud* (College Station: Texas A&M U P, 1978), 108-109.

Gwen L. Nagel

MARY NOAILLES MURFREE
(Charles Egbert Craddock)

Murfreesboro, Tenn, 24 Jan 1850-Murfreesboro, Tenn, 31 Jul 1922

Writing under the pseudonym Charles Egbert Craddock, Mary Noailles Murfree created the first local-color literature of Tennessee's Cumberland mountains. Earlier critics compared her favorably to Bret Harte and Sarah Orne Jewett; however, her reputation declined when she continued writing local-color stories long after the demand for that genre had faded. Eventually, she turned to historical novels, but they did not receive the critical acclaim of her earlier works. Murfree wrote eighteen novels and fifty short stories, but her reputation rests on four volumes: *In the Tennessee Mountains, The Prophet of the Great Smoky Mountains, In the "Stranger People's" Country,* and *Where The Battle Was Fought*, which incorporated her own recollections of the Civil War. Her major contribution to American literature was a portrayal of the beauty and grandeur of the Cumberlands in vivid contrast to the sequestered, often poignant lives of their inhabitants.

BIBLIOGRAPHIES

Bibliography of American Literature, comp Jacob Blanck. New Haven: Yale U P, 1955-1991. Primary.

Carleton, Reese M. "MNM (1850-1922): An Annotated Bibliography." *ALR*, 7 (Autumn 1974), 293-378. Primary & secondary.

BOOKS

In the Tennessee Mountains. Boston & NY: Houghton, Mifflin, 1884. Stories.

Where the Battle Was Fought: A Novel. Boston: Osgood, 1884.

Down the Ravine. Boston & NY: Houghton, Mifflin, 1885. Novel.

The Prophet of the Great Smoky Mountains. Boston & NY: Houghton, Mifflin, 1885. Novel.

In the Clouds. Boston & NY: Houghton, Mifflin, 1887. Novel.

The Story of Keedon Bluffs. Boston & NY: Houghton, Mifflin, 1888. Novel.

The Despot of Broomsedge Cove. Boston & NY: Houghton, Mifflin, 1889. Novel.

In the "Stranger People's" Country: A Novel. NY: Harper, 1891.

His Vanished Star. Boston & NY: Houghton, Mifflin, 1894. Novel.

The Phantoms of the Foot-Bridge and Other Stories. NY: Harper, 1895.

The Mystery of Witch-Face Mountain and Other Stories. Boston & NY: Houghton, Mifflin, 1895.

The Young Mountaineers: Short Stories. Boston & NY: Houghton, Mifflin, 1897.

The Juggler. Boston & NY: Houghton, Mifflin, 1897. Novel.

The Story of Old Fort Loudon. NY & London: Macmillan, 1899. Novel.

The Bushwhackers & Other Stories. Chicago & NY: Stone, 1899.

The Champion. Boston & NY: Houghton, Mifflin, 1902.

A Spectre of Power. Boston & NY: Houghton, Mifflin, 1903. Novel.

The Frontiersmen. Boston & NY: Houghton, Mifflin, 1904. Stories.

The Storm Centre: A Novel. NY & London: Macmillan, 1905.

The Amulet: A Novel. NY & London: Macmillan, 1906.

The Windfall: A Novel. NY: Duffield, 1907.

The Fair Mississippian: A Novel. Boston & NY: Houghton Mifflin, 1908.

The Raid of the Guerilla and Other Stories. Philadelphia & London: Lippincott, 1912.

The Ordeal: A Mountain Romance of Tennessee. Philadelphia & London: Lippincott, 1912. Novel.

The Story of Duciehurst: A Tale of the Mississippi. NY: Macmillan, 1914. Novel.

MANUSCRIPTS & ARCHIVES

The major collections are at the Houghton Library, Harvard U; Tennessee State Library Archives, Nashville; & Emory U Library.

BIOGRAPHY

Book

Parks, Edd Winfield. *Charles Egbert Craddock (MNM).* Chapel Hill: U North Carolina P, 1941.

CRITICAL STUDIES

Books

Carleton, Reese M. "Conflict in Direction: Realis-

tic, Romantic, and Romanticistic Elements in the Fiction of MNM." Dissertation: U Wisconsin, Madison, 1976.

Cary, Richard. *MNM.* NY: Twayne, 1967.

Articles

Cary, Richard. "MNM (1850-1922)." *ALR*, 1 (Fall 1967-1968), 79-83.

Dillingham, William B, ed. " 'When Old Baldy Spoke.' " *EUQ*, 18 (Summer 1962), 93-106. Includes previously unpublished story by MNM.

Dunn, Durwood. "MNM: A Reappraisal." *AppalJ*, 6 (Spring 1979), 197-204.

Ensor, Allison. "The Geography of MNM's *In the Tennessee Mountains*." *MissQ*, 31 (Spring 1978), 191-199.

Frank, Waldo. "Among the Southern Appalachians." *NEMag*, 24 (May 1901), 231-247.

Lanier, Doris. "MNM: An Interview." *THQ*, 31 (Fall 1972), 276-278.

Loyd, Dennis. "Tennessee's Mystery Woman Novelist." *THQ*, 29 (Fall 1970), 272-277.

Niles, Mary. "Craddock's Girls: A Look at Some Unliberated Women." *MarkhamR*, 3 (Oct 1972), 74-77.

Parks, Edd Winfield. "Craddock's First Pseudonym." *ETHSP*, no 6 (1934), 67-80.

Reeves, Paschal. "From Halley's Comet to Prohibition." *MissQ*, 21 (Fall 1968), 285-290.

Shuman, R Baird. "MM's Battle." *TSL*, 6 (1961), 33-37.

Taylor, Archer. "Proverbs and Proverbial Phrases in the Writings of MNM (Charles Egbert Craddock)." *TFSB*, 24 (Mar 1958), 11-50.

Warfel, Harry R. "Local Color and Literary Artistry: MNM's *In the Tennessee Mountains*." *SLJ*, 3 (Fall 1970), 154-163.

Wood, Ann Douglas. "The Literature of Impoverishment: The Women Local Colorists in America, 1865-1914." *WS*, 1, no 1 (1972), 3-45.

Wright, Nathalia. "A Note on the Setting of MNM's 'The "Harnt" That Walks Chilhowee.' " *MLN*, 62 (Apr 1947), 272.

Kathryn Thompson Presley

MEREDITH NICHOLSON

Crawfordsville, Ind, 9 Dec 1866-Indianapolis, Ind, 21 Dec 1947

Novelist, essayist, and poet Meredith Nicholson published more than thirty books between 1891 and 1929, among which *The Hoosiers*, a collection of essays, and *A Hoosier Chronicle*, a novel, are his most famous. In these works Nicholson celebrated the wholesome, homespun, middle-class virtues of small-town Indiana, providing a somewhat romanticized image of the Midwest that would later be attacked by such analysts of the region as Sherwood Anderson and Sinclair Lewis. An active member of the Democratic Party, Nicholson also wrote many essays on political subjects.

BIBLIOGRAPHY

Russo, Dorothy Ritter & Thelma Lois Sullivan. "MN." *Bibliographical Studies of Seven Authors of Crawfordsville, Indiana* (Indianapolis: Indiana Historical Society, 1952), 69-172. Primary.

BOOKS

Short Flights. Indianapolis: Bowen-Merrill, 1891. Poetry.

The Hoosiers. NY & London: Macmillan, 1900. Rev "Centennial Edition," 1915. Essays.

The Main Chance. Indianapolis: Bobbs-Merrill, 1903. Novel.

Zelda Dameron. Indianapolis: Bobbs-Merrill, 1904. Novel.

The House of a Thousand Candles. Indianapolis: Bobbs-Merrill, 1905. Novel.

Poems. Indianapolis: Bobbs-Merrill, 1906.

The Port of Missing Men. Indianapolis: Bobbs-Merrill, 1907. Novel.

Rosalind at Red Gate. Indianapolis: Bobbs-Merrill, 1907. Novel.

The Little Brown Jug at Kildare. Indianapolis: Bobbs-Merrill, 1908; *The War of the Carolinas.* London: Nelson, 1909. Novel.

The Lords of High Decision. NY: Doubleday, Page, 1909. Novel.

The Siege of the Seven Suitors. Boston & NY: Houghton Mifflin, 1910. Novel.

Style and the Man. Indianapolis: Bobbs-Merrill, 1911. Essay.

A Hoosier Chronicle. Boston & NY: Houghton Mifflin, 1912. Novel.

The Provincial American and Other Papers. Boston & NY: Houghton Mifflin, 1912. Essays.

Otherwise Phyllis. Boston & NY: Houghton Mifflin, 1913. Novel.

The Poet. Boston & NY: Houghton Mifflin, 1914. Novel.

The Proof of the Pudding. Boston & NY: Houghton Mifflin, 1916. Novel.

The Madness of May. NY: Scribners, 1917. Novel.

A Reversible Santa Claus. Boston & NY: Houghton Mifflin, 1917. Novel.

The Valley of Democracy. NY: Scribners, 1918. Essays.

Lady Larkspur. NY: Scribners, 1919. Novel.

Blacksheep! Blacksheep! NY: Scribners, 1920. Novel.

The Man in the Street. NY: Scribners, 1921. Essays.

Best Laid Schemes. NY: Scribners, 1922. Stories.

Broken Barriers. NY: Scribners, 1922. Novel.

The Hope of Happiness. NY: Scribners, 1923. Novel.

Honor Bright: A Comedy in Three Acts, with Kenyon Nicholson. NY & London: French, 1923.

On the Antietam Battlefield. Indianapolis: Keystone, 1924. Poem.

And They Lived Happily Ever After! NY: Scribners, 1925. Novel.

The Cavalier of Tennessee. Indianapolis: Bobbs-Merrill, 1928. Novel.

Old Familiar Faces. Indianapolis: Bobbs-Merrill, 1929. Essays.

MANUSCRIPTS & ARCHIVES

The major collections are at the Beinecke Library, Yale U; the Lilly Library, Indiana U; Princeton U Library; & the Indiana Historical Society, Indianapolis.

CRITICAL STUDIES

Book

MN, American Man of Letters. NY: Scribners, 1923.

Book Sections & Articles

Baldwin, Charles C. "MN." *The Men Who Make Our Novels* (NY: Moffat, Yard, 1919), 64-68.

Banta, Richard Elwell. "MN." *Indiana Authors and Their Books: 1816-1916* (Crawfordsville, Ind: Wabash C P, 1949), 237-239.

Banta. "MN." *Hoosier Caravan: A Treasury of Indiana Life and Lore* (Bloomington: Indiana U P, 1951), 12-23.

Blake, Warren Barton. "Our Author-Diplomats." *I&WR* (3 Jul 1913), 17-19.

Dunn, Jacob P. "MN." *Indiana and Indianans* (Chicago: American Historical Society, 1919), 1526-1528.

Mitchell, Edward Bedinger. "MN's *A Hoosier Chronicle*." *Bookman*, 35 (May 1912), 313-314.

Smith, Russel E. " 'Consider the Author,' Says MN." *Writer's Monthly*, 16 (Oct 1920), 257-259.

Smith. "The Play Boy of the Wabash." *Bookman*, 52 (Oct 1920), 133-136.

Sutherland, R C. "The Kentucky Girl in Two Literary Classics." *KyHSR*, 45 (1967), 134-143.

Titus, W I, ed. "Three Letters of MN to Novelist Winston Churchill." *IMH*, 57 (Sep 1961), 249-252.

"Western Contribution to Our National Spirit: MN's Vivid Picture of the Valley of Democracy." *Our Opinion*, 65 (1918), 385-386.

Susan B. Egenolf

FRANK NORRIS

Chicago, Ill, 5 Mar 1870-San Francisco, Calif, 25 Oct 1902

Frank Norris's reputation as both a popular and serious novelist waxed rapidly between 1898, when his first novel appeared, and 1902, when he died at thirty-two. The posthumously published *The Pit* was one of the best-selling books of 1903 and Norris's greatest popular success. By the 1920s, however, *The Octopus* was regarded as a more important, pioneering work in the muckraking tradition and as a major attempt at writing "the great American novel." Like *McTeague*—now viewed as his best book—and *Vandover and the Brute*, *The Octopus* indicates the primary influence of Emile Zola: Norris's deliberate adaptations of Zolaesque themes and style have made him a major point of reference in the early history of American literary naturalism. His versatility as a writer is apparent in the adventure-romance *Moran of the Lady Letty*, in the Howellsian love-idyl *Blix*, and in short fiction resembling that produced by Rudyard Kipling, Richard Harding Davis, and Anthony Hope. But Norris's major achievement was in his mordant, post-Victorian analyses of socio-economic, cultural, and biological determinisms observable in American life at the turn of the century.

BIBLIOGRAPHIES

Bibliography of American Literature, comp Jacob Blanck. New Haven: Yale U P, 1955-1991. Primary.

Crisler, Jesse S & Joseph R McElrath, Jr. *FN: A Reference Guide*. Boston: Hall, 1974. Secondary.

Hill, John S. *The Merrill Checklist of FN*. Columbus, Ohio: Merrill, 1970. Primary & secondary.

Katz, Joseph. *A FN Collection*. Columbia: Department of English, U South Carolina, 1970. Primary.

Katz. "The Shorter Publications of FN: A Checklist." *Proof*, 3 (1973), 155-220. Primary.

Lohf, Kenneth A & Eugene P Sheehy. *FN: A Bibliography*. Los Gatos, Calif: Talisman, 1959. Primary & secondary.

McElrath, Joseph R, Jr. "FN." *ALR*, 8 (Autumn 1975), 307-319. Secondary.

McElrath. *FN and The Wave: A Bibliography*. NY: Garland, 1988. Primary.

BOOKS

Yvernelle: A Legend of Feudal France. Philadelphia: Lippincott, 1892. Poem.

Moran of the Lady Letty: A Story of Adventure off the California Coast. NY: Doubleday & McClure, 1898; *Shanghaied: A Story of Adventure off the California Coast*. London: Richards, 1899. Novel.

McTeague: A Story of San Francisco. NY: Doubleday & McClure, 1899. Novel.

Blix. NY: Doubleday & McClure, 1899; *Blix: A Love Idyll.* London: Richards, 1900. Novel.

A Man's Woman. NY: Doubleday & McClure, 1900. Novel.

The Octopus: A Story of California. NY: Doubleday, Page, 1901 (Vol 1 of "The Trilogy of the Epic of the Wheat"). Novel.

The Pit: A Story of Chicago. NY: Doubleday, Page, 1903 (Vol 2 of "The Trilogy of the Epic of the Wheat"). Novel.

A Deal in Wheat and Other Stories of the New and Old West. NY: Doubleday, Page, 1903.

The Responsibilities of the Novelist and Other Literary Essays. NY: Doubleday, Page, 1903.

The Joyous Miracle. NY: Doubleday, Page, 1906. Story.

The Third Circle. NY: Lane / London: Lane, Bodley Head, 1909. Stories.

Vandover and the Brute, ed with foreword by Charles G Norris. Garden City, NY: Doubleday, Page, 1914. Novel.

The Surrender of Santiago: An Account of the Historic Surrender of Santiago to General Shafter July 17, 1898. San Francisco: Elder, 1917. History.

Collected Writings Hitherto Unpublished in Book Form, intro by Charles G Norris. Garden City, NY: Doubleday, Doran, 1928 (Vol 10 of *The Argonaut Manuscript Limited Edition of FN's Works*).

FN: Two Poems and "Kim" Reviewed, with a bibliography by Harvey Taylor. San Francisco: Taylor, 1930.

FN of "The Wave": Stories & Sketches From the San Francisco Weekly, 1893 to 1897, ed with intro by Oscar Lewis; foreword by Charles G Norris. San Francisco: Westgate, 1931. Stories, sketches, articles, interviews & book reviews.

The Literary Criticism of FN, ed with intro by Donald Pizer. Austin: U Texas P, 1964. Essays, reviews & parodies.

A Novelist in the Making: A Collection of Student Themes and the Novels Blix and Vandover and the Brute, ed James D Hart. Cambridge: Harvard U P, 1970. Includes 45 of FN's student themes.

A Student Theme by FN, intro by Hart. Berkeley, Calif: Tanner, 1987.

LETTERS

The Letters of FN, ed Franklin Walker. San Francisco: Book Club of California, 1956.

FN: Collected Letters, ed with intro by Jesse S Crisler. San Francisco: Book Club of California, 1986.

OTHER

" 'The Great Corner in Hannibal and St. Jo': A Previously Unpublished Short Story by FN," ed John K Swensson. *ALR,* 4 (Summer 1971), 205-226.

"The Elusive Criticisms Syndicated by FN," ed Joseph Katz. *Proof,* 3 (1973), 221-251.

"The *Moran* Controversy: N's Defense of His 'Nautical Absurdities,' " ed Robert C Leitz, III. *ALR,* 15 (Spring 1982), 119-124.

"A New Short Story by FN," ed Leitz & Joseph R McElrath, Jr. *ALR,* 17 (Spring 1984), 1-11.

"FN at Del Monte: Two New *Wave* Essays From 1895," ed McElrath. *ALR,* 20 (Fall 1987), 56-70.

EDITIONS & COLLECTIONS

Complete Works of FN: Golden Gate Edition, 7 vols. NY: Doubleday, Page, 1903.

The Argonaut Manuscript Limited Edition of FN's Works, 10 vols. Garden City, NY: Doubleday, Doran, 1928; *The Complete Edition of FN,* 10 vols, 1928.

Six Essays on the Responsibilities of the Novelist. Yonkers, NY: Alicat, 1949.

McTeague: An Authoritative Text, Backgrounds and Sources, Criticism, ed with intro & notes by Donald Pizer. NY: Norton, 1977.

The Works of FN, 12 vols, ed Kenji Inoue. Tokyo: Meicho Fukyu Kai, 1983.

FN: Novels and Essays, ed with afterword & notes by Pizer. NY: Library of America, 1986.

MANUSCRIPTS & ARCHIVES

The major collections are at the U of California, Berkeley, Library; U of Virginia Library; & the Houghton Library, Harvard U.

BIOGRAPHIES

Books

Norris, Charles G. *FN, 1870-1902.* NY: Doubleday, Page, 1914.

Poncet, André. *FN (1870-1902),* 2 vols. Paris: Librairie Honore Champion, 1977.

Walker, Franklin. *FN: A Biography.* Garden City, NY: Doubleday, Doran, 1932.

Book Sections & Articles

Crisler, Jesse S. "N's 'Library.' " *FNS,* no 5 (Spring 1988), 1-11.

Crow, Charles L. "Bruce Porter's Memoir of FN." *FNS,* no 3 (Spring 1987), 1-4.

Everett, Wallace W. "FN in His Chapter." *PhiGDQ,* 52 (Apr 1930), 561-566.

Graham, D B. "FN, Actor." *BClubCalQNL,* 41 (Spring 1976), 38-40.

Katz, Joseph. "FN on the Battles of El Caney and San Juan Hill." *SAF*, 12 (Autumn 1984), 217-221.

Lewis, Oscar. *Bay Window Bohemia* (Garden City, NY: Doubleday, 1956), 197-200, passim.

Lynn, Kenneth S. "FN: Mama's Boy." *The Dream of Success: A Study of the Modern American Imagination* (Boston: Little, Brown, 1955), 158-207.

Lyon, Peter. *Success Story: The Life and Times of S. S. McClure* (NY: Scribners, 1963), passim.

Marcosson, Isaac F. *Adventures in Interviewing* (London & NY: Lane, 1920), passim.

Martin, Willard E, Jr. "FN's Reading at Harvard College." *AL*, 7 (May 1935), 203-204.

McElrath, Joseph R, Jr. "FN: A Biographical Essay." *ALR*, 11 (Autumn 1978), 219-234. Rpt Graham.

McElrath. "FN: Early Posthumous Responses." *ALR*, 12 (Spring 1979), 1-76.

Miller, Edwin Haviland. "FN's *The Pit* as Autobiography." *HSL*, 17, no 3 (1985), 18-32.

Mitchell, Mark L & Joseph R McElrath, Jr. "FN's *The Pit*: Musical Elements as Biographical Evidence." *PLL*, 23 (Spring 1987), 161-174.

Peixotto, Ernest. "Romanticist Under the Skin." *SatRL*, 9 (27 May 1933), 613-615.

Richards, Grant. *Author Hunting by an Old Literary Sports Man* (NY: Coward-McCann, 1934), 169-174, 188.

Sanchez, Nellie Van de Grift. *The Life of Mrs. Robert Louis Stevenson* (NY: Scribners, 1920), 275-278.

Ziff, Larzer. "Life Without Style: FN." *The American 1890s: Life and Times of a Lost Generation* (NY: Viking, 1966), 250-274, passim.

CRITICAL STUDIES

Books

Ahnebrink, Lars. *The Influence of Émile Zola on FN*. Uppsala, Sweden: Lundequistska Bokhandeln / Cambridge: Harvard U P, 1947.

Crisler, Jesse S. "A Critical and Textual Study of FN's *McTeague*." Dissertation: U South Carolina, 1973.

Dillingham, William B. *FN: Instinct and Art*. Lincoln: U Nebraska P, 1969.

French, Warren. *FN*. NY: Twayne, 1962.

Frohock, W M. *FN*. Minneapolis: U Minnesota P, 1968.

Graham, Don. *The Fiction of FN: The Aesthetic Context*. Columbia: U Missouri P, 1978.

Hill, John S. "FN's Heroines." Dissertation: U Wisconsin, Madison, 1960.

Hochman, Barbara. *The Art of FN, Storyteller*. Columbia: U Missouri P, 1988.

Kaplan, Charles. "FN and the Craft of Fiction." Dissertation: Northwestern U, 1952.

Lundy, Robert Donald. "The Making of *McTeague* and *The Octopus*." Dissertation: U California, Berkeley, 1956.

Marchand, Ernest. *FN: A Study*. Stanford, Calif: Stanford U P, 1942.

Pizer, Donald. *The Novels of FN*. Bloomington: Indiana U P, 1966.

Collections of Essays

Davison, Richard Allan, ed. *The Merrill Studies in The Octopus*. Columbus, Ohio: Merrill, 1969.

Graham, Don, ed. *Critical Essays on FN*. Boston: Hall, 1980.

McElrath Joseph R, Jr & Katherine S Knight, eds. *FN: The Critical Reception*. NY: Burt Franklin, 1981.

Special Journals

Frank Norris Studies (semiannually, 1986-   ). Includes checklists.

Book Sections & Articles

Ahnebrink, Lars. *The Beginnings of Naturalism in American Fiction* (Uppsala, Sweden: U Uppsala / Cambridge: Harvard U P, 1950), passim.

Berthoff, Warner. "FN, Stephen Crane." *The Ferment of Realism: American Literature, 1884-1919* (NY: Free P, 1965), 223-235.

Budd, Louis J. "Objectivity and Low Seriousness in American Naturalism." *Prospects*, 1 (1975), 41-61.

Chase, Richard "N and Naturalism." *The American Novel and Its Tradition* (Garden City, NY: Doubleday, 1957), 185-204. Excerpted Davison; *McTeague: An Authoritative Text, Backgrounds and Sources, Criticism*.

Conder, John J. "N and Hard Determinism: *McTeague*." *Naturalism in American Fiction* (Lexington: U P Kentucky, 1984), 69-85.

Cooperman, Stanley. "FN and the Werewolf of Guilt." *MLQ*, 20 (Sep 1959), 252-258.

Crow, Charles L. "The Real Vanamee and His Influence on FN's *The Octopus*." *WAL*, 9 (Summer 1974), 131-139.

Davison, Richard Allan. "FN's *The Octopus*: Some Observations on Vanamee, Shelgrim and St. Paul." *Literature and Ideas in America*, ed Robert Falk (Athens: Ohio U P, 1975), 182-203. Rpt Graham.

Dawson, Hugh J. "McTeague as Ethnic Stereotype." *ALR*, 20 (Fall 1987), 34-44.

Dillingham, William B. "The Old Folks of *McTeague*." *NCF*, 16 (Sep 1961), 169-173. Rpt *McTeague: An Authoritative Text, Backgrounds and Sources, Criticism*.

Dover, Linda A. "FN's *A Man's Woman*: The Textual Changes." *RALS*, 13 (Autumn 1983), 165-183.

Folsom, James K. "Social Darwinism or Social Protest? The 'Philosophy' of *The Octopus*." *MFS*, 8 (Winter 1962-1963), 393-400. Rpt Davison.

Folsom. "The Wheat and the Locomotive: N and Naturalistic Esthetics." *American Literary Naturalism: A Reassessment*, ed Yoshinobu Hakutani & Lewis Fried (Heidelberg: Carl Winter, 1975), 57-74.

French, Warren. "Introduction." *Vandover and the Brute* (Lincoln: U Nebraska P, 1978), vii-xvi.

Giles, James R. "Beneficial Atavism in FN and Jack London." *WAL*, 4 (Spring 1969), 15-27.

Hill, John S. "Trina Sieppe: First Lady of American Literary Naturalism." *UKCR*, 29 (Autumn 1962), 77-80.

Howard, June. *Form and History in American Literary Naturalism* (Chapel Hill: U North Carolina P, 1985), passim.

Johnson, George W. "The Frontier Behind FN's *McTeague*." *HLQ*, 26 (Nov 1962), 91-104.

Kaplan, Charles. "N's Use of Sources in *The Pit*." *AL*, 25 (Mar 1953), 75-84.

Kaplan. "Fact into Fiction in *McTeague*." *HLB*, 8 (Autumn 1954), 381-385. Rpt *McTeague: An Authoritative Text, Backgrounds and Sources, Criticism*.

Kwiat, Joseph J. "The Newspaper Experience: Crane, N, Drieser." *NCF*, 8 (Sep 1953), 99-117.

Love, Glen A. "FN's Western Metropolitans." *WAL*, 11 (Spring 1976), 3-22. Rpt Graham.

Martin, Jay. *Harvests of Change: American Literature, 1865-1914* (Englewood Cliffs, NJ: Prentice-Hall, 1967), passim.

Martin, Ronald E. "FN: Naive Omniscience and the Universe of Force." *American Literature and the Universe of Force* (Durham, NC: Duke U P, 1981), 146-183.

McElrath, Joseph R, Jr. "The Comedy of FN's *McTeague*." *SAH*, 2 (Oct 1975), 88-95.

McElrath. "FN's *Vandover and the Brute*: Narrative Technique and the Socio-Critical Viewpoint." *SAF*, 4 (Spring 1976), 27-43. Rpt Graham.

McElrath. "The Erratic Design of FN's *Moran of the Lady Letty*." *ALR*, 10 (Spring 1977), 114-124.

McElrath. "FN's *The Octopus*: The Christian Ethic as Pragmatic Response." Graham, 138-152.

McKee, Irving. "Notable Memorials to Mussel Slough." *PacHR*, 17 (Feb 1948), 19-27.

Michaels, Walter Benn. *The Gold Standard and the Logic of Naturalism* (Berkeley: U California P, 1987), passim.

Miller, Edwin Haviland. "The Art of FN in *McTeague*." *MarkhamR*, 8 (Summer 1979), 61-66.

Miller. "The Art of FN in *Vandover and the Brute*." *MarkhamR*, 10 (Summer 1981), 56-63.

Mitchell, Lee Clark. " 'Little Pictures on the Lacquered Surface': The Determining Vocabularies of N's *Vandover and the Brute*." *PLL*, 22 (Fall 1986), 386-405.

Moorty, S S. "FN and Scott Fitzgerald: Two Sides of the Same Coin." *PUASAL*, 53, part 2 (1976), 29-34.

Morace, Robert A. "FN and the Magazine Experience." *MarkhamR*, 9 (Summer 1980), 64-67.

Munn, Debra D. "The Revision of FN's *Blix*." *RALS*, 10 (Spring 1980), 47-55.

Newman, Robert D. "Supernatural Naturalism: N's Spiritualism in *The Octopus*." *FNS*, no 4 (Autumn 1987), 1-4.

Pizer, Donald. "FN and the Frontier as Popular Idea in America." *Amst*, 23 (1978), 230-239.

Pizer. "Late Nineteenth-Century American Naturalism," "FN's Definition of Naturalism," "The Significance of FN's Literary Criticism," "Synthetic Criticism and FN's *The Octopus*." *Realism and Naturalism in Nineteenth-Century American Literature* (Carbondale: Southern Illinois U P, rev 1984), 9-40, 59-69, 107-120, 154-165. "Late Nineteenth-Century American Naturalism" rpt *McTeague: An Authoritative Text, Backgrounds and Sources, Criticism*.

Poncet, André. "Anti-Racist Strategies in FN's Fiction." *Les Americains et Les Autres*, ed Serge Ricard (Aix en Provence: Publications de l'Université de Provence, 1982), 55-63.

Reninger, H Willard. "N Explains *The Octopus*: A Correlation of His Theory and Practice." *AL*, 12 (May 1940), 218-227. Rpt Davison.

Schneider, Robert W. "FN: The Naturalist as Victorian." *MASJ*, 3 (Spring 1962), 13-27.

Shroeder, John. "The Shakespearean Plots of *McTeague*." *ALR*, 14 (Autumn 1981), 289-296.

Spangler, George M. "The Structure of *McTeague*." *ES*, 59 (Feb 1978), 48-56. Rpt Graham.

Vance, William L. "Romance in *The Octopus*." *Genre*, 3 (Jun 1970), 111-136. Rpt Graham.

Walcutt, Charles C. "FN on Realism and Naturalism." *AL*, 13 (Mar 1941), 61-63.

Walcutt. "FN and the Search for Form." *American Literary Naturalism: A Divided Stream* (Minneapolis: U Minnesota P, 1956), 114-156, passim. Excerpted Davison; Graham; *McTeague: An Authoritative Text, Backgrounds and Sources, Criticism*.

Wilson, Christopher P. *The Labor of Words: Literary Professionalism in the Progressive Era* (Athens: U Georgia P, 1985), passim.

Joseph R. McElrath, Jr.

EDGAR WILSON (BILL) NYE

Shirley, Maine, 25 Aug 1850-Arden, NC, 22 Feb 1896

Edgar Wilson (Bill) Nye achieved his fame as founding editor of the *Laramie Boomerang,* a Wyoming newspaper that earned a national reputation with Nye's humorous columns. Nye produced books of comic essays and sketches and was a public lecturer, emerging as one of the most prominent figures on the lyceum circuit. For two years he joined company with Hoosier poet James Whitcomb Riley, launching the renowned lecture team billed as the "Twins of Genius." His most prestigious position as journalist was as weekly columnist for the *New York World* from 1887 to his death. Nye wrote popular burlesque histories of the United States and England, essays, and two plays for the Broadway stage, all the while producing his weekly columns, lecturing, and serving the *World* as special traveling correspondent. Bill Nye's writings were so popular that they were frequently pirated, and after Nye's death his publishers released new and reprinted editions of his works.

BIBLIOGRAPHY

Bibliography of American Literature, comp Jacob Blanck. New Haven: Yale U P, 1955-1991. Primary.

BOOKS

Bill Nye and Boomerang; or, The Tale of a Meek-Eyed Mule and Some Other Literary Gems. Chicago: Belford, Clarke, 1881. Essays, sketches & stories.

Forty Liars and Other Lies. Chicago & St Louis: Belford, Clarke, 1882. Essays, sketches & stories.

Baled Hay: A Drier Book Than Walt Whitman's "Leaves o' Grass." Chicago & NY: Belford, Clarke, 1884. Essays, sketches & stories.

Boomerang Shots, with others. London & NY: Ward, Lock, 1884. Essays, sketches & stories.

Hits and Skits. London & NY: Ward, Lock, 1884. Essays, sketches & stories.

Bill Nye's Cordwood. Chicago: Rhodes & McClure, 1887. Essays, sketches & stories.

Remarks. Chicago: Davis, 1887. Essays, sketches & stories.

Bill Nye's Chestnuts Old and New: Latest Gathering. Chicago & NY: Belford, Clarke, 1888. Essays, sketches & stories.

An Aristocrat in America: Extracts From the Diary of the Right Honorable Lord William Henry Cavendish-Bentinck-Pelham-Clinton-St. Maur-Beauchamp-DeVere, K.G. NY: Ivers, 1888. Essays, sketches & stories.

Nye and Riley's Railway Guide, with James Whitcomb Riley. Chicago & c: Dearborn, 1888. Repub as *Nye and Riley's Wit and Humor.* NY: Neely, 1896. Repub again as *On the "Shoe-String" Limited.* Chicago: Thompson & Thomas, 1905. Essays, sketches & stories by Nye; poems by Riley. Material by Nye separately repub as *Bill Nye's Grim Jokes.* Chicago: Conkey, nd.

Bill Nye's Thinks Prepared at the Instigation of the Author in Response to a Loud, Piercing and Popular Demand. Chicago & c: Dearborn, 1888. Excerpted in *Sparks From the Pen of Bill Nye.* Chicago & NY: Neely, 1891. Essays, sketches & stories.

An Almanac for 1891 by Bill Nye. NY: Privately printed, 1890. Almanac & miscellany.

Bill Nye's History of the United States. Philadelphia: Lippincott, 1894. Burlesque history.

Bill Nye's History of England From the Druids to the Reign of Henry VIII. Philadelphia: Lippincott, 1896. Burlesque history.

A Guest at the Ludlow and Other Stories. Indianapolis & Kansas City: Bowen-Merrill, 1897. Essays, sketches & stories.

The Funny Fellows Grab-Bag. By Bill Nye and Other Funny Men. NY: Ogilvie, 1903. Anecdotes, essays, sketches & stories.

LETTERS

"Letters of Riley and Bill Nye," ed Edmund H Eitel. *Harper's,* 138 (Mar 1919), 473-484.

Letters of EWN Now in the University of Wyoming Library, ed Nixon Orwin Rush. Laramie: U Wyoming Library, 1950.

OTHER

Laramie [Wyoming] *Boomerang* (1881-1883), ed EWN. Newspaper.

COLLECTIONS

The Humor of "Bill" Nye, ed with intro by John

W Gunn. Girard, Kans: Haldeman-Julius, 1924.

Bill Nye's Western Humor, ed with intro by T A Larson. Lincoln: U Nebraska P, 1968.

The Best of Bill Nye's Humor, ed with intro by Louis Hasley. New Haven, Conn: College & University P, 1972.

MANUSCRIPTS & ARCHIVES

U of Wyoming Library.

BIOGRAPHIES

Book

Nye, Frank Wilson. *Bill Nye: His Own Life Story.* NY: Century, 1926.

Book Sections & Articles

Armstrong, Paul. "History of the Post Office at Laramie, Wyoming." *AnWy,* 11 (Jan 1939), 52-60.

Burrage, Frank Sumner. "Bill Nye (1850-1896)." *AnWy,* 18 (Jan 1946), 79-87.

Chaplin, W E. "Bill Nye in Laramie." *Second Biennial Report, State Historian of Wyoming* (Sheridan, Wyo: Mills, 1921-1923), 142-158.

Chaplin. "Bill Nye." *Frontier,* 11 (Mar 1931), 223-226.

Chaplin. "Some Wyoming Editors I Have Known." *AnWy,* 18 (Jan 1946), 79-87.

Davidson, Levette J. " 'Bill' Nye and the Denver Tribune." *ColMag,* 4 (Jan 1927), 13-18.

Gibson, O N. "Bill Nye." *AnWy,* 3 (Jul 1925), 95-104.

Larson, T A. "Laramie's Bill Nye." *The Denver West-1952 Brand Book* (Denver: Westerners, 1953), 34-56.

Mead, Leon. "Eugene Field and Bill Nye: A Reminiscence and an Original Manuscript." *Bookman,* 9 (Apr 1899), 135-136.

Phelps, William Lyon, ed. *Letters of James Whitcomb Riley* (Indianapolis: Bobbs-Merrill, 1930), passim.

Revell, Peter. *James Whitcomb Riley* (NY: Twayne, 1970), passim.

Sprague, John Francis. "EWN." *Collections of the Piscataquis County Historical Society,* Vol 1 (Dover, Maine: Observer, 1910), 147-153.

Visscher, William Lightfoot. "EWN, Known as 'Bill.' " *Ten Wise Men and Some More* (Chicago: Atwell, 1909), 87-107.

Wilder, Marshall P. "Bill Nye." *The Sunny Side of the Street* (NY: Funk & Wagnalls, 1905), 321-329.

CRITICAL STUDIES

Books

Blair, Walter. "The Background of Bill Nye in American Humor." Dissertation: U Chicago, 1931.

Kesterson, David B. *Bill Nye: The Western Writings.* Boise, Idaho: Boise State U, 1976.

Kesterson. *Bill Nye.* Boston: Twayne, 1981.

Book Sections & Articles

Blair, Walter. "Burlesques in Nineteenth-Century American Humor." *AL,* 2 (Nov 1930), 236-247.

Blair. "The Popularity of Nineteenth-Century American Humorists." *AL,* 3 (May 1931), 175-194.

Blair. *Native American Humor, 1800-1900* (NY: American Book, 1937), passim.

Blair. *Horse Sense in American Humor* (Chicago: U Chicago P, 1942), 182-186.

Clarke, Mabell Shippie. "EWN." *Writer,* 9 (Mar 1896), 34-35.

Dickey, Marcus. "The Unique Combination." *The Maturity of James Whitcomb Riley* (Indianapolis: Bobbs-Merrill, 1922), 234-256.

Eaton, G D. "When Bill Nye's Humor Was Funny." *LDIBR,* 4 (Nov 1926), 769, 779.

Ford, Robert. "Bill Nye." *American Humourists* (London: Gardner, 1897), 226-238.

Hancock, Albert E. "Bill Nye and His Work," in "Bill Nye—The Inimitable: His Work and His Personality." *Booklover,* 1 (Jun 1903), 591-605.

Hollis, C Carroll. "Rural Humor of the Late Nineteenth Century." *The Comic Imagination in American Literature,* ed Louis D Rubin, Jr (New Brunswick, NJ: Rutgers U P, 1973), 165-177.

Kesterson, David B. "The Literary Comedians and the Language of Humor." *StAH,* 1 (Jun 1982), 44-51.

Kesterson. "Those *Literary* Comedians." *Critical Essays on American Humor,* ed William Bedford Clark & W Craig Turner (Boston: Hall, 1984), 167-183.

Kesterson. "The Literary Comedians: A Review of Modern Scholarship." *Amst,* 30 (1985), 167-175.

Kesterson & John L Idol, Jr. "Wealth in Their Midst: Bill Nye and Thomas Wolfe on the Asheville Vanderbilts." *TWR,* 7 (Fall 1983), 27-35.

Landon, Melville D. "Bill Nye." *Kings of the Platform and Pulpit* (Chicago: Werner, 1895), 306-330.

Lippincott, J B. "Bill Nye as Viewed by His Publisher," in "Bill Nye—The Inimitable: His Work and His Personality." *Booklover,* 1 (Jun 1903), 605.

McDougall, Walt. "Bill Nye as Seen by Walt McDougall," in "Bill Nye—The Inimitable:

His Work and His Personality." *Booklover*, 1 (Jun 1903), 604-605.

McDougall. "Pictures in the Papers." *AMercury*, 6 (Sep 1925), 67-73.

Pond, J B. *Eccentricities of Genius* (NY: Dillingham, 1900), 237-259.

Searight, Frank Thompson, ed. *The American Press*

Humorists' Book ("Bill" Nye Monument Edition) (Los Angeles: Searight, 1907), 1-48.

Sloane, David E E. *Mark Twain as a Literary Comedian* (Baton Rouge: Louisiana State U P, 1979), passim.

David B. Kesterson

THOMAS NELSON PAGE

Hanover County, Va, 23 Apr 1853-Hanover County, Va, 1 Nov 1922

Thomas Nelson Page's importance to southern literature resulted from his articulation of the myth of the South as a prelapsarian Eden. Page's plantation settings and characters embodied the postbellum nostalgia for the antebellum South; his stereotypes of the belle, the gentleman, and black southern rustics entered popular culture. His work was widely read and praised by his contemporaries who regarded him as a local colorist with an ear for dialect and an eye for customs. The recognition during the twentieth-century Southern Renascence of the flaws in the South's Edenic image caused Page's fiction to be regarded as unrealistic and evasive in its treatment of the race question in particular and plantation life in general.

BIBLIOGRAPHY

Bibliography of American Literature, comp Jacob Blanck. New Haven: Yale U P, 1955-1991. Primary.

Longest, George C. *Three Virginia Writers: Mary Johnston, TNP, and Amélie Rives Troubetzkoy: A Reference Guide*. Boston: Hall, 1978. Secondary.

BOOKS

In Ole Virginia; or, Marse Chan and Other Stories. NY: Scribners, 1887.

Befo' de War: Echoes in Negro Dialect, with A C Gordon. NY: Scribners, 1888. Stories.

Two Little Confederates. NY: Scribners, 1888. Children's novella.

On Newfound River. NY: Scribners, 1891. Augmented ed, 1906. Novella.

Elsket and Other Stories. NY: Scribners, 1891.

Among the Camps; or, Young People's Stories of the War. NY: Scribners, 1891.

The Old South: Essays Social and Political. NY: Scribners, 1892.

Pastime Stories. NY: Harper, 1894.

The Burial of the Guns. NY: Scribners, 1894. Stories.

The Old Gentleman of the Black Stock. NY: Scribners, 1897. Novella.

Two Prisoners. NY: Russell, 1898. Rev ed, 1903. Novella.

Red Rock: A Chronicle of the Reconstruction. NY: Scribners, 1898. Novel.

Santa Claus's Partner. NY: Scribners, 1899. Children's stories.

Gordon Keith. NY: Scribners, 1903. Novel.

Bred in the Bone. NY: Scribners, 1904. Stories.

The Negro: The Southerner's Problem. NY: Scribners, 1904. Essays.

The Coast of Bohemia. NY: Scribners, 1906. Poems.

Under the Crust. NY: Scribners, 1907. Stories.

The Old Dominion: Her Making and Her Manners. NY: Scribners, 1908. Essay.

Tommy Trot's Visit to Santa Claus. NY: Scribners, 1908. Children's stories.
Robert E. Lee, the Southerner. NY: Scribners, 1908. Biography.
John Marvel, Assistant. NY: Scribners, 1909. Novel.
Robert E. Lee, Man and Soldier. NY: Scribners, 1911. Biography.
The Land of the Spirit. NY: Scribners, 1913. Stories.
Italy and the World War. NY: Scribners, 1920. History.
Dante and His Influence: Studies. NY: Scribners, 1922. Essays.
Washington and Its Romance. NY: Doubleday, Page, 1923. History.
The Red Riders. NY: Scribners, 1924. Novel.

EDITION

The Novels, Stories, Sketches, and Poems of TNP, Plantation Edition, 18 vols. NY: Scribners, 1906-1912.

MANUSCRIPTS & ARCHIVES

The major collections are at Duke U Library & the C of William & Mary Library.

BIOGRAPHY

Book
Page, Rosewell. *TNP: A Memoir of a Virginia Gentleman.* NY: Scribners, 1923.

CRITICAL STUDIES

Books
Gross, Theodore L. *TNP.* NY: Twayne, 1967.

Holman, Harriet R. "The Literary Career of TNP, 1884-1910." Dissertation: Duke U, 1947.
King, Kimball. "George Washington Cable and TNP: Two Literary Approaches to the New South." Dissertation: U Wisconsin, Madison, 1964.

Book Sections & Articles
Bargainnier, Earl F. "*Red Rock:* A Reappraisal." *SoQ,* 22 (Winter 1984), 44-53.
Flusche, Michael. "TNP: The Quandary of a Literary Gentleman." *VMHB,* 84 (Oct 1976), 464-485.
Hubbell, Jay B. "TNP." *The South in American Literature* (Durham, NC: Duke U P, 1954), 795-804, 952.
King, Kimball. Introduction. *In Ole Virginia* (Chapel Hill: U North Carolina P, 1969), ix-xxxvi.
MacKethan, Lucinda Hardwick. "TNP: The Plantation Arcady." *The Dream of Arcady: Place and Time in Southern Literature* (Baton Rouge: Louisiana State U P, 1980), 36-60.
McCluskey, John. "Americanisms in the Writings of TNP." *AS,* 57 (Spring 1982), 44-47.
Roberson, John R, ed. "Two Virginia Novelists on Women's Suffrage: An Exchange of Letters Between Mary Johnston and TNP." *VMHB,* 64 (Jul 1956), 286-290.
Seidel, Kathryn Lee. "The Southern Eve." *The Southern Belle in the American Novel* (Gainesville: U P Florida / Tampa: U South Florida P, 1985), 119-134.
Wilson, Edmund. *Patriotic Gore: Studies in the Literature of the American Civil War* (NY: Oxford U P, 1962), 604-615.

Kathryn Lee Seidel

DAVID GRAHAM PHILLIPS

Madison, Ind, 31 Oct 1867-New York City, NY, 24 Jan 1911

David Graham Phillips was a popular and controversial novelist of the Progressive Era. H. L. Mencken proclaimed him the "leading American novelist" of his time. A muckraking journalist before he turned to fiction, Phillips published twenty-three novels prior to his death. *Susan Lenox, Her Fall and Rise,* the posthumously published exposé of Cincinnati slum life and New York City political corruption, is considered his major work. As the Progressive Era's zeal for reform faded during and after World War I, so did the appeal of Phillips's writings. Though his fiction and journalism continue to draw scholarly attention, Phillips is today generally regarded as a minor figure in American literary history.

BIBLIOGRAPHIES

Bibliography of American Literature, comp Jacob Blanck. New Haven: Yale U P, 1955-1991. Primary.

Ravitz, Abe C. "DGP (1867-1911)." *ALR,* 1 (Summer 1968), 24-29. Primary & secondary.

Stallings, Frank L, Jr. "DGP (1867-1911): A Critical Bibliography of Secondary Comment." *ALR,* 3 (Winter 1970), 1-35.

BOOKS

The Great God Success: A Novel (as by John Graham). NY: Stokes, 1901.

Her Serene Highness: A Novel. NY & London: Harper, 1902.

A Woman Ventures: A Novel. NY: Stokes, 1902.

Golden Fleece: The American Adventures of a Fortune Hunting Earl. NY: McClure, Phillips, 1903. Novel.

The Master-Rogue: The Confessions of a Croesus. NY: McClure, Phillips, 1903. Novel.

The Cost. Indianapolis: Bobbs-Merrill, 1904. Novel.

The Deluge. Indianapolis: Bobbs-Merrill, 1905. Novel.

The Mother-Light: A Novel (Anon). NY: Appleton, 1905.

The Plum Tree. Indianapolis: Bobbs-Merrill, 1905. Novel.

The Social Secretary. Indianapolis: Bobbs-Merrill, 1905. Novel.

The Reign of Gilt. NY: Pott, 1905. Essays.

The Fortune Hunter. Indianapolis: Bobbs-Merrill, 1906. Novel.

Light-Fingered Gentry. NY: Appleton, 1907. Novel.

The Second Generation. NY: Appleton, 1907. Novel.

Old Wives for New: A Novel. NY: Appleton, 1908.

The Worth of a Woman: A Play in Four Acts, Followed by A Point of Law: A Dramatic Incident. NY: Appleton, 1908.

The Fashionable Adventures of Joshua Craig: A Novel. NY: Appleton, 1909.

The Hungry Heart: A Novel. NY & London: Appleton, 1909.

The Husband's Story: A Novel. NY & London: Appleton, 1910.

White Magic: A Novel. NY & London: Appleton, 1910.

The Grain of Dust: A Novel. NY & London: Appleton, 1911.

The Conflict: A Novel. NY & London: Appleton, 1912.

George Helm. NY & London: Appleton, 1912. Novel.

The Price She Paid: A Novel. NY & London: Appleton, 1912.

Degarmo's Wife and Other Stories. NY & London: Appleton, 1913.

Susan Lenox, Her Fall and Rise, 2 vols. NY & London: Appleton, 1917. Novel.

The Treason of the Senate. NY: Monthly Review, 1953. Articles.

Contemporaries: Portraits in the Progressive Era, ed with intro by Louis Filler. Westport, Conn & London: Greenwood, 1981. Essays.

MANUSCRIPTS & ARCHIVES

Princeton U Library.

BIOGRAPHIES

Books

Filler, Louis. *Voice of the Democracy: A Critical Biography of DGP.* University Park: Pennsylvania State U P, 1978.

Marcosson, Isaac F. *DGP: His Life and Times.* NY: Dodd, Mead, 1932.

CRITICAL STUDIES

Book

Ravitz, Abe C. *DGP*. NY: Twayne, 1966.

Book Sections & Articles

Blotner, Joseph L. "Winston Churchill and DGP: Bosses and Lobbies." *The Political Novel* (Garden City, NY: Doubleday, 1955), 36-37.

Conn, Peter. "Restoration as Reform: DGP." *The Divided Mind* (Cambridge: Cambridge U P, 1983), 49-82.

Filler, Louis. "Hoosier DGP: 'Radical'?—'Conservative'?" *ON*, 7 (Winter 1981-1982), 325-337.

Flower, Benjamin O. "DGP, a Novelist With Democratic Ideals." *Arena*, 31 (Mar 1904), 236-243.

Harris, Frank. "DGP: The Greatest American Novelist." *Latest Contemporary Portraits* (NY: Macaulay, 1927), 17-29.

Hicks, Granville. "DGP: Journalist." *Bookman*, 73 (May 1931), 257-266.

Kazin, Alfred. "Three Pioneer Realists." *SatRL*, 20 (8 Jul 1939), 3-4, 14-15.

Lynn, Kenneth S. "DGP: The Dream Panderer." *The Dream of Success: A Study of the Modern American Imagination* (Boston: Atlantic/Little, Brown, 1955), 121-157.

McGovern, James R. "DGP and the Virility Impulse of Progressives." *NEQ*, 39 (Sep 1966), 334-355.

Mencken, H L. "The Leading American Novelist." *Smart Set*, 33 (Jan 1911), 163-164.

Miller, Gabriel. "The New Woman Gets the Old Treatment." *Screening the Novel: Rediscovered American Fiction in Film* (NY: Ungar, 1980), 19-45.

Milne, Gordon. "In the Vanguard: Churchill and P." *The American Political Novel* (Norman: U Oklahoma P, 1966), 87-103.

Underwood, John Curtis. "DGP and Results." *Literature and Insurgency* (NY: Kennerley, 1914), 179-253.

Wilson, Christopher P. "The Eternal Masculine: DGP." *The Labor of Words: Literary Professionalism in the Progressive Era* (Athens: U Georgia P, 1985), 141-167, 226-228.

Lawrence J. Oliver

ERNEST POOLE

Chicago, Ill, 23 Jan 1880-New York City, NY, 10 Jan 1950

Ernest Poole is best known as an influential socialist writer. His experience as a journalist on the Lower East Side of New York provided him with the proletarian subjects for his best work, *The Voice of the Street, The Harbor,* and *His Family,* the last of which won the first Pulitzer Prize for fiction in 1918. The acclaim for these novels, which portrayed the heroic struggle of the urban poor against nearly impossible odds, was not sustained by his later fiction; but Poole is remembered for his work in the American socialist movement, for his vivid portrayals of the lower-class world of New York, and for his contributions to the public awareness of the social problems of the American city.

BOOKS

The Plague in Its Stronghold: Tuberculosis in the New York Tenement. NY: Charity Organization Society, 1903. Essay.

Child Labor: The Street. NY: Child Labor Committee, 1903. Essay.

The Voice of the Street. NY: Barnes, 1906. Novel.

The Harbor. NY: Macmillan, 1915. Novel.

His Family. NY: Macmillan, 1917. Novel.

The Village: Russian Impressions. NY: Macmillan, 1918. Essays.

"The Dark People": Russia's Crisis. NY: Macmillan, 1918. Nonfiction.

His Second Wife. NY: Macmillan, 1918. Novel.

Blind: A Story of These Times. NY: Macmillan, 1920. Novel.

Beggars' Gold. NY: Macmillan, 1921. Novel.
Millions. NY: Macmillan, 1922. Novel.
Danger. NY: Macmillan, 1923. Novel.
The Avalanche. NY: Macmillan, 1924. Novel.
The Hunter's Moon. NY: Macmillan, 1925. Novel.
The Little Dark Man and Other Russian Sketches. NY: Macmillan, 1925. Stories.
With Eastern Eyes. NY: Macmillan, 1926. Novel.
Silent Storms. NY: Macmillan, 1927. Novel.
The Car of Croesus. NY: Macmillan, 1930. Novel.
The Destroyer. NY: Macmillan, 1931. Novel.
Nurses on Horseback. NY: Macmillan, 1932. Nonfiction.
Great Winds. NY: Macmillan, 1933. Novel.
One of Us. NY: Macmillan, 1934. Novel.
The Bridge: My Own Story. NY: Macmillan, 1940. Autobiography.
Giants Gone: Men Who Made Chicago. NY & London: McGraw-Hill, 1943. Biography.
The Great White Hills of New Hampshire. Garden City, NY: Doubleday, 1946.
The Nancy Flyer: A Stagecoach Epic. NY: Crowell, 1949. Novel.

OTHER

For Russia's Freedom by Katherine Breshkovsky; ed EP. Chicago: Kerr, 1905. Biography.

BIOGRAPHIES

Book Section & Article

"EP." *Bookman,* 41 (Apr 1915), 115-118.
Warfel, Harry R. "EP." *American Novelists of Today* (NY: American Book, 1951), 342-343.

CRITICAL STUDIES

Book

Keefer, Truman Frederick. *EP.* NY: Twayne, 1966.

Book Sections & Articles

Baldwin, Charles C. "EP." *The Men Who Make Our Novels* (NY: Dodd, Mead, rev 1924), 427-432.
Feld, Rose C. "Mr. P Ventures a Glance into the Future." *NYTBR* (3 Feb 1924), 2, 26.
Hart, John E. "Heroism Through Social Awareness: EP's *The Harbor.*" *Crit,* 9, no 3 (1967), 84-94.
Holt, Henry. "The Problem of Poverty: II. By an Aristotelian." *UnpopularR,* 6 (Oct-Dec 1916), 245-263.
Marble, Annie R. "Characterization: EP." *A Study of the Modern Novel: British and American Since 1900* (NY: Appleton, 1928), 328-330.
Mencken, H L. "A Bad Novelist." *Prejudices: First Series* (NY: Knopf, 1919), 145-148.
More, Paul Elmer. "The Problem of Poverty: I. By a Platonist." *UnpopularR,* 6 (Oct-Dec 1916), 231-245.
More. "Economic Ideals." *Shelburne Essays, Eleventh Series* (Boston: Houghton Mifflin, 1921), 235-256.
Quinn, Arthur Hobson. *American Fiction* (NY: Appleton-Century, 1936), 640-643.
Richards, Edwin B. "Introduction." *The Harbor* (NY: Macmillan, 1925), xi-xiii.
Rideout, Walter B. *The Radical Novel in the United States, 1900-1954* (Cambridge: Harvard U P, 1956), passim.
Stidger, William L. "Beggars' Gold: EP." *There Are Sermons in Books* (NY: Doran, 1922), 67-82.
Stuckey, W J. *The Pulitzer Prize Novels* (Norman: U Oklahoma P, 1966), 27-31.

Gary Beason

ELEANOR H. PORTER

Littleton, NH, 19 Dec 1868-Cambridge, Mass, 21 May 1920

Although Eleanor H. Porter had a respectable career as a writer of short stories and novels, she is chiefly remembered as the author of the literary phenomenon *Pollyanna*. This story of the girl who teaches others to be glad was republished many times, inspired theatrical and movie treatments, and spawned an industry of calendars and clubs, as well as giving a new word to the language. The book uses the theme of most of Porter's novels: static or meaningless adult lives transformed by a child. Some of her short stories, many collected and published after her death, are local-color stories, reminiscent of the work of Sarah Orne Jewett and Mary E. Wilkins Freeman. Later books, even the sequel to *Pollyanna*, approached life less simplistically, but Porter is marked as the author of one book, and while most of her works were written for an adult audience, she is classified as a children's author.

BOOKS

Cross Currents. Boston: Wilde, 1907. Novel.
The Turn of the Tide. Boston: Wilde, 1908. Novel.
The Story of Marco. Cincinnati: Jennings & Graham, 1911. Novel.
Miss Billy. Boston: Page, 1911. Novel.
Miss Billy's Decision. Boston: Page, 1912. Novel.
Pollyanna. Boston: Page, 1913. Novel.
The Sunbridge Girls at Six-Star Ranch (as by Eleanor Stuart). Boston: Page, 1913. Children's novel.
Miss Billy Married. Boston: Page, 1914. Novel.
Pollyanna Grows Up. Boston: Page, 1915. Novel.
Just David. Boston & NY: Houghton Mifflin, 1916. Novel.
Six-Star Ranch. Boston: Page, 1916. Children's novel.
The Road to Understanding. Boston & NY: Houghton Mifflin, 1917. Novel.
Oh, Money! Money. Boston & NY: Houghton Mifflin, 1918. Novel.
Dawn. Boston & NY: Houghton Mifflin, 1919; *Keith's Dark Tower.* London: Constable, 1919. Novel.

The Tie That Binds: Tales of Love and Marriage. Boston & NY: Houghton Mifflin, 1919. Stories.
Across the Years. Boston & NY: Houghton Mifflin, 1919. Stories.
The Tangled Threads: Just Stories. Boston & NY: Houghton Mifflin, 1919.
Mary-Marie. Boston & NY: Houghton Mifflin, 1920. Novel.
Sister Sue. Boston & NY: Houghton Mifflin, 1921. Novel.
Money, Love, and Kate, Together With The Story of a Nickel. NY: Doran, 1923. Novel.
Hustler Joe and Other Stories. NY: Doran, 1924.
Little Pardner and Other Stories. NY: Doran, 1926.
Just Mother and Other Stories. NY: Doran, 1927.
The Fortunate Mary, with Florence M Kingsley. Garden City, NY: Doubleday, Doran, 1928. Stories.

CRITICAL STUDIES

Book Sections & Articles
Allentuck, Marcia E. "Old Books: *Pollyana* by EHP." *GaR*, 14 (Winter 1960), 447-449.
Cadogan, Mary & Patricia Craig. *You're a Brick, Angela! A New Look at Girls' Fiction From 1839 to 1975* (London: Gollancz, 1976), 99-101, passim.
Colbron, Grace Isabel. "The Popularity of Pollyanna." *Bookman*, 41 (May 1915), 297-298.
Hart, James D. *The Popular Book* (NY: Oxford, 1950), 212-213.
Mott, Frank Luther. *Golden Multitudes: The Story of Best Sellers in the United States* (NY: Macmillan, 1947), 222, 313, 325.
Nodelman, Perry. "Progressive Utopia; or, How to Grow Up Without Growing Up." *Proceedings of the Sixth Annual Conference of the Children's Literature Association*, ed Priscilla A Ord (Villanova, Pa: Villanova U, 1980), 146-154.
Overton, Grant. "EHP." *The Women Who Make Our Novels* (NY: Dodd, Mead, rev 1928), 108-120.

Shirley Marchalonis

GENE STRATTON PORTER

Wabash City, Ind, 17 Aug 1863-Los Angeles, Calif, 6 Dec 1924

Gene Stratton Porter was the most widely read female fiction writer of her day, with a readership estimated during her lifetime at more than fifty million. Although such books as *Freckles*—works of romantic fiction aimed at young women and heavily tinged with nature lore—insured her popular reputation, Porter saw herself primarily as a naturalist who used her fiction as a vehicle to educate the public in the enjoyment and conservation of nature. Critics largely dismissed her work as "molasses fiction," idealistic and sentimental, and almost no critical study has been devoted to it.

BIBLIOGRAPHY

MacLean, David G. *GSP: A Bibliography and Collector's Guide*. Decatur, Ind: Americana, 1976. Primary & secondary.

BOOKS

The Song of the Cardinal. Indianapolis: Bobbs-Merrill, 1903. Rev ed, Garden City, NY: Doubleday, Page, 1915. Novel.

Freckles. Garden City, NY: Doubleday, Page, 1904. Novel.

At the Foot of the Rainbow. NY: Outing, 1907. Novel.

What I Have Done With Birds. Indianapolis: Bobbs-Merrill, 1907. Nonfiction.

Birds of the Bible. Cincinnati: Jennings & Graham / NY: Eaton & Mains, 1909. Nonfiction.

A Girl of the Limberlost. Garden City, NY: Doubleday, Page, 1909. Novel.

Music of the Wild. Cincinnati: Jennings & Graham / NY: Eaton & Mains, 1910. Nonfiction.

After the Flood. Indianapolis: Bobbs-Merrill, 1911. Stories.

The Harvester. Garden City, NY: Doubleday, Page, 1911. Novel.

Moths of the Limberlost. Garden City, NY: Doubleday, Page, 1912. Nonfiction.

Laddie. Garden City, NY: Doubleday, Page, 1913. Novel.

Birds of the Limberlost Especially Prepared for Katherine Minahan. Garden City, NY: Doubleday, Page, 1914. Nonfiction.

Michael O'Halloran. Garden City, NY: Doubleday, Page, 1915. Novel.

Morning Face. Garden City, NY: Doubleday, Page, 1916. Stories & poetry.

Friends in Feathers. Garden City, NY: Doubleday, Page, 1917. Nonfiction.

A Daughter of the Land. Garden City, NY: Doubleday, Page, 1918. Novel.

Homing With the Birds. Garden City, NY: Doubleday, Page, 1919. Nonfiction.

Her Father's Daughter. Garden City, NY: Doubleday, Page, 1921. Novel.

The Fire Bird. Garden City, NY & Toronto: Doubleday, Page, 1922. Poetry.

Jesus of the Emerald. Garden City, NY: Doubleday, Page, 1923. Poetry.

The White Flag. Garden City, NY: Doubleday, Page, 1923. Novel.

Wings. Garden City, NY: Garden City Publishing, 1923. Nonfiction.

The Keeper of the Bees. Garden City, NY: Doubleday, Page, 1925. Novel.

Tales You Won't Believe. Garden City, NY: Doubleday, Page, 1925. Nonfiction.

Let Us Highly Resolve. Garden City, NY: Doubleday, Page, 1927. Nonfiction.

The Magic Garden. Garden City, NY: Doubleday, Page, 1927. Novel.

BIOGRAPHIES

Books

King, Rollin Patterson. *GSP: A Lovely Light*. Chicago: Adams, 1979.

Meehan, Jeannette Porter. *Lady of the Limberlost: Life and Letters of GSP*. Garden City, NY: Doubleday, Doran, 1928.

Saxton, Eugene Francis. *Lady of the Limberlost: A Little Story of the Life and Works and Ideals of "The Bird Woman."* Garden City, NY: Doubleday, Page, 1915.

Book Section

Bailey, Flossie Enyart. *Pioneer Days in the Wabash Valley With a Review of the Life of GSP* (Logansport, Ind: Hendricks, 1933), 30-59, 74-75, 79-83.

CRITICAL STUDIES

Book
Richards, Bertrand F. *GSP*. Boston: Twayne, 1980.

Book Sections & Articles
Allen, Frederick Lewis. "Best Sellers: 1900-1935."
SatRL, 13 (7 Dec 1935), 3-4, 20, 24, 26.
Cooper, Frederic Taber. "The Popularity of GSP."
Bookman, 41 (Aug 1915), 670-671.
MacMullen, Margaret. "Love's Old Sweetish

Song." *Harper's*, 195 (Oct 1947), 371-380.
Nye, Russel. *The Unembarrassed Muse: The Popular Arts in America* (NY: Dial, 1970), 37-38.
Overton, Grant. "Naturalist vs. Novelist: GSP."
American Nights Entertainment (NY: Appleton/Doran/Doubleday, Page/Scribners, 1923), 270-292.

Mary Beth Butler

WILLIAM SYDNEY PORTER
(O. Henry)

Greensboro, NC, 11 Sep 1862-New York City, NY, 5 Jun 1910

The O. Henry award for the nation's best short stories is an annual reminder of the critical as well as popular esteem that William Sydney Porter (who wrote under the pseudonym O. Henry) enjoyed before World War I. The 300-odd stories that appeared in magazines and the *New York Sunday World* during the first decade of the twentieth century were immediately republished in volumes that have reached tens of millions of readers through countless editions and translations. Porter's critical reputation as "the Yankee Maupassant" and "one of the great masters of modern literature" rapidly deteriorated, however, in the face of postwar skepticism and critical attacks on his intrusive narrators, sentimentality, and trick endings. While Porter's importance to the American short story is universally acknowledged and he is firmly enshrined in popular culture and school anthologies, scholarly interest is found today chiefly among biographers and historians of the American Southwest and New York City, Porter's "Bagdad-by-the-Subway."

BIBLIOGRAPHIES

Bibliography of American Literature, comp Jacob Blanck. New Haven: Yale U P, 1955-1991. Primary.
Clarkson, Paul S. *A Bibliography of WSP (O. Henry)*. Caldwell, Idaho: Caxton, 1938. Primary & secondary.
Harris, Richard C. *WSP (O. Henry): A Reference Guide*. Boston: Hall, 1980. Secondary.

BOOKS

Cabbages and Kings. NY: McClure, Phillips, 1904. Stories reworked as novel.
The Four Million. NY: McClure, Phillips, 1906. Stories.
The Trimmed Lamp and Other Stories of the Four Million. NY: McClure, Phillips, 1907.
Heart of the West. NY: McClure, 1907. Stories.
The Voice of the City: Further Stories of the Four Million. NY: McClure, 1908.
The Gentle Grafter. NY: McClure, 1908. Stories.
Roads of Destiny. NY: Doubleday, Page, 1909. Stories.
Options. NY & London: Harper, 1909. Stories.
Strictly Business: More Stories of the Four Million. NY: Doubleday, Page, 1910. Stories.
Whirligigs. NY: Doubleday, Page, 1910. Stories.
Let Me Feel Your Pulse. NY: Doubleday, Page, 1910. Story.

The Two Women—The One: A Fog in Santone; The Other: A Medley of Moods. Boston: Small, Maynard, 1910. Stories.

Sixes and Sevens. Garden City, NY: Doubleday, Page, 1911. Stories.

Rolling Stones. Garden City, NY: Doubleday, Page, 1912. Stories.

Waifs and Strays. . . . Garden City, NY: Doubleday, Page, 1917. Stories with critical and biographical commentary.

O. Henryana: Seven Odds and Ends. . . . Garden City, NY: Doubleday, Page, 1920. Poetry & stories.

Postscripts, intro by Florence Stratton. NY & London: Harper, 1923. Newspaper articles.

O. Henry Encore. . . , ed Mary Sunlocks Harrell. Dallas: Upshaw, 1936. Stories & illustrations.

LETTERS

Letters to Lithopolis: From O. Henry to Mabel Wagnalls. Garden City, NY & Toronto: Doubleday, Page, 1922.

OTHER

Indian Depredations in Texas by J W Wilbarger; illustrated by WSP (as by T J Owen). Austin, Tex: Owen Engraving, 1889.

EDITIONS & COLLECTION

The Complete Writings of O. Henry, 14 vols. Garden City, NY: Doubleday, Page, 1917.

O. Henry: Biographical Edition, 18 vols. Garden City, NY: Doubleday, Doran, 1929.

The Complete Works of O. Henry, 2 vols; foreword by Harry Hansen. Garden City, NY: Doubleday, 1953.

MANUSCRIPTS & ARCHIVES

The major collections are at the Greensboro Public Library, Greensboro, NC; the Houghton Library, Harvard U; U of Virginia Library; & the Harry Ransom Humanities Research Center, U of Texas, Austin.

BIOGRAPHIES

Books

Arnett, Ethel Stephens. *O. Henry From Polecat Creek.* Greensboro, NC: Piedmont, 1962.

Coleman, Sara Lindsay. *Wind of Destiny.* Garden City, NY: Doubleday, Page, 1916.

Davis, Robert H & Arthur B Maurice. *The Caliph of Bagdad: Being Arabian Nights Flashes of the Life, Letters, and Work of O. Henry.* NY: Appleton, 1931.

Jennings, Al. *Through the Shadows With O. Henry.* NY: Fly, 1921.

Kramer, Dale. *The Heart of O. Henry.* NY: Rinehart, 1954.

Langford, Gerald. *Alias O. Henry: A Biography of WSP.* NY: Macmillan, 1957.

Long, E Hudson. *O. Henry: The Man and His Work.* Philadelphia: U Pennsylvania P, 1949.

Maltby, Frances G. *The Dimity Sweetheart: O. Henry's Own Love Story.* Richmond, Va: Dietz, 1930.

O'Connor, Richard. *O. Henry: The Legendary Life of WSP.* Garden City, NY: Doubleday, 1970.

Smith, C Alphonso. *O. Henry Biography.* Garden City, NY: Doubleday, Page, 1916. Rpt with intro by Warner Berthoff, NY: Chelsea House, 1980.

Williams, William Wash. *The Quiet Lodger of Irving Place.* NY: Dutton, 1936.

Wilson, Lollie Cave. *Hard to Forget: The Young O. Henry.* Los Angeles: Lymanhouse, 1939.

CRITICAL STUDIES

Books

Blansfield, Karen Charmaine. *Cheap Rooms and Restless Hearts: A Study of Formula in the Urban Tales of WSP.* Bowling Green, Ohio: Bowling Green State U Popular P, 1988.

Current-Garcia, Eugene. *O. Henry (WSP).* NY: Twayne, 1965.

Èjxenbaum, B M. *O. Henry and the Theory of the Short Story,* trans I R Titunik. Ann Arbor: U Michigan P, 1968.

Gallegly, Joseph. *From Alamo Plaza to Jack Harris's Saloon: O. Henry and the Southwest He Knew.* The Hague: Mouton, 1970.

Long, E Hudson. *O. Henry: American Regionalist.* Austin, Tex: Steck-Vaughn, 1969.

McQuinn, Trueman E & Jenny Lind Porter. *Time to Write: How WSP Became O. Henry.* Austin, Tex: Eakin, 1986.

Special Journal

Mentor, 11 (Feb 1923). WSP issue.

Book Sections & Articles

Abrams, Fred. "The Pseudonym 'O. Henry': A New Perspective." *SSF,* 15 (Summer 1978), 327-329.

Brooks, Cleanth, Jr & Robert Penn Warren. *Understanding Fiction* (NY: Crofts, 1943), 114-118.

Brooks, Van Wyck. "New York: O. Henry." *The Confident Years, 1885-1915* (NY: Dutton, 1952), 271-281.

Brown, Deming. "O. Henry in Russia." *RusR,* 12 (Oct 1953), 253-258.

Brown. "Jack London and O. Henry." *Soviet Attitudes Toward American Writing* (Princeton: Princeton U P, 1962), 219-238.

Clarkson, Paul S. "A Decomposition of *Cabbages and Kings.*" *AL,* 7 (May 1935), 195-202.

Evans, Walter. " 'A Municipal Report': O. Henry and Postmodernism." *TSL*, 26 (1981), 101-116.

Gates, William B. "O. Henry and Shakspere." *ShakespeareAB*, 19 (Jan 1944), 20-25.

Leacock, Stephen Butler. "The Amazing Genius of O. Henry." *Essays and Literary Studies* (NY: Lane, 1916), 233-266.

Long, E Hudson. "O. Henry as a Regional Artist." *Essays on American Literature in Honor of Jay B. Hubbell*, ed Clarence Gohdes (Durham, NC: Duke U P, 1967), 229-240.

Mais, S P B. *From Shakespeare to O. Henry: Studies in Literature* (London: Richards, 1917), 296-313.

McCreery, David J. "Imitating Life: O. Henry's 'The Shamrock and the Palm.' " *MissQ*, 34 (Spring 1981), 113-121.

McLean, Malcolm D. "O. Henry in Honduras." *ALR*, 1 (Summer 1968), 39-46.

Millstein, Gilbert. "O. Henry's New Yorkers—and Today's." *NYTM* (9 Sep 1962), 36-37, 132, 134-135.

Monteiro, George. "Hemingway, O. Henry, and the Surprise Ending." *PrS*, 47 (Winter 1973-1974), 296-302.

Ostrofsky, Martin B. "O. Henry's Use of Stereotypes in His New York City Stories: An Example of the Utilization of Folklore in Literature." *NYFQ*, 7 (Summer 1981), 41-64.

Pattee, Fred Lewis. "O. Henry and the Handbooks." *The Development of the American Short Story* (NY: Harper, 1923), 357-379.

Pavese, Cesare. "O. Henry; or, The Literary Trick." *American Literature: Essays and Opinions*, trans Edwin Fussell (Berkeley: U California P, 1970), 79-90.

Peck, Harry Thurston. "The American Storyteller XI—'O. Henry.' " *Bookman*, 31 (Apr 1910), 131-137.

Rea, John A. "The Idea for O. Henry's 'Gift of the Magi.' " *SHR*, 7 (Summer 1973), 311-314.

Saroyan, William. "O What a Man Was O. Henry." *KR*, 29 (Nov 1967), 671-675.

Tintner, Adeline R. "O. Henry and Henry James: The Author of the Four Million Views the Author of the Four Hundred." *MarkhamR*, 13 (Spring-Summer 1984), 27-31.

Van Doren, Carl. "O. Henry." *TexasR*, 2 (Jan 1917), 248-259.

Voss, Arthur. "O. Henry." *The American Short Story: A Critical Survey* (Norman: Oklahoma U P, 1973), 121-126.

Luther S. Luedtke

HOWARD PYLE

Wilmington, Del, 5 Mar 1853-Florence, Italy, 9 Nov 1911

Howard Pyle has long been acknowledged as one of America's foremost illustrators. As founder of the Brandywine school of illustration he influenced such notable students as N. C. Wyeth and Maxfield Parrish. Pyle illustrated not only his own books but more than 100 works of other authors. He was an innovator in the integration of text, illustration, and calligraphy, creating a "total book." Much of the critical writing about Pyle has been focused on his art work, but in recent years increased attention has been given to his writings for young people. In his best works Pyle recreated the legends and folk tales of medieval England, combining a romanticism that characterized the literature of his time with a realism of detail.

BIBLIOGRAPHIES

Bibliography of American Literature, comp Jacob Blanck. New Haven: Yale U P, 1955-1991. Primary.

Morse, Willard S & Gertrude Brincklé, comps. *HP: A Record of His Illustrations and Writings*. Wilmington, Del: Wilmington Society of the Fine Arts, 1921. Rpt Detroit: Singing Tree, 1969. Primary.

BOOKS

(This list omits books illustrated by HP but written by others.)

The Merry Adventures of Robin Hood of Great Renown, in Nottinghamshire. NY: Scribners, 1883. Children's stories.

Within the Capes. NY: Scribners, 1885. Novel.

Pepper & Salt; or, Seasoning for Young Folk. NY: Harper, 1886. Folk tales.

The Rose of Paradise. . . . NY: Harper, 1888. Novel.

The Wonder Clock; or, Four & Twenty Marvellous Tales. . ., with verses by Katharine Pyle. NY: Harper, 1888.

Otto of the Silver Hand. NY: Scribners, 1888. Children's novel.

Men of Iron. NY: Harper, 1892. Novel.

A Modern Aladdin; or, The Wonderful Adventure of Oliver Munier, . . . NY: Harper, 1892. Novel.

Twilight Land. NY: Harper, 1895. Folk tales.

The Story of Jack Ballister's Fortunes. . . . NY: Century, 1895. Novel.

The Garden Behind the Moon. NY: Scribners, 1895. Fairy-tale.

The Price of Blood: An Extravaganza of New York Life in 1807. Boston: Badger, 1899. Novel.

Rejected of Men: A Story of To-day. NY & London: Harper, 1903. Novel.

The Story of King Arthur and His Knights. NY: Scribners, 1903. Legends.

The Story of the Champions of the Round Table. NY: Scribners, 1905. Legends.

Stolen Treasure. NY & London: Harper, 1907. Stories.

The Story of Sir Launcelot and His Companions. NY: Scribners, 1907. Legends.

The Ruby of Kishmoor. NY & London: Harper, 1908. Novel.

The Story of the Grail and the Passing of Arthur. NY: Scribners, 1910. Legends.

OTHER

The Buccaneers and Marooners of America by Alexandre Olivier Exquemelin; ed with intro by HP. London: Unwin / NY: Macmillan, 1891.

BIOGRAPHIES

Books

Abbott, Charles D. *HP: A Chronicle*. NY: Harper, 1925.

Nesbitt, Elizabeth. *HP*. NY: Walck, 1966.

Pitz, Henry C. *HP: Writer, Illustrator, Founder of the Brandywine School*. NY: Potter, 1975.

CRITICAL STUDIES

Book

Agosta, Lucien L. *HP*. Boston: Twayne, 1987.

Special Journal

CLAQ, 8 (Summer 1983). HP issue.

Book Sections & Article

Agosta, Lucien L. "HP's Illustrations as Shorthand Icons." *Proceedings of the Thirteenth Annual*

Conference of the Children's Literature Association, ed Susan R Gannon & Ruth Anne Thompson (West Lafayette, Ind: Purdue U, 1988), 88-91.

Lawson, Robert. "HP and His Times." *Illustrators of Children's Books, 1774-1945,* comp Bertha Mahony, Louise Payson Latimer & Beulah Folmsbee (Boston: Horn Book, 1947), 103-122.

May, Jill P. "The Hero's Woods: P's *The Merry Adventures of Robin Hood* and the Female Reader." *CLAQ,* 11 (Winter 1986), 197-200.

May. "Symbolic Journeys Toward Death: George

MacDonald and HP as Fantasists." *Proceedings of the Thirteenth Annual Conference of the Children's Literature Association,* ed Susan R Gannon & Ruth Anne Thompson (West Lafayette, Ind: Purdue U, 1988), 129-134.

May. "HP." *Writers for Children: Critical Studies of Major Authors Since the Seventeenth Century,* ed Jane M Bingham (NY: Scribners, 1988), 447-454.

Mary Evelyn Tielking

EUGENE MANLOVE RHODES

Tecumseh, Nebr, 19 Jan 1869-Pacific Beach, Calif, 27 Jun 1934

Eugene Manlove Rhodes grew up in New Mexico where he ranched and wrangled horses. He published poetry and essays but is best remembered as a fiction writer whose novels and short stories depicted cowboy life in the Southwest. In many of his works of fiction he explored the corruption of the seemingly law-abiding citizen and public official and, conversely, the nobility of the lawbreaker. Rhodes has received a modicum of scholarly attention over the decades. Critics have attacked his episodic and at times digressive plots, his naive romanticism, and his sentimental heroines and one-dimensional villains. Rhodes has been praised for his accurate descriptions of the southwestern landscape, his vivid dialogue, and his depictions of the everyday life of cowboys.

BIBLIOGRAPHIES

Hutchinson, W H. "Check List of EMR's Writing." Hutchinson (1956), 392-407. Primary & secondary.

Starrett, Vincent. "The Published Writings of EMR." Rhodes, 257-260. Primary.

BOOKS

Good Men and True. NY: Holt, 1910. Novel.

Bransford in Arcadia; or, The Little Eohippus. NY: Holt, 1914. Repub as *Bransford of Rainbow Lodge* in *Romances of Navaho Land.* Novel.

The Desire of the Moth. NY: Holt, 1916. Novel.

West Is West. NY: Fly, 1917. Novel.

Stepsons of Light. Boston: Houghton Mifflin, 1921. Novel.

Say Now Shibboleth. Chicago: Bookfellows, 1921. Essays.

Copper Streak Trail. Boston: Houghton Mifflin, 1922. Novel.

Once in the Saddle and *Pasó por Aquí.* Boston: Houghton Mifflin, 1927. Novels.

The Trusty Knaves. Boston: Houghton Mifflin, 1934. Novel.

Beyond the Desert. Boston: Houghton Mifflin, 1934. Novel.

Peñalosa. Santa Fe, N Mex: Rydal, 1934. Essay.

The Proud Sheriff. Boston: Houghton Mifflin, 1935. Novel.

The Little World Waddies. Chico, Calif: Hutchinson, 1946. Stories & poetry.

The Line of Least Resistance, ed with intro by W H Hutchinson. Chico, Calif: Hurst & Yount, 1958. Novel.

COLLECTIONS

Romances of Navaho Land. NY: Grosset & Dunlap, 1920.

The Best Novels and Stories of EMR, ed Frank V
    Dearing. Boston: Houghton Mifflin, 1949.
Sunset Land. NY: Dell, 1955.
*The R Reader: Stories of Virgins, Villains, and Var-
    mints*, ed W H Hutchinson. Norman: U Okla-
    homa P, 1957.

MANUSCRIPTS & ARCHIVES

The major collections are at the Southwest Museum Library, Los Angeles; New Mexico State U
Library; Stanford U Library; Brigham Young U Library; & U of New Mexico Library.

BIOGRAPHIES

Books

Hutchinson, W H. *A Bar Cross Man: The Life and
    Personal Writings of EMR*. Norman: U Okla-
    homa P, 1956.
Hutchinson. *A Bar Cross Liar*. Stillwater, Okla:
    Redlands, 1959.
Rhodes, May Davison. *The Hired Man on Horse-
    back: My Story of EMR*. Boston: Houghton
    Mifflin, 1938.

Articles

Hutchinson, W H. "I Pay for What I Break." *WAL*,
    1 (Summer 1966), 91-96.
Hutchinson. "New Mexico Incident: An Episode in
    the Life of Western Writer EMR." *AWest*, 14
    (Nov-Dec 1977), 4-7, 59-63.

CRITICAL STUDIES

Book

Gaston, Edwin W, Jr. *EMR: Cowboy Chronicler*.
    Austin, Tex: Steck-Vaughn, 1967.

Book Sections & Articles

Busby, Mark. "EMR: Ken Kesey Passed by Here."
    WAL, 15 (Summer 1980), 83-92.
De Voto, Bernard. "The Novelist of the Cattle
    Kingdom." Rhodes, xix-xliv.
Dobie, J Frank. "Gene Rhodes: Cowboy Novelist."
    Atlantic, 183 (Jun 1949), 75-77.
Fife, Jim L. "Two Views of the American West."
    WAL, 1 (Spring 1966), 34-43.
Folsom, James K. "A Dedication to the Memory of
    EMR: 1869-1934." *Ar&W*, 11 (Winter
    1969), 310-314.
Hutchinson, W H. "Virgins, Villains, and Var-
    mints." *The R Reader*, vii-xxvi.
Hutchinson. "The Mythic West of W. H. D.
    Koerner." *AWest*, 4 (May 1967), 54-60.
Hutchinson. "The West of EMR." *Ar&W*, 9 (Au-
    tumn 1967), 211-218.
Powell, Lawrence Clark. "Southwest Classics Re-
    read: From Cattle Kingdom Come."
    Westways, 65 (Apr 1973), 30-35, 85.
Powell. "Pasó por Aquí: EMR." *Southwest Clas-
    sics: The Creative Literature of the Arid
    Lands* (Los Angeles: Ritchie, 1974), 160-174.
Skillman, Richard & Jerry C Hoke. "The Portrait
    of the New Mexican in the Fiction of ER."
    WestR, 6 (Spring 1969), 26-36.
Sonnichsen, C L. *From Hopalong to Hud* (College
    Station: Texas A&M U P, 1978), passim.
Topping, Gary. "The Rise of the Western." *JW*, 19
    (Jan 1980), 29-35.

Gwen L. Nagel

ALICE HEGAN RICE

Shelbyville, Ky, 11 Jan 1870-Louisville, Ky, 10 Feb 1942

Alice Hegan Rice's reputation as a writer of children's fiction was firmly established with the 1901 publication of her first book, *Mrs. Wiggs of the Cabbage Patch*. She followed this tale of a simple and optimistic protagonist with several other novels and stories for children, including *Lovey Mary*, the sequel to *Mrs. Wiggs*. Rice later wrote several novels concerning social problems; *Mr. Opp* was the most critically praised of these works for adults. Although most of her books are out of print, *Mrs. Wiggs of the Cabbage Patch* continues to sell steadily and remains in the canon of enduring children's literature.

BOOKS

Mrs. Wiggs of the Cabbage Patch (as by Alice Caldwell Hegan). NY: Century, 1901. Children's novel.

Lovey Mary. NY: Century, 1902. Children's novel.

Sandy. NY: Century, 1905. Children's novel.

The Christmas Lady. London: Hodder & Stoughton, 1906. Story.

Captain June. NY: Century, 1907. Children's novel.

Mr. Opp. NY: Century, 1909. Novel.

A Romance of Billy-Goat Hill. NY: Century, 1912. Novel.

The Honorable Percival. NY: Century, 1914. Novel.

Calvary Alley. NY: Century, 1917. Novel.

Miss Mink's Soldier and Other Stories. NY: Century, 1918.

Turn About Tales, with Cale Young Rice. NY: Century, 1920. Stories.

Quin. NY: Century, 1921. Novel.

Winners and Losers, with Cale Young Rice. NY & London: Century, 1925. Stories.

The Buffer: A Novel. NY & London: Century, 1929.

On Being "Clinicked" (A Bit of Talk Over the Alley Fence). Denver: Eldridge Entertainment House, 1931. Story.

Mr. Pete & Co. NY: Appleton-Century, 1933. Novel.

The Lark Legacy. NY & London: Appleton-Century, 1935. Novel.

Passionate Follies: Alternate Tales, with Cale Young Rice. NY & London: Appleton-Century, 1936. Stories.

My Pillow Book. NY & London: Appleton-Century, 1937. Stories. Includes excerpts from other authors.

Our Ernie. NY & London: Appleton-Century, 1939. Novel.

The Inky Way. NY & London: Appleton-Century, 1940. Autobiography.

Happiness Road. NY & London: Appleton-Century, 1942. Stories.

MANUSCRIPTS & ARCHIVES

The major collections are at Western Kentucky U Library; U of Kentucky, Lexington, Library; & the Houghton Library, Harvard U.

BIOGRAPHIES

Book

Rice, Cale Young. *Bridging the Years.* NY & London: Appleton-Century, 1939.

Articles

Dix, William Frederick. "Alice Caldwell Hegan." *Outlook,* 72 (6 Dec 1902), 802-804.

Ford, Mary K. "AHR's *Mr. Opp.*" *Bookman,* 29 (Jun 1909), 412-413.

Rice, Laban Lacy. "AHR—Home Maker." *FilsonCHQ,* 28, no 3 (1954), 233-238.

CRITICAL STUDIES

Article

Roach, Abby Meguire. "The Authors Club of Louisville." *FilsonCHQ,* 31, no 1 (1957), 28-37.

Thomas L. Wilmeth

MARY ROBERTS RINEHART

Allegheny, Pa, 12 Aug 1876-New York City, NY, 22 Sep 1958

After early financial success with a play, *The Bat,* Mary Roberts Rinehart became a public figure and remained popular until her death. Her writings include mysteries, romances, comedies, and nonfiction pieces of travel and autobiography. One of her enduring characters, Letitia Carberry, better known as "Tish," appeared in many humorous stories in *The Saturday Evening Post* beginning in 1910. Rinehart's mysteries usually feature unmarried, wealthy, well-educated heroines in contemporary, urban settings. Her mystery novels employ romantic subplots so that ultimately the villain is exposed and true love is expedited. Rinehart's mysteries remain popular today, but her comedies and serious novels are often marked by sentimental treatment of women's issues.

BIBLIOGRAPHY

"MRR: A Chronological Bibliography." Cohn (1980), 267-287. Primary.

BOOKS

The Circular Staircase. Indianapolis: Bobbs-Merrill, 1908. Novel.

The Man in Lower Ten. Indianapolis: Bobbs-Merrill, 1909. Novel.

When a Man Marries. Indianapolis: Bobbs-Merrill, 1909. Novel.

The Window at the White Cat. Indianapolis: Bobbs-Merrill, 1910. Novel.

The Amazing Adventures of Letitia Carberry. Indianapolis: Bobbs-Merrill, 1911. Novel.

Where There's a Will. Indianapolis: Bobbs-Merrill, 1912. Novel.

The Case of Jennie Brice. Indianapolis: Bobbs-Merrill, 1913. Novel.

The After House: A Story of Love, Mystery and a Private Yacht. Boston: Houghton Mifflin, 1914. Novel.

The Street of Seven Stars. Boston & NY: Houghton Mifflin, 1914. Novel.

K. Boston & NY: Houghton Mifflin, 1915. Novel.

Kings, Queens and Pawns: An American Woman at the Front. NY: Doran, 1915. Autobiography.

Tish. Boston & NY: Houghton Mifflin, 1916. Stories.

Through Glacier Park: Seeing America First With Howard Eaton. Boston & NY: Houghton Mifflin, 1916. Travel.

Bab: A Sub-Deb. NY: Doran, 1917. Novel.

Long Live the King! Boston & NY: Houghton Mifflin, 1917. Novel.

The Altar of Freedom. Boston: Houghton Mifflin, 1917. Essay.

The Amazing Interlude. NY: Doran, 1918. Novel.

Twenty-Three and a Half Hours' Leave. NY: Doran, 1918. Novella.

Tenting To-night: A Chronicle of Sport and Adventure in Glacier Park and the Cascade Mountains. Boston & NY: Houghton Mifflin, 1918. Travel.

Dangerous Days. NY: Doran, 1919. Novel.

Love Stories. NY: Doran, 1919. Stories.

Affinities and Other Stories. NY: Doran, 1920.

"Isn't That Just Like a Man!" bound with *"Oh! Well! You Know How Women Are!"* by Irvin S Cobb. NY: Doran / London: Hodder & Stoughton, 1920. Essay.

A Poor Wise Man. NY: Doran, 1920. Novel.

The Truce of God. NY: Doran, 1920. Novel.

The Breaking Point. NY: Doran, 1921. Novel.

More Tish. NY: Doran, 1921. Stories.

Sight Unseen and The Confession. NY: Doran, 1921. Novellas.

The Out Trail. NY: Doran, 1923. Travel.

Temperamental People. NY: Doran, 1924. Stories.

The Red Lamp. NY: Doran, 1925; *The Mystery Lamp.* London: Hodder & Stoughton, 1925. Novel.

The Bat. NY: Doran, 1926. Novel.

Nomad's Land. NY: Doran, 1926. Travel.

Tish Plays the Game. NY: Doran, 1926. Stories.

Two Flights Up. NY: Doran, 1926. Novel.

Lost Ecstasy. NY: Doran, 1927. Novel.

The Trumpet Sounds. NY: Doran, 1927. Novel.

The Romantics. NY: Farrar & Rinehart, 1929. Stories.

This Strange Adventure. NY: Doubleday, Doran, 1929. Novel.

The Door. NY: Farrar & Rinehart, 1930. Novel.

Seven Days: A Farce in Three Acts, with Avery Hopwood. NY & c: French, 1931. Play.

My Story. NY: Farrar & Rinehart, 1931. Augmented as *My Story and Seventeen New Years.* NY: Rinehart, 1948. Autobiography.

The Bat: A Play of Mystery in Three Acts, with
  Hopwood. NY & c: French, 1932.
Miss Pinkerton. NY: Farrar & Rinehart, 1932; *The
  Double Alibi.* London: Cassell, 1932. Novel.
The Album. NY: Farrar & Rinehart, 1933. Novel.
The Crime Book. NY: Farrar & Rinehart, 1933.
  Stories.
The State Versus Elinor Norton. NY: Farrar &
  Rinehart, 1933; *The Case of Elinor Norton.*
  London: Cassell, 1934. Novel.
Mr. Cohen Takes a Walk. NY: Farrar & Rinehart,
  1934. Novella.
The Doctor. NY & Toronto: Farrar & Rinehart,
  1936. Novel.
Married People. NY: Farrar & Rinehart, 1937.
  Stories.
Tish Marches On. NY: Farrar & Rinehart, 1937.
  Stories.
The Wall. NY & Toronto: Farrar & Rinehart,
  1938. Novel.
Writing Is Work. Boston: The Writer, 1939. Essay.
The Great Mistake. NY: Farrar & Rinehart, 1940.
  Novel.
Familiar Faces: Stories of People You Know. NY:
  Farrar & Rinehart, 1941. Stories.
The Haunted Lady. NY: Farrar & Rinehart, 1942.
  Novel.
Alibi for Isabel and Other Stories. NY: Farrar &
  Rinehart, 1944. *Alibi for Isabel* separately
  published, NY: Dell, 1951.
The Yellow Room. NY: Farrar & Rinehart, 1945.
  Novel.
A Light in the Window. NY: Rinehart, 1948.
  Novel.
*Episode of the Wandering Knife: Three Mystery
  Tales.* NY: Rinehart, 1950; *The Wandering
  Knife.* London: Cassell, 1951. Novellas.
The Swimming Pool. NY: Rinehart, 1952; *The
  Pool.* London: Cassell, 1952. Novel.
The Frightened Wife and Other Murder Stories.
  NY: Rinehart, 1953.

COLLECTIONS

MRR's Mystery Book. NY: Farrar & Rinehart,
  1930.
MRR's Romance Book. NY: Farrar & Rinehart,
  1931.
The Book of Tish. NY: Farrar & Rinehart, 1931.
The Best of Tish. NY: Rinehart, 1955.
The MRR Crime Book. NY: Rinehart, 1957.

MANUSCRIPTS & ARCHIVES

U of Pittsburgh Library.

BIOGRAPHIES

Books
Cohn, Jan. *Improbable Fiction: The Life of MRR.*
  Pittsburgh: U Pittsburgh P, 1980.
Disney, Dorothy Cameron & Milton MacKaye.
  MRR. NY: Rinehart, 1948.
Overton, Grant. *The Woman Behind the Door:
  MRR.* NY: Farrar & Rinehart, 1930.

Book Sections
Doran, George Henry. "MRR." *Chronicles of Bar-
  abbas* (NY: Harcourt, Brace, 1935), 187-194.
Overton, Grant. "MRR." *The Women Who Make
  Our Novels* (NY: Moffat, Yard, 1918), 54-67.
Overton. "The Vitality of MRR." *When Winter
  Comes to Main Street* (NY: Doran, 1922),
  102-117.

CRITICAL STUDIES

Book Sections & Articles
Cohn, Jan. "The Romances of MRR: Some Prob-
  lems in the Study of Popular Culture." *JPC,*
  11, no 3 (1977), 581-590.
Cohn. "MRR." *10 Women of Mystery,* ed Earl F
  Bargainnier (Bowling Green, Ohio: Bowling
  Green State U Popular P, 1981), 183-220.
Haycraft, Howard. *Murder for Pleasure: The Life
  and Times of the Detective Story* (NY:
  Appleton-Century, 1941), 87-91.
Hoffman, Arnold R. "Social History and the Crime
  Fiction of MRR." *New Dimensions in Popu-
  lar Culture,* ed Russel B Nye (Bowling Green,
  Ohio: Bowling Green U Popular P, 1972),
  153-171.
Maio, Kathleen L. "Had-I-But-Known: The Mar-
  riage of Gothic Terror and Detection." *The
  Female Gothic,* ed Julian E Fleenor (Montreal:
  Eden, 1983), 82-90.
Symons, Julian. *Mortal Consequences: A History
  From the Detective Story to the Crime Novel*
  (NY: Harper & Row, 1972), 96-99.
Walker, Nancy. "Susan and Tish: Women's Humor
  at the Turn of the Century." *TCW,* 2 (Winter
  1985), 50-54.

Nancy W. Shankle

ELIZABETH MADOX ROBERTS

Perryville, Ky, 30 Oct 1881-Orlando, Fla, 13 Mar 1941

Elizabeth Madox Roberts was known both as a poet who captured a child's sensibility and as a novelist of rural Kentucky. Her first novel, *The Time of Man*, is about a woman's discovery of herself and an existence in harmony with nature; *The Great Meadow*, her other celebrated novel, traces the lives and courage of Kentucky pioneers. Influenced by the theories of the eighteenth-century English philosopher George Berkeley, Roberts explored in her fiction the interconnection between the world of the mind and external existence. Praised for her poetic prose style, her symbolism, and her treatment of psychological themes, Roberts achieved some national recognition. After her death her works continued to receive attention from academics, and she was frequently included as one of the writers of the Southern Renascence.

BIBLIOGRAPHIES

First Printings of American Authors, Vol 2 (Detroit: Bruccoli Clark/Gale, 1978), 317-319. Primary.
"Selected Bibliography." McDowell, 169-172. Primary & secondary.

BOOKS

In the Great Steep's Garden. Colorado Springs: Gowdy-Simmons, 1915. Poetry.
Under the Tree. NY: Huebsch, 1922. Augmented ed, NY: Viking, 1930. Poetry.
The Time of Man. NY: Viking, 1926. Novel.
My Heart and My Flesh. NY: Viking, 1927. Novel.
Jingling in the Wind. NY: Viking, 1928. Novel.
The Great Meadow. NY: Viking, 1930. Novel.
A Buried Treasure. NY: Viking, 1931. Novel.
The Haunted Mirror. NY: Viking, 1932. Stories.
He Sent Forth a Raven. NY: Viking, 1935. Novel.
Black Is My Truelove's Hair. NY: Viking, 1938. Novel.
Song in the Meadow. NY: Viking, 1940. Poetry.
Not by Strange Gods. NY: Viking, 1941. Stories.

MANUSCRIPTS & ARCHIVES

The Library of Congress.

CRITICAL STUDIES

Books
Campbell, Harry Modean & Ruel E Foster. *EMR: American Novelist*. Norman: U Oklahoma P, 1956.
McDowell, Frederick P W. *EMR*. NY: Twayne, 1963.
Rovit, Earl H. *Herald to Chaos: The Novels of EMR*. Lexington: U Kentucky P, 1960.
Spears, Woodridge. "EMR: A Biographical and Critical Study." Dissertation: U Kentucky, 1953.

Collection of Essays
Adams, J Donald et al. *EMR: An Appraisal*. NY: Viking, 1938.

Special Journal
SoR, 20 (Oct 1984). EMR issue.

Book Sections & Articles
Adams, J Donald. "EMR." *VQR*, 12 (Jan 1936), 80-90.
Auchincloss, Louis. "EMR." *Pioneers & Caretakers: A Study of 9 American Women Novelists* (Minneapolis: U Minnesota P, 1965), 123-135.
Buchan, Alexander M. "EMR." *SWR*, 25 (Jul 1940), 463-481.
Davidson, Donald. "Analysis of EMR's *A Buried Treasure*." *Creative Reading*, 6 (Dec 1931), 1235-1249.
Dekker, George. *The American Historical Romance* (Cambridge: Cambridge U P, 1987), passim.
Foster, Ruel E. "An Undiscovered Source for EMR's 'On the Mountainside.' " *WVUPP*, 15 (Jun 1966), 57-61.
Hall, Wade. "Place in the Short Fiction of EMR." *KRev*, 6 (Fall-Winter 1986), 3-16.
Janney, F Lamar. "EMR." *SR*, 45 (Oct-Dec 1937), 388-410.
Kramer, Victor A. "Through Language to Self: Ellen's Journey in *The Time of Man*." *SoR*, 20 (Oct 1984), 774-784.
Lewis, Janet. "Letters From the Little Country: The Summers of 1919 and 1920." *SoR*, 20 (Oct 1984), 829-835.
McBride, Anne K. "The Poetry of Space in EMR's

The Time of Man." *SLJ*, 18 (Fall 1985), 61-72.

Niles, Mary. "Social Development in the Poetry of EMR." *MarkhamR*, 2 (Sep 1969), 16-20.

Rouse, H Blair. "Time and Place in Southern Fiction." *Southern Renascence: The Literature of the Modern South*, ed Louis D Rubin, Jr & Robert D Jacobs (Baltimore, Md: Johns Hopkins P, 1953), 126-150.

Rovit, Earl H. "Recurrent Symbols in the Novels of EMR." *BUSE*, 2 (Spring 1956), 36-54.

Seltzer, Sandra. "Some Similarities Between Three Heroines: Tess d'Urbervilles, Ellen Chesser, and Kristin Lavransdatter." *KFR*, 24 (Jul-Dec 1978), 89-102.

Simpson, Lewis P. "The Sexuality of History." *SoR*, 20 (Oct 1984), 785-802.

Slavick, William H. "Taken With a Long-Handled Spoon: The R Papers and Letters." *SoR*, 20 (Oct 1984), 752-773.

Smith, Jo Reinhard. "New Troy in the Bluegrass:

Vergilian Metaphor and *The Great Meadow.*" *MissQ*, 22 (Winter 1968-1969), 39-46.

Tate, Linda. "Against the Chaos of the World: Language and Consciousness in EMR's *The Time of Man.*" *MissQ*, 40 (Spring 1987), 95-111.

Tyree, Wade. "Time's Own River: The Three Major Novels of EMR." *MQR*, 16 (Winter 1977), 33-46.

Van Doren, Mark. "EMR: Her Mind and Style." *EJ*, 21 (Sep 1932), 521-529. Rpt *The Private Reader* by Van Doren (NY: Holt, 1942).

Wagenknecht, Edward. "The Inner Vision: EMR." *Cavalcade of the American Novel* (NY: Holt, 1952), 389-396, 547-548.

Ward, William S. "EMR." *A Literary History of Kentucky* (Knoxville: U Tennessee P, 1988), 150-159.

Warren, Robert Penn. "EMR: Life Is From Within." *SatR*, 46 (2 Mar 1963), 20-21, 38.

Gwen L. Nagel

EDWARD PAYSON ROE

Moodna, NY, 7 Mar 1838-Cornwall, NY, 19 Jul 1888

Writer and minister Edward Payson Roe became one of the most widely read American authors in the 1880s and 1890s. An estimated five million copies of his novels, including the enormously successful *Barriers Burned Away,* were sold in the United States during the last decade of the nineteenth century. Preaching didactic religious values to the middle class, Roe's novels have traditionally been slighted by critics as subliterary, unsophisticated, and rudimentary in style. In his autobiography Roe declared that his "object in writing, as in preaching," was "to do good" and to leave the final verdict to "time and the public."

BIBLIOGRAPHY

Bibliography of American Literature, comp Jacob Blanck. New Haven: Yale U P, 1955-1991. Primary.

BOOKS

Barriers Burned Away. . . . NY: Dodd & Mead, 1872. Rev ed, NY: Dodd, Mead, 1885. Novel.

Play and Profit in My Garden. NY: Dodd & Mead, 1873. Nonfiction.

What Can She Do? . . . NY: Dodd & Mead, 1873. Novel.

Opening a Chestnut Burr. NY: Dodd & Mead, 1874. Rev ed, NY: Dodd, Mead, 1884. Novel.

Gentle Woman Roused. . . . NY: National Temperance Society, 1874. Story.

From Jest to Earnest. NY: Dodd & Mead, 1875. Novel.

A Manual on the Culture of Small Fruits. Newburgh, NY: Journal Printing Establishment, 1876. Nonfiction.

Near to Nature's Heart. NY: Dodd, Mead, 1876. Novel.

A Knight of the Nineteenth Century. NY: Dodd, Mead, 1877. Novel.

A Face Illumined. . . . NY: Dodd, Mead, 1878. Novel.

Success With Small Fruits. . . . NY: Dodd, Mead, 1880. Nonfiction.

A Day of Fate. NY: Dodd, Mead, 1880. Novel.

Without a Home. NY: Dodd, Mead, 1881. Novel.

An Unexpected Result and Other Stories. NY: Dodd, Mead, 1883.

His Sombre Rivals. NY: Dodd, Mead, 1883. Novel.

A Young Girl's Wooing. NY: Dodd, Mead, 1884. Novel.

Nature's Serial Story. NY: Harper, 1885. Novel.

An Original Belle. NY: Dodd, Mead, 1885. Novel.

Driven Back to Eden. NY: Dodd, Mead, 1885. Novel.

He Fell in Love With His Wife. NY: Dodd, Mead, 1886. Novel.

The Hornet's Nest: A Story of Love and War. NY: Dodd, Mead, 1887. Novel.

The Earth Trembled. NY: Dodd, Mead, 1887. Novel.

Found Yet Lost. NY: Dodd, Mead, 1888. Stories.

"Miss Lou." NY: Dodd, Mead, 1888. Unfinished novel.

The Home Acre. NY: Dodd, Mead, 1889. Nonfiction.

Taken Alive and Other Stories With an Autobiography. NY: Dodd, Mead, 1889.

OTHER

EPR's Catalogue of Small Fruits and Grape Vines. Newburgh, NY: Journal Printing House, 1882.

EDITION & COLLECTIONS

Birthday Mottoes Selected From the Writings of EPR, ed Lyman Abbott. NY: Dodd, Mead, 1882. Also known as *The R Birthday Book.*

A Brave Little Quakeress and Other Stories. NY: Dodd, Mead, 1892.

The Works of EPR, 19 vols. NY: Collier, 1900.

BIOGRAPHIES

Book

Roe, Mary A. *EPR: Reminiscences of His Life.* NY: Collier, 1899.

Articles

Hawthorne, Julian. "EPR." *Critic,* 13 (28 Jul 1888), 43-44.

Walsh, William S. "Some Words About EPR." *Lippincott's,* 42 (Oct 1888), 497-500.

CRITICAL STUDIES

Book

Carey, Glenn O. *EPR.* Boston: Twayne, 1985.

Special Journal

Lippincott's, 42 (Oct 1888). EPR issue.

Book Sections & Articles

Arnold, Matthew. "Civilisation in the United States." *NCent,* 23 (Apr 1888), 481-496.

Boyesen, Hjalmar Hjorth. "American Literary Criticism and Its Value." *Forum,* 15 (Jun 1893), 459-466.

Cleveland, Paul R. "Is Literature Bread-Winning?" *Cosmopolitan,* 5 (Jun 1888), 312-320.

"EPR." *EOSat,* 2 (1 Aug 1885), 242-243.

Mabie, Hamilton W. "The Most Popular Novels in America." *Forum,* 16 (Dec 1893), 508-516.

Maurice, Arthur Bartlett. "Best Sellers of Yesterday: EPR's *Barriers Burned Away.*" *Bookman,* 33 (May 1911), 247-253.

Minor, Dennis E. "The New and Regenerated Adams of EPR." *MarkhamR,* 6 (Winter 1977), 21-26.

Mott, Frank Luther. *Golden Multitudes: The Story of Best Sellers in the United States* (NY: Macmillan, 1947), 147-148.

Reynolds, David S. *Faith in Fiction: The Emergence of Religious Literature in America* (Cambridge: Harvard U P, 1981), 204-206.

Roberts, Edwards. "How Mr. R Impressed His Friends." *Critic,* 13 (4 Aug 1880), 49.

"The Writings of EPR." *LitW,* 19 (4 Aug 1888), 248.

Yanwing Leung

EDGAR SALTUS

New York City, NY, 24 Jun 1856-New York City, NY, 31 Jul 1921

Edgar Saltus was a prolific writer of philosophy, history, essays, and fiction. He also compiled and edited several history books and wrote supplementary chapters to update earlier books, often using the pseudonym Archibald Wilberforce. Although he was never widely appreciated and is now largely forgotten, Saltus did occasionally attract critical attention because of his rebellion against conventional standards, his extraordinary vocabulary, and his epigrammatic style. Much of his fiction is a critique of New York society and deals with such topics as adultery, murder, and suicide.

BIBLIOGRAPHY

Bibliography of American Literature, comp Jacob Blanck. New Haven: Yale U P, 1955-1991. Primary.

BOOKS

Balzac. Boston & NY: Houghton, Mifflin, 1884. Biography.

The Philosophy of Disenchantment. Boston & NY: Houghton, Mifflin, 1885. Nonfiction.

The Anatomy of Negation. NY: Scribner & Welford, 1886. Rev ed, Chicago & c: Belford, Clarke / London: Drane, 1889. Nonfiction.

Mr. Incoul's Misadventure. NY: Benjamin & Bell, 1887. Novel.

The Truth About Tristrem Varick. Chicago & NY: Belford, Clarke, 1888. Novel.

Eden: An Episode. Chicago & c: Belford, Clarke, 1888. Novel.

A Transaction in Hearts: An Episode. Chicago & c: Belford, Clarke, 1889. Novel.

The Pace That Kills: A Chronicle. Chicago & c: Belford, Clarke / London: Drane, 1889. Novel.

A Transient Guest and Other Episodes. Chicago & c: Belford, Clarke / London: Drane, 1889. Stories.

Love and Lore. NY: Belford, 1890. Essays.

Mary Magdalen: A Chronicle. NY: Belford, 1891. Novel.

Imperial Purple. Chicago: Morrill Higgins, 1892. History.

The Facts in the Curious Case of H. Hyrtl, Esq. . . . NY: Collier, 1892. Novel.

Madam Sapphira: A Fifth Avenue Story. NY & Chicago: Neely, 1893. Novel.

Enthralled: A Story of International Life. . . . London & c: Tudor, 1894; NY: AMS, 1969. Novel.

When Dreams Come True: A Story of Emotional Life. NY & London: Transatlantic, 1895. Novel.

Purple and Fine Women. NY & London: Ainslee, 1903. Stories.

The Pomps of Satan. London: Greening, 1904; NY: Kennerley, 1906. Essays.

The Perfume of Eros: A Fifth Avenue Incident. NY: Wessels, 1905. Novel.

Vanity Square: A Story of Fifth Avenue Life. Philadelphia & London: Lippincott, 1906. Novel.

Historia Amoris: A History of Love, Ancient and Modern. NY: Kennerley, 1906; *Love Throughout the Ages.* London: Sisley, 1908. Essays.

The Lords of Ghostland: A History of the Ideal. NY: Kennerley, 1907. Essays.

Daughters of the Rich. NY: Kennerley, 1909. Novel.

The Monster. NY: Pulitzer, 1912. Novel.

Oscar Wilde: An Idler's Impression. Chicago: Brothers of the Book, 1917. Essay.

The Paliser Case. NY: Boni & Liveright, 1919. Novel.

The Imperial Orgy: An Account of the Tsars From the First to the Last. NY: Boni & Liveright, 1920. History.

The Gardens of Aphrodite. Philadelphia: Pennell Club, 1920. Essay.

The Ghost Girl. NY: Boni & Liveright, 1922. Novel.

Parnassians Personally Encountered. Cedar Rapids, Iowa: Torch, 1923. Essay.

The Uplands of Dream, ed Charles Honce. Chicago: Covici, 1925. Essays.

Victor Hugo and Golgotha. Chicago: Covici, 1925. Essays.

Poppies and Mandragora, Poems . . . With Twenty-Three Additional Poems by Marie Saltus. NY: Vinal, 1926.

OTHER

After-Dinner Stories From Balzac, trans ES (as by
  Myndart Verelst). NY: Coombes, 1886.
*Tales Before Supper From Théophile Gautier and
  Prosper Mérimée,* trans ES (as by Verelst). NY
  & Chicago: Brentano, 1887.
The Story Without a Name by Jules Barbey d'Aure-
  villy; trans ES. NY: Belford, 1891.
The Capitals of the Globe, ed ES (as by Archibald
  Wilberforce). NY: Collier, 1893.
The Lovers of the World, 3 vols, comp ES. NY:
  Collier, 1896-1897?
Spain and Her Colonies, comp ES (as by Wilber-
  force). NY: Collier, 1898.
*The Great Battles of All Nations From Marathon
  to Santiago,* ed ES (as by Wilberforce). NY:
  Collier, 1898.

COLLECTION

Wit and Wisdom From ES, ed G F Monkshood &
  George Gamble. London: Greening, 1903.

MANUSCRIPTS & ARCHIVES

The Beinecke Library, Yale U.

BIOGRAPHIES

Book
Saltus, Marie. *ES: The Man.* Chicago: Covici,
  1925.

Article
Hartmann, Sadakichi. "The ES I Knew." *Bookman,*
  58 (Sep 1923), 17-19.

CRITICAL STUDIES

Books
Sprague, Claire. *ES.* NY: Twayne, 1968.
Stephenson, Ruth D. "Literary Techniques, Back-
  ground, and Ideas of ES." Dissertation: U
  Wisconsin, Madison, 1953.

Book Sections & Articles
Brooks, Van Wyck. *The Confident Years,
  1885-1915* (NY: Dutton, 1952), passim.
Honce, Charles. "Introduction." *The Uplands of
  Dream,* xiii-xxxiii.
Kitchen, Paul H. "Sorcerer of Syllabus." *Open
  Road,* 43 (Mar 1943), 15-17.
McKitrick, Eric. "ES of the Obsolete." *AQ,* 3
  (Spring 1951), 22-35.
Mencken, H L. "ES." *Prejudices: Fifth Series* (NY:
  Knopf, 1926), 277-282.
Munson, Gorham B. "The Limbo of American Lit-
  erature." *Broom,* 2 (Jun 1922), 250-260.
Symons, Arthur. "A Note on ES: An American Au-
  thor Who Is Altogether Too Little Appreci-
  ated." *VanityF,* 13 (Mar 1920), 71.
Van Doren, Carl. "The Roving Critic." *Nation,* 114
  (11 Jan 1922), 45.
Van Vechten, Carl. "ES: A Postscript." *DD,* 2 (Oct
  1921), 162-164.
Van Vechten. "ES." *Excavations: A Book of Advo-
  cacies* (NY: Knopf, 1926), 89-128.
Warner, Beverley E. "Practical Pessimism." *NewE,*
  48 (Jun 1888), 432-442.

Lori Correll

HENRY WHEELER SHAW
(Josh Billings)
Lanesboro, Mass, 21 Apr 1818-Monterey, Calif, 14 Oct 1885

Henry Wheeler Shaw, known by the pseudonym Josh Billings, was a popular writer of comic aphorisms, almanacs, essays, and sketches. His burlesque almanacs, which sold more than 200,000 copies in their first two years, gave him a national audience as did his frequent appearances on the lecture circuit. Like other contemporary cracker-barrel humorists, he developed a style marked by rustic grammar and misspellings. Recognized in his time as an important humorist, he has been largely ignored by twentieth-century readers and accorded only historical significance by literary critics.

BIBLIOGRAPHIES

Bibliography of American Literature, comp Jacob Blanck. New Haven: Yale U P, 1955-1991. Primary.

"Selected Bibliography." Kesterson, 147-153. Primary & secondary.

BOOKS

Josh Billings, Hiz Sayings. NY: Carleton, 1866. Aphorisms, sketches & essays.

Josh Billings on Ice and Other Things. NY: Carleton / London: Hotten, 1868. Aphorisms, sketches & essays.

Josh Billings' Farmer's Allminax. NY: Carleton, annually 1870-1879. Collected & augmented as *Old Probability: Perhaps Rain—Perhaps Not.* NY: Carleton / London: Low, 1879; *Josh Billings' Old Farmer's Allminax, 1870-1879.* NY: Dillingham, 1902. Burlesque almanacs.

Josh Billings' Wit and Humor: "The World Is My Oyster." London: Routledge, 1874; *Everybody's Friend; or, Josh Billings' Encyclopedia and Proverbial Philosophy of Wit and Humor.* Hartford, Conn: American Publishing, 1874.

Josh Billings' Trump Kards: Blue Grass Philosophy. NY: Carleton / London: Low, 1877. Aphorisms, sketches & essays.

Josh Billings' Cook Book and Picktorial Proverbs. NY: Carleton / London: Low, 1880. Rev as *Josh Billings Struggling With Things,* 1881.

OTHER

Josh Billings' Spice Box, ed HWS. Periodical collection of humor published in 1874 and thereafter by various NY publishers.

EDITION & COLLECTION

Josh Billings: His Works, Complete. NY: Carleton / London: Hotten, 1876. Repub as *The Complete Works of Josh Billings.* NY: Dillingham, 1888.

Uncle Sam's Uncle Josh, ed Donald Day. Boston: Little, Brown, 1953.

BIOGRAPHIES
Books
Clemens, Cyril. *Josh Billings, Yankee Humorist.* Webster Groves, Mo: International Mark Twain Society, 1932.

Smith, Francis S. *Life and Adventures of Josh Billings.* NY: Carleton, 1883.

Book Sections
Fatout, Paul. *Mark Twain on the Lecture Circuit* (Bloomington: Indiana U P, 1960), passim.

Paine, Albert Bigelow. *Mark Twain: A Biography* (NY: Harper, 1912), passim.

CRITICAL STUDIES
Book
Kesterson, David B. *Josh Billings (HWS).* NY: Twayne, 1973.

Book Sections & Articles
Bier, Jesse. " 'Literary Comedians': The Civil War and Reconstruction." *The Rise and Fall of American Humor* (NY: Holt, Rinehart & Winston, 1968), 77-116.

Blair, Walter. "Literary Comedians (1855-1900)." *Native American Humor, 1800-1900* (NY: American Book, 1937), 102-124.

Blair, Walter & Hamlin Hill. "Phunny Phellows: S, Locke, and Smith." *America's Humor: From Poor Richard to Doonesbury* (NY: Oxford U P, 1978), 284-299.

Grimes, Geoffrey Allan. " 'Mules,' 'Owls,' and Other Things: Folk Material in the Tobacco

Philosophy of Josh Billings." *NYFQ*, 26 (Dec 1970), 283-296.

Jones, Joseph. "Josh Billings: Some Yankee Notions on Humor." *UTSE*, 23 (1943), 148-161.

Kesterson, David B. "Josh Billings and His Burlesque *Allminax*." *IllQ*, 35 (Nov 1972), 6-14.

Kesterson. "Josh Billings 'Defolks' Rural America." *TFSB*, 41 (Jun 1975), 57-64.

Pond, J B. "Josh Billings." *Eccentricities of Genius* (NY: Dillingham, 1900), 185-187.

Smith, Charles Henry. *The Farm and the Fireside: Sketches of Domestic Life in War and in Peace* (Atlanta: Constitution, 1891), passim.

Tandy, Jennette. "The Funny Men: Artemus Ward and Josh Billings." *Crackerbox Philosophers in American Humor and Satire* (NY: Columbia U P, 1925), 132-157.

Kreg A. Abshire

UPTON SINCLAIR

Baltimore, Md, 20 Sep 1878-Bound Brook, NJ, 25 Nov 1968

Upton Sinclair achieved fame as a protest writer and social critic with his 1906 novel *The Jungle*. Almost one hundred other books brought him an international readership between the wars. During his lifetime he may have been the most widely known American author abroad. Sinclair was primarily concerned with messages—not literature. Although literary critics faulted him for his didactic prose and simple characterizations, Sinclair's Lanny Budd novels (1940-1953) received some respect; *Dragon's Teeth*, for example, won the Pulitzer Prize for fiction in 1943. His dissent also found expression in his publishing enterprises, which kept his work in print. Literary historians are beginning to re-evaluate Sinclair's contributions as a crusader on behalf of the deprived.

BIBLIOGRAPHIES & CATALOGUES

A Catalogue of Books, Manuscripts, and Other Materials From the US Archives, the Lilly Library, Indiana University. Bloomington: Lilly Library, Indiana U, 1963. Primary & secondary.

First Printings of American Authors, Vol 5, ed Philip B Eppard (Detroit: Bruccoli Clark Layman/Gale, 1987), 293-319. Primary.

Gottesman, Ronald. *US: An Annotated Checklist*. Kent, Ohio: Kent State U P, 1973. Primary & secondary.

Gottesman & Charles L P Silet. *The Literary Manuscripts of US*. Columbus: Ohio State U P, 1972.

BOOKS

(Works credited to Ensign Clarke Fitch & Lieut. Frederick Garrison are believed to have been written by US; separately published excerpts from books are not listed here. When it is impossible to identify with certainty the first edition of an US book, all possible first editions are listed.)

The Fighting Squadron (as by Ensign Clarke Fitch). NY: Street & Smith, 1898. Children's book.

A Prisoner of Morro (as by Fitch). NY: Street & Smith, 1898. Children's book.

Court-Martialed (as by Fitch). NY: Street & Smith, 1898. Children's book.

Saved by the Enemy (as by Fitch). NY: Street & Smith, 1898. Children's book.

A Gauntlet of Fire (as by Fitch). NY: Street & Smith, 1899. Children's book.

Holding the Fort (as by Fitch). NY: Street & Smith, 1899. Children's book.

A Soldier's Pledge (as by Fitch). NY: Street & Smith, 1899. Children's book.

Wolves of the Navy; or, Clif Faraday's Search for a Traitor (as by Fitch). NY: Street & Smith, 1899. Children's book.

A Soldier Monk (as by Fitch). NY: Street & Smith, 1899. Children's book.

Springtime and Harvest: A Romance. NY: Sinclair, 1901. Repub as *King Midas: A Romance*. NY & London: Funk & Wagnalls, 1901. Novel.

The Winning of Sarenne (as by St. Clair Beall). NY: Federal Book, 1902. Novel.

A Cadet's Honor; or, Mark Mallory's Heroism (as by Lieut. Frederick Garrison). NY & London: Street & Smith, 1903. Children's book.

Off for West Point; or, Mark Mallory's Struggle (as by Garrison). NY & London: Street & Smith, 1903. Children's book.

On Guard; or, Mark Mallory's Celebration (as by Garrison). NY & London: Street & Smith, 1903). Children's book.

The West Point Rivals; or, Mark Mallory's Stratagem (as by Garrison). NY & London: Street & Smith, 1903. Children's book.

A West Point Treasure; or, Mark Mallory's Strange Find (as by Garrison). NY & London: Street & Smith, 1903). Children's book.

Bound for Annapolis (as by Fitch). NY & London: Street & Smith, 1903. Children's book.

Clif, the Naval Cadet; or, Exciting Days at Annapolis (as by Fitch). NY & London: Street & Smith, 1903. Children's book.

The Cruise of the Training Ship; or, Clif Faraday's Pluck (as by Fitch). NY & London: Street & Smith, 1903. Children's book.

From Port to Port; or, Clif Faraday in Many Waters (as by Fitch). NY & London: Street & Smith, 1903. Children's book.

A Strange Cruise; or, Clif Faraday's Yacht Chase (as by Fitch). NY & London: Street & Smith, 1903. Children's book.

The Journal of Arthur Stirling: "The Valley of the Shadow." NY: Appleton, 1903. Abridged ed, London: Heinemann, 1903. Repub, with preface by US, NY: Doubleday, Page, 1906. Novel.

Prince Hagen: A Phantasy. Boston: Page, 1903. Repub, with postscript by US, Pasadena Calif: Author, 1923. Novel.

Manassas: A Novel of the War. NY & London: Macmillan, 1904. Rev as *Theirs Be the Guilt: A Novel of the War Between the States.* NY: Twayne, 1959.

The Toy and the Man. Westwood, Mass: Ariel, 1904. Essay.

Our Bourgeois Literature. Chicago: Kerr, 1905. Essay.

The Jungle. NY: Jungle Publishing, 1906; NY: Doubleday, Page, 1906.

A Home Colony: A Prospectus. NY: Jungle Publishing, 1906. Essay.

A Captain of Industry: Being the Story of a Civilized Man. Girard, Kans: Appeal to Reason, 1906. Novella.

The Industrial Republic: A Study of the America of Ten Years Hence. NY: Doubleday, Page, 1907. Essays.

The Overman. NY: Doubleday, Page, 1907. Story.

The Metropolis. NY: Moffat, Yard, 1908. Novel.

The Moneychangers. NY: Dodge, 1908; *The Money Changers.* London: Long, 1908. Novel.

Good Health and How We Won It, with Michael Williams. NY: Stokes, 1909; *The Art of Health.* London: Health & Strength, 1909. Rev ed, London, Health & Strength, 1910. Nonfiction.

Prince Hagen: A Drama in Four Acts. NY?: Privately printed, 1910.

Samuel the Seeker. NY: Dodge, 1910. Novel.

Love's Pilgrimage. NY & London: Kennerley, 1911. Novel.

The Fasting Cure. NY & London: Kennerley, 1911. Essay.

Plays of Protest: The Naturewoman, The Machine, The Second-Story Man, Prince Hagen. NY: Kennerley, 1912.

Sylvia. Philadelphia & Chicago: Winston, 1913. Novel.

Damaged Goods: The Great Play "Les Avariés" of Brieux, Novelized With the Permission of the Author. Philadelphia: Winston, 1913.

Sylvia's Marriage. Philadelphia & Chicago: Winston, 1914; Pasadena, Calif: Author, 1914. Novel.

King Coal. Macmillan, 1917. Novel.

The Profits of Religion: An Essay in Economic Interpretation. Pasadena, Calif: Author, 1918. Repub as *The Profits of Religion: A Study of Supernaturalism as a Source of Income and a Shield to Privilege.* Girard, Kans: Haldeman-Julius, 1947.

Jimmie Higgins. NY: Boni & Liveright, 1919. Novel.

The Brass Check: A Study of American Journalism. Pasadena, Calif: Author, 1920. Nonfiction.

100%: The Story of a Patriot. Pasadena, Calif: Author, 1920; *The Spy.* London: Laurie, 1921. Novel.

The Book of Life: Mind and Body. NY: Macmillan, 1921; Pasadena, Calif: Author / Chicago: Economy, 1921. Essays.

The Crimes of the "Times": A Test of Newspaper Decency. Pasadena, Calif: Sinclair, 1921. Essay.

Debate on Socialism, with Thomas Allen McNeal. Girard, Kans: Appeal Publishing, 1921.

The Book of Life: Love and Society. Pasadena, Calif: Sinclair / Chicago: Paine, 1922. Repub as *The Book of Love.* London: Laurie, 1934. Essays.

They Call Me Carpenter: A Tale of the Second Coming. NY: Boni & Liveright, 1922. Novel.

The Goose-Step: A Study of American Education. Pasadena, Calif: Author / Chicago: Economy, 1923. Nonfiction.

Hell: A Verse Drama and Photo-Play. Pasadena, Calif: Author, 1923.

The Goslings: A Study of the American Schools. Pasadena, Calif: Sinclair, 1924.

The Pot Boiler: A Comedy in Four Acts. Girard, Kans: Haldeman-Julius, 1924.

The Millenium: A Comedy of the Year 2000, 3 vols. Girard, Kans: Haldeman-Julius, 1924. Novel.

Singing Jailbirds: A Drama in Four Acts. Pasadena, Calif: Author, 1924.

Mammonart: An Essay in Economic Interpretation. Pasadena, Calif: Author, 1925.

Bill Porter: A Drama of O. Henry in Prison. Pasadena, Calif: Author, 1925. Play.

Letters to Judd, an American Workingman. Pasadena, Calif: Author, 1926. Repub as *This World of 1949 and What to Do About It: Revised Letters to a Workingman on the Economic and Political Situation.* Girard, Kans: Haldeman-Julius, 1949.

The Spokesman's Secretary: Being the Letters of Mame to Mom. Pasadena, Calif: Author, 1926. Novel.

Oil! NY: Boni, 1927. Novel.

Money Writes! NY: Boni, 1927. Repub as *Money Writes! A Study of American Literature.* Long Beach, Calif: Author, 1927.

Boston, 2 vols. NY: Boni, 1928. Condensed as *August 22nd.* NY: Award, 1965. Novel.

Oil! Pasadena, Calif: Author, 1929. Play.

Mountain City. NY: Boni, 1930. Novel.

Mental Radio. NY: Boni, 1930; *Mental Radio: Does It Work, and How?* London: Laurie, 1930. Nonfiction.

Roman Holiday. NY: Farrar & Rinehart, 1931. Novel.

The Wet Parade. NY: Farrar & Rinehart, 1931. Novel.

Socialism and Culture. Girard, Kans: Haldeman-Julius, 1931. Essay.

American Outpost: A Book of Reminiscences. NY: Farrar & Rinehart, 1932; *Candid Reminiscences: My First Thirty Years.* London: Laurie, 1932. Autobiography.

I, Governor of California, and How I Ended Poverty. Los Angeles: Sinclair, 1933. Essay.

US Presents William Fox. Los Angeles: Author, 1933. Biography.

The Way Out: What Lies Ahead for America. NY: Farrar & Rinehart, 1933; *The Way Out: A Solution of Our Present Economic and Social Ills.* London: Laurie, 1933. Essay.

I, Candidate for Governor, and How I Got Licked. NY: Farrar & Rinehart, 1935; *How I Got Licked and Why.* London: Laurie, 1935. Nonfiction.

Depression Island. Pasadena, Calif: Author, 1935. Play.

We, People of America, and How We Ended Poverty: A True Story of the Future. Pasadena, Calif: Author, 1935. Essay.

Co-Op: A Novel of Living Together. NY & Toronto: Farrar & Rinehart, 1936.

The Gnomobile: A Gnice Gnew Gnarrative With Gnonsense, But Gnothing Gnaughty. NY: Farrar & Rinehart, 1936. Children's story.

What God Means to Me: An Attempt at a Working Religion. NY: Farrar & Rinehart, 1936. Nonfiction.

The Flivver-King: A Story of Ford-America. Detroit: United Automobile Workers of America / Pasadena, Calif: Author, 1937. Novel.

No Pasaran! (They Shall Not Pass): A Story of the Battle of Madrid. Pasadena, Calif: Author, 1937. Novel.

Little Steel. NY & Toronto: Farrar & Rinehart, 1938; *Little Steel: A Story.* London: Laurie, 1938. Novel.

Our Lady. Emmaus, Pa: Rodale, 1938; Pasadena, Calif: Author, 1938; Pasadena, Calif & NY: Author, 1938; *Our Lady: A Story.* London: Laurie, 1938. Repub as *Our Lady: A Parable for Moderns.* Hollywood, Calif: Murray & Gee, 1943. Repub as *Our Lady: A Novel.* Girard, Kans: Haldeman-Julius, 1948. Novella.

Terror in Russia? Two Views, with Eugene Lyons. NY: Smith, 1938. Essays.

Expect No Peace! Girard, Kans: Haldeman-Julius, 1939. Essays.

Marie Antoinette: A Play by US. NY: Vanguard, 1939. Repub as *Marie and Her Lover: A Play.* Girard, Kans: Haldeman-Julius, 1948.

Telling the World. London: Laurie, 1939. Essays.

Your Million Dollars. NY & Pasadena, Calif: Sinclair, 1939; *Letters to a Millionaire.* London: Laurie, 1939. Essay.

World's End. NY: Viking, 1940; NY & Pasadena, Calif: Author, 1940. Novel.

Between Two Worlds. NY: Viking, 1941; NY & Pasadena, Calif: Author, 1941. Novel.

Dragon's Teeth. NY: Viking, 1942; NY & Pasadena, Calif: Author, 1942. Novel.

Wide Is the Gate. NY: Viking, 1943. Novel.

Presidential Agent. NY: Viking, 1944; NY & Monrovia, Calif: Author, 1944. Novel.

Dragon Harvest. NY: Viking, 1945; Monrovia, Calif: Author, 1945. Novel.

A World to Win. NY: Viking, 1946; Monrovia, Calif: Author, 1946.

Presidential Mission. NY: Viking, 1947; Monrovia, Calif: Author, 1947. Novel.

One Clear Call. NY: Viking, 1948; Monrovia, Calif: Author, 1948. Novel.

A Giant's Strength: Drama in Three Acts. Monrovia, Calif: Author, 1948. Repub as *A Giant's Strength: A Three-Act Drama of the Atomic Bomb.* Girard, Kans: Haldeman-Julius, 1948.

Repub as *A Giant's Strength: A Drama in Three Acts*. London: Laurie, 1948.

O Shepherd, Speak! NY: Viking, 1949; Monrovia, Calif: Author, 1949. Novel.

The Enemy Had It Too: A Play in Three Acts. NY: Viking, 1950.

Another Pamela; or, Virtue Still Rewarded: A Story. NY: Viking, 1950. Novel.

A Personal Jesus: Portrait and Interpretation. NY & Philadelphia: Evans, 1952. Repub as *The Secret Life of Jesus*. Philadelphia: Mercury, 1962. Nonfiction.

The Return of Lanny Budd. NY: Viking, 1953. Novel.

What Didymus Did. London: Wingate, 1954. Rev as *It Happened to Didymus*. NY: Sagamore, 1958. Novel.

The Cup of Fury. Great Neck, NY: Channel, 1956. Nonfiction.

Affectionately, Eve. NY: Twayne, 1961. Novel.

The Autobiography of US. NY: Harcourt, Brace & World, 1962.

The Coal War: A Sequel to "King Coal." Boulder: Colorado Associated U P, 1976. Novel.

LETTERS

My Lifetime in Letters. Columbia: U Missouri P, 1960.

Sergei Eisenstein and Upton Sinclair: The Making and Unmaking of Que Viva Mexico!, ed Harry M Geduld & Ronald Gottesman. Bloomington & London: Indiana U P, 1970.

"US to Jack London: A Literary Friendship," ed with intro by Charles L P Silet. *JLN*, 5 (May-Aug 1972), 49-76.

OTHER

The Cry for Justice: An Anthology of the Literature of Social Protest. . . , ed US. Philadelphia: Winston, 1915.

Index to the Lanny Budd Story. NY: Viking, 1943. Includes commentary by US & others.

COLLECTION

An US Anthology, ed with intro by I O Evans. NY: Farrar & Rinehart, 1934. Augmented as *US Anthology,* intro by Irving Stone & Lewis Browne. Culver City, Calif: Murray & Gee, 1947.

MANUSCRIPTS & ARCHIVES

The Lilly Library, Indiana U.

BIOGRAPHIES

Books

Dell, Floyd. *US: A Study in Social Protest*. NY: Doran, 1927.

Harris, Leon. *US: American Rebel*. NY: Crowell, 1975.

Harte, James Lambert. *This Is US*. Emmaus, Pa: Rodale, 1938.

Book Sections & Articles

Adamic, Louis. "US: A Prophet of Red Dawn." *Open Forum*, 4 (26 Nov 1927), 1-2.

Ainsworth, Ed. "Remembering 'Uppie.' " *SatR*, 50 (30 Sep 1967), 32-33.

Becker, George J. "US: Quixote in a Flivver." *CE*, 21 (Dec 1959), 133-140.

Blinderman, Abraham. "The Social Passions of US." *ChiJF*, 25 (Spring 1967), 203-208.

Blinderman. "The Religious Idealism of US." *CraneR*, 10 (Fall 1967), 33-41.

Blinderman. "US and Higher Education." *UBSCentJ*, 1 (Sep 1978), 29-41.

Brevda, William. "Love's Coming-of-Age: The US-Harry Kemp Divorce Scandal." *NDQ*, 51 (Spring 1983), 60-77.

Cantwell, Robert. "US." *After the Genteel Tradition,* ed Malcolm Cowley (NY: Norton, 1937), 37-51.

Dell, Floyd. "The Artist in Revolt." *Bookman*, 65 (27 May 1927), 316-322.

Dreiser, Theodore. "US." *Clipper*, 1 (Sep 1940), 3-4.

Fretz, Lewis A. "US and World War I." *PolS*, 25 (Jul 1973), 2-12.

Fretz. "US and the Red Decade." *PolS*, 25 (Dec 1973), 131-143.

Gottesman, Ronald. "Louis Adamic and US: The Record of a Friendship." *AN*, 1 (1968), 41-65.

Gottesman. "Some Implications to *The Literary Manuscripts of US:* A Preview Article." *Proof*, 3 (1973), 395-410.

Grenier, Judson A. "US: A Remembrance." *CalHQ*, 48 (Jun 1969), 165-169.

Grenier. "US: The Road to California." *SCQ*, 56 (Winter 1974), 325-336.

Harris, Frank. "US." *Contemporary Portraits, Third Series* (NY: Author, 1920), 14-30.

Hicks, Granville. "The Survival of US." *CE*, 4 (Jan 1943), 213-220.

Kazin, Alfred. "US." *On Native Grounds* (NY: Reynal & Hitchcock, 1942), 116-121.

Koerner, J D. "The Last of the Muckrake Men." *SAQ*, 55 (Apr 1956), 221-232.

Lacassin, Francis. "US and Jack London: A Great Friendship . . . by Correspondence." *JLN*, 9 (Jan-Apr 1976), 1-7.

Lovett, Robert Morss. "US." *EJ*, 17 (Nov 1928), 706-714.

McWilliams, Carey. "US: Two Impressions." *Saturday Night*, 8 (24 Dec 1927), 4-5.

Remley, David A. "US and H. L. Mencken in Correspondence: 'An Illustration of How Not to Agree.' " *SCQ*, 56 (Winter 1974), 337-358.

Rolfe, Lionel. "In Search of US." *Literary L. A.* (San Francisco: Chronicle, 1981), 77-90.

Scully, Frank. "Sinclair." *Rogues' Gallery* (Hollywood, Calif: Murray & Gee, 1943), 193-209.

Soderbergh, Peter A. "US and Hollywood." *MQ,* 11 (Jan 1970), 173-191.

Swados, Harvey. "The World of US." *Atlantic,* 208 (Dec 1961), 96, 98, 100, 102.

Turner, Justin G. "Conversation With US." *ABC,* 20 (Summer 1970), 7-10.

Van Doren, Carl. "US." *Contemporary American Novelists, 1900-1920* (NY: Macmillan, 1923), 65-74.

Welland, Dennis. "US: The Centenary of an American Writer." *BJRL,* 61 (Spring 1979), 474-494.

CRITICAL STUDIES

Books

Albrecht, Alfred J. "A Rhetorical Study of US's 1934 Campaign for Governor of California." Dissertation: Indiana U, 1966.

Biella, Arnold P. "US: Crusader." Dissertation: Stanford U, 1954.

Blinderman, Abraham. "US's Criticism of Higher Education in America: A Study of 'The Goose-Step'. . . ." Dissertation: NYU, 1963.

Bloodworth, William. *US.* Boston: Twayne, 1977.

Eastman, Norton B. "US: A Social Crusader Views American Education." Dissertation: SUNY, Buffalo, 1965.

Fakir, Abu Bakr. "US: Social Critic." Dissertation: Indiana U, 1987.

Fretz, Lewis A. "US: The Don Quixote of American Reform." Dissertation: Stanford U, 1970.

Heimerdinger, Charles C. "Propagandist in the Theatre: The Career of US as an American Dramatist." Dissertation: Indiana U, 1968.

McIntosh, Clarence F. "US and the EPIC Movement, 1933-1936." Dissertation: Stanford U, 1955.

Mookerjee, R N. *Art for Social Justice: The Major Novels of US.* Metuchen, NJ: Scarecrow, 1988.

Mordell, Albert. *Haldeman-Julius and US.* Girard, Kans: Haldeman-Julius, 1950.

Riherd, James Michael. "US: Creating *World's End.*" Dissertation: U Southern California, 1978.

Scriabine, Christine B. "US: Witness to History." Dissertation: Brown U, 1973.

Smith, John Kares. "US and the Celestial Crown: The Rhetoric of 'The Dead Hand' Series." Dissertation: Northwestern U, 1974.

Suh, Suk Bong."Literature, Society, and Culture: US and *The Jungle.*" Dissertation: U Iowa, 1986.

Yoder, Jon A. *US.* NY: Ungar, 1975.

Zanger, Martin N. "The Reluctant Activist: US's Reform Activities in California, 1915-1930." Dissertation: Indiana U, 1971.

Collection of Essays

Blinderman, Abraham, ed. *Critics on US: Readings in Literary Criticism.* Coral Gables, Fla: U Miami P, 1975.

Special Journals

SCQ, 56 (Winter 1974). US issue.

Uppie Speaks: The Upton Sinclair Quarterly (1978-1986).

Upton Beall Sinclair Centenary Journal, 1 (Fall 1978).

Book Sections & Articles

Aaron, Daniel. *Writers on the Left* (NY: Harcourt, Brace & World, 1961), passim.

Adimari, Ralph. "Last of the Dime Novelists." *DNR,* 24 (15 Jun 1956), 41-44; 24 (15 Jul 1956), 51-52.

Ashton, George F. "Bellamy, Judd, and the Industrial Republic: Some Sources of the EPIC Plan." *US: USQ,* 9 (Summer 1985), 6-11.

Blake, Fay M & H Morton Newman. "US's EPIC Campaign." *CalH,* 63 (Fall 1984), 305-312.

Bloodworth, William. "S's Protagonists: Genteel or Radical?" *UBSCentJ,* 1 (Sep 1978), 55-68.

Bloodworth. "From *The Jungle* to *The Fasting Cure:* US on American Food." *JAmC,* 2 (Fall 1979), 444-453.

Brooks, Van Wyck. "US and His Novels." *Sketches in Criticism* (NY: Dutton, 1932), 291-298.

Buitenhuis, Peter. "US and the Socialist Response to World War I." *CRevAS,* 14 (Summer 1983), 121-130.

Cook, Timothy. "US's *The Jungle* and Orwell's *Animal Farm:* A Relationship Explored." *MFS,* 30 (Winter 1984), 696-703.

Dembo, L S. "The Socialist and Socialite Heroes of US." *Toward a New American Literary History: Essays in Honor of Arlin Turner,* ed Louis J Budd, Edwin H Cady & Carl L Anderson (Durham, NC: Duke U P, 1980), 164-180.

Durham, James. "US's Realistic Romanticism." *WichitaSUB,* 46 (May 1970), 3-11.

Ebon, Martin. "US's 'Mental Radio.' " *They Knew the Unknown* (NY: World, 1971), 244-252.

Filler, Louis. *Crusaders for American Liberalism* (NY: Harcourt, Brace, 1939), passim.

Filler. *Appointment at Armageddon: Muckraking and Progressivism in the American Tradition* (Westport, Conn: Greenwood, 1976), passim.

Fincher, Jack. "The Mogul, the Magnate, the Muckraker." *Los Angeles,* 30 (Jul 1985), 132-137, 252.

Folsom, Michael Brewster. "US's Escape From *The Jungle:* The Narrative Strategy and Suppressed Conclusion of America's First Prole-tarian Novel." *Prospects,* 4 (1979), 236-266.

Graham, John. "US and the Ludlow Massacre." *ColQ,* 21 (Summer 1972), 55-67.

Grenier, Judson A. "US and the Press: *The Brass Check* Reconsidered." *JQ,* 49 (Autumn 1972), 427-436.

Grenier. "Muckraking the Muckrakers: US and His Peers." *Reform and Reformers in the Progressive Era,* ed David R Colburn & George E Pozzetta (Westport, Conn: Greenwood, 1983), 71-92.

Gross, Dalton. "George Sterling's Letters to the USs: A Selection." *ABC,* 24 (Sep-Oct 1973), 16-20.

Herms, Dieter. "The Coming of Age in S Criticism." *KLit,* 6 (1977), 93-101.

Herms. "From West Point Cadet to Presidential Agent: Popular Literature Elements in US." *US: USQ,* 4 (Dec 1980), 13-19.

Herms. "The Novelist as Dramatist: A Note on US's Plays." *US: USQ,* 7 (Summer-Fall 1983), 3-11.

Hitchcock, Curtice N. "*The Brass Check,* a Study of American Journalism by US." *JPE,* 29 (Apr 1921), 336-348.

Kaplan, Lawrence. "A Utopia During the Progressive Era: The Helicon Home Colony, 1906-1907." *AmerS,* 25 (Fall 1984), 59-73.

Kimball, William J. "*Manassas:* An Early Expression of US's Socialist Leanings." *McNR,* 20 (1971-1972), 28-32.

Kress, Melville. "US: The Great Pamphlets of US." *UBSCentJ,* 1 (Sep 1978), 14-28.

Larsen, Charles E. "The EPIC Campaign of 1934." *PacHR,* 27 (May 1958), 127-147.

Leader, Leonard. "US's EPIC Switch: A Dilemma for American Socialists." *SCQ,* 62 (Winter 1980), 361-385.

Lesser, Stephen O. "Sol Lesser and US: The Record of a Friendship." *WSJHQ,* 12 (Jan 1980), 134-141.

Mansfield, Joseph. "*The Wet Parade* (1931), US: Que Viva Prohibition?" *The Modern American Novel and the Movies,* ed Gerald Peary & Roger Shatzkin (NY: Ungar, 1978), 308-316.

McIntosh, Clarence F. "The Significance of the End-Poverty-in-California Movement." *PacH,* 27 (Winter 1983), 20-25.

Mitchell, Greg. "The Greatest Movie Never Made." *AmerF,* 8 (Jan-Feb 1983), 53-58.

Mitchell. "US's EPIC Campaign." *Nation,* 239 (4-11 Aug 1984), 75-78.

Mitchell. "How Media Politics Was Born." *AH,* 39 (Sep-Oct 1988), 34-41.

Mitchell. "How Hollywood Fixed an Election." *AmerF,* 14 (Nov 1988), 26-31.

Musteikis, Antanas. "The Lithuanian Heroes of *The Jungle.*" *Lituanus,* 17 (Summer 1971), 27-38.

Powell, Lawrence Clark. "California Classics Reread: US's *Oil!*" *Westways,* 62 (Sep 1970), 14-16.

Putt, S Gorley. "World Without End: US and Lanny Budd." *Scholars of the Heart: Essays in Criticism* (London: Faber & Faber, 1962), 87-109.

Quint, Howard H. "US's Quest for Artistic Independence—1909." *AL,* 29 (May 1957), 194-202.

Rajannan, Busnagi. "US's *The Jungle* Revisited." *IJAS,* 12 (Jul 1982), 49-54.

Scriabine, Christine. "US and the Writing of *The Jungle.*" *Chicago History,* 10 (Spring 1981), 27-37.

Seib, Kenneth. "US, Poet." *US: USQ,* 5 (Dec 1981), 4-6.

Šešplaukis, Alfonsas. "Lithuanians in US's *The Jungle.*" *Lituanus,* 23 (Summer 1977), 24-31.

Singer, Donald L. "US and the California Gubernatorial Campaign of 1934." *SCQ,* 56 (Winter 1974), 375-406.

Smith, Carl S. "Into the Jungle." *Chicago and the American Literary Imagination, 1880-1920* (Chicago: U Chicago P, 1984), 164-170.

Suh, Suk Bong. "Lithuanian Wedding Traditions in US's *The Jungle.*" *Lituanus,* 33 (Winter 1987), 5-17.

Tebbetts, Terrell L. "Jurgis's Freedom: *The Jungle* as a Case for Familial Society." *LJHum,* 4 (Fall 1978), 15-20.

Wilson, Christopher P. "Would-Be Singer: US." *The Labor of Words: Literary Professionalism in the Progressive Era* (Athens: U Georgia P, 1985), 113-140.

Wilson, Edmund. "Lincoln Steffens and US." *NewR,* 72 (28 Sep 1932), 173-175.

Wolfe, Don M. "An Evening With US: 1954." *JHS,* 1 (Spring 1968), 265-267.

Yoder, Jon A. "US, Lanny, and the Liberals." *MFS,* 20 (1974-1975), 483-504.

Youdelman, Jeffrey. "In Search of Lanny Budd." *SJS,* 6 (Feb 1980), 86-94.

Young, James Harvey. "The Pig That Fell into the Privy: US's *The Jungle* and the Meat Inspection Amendments of 1906." *BHM,* 59 (Winter 1985), 467-480.

Zanger, Martin. "Politics of Confrontation: US and the Launching of the ACLU in Southern California." *PacHR,* 38 (Nov 1969), 383-406.

Zanger. "US as California's Socialist Candidate for Congress, 1920." *SCQ,* 56 (Winter 1974), 359-373.

John Ahouse & Cheryl Z. Oreovicz

CHARLES HENRY SMITH
(Bill Arp)

Lawrenceville, Ga, 15 Jun 1826-Cartersville, Ga, 24 Aug 1903

Under the pseudonym Bill Arp, Charles Henry Smith wrote more than 2,000 humorous letters for newspaper columns, most of which were published in the Atlanta *Southern Confederacy* and the *Atlanta Constitution*. Bill Arp joined Charles Farrar Browne's Artemus Ward, David Ross Locke's Petroleum V. Nasby, and Henry Wheeler Shaw's Josh Billings as one of a new breed of humorists produced by the Civil War, literary comedians whose timely epistles and lectures made capital of the comic dialect of an illiterate persona. Carrying on the humorous tradition of a cracker-barrel philosopher writing to the editor of a newspaper, Smith's Bill Arp expressed "the silent echoes of our people's thoughts" during the Civil War and Reconstruction. Bill Arp's importance lies in his immediate record of these times from the southern point of view, in the intelligence with which he gave voice to the sentiments of the average southerner, and in his insistence on the humanity and vigor of southern men and women.

BIBLIOGRAPHY

"Bibliography." Austin, 115-118. Primary & secondary.

BOOKS

Bill Arp, So Called: A Side Show of the Southern Side of the War. NY: Metropolitan Record Office, 1866. Sketches.
Bill Arp's Peace Papers. NY: Carleton, 1873. Sketches.
Bill Arp's Scrap Book: Humor and Philosophy. Atlanta: Harrison, 1884.
The Farm and the Fireside: Sketches of Domestic Life in War and in Peace. Atlanta: Constitution, 1891.
A School History of Georgia: Georgia as a Colony and a State, 1733-1893. Boston: Ginn, 1893.
Bill Arp: From the Uncivil War to Date, 1861-1903. Atlanta: Byrd, 1903. Sketches.

MANUSCRIPTS & ARCHIVES

U of Chicago Library.

BIOGRAPHIES

Book Sections & Article
Aubrey, George H. "CHS (Bill Arp)." *Men of Mark in Georgia*, Vol 3, ed William J Northen (Atlanta: Caldwell, 1911), 393-396.
Cooper, Cornelia E. "Bill Arp: The Cherokee Philosopher." *GaM*, 8 (Apr-May 1965), 12-15.
Smith, Marian Caroline. "The Home Life of Bill Arp." *Bill Arp: From the Uncivil War to Date, 1861-1903*, Memorial Edition (Atlanta: Hudgins, 1903), 5-14.
Smith. *I Remember* (Jacksonville, Fla: Ambrose, 1931), passim.

CRITICAL STUDIES

Books
Austin, James C. *Bill Arp*. NY: Twayne, 1969.
Christie, Annie M. "CHS, 'Bill Arp': A Biographical and Critical Study of a Nineteenth-Century Georgia Humorist, Politician, Homely Philosopher." Dissertation: U Chicago, 1953.

Book Sections & Articles
Austin, James C & Wayne Pike. "The Language of Bill Arp." *AS*, 48 (Spring-Summer 1973), 84-97.
Baird, Joseph H. "Bill Arp's Humor in the Bleak South." *AtlantaJ&CM* (18 Oct 1970), 18-21, 37-39.
Bier, Jesse. " 'Literary Comedians': The Civil War and Reconstruction." *The Rise and Fall of American Humor* (NY: Holt, Rinehart & Winston, 1968), 76-116.
Blair, Walter. *Native American Humor, 1800-1900* (NY: American Book, 1937), passim.
Blair & Hamlin Hill. "Phunny Phellows: Shaw, Locke, and S." *America's Humor: From Poor Richard to Doonesbury* (NY: Oxford U P, 1978), 284-299.
Blair & Raven I McDavid, Jr. "CHS." *The Mirth of a Nation: America's Great Dialect Humor* (Minneapolis: U Minnesota P, 1983), 136-143.

Budd, Louis J. "Gentlemanly Humorists of the Old South." *SFQ,* 17 (Dec 1953), 232-240.

Christie, Annie M. "Civil War Humor: Bill Arp." *CWH,* 2 (Sep 1956), 103-119.

Dutcher, Salem. "Bill Arp and Artemus Ward." *Scott's,* 1-2 (Jun 1866), 472-478.

Figh, Margaret Gillis. "Folklore in Bill Arp's Works." *SFQ,* 12 (Sep 1948), 169-175.

Figh. "Tall Talk and Folk Sayings in Bill Arp's Works." *SFQ,* 13 (Dec 1949), 206-212.

Figh. "A Word-List From 'Bill Arp' and 'Rufus Sanders.'" *PADS,* 13 (Apr 1950), 3-15.

Ginther, James E. "CHS, Alias 'Bill Arp.'" *GaR,* 4 (Winter 1950), 313-322.

Ginther. "CHS, the Creator of Bill Arp." *MTJ,* 10 (Summer 1955), 11-12, 23-24.

Hall, Wade H. "During and After the War." *Reflections of the Civil War in Southern Humor* (Gainesville: U Florida P, 1962), 1-12.

Hall. *The Smiling Phoenix: Southern Humor From 1865 to 1914* (Gainesville: U Florida P, 1965), passim.

Hubbell, Jay B. *The South in American Literature, 1607-1900* (Durham, NC: Duke U P, 1954), 683-686, passim.

Kesterson, David B. "The Literary Comedians and the Language of Humor." *StAH,* ns 1 (Jun 1982), 44-51.

Kesterson. "Those *Literary* Comedians." *Critical Essays on American Humor,* ed William Bedford Clark & W Craig Turner (Boston: Hall, 1984), 167-183.

Lenz, William E. *Fast Talk and Flush Times: The Confidence Man as a Literary Convention* (Columbia: U Missouri P, 1985), 156-157.

Lukens, Henry Clay. "American Literary Comedians." *Harper's,* 80 (Apr 1890), 783-797.

Massey, Mary Elizabeth. *Refugee Life in the Confederacy* (Baton Rouge: Louisiana State U P, 1964), passim.

McIlwaine, Shields. *The Southern Poor White From Lubberland to Tobacco Road* (NY: Cooper Square, 1970), passim.

Parker, David B, Jr. "Bill Arp and the North: The Misreading of a Southern Humorist." *SoSt,* 25 (Fall 1986), 257-273.

Tandy, Jennette. *Crackerbox Philosophers in American Humor and Satire* (NY: Columbia U P, 1925), passim.

William E. Lenz

F. HOPKINSON SMITH

Baltimore, Md, 23 Oct 1838-New York City, NY, 7 Apr 1915

F. Hopkinson Smith was in his lifetime a widely read writer of novels, short stories, and travel books. Before Smith began his literary career he was an engineer who worked primarily on maritime projects. Painting and sketching became the foundation for his stories and novels, many of which he illustrated himself. His painter's eye gave his writing its characteristic love of visual detail, a source of his great popularity. He devoted his life to the writing of popular stories of romance, adventure, and travel, while maintaining a profuse output of paintings, sketches, and illustrations for his own works and the works of others. The depiction of the charming and old-fashioned, of which he was so fond, lost its appeal for the reading public after Smith's death.

BIBLIOGRAPHY

Bibliography of American Literature, comp Jacob Blanck. New Haven: Yale U P, 1955-1991. Primary.

BOOKS

(This list omits books written by others and illustrated by FHS. It also omits albums and exhibition catalogues of his art.)

A Book of the Tile Club, with Earl Shinn (as by Edward Strahan). Boston & NY: Houghton Mifflin, 1886. Stories.

Well-Worn Roads of Spain, Holland, and Italy, Traveled by a Painter in Search of the Picturesque. Boston & NY: Houghton, Mifflin, 1887. Augmented ed, 1898. Travel.

Between the Extremes: A Paper Read Before the Rembrandt Club, February 8th, 1888. Brooklyn, NY: The Club, 1888.

A White Umbrella in Mexico. Boston & NY: Houghton, Mifflin, 1889. Travel.

A Paper Read at the 13th Subscription Dinner of the Hamilton Club, February 8, 1890. Subject Under Discussion: "How Shall We Train Our Wives and Children?" Brooklyn, NY: Privately printed, 1890.

Colonel Carter of Cartersville. Boston & NY: Houghton, Mifflin, 1891. Augmented as *Colonel Carter of Cartersville and Other Tales.* NY: Collier, 1891. Novel.

A Day at Laguerre's and Other Days, Being Nine Sketches. Boston & NY: Houghton Mifflin, 1892. Repub as *A Day at Laguerre's and Other Days: Nine Sketches,* 1892. Stories.

A Gentleman Vagabond and Some Others. Boston & NY: Houghton, Mifflin, 1895. Stories.

Venice of To-Day. NY: Thomas, 1895. Repub as *Gondola Days.* Boston & NY: Houghton Mifflin, 1897. Travel.

Tom Grogan. Boston & NY: Houghton, Mifflin, 1896. Novel.

Caleb West: Master Diver. Boston & NY: Houghton, Mifflin, 1898. Novel.

The Other Fellow. Boston & NY: Houghton, Mifflin, 1899. Stories.

The Fortunes of Oliver Horn. NY: Scribners, 1902. Novel.

The Under Dog. NY: Scribners, 1903. Stories.

Colonel Carter's Christmas. NY: Scribners, 1903. Novel.

At Close Range. NY: Scribners, 1905. Stories.

The Wood Fire in No. 3. NY: Scribners, 1905. Excerpted in *The Gentle Art of Dining,* 1906. Stories.

The Tides of Barnegat. NY: Scribners, 1906. Novel.

The Veiled Lady, and Other Men and Women. NY: Scribners, 1907. Stories.

Old Fashioned Folk. Boston: Privately printed, 1907. Essay.

The Romance of an Old-Fashioned Gentleman. NY: Scribners, 1907. Novel.

Peter: A Novel of Which He Is Not the Hero. NY: Scribners, 1908.

Captain Thomas A. Scott, Master Diver, One Who Was Not Afraid and Who Spoke the Truth. Boston: American Unitarian Association, 1908. Novel.

Forty Minutes Late and Other Stories. NY: Scribners, 1909.

Kennedy Square. NY: Scribners, 1911. Novel.

The Arm-Chair at the Inn. NY: Scribners, 1912. Stories.

Charcoals of New and Old New York. Garden City, NY: Doubleday, Page, 1912.

In Thackeray's London. Garden City, NY: Doubleday, Page, 1913. Travel.

In Dickens's London. NY: Scribners, 1914. Travel.

Outdoor Sketching: Four Talks Given Before the Art Institute of Chicago: The Scammon Lectures, 1914. NY: Scribners, 1915.

Felix O'Day. NY: Scribners, 1915. Novel.

Enoch Crane: A Novel Planned and Begun by F. Hopkinson Smith and Completed by F. Berkeley Smith. NY: Scribners, 1916.

OTHER

American Illustrators. NY: Scribners, 1892. Commentary by FHS.

"The Picturesque Side." *Some Artists at the Fair,* with Frank D Millet, Will H Low, J A Mitchell & W Hamilton Gibson (NY: Scribners, 1893), 100-123. Essay.

EDITION

The Novels, Stories and Sketches of FHS, Beacon

Edition, 23 vols; ed FHS. NY: Scribners, 1902-1915.

MANUSCRIPTS & ARCHIVES

The major collections are at the U of Virginia Library & Princeton U Library.

CRITICAL STUDIES

Articles

Hornberger, Theodore. "The Effect of Painting on the Fiction of FHS (1838-1915)." *SEUT,* no 23 (1943), 162-192.

Hornberger. "Painters and Painting in the Writing of FHS." *AL,* 16 (Mar 1944), 1-10.

Shelton, William Henry. "Artist Life in New York in the Days of Oliver Horn." *Critic,* 43 (Jul 1903), 31-40.

Chryseis O. Fox

HARRIET PRESCOTT SPOFFORD

Calais, Maine, 3 Apr 1835-Deer Island, near Newburyport, Mass, 14 Aug 1921

From the 1860s until her death in 1921, Harriet Prescott Spofford was one of the most widely published American authors. Best known for her poetry and short fiction, Spofford also wrote five novels and eight novellas. The scenery, legends, and people of New England supplied much of the material for her writing. Critics have often viewed Spofford's writing as progressing from romanticism to the realism of her last collection of stories, *The Elder's People;* nonetheless, her works contained both romantic and realistic elements throughout her career. Her evolution lay instead in her observations of the daily lives of turn-of-the-century women. Spofford employed domestic imagery to capture character through setting and such inanimate objects as jewelry and furniture.

BIBLIOGRAPHY

Bibliography of American Literature, comp Jacob Blanck. New Haven: Yale U P, 1955-1991. Primary.

BOOKS

Sir Rohan's Ghost: A Romance (Anon). Boston: Tilton, 1860. Novel.

The Amber Gods and Other Stories. Boston: Ticknor & Fields, 1863.

Azarian: An Episode. Boston: Ticknor & Fields, 1864. Novel.

New-England Legends. Boston: Osgood, 1871. Essays.

The Thief in the Night. Boston: Roberts, 1872. Novel.

Art Decoration Applied to Furniture. NY: Harper, 1878. Essays.

The Servant Girl Question. Boston: Houghton, Mifflin, 1881. Essays.

Poems. Boston & NY: Houghton, Mifflin, 1882.

The Marquis of Carabas. Boston: Roberts, 1882. Novel.

Hester Stanley at St. Marks. Boston: Roberts, 1882. Novella.

Ballads About Authors. Boston: Lothrop, 1887. Poetry.

A Lost Jewel. Boston: Lee & Shepard / NY: Dillingham, 1891. Novella.

House and Hearth. NY: Dodd, Mead, 1891. Essays.

A Scarlet Poppy and Other Stories. NY: Harper, 1894.

A Master Spirit. NY: Scribners, 1896. Novella.

An Inheritance. NY: Scribners, 1897. Novella.

In Titian's Garden and Other Poems. Boston: Copeland & Day, 1897.

Stepping-Stones to Happiness. NY: Christian Herald, 1897. Essays.

Priscilla's Love-Story. Chicago & NY: Stone, 1898. Novella.

Hester Stanley's Friends. Boston: Little, Brown, 1898. Stories.

The Maid He Married. Chicago & NY: Stone, 1899. Novella.

Old Madame & Other Tragedies. Boston: Badger, 1900. Stories.

The Children of the Valley. NY: Crowell, 1901. Novella.

The Great Procession and Other Verses For and About Children. Boston: Badger, 1902.

That Betty. NY & c: Revell, 1903. Novella.

Four Days of God. Boston: Badger, 1905. Essays.

Old Washington. Boston: Little, Brown, 1906. Stories.

The Fairy Changeling: A Flower and Fairy Play. Boston: Badger, 1911.

The Making of a Fortune: A Romance. NY & London: Harper, 1911. Novel.

The King's Easter. Boston: World Peace Foundation, 1912. Story.

A Little Book of Friends. Boston: Little, Brown, 1916. Essays.

The Elder's People. Boston & NY: Houghton Mifflin, 1920. Stories.

MANUSCRIPTS & ARCHIVES

Essex Institute, Salem, Mass.

BIOGRAPHIES

Book

Halbeisen, Elizabeth K. "HPS: A Romantic Survival." Dissertation: U Pennsylvania, 1934.

Book Sections & Articles

Bacon, Edwin M. *Literary Pilgrimages in New England* (NY: Silver, Burdett, 1902), 65-70.

Cooke, Rose Terry. "HPS." *Our Famous Women* (Hartford, Conn: Worthington, 1884), 521-538.

"HPS." *Book Buyer,* ns 6 (Aug 1889), 235-236.

Morrison, Mary Gray. "Memories of Mrs. S." *Bookman,* 62 (Nov 1925), 315-318.

Stoddard, R H et al. *Poets' Homes,* Vol 1 (Boston: Lothrop, 1879), 196-229.

Winslow, Helen M. *Literary Boston of To-day* (Boston: Page, 1903), 114-117.

CRITICAL STUDIES

Books Sections & Articles

Bartlett, Albert L. "Some Annals of Old Haverhill." *NEMag,* ns 2 (Jul 1890), 505-507.

Dalke, Anne. " 'Circumstance' and the Creative Woman: HPS." *ArQ,* 41 (Spring 1985), 71-85.

Goodwin, Etta Ramsdale. "The Literary Women of Washington." *Chautauquan,* 27 (Sep 1898), 579-586.

Hopkins, Alphonso A. "HPS." *Waifs, and Their Authors* (Boston: Lothrop, 1879), 303-316.

Hopkins, F M. "American Poets of Today: HPS." *CurrentL,* 25 (Feb 1899), 122-123.

"Miss Prescott's *Azarian.*" *NAR,* 100 (Jan 1865), 268-277.

Shinn, Thelma J. "HPS: A Reconsideration." *TCW,* 1 (Summer 1984), 36-45.

St Armand, Barton Levi. " 'I Must Have Died at Ten Minutes Past One': Posthumous Reverie in HPS's 'The Amber Gods.' " *The Haunted Dusk: American Supernatural Fiction, 1820-1920,* ed Howard Kerr, John W Crowley & Charles L Crow (Athens: U Georgia P, 1983), 99-119.

Ward, Elizabeth Stuart Phelps. "Stories That Stay." *Century,* ns 81 (Nov 1910), 118-123.

Heather Stone

FRANK R. STOCKTON

Philadelphia, Pa, 5 Apr 1834-Washington, DC, 20 Apr 1902

Frank R. Stockton contributed many stories to the children's magazines *Hearth and Home* and *St. Nicholas*, for both of which he served as an editor, and he published much adult fiction in *Scribner's Magazine*. Although he is best remembered for the story "The Lady, or the Tiger?" Stockton also enjoyed success with such humorous novels as *Rudder Grange* and *The Casting Away of Mrs. Lecks and Mrs. Aleshine*. Highly regarded by his contemporaries for his inventiveness, Stockton experimented with fantasy stories and novels, several of which are considered precursors of modern science fiction. He also produced several works in the mystery and detective genre.

BIBLIOGRAPHIES & CATALOGUE

"Bibliography." Griffin, 149-173. Primary & secondary.

Bibliography of American Literature, comp Jacob Blanck. New Haven: Yale U P, 1955-1991. Primary.

Clark, Lucy T & Marjorie D Carver. *FRS: A Checklist of Printed and Manuscript Works of FRS in the Library of the University of Virginia*. Charlottesville: U Virginia P, 1963.

BOOKS

A Northern Voice for the Dissolution of the Union of the United States of America (Anon). Npl: npub, 1860.

Ting a Ling. NY: Hurd & Houghton, 1870. Repub as *Ting-a-Ling Tales*. NY: Scribners, 1882. Stories.

Round-About Rambles in Lands of Fact and Fancy. NY: Scribner, Armstrong, 1872. Stories & essays.

The Home: Where It Should Be and What to Put in It, with Marian Stockton. NY: Putnam, 1873. Nonfiction.

What Might Have Been Expected. NY: Dodd & Mead, 1874. Story.

Tales Out of School. NY: Scribner, Armstrong, 1876. Stories.

Rudder Grange. NY: Scribners, 1879. Rev ed, 1879. Novel.

A Jolly Fellowship. NY: Scribners, 1880. Novel.

The Floating Prince and Other Fairy Tales. NY: Scribners, 1881. Stories.

The Lady, or the Tiger? and Other Stories. NY: Scribners, 1884. Augmented ed, Edinburgh: Douglas, 1884.

The Story of Viteau. NY: Scribners, 1884. Novel.

The Late Mrs. Null. NY: Scribners, 1886. Novel.

The Christmas Wreck and Other Stories. NY: Scribners, 1886. Repub as *A Borrowed Month and Other Stories*. Edinburgh: Douglas, 1887.

The Casting Away of Mrs. Lecks and Mrs. Aleshine. NY: Century, 1886. Novel.

The Bee-Man of Orn and Other Fanciful Tales. NY: Scribners, 1887. Stories.

The Hundredth Man. NY: Century, 1887. Novel.

The Dusantes: A Sequel to "The Casting Away of Mrs. Lecks and Mrs. Aleshine." NY: Century, 1888. Novel.

Amos Kilbright: His Adscititious Experience, With Other Stories. NY: Scribners, 1888.

The Great War Syndicate. NY: Collier, 1889. Novel.

Personally Conducted. NY: Scribners, 1889. Travel.

The Stories of the Three Burglars. NY: Dodd, Mead, 1889.

The Merry Chanter. NY: Century, 1890; *The Schooner "Merry Chanter."* London: Low, 1890. Novel.

Ardis Claverden. NY: Dodd, Mead, 1890. Novel.

The Cosmic Bean; or, The Great Show in Kobol-Land. London: Black & White, 1891. Repub as *The Great Show in Kobol-land*. London: Osgood, McIlvaine, 1891. Story.

The Rudder Grangers Abroad and Other Stories. NY: Scribners, 1891.

The Squirrel Inn. NY: Century, 1891. Novel.

The House of Martha. Boston & NY: Houghton, Mifflin, 1891. Novel.

My Terminal Moraine. . . . NY: Collier, 1892. Story.

The Clocks of Rondaine and Other Stories. NY: Scribners, 1892.

The Watchmaker's Wife and Other Stories. NY: Scribners, 1893; *The Shadrach and Other Stories*. London: Allen, 1893.

Pomona's Travels. NY: Scribners, 1894. Novel.

The Adventures of Captain Horn. NY: Scribners, 1895. Novel.

The Spirit of Washington, a Paper Prepared and Read Before the Washington Association of New Jersey. . . . Morristown, NJ: npub, 1895.

Stories of New Jersey. NY & c: American Book, 1896. Repub as *New Jersey, From the Discovery of the Scheyibi to Recent Times.* NY: Appleton, 1896. Nonfiction.

Mrs. Cliff's Yacht. NY: Scribners, 1896. Novel.

Captain Chap; or, The Rolling Stones. Philadelphia: Lippincott, 1897. Novel.

A Story-Teller's Pack. NY: Scribners, 1897. Stories.

The Great Stone of Sardis: A Novel. NY & London: Harper, 1898.

The Girl at Cobhurst. NY: Scribners, 1898. Novel.

Buccaneers and Pirates of Our Coasts. NY & London: Macmillan, 1898. Nonfiction.

The Associate Hermits. NY & London: Harper, 1899. Novel.

The Vizier of the Two-Horned Alexander. NY: Century, 1899. Novel.

The Young Master of Hyson Hall. London: Chatto & Windus, 1899; Philadelphia: Lippincott, 1900. Novel.

Afield and Afloat. NY: Scribners, 1900. Stories.

A Bicycle of Cathay: A Novel. NY & London: Harper, 1900.

Kate Bonnet: The Romance of a Pirate's Daughter. NY: Appleton, 1902. Novel.

John Gayther's Garden and the Stories Told Therein. NY: Scribners, 1902. Stories.

The Captain's Toll-Gate, With a Memorial Sketch by Mrs. Stockton and a Bibliography. NY: Appleton, 1903. Novel.

The Lost Dryad. Riverside, Conn: United Workers of Greenwich, 1912. Story.

The Poor Count's Christmas. NY: Stokes, 1927. Story.

EDITION & COLLECTIONS

Fanciful Tales, ed Julia Elizabeth Langworthy. NY: Scribners, 1894.

A Chosen Few: Short Stories. NY: Scribners, 1895.

The Novels and Stories of FRS, Shenandoah Edition, 23 vols. NY: Scribners, 1899-1904.

The Queen's Museum, and Other Fanciful Tales. NY: Scribners, 1906.

The Magic Egg and Other Stories. NY: Scribners, 1907.

The Reformed Pirate: Stories From The Floating Prince, Ting-a-Ling Tales & The Queen's Museum. NY & London: Scribners, 1936.

The Best Short Stories of FRS. NY: Scribners, 1957.

The Storyteller's Pack: A FRS Reader. NY: Scribners, 1968.

The Science Fiction of FRS, ed with intro by Richard Gid Powers. Boston: Gregg, 1976.

MANUSCRIPTS & ARCHIVES

U of Virginia Library.

BIOGRAPHIES

Book

Griffin, Martin I J. *FRS: A Critical Biography.* Philadelphia: U Pennsylvania P, 1939. Repub Port Washington, NY: Kennikat, 1965.

Article

Stockton, Marian Edwards. "Memorial Sketch of FRS." *The Capain's Toll-Gate,* i-xxxii.

CRITICAL STUDIES

Book

Golemba, Henry L. *FRS.* Boston: Twayne, 1981.

Book Section & Articles

Bowen, Edwin W. "FRS." *SR,* 11 (Oct 1903), 474-478.

Bowen. "The Fiction of FRS." *SR,* 28 (Jul 1920), 452-462.

Fox, Robert C. "Before the *Nautilus.*" *AmNeptune,* 20 (Jul 1960), 174-176.

Howells, William Dean. "S's Stories." *Atlantic,* 59 (Jan 1887), 130-132.

Howells. "Life and Letters." *HarW,* 41 (29 May 1897), 538.

Howells. "Mr. S and All His Works." *Book Buyer,* 20 (Feb 1900), 19-21.

Howells. "S's Novels and Stories." *Atlantic,* 87 (Jan 1901), 136-138.

Mabie, H W. "FRS." *Book Buyer,* 24 (Jun 1902), 355-356.

Marble, Annie Russell. "Pseudonyms and Sobriquets." *Bookman,* 71 (Mar 1930), 58-64.

Pforzheimer, Walter L. "The Lady, the Tiger, and the Author." *Colophon,* ns 1 (Autumn 1935), 261-270.

Werner, William L. "The Escapes of FS." *Essays in Honor of A. Howry Espenshade* (NY: Nelson, 1937), 21-45.

David C. Owens

BOOTH TARKINGTON

Indianapolis, Ind, 29 Jul 1869-Indianapolis, Ind, 19 May 1946

Although he was one of the most respected, popular, and well-paid writers of the early 1920s, Booth Tarkington has since suffered a diminished reputation and readership. He moved easily among short stories, essays, plays, and novels—publishing more than forty-five books and writing more than twenty plays. Tarkington achieved popular success with the publication of his first novel, *The Gentleman From Indiana*, and books recounting the escapades of Penrod, an adventurous boy; he earned critical praise for *The Magnificent Ambersons* and *Alice Adams*, both of which won Pulitzer Prizes. Although much of his work leaned toward social criticism, his genteel approach to modern issues made him seem less "modern" than other writers of the 1920s, who grappled with an increasingly depersonalized modern society. Yet Tarkington remains one of the most significant minor writers in American literature.

BIBLIOGRAPHIES

"Additions to the T Bibliography." *PULC*, 16 (Winter 1955), 89-94. Primary.

First Printings of American Authors, Vol 1 (Detroit: Bruccoli Clark/Gale, 1977), 369-375. Primary.

Russo, Dorothy Ritter & Thelma L Sullivan. *A Bibliography of BT, 1869-1946*. Indianapolis: Indiana Historical Society, 1949. Primary.

BOOKS

The Gentleman From Indiana. NY: Doubleday & McClure, 1899. Novel.

Monsieur Beaucaire. NY: McClure, Phillips, 1900. Novel.

The Two Vanrevels. NY: McClure, Phillips, 1902. Novel.

Cherry. NY & London: Harper, 1903. Novel.

In the Arena: Stories of Political Life. NY: McClure, Phillips, 1905. Stories.

The Beautiful Lady. NY: McClure, Phillips, 1905. Novel.

The Conquest of Canaan. NY & London: Harper, 1905. Novel.

His Own People. NY: Doubleday, Page, 1907. Novel.

The Guest of Quesnay. NY: McClure, 1908. Novel.

The Man From Home, with Harry Leon Wilson. NY & London: Harper, 1908. Play.

Beasley's Christmas Party. NY & London: Harper, 1909. Novel.

Beauty and the Jacobin: An Interlude of the French Revolution. NY & London: Harper, 1912. Novel.

The Flirt. Garden City, NY: Doubleday, Page, 1913. Novel.

Penrod. Garden City, NY: Doubleday, Page, 1914. Novel.

The Turmoil. NY & London: Harper, 1915. Novel.

Seventeen. NY & London: Harper, 1916. Novel.

Penrod and Sam. Garden City, NY: Doubleday, Page, 1916. Novel.

The Magnificent Ambersons. Garden City, NY: Doubleday, Page, 1918. Novel.

Ramsey Milholland. Garden City, NY: Doubleday, Page, 1919. Novel.

The Gibson Upright, with Wilson. Garden City, NY: Doubleday, Page, 1919. Play.

Alice Adams. Garden City, NY & Toronto: Doubleday, Page, 1921. Novel.

Harlequin and Columbine. Garden City, NY & Toronto: Doubleday, Page, 1921. Stories.

Clarence: A Comedy in Four Acts. NY & London: French, 1921. Play.

The Country Cousin: A Comedy in Four Acts, with Julian Street. NY & London: French, 1921. Play.

The Intimate Strangers: A Comedy in Three Acts. NY & London: French, 1921. Play.

The Ghost Story: A One-Act Play for Persons of No Great Age. Cincinnati: Kidd, 1922.

Gentle Julia. Garden City, NY & Toronto: Doubleday, Page, 1922. Novel.

The Wren: A Comedy in Three Acts. NY & London: French, 1922. Play.

The Trysting Place: A Farce in One Act. Cincinnati: Kidd, 1923. Play.

The Fascinating Stranger and Other Stories. Garden City, NY: Doubleday, Page, 1923.

The Collector's Whatnot (as by Cornelius Obenchain Van Loot), with Kenneth Roberts as Milton Kilgallen & Hugh MacNair Kahler as Murgatroyd Elphinstone. Boston & NY: Houghton Mifflin, 1923. Essays.

The Midlander. Garden City, NY: Doubleday, Page, 1924. Repub as *National Avenue* in *Growth.*

Tweedles: A Comedy, with Wilson. NY & London: French, 1924. Play.

Women. Garden City, NY: Doubleday, Page, 1925. Novel.

Bimbo, the Pirate: A Comedy. NY & London: Appleton, 1926. Play.

Looking Forward and Others. Garden City, NY: Doubleday, Page, 1926. Essays.

The Plutocrat. Garden City, NY: Doubleday, Page, 1927. Novel.

Station YYYY. NY & London: Appleton, 1927. Play.

The Travelers. NY & London: Appleton, 1927. Play.

Claire Ambler. Garden City, NY: Doubleday, Doran, 1928. Novel.

The World Does Move. Garden City, NY: Doubleday, Doran, 1928. Essays.

Young Mrs. Greeley. Garden City, NY: Doubleday, Doran, 1929. Novel.

Penrod Jashber. Garden City, NY: Doubleday, Doran, 1929. Novel.

Mirthful Haven. Garden City, NY: Doubleday, Doran, 1930. Novel.

How's Your Health? A Comedy in Three Acts, with Wilson. NY & c: French, 1930. Play.

Mary's Neck. Garden City, NY: Doubleday, Doran, 1932. Novel.

Wanton Mally. Garden City, NY: Doubleday, Doran, 1932. Novel.

Presenting Lily Mars. Garden City, NY: Doubleday, Doran, 1933. Novel.

Little Orvie. Garden City, NY: Doubleday, Doran, 1934. Novel.

The Help Each Other Club. NY & London: Appleton-Century, 1934. Play.

Mister Antonio: A Play in Four Acts. NY & c: French, 1935.

Mr. White, The Red Barn, Hell, and Bridewater. Garden City, NY: Doubleday, Doran, 1935. Stories.

The Lorenzo Bunch. Garden City, NY: Doubleday, Doran, 1936. Novel.

Rumbin Galleries. Garden City, NY: Doubleday, Doran, 1937. Novel.

Some Old Portraits: A Book About Art and Human Beings. NY: Doubleday, Doran, 1939. Essays.

The Heritage of Hatcher Ide. NY: Doubleday, Doran, 1941. Novel.

The Fighting Littles. Garden City, NY: Doubleday, Doran, 1941. Novel.

Kate Fennigate. Garden City, NY: Doubleday, Doran, 1943. Novel.

Image of Josephine. Garden City, NY: Doubleday, Doran, 1945. Novel.

Lady Hamilton and Her Nelson. NY: House of Books, 1945. Play.

The Show Piece, intro by Susanah Tarkington. Garden City, NY: Doubleday, 1947. Unfinished novel.

Three Selected Short Novels. Garden City, NY: Doubleday, 1947.

LETTERS

Your Amiable Uncle: Letters to His Nephews. Indianapolis & NY: Bobbs-Merrill, 1949.

"T's New York Literary Debut: Letters Written to His Family in 1899," ed James Woodress. *PULC,* 16 (Winter 1955), 54-79.

On Plays, Playwrights, and Playgoers: Selections From the Letters of BT to George C. Tyler and John Peter Toohey, 1918-1925, ed Alan S Downer. Princeton: Princeton U Library, 1959.

EDITIONS & COLLECTIONS

The Works of BT, Autograph Edition, 27 vols. Garden City, NY: Doubleday, Page/Doubleday, Doran, 1918-1932.

The Works of BT, Seaweed Edition, 27 vols. Garden City, NY: Doubleday, Page/Doubleday, Doran, 1922-1932.

Growth. Garden City, NY: Doubleday, Page, 1927.

Penrod, His Complete Story: Penrod, Penrod and Sam, Penrod Jashber. Garden City, NY: Doubleday, Doran, 1931.

The Gentleman From Indianapolis—A Treasury of BT, ed John Beecroft. Garden City, NY: Doubleday, 1957.

MANUSCRIPTS & ARCHIVES

Princeton U Library.

BIOGRAPHIES

Books

Dickinson, Asa Don. *BT: A Sketch.* Garden City, NY: Doubleday, Page, 1926.

Mayberry, Susanah. *My Amiable Uncle: Recollections About BT,* intro by James Woodress. West Lafayette, Ind: Purdue U P, 1983.

Woodress, James. *BT: Gentleman From Indiana.* NY: Lippincott, 1955.

CRITICAL STUDIES

Books

Fennimore, Keith J. *BT.* NY: Twayne, 1974.

Holliday, Robert Cortes. *BT.* Garden City, NY: Doubleday, Page, 1918.

Book Sections & Articles

Anderson, David D. "The Boy's World of BT." *MMisc,* 1 (Fall 1974), 35-42.

Cary, Richard. "Jewett, T, and the Maine Line." *CLQ*, Series 4 (Feb 1956), 89-95.

Currie, Barton. "An Editor in Pursuit of BT." *PULC*, 16 (Winter 1955), 80-88.

Downer, Alan S. "BT as Playwright." *PULC*, 19 (Winter 1958), 103-104.

Drake, R Y. "BT Reconsidered: The Last of the Innocents." *NatlRep*, 11 (29 Jul 1961), 58-60.

Hamblen, Abigail Ann. "Two Almost-Forgotten Innocents." *Cresset*, 30 (Oct 1967), 16-17.

Hamblen. "BT's Classic of Adolescence." *SHR*, 3 (Summer 1969), 225-231.

Hellman, John M, Jr. "BT." *ALR*, 8 (Autumn 1975), 325-327.

LeGates, Charlotte. "The Family in BT's *Growth* Trilogy." *Midamerica*, 6 (1979), 88-99.

Noverr, Douglas A. "Change, Growth and the Human Dilemma in BT's *The Magnificent Ambersons*." *SSMLN*, 11 (Spring 1981), 14-32.

Quinn, Arthur Hobson. "BT and the Later Romance." *American Fiction* (NY: Appleton-Century, 1936), 596-622.

Rowlette, Robert. "T in Defense of Howells and Realism: A Recovered Letter." *BSUF*, 14 (Summer 1973), 64-65.

Schwartz, Nancy L. "*Alice Adams* (1921), BT: From American Tragedy to Small-Town Dream-Come-True." *The Classic American Novel and the Movies* (NY: Ungar, 1977), 218-225.

Scott, Winfield Townley. "T and the 1920's." *ASch*, 26 (Spring 1957), 181-194.

Seelye, John D. "That Marvelous Boy—Penrod Once Again." *VQR*, 37 (Autumn 1961), 591-604.

Sorkin, Adam J. " 'She Doesn't Last, Apparently': A Reconsideration of BT's *Alice Adams*." *AL*, 46 (May 1974), 182-199.

Sorkin. "Chance, Bigness and the Romance of Reality in BT's *Growth*." *PaEng*, 10 (Fall 1983), 33-44.

Van Doren, Carl. "Tradition and Transition: Stream of Fiction." *The American Novel, 1789-1939* (NY: Macmillan, 1940), 260-280.

Van Nostrand, Albert. "The Plays of BT." *PULC*, 17 (Autumn 1955), 13-39.

Wagenknecht, Edward. "BT, Success." *Cavalcade of the American Novel* (NY: Holt, 1952), 244-251.

Wilson, William Edward. "The Titan and the Gentleman." *AR*, 23 (Spring 1963), 25-34.

Woodress, James. "BT's Attack on American Materialism." *GaR*, 8 (Winter 1954), 440-446.

Woodress. "The T Papers." *PULC*, 16 (Winter 1955), 45-53.

Woodress. "Popular Taste in 1899: BT's First Novel." *Essays in American and English Literature Presented to Bruce Robert McElderry, Jr* (Athens: Ohio U P, 1967), 108-121.

Mark E. Williams

MAURICE THOMPSON

Fairfield, Ind, 9 Sep 1844-Crawfordsville, Ind, 15 Feb 1901

Although Maurice Thompson wrote poetry, criticism, natural history, and essays on geology and archery, he is best known for his historical romance *Alice of Old Vincennes,* which became a best-seller. His short stories, collected in *Hoosier Mosaics, Stories of Indiana,* and *Stories of the Cherokee Hills,* stress the regional details and dialects of the local-color tradition. Thompson's work was limited by his condemnation of realism, and he turned instead to the nostalgia and romanticism inspired by Sir Walter Scott.

BIBLIOGRAPHY

Bibliography of American Literature, comp Jacob Blanck. New Haven: Yale U P, 1955-1991. Primary.

Russo, Dorothy Ritter & Thelma Lois Sullivan. "[James] MT." *Bibliographical Studies of Seven Authors of Crawfordsville, Indiana* (Indianapolis: Indiana Historical Society, 1952), 173-283. Primary.

BOOKS

Hoosier Mosaics. NY: Hale, 1875. Stories.

The Witchery of Archery: A Complete Manual of Archery. . . . NY: Scribners, 1878. Augmented ed, ed Robert P Elmer, Pinehurst, NC: Archers, 1928.

How to Train in Archery. . . , with Will H Thompson. NY: Horsman, 1879. Manual.

A Tallahassee Girl (Anon). Boston: Osgood, 1882. Novel.

His Second Campaign (Anon). Boston: Osgood, 1883. Novel.

Songs of Fair Weather. Boston: Osgood, 1883. Poetry.

A Red-headed Family. NY: Alden, 1885. Essay.

At Love's Extremes. NY: Cassell, 1885. Repub as *Milly: At Love's Extremes.* NY: New Amsterdam Book, 1901. Novel.

By-Ways and Bird Notes. NY: Alden, 1885. Essays.

A Banker of Bandersville: A Novel. NY: Cassell, 1886.

Sylvan Secrets in Bird-Songs and Books. NY: Alden, 1887. Essays.

A Fortnight of Folly. NY: Alden, 1888. Novel.

The Story of Louisiana. Boston: Lothrop, 1888. History.

Poems. Boston & NY: Houghton, Mifflin, 1892.

The King of Honey Island: A Novel. NY: Bonner, 1893. Novel.

The Ethics of Literary Art: The Carew Lectures for 1893, Hartford Theological Seminary. Hartford, Conn: Hartford Seminary, 1893.

Lincoln's Grave. Cambridge & Chicago: Stone & Kimball, 1894. Poetry.

The Ocala Boy: A Story of Florida Town and Forest. Boston: Lothrop, 1895. Novel.

Stories of Indiana. NY & c: American Book, 1898.

Stories of the Cherokee Hills. Boston & NY: Houghton, Mifflin, 1898.

Alice of Old Vincennes. Indianapolis: Bowen-Merrill, 1900. Novel.

My Winter Garden: A Nature-Lover Under Southern Skies. NY: Century, 1900. Essays.

Sweetheart Manette. Philadelphia & London: Lippincott, 1901. Novel.

Rosalynde's Lovers. Indianapolis: Bowen-Merrill, 1901. Novel.

OTHER

The Boys' Book of Sports and Outdoor Life, ed MT. NY: Century, 1886.

EDITION

Alice of Old Vincennes. Bloomington: Indiana U P, 1985.

MANUSCRIPTS & ARCHIVES

The Lilly Library, Indiana U.

BIOGRAPHY

Book

Schumacher, George A. *MT: Archer and Author.* NY: Vantage, 1968.

CRITICAL STUDIES

Book

Wheeler, Otis B. *The Literary Career of MT.* Baton Rouge: Louisiana State U P, 1965.

Book Sections & Articles

Fertig, Walter L. "MT as a Spokesman for the New South." *IMH,* 60 (Dec 1964), 323-330.

Fertig. "MT and *A Modern Instance*." *AL*, 38 (Mar 1966), 103-111.

Fertig. "MT's Primitive Baptist Heritage." *IMH*, 64 (Mar 1968), 1-12.

Fertig. "MT at War With the Realists." *ON*, 1 (Sep 1975), 239-251.

Gaither, Mary E. "Introduction." *Alice of Old Vincennes* (Bloomington: Indiana U P, 1985), ix-xxiv.

Krout, Mary H. "MT at Home." *Independent*, 53 (21 Feb 1901), 416-418.

Moore, Rayburn S. "The Old South and the New: Paul Hamilton Hayne and MT." *SLJ*, 5 (Fall 1972), 108-122.

Moore. *Paul Hamilton Hayne* (NY: Twayne, 1972), passim.

Moore, ed. *A Man of Letters in the Nineteenth-Century South: Selected Letters of Paul Hamilton Hayne* (Baton Rouge: Louisiana State U P, 1982), passim.

Scharnhorst, Gary F. "MT's Regional Critique of William Dean Howells." *ALR*, 9 (Winter 1976), 57-63.

Scharnhorst. "William Dean Howells and MT: At War Over Realism?" *ON*, 5 (Fall 1979), 291-302.

Simms, L Moody, Jr. "MT Recalls Paul Hamilton Hayne." *SoSt*, 16 (Spring 1977), 91-97.

James Nagel

ALBION WINEGAR TOURGÉE

Williamsfield, Ohio, 2 May 1838-Bordeaux, France, 21 May 1905

Albion Winegar Tourgée was one of the most prolific and widely read American novelists and political essayists of the second half of the nineteenth century. Tourgée's most famous novel, *A Fool's Errand*, which was based on his experiences while living in North Carolina, sold 150,000 copies in the year of its publication. Although Tourgée rejected the realism of many of his contemporaries in favor of a more sentimental and polemic style, modern scholars study him for the historical interest of his fiction, claiming that he realistically portrayed the postbellum South and the social problems during Reconstruction.

BIBLIOGRAPHIES & CATALOGUE

Bibliography of American Literature, comp Jacob Blanck. New Haven: Yale U P, 1955-1991. Primary.

Ealy, Marguerite & Sanford E Marovitz. "AWT (1838-1905)." *ALR*, 8 (Winter 1975), 53-80. Primary.

First Printings of American Authors, Vol 1 (Detroit: Bruccoli Clark/Gale, 1977), 387-390. Primary.

Keller, Dean H. "An Index To the AWT Papers in the Chautauqua County Historical Society, Westfield, New York." *KSB*, 7 (May 1964).

Keller. "A Checklist of the Writings of AWT (1838-1905)." *SB*, 18 (1965), 269-279.

BOOKS

Book of Forms, Prepared by Commissioners of the Code, with Victor C Barringer & William B Rodman. Raleigh, NC: npub, 1868.

The Code of Civil Procedure of North Carolina, to Special Proceedings, with Barringer & Rodman. Raleigh, NC: Paige, 1868.

A Plan for the Organization of the Judiciary Department, Proposed by AWT, of Guilford, as a Section of the Constitution. Raleigh, NC: npub, 1868.

Toinette: A Novel (as by Henry Churton). NY: Ford, 1874. Abridged as *Toinette: A Tale of the South*. NY: Fords, Howard, & Hulbert, 1879. Rev as *A Royal Gentleman* in *A Royal*

Gentleman and Zouri's Christmas. NY: Fords, Howard, & Hulbert, 1881.

The "C" Letters, as Published in "The North State." Greensboro, NC: "The North State," 1878.

The Code of Civil Procedure of North Carolina, With Notes and Decisions. Raleigh, NC: Nichols, 1878.

A Digest of Cited Cases in the North Carolina Reports, . . . and a Careful Synopsis of Each Modification, Extension or Reversal. Raleigh, NC: Williams, 1879.

Figs and Thistles: A Western Story. NY: Fords, Howard, & Hulbert, 1879. Novel.

Statutory Adjudications in the North Carolina Reports, With a Supplement to "The Code With Notes and Decisions," and an Index of Parallel References. Raleigh, NC: Williams, 1879.

A Fool's Errand. By One of the Fools (Anon). NY: Fords, Howard, & Hulbert, 1879. Rev & augmented in The Invisible Empire: Part I. A New, Illustrated, and Enlarged Edition of A Fool's Errand . . . Part II. A Concise Review of Recent Events. . . . NY: Fords, Howard, & Hulbert / Boston: Thompson / Chicago: Weston Hulbert / St Louis: Scammell / San Francisco: Bancroft, 1880. The Invisible Empire separately published, Ridgeway, NJ: Gregg, 1968. Novels.

Bricks Without Straw. NY: Fords, Howard, & Hulbert / London: Low / Montreal: Dawson, 1880. Novel.

John Eax and Mamelon; or, The South Without the Shadow. NY: Fords, Howard, & Hulbert, 1882. Novel.

Hot Plowshares: A Novel. NY: Fords, Howard, & Hulbert, 1883.

An Appeal to Caesar. NY: Fords, Howard, & Hulbert, 1884. Nonfiction.

A Man of Destiny (as by Siva). Chicago & NY: Belford, Clarke, 1885. Nonfiction.

The Veteran and His Pipe (Anon). Chicago & NY: Belford, Clarke, 1886. Nonfiction.

Button's Inn. Boston: Roberts, 1887. Novel.

Black Ice. NY: Fords, Howard, & Hulbert, 1888. Novel.

Letters to a King. Cincinnati: Cranston & Stowe / NY: Phillips & Hunt, 1888. Nonfiction.

''89, Edited From the Original Manuscript (as by Edgar Henry). NY & c: Cassell, 1888. Novel.

With Gauge & Swallow, Attorneys. Philadelphia: Lippincott, 1889. Stories.

Murvale Eastman: Christian Socialist. NY: Fords, Howard, & Hulbert / London: Low, Marston, Searle, & Rivington, 1890. Novel.

Pactolus Prime. NY: Cassell, 1890. Novel.

A Son of Old Harry: A Novel. NY: Bonner, 1891.

Out of the Sunset Sea. NY: Merrill & Baker, 1893. History.

An Outing With the Queen of Hearts. NY: Merrill & Baker, 1894. Nonfiction.

The Mortgage on the Hip-Roof House. Cincinnati, Ohio: Curts & Jennings / NY: Eaton & Mains, 1896. Novel.

The Story of a Thousand, Being a History of the Service of the 105th Ohio Volunteer Infantry, in the War for the Union From August 21, 1862 to June 6, 1865. Buffalo, NY: McGerald, 1896.

The War of the Standards: Coin and Credit Versus Coin Without Credit. NY & London: Putnam, 1896. Nonfiction.

The Man Who Outlived Himself. NY: Fords, Howard, & Hulbert, 1898. Stories.

A Fool's Errand, with Steele MacKay; ed Dean H Keller. Metuchen, NJ: Scarecrow, 1969. Play.

A Golden Wedding Fancy: An Unpublished Poem. Kent, Ohio: Costmary, 1971.

DIARY

"A Civil War Diary of AWT," ed Dean H Keller. OhH, 74 (Spring 1965), 99-131.

MANUSCRIPTS & ARCHIVES

The Chautauqua County Historical Society, Westfield, NY.

BIOGRAPHIES

Books

Dibble, Roy F. AWT. NY: Lemcke & Buechner, 1921.

Olsen, Otto H. Carpetbagger's Crusade: The Life of AWT. Baltimore, Md: Johns Hopkins P, 1965.

Book Sections & Articles

Arnett, Ethel Stephens. Greensboro, North Carolina, the County Seat of Guilford (Chapel Hill: U North Carolina P, 1952), passim.

Hamilton, J G de Roulac, ed. The Correspondence of Jonathan Worth, Vol 2 (Raleigh, NC: Edwards & Broughton, 1909), passim.

Hamilton. Reconstruction in North Carolina (NY: Columbia U P, 1914), passim.

Kaplan, Sidney. "AT: Attorney for the Segregated." JNH, 49 (Apr 1964), 128-133.

Keller, Dean H. "AWT as Editor of The Basis." NiagF, 12 (Spring 1965), 24-28.

Nye, Russel B. "Judge T and Reconstruction." OSA&HQ (Apr 1941), 101-114.

Olsen, Otto H. "AWT: Carpetbagger." NCHR, 40 (Oct 1963), 434-454.

Weissbuch, Ted N. "AWT: Propagandist and Critic of Reconstruction." OHQ, 70 (Jan 1961), 27-44.

CRITICAL STUDIES

Books

Gross, Theodore L. *AWT*. NY: Twayne, 1963.

Hillger, Martin E. "AWT: Critic of Society." Dissertation: Indiana U, 1959.

Book Sections & Articles

Aaron, Daniel. *The Unwritten War: American Writers and the Civil War* (NY: Knopf, 1973), 193-205.

Becker, George J. "AWT: Pioneer in Social Criticism." *AL*, 19 (Mar 1947), 59-72.

Cowie, Alexander. *The Rise of the American Novel* (NY: American Book, 1948), 521-535, passim.

Franklin, John Hope. "Introduction." *A Fool's Errand* (Cambridge: Harvard U P, 1961), vii-xxviii.

Gross, Theodore L. "The Negro in the Literature of the Reconstruction." *Phylon*, 22 (Spring 1961), 5-14.

Gross. "AWT: Reporter of the Reconstruction." *MissQ*, 16 (Summer 1963), 111-127.

Gross. "The Fool's Errand of AWT." *Phylon*, 24 (Fall 1963), 240-254.

Keller, Dean H. "AT and a National Education Program." *PJE*, 41 (Jul 1963), 131-135.

Lewis, Richard O. "Romanticism in the Fiction of Charles W. Chesnutt: The Influence of Dickens, Scott, T, and Douglass." *CLAJ*, 26 (Dec 1982), 145-171.

Lively, Robert A. *Fiction Fights the Civil War* (Chapel Hill: U North Carolina P, 1957), passim.

Magdol, Edward. "A Note of Authenticity: Eliab Hill and Nimbus Ware in *Bricks Without Straw*." *AQ*, 22 (Winter 1970), 907-911.

Olenick, Monte M. "AWT: Radical Republican Spokesman of the Civil War Crusade." *Phylon*, 23 (Winter 1962), 332-345.

Olsen, Otto H. "T on Reconstruction: A Revisionist Document of 1892." *Serif*, 2 (Sep 1965), 21-28.

Olsen. "Introduction." *Bricks Without Straw* (Baton Rouge: Louisiana State U P, 1969), vii-xx.

Simms, L Moody, Jr. "AWT on the Fictional Use of the Post-Civil War South." *SoSt*, 17 (Winter 1978), 399-409.

Simms. "AWT on Literary Realism." *RALS*, 8 (1978), 168-173.

Sommer, Robert F. "The Fools Errant in AWT's Reconstruction Novels." *Mid-HudsonLS*, 5 (1982), 71-79.

Toth, Margaret. "AWT, '62." *URLB*, 8 (Spring 1953), 57-62.

Wilcox, Owen N. "AWT: Another Lawyer-Novelist of the Western Reserve." *Brief*, 7 (Jan 1948), 7-54.

Wilson, Edmund. *Patriotic Gore: Studies in the Literature of the American Civil War* (NY: Oxford U P, 1962), 529-548, passim.

Troy L. Headrick

LEW WALLACE

Brookville, Ind, 10 Apr 1827-Crawfordsville, Ind, 15 Feb 1905

A major-general in the Union Army during the Civil War, Lew Wallace was also an eminent lawyer, statesman, and diplomat. He reached a wide audience with the publication of his first book, *The Fair God,* a historical romance about the conquest of Mexico. Wallace's popularity as a writer increased with the appearance of his best-known novel, *Ben-Hur,* in 1880. The dramatic story of the conversion to Christianity of an aristocratic young Jew during the life of Christ, *Ben-Hur* sold 300,000 copies in ten years, was translated into many foreign languages, and had successful stage and film adaptations.

BIBLIOGRAPHIES

Bibliography of American Literature, comp Jacob Blanck. New Haven: Yale U P, 1955-1991. Primary.

Russo, Dorothy Ritter & Thelma Lois Sullivan. "LW." *Bibliographical Studies of Seven Authors of Crawfordsville, Indiana* (Indianapolis: Indiana Historical Society, 1952), 305-416. Primary.

BOOKS

The Fair God; or, The Last of the 'Tzins: A Tale of the Conquest of Mexico. Boston: Osgood, 1873. Novel.

Commodus: An Historical Play. Crawfordsville, Ind: Privately printed, 1876. Rev ed, 1877. Verse play.

Ben-Hur: A Tale of the Christ. NY: Harper, 1880. Excerpted in *The First Christmas.* NY & London: Harper, 1899. Novel.

Life of Gen. Ben Harrison, bound with *Life of Hon. Levi P. Morton* by George Alfred Townsend. Philadelphia & c: Hubbard / Boston: Guernsey / Cincinnati, Ohio: Morris / Denver: Perry / San Francisco: Bancroft, 1888. *Life of Gen. Ben Harrison,* separately published, Philadelphia & c: Hubbard / San Francisco: Bancroft, 1888.

Speech of Gen. LW on the Democratic Party and the Solid South. . . . Crawfordsville, Ind: Crawfordsville Journal, 1888.

The Boyhood of Christ. NY: Harper, 1889. Story.

The Prince of India; or, Why Constantinople Fell, 2 vols. NY: Harper, 1893. Novel.

The Wooing of Malkatoon, Commodus. NY & London: Harper, 1898. Poetry.

Address of Gen. LW at the Dedication of Indiana's Monuments on the Battlefield of Shiloh, Tennessee. . . . Crawfordsville, Ind: News-Review, 1903.

LW: An Autobiography, 2 vols. NY & London: Harper, 1906.

MANUSCRIPTS & ARCHIVES

The Indiana Historical Society, Indianapolis.

BIOGRAPHIES

Books

McKee, Irving. *"Ben-Hur" Wallace: The Life of General LW.* Berkeley: U California P, 1947.

Morsberger, Robert E & Katherine M. *LW: Militant Romantic.* NY: McGraw-Hill, 1980.

Book Sections & Articles

"General LW." *Harper's,* 30 (6 Mar 1886), 145, 151.

Howard, Oliver Otis. "LW: An Autobiography." *NAR,* 183 (21 Dec 1906), 1294-1299.

Krout, Mary H. "Personal Reminiscences of LW." *Harper's,* 49 (18 Mar 1905), 406-409.

"LW: Hoosier Governor of Territorial New Mexico, 1878-81." *NMHistR,* 60 (Apr 1985), 129-158.

McKee, Irving. "The Early Life of LW." *IMH,* 37 (Sep 1941), 205-216.

Nicholson, Meredith. "The Provincial American." *Atlantic,* 107 (Mar 1911), 311-319.

Peterson, C V. "General LW." *PhiGDQ,* 27 (Mar 1905), 388-406.

Richardson, Lyon N. "Men of Letters and the Hayes Administration." *NEQ,* 15 (Mar 1942), 110-141.

CRITICAL STUDIES

Book

Waldhart, Enid Spring. "The Defensive Rhetoric of General LW, 1845-1905." Dissertation: Indiana U, 1976.

Articles

Forbes, John P. "LW, Romantic." *IMH,* 44 (Dec 1948), 385-392.

Kennedy, George A. "Fin-de-Siècle Classicism: Henry Adams and Thorstein Veblen, LW and W. D. Howells." *CML,* 8 (Fall 1987), 15-21.

Morsberger, Robert E & Katherine M. " 'Christ and a Horse Race': *Ben-Hur* on Stage." *JPC,* 8 (Winter 1974), 489-502.

Phy, Allene Stuart. "LW and *Ben-Hur.*" *Romantist,* 6-8 (1982-1984), 2-10.

Theisen, Lee Scott. " 'My God, Did I Set All of This in Motion?' General LW and *Ben-Hur.*" *JPC,* 18 (Fall 1984), 33-41.

Towne, Jackson E. "LW's *Ben-Hur.*" *NMHistR,* 36 (Jan 1961), 62-69.

"Was LW 'An Oriental With Medieval Tastes'?" *Review of Reviews,* 31 (Apr 1905), 480-481.

Winterich, J T. "*Ben-Hur.*" *PW,* 139 (15 Feb 1941), 860-862.

J. Pritchard

ELIZABETH STUART PHELPS WARD

Boston, Mass, 31 Aug 1844-Newton, Mass, 28 Jan 1911

After an apprenticeship writing juvenile novels, Elizabeth Stuart Phelps began producing the fiction with which she is now most closely identified. *The Gates Ajar* in 1869 was the first of her immensely popular novels envisioning a compensatory heavenly afterlife. The second-best seller of the nineteenth century, it was surpassed in sales only by Harriet Beecher Stowe's *Uncle Tom's Cabin.* Now even more well known are Phelps's writings, both fiction and nonfiction, in support of various social causes: better labor conditions, antivivisectionism, and women's issues. Most of Phelps's novels were also published serially in influential magazines. Following her marriage in 1888 Phelps began signing her name Elizabeth Stuart Phelps Ward. Readers until the 1970s usually focused on Phelps as a religious writer; since then, critics have been more interested in her feminist themes.

BIBLIOGRAPHY

Bibliography of American Literature, comp Jacob Blanck. New Haven: Yale U P, 1955-1991. Primary.

BOOKS

Ellen's Idol (Anon). Boston: Massachusetts Sabbath School Society, 1864. Children's novel.

Up Hill; or, Life in the Factory (Anon). Boston: Hoyt, 1865. Novel.

Mercy Gliddon's Work. Boston: Hoyt, 1865. Children's novel.

Tiny. Boston: Massachusetts Sabbath School Society, 1866. Children's novel.

Gypsy Breynton. Boston: Graves & Young, 1866. Children's novel.

Gypsy's Cousin Joy. Boston: Graves & Young, 1866. Children's novel.

Gypsy's Sowing and Reaping. Boston: Graves & Young, 1866. Children's novel.

Tiny's Sunday Nights. Boston: Massachusetts Sabbath School Society, 1866. Children's novel.

Gypsy's Year at the Golden Crescent. Boston: Graves & Young, 1867. Children's novel.

I Don't Know How. Boston: Massachusetts Sabbath School Society, 1868. Children's novel.

The Gates Ajar. Boston: Fields, Osgood, 1869. Novel.

Men, Women, and Ghosts. Boston: Fields, Osgood, 1869. Stories.

Hedged In. Boston: Fields, Osgood, 1870. Novel.

The Trotty Book. Boston: Fields, Osgood, 1870; *That Dreadful Boy Trotty: What He Did and What He Said.* London: Ward, Lock, 1877. Children's novel.

The Silent Partner. Boston: Osgood / London: Sampson Low, 1871. Novel.

What to Wear? Boston: Osgood, 1873. Essay.

Trotty's Wedding Tour, and Story-book. London: Sampson Low, Marston, Low, & Searle, 1873; Boston: Osgood, 1874. Children's novel.

Poetic Studies. Boston: Osgood, 1875. Poems.

The Story of Avis. Boston: Osgood, 1877. Novel.

My Cousin and I: A Story in Two Parts. London: Sunday School Union, nd. Stories.

Old Maids' Paradise. London: Clarke, 1879; *An Old Maid's Paradise.* Boston: Houghton, Mifflin, 1885. Novel.

Sealed Orders. Boston: Houghton, Osgood, 1879. Stories.

Friends: A Duet. Boston: Houghton, Mifflin, 1881. Novel.

Doctor Zay. Boston & NY: Houghton, Mifflin, 1882. Novel.

Beyond the Gates. Boston & NY: Houghton, Mifflin, 1883. Novel.

Songs of the Silent World and Other Poems. Boston & NY: Houghton, Mifflin, 1885.

Burglars in Paradise. Boston & NY: Houghton, Mifflin, 1886. Novel.

The Madonna of the Tubs. Boston & NY: Houghton, Mifflin, 1887. Novel.

The Gates Between. Boston & NY: Houghton, Mifflin, 1887. Novel.

Jack the Fisherman. Boston & NY: Houghton, Mifflin, 1887. Novel.

The Struggle for Immortality. Boston & NY: Houghton, Mifflin, 1889. Essays.

The Master of the Magicians, with Herbert D Ward. Boston & NY: Houghton, Mifflin, 1890. Novel.

Come Forth! with Herbert D Ward. London: Heinemann, 1890; *Come Forth.* Boston & NY: Houghton, Mifflin, 1891. Novel.

Austin Phelps: A Memoir. NY: Scribners, 1891.

A Lost Hero, with Herbert D Ward. Boston: Roberts, 1891. Children's novel.

Fourteen to One. Boston & NY: Houghton, Mifflin, 1891. Stories.

Donald Marcy. Boston & NY: Houghton, Mifflin, 1893. Children's novel.

A Singular Life. Boston & NY: Houghton, Mifflin, 1895. Novel.

The Supply at Saint Agatha's. Boston & NY: Houghton, Mifflin, 1896. Novella.

Chapters From a Life. Boston & NY: Houghton, Mifflin, 1896. Autobiography.

The Story of Jesus Christ: An Interpretation. Boston & NY: Houghton, Mifflin, 1897.

Loveliness: A Story. Boston & NY: Houghton, Mifflin, 1899.

The Successors of Mary the First. Boston & NY: Houghton, Mifflin, 1901. Novel.

Within the Gates. Boston & NY: Houghton, Mifflin, 1901. Play.

Avery. Boston & NY: Houghton, Mifflin, 1902. Novel.

Confessions of a Wife (as by Mary Adams). NY: Century, 1902. Novel.

Trixy. Boston & NY: Houghton, Mifflin, 1904. Novel.

The Man in the Case. Boston & NY: Houghton, Mifflin, 1906. Novel.

Walled In: A Novel. NY & London: Harper, 1907.

Though Life Us Do Part. Boston & NY: Houghton Mifflin, 1908. Novel.

Jonathan and David. NY & London: Harper, 1909. Story.

The Oath of Allegiance and Other Stories. Boston & NY: Houghton Mifflin, 1909.

The Empty House and Other Stories. Boston & NY: Houghton Mifflin, 1910; *A Deserted House and Other Stories.* London: Constable, 1911.

Comrades. NY & London: Harper, 1911. Story.

OTHER

"The Married Daughter." *The Whole Family: A Novel by Twelve Authors* (NY & London: Harper, 1908), 185-218.

BIOGRAPHY

Book

Bennett, Mary Angela. "ESP, 1844-1911: A Critical Biography." Dissertation: U Pennsylvania, 1938.

CRITICAL STUDIES

Books

Coultrap-McQuin, Susan Margaret. "ESP: The Cultural Context of a Nineteenth-Century Professional Writer." Dissertation: U Iowa, 1979.

Kelly, Lori Duin. *The Life and Works of ESP, Victorian Feminist Writer.* Troy, NY: Whitston, 1982.

Kessler, Carol Farley. *ESP.* Boston: Twayne, 1982.

Book Sections & Articles

Cogan, Frances B. "Weak Fathers and Other Beasts: An Examination of the American Male in Domestic Novels, 1850-1870." *AmerS,* 25, no 2 (1984), 5-20.

Donovan, Josephine. *New England Local Color Literature: A Women's Tradition* (NY: Ungar, 1983), passim.

Douglas, Ann. *The Feminization of American Culture* (NY: Knopf, 1977), passim.

Fetterley, Judith. " 'Checkmate': ESP's *The Silent Partner.*" *Legacy,* 3 (Fall 1986), 17-29.

Habegger, Alfred. "Nineteenth-Century American Humor: Easygoing Males, Anxious Ladies, and Penelope Lapham." *PMLA,* 91 (Oct 1976), 884-899.

Habegger. "John William De Forest vs. ESP." *Gender, Fantasy, and Realism in American Literature* (NY: Columbia U P, 1982), 38-55, passim.

Huf, Linda. "*The Story of Avis* (1877): Scenes From a Marriage, by ESP." *A Portrait of the Artist as a Young Woman: The Writer as Heroine in American Literature* (NY: Ungar, 1983), 37-57.

Kessler, Carol Farley. "A Literary Legacy: ESP, Mother and Daughter." *Frontiers,* 5 (Fall 1980), 28-33.

Kessler. "The Heavenly Utopia of ESP." *Women and Utopia: Critical Interpretations,* ed Marleen Barr & Nicholas D Smith (Lanham, Md: U P America, 1983), 85-95.

Masteller, Jean Carwile. "The Women Doctors of Howells, P, and Jewett." *Critical Essays on Sarah Orne Jewett,* ed Gwen L Nagel (Boston: Hall, 1984), 135-147.

Rees, Robert A. "*Captain Stormfield's Visit to Heaven* and *The Gates Ajar.*" *ELN,* 7 (Mar 1970), 197-202.

Shapiro, Ann R. "Work and the Bridging of Social Class: ESP, *The Silent Partner* (1871)." *Unlikely Heroines: Nineteenth-Century American Women Writers and the Woman Question* (NY: Greenwood, 1987), 37-51.

Smith, Helen Sootin. "Introduction." *The Gates Ajar* (Cambridge: Harvard U P, 1964), v-xxxiii.

Stansell, Christine. "ESP: A Study in Female Rebellion." *MR,* 13 (Winter-Spring 1972), 239-256.

St Armand, Barton Levi. "Paradise Deferred: The Image of Heaven in the Works of Emily Dickinson and ESP." *AQ,* 29 (Spring 1977), 55-78.

Stewart, Grace. *A New Mythos: The Novel of the Artist as Heroine, 1877-1977* (Montreal: Eden P Women's Publications, 1981), 76-81, 110-112.

Ward, Susan. "The Career Woman Fiction of ESP." *Nineteenth-Century Women Writers of the English-Speaking World,* ed Rhoda B Nathan (NY: Greenwood, 1986), 209-219.

Welter, Barbara. "Defenders of the Faith." *Dimity Convictions: The American Woman in the Nineteenth Century* (Athens: Ohio U P, 1976), 111-120.

Wood, Ann Douglas. " 'Fashionable Diseases': Women's Complaints and Their Treatment in Nineteenth-Century America." *JIH,* 4 (Summer 1973), 25-52. Rpt *The Private Side of American History: Readings in Everyday Life,* ed Thomas R Frazier (NY: Harcourt Brace Jovanovich, 1979).

Pamela R. Matthews

EDWARD NOYES WESTCOTT

Syracuse, NY, 27 Sep 1846-Syracuse, NY, 31 Mar 1898

Edward Noyes Westcott spent most of his life as a banker. When ill health forced him into premature retirement, he began writing his only novel, *David Harum: A Story of American Life,* about a small-town banker. Although Westcott did not live to see it published, the novel was an immediate success, encouraging the posthumous publication of *The Teller: A Story.* Readers were charmed by Harum, and it is for his colorful characters that Westcott is chiefly remembered.

BIBLIOGRAPHY

Bibliography of American Literature, comp Jacob Blanck. New Haven: Yale U P, 1955-1991. Primary.

BOOKS

David Harum: A Story of American Life. NY: Appleton, 1898. Augmented ed, NY: Dover, 1960. Excerpted in *The Christmas Story From David Harum,* ed William H Crane. NY: Appleton, 1900. Novel.
The Teller: A Story. NY: Appleton, 1901. Novella & letters.

MANUSCRIPTS & ARCHIVES

The major collections are at Syracuse U Library, Columbia U Library & the Syracuse Public Library.

BIOGRAPHY

Book Section
"Preface." *The Christmas Story From David Harum,* v-ix.

CRITICAL STUDIES

Book
Vance, Arthur T. *The Real David Harum.* NY: Baker & Taylor, 1900.

Special Journal
SyracuseL, 11 (Feb 1918). *David Harum* issue.

Book Sections & Articles
Case, Richard G. "The Westcotts and David Harum." *Courier,* 10 (Winter 1973), 3-14.
Glassie, Henry. "The Use of Folklore in *David Harum.*" *NYFQ,* 23 (Sep 1967), 163-185.
Heermans, Forbes. "Introduction." *David Harum: A Story of American Life* (1898), v-viii.
Hitchcock, Helen Sargent. "David Harum Philosophizes Again." *NYTM* (17 Jul 1938), 10, 16.
Parks, Carrie Belle. "Introduction." *David Harum: A Story of American Life* (NY: Appleton, 1931), vii-xix.

Barbara Bell

EDITH WHARTON

New York City, NY, 24 Jan 1862-St. Brice-sous-Forêt, France, 11 Aug 1937

Although some of her contemporaries complained that her works lacked warmth or were overly imitative of the novels of Henry James, Edith Wharton was among the most widely admired American writers of fiction during the first three decades of the twentieth century. After her death critics generally assigned her a high place within the second rank of American writers. To some extent her work was overshadowed by the more daring experiments in fictional form of such modernists as Ernest Hemingway and William Faulkner; critics of the 1930s also felt uncomfortable with her emphasis on high society. Nevertheless, her major works, *The House of Mirth, Ethan Frome* and *The Age of Innocence*, continued to attract attention and earn admiration. The publication of R. W. B. Lewis's biography in 1975 and the advent of feminist criticism stirred a revival of interest in her life and works. Wharton is now widely recognized as one of the two or three most important American women writers of fiction and praised for her social analysis, satiric wit, stylistic grace, and psychological depth.

BIBLIOGRAPHIES

Bendixen, Alfred. "A Guide to W Criticism, 1974-1983." *EWhN*, 2 (Fall 1985), 1-8. Secondary.

Brenni, Vito J. *EW: A Bibliography.* Morgantown: West Virginia U Library, 1966. Primary.

Davis, Lavinia. *A Bibliography of the Writings of EW.* Portland, Maine: Southworth, 1933. Primary.

First Printings of American Authors, Vol 3 (Detroit: Bruccoli Clark/Gale, 1978), 341-356. Primary.

Schriber, Mary Suzanne. "EW and the French Critics, 1906-1937." *ALR*, 13 (Spring 1980), 61-72. Secondary.

Springer, Marlene. *EW and Kate Chopin: A Reference Guide.* Boston: Hall, 1976. Secondary.

Springer & Joan Gilson. "EW: A Reference Guide Updated." *RALS*, 14 (Spring-Autumn 1984), 85-111. Secondary.

Tuttleton, James W. "EW." *American Women Writers: Bibliographical Essays,* ed Maurice Duke, Jackson R Bryer & M Thomas Inge (West-

port, Conn: Greenwood, 1983), 71-107. Secondary.

BOOKS

Verses (Anon). Newport, RI: Hammett, 1878.

The Decoration of Houses, with Ogden Codman, Jr. NY: Scribners, 1897. Nonfiction.

The Greater Inclination. NY: Scribners, 1899. Stories.

The Touchstone. NY: Scribners, 1900; *A Gift From the Grave.* London: Murray, 1900. Novel.

Crucial Instances. NY: Scribners, 1901. Stories.

The Valley of Decision, 2 vols. NY: Scribners, 1902. Novel.

Sanctuary. NY: Scribners, 1903. Novel.

The Descent of Man and Other Stories. NY: Scribners, 1904.

Italian Villas and Their Gardens. NY: Century, 1904. Nonfiction.

Italian Backgrounds. NY: Scribners, 1905. Nonfiction.

The House of Mirth. NY: Scribners, 1905. Novel.

The Fruit of the Tree. NY: Scribners, 1907. Novel.

Madame de Treymes. NY: Scribners, 1907. Novel.

The Hermit and the Wild Woman and Other Stories. NY: Scribners, 1908.

A Motor-Flight Through France. NY: Scribners, 1908. Nonfiction.

Artemis to Actaeon and Other Verse. NY: Scribners, 1909.

Tales of Men and Ghosts. NY: Scribners, 1910. Stories.

Ethan Frome. NY: Scribners, 1911. Novel.

The Reef. NY: Appleton, 1912. Novel.

The Custom of the Country. NY: Scribners, 1913. Novel.

Fighting France From Dunkerque to Belfort. NY: Scribners, 1915. Nonfiction.

Xingu and Other Stories. NY: Scribners, 1916.

Summer: A Novel. NY: Appleton, 1917.

The Marne. NY: Appleton, 1918. Novel.

French Ways and Their Meaning. NY & London: Appleton, 1919. Nonfiction.

In Morocco. NY: Scribners, 1920. Nonfiction.

The Age of Innocence. NY & London: Appleton, 1920. Novel.

The Glimpses of the Moon. NY & London: Appleton, 1922. Novel.

A Son at the Front. NY: Scribners, 1923. Novel.

Old New York: False Dawn (The 'Forties). NY &
London: Appleton, 1924. Novella.
Old New York: The Old Maid (The 'Fifties). NY
& London: Appleton, 1924. Novella.
Old New York: The Spark (The 'Sixties). NY &
London: Appleton, 1924. Novella.
Old New York: New Year's Day (The 'Seventies).
NY & London: Appleton, 1924. Novella.
The Mother's Recompense. NY & London: Apple-
ton, 1925. Novel.
The Writing of Fiction. NY & London: Scribners,
1925. Nonfiction.
Here and Beyond. NY & London: Appleton, 1926.
Stories.
Twelve Poems. London: Medici Society, 1926.
Twilight Sleep. NY & London: Appleton, 1927.
Novel.
The Children. NY & London: Appleton, 1928.
Repub as *The Marriage Playground.* NY:
Grosset & Dunlap, 1930. Novel.
Hudson River Bracketed. NY & London: Apple-
ton, 1929. Novel.
Certain People. NY & London: Appleton, 1930.
Stories.
The Gods Arrive. NY & London: Appleton, 1932.
Novel.
Human Nature. NY & London: Appleton, 1933.
Stories.
A Backward Glance. NY & London: Appleton-
Century, 1934. Autobiography.
The World Over. NY & London: Appleton-
Century, 1936. Stories.
Ghosts. NY & London: Appleton-Century, 1937.
Stories.
The Buccaneers. NY & London: Appleton-Century,
1938. Unfinished novel.
The Collected Short Stories of EW, 2 vols, ed with
intro by R W B Lewis. NY: Scribners, 1968.
Fast and Loose, a Novelette (as by David Olivieri),
ed with intro by Viola Winner Hopkins.
Charlottesville: U P Virginia, 1977.
The House of Mirth: The Play of the Novel, with
Clyde Fitch; ed with intro by Glenn Loney.
Rutherford, NJ & c: Fairleigh Dickinson U P /
London & Toronto: Associated U Presses,
1981.

LETTERS

The Letters of EW, ed with intro by R W B &
Nancy Lewis. NY: Scribners, 1988.

OTHER

The Joy of Living by Hermann Sudermann; trans
EW. NY: Scribners, 1902. Play.
The Book of the Homeless, ed EW. NY: Scribners,
1916. Miscellany.
Eternal Passion in English Poetry, ed EW & Robert
Norton, with Gaillard Lapsley; preface by

EW. NY & London: Appleton-Century, 1939.
Poetry.

EDITION & COLLECTIONS

An EW Treasury, ed with intro by Arthur Hobson
Quinn. NY: Appleton-Century-Crofts, 1950.
The Best Short Stories of EW, ed with intro by
Wayne Andrews. NY: Scribners, 1958.
The EW Reader, ed with intro by Louis Auchin-
closs. NY: Scribners, 1965.
*EW's Ethan Frome: The Story With Sources and
Commentary,* ed Blake Nevius. NY: Scribners,
1968.
The EW Omnibus, ed Gore Vidal. NY: Scribners,
1978.

MANUSCRIPTS & ARCHIVES

The major collections are at the Beinecke Library,
Yale U; Princeton U Library; the Houghton Library, Harvard U; the Lilly Library, Indiana U; &
the Harry Ransom Humanities Research Center, U
of Texas, Austin.

BIOGRAPHIES

Books
Auchincloss, Louis. *EW: A Woman in Her Time.*
NY: Viking, 1971.
Lewis, R W B. *EW: A Biography.* NY: Harper &
Row, 1975.
Lubbock, Percy. *Portrait of EW.* NY: Appleton-
Century, 1947.

CRITICAL STUDIES

Books
Ammons, Elizabeth. *EW's Argument With America.*
Athens: U Georgia P, 1980.
Auchincloss, Louis. *EW.* Minneapolis: U Minnesota
P, 1961.
Bell, Millicent. *EW and Henry James: The Story of
Their Friendship.* NY: Braziller, 1965.
Brown, E K. *EW: Etude Critique.* Paris: Librairie E
Droz, 1935.
Fryer, Judith. *Felicitous Space: The Imaginative
Structures of EW and Willa Cather.* Chapel
Hill: U North Carolina P, 1986.
Gimbel, Wendy. *EW: Orphancy and Survival.* NY:
Praeger, 1984.
Lawson, Richard H. *EW and German Literature.*
Bonn: Bouvier, 1974.
Lawson. *EW.* NY: Ungar, 1977.
Lindberg, Gary H. *EW and the Novel of Manners.*
Charlottesville: U P Virginia, 1975.
McDowell, Margaret B. *EW.* Boston: Twayne,
1976.
Nevius, Blake. *EW: A Study of Her Fiction.* Berke-
ley: U California P, 1953.

Rae, Catherine M. *EW's New York Quartet*. Lanham, Md: U P America, 1984.

Walton, Geoffrey. *EW: A Critical Interpretation*. Rutherford, NJ: Fairleigh Dickinson U P, 1970.

Wershoven, Carol. *The Female Intruder in the Novels of EW*. Rutherford, NJ: Fairleigh Dickinson U P, 1982.

Wolff, Cynthia Griffin. *A Feast of Words: The Triumph of EW*. NY: Oxford U P, 1977.

Collection of Essays

Bloom, Harold, ed. *EW*. NY: Chelsea House, 1986.

Howe, Irving, ed. *EW: A Collection of Critical Essays*. Englewood Cliffs, NJ: Prentice-Hall, 1962.

Special Journals

CollL, 14 (Fall 1987). EW issue.

Edith Wharton Newsletter (semiannually, 1984-   ).

LCUT, ns 31 (1985). EW issue.

Book Sections & Articles

Ammons, Elizabeth. "New Literary History: EW and Jessie Redmon Fauset." *CollL*, 14 (Fall 1987), 207-218.

Bernard, Kenneth. "Imagery and Symbolism in *Ethan Frome*." *CE*, 23 (Dec 1961), 178-184. Rpt *EW's Ethan Frome: The Story With Sources and Commentary*.

Blackall, Jean Frantz. "EW's Art of Ellipsis." *JNT*, 17 (Spring 1987), 145-162.

Bloom, Lillian D. "On Daring to Look Back With W and Cather." *Novel*, 10 (Winter 1977), 167-178.

Blum, Virginia L. "EW's Erotic Other World." *L&P*, 33, no 1 (1987), 12-29.

Brennan, Joseph X. "*Ethan Frome*: Structure and Metaphor." *MFS*, 7 (Winter 1961-1962), 347-356.

Brown, E K. "EW." *The Art of the Novel*, ed Pelham Edgar (NY: Macmillan, 1933), 196-205. Rpt Howe.

Buitenhuis, Peter. "EW and the First World War." *AQ*, 18 (Fall 1966), 493-505.

Candido, Joseph. "EW's Final Alterations of *The Age of Innocence*." *SAF*, 6 (Spring 1978), 21-31.

Coard, Robert L. "EW's Influence on Sinclair Lewis." *MFS*, 31 (Autumn 1985), 511-527.

Cohn, Jan. "The Houses of Fiction: Domestic Architecture in Howells and EW." *TSLL*, 15 (Fall 1973), 537-549.

Coxe, Louis O. "What EW Saw in Innocence." *NewR*, 132 (27 Jun 1955), 16-18. Rpt Howe.

Crowley, John W. "The Unmastered Streak: Feminist Themes in W's *Summer*." *ALR*, 15 (Spring 1982), 86-96.

Dahl, Curtis. "EW's *The House of Mirth*: Sermon on a Text." *MFS*, 21 (Winter 1975-1976), 572-576.

Dimock, Wai-chee. "Debasing Exchange: EW's *The House of Mirth*." *PMLA*, 100 (Oct 1985), 783-792. Rpt Bloom.

Dixon, Roslyn. "Reflecting Vision in *The House of Mirth*." *TCL*, 33 (Spring 1987), 211-222.

Dupree, Ellen Phillips. "W, Lewis and the Nobel Prize Address." *AL*, 56 (May 1984), 262-270.

Eggenschwiler, David. "The Ordered Disorder of *Ethan Frome*." *SNNTS*, 9 (Fall 1977), 237-246.

Fetterley, Judith. " 'The Temptation to Be a Beautiful Object.' " *SAF*, 5 (Autumn 1977), 199-211.

Friedman, Henry J. "The Masochistic Character in the Work of EW." *SIP*, 5 (Aug 1973), 313-329.

Funston, Judith E. " 'Xingu' : EW's Velvet Gauntlet." *SAF*, 12 (Autumn 1984), 227-234.

Gargano, James W. "EW's *The Reef*: The Genteel Woman's Quest for Knowledge." *Novel*, 10 (Fall 1976), 40-48.

Gargano. "Tableaux of Renunciation: W's Use of *The Shaughran* in *The Age of Innocence*." *SAF*, 15 (Spring 1987), 1-11.

Gilbert, Sandra M. "Life's Empty Pack: Notes Toward a Literary Daughteronomy." *CritI*, 11 (Mar 1985), 355-384.

Hopkins, Viola. "The Ordering Style of *The Age of Innocence*." *AL*, 30 (Nov 1958), 345-357.

Hovey, R B. "*Ethan Frome*: A Controversy About Modernizing It." *ALR*, 19 (Fall 1986), 4-20.

Howe, Irving. "The Achievement of EW." *Encounter*, 19 (Jul 1962), 45-52. Rpt Howe.

Jessup, Josephine Lurie. "EW: Drawing-Room Devotee." *The Faith of Our Feminists: A Study in the Novels of EW, Ellen Glasgow, Willa Cather* (NY: Smith, 1950), 14-33, passim.

Kaplan, Amy. "EW's Profession of Authorship." *ELH*, 53 (Summer 1986), 433-457.

Kazin, Alfred. "The Lady and the Tiger: EW and Theodore Dreiser." *VQR*, 17 (Winter 1941), 101-119. Rpt as "Two Educations: EW and Theodore Dreiser." *On Native Grounds* by Kazin (NY: Reynal & Hitchcock, 1942). Rpt as "EW," Howe.

Kronenberger, Louis. "EW's New York: Two Period Pieces." *MQR*, 4 (Winter 1965), 3-13.

Leavis, Q D. "Henry James's Heiress: The Importance of EW." *Scrutiny*, 7 (Dec 1938), 261-276. Rpt Howe.

Lewis, R W B. "Powers of Darkness." *TLS* (13 Jun 1975), 644-645.

Lidoff, Joan. "Another Sleeping Beauty: Narcissism in *The House of Mirth*." *AQ*, 32 (Winter 1980), 519-539. Rpt *American Realism: New*

Essays, ed Eric J Sundquist (Baltimore, Md: Johns Hopkins U P, 1982).

McDowell, Margaret B. "EW's Ghost Stories." *Criticism*, 12 (Spring 1970), 133-152.

McDowell. "Viewing the Custom of Her Country: EW's Feminism." *ConL*, 15 (Autumn 1974), 521-538.

McDowell. "EW's *The Old Maid*: Novella/Play/ Film." *CollL*, 14 (Fall 1987), 246-262.

Michelson, Bruce. "EW's House Divided." *SAF*, 12 (Autumn 1984), 199-215.

Morante, Linda. "The Desolation of Charity Royall: Imagery in EW's *Summer*." *CLQ*, 18 (Dec 1982), 241-248.

Morrow, Nancy. "Games and Conflict in EW's *The Custom of the Country*." *ALR*, 17 (Spring 1984), 32-39.

Murphy, John J. "EW's Italian Triptych: *The Valley of Decision*." *XUS*, 4 (May 1965), 85-94.

Murphy. "The Satiric Structure of W's *The Age of Innocence*." *MarkhamR*, 2 (May 1970), 1-4.

Plante, Patricia R. "EW as a Short Story Writer." *MQ*, 4 (Jul 1963), 363-379.

Poirier, Richard. "EW: *The House of Mirth*." *The American Novel From James Fenimore Cooper to William Faulkner*, ed Wallace Stegner (NY: Basic Books, 1965), 117-132. Excerpted *A World Elsewhere* by Poirier (NY: Oxford U P, 1966).

Price, Alan. "The Composition of EW's *The Age of Innocence*. " *YULG*, 55 (Jul 1980), 22-30.

Ransom, John Crowe. "Characters and Character: A Note on Fiction." *AmR*, 6 (Jan 1936), 271-288. Rpt *EW's Ethan Frome: The Story With Sources and Commentary*.

Rose, Alan Henry. " 'Such Depths of Sad Initiation': EW and New England." *NEQ*, 50 (Sep 1977), 423-439.

Saunders, Judith P. "A New Look at the Oldest Profession in W's *New Year's Day*." *SSF*, 17 (Spring 1980), 121-126.

Schriber, Mary Suzanne. "EW and Travel Writing as Self-Discovery." *AL*, 59 (May 1987), 257-267.

Sensibar, Judith L. "EW Reads the Bachelor Type: Her Critique of Modernism's Representative Man." *AL*, 60 (Dec 1988), 575-590.

Showalter, Elaine. "The Death of the Lady (Novelist): W's *House of Mirth*." *Representations*, 9 (Winter 1985), 133-149. Rpt Bloom.

Smith, Allan Gardner. "EW and the Ghost Story." *W&L*, 1 (1980), 149-159. Rpt Bloom.

Tintner, Adeline R. " 'The Hermit and the Wild Woman': EW's 'Fictioning' of Henry James." *JML*, 4 (Sep 1974), 32-42.

Tintner. "Jamesian Structures in *The Age of Innocence* and Related Stories." *TCL*, 26 (Fall 1980), 332-347.

Tintner. "Mothers, Daughters, and Incest in the Late Novels of EW." *The Lost Tradition: Mothers and Daughters in Literature*, ed Cathy N Davidson & E M Broner (NY: Ungar, 1980), 147-156.

Tintner. "The Narrative Structure of *Old New York*: Text and Pictures in EW's Quartet of Linked Short Stories." *JNT*, 17 (Winter 1987), 76-82.

Trilling, Diana. "*The House of Mirth* Revisited." *HB*, 81 (Dec 1947), 126-127, 181-186. Rev *ASch*, 32 (Winter 1962-1963), 113-128. Rpt Howe.

Tuttleton, James W. "EW: Social Historian of Old New York." *The Novel of Manners in America* (Chapel Hill: U North Carolina P, 1972), 122-140.

Vidal, Gore. "Of Writers and Class: In Praise of EW." *Atlantic*, 241 (Feb 1978), 64-77. Rpt as "Introduction," *The EW Omnibus*.

Wegelin, Christof. "EW and the Twilight of the International Novel." *SoR*, 5 (Apr 1969), 398-418.

White, Barbara A. "EW's *Summer* and 'Woman's Fiction.' " *ELWIU*, 11 (Fall 1984), 223-235.

Wilson, Edmund. "Justice to EW." *NewR*, 95 (29 Jun 1938), 209-213. Rpt *The Wound and the Bow* by Wilson (Boston: Houghton Mifflin, 1941). Rpt Howe.

Wolff, Cynthia Griffin. " 'Cold Ethan' and 'Hot Ethan.' " *CollL*, 14 (Fall 1987), 230-245.

Alfred Bendixen

STEWART EDWARD WHITE

Grand Rapids, Mich, 12 Mar 1873-San Francisco, Calif, 18 Sep 1946

A prolific writer of best-sellers, Stewart Edward White first earned his fame with *The Blazed Trail,* a romance about the logging industry. Among White's more than fifty volumes are historical romances; novels about pioneers, miners, loggers, and fur traders; travel essays; and nonfiction works about hunting and nature. Many of his novels are parts of series, and of these "The Saga of Andy Burnett" is considered his strongest. Best known for his portraits of the outdoor adventures of manly heroes in the West and Northwest, White also wrote fiction and nonfiction about Africa. Late in his career he turned to parapsychology and psychical research.

BIBLIOGRAPHY

First Printings of American Authors, Vol 5, ed Philip B Eppard (Detroit: Bruccoli Clark Layman/Gale, 1987), 355-362. Primary.

BOOKS

The Claim Jumpers: A Romance. NY: Appleton, 1901. Novel.

The Westerners. NY: McClure, Phillips, 1901. Novel.

The Blazed Trail. NY: McClure, Phillips, 1902. Novel.

Conjuror's House: A Romance of the Free Forest. NY: McClure, Phillips, 1903. Repub as *The Call of the North.* NY: Doubleday, Page, 1919. Novel.

The Forest. NY: Outlook, 1903. Essays.

The Magic Forest: A Modern Fairy Story. NY & London: Macmillan, 1903. Children's story.

Blazed Trail Stories and Stories of the Wild Life. NY: McClure, Phillips, 1904.

The Silent Places. NY: McClure, Phillips, 1904. Novel.

The Mountains. NY: McClure, Phillips, 1904. Essays.

The Pass. NY: Outing, 1906. Essays.

The Mystery, with Samuel Hopkins Adams. NY: McClure, Phillips, 1907. Novel.

Arizona Nights. NY: McClure, 1907. Stories.

Camp and Trail. NY: Outing, 1907. Essays.

The Riverman. NY: McClure, 1908. Novel.

The Rules of the Game. NY: Doubleday, Page, 1910. Novel.

The Adventures of Bobby Orde. NY: Doubleday, Page, 1910. Children's novel.

The Cabin. Garden City, NY: Doubleday, Page, 1911. Essays.

The Sign at Six. Indianapolis: Bobbs-Merrill, 1912. Novel.

The Land of Footprints. Garden City, NY: Doubleday, Page, 1912. Essays.

Gold. Garden City, NY: Doubleday, Page, 1913. Novel.

African Camp Fires. Garden City, NY: Doubleday, 1913. Essays.

The Gray Dawn. Garden City, NY: Doubleday, Page, 1915. Novel.

The Rediscovered Country. Garden City, NY: Doubleday, Page, 1915. Essays.

The Leopard Woman. Garden City, NY: Doubleday, Page, 1916. Novel.

Simba. Garden City, NY: Doubleday, Page, 1918; *White Magic.* London & c: Hodder & Stoughton, 1918. Stories.

The Forty-Niners: A Chronicle of the California Trail and El Dorado. New Haven: Yale U P, 1918. History.

The Killer. Garden City, NY: Doubleday, Page, 1919. Augmented ed, 1920. Stories.

The Rose Dawn. Garden City, NY: Doubleday, Page, 1920. Novel.

On Tiptoe: A Romance of the Redwoods. NY: Doran, 1922. Novel.

Daniel Boone, Wilderness Scout. Garden City, NY: Doubleday, Page, 1922. Biography.

The Glory Hole. Garden City, NY: Doubleday, Page, 1924. Novel.

Skookum Chuck: A Novel. Garden City, NY: Doubleday, Page, 1925.

Credo. Garden City, NY: Doubleday, Page, 1925. Essays.

Secret Harbour. Garden City, NY: Doubleday, Page, 1926. Novel.

Lions in the Path: A Book of Adventure on the High Veldt. Garden City, NY: Doubleday, Page, 1926. Essays.

Back of Beyond. Garden City, NY: Doubleday, Page, 1927. Novel.

Why Be a Mud Turtle? Garden City, NY: Doubleday, Doran, 1928. Essays.

Dog Days, Other Times, Other Dogs: The Autobiography of a Man and His Dog Friends Through Four Decades of Changing America. Garden City, NY: Doubleday, Doran, 1930. Legends & stories.

The Shepper-Newfounder. Garden City, NY: Doubleday, Doran, 1931. Children's story.

Wild Animals. Burlingame, Calif: Workers' Shop for the Unemployed, 1932. Children's nonfiction.

The Long Rifle. Garden City, NY: Doubleday, Doran, 1932. Novel.

Ranchero. Garden City, NY: Doubleday, Doran, 1933. Novel.

Folded Hills. Garden City, NY: Doubleday, Doran, 1934. Novel.

Pole Star, with Harry DeVighne. Garden City, NY: Doubleday, Doran, 1935. Novel.

The Betty Book: Excursions into the World of Other-Consciousness, Made by Betty Between 1919 and 1936. NY: Dutton, 1937. Essays.

The Hold-Up. San Francisco: Book Club of California, 1937. Stories.

Old California in Picture and Story. Garden City, NY: Doubleday, Doran, 1937. History.

Across the Unknown, with Harwood White. NY: Dutton, 1939. Essays.

The Unobstructed Universe. NY: Dutton, 1940. Essays.

Wild Geese Calling. NY: Doubleday, Doran, 1940. Novel.

Stampede. Garden City, NY: Doubleday, Doran, 1942. Novel.

The Road I Know. NY: Dutton, 1942. Essays.

Anchors to Windward: Stability and Personal Peace—Here and Now—. NY: Dutton, 1943. Essays.

Speaking for Myself. Garden City, NY: Doubleday, Doran, 1943. Autobiography.

The Stars Are Still There. NY: Dutton, 1946. Essays.

With Folded Wings. NY: Dutton, 1947. Essays.

The Job of Living. NY: Dutton, 1948. Essays.

EDITION & COLLECTIONS

The Works of SEW, 8 vols. Garden City, NY: Doubleday, 1913. Augmented ed, 10 vols, 1916.

The Story of California. Garden City, NY: Doubleday, Page, 1927 (*Gold, The Gray Dawn, The Rose Dawn*).

The Outdoor Omnibus. NY: Grosset & Dunlap, 1936? (*The Mountains, The Cabin, The Forest*).

The Saga of Andy Burnett. Garden City, NY: Doubleday, 1947 (*The Long Rifle, Ranchero, Folded Hills, Stampede*).

MANUSCRIPTS & ARCHIVES

The major collections are at the UCLA Library; U of California, Berkeley, Library; the American Academy of Arts and Letters, New York City; & the Huntington Library, San Marino, Calif.

BIOGRAPHIES
Book Sections
Kimmell, Mrs Leslie F. "SEW: His Later Years." *The Job of Living,* xiii-xix.
Saxon, Eugene F. "SEW." *Gold* (1913), Appendix.

CRITICAL STUDIES
Books
Alter, Judy. *SEW.* Boise, Idaho: Boise State U, 1975.
Butte, Edna Rosemary. "SEW: His Life and Literary Career." Dissertation: U Southern California, 1960.

Book Sections & Articles
Baldwin, Charles C. "SEW." *The Men Who Make Our Novels* (NY: Moffat, Yard, 1919), 80-84.
Clark, Ward. "Some Representative American Story Tellers: XIII—SEW." *Bookman,* 31 (Jul 1910), 486-492.
Denison, Lindsay. "SEW." *Bookman,* 17 (May 1903), 308-311.
Lieberman, Elias. *The American Short Story* (Ridgewood, NJ: Editor, 1912), 58-63, 103-112.
Maurice, Arthur Bartlett. "The History of Their Books: VIII. SEW." *Bookman,* 69 (Aug 1929), 588-589.
Overton, Grant. "SEW and Adventure." *When Winter Comes to Main Street* (NY: Doran, 1922), 55-67. Rpt *Authors of the Day* by Overton (NY: Doran, 1924).
Powell, Lawrence Clark. "SEW." *Southwest Classics: The Creative Literature of the Arid Lands* (Tucson: U Arizona P, 1974), passim.
Underwood, John Curtis. *Literature and Insurgency* (NY: Kennerley, 1914), 254-298.
Wright, Edward. "SEW." *Bookman* (London), 46 (Apr 1914), 31-33.

Gwen L. Nagel

BRAND WHITLOCK

Urbana, Ohio, 4 Mar 1869-Cannes, France, 24 May 1934

Brand Whitlock aspired to write realistic fiction in the tradition of his mentor William Dean Howells, who called Whitlock one of the "two most hopeful figures in American literature" of the 1890s. Although he published eleven novels and more than two dozen short stories, Whitlock never enjoyed major popular or critical success. Today, he is best remembered as a leader in the midwestern progressive movement, as a reform-minded mayor of Toledo, Ohio, and as a humanitarian diplomat who led the Belgian relief effort during World War I. Whitlock's literary reputation rests largely on *The 13th District,* an early political novel; on *The Turn of the Balance,* his attack on abuses in the criminal justice system; and on his vivid portrayals of rural Ohio life in such works as *J. Hardin & Son.*

BIBLIOGRAPHY

Steffens, Eleanor S. "BW: An Essay, a Checklist, and an Annotated Bibliography." Dissertation: Case Western Reserve U, 1972. Primary & secondary.

BOOKS

The 13th District: A Story of a Candidate. Indianapolis: Bowen-Merrill, 1902. Novel.

Her Infinite Variety. Indianapolis: Bobbs-Merrill, 1904. Novel.

The Happy Average. Indianapolis: Bobbs-Merrill, 1904. Novel.

The Turn of the Balance. Indianapolis: Bobbs-Merrill, 1907. Rev ed, with intro by BW, 1924. Novel.

Abraham Lincoln. Boston: Small, Maynard, 1909. Rev ed, London & c: Nelson, 1919. Biography.

The Gold Brick. Indianapolis: Bobbs-Merrill, 1910. Stories.

On the Enforcement of Law in Cities. Toledo: Rosengarten, 1910. Essay.

The Fall Guy. Indianapolis: Bobbs-Merrill, 1912. Stories.

Forty Years of It. NY & London: Appleton, 1914. Autobiography.

Belgium: A Personal Narrative, 2 vols. NY: Appleton, 1919; *Belgium Under the German Occu-*
pation: A Personal Narrative. London: Heinemann, 1919.

J. Hardin & Son. NY & London: Appleton, 1923. Novel.

Uprooted. NY & London: Appleton, 1926. Novel.

Transplanted. NY & London: Appleton, 1927. Novel.

Big Matt. NY & London: Appleton, 1928. Novel.

La Fayette, 2 vols. NY & London: Appleton, 1929. Biography.

The Little Green Shutter. NY & London: Appleton, 1931. Novel.

Narcissus: A Belgian Legend of Van Dyck. NY & London: Appleton, 1931. Novel.

The Stranger on the Island. NY & London: Appleton, 1933. Novel.

Little Lion: Mieke, intro by Allan Nevins. NY & London: Appleton-Century, 1937. Essay.

BW's the Buckeyes: Politics and Abolitionism in an Ohio Town, 1836-1845, ed with intro by Paul W Miller. Athens: Ohio U P, 1977. Novel.

LETTERS & DIARY

The Letters and Journal of BW, ed Allan Nevins; intros by Nevins & Newton D Baker. NY & London: Appleton-Century, 1936.

MANUSCRIPTS & ARCHIVES

The Library of Congress.

BIOGRAPHIES

Books

Crunden, Robert M. *A Hero in Spite of Himself: BW in Art, Politics, & War.* NY: Knopf, 1969.

Tager, Jack. *The Intellectual as Urban Reformer: BW and the Progressive Movement.* Cleveland: P of Case Western Reserve U, 1968.

CRITICAL STUDIES

Book

Anderson, David D. *BW.* NY: Twayne, 1968.

Book Sections & Articles

Arms, George. " 'Ever Devotedly Yours': The W-Howells Correspondence." *JRUL,* 10 (Dec 1946), 1-19.

Howells, William Dean. "A Political Novelist and More." *NAR,* 192 (Jul 1910), 93-100.

Miller, Paul W. "Belgian Sources of BW's 'French' Expatriate Novels." *Midamerica,* 9 (1982), 65-75.

Miller. "Introduction." *J. Hardin & Son* (Athens: Ohio U P, 1982), xi-xxvii.

Nevins, Allan. "Introduction." *The Turn of the Bal-* *ance* (Lexington: U P Kentucky, 1970), iii-xiii.

Ravitz, Abe C. "BW's Macochee: Puritan Theo-Politics in the Midwest." *OHQ,* 68 (Jul 1959), 257-275.

Richard W. Oram

KATE DOUGLAS WIGGIN

Philadelphia, Pa, 28 Sep 1856-Harrow-on-Hill, England, 24 Aug 1923

Kate Douglas Wiggin is best remembered as the author of the children's book *Rebecca of Sunnybrook Farm.* Much of her writing is now considered didactic and sentimental, particularly her novels about poor and ailing children; but interesting portrayals of rural life, including those of single women, people in financial difficulty, and rustic eccentrics, recur throughout her work. Wiggin's primary setting was her native New England, from which she drew such material as the Maine dialect, the Shaker presence that is central to *Susanna and Sue,* and the shortage of men in rural communities as recorded in *The Old Peabody Pew.* Most of Wiggin's writing was intended for children, including a series of travel books based on her experiences in Europe.

BIBLIOGRAPHY

Bibliography of American Literature, comp Jacob Blanck. New Haven: Yale U P, 1955-1991. Primary.

BOOKS

The Story of Patsy: A Reminiscence. San Francisco: Murdock, 1883. Augmented ed, Boston: Houghton, Mifflin, 1889. Children's novella.

The Birds' Christmas Carol. San Francisco: Murdock, 1887. Children's novella.

A Summer in a Cañon: A California Story. Boston & NY: Houghton, Mifflin, 1889. Children's novella.

Timothy's Quest: A Story for Anybody, Young or Old, Who Cares to Read It. Boston & NY: Houghton, Mifflin, 1890. Excerpted in *Finding a Home.* Boston & NY: Houghton, Mifflin, 1907. Children's novel.

The Story Hour: A Book for the Home and the Kindergarten with Nora A Smith. Boston & NY: Houghton, Mifflin, 1890.

The Relation of the Kindergarten to the Public School. San Francisco: Murdock, 1891. Nonfiction.

Children's Rights: A Book of Nursery Logic, with Smith. Boston & NY: Houghton, Mifflin, 1892. Essays.

A Cathedral Courtship and Penelope's English Experiences. Boston & NY: Houghton, Mifflin, 1893. Children's novellas.

Polly Oliver's Problem: A Story for Girls. Boston & NY: Houghton, Mifflin, 1893. Children's novel.

The Village Watch-Tower. Boston & NY: Houghton, Mifflin, 1895. Stories.

Froebel's Gifts, with Smith. Boston & NY: Houghton, Mifflin, 1895. Essays.

Froebel's Occupations, with Smith. Boston & NY: Houghton, Mifflin, 1896. Essays.

Kindergarten Principles and Practice, with Smith. Boston & NY: Houghton, Mifflin, 1896.

Marm Lisa. Boston & NY: Houghton, Mifflin, 1896. Novel.

Nine Love Songs and a Carol. Boston: Houghton, Mifflin, 1896. Music.

Penelope's Progress. . . . Boston & NY: Houghton, Mifflin, 1898; *Penelope's Experiences in Scotland.* London: Gay & Bird, 1898. Children's novel.

Penelope's English Experiences (substantially rev "Holiday Edition"). Boston & NY: Houghton, Mifflin, 1900. Repub as *Penelope's Experiences in England.* London: Black, 1930. Children's novel.

Penelope's Irish Experiences. Boston & NY: Houghton, Mifflin, 1901. Children's novel.

Diary of a Goose Girl. Boston & NY: Houghton, Mifflin, 1902. Children's novel.

Half-a-dozen Housekeepers: A Story for Girls in Half-a-dozen Chapters. Philadelphia: Altemus, 1903. Children's novella.

Rebecca of Sunnybrook Farm. Boston & NY: Houghton, Mifflin, 1903. Excerpted in *The Flag-Raising,* 1907. Children's novel.

The Affair at the Inn, with Mary Findlater, Jane Findlater & Allan McAulay. Boston: Houghton, Mifflin, 1904. Novel.

A Village Stradivarius. London: Gay & Bird, 1904. Novella.

Rose o' the River. Boston & NY: Houghton, Mifflin, 1905. Novel.

New Chronicles of Rebecca. Boston & NY: Houghton, Mifflin, 1907. Excerpted in *The Flag-Raising,* 1907. Repub as *More About Rebecca of Sunnybrook Farm.* London: Black, 1930. Children's stories.

The Old Peabody Pew: A Christmas Romance of a Country Church. Boston & NY: Houghton, Mifflin, 1907. Novel.

Rebecca of Sunnybrook Farm: A State o' Maine Play in Four Acts, with Charlotte Thompson. NY: French, 1909.

Susanna and Sue. Boston & NY: Houghton Mifflin, 1909. Novel.

Robinetta, with Mary Findlater, Jane Findlater & Allan McAulay. Boston & NY: Houghton Mifflin, 1911. Novel.

Mother Carey's Chickens. Boston & NY: Houghton Mifflin, 1911; *Mother Carey.* London: Hodder & Stoughton, 1911. Children's novel.

A Child's Journey With Dickens. Boston & NY: Houghton Mifflin, 1912. Children's novella.

The Story of Waitstill Baxter. Boston & NY: Houghton Mifflin, 1913. Novel.

Bluebeard: A Musical Fantasy. . . . NY & London: Harper, 1914. Play.

The Birds' Christmas Carol: Dramatic Version, with Helen Ingersoll. Boston: Houghton Mifflin, 1914. Play.

Penelope's Postscripts: Switzerland, Venice, Wales, Devon, Home. Boston & NY: Houghton Mifflin, 1915. Children's stories.

The Girl and the Kingdom: Learning to Teach. . . . Los Angeles: City Teachers Club, 1915? Essay.

The Romance of a Christmas Card. Boston & NY: Houghton Mifflin, 1916. Children's novel.

The Old Peabody Pew. NY & London: French, 1917. Play.

Ladies-in-Waiting. Boston & NY: Houghton Mifflin, 1919. Stories.

My Garden of Memory: An Autobiography. Boston & NY: Houghton Mifflin, 1923.

The Quilt of Happiness. Boston & NY: Houghton Mifflin, 1923. Novel.

Love by Express: A Novel of California. Hollis & Buxton, Maine: Dorcas Society, 1924.

Creeping Jenny and Other New England Stories. Boston & NY: Houghton Mifflin, 1924.

Mother Carey's Chickens: A Little Comedy of Home in Three Acts, with Rachel Crothers. NY & London: French, 1925. Play.

A Thorn in the Flesh: A Monologue . . . Freely Adapted From the French of Ernest Leqouvé. NY & London: French, 1926.

The Spirit of Christmas. Boston & NY: Houghton Mifflin, 1927. Essay.

A Thanksgiving Retrospect; or, Simplicity of Life in Old New England. Boston & NY: Houghton Mifflin, 1928. Essay.

OTHER

Kindergarten Chimes: A Collection of Songs and Games Composed and Arranged for Kindergartens and Primary Schools, ed KDW. Boston: Oliver H Ditson / NY: Chas H Ditson / Philadelphia: J E Ditson / Chicago: Lyon & Healy, 1885. Augmented ed, 1887.

Hymns for Kindergartners, ed with Nora A Smith. San Francisco: Froebel Society, 1891. Children's songs.

The Kindergarten, ed KDW. NY: Harper, 1893. Essays.

Golden Numbers: A Book of Verse for Youth, ed KDW & Smith. NY: McClure, Phillips, 1902. Repub as *Golden Numbers: Poems for Children and Young People.* Boston: Houghton, Mifflin, 1902.

The Posy Ring: A Book of Verse for Children, ed KDW & Smith. NY: McClure, Phillips, 1903. Repub as *The Posy Ring: A Book of Verse for the Youngest Children.* Boston: Houghton, Mifflin, 1903. Repub as *Poems Every Child Should Know.* NY: Doubleday, Doran, 1942.

The Fairy Ring, ed KDW & Smith. NY: McClure, Phillips, 1906. Repub as *An Hour With the Fairies.* Garden City, NY: Doubleday, Page, 1911. Repub as *Fairy Stories Every Child Should Know.* NY: Doubleday, Doran, 1942.

Magic Casements: A Second Fairy Book, ed KDW & Smith. NY: McClure, 1907.

Pinafore Palace: A Book of Rhymes for the Nursery, ed KDW & Smith. NY: McClure, 1907. Excerpts separately repub as 5 books: *Baby's Friend and Nursery Heroes and Heroines; Baby's Plays and Journeys; Nursery Nonsense; Palace Bedtime; Palace Playtime.* Garden City, NY: Doubleday, Page, 1923.

Tales of Laughter: A Third Fairy Book, ed KDW & Smith. NY: McClure, 1908. Repub as *Tales of Laughter Every Child Should Know.* NY: Doubleday, Doran, 1939.

Tales of Wonder: A Fourth Fairy Book, ed KDW & Smith. NY: Doubleday, Page, 1909. Repub as *Tales of Wonder Every Child Should Know.* Garden City, NY: Doubleday, Doran, 1941?

The Arabian Nights: Their Best-Known Tales, ed KDW & Smith. NY: Scribners, 1909.

A Book of Dorcas Dishes: Family Recipes Contributed by the Dorcas Society of Hollis and Buxton, ed KDW & Smith. Npl: Privately printed, 1911.

The Talking Beasts: A Book of Fable Wisdom, ed KDW & Smith. Garden City, NY: Doubleday, Page, 1911.

Twilight Stories: More Tales for the Story Hour, ed KDW & Smith. Boston: Houghton Mifflin, 1925.

EDITION

The Writings of KDW, 10 vols. Boston & NY: Houghton Mifflin, 1917.

MANUSCRIPTS & ARCHIVES

The major collections are at Dartmouth C Library, Bowdoin C Library & Stanford U Library.

BIOGRAPHIES

Book

Smith, Nora Archibald. *KDW as Her Sister Knew Her.* Boston: Houghton Mifflin, 1925.

Book Sections & Articles

Benét, Laura. "KDW [1856-1923]." *Famous Storytellers for Young People* (NY: Dodd, Mead, 1968), 118-123.

Burnett, Frances Hodgson. "An Appreciation." *KDW: A Sketch of Her Life, With an Appreciation* (Boston: Houghton Mifflin, 1924?), 3-6.

Gibson, Ashley. "KDW." *Bookman,* 38 (Jul 1910), 149-159.

Montgomery, Elizabeth Rider. "Bread Upon the Waters: *The Birds' Christmas Carol*—Wiggin,

1888." *The Story Behind Great Stories* (NY: Dodd, Mead, 1947), 124-129.

More, Nettie A. "KDW: An Appreciation." *Overland,* 87 (Jan 1929), 18, 28.

Overton, Grant. *The Women Who Make Our Novels* (NY: Dodd, Mead, rev 1928), 345-349.

Stebbins, Lucy Ward. "KDW as a Child Knew Her." *Horn Book,* 26 (Nov-Dec 1950), 447-454.

Stebbins, Roderick. "KDW as I Knew Her." *Bookman,* 29 (Jun 1924), 404-412.

Van Westrum, Adrian Schade. "KDW, Litt.D (Bowdoin)." *Lamp,* 29 (Aug 1904-Jan 1905), 585-590.

Winter, Calvin. "KDW." *Bookman,* 32 (Nov 1910), 236-243.

CRITICAL STUDIES

Book

Benner, Helen Frances. *KDW's Country of Childhood.* Orono: U Maine P, 1956.

Book Sections & Articles

Boutwell, Edna. "KDW—The Lady With the Golden Key." *The Hewins Lectures, 1947-1962,* ed Siri Andrews (Boston: Horn Book, 1963), 297-319.

Cooper, Frederic Taber. "KDW." *Some American Story Tellers* (NY: Holt, 1911), 27-47.

Erisman, Fred. "Transcendentalism for American Youth: The Children's Books of KDW." *NEQ,* 41 (Jun 1968), 238-247.

Forman, Henry James. "KDW: A Woman of Letters." *SCQ,* 44 (Dec 1962), 273-285.

Kornfeld, Eve & Susan Jackson. "The Female Bildungsroman in Nineteenth-Century America: Parameters of a Vision." *JAmC,* 10 (Winter 1987), 69-75.

MacLeod, Anne Scott. "The *Caddie Woodlawn* Syndrome: American Girlhood in the Nineteenth Century." *A Century of Childhood, 1820-1920,* ed Mary Lynn Stevens Heininger (Rochester, NY: Strong Museum, 1984), 97-119.

Moore, Anne Carroll. *My Roads to Childhood: Views and Reviews of Children's Books* (Boston: Horn Book, 1961), passim.

Nodelman, Perry. "Progressive Utopia; or, How to Grow Up Without Growing Up." *Proceedings of the Sixth Annual Conference of the Children's Literature Association,* ed Priscilla A Ord (Villanova, Pa: Villanova U, 1980), 146-154.

Jennifer Meta Robinson

HARRY LEON WILSON

Oregon, Ill, 1 May 1867-Carmel, Calif, 29 Jun 1939

Harry Leon Wilson was a humorist who wrote nostalgic, sentimental fiction and plays, the latter in collaboration with Booth Tarkington. A typical Wilson plot involves a bumbling innocent who, thanks to the help of a "good woman," learns to make his way in the world. Portraying the modern world, albeit gently, as a Vanity Fair, Wilson drew protagonists who stand outside society—rugged individualists from the frontier or gentle eccentrics. Wilson achieved commercial success, becoming one of the most admired and best-paid contributors to *The Saturday Evening Post*. Today his reputation has declined. The few recent critical treatments examine his novels, especially *Merton of the Movies*, as exemplifications of American popular culture.

BOOKS

Zigzag Tales From the East to the West. NY: Keppler & Schwarzmann, 1894. Stories.

The Spenders: A Tale of the Third Generation. Boston: Lothrop, 1902. Novel.

The Lions of the Lord: A Tale of the Old West. Boston: Lothrop, 1903. Novel.

The Seeker. NY: Doubleday, Page, 1904. Novel.

The Boss of Little Arcady. Boston: Lothrop, Lee & Shepard, 1905. Novel.

Ewing's Lady. NY: Appleton, 1907. Novel.

The Man From Home, with Booth Tarkington. NY & London: Harper, 1908. Play.

Bunker Bean. Garden City, NY: Doubleday, Page, 1913. Novel.

Ruggles of Red Gap. Garden City, NY: Doubleday, Page, 1915. Novel.

The Man From Home. NY & London: Appleton, 1915. Novel.

Somewhere in Red Gap. Garden City, NY: Doubleday, Page, 1916. Stories.

Life. San Francisco: Bohemian Club, 1919. Play.

The Gibson Upright, with Tarkington. Garden City, NY: Doubleday, Page, 1919. Play.

Ma Pettengill. Garden City, NY: Garden City Publishing, 1919. Stories.

The Wrong Twin. Garden City, NY & Toronto: Doubleday, Page, 1921. Novel.

Merton of the Movies. Garden City, NY & Toronto: Doubleday, Page, 1922. Novel.

So This Is Golf! NY: Cosmopolitan, 1923. Comic sketch.

Oh, Doctor! NY: Cosmopolitan, 1923. Novel.

Ma Pettingill Talks. Garden City, NY: Garden City Publishing, 1923. Stories.

Professor, How Could You! NY: Cosmopolitan, 1924. Novel.

Tweedles: A Comedy, with Tarkington. NY & London: French, 1924. Play.

Cousin Jane. NY: Cosmopolitan, 1925. Novel.

Lone Tree. NY: Cosmopolitan, 1925. Novel.

How's Your Health? A Comedy in Three Acts, with Tarkington. NY & c: French, 1930. Play.

Two Black Sheep. NY: Cosmopolitan, 1931. Novel.

When in the Course—. NY: Kinsey, 1940. Novel.

OTHER

Puck: The Comic Weekly (1896-1902), ed HLW.

MANUSCRIPTS & ARCHIVES

U of California, Berkeley, Library.

CRITICAL STUDIES

Book

Kummer, George. *HLW*. Cleveland: Western Reserve U P, 1963.

Book Sections & Articles

Baldwin, Charles C. *The Men Who Make Our Novels* (NY: Dodd, Mead, rev 1924), 584-589.

Closser, Myla Jo. "HLW, an Interview." *Bookman*, 61 (Jun 1925), 458-560.

Dodd, Lee Wilson. "A Satire of the High Type." *LitR*, 2 (3 Jun 1922), 699.

"HLW Papers." *Bancroftiana*, 57 (Jan 1974), 1-3.

Havig, Alan. "Hollywood and the American Heartland." *JPFT*, 14 (Winter 1987), 167-175.

Leutrat, Jean-Louis. "Merton Gill, un homme ordinaire du cinema des années 1920." *RFEA*, 19 (Feb 1984), 19-31.

Masson, Thomas L. *Our American Humorists* (NY: Dodd, Mead, rev 1931), 303-304.

Maurice, Arthur Bartlett. "The History of Their Books: XI. HLW." *Bookman*, 70 (Jan 1930), 499-501.

Tarkington, Booth. "H. L.: A Writing Man." *SatRL*, 20 (12 Aug 1939), 10-11.

David M. Craig

OWEN WISTER

Philadelphia, Pa, 14 Jul 1860-North Kingston, RI, 14 Jul 1938

Owen Wister's literary reputation was established with the publication of *The Virginian*, which was hailed as an expression of American character. Although Wister is remembered primarily for his western fiction, he also wrote *Lady Baltimore*, a novel of manners, as well as drama, music, essays of social and political commentary, and biographies. Wister is credited with having created the cowboy hero, and *The Virginian* is praised for its contribution to the establishment of the western as a legitimate genre. There has been some renewed scholarly interest in Wister in recent years.

BIBLIOGRAPHIES

First Printings of American Authors, Vol 4 (Detroit: Bruccoli Clark/Gale, 1979), 391-397. Primary.

Marovitz, Sanford E. "OW: An Annotated Bibliography of Secondary Material." *ALR*, 7 (Winter 1974), 1-110.

Rush, N Orwin. "Fifty Years of *The Virginian*." *PBSA*, 46 (Second Quarter 1952), 99-120. Secondary.

Sherman, Dean. "OW: An Annotated Bibliography." *BB*, 28 (Jan-Mar 1971), 7-16. Primary.

BOOKS

The New Swiss Family Robinson. Cambridge, Mass: Sever, University Bookstore, 1882. Story.

The Dragon of Wantley. Philadelphia: Lippincott, 1892. Story.

Red Men and White. NY: Harper, 1896. Stories.

Lin McLean. NY & London: Harper, 1898. Stories.

The Jimmyjohn Boss and Other Stories. NY & London: Harper, 1900. Repub as *Hank's Woman*, Vol 3 of *The Writings of OW*.

Ulysses S. Grant. Boston: Small, Maynard, 1900. Biography.

The Virginian: A Horseman of the Plains. NY & London: Macmillan, 1902. Novel.

Philosophy 4: A Story of Harvard University. NY & London: Macmillan, 1903. Story.

Musk-Ox, Bison, Sheep and Goat, with Caspar Whitney & George Bird Grinnell. NY & London: Macmillan, 1904. Essays.

A Journey in Search of Christmas. NY & London: Harper, 1904. Stories.

Lady Baltimore. NY & London: Macmillan, 1906. Novel.

How Doth the Simple Spelling Bee. NY & London: Macmillan, 1907. Story.

The Seven Ages of Washington. NY: Macmillan, 1907. Biography.

Mother. NY: Dodd, Mead, 1907. Story.

Padre Ignacio. NY & London: Harper, 1911. Story.

Members of the Family. NY: Macmillan, 1911. Stories.

The Pentecost of Calamity. NY: Macmillan, 1915. Essay.

A Straight Deal; or, The Ancient Grudge. NY: Macmillan, 1920. Essay.

Indispensable Information for Infants; or, Easy Entrance to Education. NY: Macmillan, 1921. Poetry.

Neighbors Henceforth. NY: Macmillan, 1922. Essay.

Watch Your Thirst: A Dry Opera in Three Acts. NY: Macmillan, 1923.

Safe in the Arms of Croesus. NY: Macmillan, 1928. Stories.

When West Was West. NY: Macmillan, 1928. Stories.

Roosevelt, the Story of a Friendship, 1880-1919. NY: Macmillan, 1930. Biography.

Two Appreciations of John Jay Chapman. NY: Privately printed, 1934. Nonfiction.

LETTERS, DIARIES, NOTEBOOKS

OW Out West: His Journals and Letters, ed with intro by Fanny Kemble Wister. Chicago: U Chicago P, 1958.

My Dear W: The Frederic Remington-OW Letters, ed with intro by Ben Merchant Vorpahl; foreword by Wallace Stegner. Palo Alto, Calif: American West, 1972.

That I May Tell You: Journals and Letters of the W Family. Wayne, Pa: Haverford C, 1979.

OTHER

The Lady of the Lake. Cambridge, Mass: Chorus Book, 1881. Lyrics & music by OW.

Done in the Open, drawings by Frederic Remington. NY: Collier, 1902. Intro & verses by OW.

The Illustrations of Frederic Remington, ed Marta Jackson. NY: Bounty, 1970. Commentary by OW.

EDITION & COLLECTIONS

The Writings of OW, 11 vols. NY: Macmillan, 1928.

The West of OW: Selected Short Stories, ed with intro by Robert L Hough. Lincoln: U Nebraska P, 1972.

OW's West: Selected Articles, ed Robert Murray Davis. Albuquerque: U New Mexico P, 1987.

MANUSCRIPTS & ARCHIVES

The major collections are at the Library of Congress; the Houghton Library, Harvard U; & the U of Wyoming American Heritage Center.

BIOGRAPHIES

Books

Etulain, Richard W. *OW*. Boise, Idaho: Boise State U, 1973.

Payne, Darwin. *OW: Chronicler of the West, Gentleman of the East*. Dallas, Tex: Southern Methodist U P, 1985.

Rush, N Orwin. *Frederic Remington and OW: The Story of a Friendship, 1893-1909*. Tallahassee: Florida State U P, 1961.

Stokes, Frances Kemble Wister. *My Father, OW, and Ten Letters Written by OW to His Mother During His First Trip to Wyoming in 1885*, foreword by N Orwin Rush. Laramie: U Wyoming Library Association, 1952.

Book Section & Articles

Lukacs, John. "OW; or, The Decline of the West." *Philadelphia: Patricians and Philistines, 1900-1950* (NY: Farrar, Straus & Giroux, 1981), 240-257.

Marsh, Edward Clark. "Representative American Story Tellers VI: OW." *Bookman*, 27 (Jul 1908), 458-466.

Mason, Julian. "OW, Boy Librarian." *QJLC*, 26 (Oct 1969), 201-212.

Robinson, Forrest G. "The Roosevelt-W Connection: Some Notes on the West and the Uses of History." *WAL*, 14 (Summer 1979), 95-114.

Vorpahl, Ben Merchant. "Ernest Hemingway and OW: Finding the Lost Generation." *LCUT*, 36 (Spring 1970), 126-137.

Vorpahl. "Henry James and OW." *PMHB*, 95 (Jul 1971), 291-338.

White, John I. "*The Virginian*." *Montana*, 16 (Oct 1966), 2-11.

CRITICAL STUDIES

Books

Cobbs, John L. *OW*. Boston: Twayne, 1984.

Watkins, George Thomas, II. "OW and the American West: A Biographical and Critical Study." Dissertation: U Illinois, Urbana, 1959.

White, G Edward. *The Eastern Establishment and the Western Experience: The West of Frederic Remington, Theodore Roosevelt, and OW*. New Haven, Conn: Yale U P, 1968.

Book Sections & Articles

Boatright, Mody C. "The American Myth Rides the Range: OW's Man on Horseback." *SWR*, 36 (Summer 1951), 157-163.

Bode, Carl. "Henry James and OW." *AL*, 26 (May 1954), 250-252.

Bold, Christine. "How the Western Ends: Fenimore Cooper to Frederic Remington." *WAL*, 17 (Summer 1982), 117-135.

Branch, Douglas. *The Cowboy and His Interpreters* (NY: Cooper Square, rpt 1961), 192-200.

Cady, Edwin H. *The Light of Common Day: Realism in American Fiction* (Bloomington: Indiana U P, 1971), passim.

Cobbs, John L. "Charleston: The Image of Aristocracy in OW's *Lady Baltimore*." *SCR*, 9 (Nov 1976), 44-51.

Cooper, Frederic Taber. "OW." *Some American Story Tellers* (NY: Holt, 1911), 265-294.

Donahue, John. "Nature in *Don Segundo Sombra* and *The Virginian*." *GPQ*, 7 (Summer 1987), 166-177.

Folsom, James K. *The American Western Novel* (New Haven, Conn: College & University P, 1966), passim.

Frantz, Joe B & Julian Ernest Choate, Jr. *The American Cowboy: The Myth & the Reality* (Norman: U Oklahoma P, 1955), passim.

Heatherington, Madelon E. "Romance Without Women: The Sterile Fiction of the American West." *GaR*, 33 (Fall 1979), 643-656.

Houghton, Donald E. "Two Heroes in One: Reflections Upon the Popularity of *The Virginian*." *JPC*, 4 (Fall 1970), 497-506.

Hubbell, Jay B. "OW's Work." *SAQ*, 29 (Oct 1930), 440-443.

Kaye, Frances W. "Cooper, Sarmiento, W, and Hernández: The Search for a New World Literary Hero." *CLAJ*, 19 (Mar 1976), 404-411.

Kaye. "The 49th Parallel and the 98th Meridian: Some Lines for Thought." *Mosaic*, 14 (Spring 1981), 165-175.

Lambert, Neal. "OW—The 'Real Incident' and the 'Thrilling Story.' " *The American West: An Appraisal*, ed Robert G Ferris (Santa Fe: Museum of New Mexico P, 1963), 191-200.

Lambert. "OW's 'Hank's Woman': The Writer and His Comment." *WAL*, 4 (Spring 1969), 39-50.

Lambert. "OW's Lin McLean: The Failure of the Vernacular Hero." *WAL*, 5 (Fall 1970), 219-232.

Lambert. "The Values of the Frontier: OW's Final Assessment." *SDR*, 9 (Spring 1971), 76-87.

Lambert. "OW's Virginian: The Genesis of a Cultural Hero." *WAL*, 6 (Summer 1971), 99-107.

Lewis, Marvin. "OW: Caste Imprints in Western Letters." *ArQ*, 10 (Summer 1954), 147-156.

Marovitz, Sanford E. "Testament of a Patriot: The Virginian, the Tenderfoot, and OW." *TSLL*, 15 (Fall 1973), 551-575.

Marovitz. "Unseemly Realities in OW's Western/ American Myth." *ALR*, 17 (Autumn 1984), 209-215.

Mason, Julian. "OW and the South." *SHR*, 6 (Winter 1972), 23-34.

Mason. "OW: Champion of Old Charleston." *QJLC*, 29 (Jul 1972), 162-185.

Mason. "OW and World War I: Appeal for Pentecost." *PMHB*, 101 (Jan 1977), 89-102.

Mitchell, Lee Clark. " 'When You Call Me That . . .': Tall Talk and Male Hegemony in *The Virginian*." *PMLA*, 102 (Jan 1987), 66-77.

Mogen, David. "OW's Cowboy Heroes." *SwAL*, 5 (1975), 47-61.

Murphy, John J. "The Virginian and Ántonia Shimerda: Different Sides of the Western Coin." *Women and Western American Literature*, ed Helen Winter Stauffer & Susan J Rosowski (Troy, NY: Whitston, 1982), 162-178.

Nesbitt, John D. "OW's Achievement in Literary Tradition." *WAL*, 18 (Fall 1983), 199-208.

Robinson, Forrest G. "The Virginian and Molly in Paradise: How Sweet Is It?" *WAL*, 21 (Spring 1986), 27-38.

Rowe, Anne E. *The Enchanted Country: Northern Writers in the South, 1865-1910* (Baton Rouge: Louisiana State U P, 1978), 96-122, passim.

Scafella, Frank. "*The Sun Also Rises*: OW's 'Garbage Pail,' Hemingway's Passage of the 'Human Soul.' " *HemR*, 6 (Fall 1986), 101-111.

Scharnhorst, Gary. "The Virginian as a Founding Father." *ArQ*, 40 (Autumn 1984), 227-241.

Simms, L Moody, Jr. "*Lady Baltimore*: OW and the Southern Race Question." *Serif*, 7 (Jun 1970), 23-26.

Stegner, Wallace. "OW: Creator of the Cowboy Myth." *AWest*, 21 (Jan-Feb 1984), 48-52.

Swaim, Elizabeth A. "OW's *Roosevelt*: A Case Study in Post-Production Censorship." *SB*, 27 (1974), 290-293.

Trimmer, Joseph F. "*The Virginian*: Novel and Films." *IllQ*, 35 (Dec 1972), 5-18.

Vorpahl, Ben Merchant. " 'Very Much Like a Firecracker': OW on Mark Twain." *WAL*, 6 (Summer 1971), 83-98.

Walker, Don D. "W, Roosevelt, and James: A Note on the Western." *AQ*, 12 (Fall 1960), 358-366.

White, John I. "OW and the Dogies." *JAF*, 82 (Jan-Mar 1969), 66-69.

Gary E. Lovan

CONSTANCE FENIMORE WOOLSON

Claremont, NH, 5 Mar 1840-Venice, Italy, 24 Jan 1894

Unlike the local colorists to whom she is often compared, Constance Fenimore Woolson extended her range beyond one locality. *Castle Nowhere,* her first collection, sets its stories along the shores of the Great Lakes; *Rodman the Keeper,* perhaps her strongest volume, sketches the defeated South with sympathy. Woolson's later stories take on an international theme, exploring the contrasts between American and European society. Her best sketches often depict communities isolated by ruin, defeat, or natural solitude. Henry James thought Woolson's attitude toward women fundamentally conservative; recent feminist criticism addressing her female artist-figures has challenged that assessment.

BIBLIOGRAPHIES & CATALOGUE

"Bibliography." Kern, 180-194. Primary & secondary.

Bibliography of American Literature, comp Jacob Blanck. New Haven: Yale U P, 1955-1991. Primary.

A Catalogue of Memorabilia Relating to CFW, Preserved in Woolson House, Rollins College, Winter Park, Fla. Winter Park, Fla: Rollins C, 1938.

"Selected Bibliography." Moore, 163-165. Primary & secondary.

BOOKS

The Old Stone House (as by Anne March). Boston: Lothrop / Dover, NH: Day, 1873. Children's novel.

Castle Nowhere: Lake-Country Sketches. Boston: Osgood, 1875. Stories.

Two Women: 1862. A Poem. NY: Appleton, 1877.

Rodman the Keeper: Southern Sketches. NY: Appleton, 1880. Stories.

Anne: A Novel. NY: Harper, 1882.

For the Major: A Novelette. NY: Harper, 1883.

East Angels: A Novel. NY: Harper, 1886.

Jupiter Lights: A Novel. NY: Harper, 1889.

Horace Chase: A Novel. NY: Harper, 1894.

The Front Yard and Other Italian Stories. NY: Harper, 1895.

Dorothy and Other Italian Stories. NY: Harper, 1896.

Mentone, Cairo, and Corfu. NY: Harper, 1896. Travel.

CFW, Vol 2 of *Five Generations (1785-1923), Being Scattered Chapters From the History of the Cooper, Pomeroy, Woolson and Benedict Families, With Extracts From Their Letters and Journals, as Well as Articles and Poems by CFW,* ed Clare Benedict. London: Ellis, 1930.

LETTERS

"Some New Letters of CFW," ed Jay B Hubbell. *NEQ,* 14 (Dec 1941), 715-735.

"Appendix: Four Letters From CFW to Henry James." *Henry James: Letters, Vol. 3, 1883-1895,* ed Leon Edel (Cambridge: Harvard U P, 1980), 523-562.

" 'Always, Your Attached Friend': The Unpublished Letters of CFW to John and Clara Hay," ed Alice Hall Petry. *BBr,* 29-30 (1983), 11-107.

COLLECTIONS

For the Major, and Selected Short Stories, ed Rayburn S Moore. New Haven, Conn: College & University P, 1967.

Women Artists, Women Exiles: "Miss Grief" and Other Stories, ed Joan Myers Weimer. New Brunswick, NJ: Rutgers U P, 1988.

MANUSCRIPTS & ARCHIVES

The major collections are at Rollins C Library; the Western Reserve Historical Society; the Houghton Library, Harvard U; & the Beinecke Library, Yale U.

BIOGRAPHIES

Book Sections

Edel, Leon. *Henry James: The Conquest of London, 1870-1881* & *Henry James: The Middle Years, 1882-1895* (Philadelphia: Lippincott, 1962), passim.

Strouse, Jean. *Alice James: A Biography* (Boston: Houghton Mifflin, 1980), passim.

CRITICAL STUDIES

Books

Gingras, Robert. "CFW's Literary Achievement as a Short Story Writer." Dissertation: Florida State U, 1980.

Kennedy, Elizabeth Marie. "CFW and Henry James: Friendship and Reflections." Dissertation: Yale U, 1983.

Kern, John Dwight. *CFW: Literary Pioneer*. Philadelphia: U Pennsylvania P, 1934.

Moore, Rayburn S. *CFW*. NY: Twayne, 1963.

Stephan, Peter Morris. "Comparative Value Systems in the Fiction of CFW." Dissertation: U New Mexico, 1976.

Weddell, Anna Louise. "Internationalism in the European Short Stories of CFW." Dissertation: Texas A&M U, 1974.

Book Sections & Articles

Brooks, Van Wyck. *The Times of Melville and Whitman* (NY: Dutton, 1947), passim.

Dean, Sharon. "CFW and Henry James: The Literary Relationship." *MSE*, 7, no 3 (1980), 1-9.

Dean. "CFW's Southern Sketches." *SoSt*, 25 (Fall 1986), 274-283.

Helmick, Evelyn Thomas. "CFW: First Novelist of Florida." *Carrell*, 10 (Dec 1969), 8-18.

James, Henry. "Miss CFW." *HarW*, 31 (12 Feb 1887), 114-115. Rpt as "Miss W." *Partial Portraits* by James (London: Macmillan, 1888).

Kitterman, Mary P Edwards. "Henry James and the Artist-Heroine in the Tales of CFW." *Nineteenth-Century Women Writers of the English-Speaking World*, ed Rhoda B Nathan (NY: Greenwood, 1986), 45-59.

Lupold, Harry Forrest. "CFW and the Genre of Regional Fiction." *OhioanaQ*, 29 (Winter 1986), 132-136.

Monteiro, George. "William Dean Howells: Two Mistaken Attributions." *PBSA*, 56 (Second Quarter 1962), 254-257.

Moore, Rayburn S. "The Strange Irregular Rhythm of Life: James's Late Tales and CW." *SAB*, 41 (Nov 1976), 86-93.

Pattee, Fred Lewis. *The Development of the American Short Story* (NY: Harper, 1923), 250-255, 264, 332.

Pattee. "CFW and the South." *SAQ*, 38 (Apr 1939), 130-141.

Richardson, Lyon N. "CFW, 'Novelist Laureate' of America." *SAQ*, 39 (Jan 1940), 18-36.

Rowe, Anne E. *The Enchanted Country: Northern Writers in the South, 1865-1910* (Baton Rouge: Louisiana State U P, 1978), passim.

Simms, L Moody, Jr. "CFW on Southern Literary Taste." *MissQ*, 22 (Fall 1969), 362-366.

Torsney, Cheryl B. "In Anticipation of the Fiftieth Anniversary of Woolson House." *Legacy*, 2 (Fall 1985), 72-73.

Torsney. Introduction. " 'Miss Grief ' by CFW." *Legacy*, 4 (Spring 1987), 11-13.

Wagenknecht, Edward. *Cavalcade of the American Novel* (NY: Holt, 1952), passim.

Weimer, Joan Myers. "Women Artists as Exiles in the Fiction of CFW." *Legacy*, 3 (Fall 1986), 3-15.

Weimer. "Introduction." *Women Artists, Women Exiles: "Miss Grief " and Other Stories*, ix-xliii.

White, Robert L. "Cultural Ambivalence in CFW's Italian Tales." *TSL*, 12 (1967), 121-129.

Wood, Ann Douglas. "The Literature of Impoverishment: The Women Local Colorists in America, 1865-1914." *WS*, 1, no 1 (1972), 3-45.

Pamela R. Matthews & Mary Loeffelholz

HAROLD BELL WRIGHT

Rome, NY, 4 May 1872-La Jolla, Calif, 24 May 1944

Between 1895 and 1926 Harold Bell Wright's novels earned him immense popularity in America. At a time of upheaval caused by urbanization, industrialization, and a world war, Wright provided an unsettled public with a message that Christianity was the hope for mankind, the ideal American home would survive, and a life close to nature was morally beneficial. Wright's novels also revolutionized the publishing industry. Using mail-order and other advertising techniques, his publishers found in middle-class America a vast market. Literary critics scorned his work as poorly written, melodramatic, and dripping with sentimentality and unconvincing characters. By the end of World War I, the reading public also lost interest in Wright, and his popularity declined.

BIBLIOGRAPHIES

DeGruson, Gene. *Kansas Authors of Best Sellers: A Bibliography of the Works of Martin and Osa Johnson, Margaret Hill McCarter, Charles M. Sheldon, and HBW.* Pittsburg: Porter Library, Kansas State C of Pittsburg, 1970. Primary & secondary.

First Printings of American Authors, Vol 2 (Detroit: Bruccoli Clark/Gale, 1978), 395-397. Primary.

BOOKS

That Printer of Udell's: A Story of the Middle West. Chicago: Book Supply, 1903. Novel.

The Shepherd of the Hills. Chicago: Book Supply, 1907. Novel.

The Calling of Dan Matthews. Chicago: Book Supply, 1909. Novel.

The Uncrowned King. Chicago: Book Supply, 1910. Novel.

The Winning of Barbara Worth. Chicago: Book Supply, 1911. Novel.

Their Yesterdays. Chicago: Book Supply, 1912. Novel.

The Eyes of the World. Chicago: Book Supply, 1914. Novel.

When a Man's a Man. Chicago: Book Supply, 1916. Novel.

The Re-creation of Brian Kent. Chicago: Book Supply, 1919. Novel.

On a Portrait of a Woman Painted by Hovsep Pushman. Npl: npub, 1919. Essay.

Helen of the Old House. NY & London: Appleton, 1921. Novel.

The Mine With the Iron Door. NY & London: Appleton, 1923. Novel.

A Son of His Father. NY & London: Appleton, 1925. Novel.

God and the Groceryman. NY & London: Appleton, 1927. Novel.

Exit. NY & London: Appleton, 1930. Novel.

The Devil's Highway, with Gilbert Munger Wright (as by John Lebar). NY & London: Appleton, 1932. Novel.

Ma Cinderella. NY & London: Harper, 1932. Novel.

To My Sons. NY & London: Harper, 1934. Autobiography.

The Man Who Went Away. NY & London: Harper, 1942. Novel.

OTHER

Long Ago Told (Huh-Kew Ah-Kah): Legends of the Papago Indians, arranged by HBW. NY & London: Appleton, 1929.

MANUSCRIPTS & ARCHIVES

UCLA Library.

BIOGRAPHIES

Books

Hawthorne, Hildegarde. *HBW: The Man Behind the Novels.* NY: Appleton, nd.

Tagg, Lawrence V. *HBW: Storyteller to America.* Tucson: Westernlore, 1986.

Book Sections & Articles

Baldwin, Charles C. "HBW." *The Men Who Make Our Novels* (NY: Dodd, Mead, rev 1924), 601-612.

Hawthorne, Hildegarde. "The Wright American." *Bookman,* 56 (Feb 1923), 710-713.

Jones, Charles T. "Brother Hal: The Preaching Career of HBW." *MoHR,* 78 (Jul 1984), 387-413.

Langdon, Thomas C. "HBW: Citizen of Tucson." *JArH,* 16 (Spring 1975), 77-98.

Millard, Bailey. "The Personality of HBW." *Bookman*, 44 (Jan 1917), 463-469.

Mott, Frank Luther. "HBW." *Golden Multitudes: The Story of Best Sellers of the United States* (NY: Macmillan, 1947), 225-233.

Overton, Grant. "HBW." *American Nights Entertainment* (NY: Appleton/Doran/Doubleday, Page/Scribners, 1923), 119-138. Rpt *Authors of the Day* by Overton (Freeport, NY: Doran, 1924).

Reynolds, Elsbery W. "HBW: A Biography." *The Re-creation of Brian Kent*, 345-352.

Tagg, Lawrence V. "A Dedication to the Memory of HBW, 1872-1944." *Ar&W*, 22 (Winter 1980), 302-306.

CRITICAL STUDIES

Book

Ferré, John P. *A Social Gospel for Millions: The Religious Bestsellers of Charles Sheldon, Charles Gordon, and HBW*. Bowling Green, Ohio: Bowling Green State U Popular P, 1988.

Book Section & Articles

Boynton, H W. "A Word on the 'Genteel Critic.'" *Dial*, 59 (14 Oct 1915), 303-306.

Cooper, Frederic Taber. "The Popularity of HBW." *Bookman*, 40 (Jan 1915), 498-500.

Gaston, Edwin W, Jr. *The Early Novel of the Southwest* (Albuquerque: U New Mexico P, 1961), passim.

Ifkovic, Edward. "HBW and the Minister of Man: The Domestic Romancer at the End of the Genteel Age." *MarkhamR*, 4 (Feb 1974), 21-26.

Kenamore, Clair. "A Curiosity in Best-Seller Technique." *Bookman*, 47 (Jul 1918), 538-544.

Kinkead, Joyce. "The Western Sermons of HBW." *JAmC*, 7 (Fall 1984), 85-87.

Oehlschlaeger, Fritz H. "Civilization as Emasculation: The Threatening Role of Women in the Frontier Fiction of HBW and Zane Grey." *MQ*, 22 (Summer 1981), 346-360.

Randall, Dale B J. "The 'Seer' and 'Seen' Themes in *Gatsby* and Some of Their Parallels in Eliot and W." *TCL*, 10 (Jul 1964), 51-63.

Sally Dee Wade

ELIZABETH (LILLIE) BUFFUM CHACE WYMAN

Valley Falls, RI, 10 Dec 1847-Newtonville, Mass, 10 Jan 1929

Lillie Wyman is best remembered for *Poverty Grass,* a collection of eight short stories of local color and realistic social commentary. Her essays and stories, which appeared in popular magazines, advocated prohibition, equal rights for women, and acceptance of all ethnic and racial groups. Wyman's most important literary contributions are her realistic portrayals of conditions in New England factory villages and her depictions of social reform and inner growth.

BOOKS

Poverty Grass. Boston & NY: Houghton, Mifflin, 1886. Stories.
American Chivalry. Boston: Clarke, 1913. Biographical sketches.
Interludes and Other Verses. Boston: Clarke, 1913. Poetry.
Elizabeth Buffum Chace, 1806-1899: Her Life and Environment, 2 vols, with Arthur Crawford Wyman. Boston: Clarke, 1914. Biography.

The Strange Case of Edgar Allan Poe. Boston: npub, 1923. Criticism.
Gertrude of Denmark: An Interpretation of Hamlet. Boston: Jones, 1924. Novel.
A Grand Army Man of Rhode Island. Newton, Mass: Graphic, 1925. Biography.
Syringa at the Gate. Boston: Jones, 1926. Poetry.

MANUSCRIPTS & ARCHIVES

The major collections are at Howard U Library, the Boston Public Library & Brown U Library.

CRITICAL STUDIES

Articles
Howells, William Dean. "Editor's Study." *Harper's,* 74 (Feb 1887), 482-483.
"Notes: Recent Novels." *Nation,* 43 (30 Dec 1886), 547-549.

James Nagel

Chronology of American Fiction and Authors, 1866-1918

The following chronology lists significant fiction by authors who appear in *Bibliography of American Fiction: 1866-1918* and by others who were omitted because their most significant works of fiction were published either before 1866 or after 1918 or because their reputations are based primarily on contributions in another genre. The dates of publication are for the first American editions. The chronology also records birth (b.) and death (d.) dates of writers covered in the bibliography.

1866 George Ade b. (d. 1944)
George Barr McCutcheon b. (d. 1928)
Meredith Nicholson b. (d. 1947)
Mary Mapes Dodge, *Hans Brinker; or, The Silver Skates*
David Ross Locke (Petroleum V. Nasby), *Nasby. Divers Views, . . .*
Henry Wheeler Shaw (Josh Billings), *Josh Billings, Hiz Sayings*
Charles Henry Smith (Bill Arp), *Bill Arp, So Called*
Every Saturday (Boston), 1866-1874
The Galaxy (New York), 1866-1878

1867 Charles Farrar Browne (Artemus Ward) d. (b. 1834)
Finley Peter Dunne b. (d. 1936)
David Graham Phillips b. (d. 1911)
Harry Leon Wilson b. (d. 1939)
Henry Ward Beecher, *Norwood; or, Village Life in New England*
Samuel Langhorne Clemens (Mark Twain), *The Celebrated Jumping Frog of Calaveras County and Other Sketches*
John William De Forest, *Miss Ravenel's Conversion From Secession to Loyalty*
Augusta Jane Evans, *St. Elmo*
George Washington Harris, *Sut Lovingood Yarns: Spun by a "Nat'ral Born Durn'd Fool."*
Bret Harte, *Condensed Novels and Other Papers*
Sidney Lanier, *Tiger-Lilies*
Elizabeth Stoddard, *Temple House*
The Southern Review (Baltimore), 1867-1879

1868 Mary Austin b. (d. 1934)
Robert Herrick b. (d. 1938)
Eleanor H. Porter b. (d. 1920)
Louisa May Alcott, *Little Women*
Horatio Alger, Jr., *Ragged Dick*
John Esten Cooke, *Fairfax*
Lippincott's Magazine (Philadelphia), 1868-1916
Overland Monthly (San Francisco), 1868-1875; 1883-1935
Putnam's Magazine (New York), 1868-1906
Vanity Fair (New York), 1868-1936

1869 George Randolph Chester b. (d. 1924)
Olive Tilford Dargan b. (d. 1968)
Eugene Manlove Rhodes b. (d. 1934)
Booth Tarkington b. (d. 1946)
Brand Whitlock b. (d. 1934)
Horatio Alger, Jr., *Rough and Ready*
Samuel Langhorne Clemens (Mark Twain), *The Innocents Abroad*
Harriet Beecher Stowe, *Oldtown Folks*
Elizabeth Stuart Phelps Ward, *The Gates Ajar*
Appleton's Journal (New York), 1869-1881

1870 Mary Johnston b. (d. 1936)
Joseph C. Lincoln b. (d. 1944)
Frank Norris b. (d. 1902)
Alice Hegan Rice b. (d. 1942)
Louisa May Alcott, *An Old-Fashioned Girl*
Thomas Bailey Aldrich, *The Story of a Bad Boy*
Bret Harte, *The Luck of Roaring Camp and Other Sketches*
The Literary World (Boston), 1870-1904
Scribner's Monthly (New York), 1870-1881
Dodd & Mead, publishers, founded

1871 Samuel Hopkins Adams b. (d. 1958)
Winston Churchill b. (d. 1947)
Stephen Crane b. (d. 1900)
Theodore Dreiser b. (d. 1945)
James Weldon Johnson b. (d. 1938)
Louisa May Alcott, *Little Men*
Edward Eggleston, *The Hoosier School-Master*
Richard Malcolm Johnston (as by Philemon Perch), *Dukesborough Tales*
Harriet Prescott Spofford, *New-England Legends*
Elizabeth Stuart Phelps Ward, *The Silent Partner*

Southern Magazine (Charleston), 1871-1875

1872 Zane Grey b. (d. 1939)
Sutton Elbert Griggs b. (d. 1930)
Harold Bell Wright b. (d. 1944)
Samuel Langhorne Clemens (Mark Twain), *Roughing It*
John William De Forest, *Kate Beaumont*
William Dean Howells, *Their Wedding Journey*
Edward Payson Roe, *Barriers Burned Away*
Publisher's Weekly (New York), 1872-

1873 Guy Wetmore Carryl b. (d. 1904)
Willa Cather b. (d. 1947)
Ellen Glasgow b. (d. 1945)
Stewart Edward White b. (d. 1946)
Louisa May Alcott, *Work*
Thomas Bailey Aldrich, *Marjorie Daw and Other People*
Samuel Langhorne Clemens (Mark Twain) &
    Charles Dudley Warner, *The Gilded Age*
Edgar Fawcett, *Purple and Fine Linen*
Bret Harte, *Mrs. Skaggs's Husbands and Other Sketches*
Marietta Holley (Josiah Allen's Wife), *My Opinions and Betsy Bobbet's*
William Dean Howells, *A Chance Acquaintance*
St. Nicholas (New York), 1873-1940
Woman's Home Companion (Springfield, Ohio),
    1873-1957
Henry Holt, publishers, founded

1874 Thornton W. Burgess b. (d. 1965)
Zona Gale b. (d. 1938)
Hjalmar Hjorth Boyesen, *Gunnar*
Rebecca Harding Davis, *John Andross*
Edward Eggleston, *The Circuit Rider*
Chautauqua Assembly founded

1875 Edgar Rice Burroughs b. (d. 1950)
Alice Moore Dunbar-Nelson b. (d. 1935)
John William De Forest, *Honest John Vane*
Bret Harte, *Tales of the Argonauts and Other Sketches*
William Dean Howells, *A Foregone Conclusion*
Henry James, *A Passionate Pilgrim and Other Tales*
Maurice Thompson, *Hoosier Mosaics*
Constance Fenimore Woolson, *Castle Nowhere: Lake-Country Sketches*

1876 Sherwood Anderson b. (d. 1941)
Irvin S. Cobb b. (d. 1944)
Susan Glaspell b.? (d. 1948)
Jack London b. (d. 1916)
Mary Roberts Rinehart b. (d. 1958)
Samuel Langhorne Clemens (Mark Twain), *The Adventures of Tom Sawyer*
Helen Hunt Jackson, *Mercy Philbrick's Choice*
Henry James, *Roderick Hudson*

Edward Payson Roe, *Near to Nature's Heart*
Frank Leslie's Popular Monthly (New York),
    1876-1904
Thomas Y. Crowell, publishers, founded

1877 Rex Beach b. (d. 1949)
Henry James, *The American*
Sarah Orne Jewett, *Deephaven*
Edward Payson Roe, *A Knight of the Nineteenth Century*
Elizabeth Stuart Phelps Ward, *The Story of Avis*
Puck (New York), 1877-1918

1878 James Oliver Curwood b. (d. 1927)
Owen Johnson b. (d. 1952)
Don Marquis b. (d. 1937)
Upton Sinclair b. (d. 1968)
Anna Katharine Green, *The Leavenworth Case*
Henry James, *The Europeans*

1879 James Branch Cabell b. (d. 1958)
Dorothy Canfield Fisher b. (d. 1958)
Katharine Fullerton Gerould b. (d. 1944)
George Washington Cable, *Old Creole Days*
William Dean Howells, *The Lady of the Aroostook*
Henry James, *Daisy Miller*
Frank R. Stockton, *Rudder Grange*
Albion Winegar Tourgée, *A Fool's Errand*

1880 Joseph Hergesheimer b. (d. 1954)
Peter B. Kyne b. (d. 1957)
Ernest Poole b. (d. 1950)
Henry Adams (Anon), *Democracy: An American Novel*
George Washington Cable, *The Grandissimes*
Lucretia Peabody Hale, *The Peterkin Papers*
Harriett M. Lothrop (Margaret Sidney), *Five Little Peppers and How They Grew*
Albion Winegar Tourgée, *Bricks Without Straw*
Lew Wallace, *Ben-Hur: A Tale of the Christ*
Constance Fenimore Woolson, *Rodman the Keeper: Southern Sketches*
The Dial (Chicago), 1880-1929
Houghton, Mifflin and Co., publishers, founded

1881 Clarence Budington Kelland b. (d. 1964)
William McFee b. (d. 1966)
Elizabeth Madox Roberts b. (d. 1941)
George Washington Cable, *Madame Delphine*
Rose Terry Cooke, *Somebody's Neighbors*
Joel Chandler Harris, *Uncle Remus: His Songs and His Sayings*
Henry James, *The Portrait of a Lady; Washington Square*
The Century Illustrated Magazine (New York),
    1881-1930

1882 Samuel Langhorne Clemens (Mark Twain),
    The Prince and the Pauper

F. Marion Crawford, *Mr. Isaacs: A Tale of Modern India*
William Dean Howells, *A Modern Instance*
Elizabeth Stuart Phelps Ward, *Dr. Zay*

1883 Sherwood Bonner d. (b. 1849)
Clarence E. Mulford b. (d. 1956)
Edward Eggleston, *The Hoosier School-Boy*
Mary Hallock Foote, *The Led-Horse Claim*
Joel Chandler Harris, *Nights With Uncle Remus*
E. W. Howe, *The Story of a Country Town*
Howard Pyle, *The Merry Adventures of Robin Hood*
Constance Fenimore Woolson, *For the Major*
Ladies Home Journal (Philadelphia), 1883-1968
Life (New York), 1883-1936

1884 Earl Derr Biggers b. (d. 1933)
Oscar Micheaux b. (d. 1951)
Henry Adams (as by Frances Snow Compton), *Esther*
Sherwood Bonner, *Suwanee River Tales*
Edgar Fawcett, *An Ambitious Woman*
Helen Hunt Jackson, *Ramona*
Sarah Orne Jewett, *A Country Doctor*
Mary Noailles Murfree, *In the Tennessee Mountains*
Bill Nye, *Baled Hay: A Drier Book Than Walt Whitman's "Leaves o' Grass"*
Frank R. Stockton, *The Lady, or the Tiger? and Other Stories*

1885 Helen Hunt Jackson d. (b. 1830)
Henry Wheeler Shaw (Josh Billings) d. (b. 1818)
George Washington Cable, *Dr. Sevier*
Samuel Langhorne Clemens (Mark Twain), *Adventures of Huckleberry Finn*
Rose Terry Cooke, *Root-Bound and Other Sketches*
F. Marion Crawford, *Zoroaster*
Oliver Wendell Holmes, *A Mortal Antipathy*
William Dean Howells, *The Rise of Silas Lapham*
Sarah Orne Jewett, *A Marsh Island*
Mary Noailles Murfree, *The Prophet of the Great Smoky Mountains*

1886 Frances Hodgson Burnett, *Little Lord Fauntleroy*
William Dean Howells, *Indian Summer*
Henry James, *The Bostonians*
Sarah Orne Jewett, *A White Heron and Other Stories*
Elizabeth (Lillie) Buffum Chace Wyman, *Poverty Grass*
Cosmopolitan Magazine (New York), 1886-
The Forum (New York), 1886-1940

1887 Alice Brown, *Fools of Nature*
Harold Frederic, *Seth's Brother's Wife*

Mary E. Wilkins Freeman, *A Humble Romance and Other Stories*
Alice French (Octave Thanet), *Knitters in the Sun*
Joel Chandler Harris, *Free Joe and Other Georgian Sketches*
Marietta Holley (Josiah Allen's Wife), *Samantha at Saratoga*
Joseph Kirkland, *Zury: The Meanest Man in Spring County*
Thomas Nelson Page, *In Ole Virginia; or, Marse Chan and Other Stories*
Scribner's Magazine (New York), 1887-1939

1888 Louisa May Alcott d. (b. 1832)
David Ross Locke (Petroleum V. Nasby) d. (b. 1833)
Edward Payson Roe d. (b. 1838)
Edward Bellamy, *Looking Backward, 2000-1887*
Margaret Deland, *John Ward, Preacher*
Grace King, *Monsieur Motte*
Collier's (Springfield, Ohio), 1888-1957

1889 Jane Goodwin Austin, *Standish of Standish*
Mary Hartwell Catherwood, *The Romance of Dollard*
Samuel Langhorne Clemens (Mark Twain), *A Connecticut Yankee in King Arthur's Court*
Lafcadio Hearn, *Chita: A Memory of Last Island*
William Dean Howells, *Annie Kilburn*
Constance Fenimore Woolson, *Jupiter Lights*
The Arena (Boston), 1889-1909

1890 Kate Chopin, *At Fault*
Ignatius Donnelly (as by Edmund Boisgilbert, M.D.), *Caesar's Column*
Constance Cary Harrison, *The Anglomaniacs*
William Dean Howells, *A Hazard of New Fortunes*
Literary Digest (New York), 1890-1938
The Smart Set (New York), 1890-1930

1891 Ambrose Bierce, *Tales of Soldiers and Civilians*
Hjalmar Hjorth Boyesen, *The Mammon of Unrighteousness*
H. C. Bunner, *"Short Sixes"*
Rose Terry Cooke, *Huckleberries Gathered From New England Hills*
Richard Harding Davis, *Gallegher and Other Stories*
Mary E. Wilkins Freeman, *A New England Nun and Other Stories*
Hamlin Garland, *Main-Travelled Roads*
Mary Noailles Murfree, *In the "Stranger People's" Country*
F. Hopkinson Smith, *Colonel Carter of Cartersville*

1892 Rose Terry Cooke, d. (b. 1827)
Richard Harding Davis, *Van Bibber and Others*
Mary Hallock Foote, *The Chosen Valley*

Joel Chandler Harris, *Uncle Remus and His Friends*
William Dean Howells, *The Quality of Mercy*
Grace King, *Tales of a Time and Place*
Godey's Magazine (New York), 1892-1898
The Sewanee Review (Sewanee, Tenn.), 1892-
The Yale Review (New Haven), 1892-

1893 Joseph Kirkland d. (b. 1830)
Stephen Crane, *Maggie: A Girl of the Streets*
Alice French (Octave Thanet), *Stories of a Western Town*
Henry Blake Fuller, *The Cliff-Dwellers*
Hamlin Garland, *Prairie Folks*
Henry James, *The Real Thing and Other Tales*
McClure's Magazine (New York), 1893-1929

1894 Jane Goodwin Austin d. (b. 1831)
Constance Fenimore Woolson d. (b. 1840)
Gertrude Atherton, *Before the Gringo Came*
George Washington Cable, *John March, Southerner*
Kate Chopin, *Bayou Folk*
Samuel Langhorne Clemens (Mark Twain), *The Tragedy of Pudd'nhead Wilson and The Comedy of Those Extraordinary Twins*
Paul Leicester Ford, *The Honorable Peter Stirling and What People Thought of Him*
Mary Wilkins Freeman, *Pembroke*
Brander Matthews, *Vignettes of Manhattan*
Harriet Prescott Spofford, *A Scarlet Poppy and Other Stories*
The Chap Book (Chicago), 1894-1898

1895 Hjalmar Hjorth Boyesen d. (b. 1848)
James Lane Allen, *A Kentucky Cardinal*
John Kendrick Bangs, *The Idiot*
Alice Brown, *Meadow-Grass: Tales of New England Life*
Robert W. Chambers, *The King in Yellow*
Stephen Crane, *The Red Badge of Courage*
Alice Moore Dunbar-Nelson, *Violets and Other Tales*
Hamlin Garland, *Rose of Dutcher's Coolly*
Constance Fenimore Woolson, *The Front Yard and Other Italian Stories*
The Bookman (New York), 1895-1933

1896 H. C. Bunner d. (b. 1855)
Bill Nye d. (b. 1850)
James Lane Allen, *Summer in Arcady*
Abraham Cahan, *Yekl: A Tale of the New York Ghetto*
Samuel Langhorne Clemens (Mark Twain), *Personal Recollections of Joan of Arc*
Stephen Crane, *The Little Regiment and Other Episodes of the American Civil War*
Harold Frederic, *The Damnation of Theron Ware*
Sarah Orne Jewett, *The Country of the Pointed Firs*
The Macmillan Co., publishers, founded

1897 Mary Hartwell Catherwood, *The Spirit of an Illinois Town and The Little Renault*
Kate Chopin, *A Night in Acadie*
Richard Harding Davis, *Soldiers of Fortune*
Ellen Glasgow, *The Descendant*
Henry James, *What Maisie Knew*
Alfred Henry Lewis, *Wolfville*
Richard Malcolm Johnston, *Old Times in Middle Georgia*
S. Weir Mitchell, *Hugh Wynne: Free Quaker*
Doubleday & McClure, publishers, founded

1898 Edward Bellamy d. (b. 1850)
Harold Frederic d. (b. 1856)
Richard Malcolm Johnston d. (b. 1822)
Edward Noyes Westcott d. (b. 1846)
Gertrude Atherton, *The Californians*
Stephen Crane, *The Open Boat and Other Tales of Adventure*
Finley Peter Dunne, *Mr. Dooley in Peace and in War*
Henry James, *The Two Magics: The Turn of the Screw, Covering End*
Mary Johnston, *Prisoners of Hope*
Charles Major, *When Knighthood Was in Flower*
Brander Matthews, *Outlines in Local Color*
S. Weir Mitchell, *The Adventures of François*
Frank Norris, *Moran of the Lady Letty*
Thomas Nelson Page, *Red Rock*
Edward Noyes Westcott, *David Harum: A Story of American Life*
National Institute of Arts and Letters founded

1899 Horatio Alger, Jr. d. (b. 1832)
Alice Brown, *Tiverton Tales*
Charles Waddell Chesnutt, *The Wife of His Youth and Other Stories of the Color Line; The Conjure Woman*
Kate Chopin, *The Awakening*
Winston Churchill, *Richard Carvel*
Margaret Deland, *Old Chester Tales*
Alice Moore Dunbar-Nelson, *The Goodness of St. Rocque and Other Stories*
Charlotte Perkins Gilman, *The Yellow Wall-paper*
Sutton Elbert Griggs, *Imperium in Imperio*
Henry James, *The Awkward Age*
Frank Norris, *McTeague*
Booth Tarkington, *The Gentleman From Indiana*
Pearson's Magazine (New York), 1899-1925

1900 Stephen Crane d. (b. 1871)
Lucretia Peabody Hale d. (b. 1820)
George Ade, *Fables in Slang*
Irving Bacheller, *Eben Holden*
L. Frank Baum, *The Wonderful Wizard of Oz*
Charles Waddell Chesnutt, *The House Behind the Cedars*

Samuel Langhorne Clemens (Mark Twain), *The Man That Corrupted Hadleyburg and Other Stories and Essays*
Stephen Crane, *Whilomville Stories*
Theodore Dreiser, *Sister Carrie*
Paul Laurence Dunbar, *The Love of Landry*
Ellen Glasgow, *The Voice of the People*
Robert Herrick, *The Web of Life*
Pauline Elizabeth Hopkins, *Contending Forces*
Mary Johnston, *To Have and to Hold*
Maurice Thompson, *Alice of Old Vincennes*
Harper's New Monthly Magazine (New York), 1900-1925

1901 Ignatius Donnelly d. (b. 1831)
Maurice Thompson d. (b. 1844)
Charles Waddell Chesnutt, *The Marrow of Tradition*
Charles Major, *The Bears of Blue River*
George Barr McCutcheon, *Graustark*
Frank Norris, *The Octopus*
David Graham Phillips (as by John Graham), *The Great God Success*
Alice Hegan Rice, *Mrs. Wiggs of the Cabbage Patch*

1902 Mary Hartwell Catherwood d. (b. 1847)
Edward Eggleston d. (b. 1837)
Paul Leicester Ford d. (b. 1865)
Bret Harte d. (b. 1836)
Frank Norris d. (b. 1870)
Frank R. Stockton d. (b. 1834)
Thomas Dixon, *The Leopard's Spots*
Paul Laurence Dunbar, *The Sport of the Gods*
Sutton Elbert Griggs, *Unfettered*
Emerson Hough, *The Mississippi Bubble*
Henry James, *The Wings of the Dove*
Edith Wharton, *The Valley of Decision*
Stewart Edward White, *The Blazed Trail*
Brand Whitlock, *The 13th District*
Owen Wister, *The Virginian*
South Atlantic Quarterly (Durham, N.C.), 1902-
B. W. Huebsch, publishers, founded

1903 Charles Henry Smith (Bill Arp) d. (b. 1826)
Andy Adams, *The Log of a Cowboy*
Guy Wetmore Carryl, *The Lieutenant-Governor*
John Fox, Jr., *The Little Shepherd of Kingdom Come*
Henry James, *The Ambassadors*
Jack London, *The Call of the Wild*
George Barr McCutcheon (as by Richard Greaves), *Brewster's Millions*
Frank Norris, *The Pit*
Kate Douglas Wiggin, *Rebecca of Sunnybrook Farm*
Bobbs-Merrill, publishers, founded

1904 Guy Wetmore Carryl d. (b. 1873)
Kate Chopin d. (b. 1851)

Edgar Fawcett d. (b. 1847)
Lafcadio Hearn d. (b. 1850)
Ellen Glasgow, *The Deliverance*
Henry James, *The Golden Bowl*
Joseph C. Lincoln, *Cap'n Eri: A Story of the Coast*
Jack London, *The Sea-Wolf*
Mary Noailles Murfree, *The Frontiersmen*
Gene Stratton Porter, *Freckles*
William Sydney Porter (O. Henry), *Cabbages and Kings*
American Academy of Arts and Letters founded

1905 Mary Mapes Dodge d. (b. 1831?)
Henry Harland d. (b. 1861)
Albion Winegar Tourgée d. (b. 1838)
Lew Wallace d. (b. 1827)
Mary Austin, *Isidro*
Rex Beach, *The Spoilers*
Frances Hodgson Burnett, *A Little Princess*
Willa Cather, *The Troll Garden*
Thomas Dixon, *The Clansman*
Edgar Saltus, *The Perfume of Eros*
Edith Wharton, *The House of Mirth*

1906 John William De Forest d. (b. 1826)
Jack London, *White Fang*
Ernest Poole, *The Voice of the Street*
William Sidney Porter (O. Henry), *The Four Million*
Upton Sinclair, *The Jungle*
Harriet Prescott Spofford, *Old Washington*
American Magazine (New York), 1906-1956
Mitchell Kennerley, publishers, founded

1907 Thomas Bailey Aldrich d. (b. 1836)
Jack London, *Love of Life and Other Stories*
Edith Wharton, *Madame de Treymes*
Brand Whitlock, *The Turn of the Balance*
Harold Bell Wright, *The Shepherd of the Hills*

1908 Joel Chandler Harris d. (b. 1848?)
Mary Austin, *Santa Lucia: A Common Story*
George Randolph Chester, *Get-Rich-Quick Wallingford*
John Fox, Jr., *The Trail of the Lonesome Pine*
Zona Gale, *Friendship Village*
Ellen Glasgow, *The Ancient Law*
Jack London, *The Iron Heel*
William McFee, *Letters From an Ocean Tramp*
Mary Roberts Rinehart, *The Circular Staircase*
George H. Doran, publishers, founded

1909 F. Marion Crawford d. (b. 1854)
Edward Everett Hale d. (b. 1822)
Sarah Orne Jewett d. (b. 1849)
Susan Glaspell, *The Glory of the Conquered*
Owen Johnson, *The Eternal Boy: Being the Story of the Prodigious Hickey*
Jack London, *Martin Eden*

Gene Stratton Porter, *A Girl of the Limberlost*
Gertrude Stein, *Three Lives*
Twentieth-Century Magazine (Boston), 1909-1913
U.S. Copyright Act passed

1910 Samuel Langhorne Clemens (Mark Twain) d.
    (b. 1835)
Rebecca Harding Davis d. (b. 1831)
William Sydney Porter (O. Henry) d. (b. 1862)
Thornton W. Burgess, *Old Mother West Wind*
Clarence E. Mulford, *Hopalong Cassidy*
Eugene Manlove Rhodes, *Good Men and True*
Harold Bell Wright, *The Uncrowned King*

1911 David Graham Phillips d. (b. 1867)
Howard Pyle d. (b. 1853)
Elizabeth Stuart Phelps Ward d. (b. 1844)
Frances Hodgson Burnett, *The Secret Garden*
Theodore Dreiser, *Jennie Gerhardt*
Mary Johnston, *The Long Roll*
Edith Wharton, *Ethan Frome*
The Masses (New York), 1911-1918

1912 Willa Cather, *Alexander's Bridge*
Theodore Dreiser, *The Financier*
Zane Grey, *Riders of the Purple Sage*
James Weldon Johnson, *The Autobiography of an
    Ex-Colored Man*
Owen Johnson, *Stover at Yale*
Authors' League of America founded

1913 Charles Major d. (b. 1856)
Earl Derr Biggers, *Seven Keys to Baldpate*
Willa Cather, *O Pioneers!*
Jack London, *The Valley of the Moon*
Oscar Micheaux, *The Conquest: The Story of a
    Negro Pioneer*
Eleanor H. Porter, *Pollyanna*
Edith Wharton, *The Custom of the Country*

1914 Ambrose Bierce d.? (b. 1842)
Alfred Henry Lewis d. (b. 1857)
S. Weir Mitchell d. (b. 1829)
Edgar Rice Burroughs, *Tarzan of the Apes*
Theodore Dreiser, *The Titan*
Joseph Hergesheimer, *The Lay Anthony*
Sinclair Lewis, *Our Mr. Wrenn*
Frank Norris, *Vandover and the Brute*
Wilbur Daniel Steele, *Storm*
Booth Tarkington, *Penrod*
The Little Review (Chicago), 1914-1929
New Republic (New York), 1914-

1915 F. Hopkinson Smith d. (b. 1838)
Willa Cather, *The Song of the Lark*
Margaret Deland, *Around Old Chester*
Theodore Dreiser, *The "Genius"*
Dorothy Canfield Fisher, *The Bent Twig*
Katharine Fullerton Gerould, *The Great Tradition
    and Other Stories*
Sinclair Lewis, *The Trail of the Hawk*
Oscar Micheaux, *The Forged Note: A Romance of
    the Darker Races*
Ernest Poole, *The Harbor*
Harry Leon Wilson, *Ruggles of Red Gap*
Alfred A. Knopf, publishers, founded
Robert M. McBride, publishers, founded

1916 Richard Harding Davis d. (b. 1864)
Henry James d. (b. 1843)
Jack London d. (b. 1876)
Sherwood Anderson, *Windy McPherson's Son*
Samuel Langhorne Clemens (Mark Twain), *The
    Mysterious Stranger*
Irvin S. Cobb, *Old Judge Priest*
James Oliver Curwood, *The Grizzly King*
William Dean Howells, *The Leatherwood God*
Grace King, *The Pleasant Ways of St. Médard*
Joseph Kirkland, *Cappy Ricks; or, The Subjugation
    of Matt Peasley*
Ring W. Lardner, *You Know Me Al*
Don Marquis, *Hermione and Her Little Group of
    Serious Thinkers*
Mary Roberts Rinehart, *Tish*
Booth Tarkington, *Seventeen*

1917 Sherwood Anderson, *Marching Men*
Abraham Cahan, *The Rise of David Levinsky*
Sinclair Lewis, *The Job*
Oscar Micheaux, *The Homesteader*
Christopher Morley, *Parnassus on Wheels*
David Graham Phillips, *Susan Lenox, Her Fall and
    Rise*
Ernest Poole, *His Family*
T. S. Stribling, *The Cruise of the Dry Dock*
Edith Wharton, *Summer*
Pulitzer Prizes established

1918 Sholem Asch, *Mottke the Vagabond*
Willa Cather, *My Ántonia*
Mary E. Wilkins Freeman, *Edgewater People*
Ring W. Lardner, *Gullible's Travels, Etc.*
Wilbur Daniel Steele, *Land's End and Other Stories*
Booth Tarkington, *The Magnificent Ambersons*
O. Henry Memorial Award established

JOURNALS AND ACRONYMS IN BIBLIOGRAPHY OF AMERICAN FICTION: 1866-1918

A

ABC   American Book Collector
Accent
AFFWord: Publication of the Arizona Friends of Folklore
AH   American Heritage
AHumor   American Humor: An Interdisciplinary Newsletter
AIQ   American Indian Quarterly
AJHQ   American Jewish Historical Quarterly
AL   American Literature: A Journal of Literary History, Criticism, and Bibliography
ALA Bulletin   American Library Association Bulletin
ALR   American Literary Realism, 1870-1910
ALS   Australian Literary Studies
AltF   Alternative Futures
Amerasia   Amerasia Journal
AMercury   American Mercury
AmerF   American Film
AmerHI   American History Illustrated
America
Americana
American Fabian
AmerMag   American Magazine
AmerP   American Poetry
AmerS   American Studies
AmerSSc   American Studies in Scandinavia
AmNeptune   American Neptune
AmR   American Review
AmRofR   American Review of Reviews
AmS   American Socialist
Amst   Amerikastudien/American Studies
AN   Acta Neophilologica (Ljubijana, Yugoslavia)
AN&Q   American Notes and Queries
AnMH   Annals of Medical History
ANQ   A Quarterly Journal of Short Articles, Notes & Reviews
AnWy   Annals of Wyoming
AppalJ   Appalachian Journal
AQ   American Quarterly
AR   Antioch Review
Ar&W   Arizona and the West
Arena

Argonaut
ArielE   Ariel: A Review of International English Literature
Arizona Highways
ArmD   Armchair Detective
Army
Arnoldian
ArQ   Arizona Quarterly
AS   American Speech: A Quarterly of Linguistic Usage
ASch   American Scholar
ASInt   American Studies International
Ath   Athenaeum
AtlantaHJ   Atlanta Historical Journal
AtlantaJ&CM   Atlanta Journal and Constitution Magazine
Atlantic   Atlantic Monthly
AtlanticJ   Atlantic Journal
ATQ   American Transcendental Quarterly: A Journal of New England Writers
AudM   Audubon Magazine
AUMLA: Journal of Australasia Universities Language and Literature Association
AustinAmS   Austin-American Statesman
AWest   American West

B

BALF   Black American Literature Forum
BaltSSun   Baltimore Sunday Sun
Bancroftiana
BB   Bulletin of Bibliography
BBr   Books at Brown
BC   The Book Collector
BClubCalQNL   Book Club of California Quarterly Newsletter
BHM   Bulletin of the History of Medicine
BI   Books at Iowa
Bibliographer
Biography
Bittersweet
BJRL   Bulletin of the John Rylands University Library of Manchester
BNYPL   Bulletin of the New York Public Library
Book Buyer   The Book Buyer
Booklover   The Booklover's Magazine
Bookman

Bookman (London)
Book-Mart
BookNM   Book News Monthly
Brief   The Brief
BRMMLA   Bulletin of the Rocky Mountain Modern Language Association
Broom
BSUF   Ball State University Forum
BuR   Bucknell Review
BUSE   Boston University Studies in English
BYUS   Brigham Young University Studies

C

Cabellian
CaC   California Courier
CaH   California History
CahiersL   Cahiers de Littérature et de Poesie: Poets et Leurs Amis
CaHSQ   California Historical Society Quarterly
CalEJ   California English Journal
CalH   California History
CalHQ   California Historical Quarterly
CanadianM   Canadian Magazine
C&L   Christianity and Literature
Carrell   The Carrell: Journal of the Friends of the University of Miami Library
CathW   Catholic World
CBS   Contributions to Black Studies
CCollector   The Curwood Collector
CE   College English
CEA   CEA Critic: An Official Journal of the College English Association
CentR   Centennial Review (East Lansing, Mich.)
Century
ChaB   Chap-Book
Chautauquan   The Chautauquan
Chicago History
ChiJF   Chicago Jewish Forum
ChildL   Children's Literature: An International Journal
ChiM   Chicago Magazine
ChiR   Chicago Review
CHSB   Cincinnati Historical Society Bulletin
CL   Comparative Literature (Eugene, Oreg.)
CLAJ   College Language Association Journal
CLAQ   Children's Literature Association Quarterly
CLC   Columbia Library Columns
ClioI   CLIO: A Journal of Literature, History, and the Philosophy of History
Clipper   The Clipper
CLQ   Colby Library Quarterly
CLS   Comparative Literature Studies
Clues: A Journal of Detection
CML   Classical and Modern Literature: A Quarterly (Terre Haute, Ind.)
Collier's   Collier's Weekly
CollL   College Literature

ColMag   Colorado Magazine
Colophon
ColoredAM   Colored American Magazine
ColQ   Colorado Quarterly
ColUQ   Columbia University Quarterly
Commentary
CommonG   Common Ground
Commonweal
ConL   Contemporary Literature
ConservativeR   Conservative Review
Cosmopolitan
Country Home
Courier: Syracuse University Library Association Courier
CraneR   Crane Review
CRAS   Centennial Review of Arts & Sciences
Creative Reading
Cresset
CRevAS   Canadian Review of American Studies
Crit   Critique: Studies in Modern Fiction
Criterion
CritI   Critical Inquiry
Critic   The Critic
Criticism: A Quarterly for Literature and the Arts
CriticNY   Critic (New York)
CSM   Christian Science Monitor
CurrentHist   Current History
CurrentL   Current Literature
Current Opinion
CWH   Civil War History

D

DallasTH   Dallas Times Herald
DCLB   Dartmouth College Library Bulletin
DD   Double Dealer
DearbornInd   Dearborn Independent
Definitions
Delta   The Delta
DeltaES   Delta: Revue du Centre d'Etudes et de Recherche sur les Ecrivains du Sud aux Etats-Unis (Montpellier, France)
Dial
DicS   Dickinson Studies
DNR   Dime Novel Roundup: A Magazine Devoted to the Collecting, Preservation and Literature of the Old-Time Dime and Nickel Novels, Libraries and Popular Story Papers
Dolphin   The Dolphin: Publications of the English Department, University of Aarhus, Denmark
DQu   Dickens Quarterly
DR   Dalhousie Review
DreiserN   Dreiser Newsletter
DreiserS   Dreiser Studies
DSA   Dickens Studies Annual: Essays on Victorian Fiction

E

EA   Etudes Anglaises: Grande-Bretagne, Etats-Unis

E&S   Essays and Studies (London)
Edde
EdForum   Educational Forum
EGN   Ellen Glasgow Newsletter
EIC   Essays in Criticism: A Quarterly Journal of
    Literary Criticism (Oxford, England)
EJ   English Journal (Urbana, Ill.)
Eleusis   Eleusis of Chi Omega
ELH (formerly Journal of English Literary History)
ELN   English Language Notes (Boulder, Colo.)
ELWIU   Essays in Literature (Macomb, Ill.)
Encounter
EngR   English Record
EngRev   English Review of Salem State College
EON   Eugene O'Neill Newsletter
EOSat   Every Other Saturday
Equal Rights: Independent Feminist Weekly
ES   English Studies: A Journal of English Lan-
    guage and Literature
ESQ: A Journal of the American Renaissance
Esquire
Ethics
EThJ   Educational Theatre Journal
EthnicG   Ethnic Groups
ETHSP   East Tennessee Historical Society's Publica-
    tions
Etudes
EUQ   Emory University Quarterly
EWHM   Edgar Watson Howe Monthly
EWhN   Edith Wharton Newsletter
*Extrapolation: A Journal of Science Fiction and Fan-
    tasy*

F

FForum   Folklore Forum
FHA   Fitzgerald/Hemingway Annual
FilmH   Film History
Films in Review
FilsonCHQ   The Filson Club History Quarterly
FNS   Frank Norris Studies
FoR   Fortnightly Review
Forum
Foundations
FR   The French Review: Journal of the American
    Association of Teachers of French
FredericH   Frederic Herald
Frontier   The Frontier
Frontiers: A Journal of Women Studies
FSt   Feminist Studies

G

GaHQ   Georgia Historical Quarterly
GaM   Georgia Magazine
GaR   Georgia Review
Genre
GLB   Godey's Lady's Book

GMHCUP   General Magazine and Historical
    Chronicle of the University of Pennsylvania
GoodH   Good Housekeeping
GPQ   Great Plains Quarterly
Greyfriar: Siena Studies in Literature
GrLR   Great Lakes Review
Gunton's

H

H&H   Hound and Horn
Har   Harper's New Monthly Magazine
Harper's
HarW   Harper's Weekly
HB   Harper's Bazaar
HemR   Hemingway Review
HGP   Heritage of the Great Plains
HispR   Hispanic Review
HJM   Haldeman-Julius Monthly
HJR   Henry James Review
HLB   Harvard Library Bulletin
HLQ   Huntington Library Quarterly: A Journal
    for the History and Interpretation of English
    and American Civilization
HMo   Harvard Monthly
Horizon
Horn Book
HSL   University of Hartford Studies in Literature:
    A Journal of Interdisciplinary Criticism
HSSCQ   Historical Society of Southern California
    Quarterly
HudR   Hudson Review

I

I&WR   Independent and Weekly Review
Idler   The Idler
IHB   Indiana History Bulletin
IHJ   Illinois Historical Journal
IJAS   Indian Journal of American Studies
IJWS   International Journal of Women's Studies
IllM   Illinois Magazine
IllQ   Illinois Quarterly
ILN   Illustrated London News
IM   Irish Monthly
IMH   Indiana Magazine of History
IndEJ   Indiana English Journal
Independent   The Independent
InFl   Indiana Folklore
IntlM   International Monthly
IQB   Indiana Quarterly for Bookmen
IUB   Indiana University Bookman
IY   Idaho Yesterdays

J

JA   Jahrbuch für Amerikastudien
JAAC   Journal of Aesthetics and Art Criticism
JAC   Journal of Advanced Composition

JAF Journal of American Folklore
JAFict Journal of American Fiction
JAH Journal of American History
JAmC Journal of American Culture
JAmS Journal of American Studies
JArH Journal of Arizona History
JART Journal of the Academy of Religious Thought
JAS Journal of the Acoustical Society of American
JCMVASA Journal of the Central Mississippi Valley American Studies Association
JFI Journal of the Folklore Institute
JGE Journal of General Education
JH Jewish Heritage
JHI Journal of the History of Ideas
JHS Journal of Historical Studies
JIH Journal of Interdisciplinary History
JISHS Journal of the Illinois State Historical Society
JLEchoes Jack London Echoes
JLH The Journal of Library History, Philosophy and Comparative Librarianship
JLIBC Journal of the Long Island Book Collectors
JLN Jack London Newsletter
JML Journal of Modern Literature
JNH Journal of Negro History
JNT Journal of Narrative Technique
JOFS Journal of the Ohio Folklore Society
JPC Journal of Popular Culture
JPE Journal of Political Economy
JPFT Journal of Popular Film and Television
JQ Journalism Quarterly
JRUL Journal of the Rutgers University Libraries
JSoH Journal of Southern History
Judaism
JW Journal of the West

K

Kalki: Studies in James Branch Cabell
KCN Kate Chopin Newsletter
KentSE Kent Studies in English
KFQ Keystone Folklore Quarterly
KFR Kentucky Folklore Record: A Regional Journal of Folklore and Folklife
KHQ Kansas Historical Quarterly
KLit Kritikon Litterarum
KQ Koreana Quarterly
KR Kenyon Review
KRev Kentucky Review
KSB Kent State University Bulletin
KyHSR Kentucky Historical Society Register

L

LadiesHJ Ladies' Home Journal
LaH Louisiana History
LaHQ Louisiana Historical Quarterly
LAmer Letterature d'America: Rivista Trimestrale

Lamp The Lamp
L&B Literature and Belief
L&P Literature and Psychology (Teaneck, N.J.)
Landscape
L&U The Lion and the Unicorn: A Critical Journal of Children's Literature
LaS Louisiana Studies
LCQ Library of Congress Quarterly
LCUT Library Chronicle of the University of Texas
LDIBR Literary Digest International Book Review
LE&W Literature East and West
Legacy: A Journal of Nineteenth-Century American Women Writers
LFQ Literature/Film Quarterly
Liberty
Library (Pittsburgh)
LibraryC Library Chronicle of the University of Pennsylvania
Life
Lippincott's Lippincott's Magazine
Listener
LitD Literary Digest
LitN Literary News
LitR Literary Review: An International Journal of Contemporary Writing
Lituanus: Baltic States Quarterly of Arts & Sciences
LitW Literary World
Living Age The Living Age
LJHum Lamar Journal of the Humanities
LMonog Literary Monographs
London Collector
London Mercury
Los Angeles
LRev Little Review

M

Maclean's
Mad River Review
MARev Mid-American Review
MarkhamR Markham Review
MASJ Midcontinent American Studies Journal
Masses The Masses
MB More Books (Boston Public Library)
McNR McNeese Review
MD Modern Drama
MELUS: The Journal of the Society for the Study of the Multi-Ethnic Literature of the United States
Menckeniana: A Quarterly Review
Mentor The Mentor
MFS Modern Fiction Studies
MHM Maryland Historical Magazine
MHR Missouri Historical Review
MichA Michigan Academician
MichAQR Michigan Alumnus Quarterly Review
MichH Michigan History

Michigan Out-of-Doors
Midamerica: The Yearbook of the Society for the Study of Midwestern Literature
Mid-America: An Historical Review (Loyola University, Chicago)
Mid-HudsonLS Mid-Hudson Language Studies
MidlandM Midland Monthly
Midstream
MidwestJ Midwest Journal
MinnH Minnesota History
MinnR Minnesota Review
Mission Herald
MissQ Mississippi Quarterly: The Journal of Southern Culture
MLN (formerly Modern Language Notes)
MLQ Modern Language Quarterly
MLR The Modern Language Review
MLS Modern Language Studies
MMisc Midwestern Miscellany
ModA Modern Age
ModE Modern Eloquence
ModernQ Modern Quarterly
MoHR Missouri Historical Review
MoHSB Missouri Historical Society Bulletin
MoIll Monthly Illustrator
Montana: The Magazine of Western History
Mosaic: A Journal for the Interdisciplinary Study of Literature
MP Modern Philology: A Journal Devoted to Research in Medieval and Modern literature
MQ Midwest Quarterly: A Journal of Contemporary Thought
MQR Michigan Quarterly Review
MR Massachusetts Review: A Quarterly of Literature, the Arts and Public Affairs (Amherst, Mass.)
Ms
MSE Massachusetts Studies in English
MTC Mark Twain Circular
MTJ Mark Twain Journal
MTQ Mark Twain Quarterly
MTSB Mark Twain Society Bulletin
Munsey's Munsey's Magazine
Museum Echoes
MVHR Mississippi Valley Historical Review

N

NALF Negro American Literature Forum
N&Q Notes and Queries
NAR North American Review
NAS Norwegian-American Studies (Northfield, Minn.)
NAS&R Norwegian-American Studies and Records
Nation
Nationalist The Nationalist
NatlRep National Republic
NatM National Magazine

NCarL North Carolina Libraries
NCent Nineteenth Century
NCF Nineteenth-Century Fiction
NCHR North Carolina Historical Review
NCL Nineteenth-Century Literature
NConL Notes on Contemporary Literature
NDQ North Dakota Quarterly
NEMag New England Magazine
NEQ New England Quarterly: A Historical Review of New England Life and Letters
NevHSQ Nevada Historical Society Quarterly
NewberryLB Newberry Library Bulletin
NewC New Criterion
NewCol New Colophon
NewE New Englander
New Era
New HavenCHSP New Haven Colony Historical Society Papers
NewN New Nation
NewR New Republic
New Review (London)
Newsboy: Newsletter of the Horatio Alger Society
New Statesman
NHJ Nathaniel Hawthorne Journal
NiagF Niagara Frontier
NLH New Literary History: A Journal of Theory and Interpretation
NMAL Notes on Modern American Literature
NMHistR New Mexico Historical Review
NMoSUS Northwest Missouri State University Studies
NMQ New Mexico Quarterly
NMQR New Mexico Quarterly Review
NMW Notes on Mississippi Writers
NOQ Northwest Ohio Quarterly
NOR New Orleans Review
Novel: A Forum on Fiction (Providence, R.I.)
NR Nassau Review
Nyctalops
NYer New Yorker
NYFQ New York Folklore Quarterly
NYH New York History
NYHSQB New York Historical Society Quarterly Bulletin
NYHTB New York Herald Tribune Books
NYJ New York Journal
NYRB New York Review of Books
NYT New York Times
NYTBR New York Times Book Review
NYTM New York Times Magazine
NYWorld New York World

O

Obsidian
OhH Ohio History
OhioanaQ Ohioana Quarterly
OHQ Ohio Historical Quarterly

ON The Old Northwest: A Journal of Regional Life and Letters
Open Forum
Open Road
Orient/West
OSA&HQ Ohio State Archaeological and Historical Quarterly
Our Opinion
OUSAC Ochanomizu Studies in Arts and Culture
Outlook
Overland Overland Monthly

P

PAAS Proceedings of the American Antiquarian Society
PacH Pacific Historian
PacHR Pacific Historical Review
PacificNQ Pacific Northwest Quarterly
PacificS Pacific Studies
PacNWF Pacific Northwest Forum
PADS Publication of the American Dialect Society
PaEng Pennsylvania English
PAH Perspectives in American History
PAJHS Publications of the American Jewish Historical Society
Palimpsest
PAPA Publications of the Arkansas Philological Association
PBN Philadelphia Book News
PBSA Papers of the Bibliographical Society of America
Persimmon Hill
Personalist
Perspective
PhiGDQ Phi Gamma Delta Quarterly
Philadelphia Afro-American
Phylon: The Atlanta University Review of Race and Culture
PittsburghC The Pittsburgh Courier
PJE Peabody Journal of Education
PLL Papers on Language and Literature
PMC Putnam's Monthly Critic
PMHB Pennsylvania Magazine of History and Biography
PMHS Proceedings of the Massachusetts Historical Society
PMissHS Publications of the Mississippi Historical Society
PMLA Publications of the Modern Language Association of America
PMPA Publications of the Missouri Philological Association
PNJHS Proceedings of the New Jersey Historical Society
PoetL Poet Lore
Poetry: A Magazine of Verse
PolS Political Science

POMPA Publications of the Mississippi Philological Association
Possible Sack (University of Utah)
PP Philologica Pragensia
PQ Philological Quarterly
PR Partisan Review
Princetonian The Princetonian
Proof: The Yearbook of American Bibliographical and Textual Studies
Prospects: An Annual Journal of American Cultural Studies
PrS Prairie Schooner
Psychohistory Psychohistory Review
PsyR Psychoanalytic Review
PUASAL Proceedings of the Utah Academy of Sciences, Arts and Letters
Puck: The Comic Weekly
PULC Princeton University Library Chronicle
Putnam'sM Putnam's Magazine
PVR Platte Valley Review
PW Publishers Weekly

Q

QJLC Quarterly Journal of the Library of Congress
QQ Queen's Quarterly
QRL Quarterly Review of Literature

R

RAFI Regionalism and the Female Imagination
RALS Resources for American Literary Studies
Ramparts
R&L Religion and Literature
RDi Reader's Digest
RdM Revue des Deux Mondes
ReAL RE: Artes Liberales
Renascence: Essays on Value in Literature
Rendezvous: Journal of Arts and Letters
Representations
ResearchS Research Studies (Pullman, Wash.)
Rev Review (Blacksburg, Va.)
Reviewer
Review of Reviews
RFEA Revue Française d'Etudes Américaines
RHR Radical History Review
RLC Revue de Littérature Comparée
RLV Revue des Langues Vivantes
RMR Rocky Mountain Review of Language and Literature
Romantist The Romantist
Roundup
RQ Riverside Quarterly
RRVHR Red River Valley Historical Review
RusR Russian Review

S

SA Studi Americani (Rome, Italy)

SAB   South Atlantic Bulletin
SAF   Studies in American Fiction
SAH   Svenska Akademiens Handlingar
SAJL   Studies in American Jewish Literature
S&S   Science & Society
SanFC   San Francisco Chronicle
SanFSE&C   San Francisco Sunday Examiner & Chronicle
SAQ   South Atlantic Quarterly
SatEP   Saturday Evening Post
SatireN   Satire Newsletter
SatR   Saturday Review
SatRL   Saturday Review of Literature
Saturday Night
SB   Studies in Bibliography: Papers of the Bibliographical Society of the University of Virginia
Scando-Slav   Scando-Slavica
SCB   South Central Bulletin
SCNews   Stephen Crane Newsletter
Scott's   Scott's Monthly Magazine
SCQ   Southern California Quarterly
SCR   South Carolina Review
SCRev   South Central Review: The Journal of the South Central Modern Language Association
Scribner's   Scribner's Magazine
Scrutiny
SDR   South Dakota Review
Seacoast
SELit   Studies in English Literature (Tokyo)
Serif   The Serif
SEUT   Studies in English, University of Texas
SFQ   Southern Folklore Quarterly
SFS   Science Fiction Studies
ShakespeareAB   Shakespeare Association Bulletin
Shenandoah
SHR   Southern Humanities Review
Signal
Signs: Journal of Women in Culture & Society
SIP   Seminars in Psychiatry
SJS   San Jose Studies
SlavR   Slavic Review
SLAVR   Slavonic and East European Review
SLitI   Studies in the Literary Imagination
SLJ   Southern Literary Journal
SLM   Southern Literary Messenger
Smart Set   The Smart Set
SN   Studia Neophilologica: A Journal of Germanic and Romance Languages and Literature
SNNTS   Studies in the Novel (Denton, Tex.)
SoAR   South Atlantic Review
SoQ   The Southern Quarterly: A Journal of the Arts in the South (Hattiesburg, Miss.)
SoR   The Southern Review (Baton Rouge, La.)
SoSt   Southern Studies: An Interdisciplinary Journal of the South
Soundings: An Interdisciplinary Journal
Southern Exposure
Southern Packet   The Southern Packet
SPC   Studies in Popular Culture

SportsIllus   Sports Illustrated
SQ   Shakespeare Quarterly
SR   Sewanee Review
SS   Scandinavian Studies
SSF   Studies in Short Fiction
SSMLN   Society for the Study of Midwestern Literature Newsletter
StAH   Studies in American Humor
StanfordT   Stanford Today
StBL   Studies in Black Literature
Step Ladder (Chicago)
StHum   Studies in the Humanities (Indiana, Pa.)
St. Nicholas
Story
StoryQ   Story Quarterly
StWF   Studies in Weird Fiction
Style (DeKalb, Ill.)
Sunset
SW   Southern Workman
SwAL   Southwestern American Literature
SWR   Southwest Review
Synthesis: Bulletin du Comité National de Littérature Comparée de la République Socialiste de Roumanie (Bucharest, Romania)
SyracuseL   Syracuse Libraries

T

TASCE   Transactions of the American Society of Civil Engineers
TCL   Twentieth-Century Literature
TCW   Turn-of-the-Century Women
TexasR   Texas Review
TexSE   Texas Studies in English
TFSB   Tennessee Folklore Society Bulletin
Thalia: Studies in Literary Humor
TheatreS   Theatre Studies
Thought: A Review of Culture & Idea
THQ   Tennessee Historical Quarterly
THStud   Theatre History Studies
TLS   [London] Times Literary Supplement
Tomorrow
Topic: A Journal of the Liberal Arts (Washington, Pa.)
TQ   Texas Quarterly
TSB   Thoreau Society Bulletin
TSCPP   Transactions and Studies of the College of Physicians of Philadelphia
TSE   Tulane Studies in English
TSL   Tennessee Studies in Literature
TSLL   Texas Studies in Literature and Language
TSWL   Tulsa Studies in Women's Literature
TWA   Transactions of the Wisconsin Academy of Sciences, Arts, and Letters
Twainian
TWR   Thomas Wolfe Review

U

UBSCentJ   Upton Beall Sinclair Centenary Journal

UCC   University of California Chronicle
UKCR   University of Kansas City Review
UMCMP   University of Michigan Contributions in Modern Philology
UMSE   University of Mississippi Studies in English
Unicorn
UniversityR   University Review (Kansas City)
UnpopularR   Unpopular Review
URLB   University of Rochester Library Bulletin
US:USQ   Uppie Speaks: The Upton Sinclair Quarterly
UTQ   University of Toronto Quarterly
UTSE   University of Texas Studies in English
UWB   University of Wichita Bulletin
UWyP   University of Wyoming Publications

V

V&R   Views and Reviews
VanityF   Vanity Fair
VC   Virginia Cavalcade
Verbatim: The Language Quarterly
VLang   Visible Language: The Quarterly Concerned With All That Is Involved in Our Being Literate
VMHB: Virginia Magazine of History and Biography
VQR   Virginia Quarterly Review: A National Journal of Literature and Discussion (Richmond, Va.)
VtH   Vermont History

W

WAL   Western American Literature
W&L   Women & Literature
W&Lang   Women and Language
W&MR   William and Mary Review
WascanaR   Wascana Review
WashHQ   Washington Historical Quarterly
Washington Eagle   The Washington Eagle
WCA   The World of Comic Art
WCPMN   Willa Cather Pioneer Memorial Newsletter
WE   The Winesburg Eagle: The Official Publication of the Sherwood Anderson Society

WEBDCP&J   W. E. B. DuBois Colloquium Proceedings and Journal
WestR   Western Review
Westways
WF   Western Folklore
WHR   Western Humanities Review
WichitaSUB   Wichita State University Bulletin
WilsonLB   Wilson Library Bulletin
WIRS   Western Illinois Regional Studies
WMH   Wisconsin Magazine of History
World of Yesterday   The World of Yesterday
World Today
WPaHM   Western Pennsylvania Historical Magazine
Wren's NestN   Wren's Nest Newsletter
Writer   The Writer
Writer's Monthly
WS   Women's Studies: An Interdisciplinary Journal
WSIF   Women's Studies International Forum
WSJHQ   Western States Jewish Historical Quarterly
WSL   Wisconsin Studies in Literature
WVUPP   West Virginia University Bulletin Philological Papers
WWork   World's Work
WWR   Walt Whitman Quarterly Review

X

XUS   Xavier Review (New Orleans)

Y

Yankee   Yankee Magazine
YFS   Yale French Studies
YLM   Yale Literary Magazine
Youth's Companion
YR   Yale Review
YULG   Yale University Library Gazette

Z

ZAA   Zeitschrift für Anglistik und Amerikanistik
ZGCollector   Zane Grey Collector

Acknowledgments

The *Bibliography of American Fiction: 1866-1918* could not have been produced without the collaboration of scores of colleagues and friends who contributed in important ways to the development of this volume. In addition to the scholars whose names appear on the entries and the editors and advisers included on the masthead, many researchers and librarians devoted their time and energies to generating and checking the primary and secondary items. Without their professionalism, the results of our efforts would have been greatly diminished.

We wish to acknowledge the extraordinary cooperation given by the staff of the University of Georgia Library and the Department of English at the University of Georgia. Dr. Coburn Freer, head of the department, was truly generous in his support of this project, and Jane Wilson provided essential research assistance. The Research and Development Fund at Northeastern University provided funding for the early development of this book, and we express our sincere gratitude for that aid.

Carol Acree directed the process of verifying entries in Boston and the efforts of a staff of checkers that included Isabel Buck, Beth Fischi, Cindy Ramsey, Kelly Reed, and Jeff Westover. Mary Armato, Editorial Assistant for *Studies in American Fiction*, contributed to every stage of this volume, and we are grateful for her untiring efforts.

Work on *BAF* at the University of South Carolina was encouraged by the benevolence of Dean Carol McGinnis Kay and Prof. Bert Dillon. The checkers in Columbia included Henry Cuningham, Timothy C. Lundy, Susan A. Bunn, Sonja Launspach, Todd Stebbins, Kreg A. Abshire, and Hoke S. Greiner.

Systems manager was Charles D. Brower. Layout and graphics supervisor was Penney L. Haughton. Copy-editing supervisor was Bill Adams. Typesetting supervisor was Kathleen M. Flanagan. Information systems analyst was George F. Dodge. The production staff included Sarah A. Estes, Kathy Lawler Merlette, and John Myrick.

It would have been impossible to compile these volumes without the extraordinary cooperation of the staff of the Thomas Cooper Library, University of South Carolina. Dr. Arthur Young, Dean of the Libraries, provided every form of assistance within the purview of a scholar-librarian. The Interlibrary-Loan Department at the Cooper Library performed prodigiously: Jens Holley, Jo Cottingham, and Angie Dorman. Roger Mortimer, Special Collections and Rare Book Librarian, was consistently helpful. The Reference Department was constantly at our service.

William Cagle, Director of the Lilly Library, Indiana University, promised assistance before he was asked and provided more benefactions than could have been decently requested. His encouragement has been crucial to many scholars. Our thanks embrace the exemplary staff of this splendid institution, including Sue Presnell and Saundra Taylor.

Among our colleagues at universities throughout the United States, a few deserve particular mention for generous assistance with entries, guidance, and patience. Joel Myerson contributed the logistical direction that his vast experience in bibliography has given him. Kent P. Ljungquist generously shared with us the progress of his work on his own volume, and his insights were consistently valuable. Charles Mann added suggestions for coverage that proved essential, as did George Monteiro, Guy Rotella, and Mary Loeffelholz. Hubert McAlexander provided advice that could not have been more graciously offered nor more gratefully received. Our deepest obligations, however, are reserved for David Nordloh, Alfred Bendixen, Alan Gribben, and Harrison T. Meserole, who helped in the planning, administration, and construction of this volume. Our gratitude for their wise counsel and warm friendship is expressed in the dedication of this volume.

G.L.N.
J.N.

Index of Scholars and Critics

This index is restricted to the authors of secondary items and to the editors or contributors (of introductions, forewords, prefaces, afterwords) to primary items. It does not include items listed in the "Vade Mecum" and the "General Bibliography."